PREVIOUS YEARS' SOLVED PAPERS

Commerce

For UGC-NET/JRF

Paper I, II and III

Latest Edition

Atlantic Research Division

ATLANTIC

PUBLISHERS & DISTRIBUTORS (P) LTD

Published by
ATLANTIC
PUBLISHERS & DISTRIBUTORS (P) LTD
7/22, Ansari Road, Darya Ganj,
New Delhi-110002
Phones : +91-11-40775252, 23273880, 23275880, 23280451
Fax : +91-11-23285873
Web : www.atlanticbooks.com
E-mail : orders@atlanticbooks.com

Branch Office
5, Nallathambi Street, Wallajah Road,
Chennai-600002
Phones : +91-44-64611085, 32413319
E-mail : chennai@atlanticbooks.com

Printed in India at Nice Printing Press, A-33/3A, Site-IV,
Industrial Area, Sahibabad, Ghaziabad, U.P.

Preface

The University Grants Commission (UGC) conducts National Eligibility Test (NET) on various subjects twice every year, once each in June and December, to determine eligibility for college and university level lectureship and for award of Junior Research Fellowship (JRF), for Indian nationals in order to ensure minimum standards for the entrants in the teaching profession and research.

This Latest Edition contains previous years' solved papers (objective type questions) on the subject of Commerce, from June 2005 to July 2016. It covers all three papers (Paper I, II and III). In Paper I (General Paper on Teaching and Research Aptitude), solved papers have been included from December 2005, while in Paper II (Elective), solved papers have been included from December 2005. In Paper III (Core and Elective), solved papers of objective type questions have been included from June 2012, conforming to the existing UGC-NET pattern. In addition, five sets of Mock Tests for Paper I, II and III have been included in the book under Practice Papers. Answers have been given at the end of each set for self-check.

It will be useful for those preparing for UGC-NET/SLET/JRF in the subject of Commerce. It will give them a feel of the type of questions asked in NET in this subject, i.e. Multiple-choice, Matching type, True/False, Assertion-Reasoning type, etc. The papers included in this book will enable the students to judge their own level of competence besides adding to their knowledge. It will also help them revise the important questions in the entire syllabus and enhance their self-confidence. Suggestions for further improvement of the book are, however, welcome.

Atlantic Research Division

Contents

JUNE–2005

Note: This paper contains Fifty (50) multiple choice questions, each question carrying two (2) marks. Attempt all of them.

PAPER–II

1. In Budget estimates 2005-06 which sector has been given maximum amount of plan outlay
   (a) Energy (b) Social Services
   (c) Rural Development (d) Transport
2. The Twelfth Finance Commission was appointed by
   (a) President of India
   (b) Prime Minister of India
   (c) Parliament
   (d) Council of Ministers
3. VAT is a modern, simple and transparent tax system that will replace the existing
   (a) Corporate Tax (b) Excise Duty
   (c) Sales Tax (d) Service Tax
4. Consider the following:
   1. Irrigation 2. Roads
   3. Water supply 4. Housing
   5. Rural Electrification
   6. Rural Telecom connectivity

   Which of these are components of 'Bharat-Nirman'?
   (a) 1–2–3–4–5 (b) 1–2–3–4–6
   (c) 2–3–4–5–6 (d) 1–2–3–4–5–6
5. A Task Force has recommended the creation of a National Fund for Strategic Agriculture. Who headed this Task Force?
   (a) M.S. Swaminathan (b) Sharad Pawar
   (c) P. Chidambaram (d) None of the above
6. Transportation expenses incurred to bring a machine from the place of purchase to the place of installation is
   (a) a revenue expenditure
   (b) a capital expenditure
   (c) deferred revenue expenditure
   (d) None of the above
7. Match the items from List-I with the items in List-II

   List-I
   (A) Working-capital ratio
   (B) Cash equivalents
   (C) Margin of safety
   (D) ROI

   List-II
   (i) Cash Flow Statement
   (ii) Break-even Analysis
   (iii) Liquidity
   (iv) Solvency
   (v) Responsibility centres

Codes:	A	B	C	D
(a)	(iii)	(iv)	(ii)	(v)
(b)	(ii)	(iii)	(v)	(iv)
(c)	(iii)	(i)	(ii)	(v)
(d)	(iii)	(i)	(ii)	(iv)

8. Bottom-line growth refers to growth in
   (a) Sales (b) Turnover
   (c) Assets (d) Profit
9. If total assets = ₹ 12,00,000, sales = ₹ 24,00,000, total expenses = ₹ 21,40,000, and normal rate of return = 12%, find out residual income
   (a) ₹ 1,44,000 (b) ₹ 2,60,000
   (c) ₹ 1,16,000 (d) ₹ 2,16,000
10. X, Y and Z are three partners sharing profits and losses in the ratio, 10:6:2. A was admitted for 1/10th share. The new profit sharing ratio will be
    (a) 10:6:2:1 (b) 5:3:2:1
    (c) 5:3:1:1 (d) 10:6:2:4
11. Which of the following is correct statement?

(a) Under perfect competition, a firm determines its price where AR=MR
(b) In perfect competitive industry, a firm is in equilibrium in the short run only when its AC=AR=MR=MC
(c) The short-run supply curve has a negative slope
(d) A firm is price-taken under perfect competition

12. A consumer attains equilibrium at a point on the indifference curve where
(a) $MRX_{xy} = P_x/P_y$ (b) $MRS_{xy} > P_x/P_y$
(c) $MRS_{xy} < P_x/P_y$ (d) $MRS_{xy} = P_x P_y$

13. In Oligopoly market kinked demand curve explains
(a) Collusion among rival firms
(b) Average variable cost curves
(c) Short run average cost curve
(d) Long run average cost curve

14. Opportunity cost means
(a) Cost of a homogeneous product
(b) Cost of the last unit
(c) Cost of next best alternative
(d) Cost of all units produced

15. A normal profit
(a) is part of economic cost
(b) has to be above economic cost in order to encourage output
(c) is not a part of the economic costs that a firm incurs
(d) is irrelevant to the production division of a firm

16. Chi-square test is a
(a) Parametric Test
(b) Non-parametric Test
(c) Small Sample Test
(d) None of the above

17. β-error in hypothesis testing refers to
(a) Type-I error
(b) Type-II error
(c) Both (a) and (b) errors
(d) None of the above

18. Convenience sampling is a
(a) Probability sampling
(b) Non-probability sampling
(c) Random sampling
(d) None of the above

19. We can measure the cause and effect relationship by the help of
(a) Time series analysis
(b) Cross-sectional analysis
(c) Correlational analysis
(d) Regression analysis

20. Match the items from List-I with the items in List-II

List-I
(A) Indirect oral interview
(B) Bi-variate Analysis
(C) F-ratio
(D) Quota sampling

List-II
(i) Non-probability sampling
(ii) Variance test
(iii) Primary data
(iv) Factor Analysis
(v) Correlation

Codes:	**A**	**B**	**C**	**D**
(a)	(iii)	(v)	(ii)	(i)
(b)	(iii)	(v)	(ii)	(iv)
(c)	(i)	(v)	(ii)	(iii)
(d)	(iii)	(ii)	(iv)	(i)

21. Which is the oldest type of organisation?
(a) Line (b) Line and Staff
(c) Functional (d) Matrix

22. Managerial decisions which increase the importance of subordinates are linked with
(a) Centralised authority
(b) Decentralised authority
(c) Both (a) and (b)
(d) None of the above

23. Which of the following is not the example of only upward Communication?
(a) Reports (b) Interviews
(c) Grapevine (d) Circulars

24. The main purpose of the Control function is to
(a) Oversee work
(b) Take remedial action
(c) Punish defaulters
(d) Meet targets

25. In a formal organisational structure authority flows
(a) Upward (b) Downward
(c) Horizontal (d) None of the above

26. Which of the following is not a case of related diversification?
    (a) A refrigerator manufacturer started manufacturing air conditioners
    (b) A washing powder manufacturer started manufacturing washing machines
    (c) A bath soap trader enters washing soap market
    (d) A Television manufacturer started manufacturing VCRs

27. Lifestyle is one of the major ______ basis of segmenting a market.
    (a) socio-economic (b) demographic
    (c) psychographic (d) none of the above

28. What stage of the product Life-cycle are pricing decisions most complex?
    (a) Introductory (b) Growth
    (c) Maturity (d) Decline

29. A company is planning to develop a new packaging for its consumer product. In order to ensure that the packaging is attractive and easy to handle, the company must conduct _______ test.
    (a) association (b) engineering
    (c) dealer (d) Inquiry

30. The most important component of promotion mix to be used for industrial goods is
    (a) Personal Selling (b) Advertisement
    (c) Sales promotion (d) Publicity

31. A firm produces 1,00,000 units and sells at ₹ 10 per unit. The cost of manufacturing is ₹ 6,00,000 per annum and depreciation is ₹ 1,00,000 per annum. The depreciation tax shield will be ______ if the rate of corporate taxation is 30%.
    (a) ₹ 20,000 (b) ₹ 25,000
    (c) ₹ 30,000 (d) ₹ 1,60,000

32. In capital budgeting, the main aim is to find the project whose _____ of future cash flows is greater than the cost of the project.
    (a) Terminal value
    (b) Present value
    (c) Cumulative value
    (d) None of the above

33. Financial risk is connected with
    (a) Debt capital
    (b) Nature of investment
    (c) Type of employees
    (d) Location of factory

34. The balance sheet of a business reveals
    (a) Financial position of a business on a particular day
    (b) Financial position of the business for a particular period
    (c) Both of the above
    (d) None of the above

35. The shares issued to existing shareholders when reserves are capitalised are
    (a) Right Issue (b) Bonus shares
    (c) Preference shares (d) All the above

36. Safety and accident prevention should concern managers for all the following reasons except
    (a) Criminal liability
    (b) Human suffering of the injured workers
    (c) Retaliatory actions by workers
    (d) Work-related accident figures are staggering

37. During the formulation of plans, HR can
    (a) provide details regarding competitors' incentive plans
    (b) provide moral support
    (c) provide information on competitor's diversity
    (d) provide empowerment strategies

38. Providing employees with basic background information about the firm is
    (a) Education
    (b) Employee orientation
    (c) Colleges and universities
    (d) Required by law

39. An enterprise gets more output and mutual cooperation from its subordinate staff by adopting
    (a) motivation by leadership
    (b) motivation by participation
    (c) motivation by goals
    (d) motivation by challenge

40. The concept of Human Relations was developed by
    (a) Robert Owen (b) V.V. Giri
    (c) Elton Maya (d) Edwin B. Filippo

41. Match the following
    List I (Name of the Merging Entity)
    (A) 20th Century Finance Company

(B) Bareilly Corporation Bank
(C) Sikkim Bank
(D) Times Bank
(E) Bank of Madura

List II (Name of the Merged entity)
(i) ICICI Bank
(ii) Centurian Bank
(iii) HDFC Bank
(iv) Bank of Baroda
(v) Union Bank of India

Codes:	A	B	C	D	E
(a)	(ii)	(iv)	(v)	(iii)	(i)
(b)	(iii)	(iv)	(i)	(iii)	(v)
(c)	(v)	(iv)	(iii)	(ii)	(i)
(d)	(v)	(ii)	(i)	(iii)	(iv)

42. Inter-institutional group comprises
(a) IDBI, IDFC, ICICI Bank
(b) SBI, LIC
(c) Bank of Baroda and Punjab National Bank
(d) All of the above

43. With reference to the Micro Finance Institutions consider the following statements:
1. At present Micro Finance Institutions (MFIs) obtain finance from banks according to RBI guidelines
2. MFIs provide small scale credit to low income households and small informal businesses.

Which of these statements is/are correct?
(a) Only 1 (b) Only 2
(c) Both 1 and 2 (d) Neither 1 nor 2

44. Which one is not the part of, Migration to new capital adequacy framework based on the three pillar approach, namely
(a) Minimum capital requirements
(b) Supervisory review
(c) Market Discipline
(d) Book keeping

45. In India the basic objectives of Monetary Policy is/are
(a) Price stability and adequate credit flow
(b) Price control and command on economy
(c) Price Reduction and Credit Reduction
(d) All of the above

46. The trade theory of absolute advantage was developed by
(a) Haberler (b) David Ricardo
(c) Adam Smith (d) Alfred Marshall

47. Which of the following is not matched against its name
(a) WTO : Generally refuses quantitative restrictions on Trade
(b) IMF : To remove unfavourable Balance of Payment and provides financial assistance
(c) SAARC : Encourages Trade between South Asian Countries
(d) ASEAN : Economic Organisation of all Asian Countries

48. Physical delivery of foreign exchange has to take place in case of
(a) Forward Market (b) Spot Market
(c) Futures Market (d) Options Market

49. A letter of credit means
(a) A bank agreeing to accept and pay on due date
(b) A letter containing conditions of credit purchase or sale
(c) A letter sent by exporter to importer sanctioning credit deal
(d) A letter sent by importer to exporter sanctioning credit deal

50. Which of the following is a document of the title of sale of goods?
(a) Certificate of Origin
(b) Letter of Credit
(c) Bill of Lading
(d) Bill of Entry

ANSWERS

1. (b)	2. (a)	3. (c)	4. (d)	5. (a)
6. (b)	7. (c)	8. (d)	9. (c)	10. (b)
11. (d)	12. (a)	13. (a)	14. (c)	15. (b)
16. (b)	17. (b)	18. (b)	19. (d)	20. (a)
21. (a)	22. (b)	23. (b)	24. (b)	25. (b)
26. (b)	27. (c)	28. (c)	29. (c)	30. (a)
31. (c)	32. (b)	33. (a)	34. (a)	35. (b)
36. (b)	37. (d)	38. (b)	39. (b)	40. (c)
41. (a)	42. (a)	43. (b)	44. (d)	45. (d)
46. (c)	47. (d)	48. (b)	49. (a)	50. (c)

DECEMBER–2005

Note: This paper contains Fifty (50) multiple choice questions, each question carrying two (2) marks. Attempt all of these.

PAPER–II

1. ______ is a permanent inter-governmental body governing and regulating international trade in goods and services.
   (a) G.A.T.T. (b) EXIM Bank
   (c) W.T.O. (d) I.M.F.
2. Fiscal deficit in the Union Budget means:
   (a) The sum of budgetary deficit and net increase in internal and external borrowings
   (b) The difference between current expenditure and current revenue
   (c) The sum of monetised deficit and budgetary deficit
   (d) Net increase in Union Government borrowings from the Reserve Bank of India
3. The objective of _____ is to achieve "growth with equity".
   (a) The Ninth Plan (b) The Tenth Plan
   (c) The Eighth Plan (d) The Seventh Plan
4. The significant development in the sphere of foreign exchange was the introduction of
   (a) Foreign Exchange Regulation Act (FERA)
   (b) Foreign Exchange Management Act (FEMA)
   (c) The Export-Import Policy, 2005-06
   (d) EXIM Bank
5. The term 'industrial policy' refers to:
   (a) the rules and regulations relating to the establishment of industrial undertakings and their expansion
   (b) remove the structural, financial, fiscal, administrative, infrastructure related impediments to the efficient functioning of a market oriented economy
   (c) the culmination of liberalisation programme
   (d) increase the efficiency of public sector undertakings
6. Who are the customers of cost and management accounting?
   (a) Managers (b) Creditors
   (c) Lenders (d) Consumers
7. Which of the following is an efficiency ratio?
   (a) Price-Earning Ratio
   (b) Debt-Equity Ratio
   (c) Acid-Test Ratio
   (d) Average collection period
8. What do you mean by 'cash equivalents'?
   (a) Bank balance
   (b) Short-term highly liquid securities
   (c) Investments
   (d) Investment in debentures
9. The profits calculated by marginal costing and absorption costing are different because of:
   (a) Capital and revenue (b) Opening stock
   (c) Valuation of stock (d) Closing stock
10. Match the items from List-I with the items in List-II:
    List-I
    (A) Error of Principle
    (B) Error of Commission
    (C) Error of Omission
    (D) Compensatory error
    List-II
    (i) A purchase of ₹ 1000 has not been recorded
    (ii) Treating repair charges as addition to assets
    (iii) A sale of ₹ 563 was posted as ₹ 653
    (iv) Sales book is undercast by ₹ 1000 and return inward book is overcast by ₹ 1000

(v) Return inward book is undercast by ₹ 1000 and purchase book is overcast by ₹ 1000

Codes:	**A**	**B**	**C**	**D**
(a)	(ii)	(iii)	(i)	(iv)
(b)	(ii)	(iii)	(iv)	(v)
(c)	(iv)	(ii)	(i)	(iii)
(d)	(ii)	(iii)	(i)	(v)

11. Which of the following is not the method of forecasting demand?
    (a) Collective opinion method
    (b) Total outlay method
    (c) Expert opinion method
    (d) Controlled opinion method
12. When marginal utility is negative then total utility?
    (a) increases (b) decreases
    (c) is zero (d) is negative
13. Which of the following is a correct statement?
    (a) Decrease in input prices causes a leftward shift in the supply curve
    (b) The desire for a commodity backed by ability and willingness to pay is demand
    (c) When income increases, the demand for essential goods increases more than proportionately
    (d) The demand for a commodity is inversely related to the price of its substitutes
14. When goods in the domestic market are sold at a high price and in the foreign market at a low price, it is a situation of:
    (a) Dumping (b) Perfect competition
    (c) Oligopoly (d) Duopoly
15. Average revenue curve will not touch 0 – X axis because it cannot be:
    (a) Positive (b) Zero
    (c) Negative (d) None of the above
16. 'Parameter' refers to the characteristics of the:
    (a) Population (b) Sample
    (c) Mean (d) None of the above
17. The median of 10, 12, 14, 16, 18 will be:
    (a) 12 (b) 16 (c) 15 (d) 14
18. Probability sampling and random sampling are:
    (a) Anonymous (b) Different terms
    (c) Synonymous (d) None of the above
19. 'F' ratio refers to:
    (a) ratio between two means
    (b) ratio between two standard deviations
    (c) ratio between two correlations
    (d) ratio between two variances
20. Match the items from List-I with the items in List-II.

List-I	**List-II**
(A) t-test	(i) Secondary data
(B) Regression test	(ii) Systematic sampling
(C) Published sources	(iii) Hypothesis test
(D) Probability sampling	(iv) quota sampling
	(v) multi-variable analysis

Codes:	**A**	**B**	**C**	**D**
(a)	(v)	(ii)	(i)	(iv)
(b)	(v)	(iii)	(i)	(iv)
(c)	(iii)	(v)	(i)	(ii)
(d)	(v)	(ii)	(i)	(iv)

21. The Plan for meeting the challenges of the competitors is called a:
    (a) Programme (b) Mission
    (c) Derivative Plan (d) Strategy
22. The chief contribution of Henry Fayol to management is that he:
    (a) provided a conceptual framework
    (b) formulated the management process approach
    (c) evolved two principles of management
    (d) stressed the need for management education based on management
23. Which type of managerial decision correspond to "basic decisions"?
    (a) Mechanical decision and analytic decision
    (b) Judicious decision and adoptive decision
    (c) Judicious decision, adoptive decision and analytic decision
    (d) All of the above
24. The process of combining the main industrial unit with all other related units is called:
    (a) Divergent Lateral combination
    (b) Convergent Lateral combination
    (c) Horizontal combination
    (d) Vertical combination
25. The lack of faith and confidence of managers in subordinates is an important barrier of:

(a) Effective leadership
(b) Effective control
(c) Effective delegation
(d) Effective direction

26. Post purchase dissatisfaction in marketing is known as:
(a) Caveat emptor
(b) Cognitive dissonance
(c) Brand III loyalty
(d) None of the above

27. Needs for goods and services are more homogenous in:
(a) Industrial market (b) Consumer market
(c) Domestic market (d) None of the above

28. Marketing concept means:
(a) Firms should produce only what their predetermined consumers would be willing to buy
(b) Firms should persuade customers to buy what they have produced
(c) The consumers will buy the products which offer them the highest quality
(d) All of the above

29. The process of dividing a potential market into distinct subsets of consumers and selecting one or more segments as a target to be reached with a distinct marketing mix means:
(a) Marketing (b) Positioning
(c) Targeting (d) None of the above

30. What is the basis for segmenting vitamin market?
(a) Age (b) Place of distribution
(c) Formulation (d) All of the above

31. Financial Risk means:
(a) Risk of technical insolvency
(b) Magnify the fluctuation in EBT
(c) Both (a) and (b)
(d) None of the above

32. The financial management is concerned with the:
(a) Procurement of funds and their effective utilisation
(b) Raising of funds from the market
(c) Management of Working Funds only
(d) Investing funds in the most appropriate assets

33. M.M. Approach is similar to ____ approach.
(a) Net Income Approach
(b) Net Operating Income Approach
(c) Both (a) and (b)
(d) None of the above

34. If the sales are ₹ 6000, variable cost ₹ 3600 and fixed cost ₹ 2000, the Break-even point will be:
(a) 5000 units (b) 5400 units
(c) 6000 units (d) 4000 units

35. Which is an incorrect statement?
(a) The issue of bonus shares is subject to sanction from the SEBI
(b) The prior approval of capitalisation of reserves upto ₹ 1 crore is totally exempted
(c) Bonus issues beyond the ratio of 1:1 is not permitted
(d) Partly paid equity shares are issued as bonus shares

36. Job analysis provides information used for writing:
(a) Organisation chart (b) Policy
(c) Job Description (d) Procedure

37. Recruitment and selection involves the following except:
(a) Building a pool of candidates
(b) Completing application forms by applicants
(c) Reduction of the work force
(d) Employment planning and forecasting

38. ____ is the process of deciding how to fill the company's most important executive positions.
(a) Succession Planning
(b) Organisational Restructuring
(c) Self-directed Teams
(d) Corporate Downsizing

39. Which of the following is not necessary for promotion from within?
(a) Job Posting
(b) Advertisements
(c) Personnel Records
(d) Performance Appraisal Form

40. Performance appraisal means evaluating an employee's performance relative to:
(a) Established goods
(b) Fellow employees

(c) Job description requirements
(d) Performance standards

41. A ________ card is basically a payment mechanism which allows the holder of the card to make purchases without any immediate cash payment.
(a) ATM (b) CREDIT
(c) DEBIT (d) KISAN CREDIT

42. Which of the following is a measure of selective credit control?
(a) Bank rate policy
(b) Moral suasion
(c) Statutory cash reserve ratio
(d) Open market operations

43. Which of the following sentence is false?
(a) Nationalisation of commercial banks has achieved its objectives
(b) Prior to nationalisation, commercial banks in India were generally concerned with profit maximisation only
(c) Nationalisation has enhanced the efficiency of commercial banks
(d) Bank nationalisation in India was prompted by the necessity of credit facilities reaching the rural sector and weaker sections of the society

44. Which of the following statements is true?
(a) The currency notes issued by RBI are legal tender throughout the world
(b) The treasury bills are sold by the RBI for raising its working capital
(c) All commercial banks, including those owned by government, need a licence from the RBI to do banking business
(d) The RBI is a banker to both central and state governments

45. M. Narasimham headed:
(a) The working group constituted by the Government of India in July 1975 for the establishment of Regional Rural Banks
(b) The Committee on the Financial System, 1991
(c) The Committee on Banking Sector Reforms, 1997
(d) All of the above

46. The gains from two nations depend on:
(a) Domestic barter rates
(b) Difference in the domestic barter rates of the two countries
(c) Terms of trade
(d) Degree of absolute advantage

47. The trade theory of comparative advantage was developed by:
(a) Haberler (b) Adam Smith
(c) Alfred Marshall (d) David Ricardo

48. Which items are included in the negative list of imports out of the combination given below:
(1) Canalised items
(2) Banned items
(3) Restricted items
(4) Items of open General Licence
(a) 1, 3 and 4 (b) 2, 3 and 4
(c) 1, 2, 3 and 4 (d) 1, 2 and 3

49. If a country has deficit in balance of current account, balance of capital account will be:
(a) Zero (b) Surplus
(c) Deficit (d) None of the above

50. When custom duty is levied according to weight of goods it is known as:
(a) Excise duty (b) Ad-valorem duty
(c) Revenue duty (d) Specific duty

ANSWERS

1. (c)	2. (a)	3. (a)	4. (b)	5. (b)
6. (a)	7. (d)	8. (b)	9. (d)	10. (d)
11. (b)	12. (b)	13. (b)	14. (a)	15. (b)
16. (a)	17. (d)	18. (c)	19. (d)	20. (a)
21. (d)	22. (a)	23. (c)	24. (d)	25. (c)
26. (b)	27. (a)	28. (d)	29. (c)	30. (a)
31. (b)	32. (a)	33. (b)	34. (a)	35. (d)
36. (c)	37. (c)	38. (a)	39. (b)	40. (d)
41. (b)	42. (b)	43. (a)	44. (d)	45. (d)
46. (c)	47. (d)	48. (d)	49. (b)	50. (d)

JUNE–2006

Note: This paper contains Fifty (50) multiple choice questions, each question carrying two (2) marks. Attempt all of them.

PAPER–II

1. No planning can start without setting:
   (a) Budget (b) Objectives
   (c) Powers (d) None of the above
2. Forms of mixed Economy consist of
   (a) Public Sector (b) Private Sector
   (c) Co-operative Sector (d) None of the above
3. According to which of the following accounting principles, the owners of the business are considered as creditors?
   (a) Money Measurement (b) Cost
   (c) Dual Aspect (d) Separate Entity
4. Under how many headings, the cash flow statement shows the flow of cash & cash equivalents?
   (a) 1 (b) 2 (c) 3 (d) 4
5. All the following curves are U-shaped: except
   (a) AVC Curve (b) AFC Curve
   (c) AC Curve (d) MC Curve
6. The Cobb-Douglas production function $Q = 4\,K^{0.6}\,L^{0.3}$ Exhibits
   (a) Constant returns to scale
   (b) Increasing returns to scale
   (c) Decreasing returns to scale
   (d) None of the above
7. Multistage stratified random sampling is:
   (a) Probability Sampling
   (b) Selective Sampling
   (c) Non-Probability Sampling
   (d) None of the above
8. Which of the following are considered output units of a computer?
   (a) Floppy Disk, Dat, CD, etc.
   (b) Printers
   (c) Video Display Unit
   (d) Micro-film
9. Process of delegation of authority involves
   (a) Transfer of authority
   (b) Transfer of responsibility
   (c) Transfer of authority and responsibility
   (d) Transfer of key management functions
10. SWOT Analysis is used in which of the following managerial function?
    (a) Organising
    (b) Decision Making
    (c) Motivating
    (d) Directing and Controlling
11. Which of the following is the function of distribution channel?
    (a) Fixing prices
    (b) Communication of decisions
    (c) Promotional activities
    (d) All of the above
12. Product Lines Cover:
    (a) General retailer
    (b) One price retailer
    (c) Departmental Stores
    (d) All of the above
13. Which one of the following is not a leverage ratio?
    (a) Total debt ratio
    (b) Debt-Equity ratio
    (c) Interest Coverage ratio
    (d) Quick ratio
14. Pay-back period method is also called as:
    (a) Pay-out method (b) Pay-off method
    (c) Pay-back method (d) All of these
15. Human relations approach of Management is associated with:
    (a) Abraham Maslow
    (b) Elton Mayo
    (c) Peter Drucker
    (d) Frederick Herzberg
16. Attrition is related to:

(a) Job description
(b) Job Evaluation
(c) Resignation/Termination
(d) Promotion

17. The nationalised New Bank of India was later merged with:
(a) Central Bank of India
(b) Bank of Baroda
(c) Punjab National Bank
(d) Canara Bank

18. The first Financial Institution set up in India:
(a) IDBI (b) ICICI (c) IRBI (d) IFCI

19. Which section is not of balance of payment?
(a) Current Account
(b) Capital Account
(c) Official Reserve Account
(d) Loss Accounts

20. Which conference had given birth to International Monetary Fund?
(a) Uruguay Round Conference
(b) Round Table Conference
(c) Brettonwoods Conference
(d) Simla Conference

21. Which one of the following pairs is not correctly matched?
(a) Installation of a Machine: Installation Cost A/c
(b) Relevant Cost: Decision Making
(c) Valuation of Share: Purchase of a company
(d) Break-even Analysis: Margin of Safety

22. Which of the following is a form of organisation?
(i) Line Organisation
(ii) Staff Organisation
(iii) Functional Organisation
(iv) Committee Organisation
(a) (i), (ii), (iii) and (iv)
(b) (i), (ii) and (iv)
(c) (i), (iii) and (iv)
(d) Only (ii)

23. For profit maximization of a firm we must have
(i) MC = MR
(ii) Marginal Cost Curve cuts the average cost curve from below
(a) only (i) is true
(b) Only (ii) is true
(c) Both (i) and (ii) are wrong
(d) Both (i) and (ii) are true

24. Analysis of variance technique is normally used when
(i) Number of samples are more than two
(ii) All the samples follow Independent normal distribution with equal variance
(a) only (i) is true
(b) only (ii) is true
(c) Both (i) and (ii) are true
(d) Neither (i) nor (ii) is true

25. Which of the following Economic Systems occurred first
(a) Laissez-faire System (b) Socialism
(c) Communism (d) Capitalism

26. Arrange the following events in the order of their occurrence:
(i) Companies Act
(ii) Partnership Act
(iii) Formation of ICAI
(iv) Accounting Standard 3 (revised)
(a) (i) (ii) (iii) (iv) (b) (ii) (iii) (iv) (i)
(c) (iii) (ii) (i) (iv) (d) (ii) (iii) (i) (iv)

27. National Income may be determined through:
(a) Income Approach
(b) Expenditure Approach
(c) Productivity Approach
(d) All of the above

28. Standard Error of Mean is defined as,
(a) Standard deviation of the sampling distribution of Mean
(b) Average of sampling distribution of Mean
(c) Inter-Quartile range of sampling distribution of mean
(d) Correlation co-efficient between the sampling distribution of mean and population mean

29. Which one of the following is not involved in the characterstics of Business Ethics?
(a) Business ethics is a dynamic philosophy
(b) Business ethics is based on moral value
(c) Business ethics influenced by socio-cultural value
(d) Business ethics is not inspired by Social Welfare

30. Management of sales force involves:

(a) Selection of Salesman
(b) Remuneration to salesman
(c) Training of Salesman
(d) All of the above

31. Working Capital cycle involves the following:
(i) Acquisition of raw materials
(ii) Finished goods
(iii) Receivables
(iv) Cash
(v) Work-in-progress
Which of the sequence is correct?
(a) (iv), (iii), (i), (v), (ii)
(b) (i), (ii), (iii), (iv), (v)
(c) (i), (v), (ii), (iii), (iv)
(d) (iv), (i), (ii), (iii), (v)

32. Which of the following needs comes last in the Maslow's need hierarchy theory?
(a) Safety needs
(b) Self-Actualisation
(c) Belongingness & Love needs
(d) Self-esteem needs

33. Arrange the following banks in order in which they were established
(i) IDBI (ii) IFCI (iii) SIDBI (iv) IIBI
(a) (ii) (i) (iii) (iv) (b) (ii) (i) (iv) (iii)
(c) (i) (ii) (iii) (iv) (d) (i) (ii) (iv) (iii)

34. Arrange the following Acts in the order in which they came into force:
(i) The Monopolies & Restrictive Trade Practices Act
(ii) Indian Contract Act
(iii) The Sale of Goods Act
(iv) The Foreign Exchange Management Act

Codes:

(a)	(ii)	(iii)	(i)	(iv)
(b)	(iii)	(i)	(iv)	(ii)
(c)	(i)	(ii)	(iii)	(iv)
(d)	(iv)	(iii)	(ii)	(i)

35. Match the following
List I (Industry)
(A) Small Scale Enterprise
(B) Tiny Enterprise
(C) SME Sector Enterprise
(D) Export Oriented Small Scale Enterprise
List-II (Investment limit)
(i) ₹ 25 lakhs (ii) ₹ 10 crores
(iii) ₹ 5 crores (iv) ₹ 1 crore

Codes:	**A**	**B**	**C**	**D**
(a)	(iv)	(i)	(iii)	(ii)
(b)	(iv)	(i)	(ii)	(iii)
(c)	(iv)	(ii)	(i)	(iii)
(d)	(iv)	(ii)	(iii)	(i)

36. Match the following
List I
(A) Fixed Capital A/c
(B) Deferred Revenue Expenditure
(C) Responsibility Centre
(D) Combination Movement
List-II
(i) Residual Income
(ii) Amalgamation
(iii) Current A/c
(iv) Advertisement for a new product

Codes:	**A**	**B**	**C**	**D**
(a)	(iv)	(iii)	(i)	(ii)
(b)	(iii)	(iv)	(i)	(ii)
(c)	(iii)	(iv)	(ii)	(i)
(d)	(iii)	(i)	(iv)	(ii)

37. Match the following
List I
(A) Average Total Cost
(B) Average fixed Cost
(C) Average Variable Cost
(D) Marginal Cost
List II
(i) Variable Cost ÷ Quantity of Output
(ii) Total Cost ÷ Quantity of Output
(iii) Fixed Cost ÷ Quantity of Output
(iv) The increase in total cost that arises from extra unit of production

Codes:	**A**	**B**	**C**	**D**
(a)	(iii)	(i)	(ii)	(iv)
(b)	(i)	(ii)	(iii)	(iv)
(c)	(ii)	(iii)	(i)	(iv)
(d)	(iii)	(iv)	(ii)	(i)

38. Match the following
List I
(a) Variable (b) Discretevariable
(c) Continuous Variable (d) Sample
List-II
(i) A quantitative characteristic of an elementary unit measured on at least an interval scale and has value with in fixed finite interval
(ii) Any portion drawn from a population

(iii) A quantitative characteristic of an elementary unit that may vary from unit to unit
(iv) A variable whose values are restricted to integer values only

Codes:	A	B	C	D
(a)	(i)	(ii)	(iii)	(iv)
(b)	(iv)	(iii)	(ii)	(i)
(c)	(i)	(iii)	(iv)	(ii)
(d)	(iii)	(iv)	(i)	(ii)

39. Match the following List I with List II

List I

(A) Schneidher, Arnold E. (B) Koehter J.W.
(C) Bassett, Glenn A. (D) Berlo David K.

List II

(i) Organisational Communication
(ii) Organisational Communication Behavioural Perspective
(iii) The New Face of Communication
(iv) The Process of Communication

Codes:	A	B	C	D
(a)	(i)	(ii)	(iii)	(iv)
(b)	(i)	(iii)	(ii)	(iv)
(c)	(iv)	(iii)	(i)	(ii)
(d)	(ii)	(iii)	(i)	(iv)

40. Match the following List I with List II

List I

(A) Purchase (B) Situational
(C) Personal (D) Physical

List II

(i) Purchasing Criteria (ii) New Markets
(iii) Risk Factor (iv) Location

Codes:	A	B	C	D
(a)	(i)	(ii)	(iii)	(iv)
(b)	(ii)	(iii)	(i)	(iv)
(c)	(iii)	(i)	(ii)	(iv)
(d)	(iv)	(ii)	(iii)	(i)

41. Match the following

List I

(A) ARR (B) Pay-back method
(C) NPV (D) IRR

List II

(i) Present value of cash inflow – Present value of cash outflow
(ii) Yield on investment
(iii) Average Income / Average Investment
(iv) Investment / Annual Cash Flow

Codes:	A	B	C	D
(a)	(iii)	(iv)	(ii)	(i)
(b)	(iii)	(iv)	(i)	(ii)
(c)	(iv)	(iii)	(ii)	(i)
(d)	(iv)	(iii)	(i)	(ii)

42. Match the following

List I

(A) Personality Test (B) Achievement Test
(C) Aptitude Test (D) Situational Test

List II

(i) Skill test (ii) Job knowledge test
(iii) Group discussion (iv) Projective test

Codes:	A	B	C	D
(a)	(iv)	(ii)	(i)	(iii)
(b)	(iv)	(ii)	(iii)	(i)
(c)	(ii)	(iv)	(i)	(iii)
(d)	(i)	(iii)	(iv)	(ii)

43. Match the following

List I (Financial Institutions)

(A) ECGC (B) GIC
(C) HUDCO (D) ICICI Bank

List II (Nature of Activity)

(i) Re-insurance (ii) Housing development
(iii) A private bank (iv) Trade

Codes:	A	B	C	D
(a)	(iv)	(i)	(iii)	(ii)
(b)	(iv)	(ii)	(i)	(iii)
(c)	(i)	(iv)	(ii)	(iii)
(d)	(iv)	(i)	(ii)	(iii)

44. Match the following

List I

(A) IBRD (B) WTO (C) ADB (D) IDA

List II

(i) Uruguay Round
(ii) ECAFE
(iii) Bretton Wood
(iv) Established by World Bank

Codes:	A	B	C	D
(a)	(iii)	(i)	(ii)	(iv)
(b)	(iii)	(i)	(iv)	(ii)
(c)	(i)	(iii)	(ii)	(iv)
(d)	(i)	(ii)	(iii)	(iv)

Directions: (Q. 45 to 50): Read the following passage and answer the questions.

AGRICULTURAL INSURANCE SCHEME

More than half a dozen farm insurance schemes have been tried out in the past two and a half decades, but no one has worked. Successive insurance models proved unsustainable because they were neither economically viable, nor suited to cover the varied risks that beset crop farming. The implementing insurance companies have invariably ended up paying compensation several times the premium collected. The existing National Agricultural Insurance Scheme (NAIS), which is now sought to be replaced with its fresh avatar, has had to cope with claims of over ₹ 5,730 crore, more than three times the premium income of ₹ 1,700 crore. The parallel farm "income insurance" scheme, aimed at covering risks ranging from a drop in yield to poor prices, tried out on a pilot basis in the last few crop seasons, has also not worked.

What needs to be realised is that agricultural insurance is an inherently complicated business because of the many risks involved in farming. The formidable functional and practical problems that ensue relate to the extent of area that should constitute the unit for assessing damage, and the benchmark for assessing the loss incurred, on the basis of the income that might have accrued to the farmer in the absence of yield-reducing factors like adverse weather, pest, disease, or natural disasters.

45. Which scheme is going to be replaced by the new insurance scheme?
(a) Crop insurance scheme
(b) Agricultural insurance scheme
(c) NAIS
(d) None of the above

46. How many times of the premium income was paid as insurance claims by the existing NAIS Scheme?
(a) 1 (b) 2 (c) 3 (d) 4

47. Farm Income Insurance Scheme is aimed at covering the risk of
(a) Natural Calamities
(b) Drop in yield and poor prices
(c) Seed failure
(d) None of the above

48. Which of the following factor(s) is/are a yield reducing factor?
(a) Adverse weather (b) Natural disaster
(c) Pest and disease (d) All of the above

49. Why the Farm Insurance Schemes are unsustainable?
(a) Not covering the varied risks
(b) Farmers not paying premium
(c) No support from government
(d) None of the above

50. Which of the following is the criteria for bench marking the Agricultural Insurance Scheme?
(a) Area (b) Output
(c) Yield per acre (d) Normal Income

ANSWERS

1. (b)	2. (a)	3. (d)	4. (c)	5. (b)
6. (c)	7. (c)	8. (b)	9. (c)	10. (b)
11. (c)	12. (d)	13. (d)	14. (c)	15. (b)
16. (c)	17. (c)	18. (d)	19. (d)	20. (c)
21. (a)	22. (a)	23. (d)	24. (c)	25. (a)
26. (d)	27. (d)	28. (a)	29. (d)	30. (d)
31. (c)	32. (b)	33. (a)	34. (a)	35. (a)
36. (b)	37. (c)	38. (d)	39. (a)	40. (a)
41. (b)	42. (a)	43. (d)	44. (a)	45. (c)
46. (c)	47. (b)	48. (d)	49. (a)	50. (d)

DECEMBER–2006

Note: This paper contains Fifty (50) multiple choice questions, each question carrying two (2) marks. Attempt all of them.

PAPER–II

1. What is the target of GDP growth rate envisaged in the 10th Five year plan?
   (a) 10% (b) 9% (c) 8% (d) 11%
2. Kyoto Protocol is relating to:
   (a) Competition
   (b) Consumer Protection
   (c) Environment Protection
   (d) Atomic Energy generation
3. Which of the following should be achieved by a business firm at the earliest?
   (a) Budgeted sales (b) Break-even point
   (c) ROI (d) Market share
4. What does the lower Debtor-Turnover Ratio indicate?
   (a) Quick recovery (b) Delay in recovery
   (c) High debtors (d) None of the above
5. Price discrimination policy helps in increasing profits in case of:
   (a) Perfect competition
   (b) Monopolistic competition
   (c) Monopoly
   (d) Oligopoly
6. The nature of Cross-price elasticity of demand in case of complementary products will be:
   (a) Positive (b) Negative
   (c) (a) and (b) both (d) Zero
7. Depiction of relationship present between two variables is called:
   (a) Correlation (b) Regression
   (c) Dispersion (d) Location
8. RAM stands for:
   (a) Random Access Memory
   (b) Readable Access Memory
   (c) Read A Machine
   (d) Read A memory
9. According to David C. McClelland, an individual's major motive to work include the need for:
   (a) Achievement (b) Affiliation
   (c) Power (d) All of the above
10. In the line and staff form, the function of staff is to:
    (a) Obey the line (b) Serve the line
    (c) Inform the line (d) Advise the line
11. Branding decisions are based on:
    (a) Market Research
    (b) Assessment of customer needs
    (c) Cost of the product
    (d) (a) and (b) above
12. Which element of the promotion mix do wholesellers primarily rely on to achieve their promotional objectives?
    (a) Advertising (b) Trade Promotion
    (c) Personal Selling (d) Direct marketing
13. What are the considerations in designing capital structure of a corporate?
    (a) Trading on Equity (b) Cost of Capital
    (c) Profitability (d) All of the above
14. Which of the following methods of inventory valuation results in lower valuation of inventory and low income when inflation is on the rise?
    (a) LIFO
    (b) FIFO
    (c) Simple average method
    (d) Weighted average method
15. HRM is concerned with:
    (a) Workers (b) Managers
    (c) Field staff (d) All employees
16. The sum total of emotional and informational behaviour is called:
    (a) Motivation (b) Talent
    (c) Intuition (d) Attitude

17. NABARD has been established on the recommendation of:
(a) Talwar Committee
(b) Tandon Committee
(c) CRAFI CARD
(d) A. Shivaraman Committee

18. Reserve Bank of India is:
(a) an extension wing of Ministry of Finance, Government of India.
(b) a body Corporate, having perpetual succession and a Common Seal.
(c) an institution owned by Indian Banks Association.
(d) a Private Sector Company.

19. A Derivative is a:
(a) Derived asset
(b) Derived financial asset
(c) Derived from net assets
(d) None of the above

20. Intellectual Property Rights are pertaining to:
(a) Medicines already patented
(b) Matters published on or before 1990
(c) Import of goods and services
(d) None of the above

21. Which one of the following pairs is not correctly matched?
(a) Capital Expenditure: Transportation costs of a machine
(b) Funds Flow Statement: Working Capital
(c) Reduction of Share Capital: Reconstruction
(d) Contribution: Sales – Cost

22. Consumer attains equilibrium when he maximises his utility, given his income and market prices of two products of:
(I) Marginal rate of substitution be equal to the ratio of commodity prices i.e.
$MRS_{xy} = MU_x / MU_y = P_x / P_y$
(II) Indifference curve is convex to the origin.
(a) Only (I) is true
(b) Both (I) and (II) are true
(c) Only (II) is true
(d) Neither (I) nor (II) is true

23. **Assertion (A):** Chi-Square test is used to measure the Association between two attributes.

Reason (R): We apply non-parametric tests like Chi-Square test for data measured on week scale like Nominal Scale or Ordinal Scale.
(a) (A) is true but (R) is wrong
(b) (A) is wrong but (R) is true
(c) Both (A) and (R) are wrong
(d) Both (A) and (R) are true

24. **Assertion (A):** A manager delegates authority.

Reasoning (R): Manager wants to shrink his responsibility.
(a) Both assertion and reasoning are correct.
(b) Assertion is wrong but reasoning is correct.
(c) Assertion is correct but reasoning is wrong.
(d) Both assertion and reasoning are wrong.

25. Arrange the following concepts/acts in the order in which they came into force:
(i) Competition Act.
(ii) Foreign Exchange Management Act.
(iii) Consumer Protection Act.
(iv) Securities and Exchange Board of India Act.

Codes:

(a)	(iii)	(iv)	(ii)	(i)
(b)	(iv)	(iii)	(i)	(ii)
(c)	(i)	(ii)	(iv)	(iii)
(d)	(ii)	(i)	(iii)	(iv)

26. How are the following items arranged in the liability side of the Balance Sheet of a Company?
(i) Current Liability and Provisions
(ii) Secured Loans
(iii) Share Capital
(iv) Unsecured Loans
(v) Reserve and Surplus

Codes:

(a)	(i)	(ii)	(iii)	(iv)	(iv)
(b)	(iii)	(i)	(ii)	(iv)	(v)
(c)	(iii)	(v)	(ii)	(iv)	(i)
(d)	(iii)	(v)	(ii)	(i)	(iv)

27. Elasticity is commonly stated in the form of:
(a) 1% change (b) 5% change
(c) 5 % (d) All of these

28. Which test we normally apply for Qualitative data?
(a) 't' test (b) 'F' test
(c) χ^2 chi-square test (d) 'z' test

29. Consider the following steps of process of decision-making and select the correct sequence:
(i) Defining the problem.
(ii) Selection of best alternatives and implementation.
(iii) Considering limiting factors.
(iv) Considering alternatives.

Codes:

(a)	(i)	(ii)	(iii)	(iv)
(b)	(iii)	(i)	(iv)	(ii)
(c)	(i)	(iv)	(iii)	(ii)
(d)	(i)	(iii)	(iv)	(ii)

30. A marketing concern generally taps sources for financing its activities from:
(a) Owned Capital (b) Bank Credit
(c) Trade Credit (d) All of the above

31. Consider the following steps in the process of Capital Budgeting:
(i) Identification of investment proposals.
(ii) Fixing priorities.
(iii) Evaluation of various proposals.
(iv) Selection and preparation of Capital Budgets.
(v) Implementation.
(vi) Performance Review.

Which of the sequence is correct?

(a)	(i)	(ii)	(iii)	(iv)	(v)	(vi)
(b)	(ii)	(i)	(iii)	(iv)	(v)	(vi)
(c)	(i)	(iii)	(ii)	(iv)	(v)	(vi)
(d)	(i)	(iv)	(iii)	(ii)	(v)	(vi)

32. Arrange the following in the order in which they are practised:
(i) Promotion
(ii) Performance appraisal
(iii) Recruitment
(iv) Training and Development

(a)	(iii)	(ii)	(iv)	(i)
(b)	(iii)	(ii)	(i)	(iv)
(c)	(iii)	(i)	(iv)	(ii)
(d)	(iii)	(iv)	(ii)	(i)

33. E-banking is synonymous with:
(a) Tele Banking (b) Internet Banking
(c) Euro Banking (d) None of the above

34. Arrange the following in the order of their inception:
(i) WTO (ii) World Bank
(iii) SAFTA (iv) ADB

Codes:

(a)	(ii)	(iv)	(i)	(iii)
(b)	(iii)	(i)	(iv)	(ii)
(c)	(iv)	(iii)	(ii)	(i)
(d)	(i)	(iv)	(iii)	(ii)

35. Match the following:

List I	**List II**
A. Capital Market	(i) IRDA
B. Monetary Policy	(ii) SEBI
C. Telecom	(iii) RBI
D. Insurance	(iv) TRAI

Codes:	**A**	**B**	**C**	**D**
(a)	(ii)	(iii)	(i)	(iv)
(b)	(ii)	(iii)	(iv)	(i)
(c)	(ii)	(iv)	(iii)	(i)
(d)	(ii)	(i)	(iv)	(iii)

36. Match the following:

List I
A. Matching Principle
B. Materiality Principle
C. Conservatism Principle
D. Cost Principle

List II
(i) Ignores future profit estimations
(ii) Normal basis for valuing assets
(iii) Revenues and expenses of a particular period
(iv) Relates to relative size or importance of item or event

Codes:	**A**	**B**	**C**	**D**
(a)	(i)	(iv)	(ii)	(iii)
(b)	(ii)	(iii)	(iv)	(i)
(c)	(iii)	(iv)	(i)	(ii)
(d)	(iv)	(iii)	(ii)	(i)

37. Match the following:

Group I (Products)
(A) Food Grain (B) Air Lines
(C) Railway (D) Cars

Group II (Market Structure)
(i) Monopoly (ii) Pure Competition
(iii) Monopolistic (iv) Oligopoly

Codes:	**A**	**B**	**C**	**D**
(a)	(i)	(ii)	(iii)	(iv)
(b)	(ii)	(iv)	(i)	(iii)
(c)	(iii)	(i)	(iv)	(ii)
(d)	(iv)	(ii)	(iii)	(i)

38. Match the following:

Group I
(A) Simple Random Sampling
(B) Stratified Random Sampling
(C) Cluster Sampling
(D) Systematic Sampling

Group II
(i) Hetrogenous
(ii) Homogenous
(iii) Chronological list of units
(iv) Forest Tree type units

Codes:	A	B	C	D
(a)	(i)	(ii)	(iii)	(iv)
(b)	(iii)	(i)	(iv)	(ii)
(c)	(ii)	(i)	(iv)	(iii)
(d)	(iv)	(iii)	(ii)	(i)

39. Match List-I with List-II and select the correct answer using the codes given below the lists:

List-I (Propounder's Name)
(A) Maslow (B) Herzberg
(C) L.G. Urwick (D) McGregor

List-II (Theories)
(i) Hygene Theory (ii) X and Y Theories
(iii) Need Hierarchy (iv) Z Theory

Codes:	A	B	C	D
(a)	(i)	(ii)	(iii)	(iv)
(b)	(ii)	(i)	(iv)	(iii)
(c)	(iv)	(iii)	(ii)	(i)
(d)	(iii)	(i)	(iv)	(ii)

40. Match the following:

Part A (Market Segmentation)
(A) Psychographic (B) Demographic
(C) Behavioural (D) Geographical

Part B (Factors of Segmentation)
(i) Personality groups (ii) Occupation
(iii) Brand Loyalty (iv) Population Size

Codes:	A	B	C	D
(a)	(i)	(ii)	(iv)	(iii)
(b)	(ii)	(i)	(iii)	(iv)
(c)	(i)	(ii)	(iii)	(iv)
(d)	(ii)	(i)	(iv)	(iii)

41. Match the following:

Part I
(A) Total Debt Ratio
(B) Debt Equity Ratio
(C) Total Capital Equity Ratio
(D) Interest Coverage Ratio

Part II
(i) Total Debt / Capital Employed
(ii) Total Debt / Net Worth
(iii) Capital Employed / Net Worth
(iv) EBIT / Interest

Codes:	A	B	C	D
(a)	(i)	(ii)	(iii)	(iv)
(b)	(ii)	(i)	(iii)	(iv)
(c)	(i)	(ii)	(iv)	(iii)
(d)	(ii)	(iv)	(iii)	(i)

42. Match Items from List I with the Items in List II:

List I
(A) Psychoanalytical Theory
(B) Scientific Management Approach
(C) Subsystems of HRM
(D) Basic elements of a job

List II
(i) Strong inter linkages (ii) Personality
(iii) Task (iv) F.W. Taylor

Codes:	A	B	C	D
(a)	(ii)	(iv)	(i)	(iii)
(b)	(ii)	(iii)	(i)	(iv)
(c)	(i)	(iii)	(ii)	(iv)
(d)	(ii)	(iv)	(iii)	(i)

43. Match the following:

List I (Name of the Bank)
(A) SBI (B) SIDBI
(C) NABARD (D) EXIM BANK

List II (Year of Establishment)
(i) 1990 (ii) 1955 (iii) 1981 (iv) 1982

Codes:	A	B	C	D
(a)	(ii)	(i)	(iii)	(iv)
(b)	(i)	(ii)	(iv)	(iii)
(c)	(ii)	(iii)	(iv)	(i)
(d)	(ii)	(i)	(iv)	(iii)

44. Match the following:

List I (Export Processing Zones)
(A) Uttar Pradesh (B) Tamil Nadu
(C) West Bengal (D) Andhra Pradesh

List II (Location in City)
(i) Noida (ii) Chennai
(iii) Falta (iv) Visakhapatnam

Codes:	A	B	C	D
(a)	(iii)	(ii)	(iv)	(i)
(b)	(ii)	(i)	(iii)	(iv)
(c)	(i)	(ii)	(iii)	(iv)
(d)	(i)	(ii)	(iv)	(iii)

Read the following passage and answer the questions from 45 to 50.

"Full Convertibility"

The Prime Minister feels that the rupee's full Convertibility is an idea whose time has come, and since these things are unstoppable, we might as well prepare a road map for it. This is salutary. Of course, a road map to Convertibility is quite different from Convertibility itself. A committee headed by Dr. C. Rangarajan had prepared one such road map in 1997. The road map lost its way, thanks to the Asian financial crisis that soon broke out. As India successfully warded off the contagion, policymakers thanked the absence of full convertibility. Things have changed significantly since then. It's not just that our forex reserves have ballooned to a size that should reassure the most worry-prone of central bankers on the count of perceived adequacy. India is now recognized by the world as an economy that will sustain high growth. The combined fiscal deficit of the Centre and the States is on the way down, along a path marked by milestones of deficit reduction mandated by law. This grants the central bank the flexibility it needs in monetary policy in a regime of uncontrolled cross-border capital movements. Import duties have come down significantly, forcing companies to acquire genuine international competitiveness, and domestic tax reform lends a hand to the process. The rupee's movement against major currencies is no longer steadfastly downwards. A couple of scams and their backlash have greatly enhanced the quality of capital market regulation. All these favour Convertibility. But that is not enough. Since one economic agent's external exposure impacts another's, the system must allow the consequences of such exposure to work its way through, fast. Financial reporting must improve, the market for corporate control must work and redeployment of the assets of failed firms via liquidation must happen fast. Reconstructing bad assets cannot remain shuffling paper from one agency to another. The RBI needn't twiddle its thumbs while these needed changes get instituted. Preparing for the prospect of any Tom, Dick or Hari buying stocks on NSE means shedding its allergy to FII sub-accounts right now.

45. Why was the road map to Convertibility lost its way?
    (a) Low foreign exchange reserve
    (b) Ineffective regulatory framework
    (c) High fiscal deficit
    (d) Asian Financial Crisis

46. Which of the following factors contribute to full Convertibility?
    (a) Economy is prepared to sustain high growth.
    (b) Tax reforms and low fiscal deficit.
    (c) Good Forex reserves and an efficient Central Bank.
    (d) All of the above.

47. What we need for full Convertibility?
    (a) Political will
    (b) A Committee of Experts
    (c) More Institutional Strength
    (d) Financial reforms

48. "Financial Reporting must improve". It refers to:
    (a) Indian Economy (b) RBI
    (c) FII (d) Companies

49. Selling of doubtful debts to a third party for collection of the debts is called:
    (a) Factoring Service (b) NPA Service
    (c) FII Service (d) Restructuring Service

50. Which of the following factors has enhanced the quality of SEBI regulations?
    (a) Financial Sector Reforms
    (b) Tax Reforms
    (c) Capital Market Scams
    (d) Increasing Foreign Exchange Reserve

ANSWERS

1. (c)	2. (c)	3. (b)	4. (b)	5. (c)
6. (b)	7. (a)	8. (a)	9. (d)	10. (d)
11. (d)	12. (a)	13. (d)	14. (b)	15. (d)
16. (d)	17. (d)	18. (b)	19. (a)	20. (d)
21. (d)	22. (b)	23. (d)	24. (c)	25. (a)
26. (c)	27. (c)	28. (c)	29. (c)	30. (d)
31. (c)	32. (d)	33. (b)	34. (a)	35. (b)
36. (c)	37. (b)	38. (c)	39. (d)	40. (c)
41. (a)	42. (a)	43. (d)	44. (c)	45. (d)
46. (d)	47. (d)	48. (a)	49. (d)	50. (c)

JUNE–2007

Note: This paper contains Fifty (50) multiple choice questions, each question carrying two (2) marks. Attempt all of them.

PAPER–I

1. Teacher uses visual-aids to make learning
   (a) simple (b) more knowledgeable
   (c) quicker (d) interesting
2. The teacher's role at the higher educational level is to
   (a) provide information to students
   (b) promote self-learning in students
   (c) encourage healthy competition among students
   (d) help students to solve their personal problems
3. Which one of the following teachers would you like the most?
   (a) Punctual
   (b) Having research aptitude
   (c) Loving and having high idealistic philosophy
   (d) Who often amuses his students
4. Micro teaching is most effective for the student-teacher
   (a) during the practice-teaching
   (b) after the practice-teaching
   (c) before the practice-teaching
   (d) None of the above
5. Which is the least important factor in teaching?
   (a) Punishing the students
   (b) Maintaining discipline in the class
   (c) Lecturing in impressive way
   (d) Drawing sketches and diagrams on the blackboard
6. To test null hypothesis, a researcher uses
   (a) t test (b) ANOVA
   (c) χ^2 (d) factorial analysis
7. A research problem is feasible only when
   (a) it has utility and relevance
   (b) it is researchable
   (c) it is new and adds something to knowledge
   (d) All of the above
8. Bibliography given in a research report
   (a) shows vast knowledge of the researcher
   (b) helps those interested in further research
   (c) has no relevance to research
   (d) All of the above
9. Fundamental research reflects the ability to
   (a) Synthesise new ideals
   (b) Expound new principles
   (c) Evaluate the existing material concerning research
   (d) Study the existing literature regarding various topics
10. The study in which the investigators attempt to trace an effect is known as
    (a) Survey Research
    (b) *Ex-post Facto* Research
    (c) Historical Research
    (d) Summative Research

Read the following passage and answer the questions 11 to 15:

All political systems need to mediate the relationship between private wealth and public power. Those that fail risk a dysfunctional government captured by wealthy interests. Corruption is one symptom of such failure with private willingness-to-pay trumping public goals. Private individuals and business firms pay to get routine services and to get to the head of the bureaucratic queue. They pay to limit their taxes, avoid costly regulations, obtain contracts at inflated prices and get concessions and privatised firms at low prices. If corruption is endemic, public officials—both bureaucrats and elected officials—may redesign programs and propose public projects with few public benefits and many opportunities for private profit. Of course, corruption, in the sense of bribes, pay-offs and kickbacks, is only one type of government failure. Efforts to promote "good governance" must be broader than anti-corruption campaigns. Governments may be honest but inefficient because no one has an incentive to work productively, and narrow elites may capture the state and exert excess influence on policy. Bribery may induce the lazy to work hard and permit those not in the inner circle of cronies to obtain benefits. However, even in such cases, corruption cannot be confined to 'functional' areas. It will be a temptation whenever private benefits are positive. It may be a reasonable response to a harsh reality but, over time, it can facilitate a spiral into an even worse situation.

11. The governments which fail to focus on the relationship between private wealth and public power are likely to become
    (a) Functional (b) Dysfunctional
    (c) Normal functioning (d) Good governance
12. One important symptom of bad governance is
    (a) Corruption
    (b) High taxes
    (c) Complicated rules and regulations
    (d) High prices
13. When corruption is rampant, public officials always aim at many opportunities for
    (a) Public benefits (b) Public profit
    (c) Private profit (d) Corporate gains
14. Productivity linked incentives to public/private officials is one of the indicatives for
    (a) Efficient government
    (b) Bad governance
    (c) Inefficient government
    (d) Corruption
15. The spiralling corruption can only be contained by promoting
    (a) Private profit
    (b) Anti-corruption campaign
    (c) Good governance
    (d) Pay-offs and kickbacks
16. Press Council of India is located at
    (a) Chennai (b) Mumbai
    (c) Kolkata (d) Delhi
17. Adjusting the photo for publication by cutting is technically known as
    (a) Photo cutting (b) Photo bleeding
    (c) Photo cropping (d) Photo adjustment
18. Feedback of a message comes from
    (a) Satellite (b) Media
    (c) Audience (d) Communicator
19. Collection of information in advance before designing communication strategy is known as
    (a) Feedback (b) Feed-forward
    (c) Research study (d) Opinion poll
20. The aspect ratio of TV screen is
    (a) 4:3 (b) 4:2 (c) 3:5 (d) 2:3
21. Which is the number that comes next in the sequence?
    9, 8, 8, 8, 7, 8, 6, __
    (a) 5 (b) 6 (c) 8 (d) 4
22. If in a certain language PUNCTUAL is coded as 16598623, how would ACTUPULN be coded?
    (a) 83453612 (b) 29861635
    (c) 83453961 (d) 83453918
23. The question to be answered by factorial analysis of the quantitative data does not explain one of the following.
    (a) Is 'X' related to 'Y'?
    (b) How is 'X' related to 'Y'?
    (c) How does 'X' affect the dependent variable 'Y' at different levels of another independent variable 'K' or 'M'?
    (d) How is 'X' by 'K' related to 'M'?
24. January 12, 1980 was Saturday, what day was January 12, 1979?
    (a) Saturday (b) Friday
    (c) Sunday (d) Thursday
25. How many Mondays are there in a particular month of a particular year, if the month ends on Wednesday?
    (a) 5 (b) 4
    (c) 3 (d) None of these
26. From the given four statements, select the two which cannot be true but yet both can be false. Choose the right pair.

1. All men are mortal
2. Some men are mortal
3. No man is mortal
4. Some men are not mortal

(a) 1 and 2 (b) 3 and 4
(c) 1 and 3 (d) 2 and 4

27. A Syllogism must have
(a) Three terms (b) Four terms
(c) Six terms (d) Five terms

28. Copula is that part of proposition which denotes the relationship between
(a) Subject and predicate
(b) Known and unknown
(c) Major premise and minor premise
(d) Subject and object

29. "E" denotes
(a) Universal Negative Proposition
(b) Particular Affirmative Proposition
(c) Universal Affirmative Proposition
(d) Particular Negative Proposition

30. 'A' is the father of 'C' and 'D' is the son of 'B'. 'E' is the brother of 'A'. If 'C' is the sister of 'D' how is 'B' related to 'E'?
(a) Daughter (b) Husband
(c) Sister-in-law (d) Brother-in-law

31. Which of the following methods will you choose to prepare choropleth map of India showing urban density of population?
(a) Quartiles (b) Quintiles
(c) Mean and SD (d) Break-point

32. Which of the following methods is best suited to show on a map the types of crops being grown in a region?
(a) Choropleth (b) Chorochromatic
(c) Choroschematic (d) Isopleth

33. A ratio represents the relation between
(a) Part and Part (b) Part and Whole
(c) Whole and Whole (d) All of the above

34. Out of four numbers, the average of the first three numbers is thrice the fourth number. If the average of the four numbers is 5, the fourth number is
(a) 4.5 (b) 5 (c) 2 (d) 4

35. Circle graphs are used to show
(a) How various sections share in the whole
(b) How various parts are related to the whole
(c) How one whole is related to other wholes
(d) How one part is related to other parts

36. On the keyboard of computer each character has an "ASCII" value which stands for
(a) American Stock Code for Information Interchange
(b) American Standard Code for Information Interchange
(c) African Standard Code for Information Interchange
(d) Adaptable Standard Code for Information Change

37. Which part of the Central Processing Unit (CPU) performs calculation and makes decisions?
(a) Arithmetic Logic Unit
(b) Alternating Logic Unit
(c) Alternate Local Unit
(d) American Logic Unit

38. "Dpi" stands for
(a) Dots per inch (b) Digits per unit
(c) Dots pixel inch (d) Diagrams per inch

39. The process of laying out a document with text, graphics, headlines and photographs is involved in
(a) Deck Top Publishing
(b) Desk Top Printing
(c) Desk Top Publishing
(d) Deck Top Printing

40. Transfer of data from one application to another line is known as
(a) Dynamic Disk Exchange
(b) Dodgy Data Exchange
(c) Dogmatic Data Exchange
(d) Dynamic Data Exchange

41. Tsunami occurs due to
(a) Mild earthquakes and landslides in the oceans
(b) Strong earthquakes and landslides in the oceans
(c) Strong earthquakes and landslides in mountains
(d) Strong earthquakes and landslides in deserts

42. Which of the natural hazards have big effect on Indian people each year?
(a) Cyclones (b) Floods
(c) Earthquakes (d) Landslides

43. Comparative Environment Impact Assessment study is to be conducted for
(a) the whole year
(b) three seasons excluding monsoon
(c) any three seasons
(d) the worst season

44. Sea level rise results primarily due to
(a) Heavy rainfall
(b) Melting of glaciers
(c) Submarine volcanism
(d) Seafloor spreading

45. The plume rise in a coal based power plant depends on
1. Buoyancy
2. Atmospheric stability
3. Momentum of exhaust gases identify

Codes:
(a) Both (1) and (2) (b) Both (2) and (3)
(c) Both (1) and (3) (d) (1), (2) and (3)

46. Value education makes a student
(a) Good citizen
(b) Successful businessman
(c) Popular teacher
(d) Efficient manager

47. Networking of libraries through electronic media is known as
(a) Inflibnet (b) Libinfnet
(c) Internet (d) HTML

48. The university which telecasts interactive educational programs through its own channel is
(a) B.R. Ambedkar Open University, Hyderabad
(b) I.G.N.O.U.
(c) University of Pune
(d) Annamalai University

49. The government established the University Grants Commission by an Act of Parliament in the year
(a) 1980 (b) 1948 (c) 1950 (d) 1956

50. Universities having central campus for imparting education are called
(a) Central Universities
(b) Deemed Universities
(c) Residential Universities
(d) Open Universities

ANSWERS

1. (d)	2. (a)	3. (a)	4. (b)	5. (a)
6. (c)	7. (d)	8. (b)	9. (b)	10. (b)
11. (b)	12. (a)	13. (c)	14. (a)	15. (c)
16. (d)	17. (c)	18. (c)	19. (d)	20. (a)
21. (c)	22. (b)	23. (c)	24. (b)	25. (d)
26. (b)	27. (a)	28. (b)	29. (a)	30. (d)
31. (b)	32. (c)	33. (b)	34. (c)	35. (a)
36. (a)	37. (a)	38. (a)	39. (c)	40. (d)
41. (b)	42. (b)	43. (a)	44. (b)	45. (d)
46. (a)	47. (a)	48. (b)	49. (d)	50. (b)

PAPER–II

Note: This paper contains fifty (50) objective type questions, each question carrying two (2) marks. All questions are compulsory.

1. Small and Medium Enterprise is one which has investment in plant and machinery not exceeding:
(a) ₹ 10 crore (b) ₹ 1 crore
(c) ₹ 50 lakhs (d) ₹ 5 crore

2. FEMA signifies:
(a) Free Export Management Act
(b) Foreign Exchange Management Act
(c) Foreign Exchange Monitoring Act
(d) Free Export Marketing Act

3. Planning commission proposed to target _____ percent yearly growth rate during the 11th Five-year Plan.
(a) 8 percent (b) 9 percent
(c) 10 percent (d) 8.5 percent

4. The market for long-term loanable funds is a:
(a) Money Market (b) Capital Market
(c) Bond Market (d) None of the above

5. The pre-liberalisation era of Indian economy was under the grip of:
(a) Unemployment
(b) Under-employment
(c) Fiscal Deficit
(d) Unfavourable and alarming balance of payments

6. Insurance expense paid to bring the machine from the place of purchase to the place of installation is:
(a) Capital Expenditure
(b) Revenue Expenditure
(c) Deferred Revenue Expenditure
(d) None of the above

7. Which financial statement can be compared with a still photograph?
(a) Income statement
(b) Balance sheet
(c) Cash Flow statement
(d) Funds Flow statement

8. The working capital ratio is:
(a) Working Capital / Sales
(b) Working Capital / Total Assets
(c) Current Assets / Sales
(d) Current Assets / Current Liabilities

9. An investment centre can be evaluated by:
(a) Profit (b) Return on sales
(c) ROI (d) None of the above

10. Which cost is taken into consideration for 'make or buy' decisions?
(a) Prime cost (b) Total cost
(c) Cost of production (d) Relevant cost

11. Which of the following is not the feature of monopolistic competition?
(a) Fairly large number of firms
(b) Co-existence of efficient and inefficient firms
(c) Product homogeneity
(d) Independent price-output policy

12. Which of the following is not a condition for successful price-discrimination?
(a) Different elasticity of demand for different consumers
(b) Seller should be an MNC
(c) Location of markets at distant places
(d) Consumers ignorance and prejudices

13. Which of the following does not influence the individual demand for a product?
(a) Price of product
(b) Price of close substitute
(c) State of production technology
(d) Change in climatic conditions

14. What is the nature of Elasticity of Demand for luxury items like high-class furnitures?
(a) Unit elastic (b) Highly elastic
(c) Fairly elastic (d) Zero elastic

15. The % change in demand for a product A divided by the % change in price of product B indicates the degree of:
(a) Price Elasticity of Demand
(b) Cross Elasticity of Demand
(c) Income Elasticity of Demand
(d) Advertising Elasticity of Demand

16. t-test is a:
(a) Parametric Test
(b) Non-parametric Test
(c) Large sample test
(d) None of the above

17. The casual relationship is indicated by:
(a) Correlation
(b) Regression
(c) Association
(d) None of the above

18. Systematic sampling belongs to:
(a) Quota sampling
(b) Non-probability sampling
(c) Probability sampling
(d) None of the above

19. Match the items:
List I
A. Chi-square test
B. Annual Reports of companies
C. Multi-variate
D. Data processing
List II
(i) Secondary data (ii) Information system
(iii) Hypothesis testing (iv) Factor analysis

Codes:	A	B	C	D
(a)	(iv)	(ii)	(i)	(iii)
(b)	(iii)	(i)	(iv)	(ii)
(c)	(iii)	(iv)	(i)	(ii)
(d)	(iv)	(i)	(iii)	(ii)

20. E-Commerce relates to:
(a) B-to-B (b) C-to-C
(c) B-to-C (d) All of the above

21. Who is the father of principles of management?
(a) Fleming (b) Bavnard
(c) F.W. Taylor (d) Henry Fayol

22. What is M.B.O.?
(a) Management by Organization
(b) Multiple Business Organization

(c) Management by Objectives
(d) Multiplicity of Business Operations

23. The tool adopted to change corporate culture is:
(a) Managerial Grid
(b) Hierarchy
(c) Span of Control
(d) Seven 's' Framework

24. What does Maslow Theory of Motivation convey to management?
(a) Satisfied need is a motivator
(b) Satisfied need is no more a motivator
(c) Needs are not motivators
(d) Needs need not be considered

25. Ethics is derived from:
(a) Bible (b) Bhagavat Gita
(c) Quran (d) All of the above

26. Who propounded 4Ps of marketing?
(a) Philip Kotler
(b) Kelker
(c) McAurthy
(d) Peter F. Drucker

27. What is cognitive dissonance?
(a) Buying Behaviour
(b) Pre-purchase Behaviour
(c) Post-purchase Behaviour
(d) Buying indifference

28. Product(s) which defied PLC concept:
(a) Amrutanjan (b) Horlicks
(c) Hairpins (d) All of the above

29. Skimming price relates to:
(a) Charging competitive price
(b) Charging high initial price
(c) Charging low initial price
(d) None of the above

30. Promotion-mix includes:
(a) Advertising and personal selling
(b) Personal promotion
(c) Product improvement
(d) None of the above

31. Cost of capital does not mean:
(a) Cut-off rate decided by management
(b) Rate of interest
(c) Expectations of investors for dividend
(d) Money paid to SEBI for permission to acquire capital

32. Financial Leverage is intended to:
(a) Increase return on capital employed
(b) Increase net equity return
(c) Decrease volatility in return
(d) Increase return on capital employed and net equity

33. Budget which is directed towards long-term strategic goals is known as:
(a) Zero-based Budget (b) Capital Budget
(c) Rolling Budget (d) Master Budget

34. Which of the following is not very much relevant in dividend decision?
(a) Availability of disposable profit
(b) Investors' expectations for dividend
(c) Capital market conditions
(d) Industry practice

35. Which of the following is not an application of working capital?
(a) Day-to-day expenditure of business
(b) Current obligations for payment
(c) Expenditure in the usual course of business
(d) Expenditure to acquire capital

36. Human Resource Management emphasises:
(a) Development of people
(b) Punishment of people
(c) Adoption of people
(d) None of the above

37. Induction means:
(a) Training (b) Promotion
(c) Incentives (d) Introduction

38. Workers participation in management in any organization is:
(a) Voluntary (b) Institutional
(c) Democratic (d) All of the above

39. Employee morale relates to:
(a) Productivity (b) Attitude
(c) Empathy (d) Skills

40. Glass ceiling relates to:
(a) Ergonomics (b) Gender Bias
(c) Recruitment (d) Promotion

41. Which bank was incorporated as one of the public sector banks in India during 2004-05?
(a) ICICI Bank Ltd. (b) Yes Bank Ltd.
(c) IDBI Bank Ltd. (d) UTI Bank Ltd.

42. The short-term money market comprises:
(a) The call money market
(b) The inter-bank deposit market

(c) The bills re-discounting market
(d) All of the above

43. Annual Report on Currency and Finance is published by:
(a) SIDBI
(b) RBI
(c) Ministry of Finance
(d) None of the above

44. Bank deposit refers to:
(a) The amount of money standing to the credit of a customer of a bank
(b) A term used by the Federal Reserve to refer to the total deposits of member banks
(c) The amount of money standing to the debit of a customer of a bank
(d) All of the above

45. Which of the following is the latest buzzword among bankers?
(a) Social Banking
(b) Financial inclusion
(c) Mass Banking
(d) None of the above

46. The balance of payments account is conventionally divided into:
(a) Current Account and Capital Account
(b) Visible Account and Invisible Account
(c) Long-term Capital Account and Short-term Capital Account
(d) None of the above

47. What is Euro-III?
(a) European Currency
(b) Group of European Countries
(c) European Film Festival
(d) Pollution Control Scale

48. The Comparative Cost Theory of International Trade was developed by:
(a) David Ricardo (b) Haberlar
(c) Adam Smith (d) Alfred Marshal

49. Which institution is known as the 'soft loan window' of World Bank?
(a) IMF (b) IFC
(c) IDA (d) None of the above

50. The 21st member to join the G-20 is:
(a) Sri Lanka (b) Uzbekistan
(c) Myanmar (d) Uruguay

ANSWERS

1. (d)	2. (b)	3. (b)	4. (b)	5. (d)
6. (a)	7. (b)	8. (d)	9. (c)	10. (b)
11. (c)	12. (b)	13. (c)	14. (b)	15. (b)
16. (a)	17. (b)	18. (c)	19. (b)	20. (d)
21. (d)	22. (c)	23. (a)	24. (b)	25. (d)
26. (c)	27. (c)	28. (c)	29. (b)	30. (a)
31. (a)	32. (d)	33. (b)	34. (c)	35. (d)
36. (a)	37. (d)	38. (c)	39. (b)	40. (b)
41. (c)	42. (d)	43. (b)	44. (d)	45. (c)
46. (a)	47. (d)	48. (a)	49. (c)	50. (a)

DECEMBER–2007

Note: This paper contains Fifty (50) multiple choice questions, each question carrying two (2) marks. Attempt all of them.

PAPER–I

1. Verbal guidance is least effective in the learning of
   (a) Aptitudes (b) Skills
   (c) Attitudes (d) Relationship
2. Which is the most important aspect of the teacher's role in learning?
   (a) The development of insight into what constitutes an adequate performance
   (b) The development of insight into what constitutes the pitfalls and dangers to be avoided
   (c) The provision of encouragement and moral support
   (d) The provision of continuous diagnostic and remedial help
3. The most appropriate purpose of learning is
   (a) personal adjustment
   (b) modification of behaviour
   (c) social and political awareness
   (d) preparing oneself for employment
4. The students who keep on asking questions in the class should be
   (a) encouraged to find answer independently
   (b) advised to meet the teacher after the class
   (c) encouraged to continue questioning
   (d) advised not to disturb during the lecture
5. Maximum participation of students is possible in teaching through
   (a) discussion method (b) lecture method
   (c) audio-visual aids (d) textbook method
6. Generalised conclusion on the basis of a sample is technically known as
   (a) Data analysis and interpretation
   (b) Parameter inference
   (c) Statistical inference
   (d) All of the above
7. The experimental study is based on
   (a) The manipulation of variables
   (b) Conceptual parameters
   (c) Replication of research
   (d) Survey of literature
8. The main characteristic of scientific research is
   (a) empirical (b) theoretical
   (c) experimental (d) All of the above
9. Authenticity of a research finding is its
   (a) Originality (b) Validity
   (c) Objectivity (d) All of the above
10. Which technique is generally followed when the population is finite?
   (a) Area Sampling Technique
   (b) Purposive Sampling Technique
   (c) Systematic Sampling Technique
   (d) None of the above

Read the following passage and answer the questions 11 to 15:

Gandhi's overall social and environmental philosophy is based on what human beings need rather than what they want. His early introduction to the teachings of Jains, Theosophists, Christian sermons, Ruskin and Tolstoy, and most significantly the *Bhagavad Gita*, were to have profound impact on the development of Gandhi's holistic thinking on humanity, nature and their ecological interrelation. His deep concern for the disadvantaged, the poor and rural population created an ambience for an alternative social thinking that was at once far-sighted, local and immediate. For Gandhi was acutely aware that the demands generated by the need to feed and sustain human life, compounded by the growing industrialisation of India, far outstripped the finite resources of nature. This might nowadays appear naive or commonplace, but such pronouncements were as rare as they were heretical a century ago. Gandhi was also concerned about the destruction, under colonial and modernist designs, of the existing infrastructures which had more potential for keeping a community flourishing within ecologically-sensitive traditional patterns of subsistence, especially in the rural areas, than did the incoming Western alternatives based on nature-blind technology and the enslavement of human spirit and energies.

Perhaps the moral principle for which Gandhi is best known is that of active non-violence, derived from the traditional moral restraint of not injuring another being. The most refined expression of this value is in the great epic of the *Mahabharata*, (c. 100 BCE to 200 CE), where moral development proceeds through placing constraints on the liberties, desires and acquisitiveness endemic to human life. One's action is judged in terms of consequences and the impact it is likely to have on another. Jainas had generalised this principle to include all sentient creatures and biocommunities alike. Advanced Jaina monks and nuns will sweep their path to avoid harming insects and even bacteria. Non-injury is a non-negotiable universal prescription.

11. Which one of the following have a profound impact on the development of Gandhi's holistic thinking on humanity, nature and their ecological interrelations?
    (a) Jain teachings (b) Christian sermons
    (c) *Bhagavad Gita* (d) Ruskin and Tolstoy
12. Gandhi's overall social and environmental philosophy is based on human beings'
    (a) need (b) desire
    (c) wealth (d) welfare
13. Gandhiji's deep concern for the disadvantaged, the poor and rural population created an ambience for an alternative
    (a) rural policy (b) social thinking
    (c) urban policy (d) economic thinking
14. Colonial policy and modernisation led to the destruction of
    (a) major industrial infrastructure
    (b) irrigation infrastructure
    (c) urban infrastructure
    (d) rural infrastructure
15. Gandhi's active non-violence is derived from
    (a) Moral restraint of not injuring another being
    (b) Having liberties, desires and acquisitiveness
    (c) Freedom of action
    (d) Nature-blind technology and enslavement of human spirit and energies
16. DTH service was started in the year
    (a) 2000 (b) 2002 (c) 2004 (d) 2006
17. National Press day is celebrated on
    (a) 16th November (b) 19th November
    (c) 21st November (d) 30th November
18. The total number of members in the Press Council of India are
    (a) 28 (b) 14 (c) 17 (d) 20
19. The right to impart and receive information is guaranteed in the Constitution of India by Article
    (a) 19(2)(a) (b) 19(16) (c) 19(2) (d) 19(1)(a)
20. Use of radio for higher education is based on the presumption of
    (a) Enriching curriculum based instruction
    (b) Replacing teacher in the long run
    (c) Everybody having access to a radio set
    (d) Other means of instruction getting outdated
21. Find out the number which should come at the place of question mark which will complete the following series.
    5, 4, 9, 17, 35, ? = 139
    (a) 149 (b) 79 (c) 49 (d) 69

Questions 22 to 24 are based on the following diagram in which there are three interlocking circles I, S and P, where circle I stands for Indians, circle S for Scientists and circle P for Politicians. Different regions in the figure are lettered from a to g.

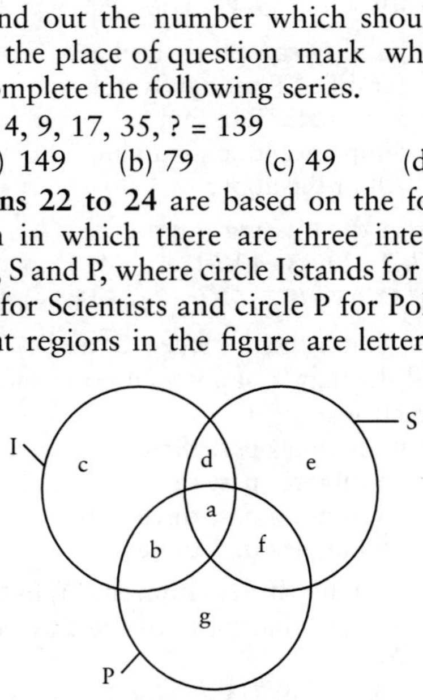

22. The region which represents Non-Indian Scientists who are Politicians.

(a) f (b) d (c) a (d) c

23. The region which represents Indians who are neither Scientists nor Politicians.
(a) g (b) c (c) f (d) a

24. The region which represents Politicians who are Indians as well as Scientists.
(a) b (b) c (c) a (d) d

25. Which number is missing in the following series?
2, 5, 10, 17, 26, 37, 50, ?
(a) 63 (b) 65 (c) 67 (d) 69

26. The function of measurement includes
(a) Prognosis (b) Diagnosis
(c) Prediction (d) All of the above

27. Logical arguments are based on
(a) Scientific reasoning
(b) Customary reasoning
(c) Mathematical reasoning
(d) Syllogistic reasoning

28. Insert the missing number 4 : 17 : : 7 : ?
(a) 48 (b) 49 (c) 50 (d) 51

29. Choose the odd word.
(a) Nun (b) Knight (c) Monk (d) Priest

30. Choose the number which is different from others in the group.
(a) 49 (b) 63 (c) 77 (d) 81

31. Probability sampling implies.
(a) Stratified Random Sampling
(b) Systematic Random Sampling
(c) Simple Random Sampling
(d) All of the above

32. Insert the missing number.
36/62, 39/63, 43/61, 48/64, ?
(a) 51/65 (b) 56/60 (c) 54/65 (d) 33/60

33. At what time between 3 and 4 O'clock will the hands of a watch point in opposite directions?
(a) 40 minutes past three
(b) 45 minutes past three
(c) 50 minutes past three
(d) 55 minutes past three

34. Mary has three children. What is the probability that none of the three children is a boy?
(a) 1/2 (b) 1/3 (c) 3/4 (d) 1

35. If the radius of a circle is increased by 50 percent. Its area is increased by
(a) 125 percent (b) 100 percent
(c) 75 percent (d) 50 percent

36. CD ROM stands for
(a) Computer Disk Read Only Memory
(b) Compact Disk Read Over Memory
(c) Compact Disk Read Only Memory
(d) Computer Disk Read Over Memory

37. The 'brain' of a computer which keeps peripherals under its control is called
(a) Common Power Unit
(b) Common Processing Unit
(c) Central Power Unit
(d) Central Processing Unit

38. Data can be saved on backing storage medium known as
(a) Compact Disk Recordable
(b) Computer Disk Rewritable
(c) Compact Disk Rewritable
(d) Computer Data Rewritable

39. RAM means
(a) Random Access Memory
(b) Rigid Access Memory
(c) Rapid Access Memory
(d) Revolving Access Memory

40. www represents
(a) who what and where
(b) weird wide web
(c) word wide web
(d) world wide web

41. Deforestation during the recent decades has led to
(a) Soil erosion (b) Landslides
(c) Loss of bio-diversity (d) All of the above

42. Which one of the following natural hazards is responsible for causing highest human disaster?
(a) Earthquakes (b) Volcanic eruptions
(c) Snowstorms (d) Tsunami

43. Which one of the following is appropriate for natural hazard mitigation?
(a) International AID
(b) Timely Warning System
(c) Rehabilitation
(d) Community Participation

44. Slums in metro city are the result of
(a) Rural to urban migration
(b) Poverty of the city-scape
(c) Lack of urban infrastructure
(d) Urban-governance

45. The great Indian Bustard bird is found in
(a) Thar Desert of India
(b) Coastal regions of India
(c) Temperate Forests in the Himalaya
(d) Tarai zones of the Himalayan Foot

46. The first Indian Satellite for serving the educational sector is known as
(a) SATEDU (b) INSAT-B
(c) EDUSAT (d) INSAT-C

47. Exclusive educational channel of IGNOU is known as
(a) Gyan Darshan (b) Gyan Vani
(c) Door Darshan (d) Prasar Bharati

48. The headquarter of Mahatma Gandhi Antarrashtriya Hindi Vishwavidyalaya is situated in
(a) Sevagram (b) New Delhi
(c) Wardha (d) Ahmedabad

49. Match List I with List II and select the correct answer using the codes given below.
List I (Institutes)
A. Central Institute of English and Foreign Languages
B. Gramodaya Vishwavidyalaya
C. Central Institute of Higher Tibetan Studies
D. IGNOU
List II (Locations)
1. Chitrakoot 2. Hyderabad
3. New Delhi 4. Dharmasala

Codes:	A	B	C	D
(a)	2	1	4	3
(b)	4	3	2	1
(c)	3	4	1	2
(d)	1	2	4	3

50. The aim of vocationalisation of education is
(a) preparing students for a vocation along with knowledge
(b) converting liberal education into vocational education
(c) giving more importance to vocational than general education
(d) making liberal education job-oriented

ANSWERS

1. (b)	2. (a)	3. (b)	4. (a)	5. (a)
6. (c)	7. (c)	8. (c)	9. (d)	10. (c)
11. (c)	12. (a)	13. (b)	14. (c)	15. (a)
16. (d)	17. (a)	18. (a)	19. (d)	20. (b)
21. (d)	22. (a)	23. (b)	24. (d)	25. (b)
26. (d)	27. (d)	28. (c)	29. (b)	30. (c)
31. (d)	32. (c)	33. (c)	34. (d)	35. (a)
36. (c)	37. (d)	38. (c)	39. (a)	40. (d)
41. (d)	42. (a)	43. (b)	44. (a)	45. (a)
46. (c)	47. (a)	48. (c)	49. (a)	50. (d)

PAPER–II

Note: This paper contains fifty (50) objective type questions, each question carrying two (2) marks. All questions are compulsory.

1. The objective of the 11th Five-year Plan approach paper is to achieve:
(a) Inclusive growth
(b) Inclusive finance
(c) Growth with equity
(d) Social justice

2. The sector owned by State or Central Government is called:
(a) Private sector (b) Public sector
(c) Joint sector (d) Co-operative sector

3. Balanced growth means:
(a) The state of an economy in which there is a constant relationship between the components of aggregate national income.
(b) The effect upon the national income of equal changes in government expenditure and revenue.
(c) A situation in which the government's planned expenditure equals its expected income.
(d) None of the above.

4. The country that is not a developing country but has not yet achieved the status of the advanced country is:
(a) Malaysia (b) South Korea
(c) Singapore (d) None of these

5. The draft Five-year Plan in India is approved by:
   (a) National Development Council
   (b) Planning Commission
   (c) Cabinet Committee
   (d) President of India
6. Which accounting principle differentiates between owners and management?
   (a) Going Concern (b) Dual Aspect
   (c) Separate Entity (d) Conservatism
7. Reducing the capital of a company is called:
   (a) Internal Reconstruction
   (b) External Reconstruction
   (c) Consolidation
   (d) None of these
8. P/V ratio shows:
   (a) Profit and Volume
   (b) Profit Earning Capability
   (c) Safety Margin
   (d) None of the above
9. The meaning of 'cash' as per AS-3 (revised is:
   (a) Cash in hand
   (b) Cash at Bank
   (c) Cash in hand and demand deposits in banks
   (d) None of the above
10. Match the items of List-I with the items in List-II:

    List-I
    A. Cash Equivalents
    B. Average Collection Period
    C. Zero-Base Budgeting
    D. Responsibility Centre

    List-II
    (i) Efficiency of managing an asset
    (ii) Controlling Government Expenditure
    (iii) Liquid Securities
    (iv) Residual Income

Codes:	A	B	C	D
(a)	(iii)	(i)	(ii)	(iv)
(b)	(iv)	(ii)	(iii)	(i)
(c)	(i)	(ii)	(iii)	(iv)
(d)	(ii)	(i)	(iii)	(iv)

11. In the short period, monopolist firm's equilibrium is at:
    (a) Break-even point (b) AR > AC
    (c) AR < AC (d) All of these
12. Price-discrimination is profitable and possible if the two markets have:
    (a) Equal Elasticity of Demand
    (b) Different Elasticity of Demand
    (c) Inelastic Demand
    (d) Highly Elastic Demand
13. Laws of increasing and constant returns are temporary phases of:
    (a) Law of Variable Proportion
    (b) Law of Diminishing Return
    (c) Law of Proportionality
    (d) Law of Diminishing Utility
14. A firm producing a large number of products will follow the pricing strategy known as:
    (a) Cost-plus pricing
    (b) Differential pricing
    (c) Product-line pricing
    (d) Price leadership
15. Cartels under oligopoly do not survive for long because of:
    (a) Inter-firm rivalry
    (b) Low profits
    (c) High cost of marketing
    (d) Heavy losses
16. F-test is a:
    (a) Probability test (b) Variance test
    (c) Factor analysis (d) None of the above
17. Regression analysis is a measure of:
    (a) Degree and direction of relationship
    (b) Degree of association
    (c) Cause and effect relationship
    (d) None of the above
18. Schedules help us in collecting:
    (a) Secondary Data (b) Qualitative Data
    (c) Primary Data (d) None of the above
19. Match the items from List-I with the items in List-II:

    List-I
    A. Random sampling B. Hypothesis testing
    C. Questionnaire D. t-test

    List-II
    (i) Structured (ii) Parametric test
    (iii) Probability sampling (iv) β-error

Codes:	A	B	C	D
(a)	(iv)	(iii)	(i)	(ii)
(b)	(iii)	(iv)	(ii)	(i)
(c)	(iii)	(i)	(iv)	(ii)
(d)	(iii)	(iv)	(i)	(ii)

20. The process of arranging records within a file is called:
(a) Ordering (b) Arranging
(c) Sequencing (d) Sorting

21. Who is the father of Scientific Management?
(a) Peter F. Drucker (b) Henry Fayol
(c) F.W. Taylor (d) Charles Babbage

22. What are K.R.As.?
(a) Key Result Areas
(b) Key Recruitment Agencies
(c) Key Real Assets
(d) Key Resourceful Areas

23. The modern organization structure usually recommended is:
(a) Tall (b) Flat
(c) Floating (d) Circular

24. Which of the following relates to interpersonal communication?
(a) Johari Window (b) Formal
(c) Body language (d) All of the above

25. Who is an independent director?
(a) Financial Institution
(b) Shareholder of the Company
(c) Nominee of Outside Agency
(d) None of the above

26. Who propounded Mega-marketing?
(a) McAurthy (b) Philip Kotler
(c) Sheth (d) Peter F. Drucker

27. On-line marketing is associated with:
(a) Segmentation (b) Product Life Cycle
(c) Distribution (d) Packing

28. Relationship marketing relates to:
(a) One-time purchase
(b) Two-time purchase
(c) Repeat purchase
(d) Continuous purchase

29. Modern marketing concept emphasizes on:
(a) Sales maximisation
(b) Customer satisfaction
(c) Profit maximisation
(d) Wealth maximisation

30. Penetration price is:
(a) Charging high price
(b) Charging low price
(c) Charging competitive price
(d) None of the above

31. Right shares enjoy preferential rights as regards:
(a) Payment of retained earnings
(b) Payment of dividend
(c) Repayment of capital in the event of winding up of the company
(d) None of the above

32. Non-performing Advance means:
(a) Non-functional assets
(b) Obsolete assets
(c) Assets transferred to company liquidator
(d) Loans becoming overdue beyond 90 days

33. Match the items of List-I with the items in List-II:

List-I
A. Capital gearing ratio
B. Fixed assets turnover
C. Return on equity
D. Acid test

List-II
(i) Profitability (ii) Short-term solvency
(iii) Activity (iv) Long-term solvency

Codes:	**A**	**B**	**C**	**D**
(a)	(iv)	(iii)	(i)	(ii)
(b)	(iv)	(iii)	(ii)	(i)
(c)	(iii)	(iv)	(i)	(ii)
(d)	(iv)	(i)	(iii)	(ii)

34. Capital structure designing has nothing to do with:
(a) Profitability (b) Solvency
(c) Flexibility (d) Transferability

35. Which of the following is the source of short-term finance?
(a) Trade Credit
(b) Bank Credit
(c) Short-term Borrowings
(d) All of the above

36. What is the operative function of Human Resource Management?
(a) Controlling (b) Organizing
(c) Procurement (d) None of the above

37. Selection means:
(a) Elimination (b) Testing
(c) Recruitment (d) None of the above

38. What is the method used to determine wage differentials?
(a) Merit rating (b) Job design
(c) Job evaluation (d) None of the above

39. Social security benefit include:
    (a) Annual bonus
    (b) Non-financial incentives
    (c) Old age pension
    (d) None of the above
40. Performance appraisal relates to:
    (a) 360 degrees appraisal
    (b) Open-door method
    (c) Autocratic method
    (d) All of the above
41. In 2005-06, which of the following banks earned the highest return on assets?
    (a) Private Sector Banks
    (b) Foreign Banks
    (c) Public Sector Banks
    (d) Scheduled Commercial Banks
42. Which of the following provides financial aid to the developing countries of Asia:
    (a) Association of South East Asian Nations
    (b) International Development Association
    (c) Asian Development Bank
    (d) None of the above
43. The merger of ______ and ________ was the first M and A activity after liberalization.
    (a) Times Bank and HDFC Bank
    (b) New Bank of India and Punjab National Bank
    (c) ICICI and ICICI Bank
    (d) GTB and Oriental Bank of Commerce
44. The first Development Bank IFCI was established in:
    (a) 1948 (b) 1947 (c) 1949 (d) 1950
45. The number of approved stock exchanges in India is:
    (a) 24 (b) 21 (c) 18 (d) 15
46. "Happiness Index" or "Happy Planet Index" has been evolved jointly by the "New Economic Foundation" and "Friends of Earth". Both are located in:
    (a) U.K. (b) U.S.A.
    (c) Australia (d) Europe
47. The amount of gold, reserve currencies and special drawing rights available for the finance of international trade is known as
    (a) International Liquidity
    (b) Special Drawing Rights
    (c) International Monetary Fund
    (d) None of the above
48. The Double Taxation Avoidance Convention (DTAC) pact was signed between:
    (a) India and China
    (b) India, Serbia and Montenegro
    (c) Australia and China
    (d) None of the above
49. 'International Trade Theory' was the contribution of:
    (a) Bertic Ohlin (b) Arthur Okun
    (c) Adam Smith (d) None of the above
50. Which of the following is not matched against its name?
    (a) **ASEAN:** Economic co-operation amongst all Asian Countries
    (b) **IMF:** To remove unfavourable balance of payment and to provide financial assistance
    (c) **WTO:** Does not allow quantitative restrictions on trade
    (d) **SAARC:** Encourages trade between South Asian Countries

ANSWERS

1. (a)	2. (b)	3. (d)	4. (b)	5. (a)
6. (c)	7. (a)	8. (a)	9. (d)	10. (a)
11. (d)	12. (b)	13. (a)	14. (d)	15. (a)
16. (b)	17. (a)	18. (c)	19. (d)	20. (c)
21. (c)	22. (a)	23. (b)	24. (a)	25. (c)
26. (b)	27. (c)	28. (c)	29. (b)	30. (b)
31. (d)	32. (d)	33. (a)	34. (b)	35. (d)
36. (d)	37. (d)	38. (c)	39. (c)	40. (a)
41. (c)	42. (c)	43. (c)	44. (a)	45. (a)
46. (a)	47. (a)	48. (b)	49. (a)	50. (a)

JUNE–2008

Note: This paper contains Fifty (50) multiple choice questions, each question carrying two (2) marks. Attempt all questions.

PAPER–I

1. The teacher has been glorified by the phrase "Friend, philosopher and guide" because
   (a) He has to play all vital roles in the context of society
   (b) He transmits the high value of humanity to students
   (c) He is the great reformer of the society
   (d) He is a great patriot
2. The most important cause of failure for teacher lies in the area of
   (a) interpersonal relationship
   (b) lack of command over the knowledge of the subject
   (c) verbal ability
   (d) strict handling of the students
3. A teacher can establish rapport with his students by
   (a) becoming a figure of authority
   (b) impressing students with knowledge and skill
   (c) playing the role of a guide
   (d) becoming a friend to the students
4. Education is a powerful instrument of
   (a) Social transformation
   (b) Personal transformation
   (c) Cultural transformation
   (d) All of the above
5. A teacher's major contribution towards the maximum self-realisation of the student is affected through
   (a) Constant fulfilment of the students' needs
   (b) Strict control of classroom activities
   (c) Sensitivity to students' needs, goals and purposes
   (d) Strict reinforcement of academic standards
6. Research problem is selected from the stand point of
   (a) Researcher's interest
   (b) Financial support
   (c) Social relevance
   (d) Availability of relevant literature
7. Which one is called non-probability sampling?
   (a) Cluster sampling
   (b) Quota sampling
   (c) Systematic sampling
   (d) Stratified random sampling
8. Formulation of hypothesis may not be required in
   (a) Survey method
   (b) Historical studies
   (c) Experimental studies
   (d) Normative studies
9. Field-work based research is classified as
   (a) Empirical (b) Historical
   (c) Experimental (d) Biographical
10. Which of the following sampling method is appropriate to study the prevalence of AIDS amongst male and female in India in 1976, 1986, 1996 and 2006?
   (a) Cluster sampling
   (b) Systematic sampling
   (c) Quota sampling
   (d) Stratified random sampling

Read the following passage and answer the questions 11 to 15:

The fundamental principle is that Article 14 forbids class legislation but permits reasonable classification for the purpose of legislation which classification must satisfy the twin tests of classification being founded on an intelligible differentia which distinguishes persons or things that are grouped together from those that are left out of the group and that differentia must have a rational nexus to the object sought to be achieved by the Statute in question. The thrust of

Article 14 is that the citizen is entitled to equality before law and equal protection of laws. In the very nature of things the society being composed of unequals a welfare State will have to strive by both executive and legislative action to help the less fortunate in society to ameliorate their condition so that the social and economic inequality in the society may be bridged. This would necessitate a legislative application to a group of citizens otherwise unequal and amelioration of whose lot is the object of state affirmative action. In the absence of the doctrine of classification such legislation is likely to flounder on the bedrock of equality enshrined in Article 14. The Court realistically appraising the social and economic inequality and keeping in view the guidelines on which the State action must move as constitutionally laid down in Part IV of the Constitution evolved the doctrine of classification. The doctrine was evolved to sustain a legislation or State action designed to help weaker sections of the society or some such segments of the society in need of succour. Legislative and executive action may accordingly be sustained if it satisfies the twin tests of reasonable classification and the rational principle correlated to the object sought to be achieved.

The concept of equality before the law does not involve the idea of absolute equality among human beings which is a physical impossibility. All that Article 14 guarantees is a similarity of treatment contra-distinguished from identical treatment. Equality before law means that among equals the law should be equal and should be equally administered and that the likes should be treated alike. Equality before the law does not mean that things which are different shall be as though they are the same. It of course means denial of any special privilege by reason of birth, creed or the like. The legislation as well as the executive government, while dealing with diverse problems arising out of an infinite variety of human relations must of necessity have the power of making special laws, to attain any particular object and to achieve that object it must have the power of selection or classification of persons and things upon which such laws are to operate.

11. Right to equality, one of the fundamental rights, is enunciated in the constitution under Part III, Article
    (a) 12 (b) 13 (c) 14 (d) 15
12. The main thrust of Right to equality is that it permits
    (a) class legislation
    (b) equality before law and equal protection under the law
    (c) absolute equality
    (d) special privilege by reason of birth
13. The social and economic inequality in the society can be bridged by
    (a) executive and legislative action
    (b) universal suffrage
    (c) identical treatment
    (d) None of the above
14. The doctrine of classification is evolved to
    (a) Help weaker sections of the society
    (b) Provide absolute equality
    (c) Provide identical treatment
    (d) None of the above
15. While dealing with diverse problems arising out of an infinite variety of human relations, the government
    (a) must have the power of making special laws
    (b) must not have any power to make special laws
    (c) must have power to withdraw equal rights
    (d) None of the above
16. Communication with oneself is known as
    (a) Group communication
    (b) Grapevine communication
    (c) Interpersonal communication
    (d) Intrapersonal communication
17. Which broadcasting system for TV is followed in India?
    (a) NTSE (b) PAL (c) SECAM (d) NTCS
18. All India Radio before 1936 was known as
    (a) Indian Radio Broadcasting
    (b) Broadcasting Service of India
    (c) Indian State Broadcasting Service
    (d) All India Broadcasting Service
19. The biggest news agency of India is
    (a) PTI (b) UNI
    (c) NANAP (d) Samachar Bharati

20. Prasar Bharati was launched in the year
(a) 1995 (b) 1997 (c) 1999 (d) 2001

21. A statistical measure based upon the entire population is called parameter while measure based upon a sample is known as
(a) Sample parameter (b) Inference
(c) Statistics (d) None of these

22. The importance of the correlation co-efficient lies in the fact that
(a) There is a linear relationship between the correlated variables
(b) It is one of the most valid measure of statistics
(c) It allows one to determine the degree or strength of the association between two variables
(d) It is a non-parametric method of statistical analysis

23. The F-test
(a) is essentially a two-tailed test
(b) is essentially a one-tailed test
(c) can be one tailed as well as two tailed depending on the hypothesis
(d) can never be a one-tailed test

24. What will be the next letter in the following series
DCXW, FEVU, HGTS, _____
(a) AKPO (b) JBYZ (c) JIRQ (d) LMRS

25. The following question is based on the diagram given below. If the two small circles represent formal classroom education and distance education and the big circle stands for university system of education, which figure represents the university systems.

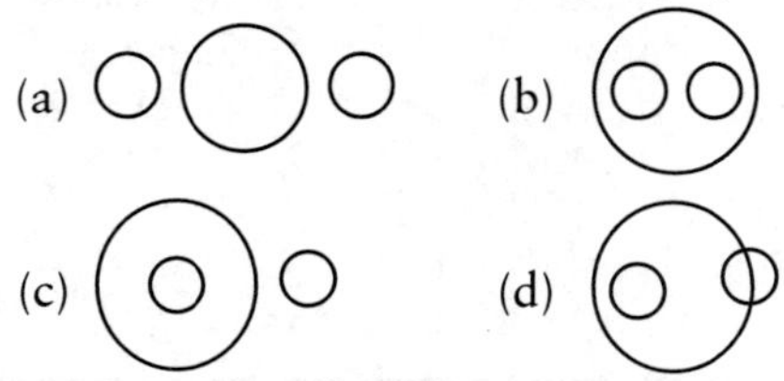

26. The statement, 'To be non-violent is good' is a
(a) Moral judgement (b) Factual judgement
(c) Religious judgement (d) Value judgement

27. **Assertion (A):** Man is a rational being.
Reason (R): Man is a social being.
(a) Both (A) and (R) are true and (R) is the correct explanation of (A)
(b) Both (A) and (R) are true but (R) is not the correct explanation of (A)
(c) (A) is true but (R) is false
(d) (A) is false but (R) is true

28. Value Judgements are
(a) Factual Judgements
(b) Ordinary Judgements
(c) Normative Judgements
(d) Expression of public opinion

29. Deductive reasoning proceeds from
(a) general to particular
(b) particular to general
(c) one general conclusion to another general conclusion
(d) one particular conclusion to another particular conclusion

30. AGARTALA is written in code as 14168171, the code for AGRA is
(a) 1641 (b) 1416 (c) 1441 (d) 1461

31. Which one of the following is the most comprehensive source of population data?
(a) National Family Health Surveys
(b) National Sample Surveys
(c) Census
(d) Demographic Health Surveys

32. Which one of the following principles is not applicable to sampling?
(a) Sample units must be clearly defined
(b) Sample units must be dependent on each other
(c) Same units of sample should be used throughout the study
(d) Sample units must be chosen in a systematic and objective manner

33. If January 1st, 2007 is Monday, what was the day on 1st January 1995?
(a) Sunday (b) Monday
(c) Friday (d) Saturday

34. Insert the missing number in the following series
4 16 8 64 ? 256
(a) 16 (b) 24 (c) 32 (d) 20

35. If an article is sold for ₹ 178 at a loss of 11%; what would be its selling price in order to earn a profit of 11%?
(a) ₹ 222.50 (b) ₹ 267 (c) ₹ 222 (d) ₹ 220

36. WYSIWYG—describes the display of a document on screen as it will actually print
(a) What you state is what you get
(b) What you see is what you get
(c) What you save is what you get
(d) What you suggest is what you get

37. Which of the following is not a Computer language?
(a) PASCAL (b) UNIX
(c) FORTRAN (d) COBOL

38. A keyboard has at least
(a) 91 keys (b) 101 keys
(c) 111 keys (d) 121 keys

39. An E-mail address is composed of
(a) two parts (b) three parts
(c) four parts (d) five parts

40. Corel Draw is a popular
(a) Illustration program
(b) Programming language
(c) Text program
(d) None of the above

41. Human ear is most sensitive to noise in which of the following ranges
(a) 1-2 kHz (b) 100-500 Hz
(c) 10-12 kHz (d) 13-16 kHz

42. Which one of the following units is used to measure intensity of noise?
(a) Decible (b) Hz (c) Phon (d) Watts/m^2

43. If the population growth follows a logistic curve, the maximum sustainable yield
(a) is equal to half the carrying capacity
(b) is equal to the carrying capacity
(c) depends on growth rates
(d) depends on the initial population

44. Chemical weathering of rocks is largely dependent upon
(a) high temperature (b) strong wind action
(c) heavy rainfall (d) glaciation

45. Structure of earth's system consists of the following: Match List I with List II and give the correct answer.

List I (Zone)
A. Atmosphere B. Biosphere
C. Hydrosphere D. Lithosphere

List II (Chemical Character)
1. Inert gases
2. Salt, freshwater, snow and ice
3. Organic substances, skeleton matter
4. Light silicates

Codes:	A	B	C	D
(a)	2	3	1	4
(b)	1	3	2	4
(c)	2	1	3	4
(d)	3	1	2	4

46. NAAC is an autonomous institution under the aegis of
(a) ICSSR (b) CSIR (c) AICTE (d) UGC

47. National Council for Women's Education was established in
(a) 1958 (b) 1976 (c) 1989 (d) 2000

48. Which one of the following is not situated in New Delhi?
(a) Indian Council of Cultural Relations
(b) Indian Council of Scientific Research
(c) National Council of Educational Research and Training
(d) Indian Institute of Advanced Studies

49. Autonomy in higher education implies freedom in
(a) Administration
(b) Policy-making
(c) Finance
(d) Curriculum development

50. Match List I with List II and select the correct answer from the code given below

List I (Institutions)
A. Dr. Hari Singh Gour University
B. S.N.D.T. University
C. M.S. University
D. J.N. Vyas University

List II (Locations)
1. Mumbai 2. Baroda
3. Jodhpur 4. Sagar

Codes:	A	B	C	D
(a)	4	1	2	3
(b)	1	2	3	4
(c)	3	1	2	4
(d)	2	4	1	3

ANSWERS

1. (b)	2. (b)	3. (b)	4. (d)	5. (c)
6. (c)	7. (b)	8. (b)	9. (a)	10. (d)
11. (c)	12. (b)	13. (a)	14. (a)	15. (a)
16. (d)	17. (b)	18. (c)	19. (a)	20. (b)

21. (a)	22. (c)	23. (c)	24. (c)	25. (b)
26. (a)	27. (b)	28. (c)	29. (a)	30. (d)
31. (c)	32. (b)	33. (d)	34. (a)	35. (c)
36. (b)	37. (b)	38. (b)	39. (a)	40. (a)
41. (b)	42. (a)	43. (a)	44. (c)	45. (b)
46. (d)	47. (a)	48. (d)	49. (c)	50. (a)

PAPER–II

Note: This paper contains fifty (50) objective type questions, each question carrying two (2) marks. All questions are compulsory.

1. The choice of distribution channel is affected by:
   (a) Market consideration
   (b) Product consideration
   (c) Middle man consideration
   (d) All of the above
2. Who is the custodian of monetary reserves in India?
   (a) SBI (b) SIDBI (c) NABARD (d) RBI
3. Who is the fiscal agent and advisor to government in monetary and financial matters in India?
   (a) SBI (b) IDBI (c) ICICI (d) RBI
4. During the depression, it is advisable to:
   (a) Lower Bank Rate and purchase securities in the market
   (b) Increase Bank Rate and purchase securities in the open market
   (c) Decrease Bank Rate and sell securities in the open market
   (d) Increase Bank Rate and sell securities in the open market
5. Nationalization of banks aimed at all of the following except:
   (a) Removal of control by a few
   (b) Provision of control by a few
   (c) Provision of adequate credit for agriculture, small industry and export units
   (d) Encouragement of a new class of entrepreneur
6. The portion of total deposits of a commercial bank which it has to keep with RBI in the form of cash reserves is termed as:
   (a) CRR (b) SLR
   (c) Bank Rate (d) Repo Rate
7. The emphasis of Human Resource Management is:
   (a) Development (b) Punishment
   (c) Promotion (d) Demotion
8. The purpose of job evaluation is:
   (a) Training (b) Promotion
   (c) Wage fixation (d) Transfer
9. Induction means:
   (a) Training
   (b) Orientation
   (c) Introducing the employee
   (d) Certification
10. Labour productivity means:
   (a) output is greater than input
   (b) output is less than input
   (c) output is equal to input
   (d) output is negative
11. Which of the following relates to performance appraisal?
   (a) Task method (b) Price method
   (c) M.B.O. (d) Link method
12. Capital structure represents:
   (a) Ratio between different forms of capital
   (b) All liabilities
   (c) All assets
   (d) Assets and liabilities
13. The item, closing inventory, is shown in the balance sheet under:
   (a) Fixed Assets
   (b) Current Assets
   (c) Current Liabilities
   (d) Miscellaneous Expenditure
14. Trading on Equity means:
   (a) Trading on arrears funds
   (b) Trading on borrowed funds
   (c) Trading on family funds
   (d) Trading on friends funds
15. Marketing process involves:
   (a) Time utility (b) Place utility
   (c) Right utility (d) All of the above

16. Which of the following activities are covered under physical distribution?
(a) Inventory (b) Packaging
(c) Transportation (d) All of the above

17. Which of the following step comes first in the selection process?
(a) Test (b) Application blank
(c) Screening (d) Medical examination

18. M-M Theory in perfect market suggests that dividend payment:
(a) has a positive impact on the value of a firm
(b) has no impact on the value of a firm
(c) has a negative impact on the value of a firm
(d) has negligible impact on the firm

19. To manage "is the forecast and plan, to organise, to command, to co-ordinate and to control". These are the words of:
(a) Koontz and O'Donnel
(b) Henry Fayol
(c) F.W. Taylor
(d) Peter F. Drucker

20. Chunk sampling is known as:
(a) Quota sampling
(b) Convenience sampling
(c) Judgement sampling
(d) Cluster sampling

21. The first electronic computer system was developed in:
(a) 1920 (b) 1930 (c) 1935 (d) 1940

22. When management pays attention to more important areas looked after by lower level of management, this is known as:
(a) MBO
(b) Management by exception
(c) Unity of command
(d) Critical path method

23. Policy making is an important part of the process of:
(a) Planning (b) Coordinating
(c) Organising (d) Motivating

24. Which of the management functions are closely related?
(a) Planning and organization
(b) Staffing and control
(c) Planning and control
(d) Planning and staffing

25. "Grapevine" is a term used in relation to:
(a) formal
(b) informal communication
(c) Both formal and informal communication
(d) this term is not used in relation to communication

26. The function of "staff" in an organisation is:
(a) take advice from the line
(b) advice the line
(c) hold authority and responsibility
(d) fix responsibility for performance of tasks in a definite manner upon certain individuals

27. Break-Even analysis deals with:
(a) relationship between cost and cost mix
(b) relationship between cost, output and profits
(c) relationship between cost and sales
(d) relationship between profit and sales

28. Dissolution of firm takes place:
(a) By the death or insolvency of any one partner
(b) The retirement of any one partner
(c) By the expiry of term
(d) By the insolvency of all but one partner

29. X Ltd. purchased land and building worth ₹ 28,80,000 and in lieu issued debentures of ₹ 100 each at a discount of 4%. What are the number of debentures issued ?
(a) 28,800 (b) 30,000
(c) 32,000 (d) 34,000

30. X, Y and Z are partners in the ratio of $\frac{1}{2}:\frac{2}{5}:\frac{1}{10}$. What will be new ratio of the remaining partners if X retires:
(a) 2 : 1 (b) 4 : 1 (c) 5 : 1 (d) 3 : 1

31. Match items in List-I with items in List-II.

List I	List II
A. Mega Marketing	(i) Advertising
B. Skimming Price	(ii) Post Purchase Behaviour
C. Promotion mix	(iii) High Price
D. Customer dissonance	(iv) Philip Kotler

Codes:	A	B	C	D
(a)	(iv)	(iii)	(i)	(ii)
(b)	(i)	(ii)	(iii)	(iv)
(c)	(iii)	(i)	(iv)	(ii)
(d)	(ii)	(iv)	(iii)	(i)

32. Match the following:

List I

A. Merchandise exports
B. Merchandise imports
C. Investment Income
D. Balance of Payments Deficits

List II

(i) Purchase of foreign goods
(ii) Sales of goods abroad
(iii) Largely caused by excess of imports over exports in merchandise
(iv) B/E analysis

Codes:	A	B	C	D
(a)	(i)	(ii)	(iii)	(iv)
(b)	(ii)	(iii)	(iv)	(i)
(c)	(ii)	(i)	(iv)	(iii)
(d)	(iii)	(iv)	(ii)	(i)

33. Match items in List-I with items in List-II:

List-I

A. ABC analysis B. ROI
C. Contribution Margin D. NPV

List-II

(i) Profitability (ii) Inventory control
(iii) Project evaluation (iv) B/E analysis

Codes:	A	B	C	D
(a)	(iii)	(ii)	(i)	(iv)
(b)	(ii)	(i)	(iv)	(iii)
(c)	(iv)	(ii)	(i)	(iii)
(d)	(i)	(iii)	(ii)	(iv)

34. Match the following:

List-I

A. Going Concern Concept
B. Consistency
C. Cost principle
D. Materiality

List-II

(i) The same accounting method used by a firm from one period to another
(ii) Relates to the relative size or importance of an item or event
(iii) An inappropriate assumption for a firm undergoing bankruptcy
(iv) The normal basis used to account for assets

Codes:	A	B	C	D
(a)	(i)	(ii)	(iii)	(iv)
(b)	(iv)	(iii)	(ii)	(i)
(c)	(iii)	(ii)	(iv)	(i)
(d)	(iii)	(i)	(iv)	(ii)

35. Match the following:

List-I

A. Smoothed Frequency Curve
B. Histogram
C. Bar diagram
D. Ogives

List-II

(i) To determine and portray the number of proportions of cases
(ii) It is one dimensional
(iii) It is two dimensional
(iv) Can be drawn through various points of polygon

Codes:	A	B	C	D
(a)	(i)	(ii)	(iii)	(iv)
(b)	(ii)	(iii)	(iv)	(i)
(c)	(iii)	(iv)	(ii)	(i)
(d)	(iv)	(iii)	(ii)	(i)

36. Match the following:

List-I

A. Merchandise Inventory
B. Comparability Quality
C. Net Realisable Value
D. Raw Materials Inventory

List-II

(i) Prevents arbitrary changes from one accounting or measurement approach from one period to another
(ii) Inventory of a retailer or wholesaler
(iii) Item acquired by purchase, growth or extraction of natural sources for further processing
(iv) Estimated selling price of product in the ordinary course of business

Codes:	A	B	C	D
(a)	(i)	(ii)	(iii)	(iv)
(b)	(ii)	(i)	(iv)	(iii)
(c)	(iii)	(ii)	(i)	(iv)
(d)	(iv)	(i)	(ii)	(iii)

37. Match the following:

List-I

A. Maxi-min principle
B. Mini-max principle
C. Max-max principle
D. Min-min principle

List-II

(i) take minimum pay-off of each action and whichever is minimum is best action

(ii) take maximum pay-off of each action and whichever is maximum is best action
(iii) take maximum pay-off of each action and whichever is minimum is best action
(iv) take minimum pay-off of each action and whichever is maximum is best action

Codes:	A	B	C	D
(a)	(i)	(ii)	(iii)	(iv)
(b)	(ii)	(iii)	(iv)	(i)
(c)	(iii)	(iv)	(i)	(ii)
(d)	(iv)	(iii)	(ii)	(i)

38. The hypothesis testing consists of following steps:
(i) Establish a level of significance, prior to sampling
(ii) Defining the rejection or critical regions
(iii) State the hypothesis
(iv) Determination of a suitable test statistic
Which of the sequence is correct?
(a) (ii), (iii), (iv), (i) (b) (iii), (i), (iv), (ii)
(c) (iii), (ii), (iv), (i) (d) (iv), (iii), (ii), (i)

39. Which of the following liabilities are taken into account for acid test ratio?
(i) Trade Creditors
(ii) Bank Overdraft
(iii) Bills Payable
(iv) Outstanding Expenses
(v) Redeemable debentures
(a) (i), (ii), (iii) and (iv) (b) (i) and (ii) only
(c) (i), (iii) and (iv) (d) All of the above

40. Statements:
(i) Employee development is more future oriented and more concerned with education than employee training.
(ii) Apprenticeship programme is one which is widely used off the job training.
(a) Both correct
(b) Both incorrect
(c) (i) incorrect, (ii) correct
(d) (i) correct, (ii) incorrect

41. For profit maximization of a firm we must have:
(i) MC = MR
(ii) Marginal cost curve cuts the average cost curve from below
(a) Only (i) is correct (b) Only (ii) is correct
(c) Both incorrect (d) Both correct

42. Statements:
(i) Fringe benefits, nowadays are a significant component of 'compensation.'
(ii) Under piece-rate plan, employees are paid at a stipulated rate per hour of work done by the employee.
(a) Both are correct
(b) Both are incorrect
(c) (i) incorrect, (ii) correct
(d) (i) correct, (ii) incorrect

43. Statements:
(i) The objective of Finance function is Wealth maximisation.
(ii) The objective of Finance function is Profit maximisation
(a) Both correct
(b) Both incorrect
(c) (i) correct, (ii) incorrect
(d) (i) incorrect, (ii) correct

44. Statements:
(i) Dividends can be paid only when there are profits.
(ii) Dividends can be paid when there are losses.
(a) Both are correct
(b) Both are incorrect
(c) (i) is incorrect, (ii) is correct
(d) (i) is correct, (ii) is incorrect

45. Statements:
(i) The greater a firms degree of operating leverage, the more its EBIT will vary with respect to fluctuations in sales.
(ii) The greater a firms degree of operating leverage, the less its EBIT will vary with fluctuations in sales.
(a) Both correct
(b) Both incorrect
(c) (i) correct, (ii) incorrect
(d) (i) incorrect, (ii) correct

46. The Indian insurance industry has come a long way. From being providers of tax planning instruments to introducing concepts of retirement planning, wealth creation, etc., customers are strengthening their ties with this industry every passing day. Today life insurance is among the fastest growing industries in India. Inspired by tremendous growth in the life insurance sector, many comparisons—product

features, charge structures, returns etc.—have been drawn between life insurance and other financial services, mostly mutual funds. These comparisons resulted in emergence of ULIPs as a preferred product and in fact they display some similarities with MFs.

The individual policyholders or retail customers buy the product when he or she wants to systematically provide towards a specific important goal. They take money regularly out of their monthly or annual income to make contribution for their goal—children education, health etc. Thus investment policies of life insurance companies are designed to enable policy holders meet their respective financial goals, while ensuring that the government is adequately funded for long term projects.

46. Which of the following products are provided by Indian insurance industry?
(a) Tax Planning
(b) Wealth-Creation
(c) Retirement Planning
(d) All of the above

47. Who is the majority investor in insurance companies?
(a) Individual Policyholder or Retail Customer
(b) Corporate Sector
(c) Government Sector
(d) Semi-Government Sector

48. Which of the following is the primary objective of insurance companies to invest savings of customers?
(a) Steady increments
(b) Risky investments
(c) Short-term investments
(d) Medium-term investments

49. Which type of customer-behaviour is observed for making investment in insurance companies?
(a) One-time savings
(b) Regular small-savings
(c) Savings on sudden-gain
(d) Retirement-savings only

50. Insurance Companies and Mutual Funds both provide to customers:
(a) Insurance Policies only (b) ULIPs
(c) Bonds (d) Loans

ANSWERS

1. (d)	2. (d)	3. (d)	4. (a)	5. (b)
6. (a)	7. (a)	8. (c)	9. (b)	10. (c)
11. (c)	12. (a)	13. (b)	14. (b)	15. (d)
16. (d)	17. (b)	18. (b)	19. (b)	20. (b)
21. (d)	22. (a)	23. (a)	24. (b)	25. (b)
26. (b)	27. (c)	28. (d)	29. (b)	30. (b)
31. (a)	32. (c)	33. (b)	34. (d)	35. (d)
36. (b)	37. (c)	38. (b)	39. (a)	40. (d)
41. (d)	42. (d)	43. (a)	44. (d)	45. (b)
46. (d)	47. (a)	48. (a)	49. (b)	50. (b)

DECEMBER–2008

Note: This paper contains Fifty (50) multiple choice questions, each question carrying two (2) marks. Attempt all questions.

PAPER–I

1. According to Swami Vivekananda, teacher's success depends on
   (a) His renunciation of personal gain and service to others
   (b) His professional training and creativity
   (c) His concentration on his work and duties with a spirit of obedience to God
   (d) His mastery on the subject and capacity in controlling the students
2. Which of the following teacher will be liked most?
   (a) A teacher of high idealistic attitude
   (b) A loving teacher
   (c) A teacher who is disciplined
   (d) A teacher who often amuses his students
3. A teacher's most important challenge is
   (a) To make students do their home work
   (b) To make teaching-learning process enjoyable
   (c) To maintain discipline in the class-room
   (d) To prepare the question paper
4. Value-education stands for
   (a) making a student healthy
   (b) making a student to get a job
   (c) inculcation of virtues
   (d) all-round development of personality
5. When a normal student behaves in an erratic manner in the class, you would
   (a) pull up the student then and there
   (b) talk to the student after the class
   (c) ask the student to leave the class
   (d) ignore the student
6. The research is always
   (a) verifying the old knowledge
   (b) exploring new knowledge
   (c) filling the gap between knowledge
   (d) All of these
7. The research that applies the laws at the time of field study to draw more and more clear ideas about the problem is
   (a) Applied research (b) Action research
   (c) Experimental research (d) None of these
8. When a research problem is related to heterogeneous population, the most suitable sampling method is
   (a) Cluster Sampling
   (b) Stratified Sampling
   (c) Convenient Sampling
   (d) Lottery Method
9. The process not needed in experimental research is:
   (a) Observation
   (b) Manipulation and replication
   (c) Controlling
   (d) Reference collection
10. A research problem is not feasible only when
    (a) it is researchable
    (b) it is new and adds something to knowledge
    (c) it consists of independent and dependent variables
    (d) it has utility and relevance

Read the following passage carefully and answer the questions 11 to 15:

Radically changing monsoon patterns, reduction in the winter rice harvest and a quantum increase in respiratory diseases all part of the environmental doomsday scenario which is reportedly playing out in South Asia. According to a United Nations Environment Program report, a deadly three-kilometer deep blanket of pollution comprising a fearsome, cocktail of ash, acids, aerosols and other particles has enveloped in this region. For India, already struggling to cope with a drought, the implication of this are devastating and further crop failure will amount to a life and death question for many Indians. The increase in premature deaths will have adverse social and economic consequences and a rise in morbidities will place an unbearable burden on our crumbling health system. And there is no one to blame but ourselves. Both official and corporate India has always been allergic to any mention of clean technology. Most mechanical two wheelers roll of the assembly line without proper pollution control system. Little effort is made for R&D on simple technologies, which could make a vital difference to people's lives and the environment.

However, while there is no denying that South Asia must clean up its act, skeptics might question the timing of the haze report. The Kyoto meet on climate change is just two weeks away and the stage is set for the usual battle between the developing world and the West, particularly the Unites States of America. President Mr. Bush has adamantly refused to sign any protocol, which would mean a change in American consumption level. U.N. environment report will likely find a place in the U.S. arsenal as it plants an accusing finger towards controls like India and China. Yet the U.S.A. can hardly deny its own dubious role in the matter of erasing trading quotas.

Richer countries can simply buy up excess credits from poorer countries and continue to pollute. Rather than try to get the better of developing countries, who undoubtedly have taken up environmental shortcuts in their bid to catch up with the West, the USA should take a look at the environmental profigacy, which is going on within. From opening up virgin territories for oil exploration to relaxing the standards for drinking water, Mr. Bush's policies are not exactly beneficial, not even to America's interests. We realise that we are all in this together and that pollution anywhere should be a global concern otherwise there will only be more tunnels at the end of the tunnel.

11. Both official and corporate India is allergic to
    (a) Failure of Monsoon
    (b) Poverty and Inequality
    (c) Slowdown in Industrial Production
    (d) Mention of Clean Technology
12. If the rate of premature death increases it will
    (a) Exert added burden on the crumbling economy
    (b) Have adverse social and economic consequences
    (c) Make positive effect on our effort to control population
    (d) Have less job aspirants in the society
13. According to the passage, the two-wheeler industry is not adequately concerned about
    (a) Passenger safety on the roads
    (b) Life cover insurance of the vehicle owner
    (c) Pollution control system in the vehicle
    (d) Rising cost of the two wheelers
14. What could be the reason behind timing of the haze report just before the Kyoto meet?
    (a) United Nations is working hand-in-glove with U.S.A.
    (b) Organisers of the forthcoming meet to teach a lesson to the U.S.A.
    (c) Drawing attention of the world towards devastating effects of environment degradation.
    (d) U.S.A. wants to use it as a handle against the developing countries in the forthcoming meet.
15. Which of the following is the indication of environmental degradation in South Asia?
    (a) Social and economic inequality
    (b) Crumbling health care system
    (c) Inadequate pollution control system
    (d) Radically changing monsoon pattern
16. Community Radio is a type of radio service that caters to the interest of
    (a) Local audience (b) Education
    (c) Entertainment (d) News
17. Orcut is a part of
    (a) Intrapersonal Communication
    (b) Mass Communication
    (c) Group Communication
    (d) Interpersonal Communication
18. Match List I with List II and select the correct answer using the codes given below.

    List I (Artists)

    A. Amrita Shergill

    B. T. Swaminathan Pillai

C. Bhimsen Joshi
D. Padma Subramaniyam

List II (Art)

1. Flute 2. Classical Song
3. Painting 4. Bharat Natyam

Codes:	A	B	C	D
(a)	3	1	2	4
(b)	2	3	1	4
(c)	4	2	3	1
(d)	1	4	2	3

19. Which is not correct in latest communication award?
(a) Salman Rushdie - Booker's Prize—July 20, 2008
(b) Dilip Sanghavi - Business Standard CEO Award, July 22, 2008
(c) Tapan Sinha - Dada Saheb Falke Award, July 21, 2008
(d) Gautam Ghosh - Osians Lifetime Achievement Award, July 11, 2008

20. Firewalls are used to protect a communication network system against
(a) Unauthorised attacks
(b) Virus attacks
(c) Data-driven attacks
(d) Fire-attacks

21. Insert the missing number in the following 2/7, 4/7, ?, 11/21, 16/31›
(a) 10/8 (b) 6/10 (c) 5/10 (d) 7/13

22. In a certain code, GAMESMAN is written as AGMEMSAN. How would DISCLOSE be written in that code?
(a) IDSCOLSE (b) IDCSOLES
(c) IDSCOLES (d) IDSCLOSE

23. The letters in the first set have a certain relationship. On the basis of this relationship mark the right choice for the second set : AST : BRU :: NQV: ?
(a) ORW (b) MPU
(c) MRW (d) OPW

24. On what dates of April, 1994 did Sunday fall?
(a) 2, 9, 16, 23, 30 (b) 3, 10, 17, 24
(c) 4, 11, 18, 25 (d) 1, 8, 15, 22, 29

25. Find out the wrong number in the sequence 125, 127, 130, 135, 142, 153, 165
(a) 130 (b) 142 (c) 153 (d) 165

26. There are five books A, B, C, D and E. The book C lies above D, the book E is below A and B is below E. Which is at the bottom?
(a) E (b) B (c) A (d) C

27. Logical reasoning is based on
(a) Truth of involved propositions
(b) Valid relation among the involved propositions
(c) Employment of symbolic language
(d) Employment of ordinary language

28. Two propositions with the same subject and predicate terms but different in quality are
(a) Contradictory (b) Contrary
(c) Subaltern (d) Identical

29. The premises of a valid deductive argument
(a) Provide some evidence for its conclusion
(b) Provide no evidence for its conclusion
(c) Are irrelevant for its conclusion
(d) Provide conclusive evidence for its conclusion

30. Syllogistic reasoning is
(a) Deductive (b) Inductive
(c) Experimental (d) Hypothetical

Study the following Venn diagram and answer questions nos. 31 to 33.

Three circles representing GRADUATES, CLERKS and GOVERNMENT EMPLOYEES are intersecting. The intersections are marked A, B, C, e, f, g and h. Which part best represents the statements in questions 31 to 33?

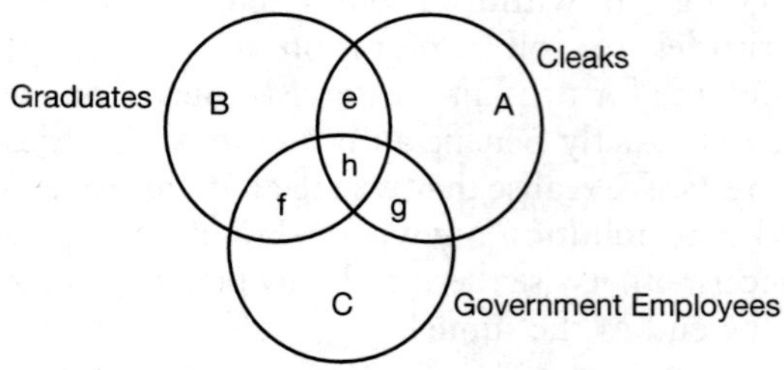

31. Some Graduates are Government employees but not as Clerks.
(a) h (b) g (c) f (d) e

32. Clerks who are graduates as well as government employees.
(a) e (b) f (c) g (d) h

33. Some graduates are Clerks but not Government employees.
(a) f (b) g (c) h (d) e

Study the following graph and answer questions numbers from 34 to 35

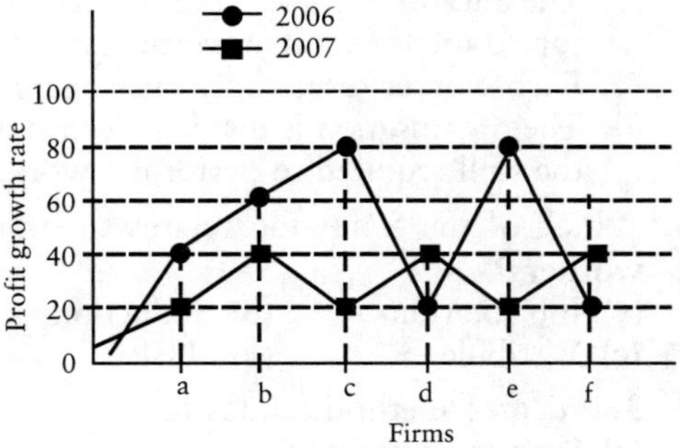

34. Which of the firms got maximum profit growth rate in the year 2006?
(a) ab (b) ce (c) cd (d) ef

35. Which of the firms got maximum profit growth rate in the year 2007?
(a) bdf (b) acf (c) bed (d) ace

36. The accounting software 'Tally' was developed by
(a) HCL (b) TCS (c) Infosys (d) Wipro

37. Errors in computer programs are called
(a) Follies (b) Mistakes
(c) Bugs (d) Spam

38. HTML is basically used to design
(a) Webpage (b) Website
(c) Graphics (d) Tables and Frames

39. 'Micro Processing' is made for
(a) Computer (b) Digital System
(c) Calculator (d) Electronic Goods

40. Information, a combination of graphics, text, sound, video and animation is called
(a) Multiprogram (b) Multifacet
(c) Multimedia (d) Multiprocess

41. Which of the following pairs regarding typical composition of hospital wastes is incorrect?
(a) Plastic - 9-12%
(b) Metals - 1-2%
(c) Ceramic - 8-10%
(d) Biodegradable - 35-40%

42. Freshwater achieves its greatest density at
(a) –4°C (b) 0°C (c) 4°C (d) –2.5°C

43. Which one of the following is not associated with earthquakes?
(a) Focus (b) Epicenter
(c) Seismograph (d) Swells

44. The tallest trees in the world are found in the region
(a) Equatorial region
(b) Temperate region
(c) Monsoon region
(d) Mediterranean region

45. Match List I with List II and select the correct answer from the codes given below.

List I (National Parks)
A. Periyar
B. Nandan Kanan
C. Corbett National Park
D. Sariska Tiger Reserve

List II (States)
1. Orissa 2. Kerala
3. Rajasthan 4. Uttarakhand

Codes:	**A**	**B**	**C**	**D**
(a)	2	1	4	3
(b)	1	2	4	3
(c)	3	2	1	4
(d)	1	2	3	4

46. According to Radhakrishnan Commission, the aim of Higher Education is
(a) To develop the democratic values, peace and harmony
(b) To develop great personalities who can give their contributions in politics, administration, industry and commerce
(c) Both (a) and (b)
(d) None of these

47. The National Museum at New Delhi is attached to
(a) Delhi University
(b) a Deemed University
(c) a Subordinate Office of the JNU
(d) Part of Ministry of Tourism and Culture

48. Match List I with List II and select the correct answer from the code given below.

List I (Institutions)	**List II (Locations)**
A. National Law Institute	1. Shimla
B. Indian Institute of Advanced Studies	2. Bhopal

C. National Judicial Academy — 3. Hyderabad
D. National Savings Institute — 4. Nagpur

Codes:	A	B	C	D
(a)	3	2	4	1
(b)	1	2	3	4
(c)	4	3	1	2
(d)	3	1	2	4

49. Election of Rural and Urban local bodies are conducted and ultimately supervised by
(a) Election Commission of India
(b) State Election Commission
(c) District Collector and District Magistrate
(d) Concerned Returning Officer

50. Which opinion is not correct?
(a) Education is a subject of concurrent list of VII schedule of Constitution of India
(b) University Grants Commission is a statutory body
(c) Patent, inventions, design, copyright and trade marks are the subject of concurrent list
(d) Indian Council of Social Science Research is a statutory body related to research in social sciences

ANSWERS

1. (d)	2. (c)	3. (b)	4. (c)	5. (b)
6. (d)	7. (a)	8. (b)	9. (d)	10. (b)
11. (d)	12. (b)	13. (c)	14. (c)	15. (d)
16. (a)	17. (d)	18. (a)	19. (b)	20. (a)
21. (d)	22. (a)	23. (d)	24. (b)	25. (d)
26. (b)	27. (b)	28. (a)	29. (d)	30. (a)
31. (c)	32. (d)	33. (d)	34. (b)	35. (a)
36. (b)	37. (c)	38. (a)	39. (a)	40. (c)
41. (d)	42. (c)	43. (d)	44. (b)	45. (a)
46. (c)	47. (d)	48. (d)	49. (b)	50. (c)

PAPER–II

Note: This paper contains fifty (50) objective type questions, each question carrying two (2) marks. All questions are compulsory.

1. Job analysis provides information used for:
(a) Organisation chart (b) Policy
(c) Procedure (d) Promotion

2. In functional organisation:
(a) The organisation is divided according to the type of work involved.
(b) The authority flows from the man at the top to the lowest man vertically.
(c) Each worker serves only one supervisor.
(d) The organisation is divided according to the skill required to perform a work.

3. Which of the following relates to training workers?
(a) Job rotation (b) Induction
(c) Vestibule (d) Task

4. 360 degree method relates to:
(a) Performance appraisal
(b) Organisation climate
(c) Employees morale
(d) Retrenchment method

5. Human relations approach of management is associated with:
(a) Abraham Maslow (b) Peter F. Drucker
(c) Elton Mayo (d) Herzberg

6. Attrition is related to:
(a) Job description
(b) Resignation/Termination
(c) Job evaluation
(d) Merit rating

7. The economic reforms have failed to:
(a) Keep fiscal deficits to the targeted levels.
(b) Fully implement industrial deregulation.
(c) Fully open the economy to trade.
(d) All of the above.

8. Which of the following developments was not noticed during 1991 (economic reforms)?
(a) National debt was nearly 60 percent of the GNP of India.
(b) Inflation crossed double digits.
(c) Foreign reserves were maintained at a very high level.
(d) None of the above.

9. Which of the following statements is incorrect?
(a) Even monopolistic can earn losses.
(b) Firms in a perfectly competitive market are price takers.

(c) It is always beneficial for a firm in a perfectly competitive market to discriminate prices.
(d) Kinked demand curve is related to an oligopolistic market.

10. Which of the following is the best general definition of the study of economics?
(a) Inflation and unemployment in a growing economy.
(b) The best way to invest in the stock market.
(c) Business decision making under foreign competition.
(d) Individual and social choice in the face of scarcity.

11. Which of the following statements is correct?
(a) Under zamindari system, farmers directly paid land revenue to the state.
(b) At present, income tax revenues from the agriculture sector are negligible.
(c) Commercial banks are providing loans to the agriculture sector at zero interest rate.
(d) None of the above.

12. Which of the following statements is incorrect?
(a) About 80 per cent of agricultural area has irrigation facilities.
(b) About two third area is rain-fed in India.
(c) Productivity per worker in agriculture is much lower than that in industry.
(d) Cropping pattern is quite skewed in India.

13. Abolition of intermediaries and tenancy reforms are both parts of:
(a) Industrial reforms in India.
(b) External sector reforms in India.
(c) Land reforms in India.
(d) Banking reforms in India.

14. Which of the following is not a measure of dispersion?
(a) Skewness (b) Mean Deviation
(c) Standard Deviation (d) QuartileDeviation

15. The immediate solvency ratio is:
(a) Current Ratio
(b) Quick Ratio
(c) Debtors Turnover Ratio
(d) Stock Turnover Ratio

16. The Foreign Exchange Management Act (FEMA) was implemented in the year:
(a) 1996 (b) 1997 (c) 1998 (d) 1999

17. SEZ Policy in India is motivated by the experience of:
(a) Japan (b) China
(c) USA (d) Germany

18. In order to control credit:
(a) CRR should be increased and Bank Rate should be decreased.
(b) CRR should be decreased and Bank Rate should be decreased.
(c) CRR should be increased and Bank Rate should be increased.
(d) CRR should be decreased and Bank Rate should be increased.

19. In order to control credit in the country, the RBI may:
(a) Buy Securities in the open market.
(b) Sell Securities in the open market.
(c) Reduce CRR.
(d) Reduce Bank Rate.

20. Which bank is called the 'Bank of Issue'?
(a) RBI (b) SBI (c) IDBI (d) ICICI

21. In order to encourage investment in the country, the RBI may:
(a) Reduce CRR
(b) Increase CRR
(c) Sell Securities in the open market
(d) Increase Bank Rate

22. The term 'funds' as used in 'funds flow statement' means:
(a) Cash
(b) Current Assets
(c) Current Liabilities
(d) Current Assets minus Current Liabilities

23. What is the "Fundamental Premise of Economics"?
(a) Individuals are capable of establishing goals and acting in a manner consistent with achievement of those goals.
(b) Natural resources will always be scare.
(c) Individuals choose the alternative for which they believe the net gains to be the greatest.
(d) No matter what the circumstances, individuals choice always involve a trade-off.

24. The consumer is in equilibrium at a point where the budget line:

(a) Is below an indifference curve
(b) Is above an indifference curve
(c) Is tangent to an indifference curve
(d) Cuts an indifference curve

25. Which of the following statements is correct concerning the relationships among the firm's functions?
(a) TC = TFC – TVC
(b) TVC = TFC – TC
(c) TFC = TC – TVC
(d) TC = TVC – TFC

26. In perfect competition in the long run there will be no
(a) Normal profits
(b) Supernormal profits
(c) Production
(d) Costs

27. An indifference curve slopes down towards right since more of one commodity and less of another result in:
(a) Same satisfaction
(b) Greater satisfaction
(c) Maximum satisfaction
(d) Decreasing expenditure

28. Which of the following results in the flow of funds?
(a) Creditors issued bills payable
(b) Loss on the sale of machinery
(c) Transfer to general reserve
(d) Building sold on credit

29. If net profit is ₹ 25,000/- after writing off preliminary expenses of ₹ 5000/- then the funds from operation will be:
(a) ₹ 25,000/- (b) ₹ 30,000/-
(c) ₹ 20,000/- (d) ₹ 10,000/-

30. Which of the following is a non-current liability?
(a) Bills payable (b) Sundry creditors
(c) Bank overdraft (d) Long term loans

31. Match the following:

List I
A. Indira Awas Yojana
B. Sampoorna Grameen Yojana
C. Pradhan Mantri Gram Sadak Yojana
D. Swaran Jayanti Gram Swarozgar Yojana

List II
(i) This programme was launched in 2001. This programme aims at providing wage employment in rural areas and food security to the people.
(ii) This is a major scheme for construction of houses to be given to the poor, free of cost.
(iii) This was introduced in April 1999 as a result of restructuring and combining the Integrated Rural Development Programme.
(iv) This was introduced in December 2000 to provide road-connectivity through good all weather roads to unconnected villages.

Codes:	A	B	C	D
(a)	(ii)	(i)	(iv)	(iii)
(b)	(i)	(ii)	(iv)	(iii)
(c)	(iii)	(iv)	(ii)	(i)
(d)	(iv)	(iii)	(ii)	(i)

32. Match the following:

List I	List II
(A) WTO	(i) Provides loans to address short-term balance of payments problems.
(B) RBI	(ii) Multilateral trade negotiating body.
(C) IMF	(iii) Facilitating lending and borrowing for reconstruction and development.
(D) IBRD	(iv) Central Bank of India.

Codes:	A	B	C	D
(a)	(ii)	(iv)	(i)	(iii)
(b)	(iv)	(iii)	(ii)	(i)
(c)	(iii)	(ii)	(iv)	(i)
(d)	(i)	(ii)	(iii)	(iv)

33. Match the items in List I with items in List II:

List-I	List-II
A. Margin of Safety	(i) Earning Power
B. ROI	(ii) Cash Flow statement
C. Current Ratio	(iii) Break Even analysis
D. Cash Equivalents	(iv) Solvency

Codes:	A	B	C	D
(a)	(ii)	(iv)	(i)	(iii)
(b)	(iv)	(iii)	(ii)	(i)
(c)	(iii)	(ii)	(iv)	(i)
(d)	(i)	(ii)	(iii)	(iv)

34. Match the items in List I with items in List II:

List-I	**List-II**
A. Theory X	(i) Participative
B. Theory Y	(ii) Autocratic
C. Theory Z	(iii) Democratic

Codes:	**A**	**B**	**C**
(a)	(i)	(ii)	(iii)
(b)	(ii)	(iii)	(i)
(c)	(iii)	(i)	(ii)
(d)	(ii)	(i)	(iii)

35. Match the items in List I with items in List II :

List I	**List II**
A. Peter F. Drucker	(i) Unity of command
B. Henry Fayol	(ii) Achievement Motivation
C. McAurthy	(iii) M.B.O.
D. McLeland	(iv) 4 Ps of marketing

36. Match the following:

List I (***Decisions regarding branding***)

A. Diversification B. Quality
C. Variety D. Packing

List II (***Explanation***)

(i) Preservation of product
(ii) Production of one or more products
(iii) Finding of new products in same line
(iv) Various product

Codes:	**A**	**B**	**C**	**D**
(a)	(ii)	(iv)	(i)	(iii)
(b)	(iii)	(ii)	(iv)	(i)
(c)	(iii)	(i)	(iv)	(ii)
(d)	(iv)	(iii)	(ii)	(i)

37. Statements:
   (i) Overcapitalisation is desirable.
   (ii) Undercapitalisation is more desirable.
   (a) Both are correct
   (b) Both are incorrect
   (c) (i) is correct (ii) is incorrect
   (d) (ii) is correct (i) is incorrect

38. Statements:
   (i) High morale leads to high productivity.
   (ii) High morale need not necessarily lead to high productivity
   (a) Both are correct
   (b) Both are incorrect
   (c) (i) is correct (ii) is incorrect
   (d) (i) is incorrect (ii) is correct

39. Statements:
   (i) Maslows theory conveys hygiene factors.
   (ii) Maslows theory conveys satisfied need is no more a motivator.
   (a) (i) is correct (ii) is incorrect
   (b) (ii) is correct (i) is incorrect
   (c) Both are correct
   (d) Both are incorrect

40. Statements:
   (i) Agency theory relates to the relationship between management and employees.
   (ii) Agency theory relates to middlemen.
   (a) Both are correct
   (b) Both are incorrect
   (c) (i) is correct (ii) is incorrect
   (d) (ii) is correct (i) is incorrect

41. Statements:

   Assertion (A): Demand for a commodity refers to quantity of the commodity demanded at a certain price during any particular period of time.

   Reason (R): Contraction of demand is the result of increase in the price of the good concerned.

   (a) Both (A) and (R) are correct
   (b) Both (A) and (R) are incorrect
   (c) (A) is correct but (R) is incorrect
   (d) (A) is incorrect but (R) is correct

42. A leader uses the following methods:
   (i) Uses criticism
   (ii) Encourages growth
   (iii) Sets objectives
   (iv) Gives orders and directions

   Which of these methods are used by a democratic leader?

   (a) (i) and (ii) (b) (iii) and (iv)
   (c) (ii) and (iii) (d) (i), (ii) and (iv)

43. In the technique of MBO:
   (i) Overall objectives are set at the top of the organisational hierarchy
   (ii) Individual objectives coincide with objectives of the organisation
   (iii) Performance should be evaluated periodically
   (iv) Objectives are decided at the subordinate level

   (a) (i) and (ii) (b) (i), (ii) and (iii)
   (c) (i) and (iii) (d) (i), (ii), (iii) and (iv)

44. Staffing includes:

(i) Training (ii) Appraisal
(iii) Placement (iv) Directing
(a) (i) and (iii) (b) (i), (ii) and (iii)
(c) (ii) and (iii) (d) (i), (ii), (iii) and (iv)

45. Working capital cycle involves the following:
(i) Acquisition of Raw material
(ii) Finished goods (iii) Receivables
(iv) Cash (v) Work-in-progress
Which of the sequence is correct?
(a) (iv), (iii), (i), (v), (ii)
(b) (i), (ii), (iii), (iv), (v)
(c) (i), (v), (ii), (iii), (iv)
(d) (iv), (i), (ii), (iii), (v)

Directions (Nos. 46 to 50): Read the following passage and answer the questions.

Accounting is the process of identifying, measuring and communicating economic information to permit informed judgements and decisions by the users of the information. It primarily focusses on measurement, analysis, interpretation and use of information. As an information system, accounting links an information source, a channel of communication and set of receivers. Accounting system should be designed to classify financial information on a basis suitable for decision-making purposes and to process the tremendous quantities of data efficiently and accurately. Financial accounting is concerned with providing information to external users and it is oriented towards the preparation of final statements which summarises the results of operations for selected periods of time and show the financial position of business at particular date. Management accounting is concerned with providing information to managers to carry out their responsibilities and functions such as planning, execution, control and decision-making. The end product of the financial accounting process is a set of reports called financial statement, such as, profit and loss account, balance-sheet and statement of changes in financial position. Profit & loss account shows the results of operations for a period of time, balance sheet shows finanical position on certain date and statement of changes in financial position shows where the financial resources have come and where they have gone.

46. A list of assets, liabilities and owner's equity of a business enterprise as of a specific date is:
(a) Income Statement
(b) Cash Flow Statement
(c) Balance Sheet
(d) Profit and Loss Account

47. The balance sheet is related to the income statement in the same way that:
(a) A point in time is related to a period of time
(b) A period of time is related to a point in time
(c) A point in time is related to another point in time
(d) A period of time is related to another period of time

48. The properties own by a business enterprise are called:
(a) Assets (b) Liabilities
(c) Capital (d) Owner's Equity

49. Which of the following is an important reason for studying accounting?
(a) The information provided by accounting is useful in making many economic decisions.
(b) Accounting plays an important role in society.
(c) The study of accounting could lead to a challenging career.
(d) All of the above.

50. Statement of changes in financial position shows:
(a) Sources and uses of funds
(b) Assets and Liabilities
(c) Income and Expenses
(d) Losses and Gains

ANSWERS

1. (c)	2. (a)	3. (a)	4. (a)	5. (c)
6. (b)	7. (d)	8. (c)	9. (c)	10. (d)
11. (b)	12. (a)	13. (c)	14. (a)	15. (b)
16. (d)	17. (b)	18. (c)	19. (b)	20. (a)
21. (a)	22. (d)	23. (c)	24. (c)	25. (c)
26. (b)	27. (a)	28. (d)	29. (b)	30. (d)
31. (a)	32. (a)	33. (b)	34. (d)	35. (d)
36. (b)	37. (c)	38. (a)	39. (b)	40. (d)
41. (a)	42. (b)	43. (b)	44. (d)	45. (c)
46. (c)	47. (a)	48. (a)	49. (d)	50. (a)

JUNE–2009

Note: This paper contains Fifty (50) multiple choice questions, each question carrying two (2) marks. Attempt all questions.

PAPER–I

1. Good evaluation of written material should not be based on
   (a) Linguistic expression
   (b) Logical presentation
   (c) Ability to reproduce whatever is read
   (d) Comprehension of subject
2. Why do teachers use teaching aid?
   (a) To make teaching fun-filled
   (b) To teach within understanding level of students
   (c) For students' attention
   (d) To make students attentive
3. Attitudes, concepts, skills and knowledge are products of
   (a) Learning (b) Research
   (c) Heredity (d) Explanation
4. Which among the following gives more freedom to the learner to interact?
   (a) Use of film
   (b) Small group discussion
   (c) Lectures by experts
   (d) Viewing country-wide classroom program on TV
5. Which of the following is not a product of learning?
   (a) Attitudes (b) Concepts
   (c) Knowledge (d) Maturation
6. How can the objectivity of the research be enhanced?
   (a) Through its impartiality
   (b) Through its reliability
   (c) Through its validity
   (d) All of these
7. Action-research is
   (a) An applied research
   (b) A research carried out to solve immediate problems
   (c) A longitudinal research
   (d) All of the above
8. The basis on which assumptions are formulated
   (a) Cultural background of the country
   (b) Universities
   (c) Specific characteristics of the castes
   (d) All of these
9. Which of the following is classified in the category of the developmental research?
   (a) Philosophical research
   (b) Action research
   (c) Descriptive research
   (d) All of the above
10. We use Factorial Analysis
   (a) To know the relationship between two variables
   (b) To test the Hypothesis
   (c) To know the difference between two variables
   (d) To know the difference among the many variables

Read the following passage and answer the questions 11 to 15:

While the British rule in India was detrimental to the economic development of the country, it did help in starting of the process of modernising Indian society and formed several progressive institutions during that process. One of the most beneficial institutions, which were initiated by the British, was democracy. Nobody can dispute that despite its many shortcomings, democracy was and is far better alternative to the arbitrary rule of the rajas and nawabs, which prevailed in India in the pre-British days.

However, one of the harmful traditions of British democracy inherited by India was that of conflict instead of cooperation between elected members. This was its essential feature. The party, which got the support of the majority of elected members, formed the government while the others constituted a standing opposition. The existence of the opposition to those in power was and is regarded as a hallmark of democracy.

In principle, democracy consists of rule by the people; but where direct rule is not possible, it's rule by persons elected by the people. It is natural that there would be some differences of opinion among the elected members as in the rest of the society.

Normally, members of any organisations have differences of opinion between themselves on different issues but they manage to work on the basis of a consensus and they do not normally form a division between some who are in majority and are placed in power, while treating the others as in opposition.

The members of an organisation usually work on consensus. Consensus simply means that after an adequate discussion, members agree that the majority opinion may prevail for the time being. Thus persons who form a majority on one issue and whose opinion is allowed to prevail may not be on the same side if there is a difference on some other issue.

It was largely by accident that instead of this normal procedure, a two-party system came to prevail in Britain and that is now being generally taken as the best method of democratic rule.

Many democratically inclined persons in India regret that such a two-party system was not brought about in the country. It appears that to have two parties in India—of more or less equal strength—is a virtual impossibility. Those who regret the absence of a two-party system should take the reasons into consideration.

When the two-party system got established in Britain, there were two groups among the rules (consisting of a limited electorate) who had the same economic interests among themselves and who therefore formed two groups within the selected members of Parliament.

There were members of the British aristocracy (which landed interests and consisting of lord, barons, etc.) and members of the new commercial class consisting of merchants and artisans. These groups were more or less of equal strength and they were able to establish their separate rule at different times.

Answer the following questions:

11. In pre-British period, when India was ruled by the independent rulers
    (a) Peace and prosperity prevailed in the society
    (b) People were isolated from political affairs
    (c) Public opinion was inevitable for policy making
    (d) Law was equal for one and all
12. What is the distinguishing feature of the democracy practised in Britain?
    (a) End to the rule of might is right.
    (b) Rule of the people, by the people and for the people.
    (c) It has stood the test of time.
    (d) Cooperation between elected members.
13. Democracy is practised where
    (a) Elected members form a uniform opinion regarding policy matter.
    (b) Opposition is more powerful than the ruling combine.
    (c) Representatives of masses.
    (d) None of these.
14. Which of the following is true about the British rule in India?
    (a) It was behind the modernisation of the Indian society.
    (b) India gained economically during that period.
    (c) Various establishments were formed for the purpose of progress.
    (d) None of these.
15. Who became the members of the new commercial class during that time?
    (a) British Aristocrats
    (b) Lord and Barons
    (c) Political Persons
    (d) Merchants and Artisans
16. Which one of the following Telephonic Conferencing with a radio link is very popular throughout the world?
    (a) TPS (b) Telepresence
    (c) Video conference (d) Video teletext

17. Which is not 24 hours news channel?
(a) NDTV 24×7 (b) ZEE News
(c) Aajtak (d) Lok Sabha Channel

18. The main objective of FM station in radio is
(a) Information, Entertainment and Tourism
(b) Entertainment, Information and Interaction
(c) Tourism, Interaction and Entertainment
(d) Entertainment only

19. In communication chatting in internet is
(a) Verbal communication
(b) Non-verbal communication
(c) Parallel communication
(d) Grapevine communication

20. Match List I with List II and select the correct answer using the codes given below:
List I (Artists)
A. Pandit Jasraj B. Kishan Maharaj
C. Ravi Shankar D. Udai Shankar
List II (Art)
1. Hindustani vocalist 2. Sitar
3. Tabla 4. Dance

Codes:	A	B	C	D
(a)	1	2	3	4
(b)	1	3	4	2
(c)	1	3	2	4
(d)	3	2	1	4

21. Insert the missing number in the following.
3, 8, 18, 23, 33, ?, 48
(a) 37 (b) 40 (c) 38 (d) 45

22. In a certain code, CLOCK is written as KCOLC. How would STEPS be written in that code?
(a) SPEST (b) SPSET (c) SPETS (d) SEPTS

23. The letters in the first set have a certain relationship. On the basis of this relationship mark the right choice for the second set
BDFH : OMKI :: GHIK : ?
(a) FHJL (b) RPNL (c) LNPR (d) LJHF

24. What was the day of the week on 1st January 2001?
(a) Friday (b) Monday
(c) Sunday (d) Wednesday

25. Find out the wrong number in the sequence.
52, 51, 48, 43, 34, 27, 16
(a) 27 (b) 34 (c) 43 (d) 48

26. In a deductive argument conclusion is
(a) Summing up of the premises
(b) Not necessarily based on premises
(c) Entailed by the premises
(d) Additional to the premises

27. 'No man are mortal' is contradictory of
(a) Some man are mortal
(b) Some man are not mortal
(c) All men are mortal
(d) No mortal is man

28. A deductive argument is valid if
(a) premises are false and conclusion is true
(b) premises are false and conclusion is also false
(c) premises are true and conclusion is false
(d) premises are true and conclusion is true

29. Structure of logical argument is based on
(a) Formal validity
(b) Material truth
(c) Linguistic expression
(d) Aptness of examples

30. Two ladies and two men are playing bridge and seated at North, East, South and West of a table. No lady is facing East. Persons sitting opposite to each other are not of the same sex. One man is facing South. Which direction are the ladies facing to?
(a) East and West (b) North and West
(c) South and East (d) None of these

Questions 31 and 32 are based on the following Venn diagram in which there are three intersecting circles representing Hindi knowing persons, English knowing persons and persons who are working as teachers. Different regions so obtained in the figure are marked as a, b, c, d, e, f and g.

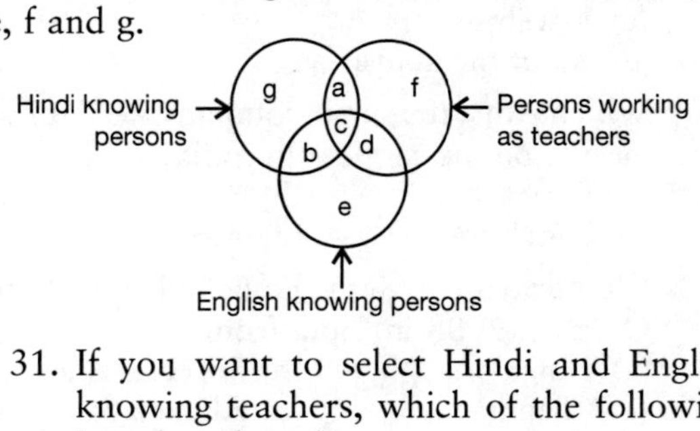

31. If you want to select Hindi and English knowing teachers, which of the following is to be selected?
(a) g (b) b (c) c (d) e

32. If you want to select persons, who do not know English and are not teachers, which of the region is to be selected?
(a) e (b) g (c) b (d) a

Study the following graph carefully and answer questions 33 to 35.

Export of Engineering Goods

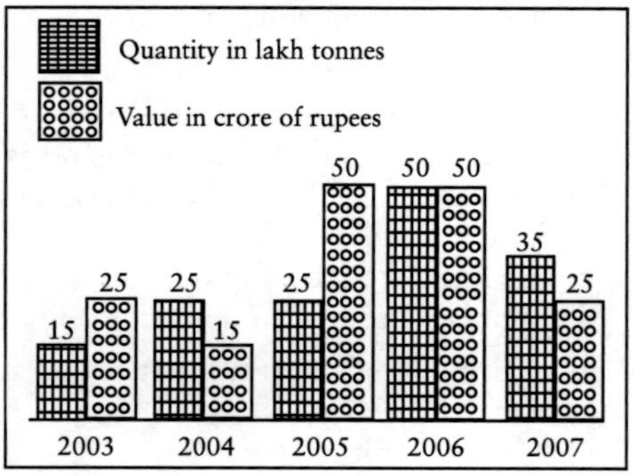

33. In which year the quantity of engineering goods' exports was maximum?
(a) 2005 (b) 2006 (c) 2004 (d) 2007

34. In which year the value of engineering goods decreased by 50 percent compared to the previous year?
(a) 2004 (b) 2007 (c) 2005 (d) 2006

35. In which year the quantity of exports was 100 percent higher than the quantity of previous year?
(a) 2004 (b) 2005 (c) 2006 (d) 2007

36. What do you need to put your web pages on the www?
(a) A connection to internet
(b) A web browser
(c) A web server
(d) All of the above

37. Which was the first company to launch mobile phone services in India?
(a) Essar (b) BPL
(c) Hutchison (d) Airtel

38. Chandrayan I was launched on 22nd October, 2008 in India from
(a) Bangalore (b) Sri Harikota
(c) Chennai (d) Ahmedabad

39. What is blog?
(a) Online music
(b) Intranet
(c) A personal or corporate website in the form of an online journal
(d) A personal or corporate Google search

40. Which is not online Indian Matrimonial website?
(a) www.jeevansathi.com
(b) www.bharatmatrimony.com
(c) www.shaadi.com
(d) www.u.k.singlemuslim.com

41. Environmental impact assessment is an objective analysis of the probable changes in
(a) physical characteristics of the environment
(b) biophysical characteristics of the environment
(c) socio-economic characteristics of the environment
(d) All the above

42. Bog is a wetland that receives water from
(a) nearby water bodies (b) melting
(c) Only rainfall (d) Only sea

43. Which of the following regions is in the very high risk zone of earthquakes?
(a) Central Indian Highland
(b) Coastal region
(c) Himalayan region
(d) Indian desert

44. Match List I with List II and select the correct answer using the codes given below.

List I (Institutes)
A. Central Arid Zone Institute
B. Space Application Centre
C. Indian Institute of Public Administration
D. Headquarters of Indian Science Congress

List II (Cities)
1. Kolkata 2. New Delhi
3. Ahmedabad 4. Jodhpur

Codes:	**A**	**B**	**C**	**D**
(a)	4	3	2	1
(b)	4	2	1	3
(c)	3	1	2	4
(d)	1	2	4	3

45. Indian coastal areas experienced Tsunami disaster in the year
(a) 2005 (b) 2004 (c) 2006 (d) 2007

46. The Kothari Commission's report was entitled on
(a) Education and National Development
(b) Learning to be adventure
(c) Diversification of Education
(d) Education and socialisation in democracy

47. Which of the following is not a dual mode university?
(a) Delhi University
(b) Bangalore University
(c) Madras University
(d) Indira Gandhi National Open University

48. Which part of the Constitution of India is known as "Code of Administrators"?
(a) Part I (b) Part II
(c) Part III (d) Part IV

49. Which article of the Constitution provides safeguards to Naga Customary and their social practices against any act of Parliament?
(a) Article 371A (b) Article 371B
(c) Article 371C (d) Article 263

50. Which one of the following is not the tool of good governance?
(a) Right to Information
(b) Citizens' Charter
(c) Social Auditing
(d) Judicial Activism

ANSWERS

1. (a)	2. (a)	3. (a)	4. (b)	5. (d)
6. (d)	7. (b)	8. (a)	9. (d)	10. (d)
11. (b)	12. (d)	13. (a)	14. (c)	15. (a)
16. (b)	17. (d)	18. (b)	19. (b)	20. (c)
21. (c)	22. (c)	23. (b)	24. (b)	25. (b)
26. (c)	27. (c)	28. (d)	29. (b)	30. (b)
31. (c)	32. (b)	33. (b)	34. (b)	35. (c)
36. (d)	37. (d)	38. (b)	39. (c)	40. (d)
41. (d)	42. (a)	43. (b)	44. (a)	45. (b)
46. (a)	47. (d)	48. (d)	49. (a)	50. (d)

DECEMBER–2009

Note: This paper contains Sixty (60) multiple choice questions, each question carrying two (2) marks. Candidate is expected to answer any Fifty (50) questions. In case more than Fifty (50) questions are attempted, only the first Fifty (50) questions will be evaluated.

PAPER–I

1. The university which telecasts interaction educational programs through its own channel is
   (a) Osmania University
   (b) University of Pune
   (c) Annamalai University
   (d) Indira Gandhi National University (IGNOU)

2. Which of the following skills are needed for present-day teacher to adjust effectively with the classroom teaching?
   1. Knowledge of technology
   2. Use of technology in teaching learning
   3. Knowledge of students' needs
   4. Content mastery

   (a) 1 and 3 (b) 2 and 3
   (c) 2, 3 and 4 (d) 2 and 4

3. Who has signed as MoU for Accreditation of Teacher Education Institutions in India?
   (a) NAAC and UGC
   (b) NCTE and NAAC
   (c) UGC and NCTE
   (d) NCTE and IGNOU

4. The primary duty of the teacher is to
   (a) raise the intellectual standard of the students
   (b) improve the physical standard of the students
   (c) help all-round development of the students
   (d) imbibe value system in the students

5. Micro teaching is more effective
   (a) during the preparation for teaching-practice
   (b) during the teaching-practice
   (c) after the teaching-practice
   (d) always

6. What quality the students like the most in a teacher?
   (a) Idealist philosophy (b) Compassion
   (c) Discipline (d) Entertaining

7. A null hypothesis is
   (a) when there is no difference between the variables
   (b) the same as research hypothesis
   (c) subjective in nature
   (d) when there is difference between the variables

8. The research which is exploring new facts through the study of the past is called
   (a) Philosophical research
   (b) Historical research
   (c) Mythological research
   (d) Content analysis

9. Action research is
   (a) An applied research
   (b) A research carried out to solve immediate problems
   (c) A longitudinal research
   (d) Simulative research

10. The process not needed in Experimental Researches is
    (a) Observation (b) Manipulation
    (c) Controlling (d) Content Analysis

11. Manipulation is always a part of
    (a) Historical research
    (b) Fundamental research
    (c) Descriptive research
    (d) Experimental research

12. Which correlation co-efficient best explains the relationship between creativity and intelligence?
    (a) 1.00 (b) 0.6 (c) 0.5 (d) 0.3

Read the following passage and answer the Question Nos. 13 to 18:

The decisive shift in British Policy really came about under mass pressure in the autumn and winter of 1945 to 46—the months which Penderel Moon while editing *Wavell's Journal* has perceptively described as "The Edge of a Volcano". Very foolishly, the British initially decided to hold public trials of several hundreds of the 20,000 I.N.A. prisoners (as well as dismissing from service and detaining without trial no less than 7,000). They compounded the folly by holding the first trial in the Red Fort, Delhi in November 1945, and putting on the dock together a Hindu, a Muslim and a Sikh (P.K. Sehgal, Shah Nawaz, Gurbaksh Singh Dhillon). Bhulabhai Desai, Tejbahadur Sapru and Nehru appeared for the defence (the latter putting on his barrister's gown after 25 years), and the Muslim League also joined the countrywide protest. On 20 November, an Intelligence Bureau note admitted that "there has seldom been a matter which has attracted so much Indian public interest and, it is safe to say, sympathy...this particular brand of sympathy cuts across communal barriers". A journalist (B. Shiva Rao) visiting the Red Fort prisoners on the same day reported that "There is not the slightest feeling among them of Hindu and Muslim.... A majority of the men now awaiting trial in the Red Fort is Muslim. Some of these men are bitter that Mr. Jinnah is keeping alive a controversy about Pakistan." The British became extremely nervous about the I.N.A. spirit spreading to the Indian Army, and in January the Punjab Governor reported that a Lahore reception for released I.N.A. prisoners had been attended by Indian soldiers in uniform.

13. Which heading is more appropriate to assign to the above passage?
(a) *Wavell's Journal*
(b) Role of Muslim League
(c) I.N.A. Trials
(d) Red Fort Prisoners

14. The trial of P.K. Sehgal, Shah Nawaz and Gurbaksh Singh Dhillon symbolises
(a) communal harmony
(b) threat to all religious persons
(c) threat to persons fighting for the freedom
(d) British reaction against the natives

15. I.N.A. stands for
(a) Indian National Assembly
(b) Indian National Association
(c) Inter-national Association
(d) Indian National Army

16. "There has seldom been a matter which has attracted so much Indian Public Interest and, it is safe to say, sympathy... this particular brand of sympathy cuts across communal barriers." Who sympathises to whom and against whom?
(a) Muslims sympathised with Shah Nawaz against the British
(b) Hindus sympathised with P.K. Sehgal against the British
(c) Sikhs sympathised with Gurbaksh Singh Dhillon against the British
(d) Indians sympathised with the persons who were to be trialled

17. The majority of people waiting for trial outside the Red Fort and criticising Jinnah were the
(a) Hindus (b) Muslims
(c) Sikhs (d) Hindus and Muslims both

18. The sympathy of Indian soldiers in uniform with the released I.N.A. prisoners at Lahore indicates
(a) Feeling of Nationalism and Fraternity
(b) Rebellion nature of Indian soldiers
(c) Simply to participate in the reception party
(d) None of the above

19. The country which has the distinction of having the two largest circulated newspapers in the world is
(a) Great Britain (b) The United States
(c) Japan (d) China

20. The chronological order of non-verbal communication is
(a) Signs, symbols, codes, colours
(b) Symbols, codes, signs, colours
(c) Colours, signs, codes, symbols
(d) Codes, colours, symbols, signs

21. Which of the following statements is not connected with communication?
(a) Medium is the message.
(b) The world is an electronic cocoon.
(c) Information is power.
(d) Telepathy is technological.

22. Communication becomes circular when
(a) the decoder becomes an encoder
(b) the feedback is absent
(c) the source is credible
(d) the channel is clear

23. The site that played a major role during the terrorist attack on Mumbai (26/11) in 2008 was
(a) Orkut (b) Facebook
(c) Amazon.com (d) Twitter

24. **Assertion (A):** For an effective classroom communication at times it is desirable to use the projection technology.
Reason (R): Using the projection technology facilitates extensive coverage of course contents.
(a) Both (A) and (R) are true, and (R) is the correct explanation.
(b) Both (A) and (R) are true, but (R) is not the correct explanation.
(c) (A) is true, but (R) is false.
(d) (A) is false, but (R) is true.

25. January 1, 1995 was a Sunday. What day of the week lies on January 1, 1996?
(a) Sunday (b) Monday
(c) Wednesday (d) Saturday

26. When an error of 1% is made in the length and breadth of a rectangle, the percentage error (%) in the area of a rectangle will be
(a) 0 (b) 1 (c) 2 (d) 4

27. The next number in the series 2, 5, 9, 19, 37, ? will be
(a) 74 (b) 75
(c) 76 (d) None of these

28. There are 10 true-false questions in an examination. Then these questions can be answered in
(a) 20 ways (b) 100 ways
(c) 240 ways (d) 1024 ways

29. What will be the next term in the following? DCXW, FEVU, HGTS, ?
(a) AKPO (b) ABYZ (c) JIRQ (d) LMRS

30. Three individuals X, Y, Z hired a car on a sharing basis and paid ₹ 1,040. They used it for 7, 8, 11 hours, respectively. What are the charges paid by Y?
(a) ₹ 290 (b) ₹ 320 (c) ₹ 360 (d) ₹ 440

31. Deductive argument involves
(a) sufficient evidence
(b) critical thinking
(c) seeing logical relations
(d) repeated observation

32. Inductive reasoning is based on or presupposes
(a) uniformity of nature
(b) God created the world
(c) unity of nature
(d) laws of nature

33. To be critical, thinking must be
(a) practical
(b) socially relevant
(c) individually satisfying
(d) analytical

34. Which of the following is an analogous statement?
(a) Man is like God
(b) God is great
(c) Gandhiji is the Father of the Nation
(d) Man is a rational being

Questions from 35-36 are based on the following diagram in which there are three intersecting circles. H representing The Hindu, I representing Indian Express and T representing The Times of India. A total of 50 persons were surveyed and the number in the Venn diagram indicates the number of persons reading the newspapers.

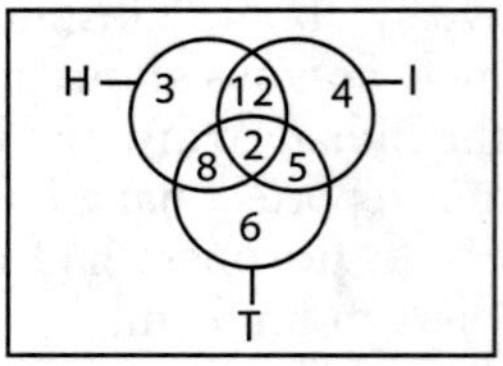

35. How many persons would be reading at least two newspapers?
(a) 23 (b) 25 (c) 27 (d) 29

36. How many persons would be reading almost two newspapers?
(a) 23 (b) 25 (c) 27 (d) 48

37. Which of the following graphs does not represent regular (periodic) behaviour of the variable f(t)?

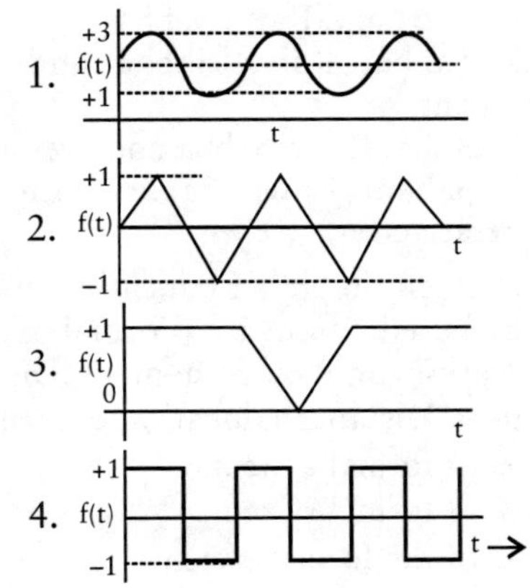

(a) 1 (b) 2
(c) 3 (d) 4

Study the following graph and answer the questions 38 to 40.

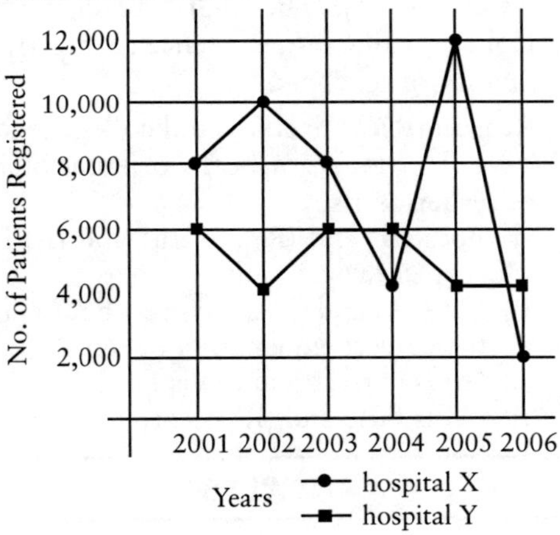

38. In which year total number of patients registered in hospital X and hospital Y was the maximum?
(a) 2003 (b) 2004 (c) 2005 (d) 2006

39. What is the maximum dispersion in the registration of patients in the two hospitals in a year?
(a) 8000 (b) 6000 (c) 4000 (d) 2000

40. In which year there was maximum decrease in registration of patients in hospital X?
(a) 2003 (b) 2004 (c) 2005 (d) 2006

41. Which of the following sources of data is not based on primary data collection?
(a) Census of India
(b) National Sample Survey
(c) Statistical Abstracts of India
(d) National Family Health Survey

42. Which of the four data sets have more dispersion?

(a)	88	91	90	92	89	91
(b)	0	1	1	0	−1	−2
(c)	3	5	2	4	1	5
(d)	0	5	8	10	−2	−8

43. Which of the following is not related to information security on the Internet?
(a) Data Encryption
(b) Water Marking
(c) Data Hiding
(d) Information Retrieval

44. Which is the largest unit of storage among the following?
(a) Terabyte (b) Megabyte
(c) Kilobyte (d) Gigabyte

45. Bit stands for
(a) binary information term
(b) binary digit
(c) binary tree
(d) Bivariate Theory

46. Which one of the following is not a linear data structure?
(a) Array (b) Binary Tree
(c) Queue (d) Stack

47. Which one of the following is not a network device?
(a) Router (b) Switch (c) Hub (d) CPU

48. A compiler is used to convert the following to object code which can be executed
(a) High-level language
(b) Low-level language
(c) Assembly language
(d) Natural language

49. The great Indian Bustard bird is found in
(a) Thar Desert of Rajasthan
(b) Malabar Coast
(c) Coastal regions of India
(d) Delta regions

50. The Sagarmanthan National Park has been established to preserve the eco-system of which mountain peak?
(a) Kanchenjunga (b) Mount Everest
(c) Annapurna (d) Dhaulavira

51. Maximum soot is released from

(a) Petrol vehicles
(b) CNG vehicles
(c) Diesel vehicles
(d) Thermal Power Plants

52. Surface Ozone is produced from
(a) Transport sector
(b) Cement plants
(c) Textile industry
(d) Chemical industry

53. Which one of the following non-conventional energy sources can be exploited most economically?
(a) Solar (b) Wind
(c) Geo-thermal
(d) Ocean Thermal Energy Conversion (OTEC)

54. The most recurring natural hazard in India is
(a) Earthquakes (b) Floods
(c) Landslides (d) Volcanoes

55. The recommendation of National Knowledge Commission for the establishment of 1500 universities is to
(a) create more teaching jobs
(b) ensure increase in student enrolment in higher education
(c) replace or substitute the privately managed higher education institutions by public institutions
(d) enable increased movement of students from rural areas to urban areas

56. According to Article 120 of the Constitution of India, the business in Parliament shall be transacted in
(a) Only English
(b) Only Hindi
(c) Both English and Hindi
(d) All the languages included in Eighth Schedule of the Constitution

57. Which of the following is more interactive and student centric?
(a) Seminar
(b) Workshop
(c) Lecture
(d) Group Discussion

58. The Parliament in India is composed of
(a) Lok Sabha and Rajya Sabha
(b) Lok Sabha, Rajya Sabha and Vice-President
(c) Lok Sabha, Rajya Sabha and President
(d) Lok Sabha, Rajya Sabha with their Secretariats

59. The enrolment in higher education in India is contributed both by Formal System of Education and by System of Distance Education. Distance education contributes
(a) 50% of formal system
(b) 25% of formal system
(c) 10% of the formal system
(d) Distance education system's contribution is not taken into account while considering the figures of enrolment in higher education

60. **Assertion (A):** The UGC Academic Staff Colleges came into existence to improve the quality of teachers.

Reason (R): University and college teachers have to undergo both orientation and refresher courses.
(a) Both (A) and (R) are true and (R) is the correct explanation.
(b) Both (A) and (R) are correct but (R) is not the correct explanation of (A).
(c) (A) is correct and (R) is false.
(d) (A) is false and (R) is correct.

ANSWERS

1. (d)	2. (c)	3. (b)	4. (c)	5. (b)
6. (c)	7. (a)	8. (b)	9. (b)	10. (b)
11. (c)	12. (b)	13. (c)	14. (a)	15. (d)
16. (d)	17. (b)	18. (a)	19. (c)	20. (a)
21. (d)	22. (a)	23. (a)	24. (a)	25. (b)
26. (c)	27. (b)	28. (d)	29. (c)	30. (b)
31. (c)	32. (a)	33. (b)	34. (a)	35. (c)
36. (d)	37. (c)	38. (c)	39. (a)	40. (d)
41. (c)	42. (d)	43. (d)	44. (a)	45. (b)
46. (b)	47. (d)	48. (a)	49. (a)	50. (b)
51. (d)	52. (a)	53. (a)	54. (b)	55. (b)
56. (c)	57. (d)	58. (c)	59. (b)	60. (a)

PAPER–II

Note: This paper contains fifty (50) objective type questions, each question carrying two (2) marks. All questions are compulsory.

1. If the amount claimed by a consumer as compensation is ₹ 89 lacs, the case under The Consumer Protection Act shall be filed with
   (a) District Consumer Redressal Forum
   (b) State Consumer Disputes Redressal Commission
   (c) National Consumer Disputes Redressal Commission
   (d) Supreme Court
2. Which of the following does not fall within the jurisdiction of MRTP Commission?
   (a) Prevention of Monopolistic Trade Practices.
   (b) Prevention of Restrictive Trade Practices.
   (c) Prohibition of Unfair Trade Practices.
   (d) Regulation of Combinations.
3. Which of the following is not a part of the economic environment of business?
   (a) Competitive Environment
   (b) Economic System
   (c) Changes in Patent Laws
   (d) None of these
4. Laissez faire policy is adopted in
   (a) Socialistic economic system
   (b) Capitalistic economic system
   (c) Mixed economic system
   (d) Communist economic system
5. Relaxing the restrictions and controls imposed on business and industry means
   (a) Liberalisation (b) Privatisation
   (c) Globalisation (d) None of these
6. A variable such as activity that causes cost over a given time is
   (a) Cost Driver (b) Cost Behaviour
   (c) Cost Centre (d) None of the above
7. The concept of budget that requires all levels to work from scratch is
   (a) Flexible Budget (b) Total Budget
   (c) Master Budget (d) Zero Base Budget
8. Accounting Standard on the "Effect of Changes in Foreign Exchange Rates" is
   (a) AS 11 (b) AS 13
   (c) AS 18 (d) None of the above
9. Land is not depreciable asset because
   (a) Its value always increases
   (b) There is no maintenance required
   (c) Life of land is unlimited
   (d) None of the above
10. The sales at which a firm would earn profit after tax @ 8% of sales, if fixed cost is ₹ 45,000; selling price ₹ 50 per unit, variable cost ₹ 30 per unit and tax rate 20%:
    (a) ₹ 90,000 (b) ₹ 1,50,000
    (c) ₹ 1,68,000 (d) None of the above
11. The elasticity of demand for luxury goods is
    (a) Infinite (b) More than one
    (c) Less than one (d) Equal to one
12. Profits are maximised at a point where
    (a) MR = MC (b) MR < MC
    (c) MR > MC (d) AC > MC
13. The concept of "consumer surplus" was introduced and developed by
    (a) E.A.G. Robinson (b) J.M. Keynes
    (c) Lionel Robbins (d) Alfred Marshall
14. In Law of Variable Proportions, initially when MP rises
    (a) TP rises at a decreasing rate.
    (b) TP rises at an increasing rate.
    (c) AP rises less than proportionately.
    (d) AP rises more than proportionately.
15. Which one of the following statements is correct?
    (a) Monopolist charges the maximum possible price.
    (b) Monopolist always makes (economic) profit.
    (c) Monopolist operates on an inelastic demand curve.
    (d) None of the above.
16. The Central Processing Unit of a computer consists of
    (a) Input, Output and Processing.
    (b) Control Unit, Primary Storage and Secondary Storage.
    (c) Control Unit, Arithmetic-logic Unit and Primary Storage.
    (d) None of the above.

17. If the sample size increases, the sampling error
(a) Decreases (b) Increases
(c) Remains constant (d) None of the above

18. Goodness of fit of a distribution is tested by
(a) t-test (b) Chi-square test
(c) F-test (d) None of these

19. Probability of rejecting the null hypothesis when it is true, is called
(a) Type-II-error (b) Type-I-error
(c) Standard error (d) None of these

20. Standard error of mean is defined as
(a) standard deviation of the sampling distribution of mean.
(b) standard deviation of data.
(c) inter-quartile range of the data.
(d) none of these.

21. Who first propounded the principle of 'unity of command'?
(a) F.W. Taylor (b) Elton Mayo
(c) Peter F. Drucker (d) Henry Fayol

22. Which element is not necessary in each objective under MBO Approach?
(a) Time element (b) Cost element
(c) Human Relation element
(d) Measurable element

23. Techniques of managerial control are useful in
(a) selection of plant location
(b) identifying appropriate technology
(c) profit planning
(d) conducting shareholders' meeting

24. The function of attracting, acquiring, retaining and developing human resources in an organisation is called
(a) recruitment (b) induction
(c) training and development (d) staffing

25. In terms of Blake-Mouton's managerial grid approach, a production oriented leader will be one who adopts
(a) 1.1 style (b) 9.1 style
(c) 9.9 style (d) 5.5 style

26. The strategy of introducing a product with high introductory price is called
(a) penetration strategy (b) skimming strategy
(c) pull strategy (d) push strategy

27. The concept of four Ps as elements of marketing mix was given by
(a) Philip Kotler (b) W.J. Stanton
(c) E.J. McCarthy (d) Bruce J. Walker

28. Which out of the following is not a type of non-store retailing?
(a) Limited line stores (b) Automatic vending
(c) Direct selling (d) Telemarketing

29. A product line strategy wherein a company adds a higher priced product to a line in order to attract a broader market which helps the sale of its existing lower priced products is called
(a) Trading up (b) Trading down
(c) Life cycle extension
(d) Product line extension

30. Which of the following is not a tool of sales promotion?
(a) Sales contests (b) Free gifts
(c) Point of purchase display
(d) Public Relations

31. Use of fixed interest securities in the capital structure is called
(a) operating leverage (b) financial leverage
(c) overall leverage (d) None of the above

32. If NPV is positive, the IRR will be
(a) Positive (b) $K = R$
(c) $K < R$ (d) None of the above

33. According to Walter, firm should pay 100% dividend if
(a) $r > k$ (b) $r = k$
(c) $r < k$ (d) None of the above

34. Sensitivity analysis is performed to
(a) Ascertain risk
(b) Determine profitability
(c) Build scenario for risk profile
(d) None of the above

35. Right shares enjoy preferential rights with regard to
(a) Payment of dividend
(b) Payment of retained earnings
(c) Repayment of capital
(d) None of the above

36. The Industrial Disputes Act, 1947 provides the following industrial relations machinery for resolution of conflicts except
(a) Conciliation (b) Arbitration
(c) Negotiations (d) Adjudication

37. Job evaluation is a technique which aims at
    (a) Establishing fair and equitable pay structure.
    (b) Analysing requirement of updating technology.
    (c) Assessing safety requirement of jobs.
    (d) Improving productivity.

38. Induction is an integral part of
    (a) Training (b) Selection
    (c) Recruitment (d) None of the above

39. PIP test seeks to measure
    (a) IQ
    (b) Personality, Interest and Preferences
    (c) Quality of a product
    (d) Preferred Investment Plans

40. The Government of India introduced "The Workers' Participation in Management" Bill in Parliament in
    (a) 1983 (b) 1988 (c) 1990 (d) 1981

41. The features of the Commercial Paper are
    (a) It is an unsecured money market instrument issued in the form of promissory note.
    (b) The highly rated corporate borrowers can raise short term funds through this instrument.
    (c) It is an additional instrument to the investing community.
    (d) All of the above.

42. Banking ombudsman may reject the complaint
    (a) immediately after receipt.
    (b) after hearing both parties.
    (c) at any stage.
    (d) None of the above.

43. Which of the following entities provide "Take out Finance" to banks engaged in financing of infrastructure projects?
    (a) ICICI (b) SIDBI (c) IDFC (d) RBI

44. Currency chest balance will be periodically verified by
    (a) Bank's own officials
    (b) RBI officials
    (c) Both (a) and (b)
    (d) Officials of AG's office

45. SEBI is
    (a) Regulatory Authority
    (b) Statutory Authority
    (c) Both (a) and (b)
    (d) None of these

46. The International Monetary Fund has estimated India's contribution to World Gross Domestic Product in Purchasing Power Parity (PPP) terms for 2007
    (a) 4.6 percent (b) 6.4 percent
    (c) 7.1 percent (d) 8.9 percent

47. The World Bank is known as
    (a) IMF (b) IDA (c) IFC (d) IBRD

48. "De-coupling" denotes
    (a) Indian market may be cut off from global markets so that it may not be affected by global volatility.
    (b) separating the birds affected by bird-flu.
    (c) that markets are independent.
    (d) None of the above.

49. Which of the country's banking have been brought under "Sanctions by U.S.A. recently"?
    (a) Iraq (b) North Korea
    (c) Pakistan (d) Iran

50. How many member countries are there in the "World Customs Organisation"?
    (a) 160 (b) 162 (c) 172 (d) 180

ANSWERS

1. (b)	2. (d)	3. (b)	4. (b)	5. (a)
6. (a)	7. (c)	8. (a)	9. (a)	10. (d)
11. (a)	12. (a)	13. (d)	14. (b)	15. (a)
16. (c)	17. (a)	18. (b)	19. (b)	20. (a)
21. (d)	22. (c)	23. (c)	24. (d)	25. (c)
26. (b)	27. (c)	28. (a)	29. (a)	30. (d)
31. (b)	32. (c)	33. (b)	34. (a)	35. (d)
36. (d)	37. (a)	38. (a)	39. (b)	40. (c)
41. (d)	42. (c)	43. (c)	44. (c)	45. (c)
46. (a)	47. (d)	48. (a)	49. (d)	50. (c)

JUNE–2010

Note: This paper contains Sixty (60) multiple-choice questions, each question carrying two (2) marks. Candidate is expected to answer any Fifty (50) questions. In case more than Fifty (50) questions are attempted, only the first Fifty (50) questions will be evaluated.

PAPER–I

1. Which one of the following is the most important quality of a good teacher?
   (a) Punctuality and sincerity
   (b) Content mastery
   (c) Content mastery and reactive
   (d) Content mastery and sociable
2. The primary responsibility for the teacher's adjustment lies with
   (a) The children
   (b) The principal
   (c) The teacher himself
   (d) The community
3. As per the NCTE norms, what should be the staff strength for a unit of 100 students at B.Ed. level?
   (a) 1 + 7 (b) 1 + 9 (c) 1 + 10 (d) 1 + 5
4. Research has shown that the most frequent symptom of nervous instability among teachers is
   (a) Digestive upsets (b) Explosive behaviour
   (c) Fatigue (d) Worry
5. Which one of the following statements is correct?
   (a) Syllabus is an annexure to the curriculum.
   (b) Curriculum is the same in all educational institutions.
   (c) Curriculum includes both formal and informal education.
   (d) Curriculum does not include methods of evaluation.
6. A successful teacher is one who is
   (a) Compassionate and disciplinarian
   (b) Quite and reactive
   (c) Tolerant and dominating
   (d) Passive and active

Read the following passage carefully and answer the questions 7 to 12.

The phrase "What is it like?" stands for a fundamental thought process. How does one go about observing and reporting on things and events that occupy segments of earth space? Of all the infinite variety of phenomena on the face of the earth, how does one decide what phenomena to observe? There is no such thing as a complete description of the earth or any part of it, for every microscopic point on the earth's surface differs from every other such point. Experience shows that the things observed are already familiar, because they are like phenomena that occur at home or because they resemble the abstract images and models developed in the human mind.

How are abstract images formed? Humans alone among the animals possess language; their words symbolise not only specific things but also mental images of classes of things. People can remember what they have seen or experienced because they attach a word symbol to them.

During the long record of our efforts to gain more and more knowledge about the face of the earth as the human habitat, there has been a continuing interplay between things and events. The direct observation through the senses is described as a percept; the mental image is described as a concept. Percepts are what some people describe as reality, in contrast to mental images, which are theoretical, implying that they are not real.

The relation of Percept to Concept is not as simple as the definition implies. It is now quite clear that people of different cultures or even individuals in the same culture develop different mental images of reality and what they perceive is a reflection of these preconceptions. The direct observation of things and events on the face of the earth is so clearly a function of the mental images of the mind of the observer that the whole idea of reality must be reconsidered.

Concepts determine what the observer perceives, yet concepts are derived from the generalisations of previous percepts. What happens is that the educated observer is taught to accept a set of concepts and then sharpens or changes these concepts during a professional career. In any one field of scholarship, professional opinion at one time determines what concepts and procedures are acceptable, and these form a kind of model of scholarly behaviour.

7. The problem raised in the passage reflects on
   (a) thought process
   (b) human behaviour
   (c) cultural perceptions
   (d) professional opinion
8. According to the passage, human beings have mostly in mind
   (a) Observation of things
   (b) Preparation of mental images
   (c) Expression through language
   (d) To gain knowledge
9. Concept means
   (a) A mental image
   (b) A reality
   (c) An idea expressed in language form
   (d) All the above
10. The relation of Percept to Concept is
    (a) Positive (b) Negative
    (c) Reflective (d) Absolute
11. In the passage, the earth is taken as
    (a) The Globe
    (b) The Human Habitat
    (c) A Celestial Body
    (d) A Planet
12. Percept means
    (a) Direct observation through the senses
    (b) A conceived idea
    (c) Ends of a spectrum
    (d) An abstract image
13. Action research means
    (a) A longitudinal research
    (b) An applied research
    (c) A research initiated to solve an immediate problem
    (d) A research with socio-economic objective
14. Research is
    (a) Searching again and again
    (b) Finding solution to any problem
    (c) Working in a scientific way to search for truth of any problem
    (d) None of the above
15. A common test in research demands much priority on
    (a) Reliability (b) Usability
    (c) Objectivity (d) All of the above
16. Which of the following is the first step in starting the research process?
    (a) Searching sources of information to locate problem
    (b) Survey of related literature
    (c) Identification of problem
    (d) Searching for solutions to the problem
17. If a researcher conducts a research on finding out which administrative style contributes more to institutional effectiveness? This will be an example of
    (a) Basic Research (b) Action Research
    (c) Applied Research (d) None of the above
18. Normal Probability Curve should be
    (a) Positively skewed
    (b) Negatively skewed
    (c) Leptokurtic skewed
    (d) Zero skewed
19. In communication, a major barrier to reception of messages is
    (a) audience attitude
    (b) audience knowledge
    (c) audience education
    (d) audience income
20. Post-modernism is associated with
    (a) Newspapers (b) Magazines
    (c) Radio (d) Television
21. Didactic communication is
    (a) intra-personal (b) inter-personal
    (c) organisational (d) relational
22. In communication, the language is
    (a) the non-verbal code
    (b) the verbal code
    (c) the symbolic code
    (d) the iconic code

23. Identify the correct sequence of the following:
    (a) Source, channel, message, receiver
    (b) Source, receiver, channel, message
    (c) Source, message, receiver, channel
    (d) Source, message, channel, receiver
24. **Assertion (A):** Mass media promote a culture of violence in the society.
    Reason (R): Because violence sells in the market as people themselves are violent in character.
    (a) Both (A) and (R) are true and (R) is the correct explanation of (A).
    (b) Both (A) and (R) are true, but (R) is not the correct explanation of (A).
    (c) (A) is true, but (R) is false.
    (d) Both (A) and (R) are false.
25. When an error of 1% is made in the length of a square, the percentage error in the area of a square will be
    (a) 0 (b) 1/2 (c) 1 (d) 2
26. On January 12, 1980, it was a Saturday. The day of the week on January 12, 1979 was
    (a) Thursday (b) Friday
    (c) Saturday (d) Sunday
27. If water is called food, food is called tree, tree is called earth, earth is called world, which of the following grows a fruit?
    (a) Water (b) Tree
    (c) World (d) Earth
28. E is the son of A, D is the son of B, E is married to C, C is the daughter of D. How is D related to E?
    (a) Brother (b) Uncle
    (c) Father-in-law (d) Brother-in-law
29. If INSURANCE is coded as ECNARUSNI, how HINDRANCE will be coded?
    (a) CADNIHWCE (b) HANODEINR
    (c) AENIRHDCN (d) ECNARDNIH
30. Find the next number in the following series:
    2, 5, 10, 17, 26, 37, 50, ?
    (a) 63 (b) 65 (c) 67 (d) 69
31. Which of the following is an example of circular argument?
    (a) God created man in his image and man created God in his own image.
    (b) God is the source of a scripture and the scripture is the source of our knowledge of God.
    (c) Some of the Indians are great because India is great.
    (d) Rama is great because he is Rama.
32. Lakshmana is a morally good person because
    (a) he is religious (b) he is educated
    (c) he is rich (d) he is rational
33. Two statements I and II given below are followed by two conclusions (A) and (B). Supposing the statements are true, which of the following conclusions can logically follow?
    Statements:
    I. Some religious people are morally good.
    II. Some religious people are rational.
    Conclusions:
    A. Rationally religious people are good morally.
    B. Non-rational religious persons are not morally good.
    (a) Only (A) follows
    (b) Only (B) follows
    (c) Both (A) and (B) follow
    (d) Neither (A) nor (B) follows
34. Certainty is
    (a) an objective fact
    (b) emotionally satisfying
    (c) logical
    (d) ontological

Questions from 35 to 36 are based on the following diagram in which there are three intersecting circles I, S and P where circle I stands for Indians, circle S stands for Scientists and circle P for Politicians. Different regions of the figure are lettered from a to g.

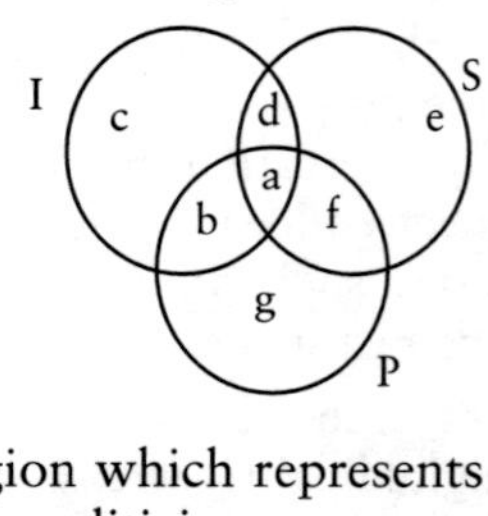

35. The region which represents non-scientists who are politicians.

(a) f (b) d (c) a (d) c

36. The region which represents politicians who are Indians as well as scientists.
(a) b (b) c (c) a (d) d

37. The population of a city is plotted as a function of time (years) in graphic form below:

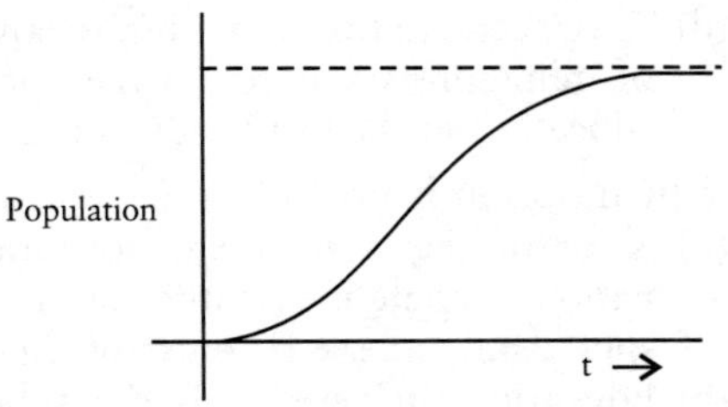

Which of the following inference can be drawn from above plot?
(a) The population increases exponentially.
(b) The population increases in parabolic fashion.
(c) The population initially increases in a linear fashion and then stabilises.
(d) The population initially increases exponentially and then stabilises.

In the following chart, the price of logs is shown in per cubic metre and that of Plywood and Saw Timber in per tonnes. Study the chart and answer the following questions 38, 39 and 40.

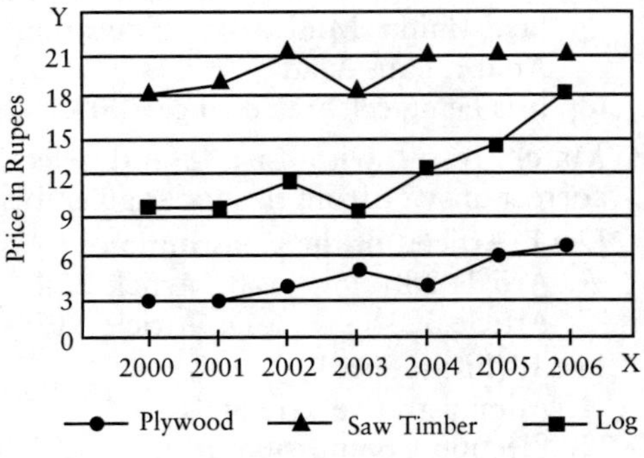

38. Which product shows the maximum percentage increase in price over the period?
(a) Saw timber (b) Plywood
(c) Log (d) None of these

39. What is the maximum percentage increase in price per cubic metre of log?
(a) 6 (b) 12
(c) 18 (d) None of these

40. In which year the prices of two products decreased and that of the third increased?
(a) 2000 (b) 2002 (c) 2003 (d) 2006

41. Which one of the following is the oldest Archival source of data in India?
(a) National Sample Surveys
(b) Agricultural Statistics
(c) Census
(d) Vital Statistics

42. In a large random data set following normal distribution, the ratio (%) of number of data points which are in the range of (mean ± standard deviation) to the total number of data points, is
(a) ~ 50% (b) ~ 67% (c) ~ 97% (d) ~ 47%

43. Which number system is usually followed in a typical 32-bit computer?
(a) 2 (b) 8 (c) 10 (d) 16

44. Which one of the following is an example of Operating System?
(a) Microsoft Word (b) Microsoft Excel
(c) Microsoft Access (d) Microsoft Windows

45. Which one of the following represent the binary equivalent of the decimal number 23?
(a) 01011 (b) 10111
(c) 10011 (d) None of these

46. Which one of the following is different from other members?
(a) Google (b) Windows
(c) Linux (d) Mac

47. Where does a computer add and compare its data?
(a) CPU (b) Memory
(c) Hard disk (d) Floppy disk

48. Computers on an internet are identified by
(a) e-mail address
(b) street address
(c) IP address
(d) None of the above

49. The Right to Information Act, 2005 makes the provision of
(a) Dissemination of all types of information by all Public authorities to any person

(b) Establishment of Central, State and District Level Information Commissions as an appellate body
(c) Transparency and accountability in Public authorities
(d) All of the above

50. Which type of natural hazards cause maximum damage to property and lives?
(a) Hydrological (b) Hydro-meteorological
(c) Geological (d) Geo-chemical

51. Dioxins are produced from
(a) Wastelands (b) Power plants
(c) Sugar factories (d) Combustion of plastics

52. The slogan "A tree for each child" was coined for
(a) Social forestry program
(b) Clean Air program
(c) Soil conservation program
(d) Environmental protection program

53. The main constituents of biogas are
(a) Methane and Carbon dioxide
(b) Methane and Nitric oxide
(c) Methane, Hydrogen and Nitric oxide
(d) Methane and Sulphur dioxide

54. **Assertion (A):** In the world as a whole, the environment has degraded during past several decades.

Reason (R): The population of the world has been growing significantly.
(a) (A) is correct, (R) is correct and (R) is the correct explanation of (A).
(b) (A) is correct, (R) is correct and (R) is not the correct explanation of (A).
(c) (A) is correct, but (R) is false.
(d) (A) is false, but (R) is correct.

55. Climate change has implications for
1. soil moisture 2. forest fires
3. biodiversity 4. groundwater

Identify the correct combination according to the code:

Codes:
(a) 1 and 3 (b) 1, 2 and 3
(c) 1, 3 and 4 (d) 1, 2, 3 and 4

56. The accreditation process by National Assessment and Accreditation Council (NAAC) differs from that of National Board of Accreditation (NBA) in terms of
(a) Disciplines covered by both being the same, there is duplication of efforts.
(b) One has institutional grading approach and the other has program grading approach.
(c) Once get accredited by NBA or NAAC, the institution is free from renewal of grading, which is not a progressive decision.
(d) This accreditation amounts to approval of minimum standards in the quality of education in the institution concerned.

57. Which option is not correct?
(a) Most of the educational institutions of national repute in scientific and technical sphere fall under 64th entry of Union list.
(b) Education, in general, is the subject of concurrent list since 42nd Constitutional Amendment Act 1976.
(c) Central Advisory Board on Education (CABE) was first established in 1920.
(d) India had implemented the right to Free and Compulsory Primary Education in 2002 through 86th Constitutional Amendment.

58. Which statement is not correct about the "National Education Day" of India?
(a) It is celebrated on 5th September every year.
(b) It is celebrated on 11th November every year.
(c) It is celebrated in the memory of India's first Union Minister of Education, Dr. Abul Kalam Azad.
(d) It is being celebrated since 2008.

59. Match List I with List II and select the correct answer from the codes given below:

List I (Articles of the Constitution)
A. Article 280 B. Article 324
C. Article 323 D. Article 315

List II (Institutions)
1. Administrative Tribunals
2. Election Commission of India
3. Finance Commission at Union level
4. Union Public Service Commission

Codes:	**A**	**B**	**C**	**D**
(a)	1	2	3	4
(b)	3	2	1	4
(c)	2	3	4	1
(d)	2	4	3	1

60. Deemed Universities declared by UGC under Section 3 of the UGC Act 1956, are not permitted to
   (a) offer programs in higher education and issue degrees
   (b) give affiliation to any institute of higher education
   (c) open off-campus and off-shore campus anywhere in the country and overseas respectively without the permission of the UGC
   (d) offer distance education programs without the approval of the Distance Education Council

ANSWERS

1. (b)	2. (c)	3. (c)	4. (b)	5. (c)
6. (a)	7. (c)	8. (a)	9. (a)	10. (c)
11. (b)	12. (a)	13. (c)	14. (c)	15. (d)
16. (c)	17. (c)	18. (d)	19. (c)	20. (d)
21. (b)	22. (b)	23. (d)	24. (d)	25. (d)
26. (b)	27. (c)	28. (c)	29. (d)	30. (b)
31. (c)	32. (d)	33. (d)	34. (c)	35. (a)
36. (d)	37. (a)	38. (c)	39. (d)	40. (b)
41. (c)	42. (b)	43. (a)	44. (d)	45. (b)
46. (b)	47. (a)	48. (c)	49. (d)	50. (c)
51. (d)	52. (d)	53. (a)	54. (b)	55. (d)
56. (c)	57. (a)	58. (a)	59. (b)	60. (b)

PAPER–II

Note: This paper contains fifty (50) objective type questions, each question carrying two (2) marks. All questions are compulsory.

1. The concept of Small Scale Industries (SSIs) was brought to fore by the
   (a) Industrial Policy Resolution, 1948
   (b) Industrial Policy Resolution, 1956
   (c) Industrial Policy Statement, 1977
   (d) None of the above

2. Which combination of the following factors has driven globalisation in the recent past?
   I. Growth of multinational corporations.
   II. Internationalisation of finance.
   III. Increased international trade.
   (a) I and II (b) I and III
   (c) II and III (d) I, II and III

3. **Assertion (A):** Privatisation process leads to change in management with change in ownership.
   Reason (R): Change in management is not a necessary condition for the process of privatisation.
   Which one of the following is correct combination?
   Codes:
   (a) Both (A) and (R) are correct.
   (b) (A) is correct, but (R) is incorrect.
   (c) (A) is incorrect, but (R) is correct.
   (d) Both (A) and (R) are incorrect.

4. Match the following two lists of statements.
   List I
   A. When one company purchases another one.
   B. Merger between two companies having no common business areas.
   C. Merger between two companies that sell the same products in different markets.
   D. Two companies are bought and combined under new entity.
   List II
   1. Conglomeration merger
   2. Consolidation merger
   3. Purchase merger
   4. Market extension merger

Codes:	**A**	**B**	**C**	**D**
(a)	1	2	3	4
(b)	2	3	1	4
(c)	3	1	4	2
(d)	3	4	1	2

5. In which of the industrial policies were the following major changes introduced?
   — Liberalisation of licensed capacity.
   — Relaxation of industrial licensing.
   — Industrialisation of backward areas.
   (a) Industrial Policy Resolution, 1956.
   (b) Industrial Policy Statement, 1977.
   (c) Industrial Policy of 1980.
   (d) Industrial Policy of 1991.

6. Which of the following is not an Accounting concept?
   (a) Matching concept
   (b) Dual Aspect concept

(c) True and Fair concept
(d) Going concern concept

7. Deficiency/Surplus Account in liquidation of a company is called
(a) List – C (b) List – D
(c) List – G (d) List – H

8. Which of the following statements is not correct?
(a) P/V ratio can be improved by reducing fixed cost.
(b) Contribution is also known as Gross margin.
(c) P/V ratio can be improved by increasing the selling price.
(d) Margin of safety can be improved by reducing fixed cost.

9. In the context of Standard Costing; Basic Standard is established for
(a) short period (b) current period
(c) indefinite period (d) pre-defined period

10. Read the following statements:
(i) Marginal costing and absorption costing are the same.
(ii) For decision making, absorption costing is more suitable than marginal costing.
(iii) Cost-volume-profit relationships also denote break-even point.
(iv) Marginal costing is based on the distinction between fixed and variable costs.
Which of the following combinations gives true statements with regard to above?
(a) (i) & (ii) (b) (ii) & (iii)
(c) (iii) & (iv) (d) (iv) & (ii)

11. A consumer consuming two goods will be in equilibrium, when the marginal utilities from both goods are
(a) maximum possible positive
(b) minimum possible positive
(c) equal
(d) zero

12. Total production will be maximum when
(a) Marginal production is maximum.
(b) Average production is maximum.
(c) Marginal production is zero.
(d) Average production is equal to the marginal production.

13. Which one of the following is not matched properly?

List I
1. High initial price to be lowered later
2. Prices to be proportional to cost
3. Prices to be increased for providing profit
4. Prices to be different in different markets

List II
A. Product line pricing
B. Differential pricing
C. Pioneer pricing
D. Incremental pricing

(a) 1 and C (b) 2 and A
(c) 3 and D (d) 4 and B

14. As per indifference curve and price line, a consumer will not be in equilibrium when
(a) Ratios of marginal utilities and prices of the respective goods are equal.
(b) Ratio of marginal utilities of the two goods is equal to the ratio of their respective prices.
(c) The marginal rate of substitution is equal to the ratio of prices of the two goods.
(d) The marginal rate of substitution is decreasing.

15. Under kinked demand model, the demand curve for the firm's product is drawn on the assumption that
(a) All rivals charge the same price which is charged by the oligopolist.
(b) All rivals charge a price independent of the price charged by the oligopolist.
(c) All rivals follow the oligopolist upto certain price but beyond that they do not.
(d) All oligopolists charge the price as independent sellers.

16. A graph of a cumulative frequency distribution is called
(a) Ogive (b) Frequency polygon
(c) Pie diagram (d) Histogram

17. Which of the following tests is used to test the significance of the coefficient of association ?
(a) Z-test (b) t-test (c) χ^2-test (d) F-test

18. The total area of a normal distribution between average value ± 1.96 of standard deviation is
(a) 95.45 % (b) 95 %
(c) 99 % (d) 68.34 %

19. Which of the following is a relative measure of dispersion?

(a) Standard deviation
(b) Variance
(c) Co-efficient of variation
(d) None of the above

20. ERP includes (i) SAP, and/or (ii) Resource Planning.
(a) Both (i) and (ii) (b) Only (i)
(c) Only (ii) (d) None of the above

21. Which one of the following was not main contribution of F.W. Tailor?
(a) Scientific management
(b) Time and motion studies
(c) Differential wage plan
(d) Modern management

22. Match the items of List-I with items of List-II.

List-I	List-II
A. Hygiene theory	(i) Abraham H. Maslow
B. Theory of 'X' and 'Y'	(ii) Victor Vroom
C. Expectancy Theory	(iii) Fredrick Herzberg
	(iv) Doughlas Mcgregor

Codes:	A	B	C
(a)	iii	iv	ii
(b)	i	iv	ii
(c)	iii	ii	iv
(d)	i	ii	iv

23. Which of the following combinations consists of correct statements?
(i) Control and planning are interlinked.
(ii) Control is not meant for men, but for activities.
(iii) Control is a circular movement.
(a) (i) and (ii) (b) (i) and (iii)
(c) (ii) and (iii) (d) (i), (ii) and (iii)

24. Staffing includes
(i) Training (ii) Appraisal
(iii) Placement (iv) Directing
Which of the following is correct?
(a) (i) and (iii) (b) (i), (ii) and (iii)
(c) (ii) and (iii) (d) (i), (ii), (iii) and (iv)

25. **Assertion (A):** Management is a continuous process involving the integration of all functions.
Reason (R): Managers first plan, then organise and finally perform the function of controlling.
Read the above statements and select the correct answer from the code below:
Codes:
(a) Both (A) and (R) are correct; and (R) is correct explanation of (A).
(b) Both (A) and (R) are correct, but (R) is not a correct explanation of (A).
(c) (A) is correct, but (R) is incorrect.
(d) (A) is incorrect, but (R) is correct.

26. Exchange concept of marketing deals with
(a) Exchange of products between sellers and buyers covering distribution and price aspects.
(b) Mere appendage to production.
(c) Achieving marketing success through product attributes.
(d) Aggressively promote and push the products.

27. Who coined the expression "Marketing Mix"?
(a) Henry Fayol (b) James Culliton
(c) Peter Drucker (d) Abraham Maslow

28. Road blocking advertisement refers to
(a) Advertising a product by blocking the road.
(b) Creating big blocks for advertising a product.
(c) Advertising a product on multiple TV channels at the same time.
(d) None of the above.

29. Match the following:
List I
A. Market segmentation
B. Skimming price
C. Multilevel marketing
D. Sales management
List II
(i) Pricing high of a new product initially.
(ii) Process of disaggregating a market into a number of submarkets.
(iii) Translation of the marketing plan into marketing performance.
(iv) Modified version of direct marketing.

Codes:	A	B	C	D
(a)	ii	i	iv	iii
(b)	iii	i	ii	iv
(c)	i	ii	iii	iv
(d)	iv	ii	iii	i

30. Which of the following buying process sequence is correct?
   1. Adoption 2. Legitimization
   3. Attitude 4. Awareness
   (a) 4, 3, 2, 1 (b) 2, 3, 4, 1
   (c) 1, 2, 3, 4 (d) 3, 4, 2, 1

31. Discounted cash flow criteria for investment appraisal does not include
   (a) Net present value
   (b) Benefit-cost ratio
   (c) Accounting rate of return
   (d) Internal rate of return

32. Working capital represents the portion of current assets financed through long term funds. This indicates (1) net working capital and/or (2) gross working capital.
   (a) (1) is correct
   (b) (2) is correct
   (c) Both (1) and (2) are correct
   (d) Neither of the two is correct

33. Dividend policy of a company mainly concerns with
   (i) dividend payout and/or
   (ii) stability of dividend.
   (a) Only (i) is correct.
   (b) Only (ii) is correct.
   (c) Both (i) and (ii) are correct.
   (d) Both (i) and (ii) are incorrect.

34. Match the following:

   List I
   A. The presence of fixed cost in the cost structure of a firm.
   B. The presence of fixed return funds in the capital structure of a firm.
   C. Impact of changes in sales on the earnings available to shareholders.

   List II
   1. Superleverage 2. Operating leverage
   3. Financial leverage

Codes:	**A**	**B**	**C**
(a)	1	2	3
(b)	2	3	1
(c)	3	2	1
(d)	1	3	2

35. Which one of the following is not used to estimate cost of equity capital?
   (a) External yield criterion
   (b) Dividend plus growth rate
   (c) Equity capitalisation approach
   (d) Capital asset pricing model

36. Which of the following is not a Central Trade Union in India?
   (a) B.M.S. (b) I.L.O.
   (c) INTUC (d) AITUC

37. Sequence the following in which they are practised:
   (i) Promotion
   (ii) Performance appraisal
   (iii) Recruitment
   (iv) Training and Development
   (a) (iii), (ii), (iv) (i) (b) (iii), (ii), (i), (iv)
   (c) (iii), (i), (iv), (ii) (d) (iii), (iv), (ii), (i)

38. Which one of the following purposes is not served by performance evaluation?
   (a) Decisions about promotions, transfers and terminations.
   (b) Centralisation and decentralisation of decision making authority.
   (c) Identification of training and development needs.
   (d) Criterion against which selection and development programmes are validated.

39. Who has introduced the "Seven Point Plan" for taking the best interview method?
   (a) Milton L. Blum (b) F.E. Burt
   (c) Prof. A. Rozar (d) Filippo

40. The last stage in a grievance redressal procedure is handled by
   (a) Union
   (b) Voluntary Arbitrator
   (c) H.R. Department
   (d) Grievance Committee

41. The Commercial Banks in India are governed by
   (a) Reserve Bank of India Act, 1934
   (b) Indian Companies' Act, 1956
   (c) Indian Banking Regulation Act, 1949
   (d) Securities and Exchange Board of India Act, 1992

42. Which of the following limits the power of credit creation by Commercial Banks?
   (a) Fiscal Policy (b) Banking Laws
   (c) Business Pessimism (d) None of the above

43. Match the following with the years of establishment/nationalisation.

List I
(a) Reserve Bank of India
(b) Nationalisation of 14 Major Commercial Banks
(c) Nationalisation of 6 Commercial Banks
(d) Regional Rural Banks

List II
(i) 1975 (ii) 1935 (iii) 1969 (iv) 1980

Codes:	A	B	C	D
(a)	i	iii	ii	iv
(b)	iii	ii	iv	i
(c)	iv	iii	i	ii
(d)	ii	iii	iv	i

44. Capital adequacy norm helps banks
(i) For strengthening capital base of banks.
(ii) For sanctioning more loans.
(a) Both (i) and (ii) are correct.
(b) Both (i) and (ii) are incorrect.
(c) (i) is correct, but (ii) is incorrect.
(d) (i) is incorrect, but (ii) is correct.

45. Which one of the following is the main objective of Unit Trust of India?
(a) To mobilize the savings of high income groups.
(b) To mobilize the savings of low and high income groups.
(c) To mobilize the savings of corporates.
(d) To mobilize the savings of low and middle income groups.

46. Which of the following is the basic objective of the World Bank?
(a) To provide social services
(b) To provide financial assistance
(c) To promote economic growth
(d) To eradicate poverty

47. Which of the following is not an International Financial Institution?
(a) I.C.I.C.I. (b) I.M.F.
(c) I.D.A. (d) World Bank

48. In balance of payment accounts, all goods exported and imported are recorded in ________.
(a) Capital Account
(b) Visible Account
(c) Invisible Account
(d) Merchandise Account

49. The devaluation of currency of a country is done when ________.
(i) It has adverse balance of payments.
(ii) It has favourable balance of payments.
(a) Both (i) and (ii) are correct.
(b) Both (i) and (ii) are incorrect.
(c) Only (i) is correct.
(d) Only (ii) is correct.

50. Match the following with the year of establishment:

List I
A. World Trade Organisation
B. Uruguay Round Negotiation
C. W.T.O.-Trade Policy Review Body
D. The Patents (Amendment) Act.

List II
i. 1993 ii. 1995 iii. 1997 iv. 1999

Codes:	A	B	C	D
(a)	i	iii	iv	ii
(b)	i	iv	iii	ii
(c)	ii	i	iii	iv
(d)	iv	ii	i	iii

ANSWERS

1. (c)	2. (d)	3. (b)	4. (c)	5. (d)
6. (c)	7. (d)	8. (b)	9. (d)	10. (c)
11. (c)	12. (c)	13. (b)	14. (d)	15. (c)
16. (a)	17. (c)	18. (b)	19. (c)	20. (a)
21. (a)	22. (a)	23. (a)	24. (b)	25. (a)
26. (a)	27. (b)	28. (c)	29. (a)	30. (a)
31. (b)	32. (c)	33. (c)	34. (b)	35. (a)
36. (b)	37. (d)	38. (b)	39. (c)	40. (b)
41. (c)	42. (d)	43. (d)	44. (c)	45. (d)
46. (b)	47. (a)	48. (b)	49. (c)	50. (c)

DECEMBER–2010

Note: This paper contains Sixty (60) multiple choice questions, each question carrying two (2) marks. Candidate is expected to answer any Fifty (50) questions. In case more than Fifty (50) questions are attempted, only the first Fifty (50) questions will be evaluated.

PAPER–I

1. Which of the following variables cannot be expressed in quantitative terms?
   (a) Socio-economic Status
   (b) Marital Status
   (c) Numerical Aptitude
   (d) Professional Attitude
2. A doctor studies the relative effectiveness of two drugs of dengue fever. His research would be classified as
   (a) Descriptive Survey
   (b) Experimental Research
   (c) Case Study
   (d) Ethnography
3. The term 'phenomenology' is associated with the process of
   (a) Qualitative Research
   (b) Analysis of Variance
   (c) Correlational Study
   (d) Probability Sampling
4. The 'Sociogram' technique is used to study
   (a) Vocational Interest
   (b) Professional Competence
   (c) Human Relations
   (d) Achievement Motivation

Read the following passage carefully and answer questions from 5 to 10.

It should be remembered that the nationalist movement in India, like all nationalist movements, was essentially a bourgeois movement. It represented the natural historical stage of development, and to consider it or to criticise it as a working-class movement is wrong. Gandhi represented that movement and the Indian masses in relation to that movement to a supreme degree, and he became the voice of Indian people to that extent. The main contribution of Gandhi to India and the Indian masses has been through the powerful movements which he launched through the National Congress. Through nation-wide action he sought to mould the millions, and largely succeeded in doing so, and changing them from a demoralised, timid and hopeless mass, bullied and crushed by every dominant interest, and incapable of resistance, into a people with self-respect and self-reliance, resisting tyranny, and capable of united action and sacrifice for a larger cause.

Gandhi made people think of political and economic issues and every village and every bazaar hummed with argument and debate on the new ideas and hopes that filled the people. That was an amazing psychological change. The time was ripe for it, of course, and circumstances and world conditions worked for this change. But a great leader is necessary to take advantage of circumstances and conditions. Gandhi was that leader, and he released many of the bonds that imprisoned and disabled our minds, and none of us who experienced it can ever forget that great feeling of release and exhilaration that came over the Indian people.

Gandhi has played a revolutionary role in India of the greatest importance because he knew how to make the most of the objective conditions and could reach the heart of the masses, while groups with a more advanced ideology functioned largely in the air because they did not fit in with those conditions and could therefore not evoke any substantial response from the masses.

It is perfectly true that Gandhi, functioning in the nationalist plane, does not think in terms of the conflict of classes, and tries to compose their differences. But the action he has indulged and taught the people has inevitably raised mass consciousness tremendously and made social issues vital. Gandhi and the Congress must be judged by the policies they pursue and the action they indulge in. But behind this, personality counts and colours those policies and activities. In the case of very exceptional person like Gandhi the question of personality becomes especially important in order to understand and appraise him. To us he has represented the spirit and honour of India, the yearning of her sorrowing millions to be rid of their innumerable burdens, and an insult to him by the British Government or others has been an insult to India and her people.

5. Which one of the following is true of the given passage?
   (a) The passage is a critique of Gandhi's role in Indian movement for independence
   (b) The passage hails the role of Gandhi in India's freedom movement
   (c) The author is neutral on Gandhi's role in India's freedom movement
   (d) It is an account of Indian National Congress's support to the working-class movement
6. The change that the Gandhian movement brought among the Indian masses was
   (a) Physical (b) Cultural
   (c) Technological (d) Psychological
7. To consider the nationalist movement or to criticise it as a working-class movement was wrong because it was a
   (a) historical movement
   (b) voice of the Indian people
   (c) bourgeois movement
   (d) movement represented by Gandhi
8. Gandhi played a revolutionary role in India because he could
   (a) preach morality
   (b) reach the heart of Indians
   (c) see the conflict of classes
   (d) lead the Indian National Congress
9. Groups with advanced ideology functioned in the air as they did not fit in with
   (a) objective conditions of masses
   (b) the Gandhian ideology
   (c) the class consciousness of the people
   (d) the differences among masses
10. The author concludes the passage by
    (a) criticising the Indian masses
    (b) the Gandhian movement
    (c) pointing out the importance of the personality of Gandhi
    (d) identifying the sorrows of millions of Indians
11. Media that exist in an interconnected series of communication—points are referred to as
    (a) Networked media (b) Connective media
    (c) Nodal media (d) Multimedia
12. The information function of mass communication is described as
    (a) diffusion (b) publicity
    (c) surveillance (d) diversion
13. An example of asynchronous medium is
    (a) Radio (b) Television
    (c) Film (d) Newspaper
14. In communication, connotative words are
    (a) explicit (b) abstract
    (c) simple (d) cultural
15. A message beneath a message is labelled as
    (a) embedded text (b) internal text
    (c) inter-text (d) sub-text
16. In analogue mass communication, stories are
    (a) static (b) dynamic
    (c) interactive (d) exploratory
17. Determine the relationship between the pair of words ALWAYS : NEVER and then select from the following pair of words which have a similar relationship
    (a) often : rarely
    (b) frequently : occasionally
    (c) constantly : frequently
    (d) intermittently : casually
18. Find the wrong number in the sequence
    52, 51, 48, 43, 34, 27, 16
    (a) 27 (b) 34 (c) 43 (d) 48
19. In a certain code, PAN is written as 31 and PAR as 35, then PAT is written in the same code as
    (a) 30 (b) 37 (c) 39 (d) 41
20. The letters in the first set have certain relationship. On the basis of this relationship, make the right choice for the second set:

AF : IK : : LQ : ?
(a) MO (b) NP (c) OR (d) TV

21. If 5472 = 9, 6342 = 6, 7584 = 6, what is 9236?
(a) 2 (b) 3 (c) 4 (d) 5

22. In an examination, 35% of the total students failed in Hindi, 45% failed in English and 20% in both. The percentage of those who passed in both subjects is
(a) 10 (b) 20 (c) 30 (d) 40

23. Two statements I and II given below are followed by two conclusions (A) and (B). Supposing the statements are true, which of the following conclusions can logically follow?

Statements:
I. Some flowers are red.
II. Some flowers are blue.

Conclusions:
(A) Some flowers are neither red nor blue.
(B) Some flowers are both red and blue.
(a) Only (A) follows
(b) Only (B) follows
(c) Both (A) and (B) follow
(d) Neither (A) nor (B) follows

24. If the statement 'all students are intelligent' is true, which of the following statements are false?
(i) No students are intelligent.
(ii) Some students are intelligent.
(iii) Some students are not intelligent.
(a) (i) and (ii) (b) (i) and (iii)
(c) (ii) and (iii) (d) Only (i)

25. A reasoning where we start with certain particular statements and conclude with a universal statement is called
(a) Deductive Reasoning
(b) Inductive Reasoning
(c) Abnormal Reasoning
(d) Transcendental Reasoning

26. What is the smallest number of ducks that could swim in this formation—two ducks in front of a duck, two ducks behind a duck and a duck between two ducks?
(a) 5 (b) 7 (c) 4 (d) 3

27. Mr. A, Miss B, Mr. C and Miss D are sitting around a table and discussing their trades.
(i) Mr. A sits opposite to the cook.
(ii) Miss B sits right to the barber.
(iii) The washerman sits right to the barber.
(iv) Miss D sits opposite to Mr. C.

What are the trades of A and B?
(a) Tailor and barber
(b) Barber and cook
(c) Tailor and cook
(d) Tailor and washerman

28. Which one of the following methods serve to measure correlation between two variables?
(a) Scatter Diagram
(b) Frequency Distrubution
(c) Two-way Table
(d) Coefficient of Rank Correlation

29. Which one of the following is not an Internet Service Provider (ISP)?
(a) MTNL (b) BSNL
(c) ERNET India (d) Infotech India Ltd.

30. The hexadecimal number system consists of the symbols
(a) 0 – 7 (b) 0 – 9, A – F
(c) 0 – 7, A – F (d) None of these

31. The binary equivalent of $(-15)_{10}$ is (2's complement system is used)
(a) 11110001 (b) 11110000
(c) 10001111 (d) None of these

32. 1 GB is equal to
(a) 2^{30} bits (b) 2^{30} bytes
(c) 2^{20} bits (d) 2^{20} bytes

33. The set of computer programs that manage the hardware/software of a computer is called
(a) Compiler system (b) Operation system
(c) Operating system (d) None of these

34. SMIME in Internet technology stands for
(a) Secure Multipurpose Internet Mail Extension
(b) Secure Multimedia Internet Mail Extension
(c) Simple Multipurpose Internet Mail Extension
(d) Simple Multimedia Internet Mail Extension

35. Which of the following is not covered in 8 missions under the Climate Action Plan of Government of India?

(a) Solar power
(b) Waste to energy conversion
(c) Afforestation
(d) Nuclear energy

36. The concentration of Total Dissolved Solids (TDS) in drinking water should not exceed
(a) 500 mg/L (b) 400 mg/L
(c) 300 mg/L (d) 200 mg/L

37. 'Chipko' movement was first started by
(a) Arundhati Roy (b) Medha Patkar
(c) Ila Bhatt (d) Sunderlal Bahuguna

38. The constituents of photochemical smog responsible for eye irritation are
(a) SO_2 and O_3 (b) SO_2 and NO_2
(c) HCHO and PAN (d) SO_2 and SPM

39. **Assertion (A):** Some carbonaceous aerosols may be carcinogenic.
Reason (R): They may contain polycyclic aromatic hydrocarbons (PAHs).
(a) Both (A) and (R) are correct and (R) is the correct explanation of (A).
(b) Both (A) and (R) are correct but (R) is not the correct explanation of (A).
(c) (A) is correct, but (R) is false.
(d) (A) is false, but (R) is correct.

40. Volcanic eruptions affect
(a) atmosphere and hydrosphere
(b) hydrosphere and biosphere
(c) lithosphere, biosphere and atmosphere
(d) lithosphere, hydrosphere and atmosphere

41. India's first Defence University is in the State of
(a) Haryana (b) Andhra Pradesh
(c) Uttar Pradesh (d) Punjab

42. Most of the universities in India
(a) conduct teaching and research only
(b) affiliate colleges and conduct examinations
(c) conduct teaching/research and examinations
(d) promote research only

43. Which one of the following is not a Constitutional Body?
(a) Election Commission
(b) Finance Commission
(c) Union Public Service Commission
(d) Planning Commission

44. Which one of the following statements is not correct?
(a) Indian Parliament is supreme.
(b) The Supreme Court of India has the power of judicial review.
(c) There is a division of powers between the Centre and the States.
(d) There is a Council of Ministers to aid and advise the President.

45. Which one of the following statements reflects the republic character of Indian democracy?
(a) Written constitution
(b) No State religion
(c) Devolution of power to local government institutions
(d) Elected President and directly or indirectly elected Parliament

46. Who among the following appointed by the Governor can be removed by only the President of India?
(a) Chief Minister of a State
(b) A member of the State Public Service Commission
(c) Advocate-General
(d) Vice Chancellor of a State University

47. If two small circles represent the class of the 'men' and the class of the 'plants' and the big circle represents 'mortality', which one of the following figures represent the proposition 'All men are mortal?.'

(a) 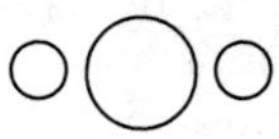 (b) 

(c) 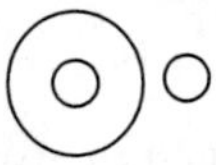 (d) 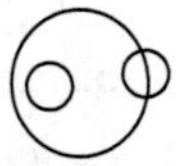

The following table presents the production of electronic items (TVs and LCDs) in a factory during the period from 2006 to 2010. Study the table carefully and answer the questions from 48 to 52:

Year	2006	2007	2008	2009	2010
TVs	6000	9000	13000	11000	8000
LCDs	7000	9400	9000	10000	12000

48. In which year, the total production of electronic items is maximum?
(a) 2006 (b) 2007 (c) 2008 (d) 2010

49. What is the difference between averages of production of LCDs and TVs from 2006 to 2008?
 (a) 3000 (b) 2867
 (c) 3015 (d) None of these
50. What is the year in which production of TVs is half the production of LCDs in the year 2010?
 (a) 2007 (b) 2006 (c) 2009 (d) 2008
51. What is the ratio of production of LCDs in the years 2008 and 2010?
 (a) 4:3 (b) 3:4 (c) 1:3 (d) 2:3
52. What is the ratio of production of TVs in the years 2006 and 2007?
 (a) 6:7 (b) 7:6 (c) 2:3 (d) 3:2
53. Some students in a class exhibit great curiosity for learning. It may be because such children
 (a) Are gifted
 (b) Come from rich families
 (c) Show artificial behaviour
 (d) Create indiscipline in the class
54. The most important quality of a good teacher is
 (a) Sound knowledge of subject matter
 (b) Good communication skills
 (c) Concern for students' welfare
 (d) Effective leadership qualities
55. Which one of the following is appropriate in respect of teacher-student relationship?
 (a) Very informal and intimate
 (b) Limited to classroom only
 (c) Cordial and respectful
 (d) Indifferent
56. The academic performance of students can be improved if parents are encouraged to
 (a) supervise the work of their wards
 (b) arrange for extra tuition
 (c) remain unconcerned about it
 (d) interact with teachers frequently
57. In a lively classroom situation, there is likely to be
 (a) occasional roars of laughter
 (b) complete silence
 (c) frequent teacher-student dialogue
 (d) loud discussion among students
58. If a parent approaches the teacher to do some favour to his/her ward in the examination, the teacher should
 (a) try to help him
 (b) ask him not to talk in those terms
 (c) refuse politely and firmly
 (d) ask him rudely to go away
59. Which of the following phrases is not relevant to describe the meaning of research as a process?
 (a) Systematic Activity
 (b) Objective Observation
 (c) Trial and Error
 (d) Problem Solving
60. Which of the following is not an example of a continuous variable?
 (a) Family size (b) Intelligence
 (c) Height (d) Altitude

ANSWERS

1. (d)	2. (b)	3. (a)	4. (c)	5. (b)
6. (d)	7. (c)	8. (b)	9. (a)	10. (c)
11. (a)	12. (c)	13. (d)	14. (d)	15. (d)
16. (a)	17. (a)	18. (b)	19. (b)	20. (d)
21. (a)	22. (b)	23. (c)	24. (d)	25. (b)
26. (a)	27. (c)	28. (d)	29. (d)	30. (b)
31. (d)	32. (b)	33. (c)	34. (a)	35. (d)
36. (a)	37. (d)	38. (b)	39. (a)	40. (d)
41. (a)	42. (c)	43. (d)	44. (b)	45. (d)
46. (b)	47. (c)	48. (c)	49. (d)	50. (b)
51. (b)	52. (c)	53. (a)	54. (b)	55. (c)
56. (d)	57. (c)	58. (c)	59. (c)	60. (c)

PAPER–II

Note: This paper contains fifty (50) objective type questions, each question carrying two (2) marks. All questions are compulsory.

1. India abolished the quantitative restrictions on imports of 1429 items in 2000 and 2001 as per the commitment to which of the following?
 (a) South Asian Free Trade Association (SAFTA)

(b) General Agreement on Tariffs and Trade (GATT)
(c) World Trade Organisation (WTO)
(d) Non-Aligned Movement

2. Globalization is a term used to describe the process of removal of restrictions on which of the following?
(a) Foreign Trade
(b) Investment
(c) (a) and (b) above
(d) None of the above

3. When a company takes over another one and clearly becomes a new owner, the action is called
(a) Merger (b) Acquisition
(c) Strategic Alliance (d) None of the above

4. Match the following two lists of statements.

List-I
A. Rate at which RBI gives loans to Commercial Banks by discounting bills
B. Rate at which RBI borrows from Commercial Banks

List-II
(i) Bank rate (ii) Repo rate
(iii) Prime lending rate

Codes:	A	B
(a)	(iii)	(i)
(b)	(ii)	(i)
(c)	(i)	(ii)
(d)	(iii)	(ii)

5. The MRTP Act, 1969 was abolished in
(a) 1991 (b) 2002
(c) 2006 (d) None of the above

6. Read the following statements:
(i) Financial statements are only interim reports.
(ii) Financial statements are prepared on the basis of realizable values.
(iii) The preparation of financial statements is not an ultimate aim.
(iv) Certain assumptions are necessary to prepare financial statements.

Which of the following combinations consists of all true statements?
(a) (i), (ii) and (iii) (b) (ii), (iii) and (iv)
(c) (i), (iii) and (iv) (d) (i), (ii) and (iv)

7. Which of the following is not a subsidiary book?
(a) Purchase Book (b) Sales Book
(c) Bills Receivables Book (d) Assets Book

8. Which of the following are the applications of funds?
(i) Redemption of Preference share capital.
(ii) Payment of Dividend.
(iii) Increase in working capital.
(a) only (i) and (ii) (b) only (ii) and (iii)
(c) only (i) and (iii) (d) (i), (ii) and (iii)

9. Accounting concepts are based on
(a) Certain assumptions
(b) Certain facts and figures
(c) Certain accounting records
(d) Government guidelines

10. The main purpose of Cost Accounting is to
(a) assist management in decision making.
(b) maximise profits and minimise losses.
(c) comply norms issued by the Government of India from time to time.
(d) prepare cost accounts in line with the accounting standards.

11. The various degrees of price elasticity of demand can be shown on a single demand curve as per which one of the following ?
(a) Total outlay method
(b) Proportional method
(c) Arc method
(d) Geometrical method

12. Which one of the following is not correct about the price discrimination by a monopolist, who intends to
(a) maximise the sales/profit
(b) share the consumer's surplus
(c) increase the welfare of masses
(d) reduce the welfare of masses

13. Returns to scale involve variations in the quantities of the various factors of production
1. Simultaneously, and/or
2. Proportionately
(a) Both (1) and (2) are correct
(b) (1) is correct and (2) is incorrect
(c) (1) is incorrect and (2) is correct
(d) Both (1) and (2) are incorrect.

14. The firm under perfect competition will be in short-run equilibrium when
(a) Rising marginal cost is equal to the minimum average cost.

(b) Marginal revenue is equal to rising marginal cost.
(c) Average revenue is equal to average cost.
(d) Marginal revenue is equal to the falling marginal cost.

15. Match the following:

List-I

A. Law of demand is fully applicable
B. Law of demand is not applicable at all
C. Law of demand is partly applicable

List-II

1. Giffen goods 2. Veblon goods
3. Normal goods

Codes:	A	B	C
(a)	1	2	3
(b)	2	3	1
(c)	3	1	2
(d)	2	1	3

16. **Statement I:** The heading for columns and rows are called caption and stub respectively.
Statement II: Sturge's Rule is used to decide the nature of manifold classification.
Which of the following is correct?
(a) Both I and II are false.
(b) Both I and II are true.
(c) I is true and II is false.
(d) I is false and II is true.

17. F-test is used to test the significance of the differences between
(a) Co-efficient of correlation between two sample groups.
(b) Co-efficient of correlation among more than two sample groups.
(c) Averages between two sample groups.
(d) Averages of more than two sample groups.

18. Co-variance between two variables is
(a) The average of the product of deviations taken from their averages.
(b) A is further divided by the product of their standard deviations.
(c) A is further divided by the product of their arithmetic averages.
(d) None of the above.

19. **Statement A:** Standard error of the mean is the standard deviation of the sampling distribution of mean.
Statement B: Simple random sampling is non-probability sampling method.
Which of the following combination is correct?
(a) Both A and B are true.
(b) Both A and B are false
(c) A is true and B is false.
(d) A is false and B is true.

20. Which of the following has RDBMS?
(i) Access (ii) Excel
(a) (*i*) and (*ii*) (b) only (*i*)
(c) only (*ii*) (d) None of the above

21. In which type of organization is 'grapevine' communication used?
(a) Informal organization
(b) Formal organization
(c) Departmental organization
(d) Matrix organization

22. In management science "Grid" refers to
(a) Diverse managerial styles
(b) Co-ordination
(c) Communication
(d) Motivation

23. "SWOT" is used for
(a) Planning (b) Organising
(c) Motivating (d) Controlling

24. Which of the following pairs is not matched?

	List-I		**List-II**
(a)	Frederick Herzburg	—	Scientific
(b)	Henry Fayol	—	Modern Management
(c)	Max Weber	—	Bureaucracy
(d)	Philip Kotlar	—	Marketing

25. Which one of the following is not covered under corporate governance?
(a) Corporate social responsibility
(b) Business ethics
(c) Role of independent directors
(d) Government monitoring

26. Market gridding means
(a) establishing and running a web marketing facility.
(b) a method of survey of expert's opinion.
(c) managing brands and developing brand equity.
(d) an analytical technique which facilitates dividing a market into segments.

27. Trade Mark is:
    (a) a name, term, symbol or design which is intended to identify the goods and services of a seller.
    (b) a brand that has been given legal protection.
    (c) giving protection to the product and adding to it's aesthetics and sales appeal.
    (d) providing written information about the product.

28. Which of the following is not a part of strategic planning?
    (a) Purposes and mission
    (b) Objectives
    (c) Choice of businesses
    (d) Social responsibility

29. Attitude means
    (a) Impulses, desires and considerations of the buyer, which induces him to purchase a product
    (b) A sum total of the individuals' faith and feelings towards a product.
    (c) The customer turning to his environment/world of information around him.
    (d) Creating some relentness in the mind of an individual.

30. Match the following:

    List I
    A. Supply chain management
    B. Product positioning
    C. Marketing environment analysis
    D. Dealer training

    List II
    (i) putting the product in the mind of the prospective buyer.
    (ii) the process of gathering, filtering and analysing information relating to the marketing environment.
    (iii) improving the performance of dealers through sharpening of their sales skills and product knowledge.
    (iv) larger in scope than both physical and marketing logistics.

Codes:	A	B	C	D
(a)	(i)	(ii)	(iii)	(iv)
(b)	(iv)	(i)	(ii)	(iii)
(c)	(ii)	(iv)	(iii)	(i)
(d)	(iii)	(iv)	(i)	(ii)

31. Over capitalization may not be as a result of which one of the following?
    (a) Promotion of a company with inflated assets
    (b) Application of low capitalization rate
    (c) Shortage of capital
    (d) Liberal dividend policy

32. Which one of the following is not matched?

    List I
    (A) Interest is a deductible expense
    (B) Realised-yield approach
    (C) Extended-yield approach
    (D) Dividend capitalization approach

    List II
    (i) Cost of debt capital
    (ii) Cost of equity capital
    (iii) Retained earnings
    (iv) Cost of preference share capital

    Codes:
    (a) (A) and (i) (b) (B) and (ii)
    (c) (C) and (iii) (d) (D) and (iv)

33. The rate of discount at which NPV of a project becomes zero is also known as
    (a) Average Rate of Return
    (b) Internal Rate of Return
    (c) Alternate Rate of Return
    (d) None of the above

34. The dividend irrelevance theorem to share valuation was propounded by
    (a) James E. Walter
    (b) Myron Gordon
    (c) Modigliani and Miller
    (d) None of the above

35. **Assertion (A):** Management of working capital refers to the management of current assets and current liabilities.

    Reason (R): But the major thrust of course, is on the management of current assets; because current liabilities arise in the context of current assets.

    Codes:
    (a) Both (A) and (R) are incorrect.
    (b) (A) is correct and (R) is incorrect.
    (c) Both (A) and (R) are correct.
    (d) (A) is incorrect, but (R) is correct.

36. Business plans designed to achieve the organizational objectives is called

(a) Human Resource Planning
(b) Human Resource Forecasting
(c) Strategic Plan
(d) Corporate Development Plan

37. "360" degree method relates to
(a) Performance appraisal
(b) Organization climate
(c) Employees morale
(d) Retrenchment

38. Match the following:

List I

(A) Adam Smith (B) Karl Marx
(C) John Davidson (D) David Ricardo

List II

(i) Subsistence Theory
(ii) Wages Fund Theory
(iii) The Surplus Value Theory
(iv) Bargaining Theory

Codes:	A	B	C	D
(a)	(ii)	(iii)	(iv)	(i)
(b)	(i)	(ii)	(iii)	(iv)
(c)	(iv)	(i)	(ii)	(iii)
(d)	(iii)	(iv)	(i)	(ii)

39. Assertions:
(i) High morale leads to high productivity.
(ii) High morale need not necessarily lead to high productivity.
(a) Both (i) and (ii) are correct.
(b) Both (i) and (ii) are incorrect.
(c) (i) is correct and (ii) is incorrect.
(d) (i) is incorrect and (ii) is correct.

40. **Statements:**
(i) Fringe benefits, nowadays, are a significant component of "compensation".
(ii) Under Piece-rate plan, employees are paid at a stipulated rate per hour of work done by them.
(a) Both (i) and (ii) are correct.
(b) Both (i) and (ii) are incorrect.
(c) (i) is incorrect and (ii) is correct.
(d) (i) is correct and (ii) is incorrect.

41. Which one of the following is not an instrument of credit control in the banking system?
(a) Open market operations
(b) Moral suasion
(c) Cash Reserve Ratio
(d) Tax rates

42. Match the following with their year of establishment:

A. IDBI	(i) 1982
B. IFCI	(ii) 1964
C. NABARD	(iii) 1948
D. ICICI	(iv) 1955

Codes:	A	B	C	D
(a)	(iii)	(i)	(iv)	(ii)
(b)	(iv)	(ii)	(i)	(iii)
(c)	(ii)	(iii)	(i)	(iv)
(d)	(i)	(iii)	(iv)	(ii)

43. Which of the following is not a function of a Rural Bank?
(a) To accept deposits
(b) To waive loans
(c) To grant advances
(d) To supply inputs to farmers

44. From which date have all banks started sharing their ATM free of cost for transactions?
(a) January 1, 2009 (b) April 1, 2009
(c) July 1, 2009 (d) September 1, 2009

45. Which of the following is not the fund based business of commercial banks?
(a) D.P. Operations (b) Loans
(c) Deposits (d) Discounting of Bills

46. Foreign Exchange and foreign currencies in India are governed by
(a) SCRA Act (b) Banking Regulation Act
(c) FEMA Act (d) SEBI Act

47. The balance of payments of a country on Current Account is equal to
(a) Balance of trade plus short term capital flows.
(b) Balance of trade plus net invisible exports.
(c) Balance of payments minus capital flows.
(d) Balance of invisible trade plus imports.

48. The following table shows cost per unit of production of two goods, wheat and cloth in two countries X and Y with no transportation cost and free trade:

	X ₹	Y ₹
Wheat	50	350
Cloth	100	500

Which one of the following will take place?

(a) No trade will take place.
(b) X will export wheat and import cloth.
(c) X will export cloth and import wheat.
(d) There is no enough information to comment.

49. A debit balance of payments occurs due to
(i) Low imports and high exports
(ii) High imports and low exports.
(a) Both (i) and (ii) are correct.
(b) Both (i) and (ii) are incorrect.
(c) Only (i) is correct.
(d) Only (ii) is correct.

50. Match the following economic institutions with the year of their establishment:

A. World Bank	(i) 1946
B. International Finance Corporation	(ii) 1956
C. International Development Agency	(iii) 1960
D. Asian Development Bank	(iv) 1966

Codes:	A	B	C	D
(a)	(i)	(ii)	(iii)	(iv)
(b)	(i)	(iii)	(iv)	(ii)
(c)	(ii)	(i)	(iv)	(iii)
(d)	(iii)	(i)	(ii)	(iv)

ANSWERS

1. (c)	2. (c)	3. (b)	4. (c)	5. (b)
6. (d)	7. (d)	8. (d)	9. (a)	10. (a)
11. (d)	12. (c)	13. (c)	14. (b)	15. (c)
16. (b)	17. (d)	18. (a)	19. (c)	20. (b)
21. (a)	22. (a)	23. (a)	24. (a)	25. (d)
26. (d)	27. (a)	28. (d)	29. (a)	30. (b)
31. (c)	32. (d)	33. (b)	34. (c)	35. (c)
36. (c)	37. (a)	38. (a)	39. (c)	40. (d)
41. (d)	42. (c)	43. (d)	44. (b)	45. (a)
46. (c)	47. (b)	48. (b)	49. (c)	50. (b)

JUNE–2011

Note: This paper contains Sixty (60) multiple-choice questions, each question carrying two (2) marks. Candidate is expected to answer any Fifty (50) questions. In case more than Fifty (50) questions are attempted, only the first Fifty (50) questions will be evaluated.

PAPER–I

1. A research paper is a brief report of research work based on
   (a) Primary Data only
   (b) Secondary Data only
   (c) Both Primary and Secondary Data
   (d) None of the above
2. Newton gave three basic laws of motion. This research is categorised as
   (a) Descriptive Research
   (b) Sample Survey
   (c) Fundamental Research
   (d) Applied Research
3. A group of experts in a specific area of knowledge assembled at a place and prepared a syllabus for a new course. The process may be termed as
   (a) Seminar (b) Workshop
   (c) Conference (d) Symposium
4. In the process of conducting research "Formulation of Hypothesis" is followed by
   (a) Statement of Objectives
   (b) Analysis of Data
   (c) Selection of Research Tools
   (d) Collection of Data

Read the following passage carefully and answer questions 5 to 10:

All historians are interpreters of text if they be private letters, Government records or parish birthlists or whatever. For most kinds of historians, these are only the necessary means to understanding something other than the texts themselves, such as a political action or a historical trend, whereas for the intellectual historian, a full understanding of his chosen texts is itself the aim of his enquiries. Of course, the intellectual history is particularly prone to draw on the focus of other disciplines that are habitually interpreting texts for purposes of their own, probing the reasoning that ostensibly connects premises and conclusions. Furthermore, the boundaries with adjacent subdisciplines are shifting and indistinct: the history of art and the history of science both claim a certain autonomy, partly just because they require specialised technical skills, but both can also be seen as part of a wider intellectual history, as is evident when one considers, for example, the common stock of knowledge about cosmological beliefs or moral ideals of a period.

Like all historians, the intellectual historian is a consumer rather than a producer of 'methods'. His distinctiveness lies in which aspect of the past he is trying to illuminate, not in having exclusive possession of either a corpus of evidence or a body of techniques. That being said, it does seem that the label 'intellectual history' attracts a disproportionate share of misunderstanding.

It is alleged that intellectual history is the history of something that never really mattered. The long dominance of the historical profession by political historians bred a kind of philistinism, an unspoken belief that power and its exercise was 'what mattered'. The prejudice was reinforced by the assertion that political action was never really the outcome of principles or ideas that were 'more flapdoodle'. The legacy of this precept is still discernible in the tendency to require ideas to have 'licensed' the political class before they can be deemed worthy of intellectual attention, as if there were some reasons why the history of art or science, of philosophy or literature, were somehow of interest and significance than the history of Parties or Parliaments. Perhaps in recent years the mirror-image of this philistinism has been more common in the claim that ideas of any one is of systematic expression or sophistication do not matter, as if they were only held by a minority.

Answer the following questions:

5. An intellectual historian aims to fully understand
   (a) the chosen texts of his own
   (b) political actions
   (c) historical trends
   (d) his enquiries
6. Intellectual historians do not claim exclusive possession of
   (a) conclusions
   (b) any corpus of evidence
   (c) distinctiveness
   (d) habitual interpretation
7. The misconceptions about intellectual history stem from
   (a) a body of techniques
   (b) the common stock of knowledge
   (c) the dominance of political historians
   (d) cosmological beliefs
8. What is philistinism?
   (a) Reinforcement of prejudice
   (b) Fabrication of reasons
   (c) The hold of land-owning classes
   (d) Belief that power and its exercise matter
9. Knowledge of cosmological beliefs or moral ideas of a period can be drawn as part of
   (a) literary criticism
   (b) history of science
   (c) history of philosophy
   (d) intellectual history
10. The claim that ideas of any one is of systematic expression do not matter, as if they were held by a minority, is
    (a) to have a licensed political class
    (b) a political action
    (c) a philosophy of literature
    (d) the mirror-image of philistinism
11. Public communication tends to occur within a more
    (a) complex structure
    (b) political structure
    (c) convenient structure
    (d) formal structure
12. Transforming thoughts, ideas and messages into verbal and non-verbal signs is referred to as
    (a) channelisation (b) mediation
    (c) encoding (d) decoding
13. Effective communication needs a supportive
    (a) economic environment
    (b) political environment
    (c) social environment
    (d) multi-cultural environment
14. A major barrier in the transmission of cognitive data in the process of communication is an individual's
    (a) personality (b) expectation
    (c) social status (d) coding ability
15. When communicated, institutionalised stereotypes become
    (a) myths (b) reasons
    (c) experiences (d) convictions
16. In mass communication, selective perception is dependent on the receiver's
    (a) competence (b) pre-disposition
    (c) receptivity (d) ethnicity
17. Determine the relationship between the pair of words NUMERATOR : DENOMINATOR and then select the pair of words from the following which have a similar relationship:
    (a) fraction : decimal (b) divisor : quotient
    (c) top : bottom (d) dividend : divisor
18. Find the wrong number in the sequence
    125, 127, 130, 135, 142, 153, 165
    (a) 130 (b) 142 (c) 153 (d) 165
19. If HOBBY is coded as IOBY and LOBBY is coded as MOBY; then BOBBY is coded as
    (a) BOBY (b) COBY (c) DOBY (d) OOBY
20. The letters in the first set have certain relationship. On the basis of this relationship, make the right choice for the second set
    K/T : 11/20 :: J/R : ?
    (a) 10/8 (b) 10/18 (c) 11/19 (d) 10/19
21. If A = 5, B = 6, C = 7, D = 8 and so on, what do the following numbers stand for?
    17, 19, 20, 9, 8
    (a) Plane (b) Moped
    (c) Motor (d) Tonga
22. The price of oil is increased by 25%. If the expenditure is not allowed to increase, the ratio between the reduction in consumption and the original consumption is

(a) 1:3 (b) 1:4 (c) 1:5 (d) 1:6

23. How many 8s are there in the following sequence which are preceded by 5 but not immediately followed by 3?
5 8 3 7 5 8 6 3 8 5 4 5 8 4 7 6
5 5 8 3 5 8 7 5 8 2 8 5
(a) 4 (b) 5 (c) 7 (d) 3

24. If a rectangle were called a circle, a circle a point, a point a triangle and a triangle a square, the shape of a wheel is
(a) Rectangle (b) Circle
(c) Point (d) Triangle

25. Which one of the following methods is best suited for mapping the distribution of different crops as provided in the standard classification of crops in India?
(a) Pie diagram
(b) Chorochromatic technique
(c) Isopleth technique
(d) Dot method

26. Which one of the following does not come under the methods of data classification?
(a) Qualitative (b) Normative
(c) Spatial (d) Quantitative

27. Which one of the following is not a source of data?
(a) Administrative records
(b) Population census
(c) GIS
(d) Sample survey

28. If the statement 'some men are cruel' is false, which of the following statements/statement are/is true?
(i) All men are cruel.
(ii) No men are cruel.
(iii) Some men are not cruel.
(a) (i) and (iii) (b) (i) and (ii)
(c) (ii) and (iii) (d) Only (iii)

29. The octal number system consists of the following symbols
(a) 0 – 7 (b) 0 – 9
(c) 0 – 9, A – F (d) None of the above

30. The binary equivalent of $(-19)_{10}$ in signed magnitude system is
(a) 11101100 (b) 11101101
(c) 10010011 (d) None of these

31. DNS in internet technology stands for
(a) Dynamic Name System
(b) Domain Name System
(c) Distributed Name System
(d) None of these

32. HTML stands for
(a) Hyper Text Markup Language
(b) Hyper Text Manipulation Language
(c) Hyper Text Managing Links
(d) Hyper Text Manipulating Links

33. Which of the following is type of LAN?
(a) Ethernet (b) Token Ring
(c) FDDI (d) All of the above

34. Which of the following statements is true?
(a) Smart cards do not require an operating system.
(b) Smart cards and PCs use some operating system.
(c) COS is smart card operating system.
(d) The communication between reader and card is in full duplex mode.

35. The Ganga Action Plan was initiated during the year
(a) 1986 (b) 1988 (c) 1990 (d) 1992

36. Identify the correct sequence of energy sources in order of their share in the power sector in India.
(a) Thermal > nuclear > hydro > wind
(b) Thermal > hydro > nuclear > wind
(c) Hydro > nuclear > thermal > wind
(d) Nuclear > hydro > wind > thermal

37. Chromium as a contaminant in drinking water in excess of permissible levels, causes
(a) Skeletal damage
(b) Gastrointestinal problem
(c) Dermal and nervous problems
(d) Liver/Kidney problems

38. The main precursors of winter smog are
(a) N_2O and hydrocarbons
(b) NO_x and hydrocarbons
(c) SO_2 and hydrocarbons
(d) SO_2 and ozone

39. Flash floods are caused when
(a) the atmosphere is convectively unstable and there is considerable vertical wind shear
(b) the atmosphere is stable

(c) the atmosphere is convectively unstable with no vertical windshear
(d) winds are catabatic

40. In mega cities of India, the dominant source of air pollution is
(a) transport sector (b) thermal power
(c) municipal waste (d) commercial sector

41. The first Open University in India was set up in the State of
(a) Andhra Pradesh (b) Delhi
(c) Himachal Pradesh (d) Tamil Nadu

42. Most of the Universities in India are funded by
(a) the Central Government
(b) the State Governments
(c) the University Grants Commission
(d) Private bodies and Individuals

43. Which of the following organisations looks after the quality of Technical and Management education in India?
(a) NCTE (b) MCI
(c) AICTE (d) CSIR

44. Consider the following statements: Identify the statement which implies natural justice.
(a) The principle of natural justice is followed by the Courts.
(b) Justice delayed is justice denied.
(c) Natural justice is an inalienable right of a citizen.
(d) A reasonable opportunity of being heard must be given.

45. The President of India is
(a) the Head of State
(b) the Head of Government
(c) both Head of the State and the Head of the Government
(d) None of the above

46. Who among the following holds office during the pleasure of the President of India?
(a) Chief Election Commissioner
(b) Comptroller and Auditor General of India
(c) Chairman of the Union Public Service Commission
(d) Governor of a State

Questions 47 to 49 are based upon the following diagram in which there are three interlocking circles A, P and S where A stands for Artists, circle P for Professors and circle S for Sportspersons. Different regions in the figure are lettered from *a* to *g*:

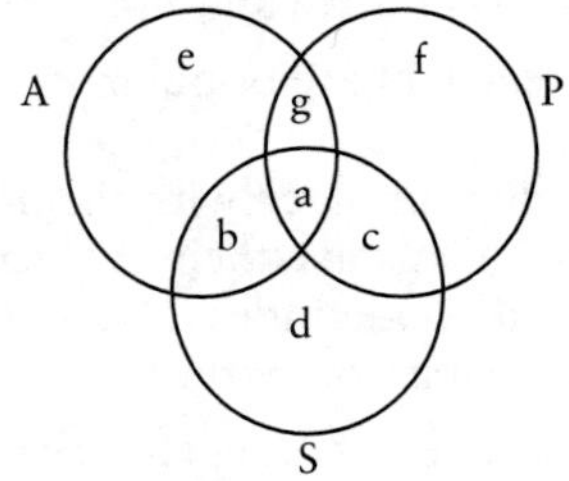

47. The region which represents artists who are neither sportsmen nor professors.
(a) *d* (b) *e* (c) *b* (d) *g*

48. The region which represents professors, who are both artists and sportspersons.
(a) *a* (b) *c* (c) *d* (d) *g*

49. The region which represents professors, who are also sportspersons, but not artists.
(a) *e* (b) *f* (c) *c* (d) *g*

Questions 50 to 52 are based on the following data:

Measurements of some variable X were made at an interval of 1 minute from 10 A.M. to 10:20 A.M. The data, thus, obtained is as follows:

X: 60, 62, 65, 64, 63, 61, 66, 65, 70, 68
63, 62, 64, 69, 65, 64, 66, 67, 66, 64

50. The value of X, which is exceeded 10% of the time in the duration of measurement, is
(a) 69 (b) 68 (c) 67 (d) 66

51. The value of X, which is exceeded 90% of the time in the duration of measurement, is
(a) 63 (b) 62 (c) 61 (d) 60

52. The value of X, which is exceeded 50% of the time in the duration of measurement, is
(a) 66 (b) 65 (c) 64 (d) 63

53. For maintaining an effective discipline in the class, the teacher should
(a) Allow students to do what they like.
(b) Deal with the students strictly.
(c) Give the students some problem to solve.
(d) Deal with them politely and firmly.

54. An effective teaching aid is one which
(a) is colourful and good looking
(b) activates all faculties
(c) is visible to all students
(d) easy to prepare and use

55. Those teachers are popular among students who
(a) develop intimacy with them
(b) help them solve their problems
(c) award good grades
(d) take classes on extra tuition fee

56. The essence of an effective classroom environment is
(a) a variety of teaching aids
(b) lively student-teacher interaction
(c) pin-drop silence
(d) strict discipline

57. On the first day of his class, if a teacher is asked by the students to introduce himself, he should
(a) ask them to meet after the class
(b) tell them about himself in brief
(c) ignore the demand and start teaching
(d) scold the student for this unwanted demand

58. Moral values can be effectively inculcated among the students when the teacher
(a) frequently talks about values
(b) himself practices them
(c) tells stories of great persons
(d) talks of Gods and Goddesses

59. The essential qualities of a researcher are
(a) spirit of free enquiry
(b) reliance on observation and evidence
(c) systematisation or theorising of knowledge
(d) All of the above

60. Research is conducted to
1. Generate new knowledge
2. Not to develop a theory
3. Obtain research degree
4. Reinterpret existing knowledge

Which of the above are correct?
(a) 1, 3 & 2 (b) 3, 2 & 4
(c) 2, 1 & 3 (d) 1, 3 & 4

ANSWERS

1. (c)	2. (c)	3. (b)	4. (c)	5. (a)
6. (b)	7. (c)	8. (d)	9. (d)	10. (d)
11. (d)	12. (c)	13. (d)	14. (c)	15. (d)
16. (b)	17. (d)	18. (d)	19. (b)	20. (b)
21. (b)	22. (c)	23. (a)	24. (c)	25. (a)
26. (b)	27. (a)	28. (b)	29. (a)	30. (d)
31. (b)	32. (a)	33. (d)	34. (c)	35. (a)
36. (b)	37. (d)	38. (c)	39. (a)	40. (a)
41. (a)	42. (c)	43. (c)	44. (d)	45. (b)
46. (d)	47. (b)	48. (a)	49. (c)	50. (c)
51. (b)	52. (d)	53. (d)	54. (b)	55. (b)
56. (b)	57. (b)	58. (b)	59. (d)	60. (d)

PAPER–II

Note: This paper contains fifty (50) objective type questions, each question carrying two (2) marks. All questions are compulsory.

1. Match the following components of Business Environment:

List I	List II
A. Economic Environment	(i) Exim Policy
B. Social Environment	(ii) Customs
C. Political Environment	(iii) Social Values
D. Legal Environment	(iv) Business Law and Banking

Codes:	A	B	C	D
(a)	(i)	(ii)	(iii)	(iv)
(b)	(iii)	(iv)	(ii)	(i)
(c)	(iii)	(i)	(ii)	(iv)
(d)	(i)	(ii)	(iv)	(iii)

2. Planning is a ______ process.
(a) Goal-oriented (b) Flexible
(c) Time-bound (d) All of the above

3. Which among the following have not been opened for private sector participation?
(a) Power Sector
(b) Telecommunication Sector
(c) Education Sector
(d) Railways

4. VAT is imposed
(a) Directly on consumers
(b) On final stage of production
(c) On all stages from production to final sales
(d) None of the above

5. In which of the following countries the Industrial Revolution took place first?

(a) France (b) Germany
(c) England (d) U.S.A.

6. Accounting Standards Board of India was established in the year
(a) 1970 (b) 1972 (c) 1973 (d) 1977

7. X and Y are partners in a firm. They withdrew @ ₹ 1,500 and ₹ 1,000 respectively on 15th day of every months for all the twelve months during 2009. Interest on drawings is chargeable @ 10% per annum. What would be the interest on drawings respectively?
(a) ₹ 1,800 and ₹ 1,200
(b) ₹ 900 and ₹ 600
(c) ₹ 18,000 and ₹ 12,000
(d) ₹ 150 and ₹ 100

8. If the purchase consideration is calculated by adding the various payments to be made, the method is called
(a) Lump-sum method
(b) Net-worth method
(c) Net-payments method
(d) Value of shares method

9. The following relate to the shares of a company. What is the correct order?
(a) Issue, Application, Call and Forfeiture.
(b) Application, Call, Forfeiture and Issue.
(c) Call, Issue, Application and Forfeiture.
(d) Forfeiture, Application, Issue and Call.

10. The final accounts of a manufacturing company generally include the following statement:
(i) Balance Sheet
(ii) Manufacturing Account
(iii) Profit and Loss Account
(iv) Trading Account
(v) Profit and Loss Appropriation Account
The correct sequence in which the statements are prepared is:
(a) (i), (ii), (iii), (iv), (v)
(b) (ii), (iv), (iii), (v), (i)
(c) (v), (ii), (iv), (iii), (i)
(d) (i), (iv), (iii), (ii), (v)

11. The theory of Revealed Preference was propounded by
(a) A. Marshall (b) P.F. Drucker
(c) Paul Samuelson (d) J.R. Hicks

12. Which of the following concepts is considered as a myth?
(a) Oligopoly
(b) Perfect competition
(c) Monopoly
(d) Imperfect competition

13. A perfectly competitive market in the short run will be in equilibrium where
(a) MC = AC (b) MC = MR
(c) MC = Zero (d) None of the above

14. Match the following:

List I	List II
(A) Perfect competition	(i) No control
(B) Monopolistic competition	(ii) Some Control
(C) Oligopoly	(iii) Practically Some Control
(D) Monopoly	(iv) Usual control

Codes:	A	B	C	D
(a)	(i)	(ii)	(iii)	(iv)
(b)	(ii)	(iii)	(iv)	(i)
(c)	(iii)	(ii)	(iv)	(i)
(d)	(iv)	(iii)	(ii)	(i)

15. **Statement (A):** The demand for the product of a firm under Oligopoly is at prices higher than the prevailing market prices.
Reason (R): The Oligopolistic firm faces a kinked demand curve.
(a) Both (A) and (R) are false.
(b) Both (A) and (R) are true, but (R) is not the correct explanation of (A).
(c) (A) is true, but (R) is false.
(d) (A) is false, but (R) is true.

16. In a factory, there are 1000 workers consisting of 400 A-Grade workers and 600 B-Grade workers. In A-Grade, 300 are male workers; and in B-Grade, only 200 are male workers. How many female workers are there in the factory?
(a) 300 (b) 400 (c) 500 (d) 600

17. When a population is heterogeneous, it is divided into groups, so that there is homogeneity within the group and heterogeneity between the groups, and some items are selected at random from each group. It is a case of
(a) Cluster Random Sampling
(b) Systematic Random Sampling

(c) Quota Sampling
(d) Stratified Random Sampling

18. Which one among the following is a small sample?
(a) 5 (b) 10
(c) 29 (d) All the above

19. Which one of the following softwares is used for Research Analysis?
(a) SAP (b) ERP (c) SPSS (d) TALLY

20. Which one of the following is a DataBase Management System?
(a) MS Access (b) MS Excel
(c) MS Outlook (d) None of the above

21. Match the following:

	List I		List II
(A)	Maslow	(i)	Hygiene Theory
(B)	Herzberg	(ii)	X and Y Theory
(C)	Ouchi	(iii)	Need Hierarchy Theory
(D)	McGregor	(iv)	Z Theory

Codes:	A	B	C	D
(a)	(i)	(ii)	(iii)	(iv)
(b)	(ii)	(i)	(iv)	(iii)
(c)	(iv)	(iii)	(ii)	(i)
(d)	(iii)	(i)	(iv)	(ii)

22. Consider the following steps in the decision making process; and select the correct sequence:
(i) Defining the problem
(ii) Considering alternatives
(iii) Considering limiting factors
(iv) Selection of the best alternative and implementation
(a) (i), (ii), (iii), (iv) (b) (iii), (i), (iv), (ii)
(c) (i), (iv), (iii), (ii) (d) (i), (iii), (iv), (ii)

23. "Unity of Objectives" principle states that there should be
(a) Only one objective
(b) Pre-determined objectives
(c) Coordination among objectives
(d) None of the above

24. The concept of M.B.O. originally came from
(a) F.W. Taylor (b) A.H. Maslow
(c) Henry Fayol (d) Peter F. Drucker

25. Which one is the most important principle of Business Ethics?
(a) Principle of unity of direction.
(b) Principle of proportional judgement.
(c) Principle of scalar chain.
(d) Principle of span of control.

26. Match the following statements with their authors:

(A)	"Marketing is the delivery of standard of living."	(i)	Peter F. Drucker
(B)	"Marketing comprises both buying and selling activities."	(ii)	Philip Kotler
(C)	"Marketing is human activity directed at satisfying needs and wants through exchange process."	(iii)	Paul Mazur
(D)	"Marketing is a process which converts a resource, distinct knowledge into a contribution of economic value in the market place."	(iv)	Pyle

Codes:	A	B	C	D
(a)	(iv)	(iii)	(i)	(ii)
(b)	(iv)	(ii)	(iii)	(i)
(c)	(iii)	(iv)	(ii)	(i)
(d)	(i)	(ii)	(iv)	(iii)

27. Which one of the following is not the mode of Direct Distribution System?
(a) Trading mediators
(b) Vending machines
(c) Own sales depot
(d) Franchise shops

28. Which one of the following is matched correctly?
(a) Consumer Promotion – Sales Meetings
(b) Dealer Promotion – Display Allowance
(c) Internal Sales Promotion – Free Samples
(d) None of the above

29. **Statement (A):** "The Electronic Media has a strong impact on consumers' behaviour in India."

Reason (R): "Most of the Indian consumers take their decision with the help of Electronic Media."
(a) Statement (A) is correct, but Reason (R) is false.

(b) Reason (R) is correct, but Statement (A) is false.
(c) Both Statement (A) and Reason (R) are false.
(d) Both Statement (A) and Reason (R) are correct.

30. Road blocking advertisement is
(a) Advertising a product by blocking a road.
(b) Putting an advertisement on a blocked road.
(c) A technique of gathering potential customers on the road.
(d) Advertising a product on all similar TV/ Radio channels at the same time.

31. Read the following statements:
(i) "Working Capital is the amount of funds necessary to cover the cost of operating the enterprise."
(ii) "Circulating capital means current assets of a company that are changed in the ordinary course of business from one form to another."
(a) (i) and (ii) both are correct.
(b) (i) and (ii) both are false.
(c) (i) is correct, but (ii) is false.
(d) (i) is false, but (ii) is correct.

32. Examine the following statements:
(i) Pay-Back Period method measures the true profitability of a project.
(ii) Capital Rationing and Capital Budgeting mean the same thing.
(iii) Internal Rate of Return and Time Adjusted Rate of Return are the same thing.
(iv) Rate of Return Method takes into account the time value of money.
(a) (i), (ii) and (iii) are correct.
(b) (ii) and (iii) are correct.
(c) Only (iii) is correct.
(d) All (i), (ii), (iii) and (iv) are false.

33. Which one of the following is correct?
(i) A ratio is an arithmetical relationship of one number to another number.
(ii) Liquid ratio is also known as acid test ratio.
(iii) Rule of thumb for current ratio is 2 : 1.
(iv) Debt equity ratio is the relationship between outsiders' fund and shareholders' fund.
(a) All (i), (ii), (iii) and (iv) are correct.
(b) Only (i), (ii) and (iii) are correct.
(c) Only (ii), (iii) and (iv) are correct.
(d) Only (ii) and (iii) are correct.

34. The basic objective of Financial Management is
(a) Maximization of profits.
(b) Profit Planning of the organization.
(c) Maximization of shareholders' wealth.
(d) Ensuring financial discipline in the organization.

35. Which of the following term is used to represent the proportionate relationship between debt and equity?
(a) Cost of Capital (b) Capital Budgeting
(c) Assets Structure (d) Capital Structure

36. HRM is amalgam of
(a) Job analysis, recruitment and selection.
(b) Social behaviour and business ethics.
(c) Organizational behaviour, personnel management and industrial relation.
(d) Employer and employees.

37. Recruitment is concerned with the process of
(a) Selection of right candidate.
(b) Developing a pool of potential employees.
(c) Inviting applications for jobs.
(d) None of the above.

38. The mechanism to identify employees growth potentials is done through
(a) Job enrichment
(b) Job evaluation
(c) Job assessment centre
(d) Position description

39. An interview conducted at the time of an employee leaving the organization is called
(a) Exit interview
(b) Feedback interview
(c) Convincing interview
(d) Directed interview

40. **Statement (A):** A Manager delegates authority.
Reason (R): The Manager wants to shirk his responsibility.
(a) Both Statement (A) and Reason (R) are correct.

(b) Both Statement (A) and Reason (R) are false.
(c) Statement (A) is correct, but Reason (R) is false.
(d) Statement (A) is false, but Reason (R) is correct.

41. Match the following:

List-I	List-II
(A) Unit Trust of India	(i) 1921
(B) Banking Regulation Act	(ii) 1949
(C) Imperial Bank of India	(iii) 1964
(D) NABARD	(iv) 1982

Codes:	A	B	C	D
(a)	(i)	(iii)	(ii)	(iv)
(b)	(iv)	(i)	(ii)	(iii)
(c)	(ii)	(iv)	(iii)	(i)
(d)	(iii)	(ii)	(i)	(iv)

42. Capital Adequacy Norms declared in the year, 1996, is applicable to
(a) Foreign Banks
(b) Co-operative Banks
(c) Private Sector Banks
(d) Nationalized Bank

43. Which one of the following is used for International Money Transfer?
(a) RTGS (b) NEFT
(c) SWIFT (d) None of the above

44. In order to control credit and investment, the Central Bank of a country should
(a) Sell securities in the open market and hike the Cash Reserve Ratio.
(b) Buy securities from the open market and lower the Cash Reserve Ratio.
(c) Buy securities from the open market and hike the Cash Reserve Ratio.
(d) Sell securities in the open market and lower the Cash Reserve Ratio.

45. India has been witnessing high rate of inflation because
(a) Public expenditure and money supply both are continuously increasing.
(b) The agricultural and industrial sectors have not performed adequately.
(c) Both agricultural and administered prices have been hiked.
(d) All of the above.

46. In India ________ has a predominant share in the debt market.
(a) Government Securities
(b) Corporate Deposits
(c) Corporate Equities
(d) Global Depository Receipts

47. Which type of elasticity plays a crucial role in determining international trade?
(a) Elasticity of demand
(b) Price elasticity of demand
(c) Income elasticity of demand
(d) Cross elasticity of demand

48. DFEC stands for
(a) Direct Foreign Exchange Control
(b) Direct Finance Exchange Control
(c) Duty Free Export Credit
(d) Duty Free Exchange Credit

49. Suppose a Canadian firm imports bananas of $ 1000 and sells them for $ 2000. The effect on GDP would be
(a) The GDP will decrease by $ 3000
(b) The GDP will increase by $ 3000
(c) The GDP will increase by $ 2000
(d) The GDP will increase by $ 1000

50. In independent India, the first major foreign exchange crisis occurred in the year ________.
(a) 1955 (b) 1956 (c) 1969 (d) 1991

ANSWERS

1. (a)	2. (d)	3. (d)	4. (c)	5. (c)
6. (d)	7. (b)	8. (c)	9. (a)	10. (b)
11. (c)	12. (b)	13. (b)	14. (a)	15. (d)
16. (c)	17. (d)	18. (d)	19. (c)	20. (a)
21. (d)	22. (a)	23. (c)	24. (d)	25. (b)
26. (c)	27. (a)	28. (b)	29. (d)	30. (d)
31. (a)	32. (c)	33. (a)	34. (c)	35. (d)
36. (c)	37. (b)	38. (a)	39. (a)	40. (c)
41. (d)	42. (d)	43. (c)	44. (a)	45. (d)
46. (a)	47. (b)	48. (c)	49. (d)	50. (b)

DECEMBER–2011

Note: This paper contains Sixty (60) multiple choice questions, each question carrying two (2) marks. Candidate is expected to answer any Fifty (50) questions. In case more than Fifty (50) questions are attempted, only the first Fifty (50) questions will be evaluated.

PAPER–I

1. Photo bleeding means
   (a) Photo cropping
   (b) Photo placement
   (c) Photo cutting
   (d) Photo colour adjustment
2. While designing communication strategy feed-forward studies are conducted by
   (a) Audience (b) Communicator
   (c) Satellite (d) Media
3. In which language the newspapers have highest circulation?
   (a) English (b) Hindi
   (c) Bengali (d) Tamil
4. Aspect ratio of TV Screen is
   (a) 4 : 3 (b) 3 : 4 (c) 2 : 3 (d) 2 : 4
5. Communication with oneself is known as
   (a) Organisational Communication
   (b) Grapevine Communication
   (c) Interpersonal Communication
   (d) Intrapersonal Communication
6. The term 'SITE' stands for
   (a) Satellite Indian Television Experiment
   (b) Satellite International Television Experiment
   (c) Satellite Instructional Television Experiment
   (d) Satellite Instructional Teachers Education
7. What is the number that comes next in the sequence?
   2, 5, 9, 19, 37, ___
   (a) 76 (b) 74 (c) 75 (d) 50
8. Find the next letter for the series MPSV.....
   (a) X (b) Y (c) Z (d) A
9. If '367' means 'I am happy'; '748' means 'you are sad' and '469' means 'happy and sad' in a given code, then which of the following represents 'and' in that code?
   (a) 3 (b) 6 (c) 9 (d) 4
10. The basis of the following classification is 'animal', 'man', 'house', 'book', and 'student':
    (a) Definite descriptions (b) Proper names
    (c) Descriptive phrases (d) Common names
11. **Assertion (A):** The coin when flipped next time will come up tails.
    Reason (R): Because the coin was flipped five times in a row, and each time it came up heads.
    Choose the correct answer from below:
    (a) Both (A) and (R) are true, and (R) is the correct explanation of (A).
    (b) Both (A) and (R) are false, and (R) is the correct explanation of (A).
    (c) (A) is doubtful, (R) is true, and (R) is not the correct explanation of (A).
    (d) (A) is doubtful, (R) is false, and (R) is the correct explanation of (A).
12. The relation 'is a sister of' is
    (a) non-symmetrical (b) symmetrical
    (c) asymmetrical (d) transitive
13. If the proposition "Vegetarians are not meat eaters" is false, then which of the following inferences is correct? Choose from the codes given below:
    1. "Some vegetarians are meat eaters" is true.
    2. "All vegetarians are meat eaters" is doubtful.
    3. "Some vegetarians are not meat eaters" is true.
    4. "Some vegetarians are not meat eaters" is doubtful.

    Codes:
    (a) 1, 2 and 3 (b) 2, 3 and 4
    (c) 1, 3 and 4 (d) 1, 2 and 4

14. Determine the nature of the following definition:
'Poor' means having an annual income of ₹ 10,000.
(a) Persuasive (b) Precising
(c) Lexical (d) Stipulative

15. Which one of the following is not an argument?
(a) If today is Tuesday, tomorrow will be Wednesday.
(b) Since today is Tuesday, tomorrow will be Wednesday.
(c) Ram insulted me so I punched him in the nose.
(d) Ram is not at home, so he must have gone to town.

16. Venn diagram is a kind of diagram to
(a) represent and assess the truth of elementary inferences with the help of Boolean Algebra of classes.
(b) represent and assess the validity of elementary inferences with the help of Boolean Algebra of classes.
(c) represent but not assess the validity of elementary inferences with the help of Boolean Algebra of classes.
(d) assess but not represent the validity of elementary inferences with the help of Boolean Algebra of classes.

17. Inductive logic studies the way in which a premise may
(a) support and entail a conclusion
(b) not support but entail a conclusion
(c) neither support nor entail a conclusion
(d) support a conclusion without entailing it

18. Which of the following statements are true? Choose from the codes given below.
1. Some arguments, while not completely valid, are almost valid.
2. A sound argument may be invalid.
3. A cogent argument may have a probably false conclusion.
4. A statement may be true or false.

Codes:
(a) 1 and 2 (b) 1, 3 and 4
(c) Only 4 (d) 3 and 4

19. If the side of the square increases by 40%, then the area of the square increases by
(a) 60% (b) 40% (c) 196% (d) 96%

20. There are 10 lamps in a hall. Each one of them can be switched on independently. The number of ways in which hall can be illuminated is
(a) 10^2 (b) 1023 (c) 2^{10} (d) 10!

21. How many numbers between 100 and 300 begin or end with 2?
(a) 100 (b) 110 (c) 120 (d) 180

22. In a college having 300 students, every student reads 5 newspapers and every newspaper is read by 60 students. The number of newspapers required is
(a) at least 30 (b) at most 20
(c) exactly 25 (d) exactly 5

The total CO_2 emissions from various sectors are 5 mmt. In the Pie Chart given below, the percentage contribution to CO_2 emissions from various sectors is indicated.

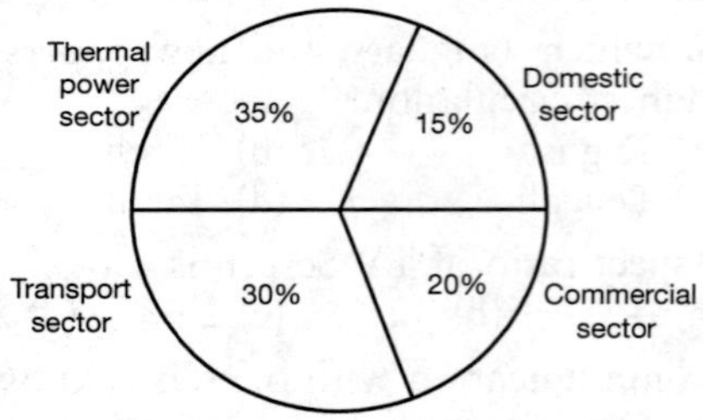

23. What is the absolute CO_2 emission from domestic sector?
(a) 1.5 mmt (b) 2.5 mmt
(c) 1.75 mmt (d) 0.75 mmt

24. What is the absolute CO_2 emission for combined thermal power and transport sectors?
(a) 3.25 mmt (b) 1.5 mmt
(c) 2.5 mmt (d) 4 mmt

25. Which of the following operating system is used on mobile phones?
(a) Windows Vista (b) Android
(c) Windows XP (d) All of the above

26. If $(y)_x$ represents a number y in base x, then which of the following numbers is smallest of all?
(a) $(1111)_2$ (b) $(1111)_8$
(c) $(1111)_{10}$ (d) $(1111)_{16}$

27. High-level programming language can be converted to machine language using which of the following?
    (a) Oracle (b) Compiler
    (c) Mat lab (d) Assembler
28. HTML is used to create
    (a) machine language program
    (b) high level program
    (c) web page
    (d) web server
29. The term DNS stands for
    (a) Domain Name System
    (b) Defense Nuclear System
    (c) Downloadable New Software
    (d) Dependent Name Server
30. IPv4 and IPv6 are addresses used to identify computers on the internet. Find the correct statement out of the following:
    (a) Number of bits required for IPv4 address is more than number of bits required for IPv6 address.
    (b) Number of bits required for IPv4 address is same as number of bits required for IPv6 address.
    (c) Number of bits required for IPv4 address is less than number of bits required for IPv6 address.
    (d) Number of bits required for IPv4 address is 64.
31. Which of the following pollutants affects the respiratory tract in humans?
    (a) Carbon monoxide
    (b) Nitric oxide
    (c) Sulphur dioxide
    (d) Aerosols
32. Which of the following pollutants is not emitted from the transport sector?
    (a) Oxides of nitrogen
    (b) Chlorofluorocarbons
    (c) Carbon monoxide
    (d) Poly aromatic hydrocarbons
33. Which of the following sources of energy has the maximum potential in India?
    (a) Solar energy (b) Wind energy
    (c) Ocean thermal energy (d) Tidal energy
34. Which of the following is not a source of pollution in soil?
    (a) Transport sector
    (b) Agriculture sector
    (c) Thermal power plants
    (d) Hydropower plants
35. Which of the following is not a natural hazard?
    (a) Earthquake (b) Tsunami
    (c) Flash floods (d) Nuclear accident
36. Ecological footprint represents
    (a) area of productive land and water to meet the resources requirement
    (b) energy consumption
    (c) CO_2 emissions per person
    (d) forest cover
37. The aim of value education to inculcate in students is
    (a) the moral values
    (b) the social values
    (c) the political values
    (d) the economic values
38. Indicate the number of Regional Offices of University Grants Commission of India.
    (a) 10 (b) 07 (c) 08 (d) 09
39. One-rupee currency note in India bears the signature of
    (a) The President of India
    (b) Finance Minister of India
    (c) Governor, Reserve Bank of India
    (d) Finance Secretary of Government of India
40. Match the List I with the List II and select the correct answer from the codes given below:

    List I (Commissions and Committees)
    A. First Administrative Reforms Commission
    B. Paul H. Appleby Committee
    C. K. Santhanam Committee
    D. Second Administrative Reforms Commission

    List II (Year)
    (i) 2005 (ii) 1962 (iii) 1966 (iv) 1953

Codes:	**A**	**B**	**C**	**D**
(a)	(i)	(iii)	(ii)	(iv)
(b)	(iii)	(iv)	(ii)	(i)
(c)	(iv)	(ii)	(iii)	(i)
(d)	(ii)	(i)	(iv)	(iii)

41. Constitutionally the registration and recognition of political parties is the function performed by

(a) The State Election Commission of respective States
(b) The Law Ministry of Government of India
(c) The Election Commission of India
(d) Election Department of the State Governments

42. The members of Gram Sabha are
(a) Sarpanch, Upsarpanch and all elected Panchas
(b) Sarpanch, Upsarpanch and Village level worker
(c) Sarpanch, Gram Sevak and elected Panchas
(d) Registered voters of Village Panchayat

43. By which of the following methods the true evaluation of the students is possible?
(a) Evaluation at the end of the course
(b) Evaluation twice in a year
(c) Continuous evaluation
(d) Formative evaluation

44. Suppose a student wants to share his problems with his teacher and he visits the teacher's house for the purpose, the teacher should
(a) contact the student's parents and solve his problem
(b) suggest him that he should never visit his house
(c) suggest him to meet the principal and solve the problem
(d) extend reasonable help and boost his morale

45. When some students are deliberately attempting to disturb the discipline of the class by making mischief, what will be your role as a teacher?
(a) Expelling those students
(b) Isolate those students
(c) Reform the group with your authority
(d) Giving them an opportunity for introspection and improve their behaviour

46. Which of the following belongs to a projected aid?
(a) Blackboard (b) Diorama
(c) Epidiascope (d) Globe

47. A teacher is said to be fluent in asking questions, if he can ask
(a) meaningful questions
(b) as many questions as possible
(c) maximum number of questions in a fixed time
(d) many meaningful questions in a fixed time

48. Which of the following qualities is most essential for a teacher?
(a) He should be a learned person
(b) He should be a well dressed person
(c) He should have patience
(d) He should be an expert in his subject

49. A hypothesis is a
(a) law (b) canon
(c) postulate (d) supposition

50. Suppose you want to investigate the working efficiency of nationalised bank in India, which one of the following would you follow?
(a) Area Sampling
(b) Multi-stage Sampling
(c) Sequential Sampling
(d) Quota Sampling

51. Controlled group condition is applied in
(a) Survey Research
(b) Historical Research
(c) Experimental Research
(d) Descriptive Research

52. Workshops are meant for
(a) giving lectures
(b) multiple target groups
(c) showcase new theories
(d) hands on training/experience

53. Which one of the following is a research tool?
(a) Graph (b) Illustration
(c) Questionnaire (d) Diagram

54. Research is not considered ethical if it
(a) tries to prove a particular point.
(b) does not ensure privacy and anonymity of the respondent.
(c) does not investigate the data scientifically.
(d) is not of a very high standard.

Read the following passage carefully and answer the questions (55 to 60):

The catalytic fact of the twentieth century is uncontrollable development, consumerist society, political materialism, and spiritual devaluation. This inordinate development has led to the transcendental 'second reality' of sacred perception that biologically transcendence is a part of human life. As the century closes, it dawns with imperative vigour that the 'first reality' of enlightened rationalism and the 'second reality' of the Beyond have to be harmonised in a worthy state of man. The *de facto* values describe what we are, they portray the 'is' of our ethic, they are *est* values (Latin *est* means is). The ideal values tell us what we ought to be, they are *esto* values (Latin *esto* 'ought to be'). Both have to be in the ebb and flow of consciousness. The ever new science and technology and the ever-perennial faith are two modes of one certainty, that is the wholeness of man, his courage to be, his share in Being.

The materialistic foundations of science have crumbled down. Science itself has proved that matter is energy, processes are as valid as facts, and affirmed the non-materiality of the universe. The encounter of the 'two cultures', the scientific and the humane, will restore the normal vision, and will be the bedrock of a 'science of understanding' in the new century. It will give new meaning to the ancient perception that quantity (measure) and quality (value) coexist at the root of nature. Human endeavours cannot afford to be humanistically irresponsible.

55. The problem raised in the passage reflects overall on
   (a) Consumerism
   (b) Materialism
   (c) Spiritual devaluation
   (d) Inordinate development
56. The *de facto* values in the passage means
   (a) What is (b) What ought to be
   (c) What can be (d) Where it is
57. According to the passage, the 'first reality' constitutes
   (a) Economic prosperity
   (b) Political development
   (c) Sacred perception of life
   (d) Enlightened rationalism
58. Encounter of the 'two cultures', the scientific and the human implies
   (a) Restoration of normal vision
   (b) Universe is both material and non-material
   (c) Man is superior to nature
   (d) Co-existence of quantity and quality in nature
59. The contents of the passage are
   (a) Descriptive (b) Prescriptive
   (c) Axiomatic (d) Optional
60. The passage indicates that science has proved that
   (a) universe is material
   (b) matter is energy
   (c) nature has abundance
   (d) humans are irresponsible

ANSWERS

1. (a)	2. (b)	3. (b)	4. (a)	5. (d)
6. (c)	7. (c)	8. (b)	9. (c)	10. (d)
11. (c)	12. (b)	13. (a)	14. (b)	15. (a)
16. (b)	17. (d)	18. (d)	19. (d)	20. (b)
21. (b)	22. (c)	23. (d)	24. (a)	25. (b)
26. (a)	27. (b)	28. (c)	29. (a)	30. (c)
31. (a)	32. (b)	33. (b)	34. (d)	35. (d)
36. (a)	37. (a)	38. (b)	39. (d)	40. (b)
41. (c)	42. (d)	43. (d)	44. (d)	45. (d)
46. (c)	47. (d)	48. (c)	49. (d)	50. (b)
51. (c)	52. (d)	53. (c)	54. (b)	55. (c)
56. (a)	57. (d)	58. (a)	59. (a)	60. (b)

PAPER–II

Note: This paper contains fifty (50) objective-type questions, each question carrying two (2) marks. All questions are compulsory.

1. By which Act, the government checks restrictive trade practices?
   (a) FEMA - 1999
   (b) Consumer Protection Act, 1986
   (c) Industrial Policy Act, 1991
   (d) None of the above
2. In which year the new Industrial Policy was announced?
   (a) 1997 (b) 1951 (c) 1991 (d) 1998
3. The Narasimham Committee made separate recommendations for the reforms of _____
   (a) Manufacturing sector
   (b) Banking sector
   (c) Agriculture sector
   (d) Insurance Sector

4. **Assertion (A):** Disinvestment tends to arouse opposition from employees.
   Reason (R): It may increase the cost of Production.
   (a) Both (A) and (R) are true.
   (b) (A) is true, but (R) is false.
   (c) Both (A) and (R) are false.
   (d) (A) is false, but (R) is true.

5. Match the following:

	Books		Authors
A.	*India and Economic Reforms*	(i)	Bhagwati, J.
B.	*Development Planning: The Indian Experience*	(ii)	Chakravarty, S.
C.	*India: Economic Development and Social Opportunity*	(iii)	Drenz, J and Amartya Sen
D.	*Fiscal Policy of Underdeveloped countries.*	(iv)	Chelliah, R.J.

Codes:	A	B	C	D
(a)	i	ii	iii	iv
(b)	ii	iii	iv	i
(c)	iii	iv	ii	i
(d)	i	iv	iii	ii

6. Which of the following accounting equations is not correct?
   (a) Assets – Liabilities = Equity
   (b) Assets – Equity = Liability
   (c) Assets + Liabilities = Equity
   (d) Liabilities + Equity = Assets

7. Which one of the following statements is correct?
   (a) Increases in liabilities are credits and decreases are debits.
   (b) Increases in assets are credits and decreases are debits.
   (c) Increases in capital are debits and decreases are credits.
   (d) Increases in expenses are credits and decreases are debits.

8. A and B are partners in a firm sharing profit and loss in the ratio of 1/8 3 : 2. They admit C into partnership for share and the new ratio between A and B is 4: 3. The sacrificing ratio is
   (a) 1 : 1 (b) 2 : 1 (c) 4 : 1 (d) 2 : 3

9. Arrange the following liabilities in the order of company balance sheet.
   (i) Bank Overdraft
   (ii) Bank Loan
   (iii) Share Capital
   (iv) Provision for Taxation
   (a) i, ii, iii, iv (b) iv, iii, ii, i
   (c) iii, ii, i, iv (d) iii, ii, iv, i

10. Intrinsic value of a share is given by:
    (a) $\frac{\text{Total net assets}}{\text{No. of shares}}$
    (b) $\frac{\text{Total assets}}{\text{No. of shares}}$
    (c) $\frac{\text{Share capital}}{\text{No. of shares}}$
    (d) $\frac{\text{Market capitalisation}}{\text{No. of shares}}$

11. When demand curve is rectangular Hyperbola, the elasticity of demand will be
    (a) Perfectly elastic (b) Unit elastic
    (c) Perfectly inelastic (d) Highly elastic

12. Opportunity cost is a term which describes:
    (a) A bargain price for a factor of production.
    (b) Cost related to an optimum level of production.
    (c) Average variable cost.
    (d) The cost of forgone opportunities.

13. Arrange the following books in order (year) in which they appeared.
    (i) *Economic Theory and Operations Analysis* by W.J. Baumol.
    (ii) *An Introduction to Positive Economics* by R.G. Lipsey.
    (iii) *Economics* by P. Samuelson.
    (iv) *Managerial Economics* by Joel Dean.
    (a) (i), (ii), (iii), (iv) (b) (iv), (iii), (i), (ii)
    (c) (ii), (iv), (i), (iii) (d) (iii), (iv), (ii), (i)

14. Marginal revenue is _____ at the quantity that generates maximum total revenue and negative beyond that point.
    (a) 0 (b) + 2 (c) + 1 (d) – 1

15. **Assertion (A):** Utility will be maximised when the marginal unit of expenditure in each direction brings the same increment of utility.

Reason (R): A consumer will try to maximise his utility.

(a) Both (A) and (R) are true.
(b) Both (A) and (R) are false.
(c) (A) is true, but (R) is false.
(d) (A) is false, but (R) is true.

16. In a predominantly illiterate area consisting of 10,000 population, data has to be collected from 10% of them. The appropriate technique for data collection would be
(a) Questionnaire (b) Schedule
(c) Interview (d) All the above

17. In a unimodal and symmetric distribution, the relationship between averages is like this.
(a) mean > median > mode
(b) mean < median < mode
(c) mean = median = mode
(d) mean > median < mode

18. Given the following tests:
(i) 'Z'-test (ii) 't'-test
(iii) 'F'-test (iv) 'χ'-test
The concept of degrees of freedom is associated with
(a) (i) and (ii) (b) (ii) and (iii)
(c) (iii) and (iv) (d) (ii), (iii) and (iv)

19. Which one of the following is not an accounting software?
(a) Tally (b) Miracle
(c) Profit (d) SPSS

20. E-marketing is ______
(a) Buying and selling of goods and services through internet.
(b) Buying of goods through internet.
(c) Selling of goods through internet.
(d) All of the above.

21. Match the items in List-I with items in List-II.

List-I	List-II
A. Peter F. Druker	i. M.B.O.
B. F.W. Taylor	ii. Scientific Management
C. Henri J. Fayol	iii. Industrial Psychology
D. Hugo Munsterberg	iv. Functional Theory

Codes:	A	B	C	D
(a)	i	ii	iii	iv
(b)	i	ii	iv	iii
(c)	iv	iii	ii	i
(d)	iii	i	iv	ii

22. The main advantage of functional organization is
(a) Simplicity (b) Specialisation
(c) Experience (d) Authority

23. Which of the following is the most democratic form of organisation?
(a) Line (b) Line and Staff
(c) Functional (d) Committee

24. Plan made in the light of a competitor's plan is known as
(a) Policy (b) Procedure
(c) Strategy (d) Under-cover plan

25. A proposed organizational change may create ______.
(a) Emotional Turmoil & Tension
(b) Problem of social displacement
(c) Fear of unknown
(d) All of the above

26. Match the following statements with their authors:

A. "Marketing mix is a pack of four sets of variables, namely; product variables, price variables, promotion variables and place variables".	(i) Wheeler
B. "The marketing mix is the set of marketing tools the firm uses to pursue its its marketing objectives in the target market."	(ii) Cundiff, Still & Govoni
C. "Marketing is the managerial process by which products are matched with markets and through which transfers of ownership are affected."	iii. McCarthy
D. "Marketing is concerned with all the resources and activities involved in the flow of goods and services from producer to consumer".	iv. Philip Kotler

Codes:	A	B	C	D
(a)	ii	iv	i	iii
(b)	i	ii	iv	iii
(c)	iv	iii	i	ii
(d)	iii	iv	ii	i

27. Which one of the following is not the mode of Direct Distribution System?
(a) Multiple shops
(b) Door to door selling
(c) Broking agent
(d) Direct mail order

28. Which one of the following is not matched correctly?

A. Sales Portfolio	– Internal Sales Promotion
B. Merchandise Allowance	– Dealer Promotion
C. Count and Recount of Stock	– Consumer Promotion
D. Advertising	– Market Promotion

29. **Assertion (A):** "Advertising plays a vital role in selling products/services."
Reason (R): "Sales promotion is incomplete without a good advertising plan."
Codes:
(a) (A) is correct, but (R) is false.
(b) (A) is false, but (R) is correct.
(c) Both (A) and (R) are correct.
(d) Both (A) and (R) are false.

30. Which one of the following contains the three elements of service marketing triangle?
(a) Management, Marketing Agency and Consumer.
(b) Marketing Agency, Government and Consumer.
(c) Management, Employees and Marketing Agency.
(d) Management, Employees and Consumer.

31. Read the following statements:
(i) "The rate of return on investment increases with the shortage of working capital."
(ii) 'Net working capital is the excess of current assets over current liabilities."
(iii) "Greater the size of the business unit, larger will be the requirement of working capital."
(iv) "Working capital is also known as circulating capital."
Which one of the following consists of the correct statements?
(a) (i), (ii) and (iii) (b) (ii), (iii) and (iv)
(c) (iii), (iv) and (i) (d) (i), (ii) and (iv)

32. Match the following:

A. Capital Budgeting	(i) Time adjusted rate of return
B. Profitability Index	(ii) Irreversible
C. Internal rate of return	(iii) Benefit/cost
D. Capital investment decisions	(iv) Planning capital Expenditure

Codes:	A	B	C	D
(a)	(iv)	(iii)	(ii)	(i)
(b)	(i)	(iv)	(ii)	(iii)
(c)	(iv)	(iii)	(i)	(ii)
(d)	(ii)	(i)	(iii)	(iv)

33. Which one of the following is correct?
(i) Liquidity ratios measure long-term solvency of a concern.
(ii) Inventory is a part of liquid assets.
(iii) Rule of thumb for acid test ratio is 2:1.
(iv) The amount of gross assets is equal to net capital employed.
(a) (i), (ii) and (iv)
(b) (ii), (iii) and (iv)
(c) (i), (ii), (iii) and (iv)
(d) None of the above

34. According to which of the following, the firm's market value is not affected by capital structure?
(a) M-M Hypothesis
(b) Net Income Approach
(c) The Traditional View
(d) None of the above

35. Modigliani and Miller's dividend policy of a firm is
(a) Relevant (b) Irrelevant
(c) Unrealistic (d) None of the above

36. The concept of quality circles is a brain child of
(a) Karou Ishikawa
(b) Munchu
(c) Japanese Union for Scientists & Engineers
(d) None of the above

37. Performance appraisal is
    (a) Morale Boosting
    (b) Training and Development Activity
    (c) Job Analysis
    (d) None of the above
38. The mechanism to identify employee's growth potentials is done through
    (a) Job enrichment
    (b) Job evaluation
    (c) Assessment centre
    (d) Position description
39. Statements:
    (i) High morale always leads to high productivity.
    (ii) High morale need not necessarily lead to high productivity.
    (a) (i) is correct, (ii) is incorrect.
    (b) (i) is incorrect, (ii) is correct.
    (c) Both are correct
    (d) Both are incorrect
40. Arrange the following in order:
    (i) Promotion
    (ii) Performance appraisal
    (iii) Recruitment
    (iv) Training and Development
    (a) (iii), (iv), (ii), (i) (b) (iii), (ii), (i), (iv)
    (c) (i), (ii), (iii), (iv) (d) (iii), (i), (ii), (iv)
41. Find out the odd one out of the following:
    (a) State Bank of India
    (b) Reserve Bank of India
    (c) Union Bank of India
    (d) Central Bank of India
42. SIDBI was set up in ______ as a wholly owned subsidiary of ______.
    (a) 1985 – EXIM (b) 1969 – RRBS
    (c) 1975 – IFCI (d) 1990 – IDBI
43. The most important reason for an investor to prefer a Bank deposit is
    (a) The credit worthiness of the Bank.
    (b) The Bank does not invest in the securities.
    (c) The Bank offers a guarantee.
    (d) All of the above.
44. Main objectives of CRR and SLR is to ensure:
    (i) Liquidity position of Bank
    (ii) Financial position of Bank
    (iii) Profit position of Bank
    (a) Only (i) is correct. (b) Only (ii) is correct.
    (c) Only (iii) is correct. (d) All are correct.
45. NABARD has taken over the entire functions of
    (a) ARDC (b) ACD of RBI
    (c) RPCD of RBI (d) All of the above
46. Which of the following is the best example of Agreement between oligopolists?
    (a) GATT (b) OPEC
    (c) WTO (d) UNIDO
47. Factor Endowment Theory of International Trade was propounded by
    (a) David Ricardo (b) Bertil-Ohlin
    (c) J.S. Mill (d) C.P. Kindleberger
48. **Assertion (A):** The British established and developed Indian Railways.
    Reason (R): The British are keenly interested in India's economic development.
    (a) Both (A) and (R) true.
    (b) Both (A) and (R) are false.
    (c) (A) is true, but (R) is false.
    (d) (A) is false, but (R) is true.
49. Which of the following is also known as World Bank?
    (a) IMF (b) IBRD (c) ADB (d) IFC
50. Special Economic Zones (SEZ) have been created first time in the
    (a) EXIM Policy – 2000
    (b) EXIM Policy – 2005
    (c) Industrial Policy – 1956
    (d) Industrial Policy – 1991

ANSWERS

1. (d)	2. (c)	3. (b)	4. (b)	5. (a)
6. (c)	7. (a)	8. (c)	9. (d)	10. (a)
11. (b)	12. (d)	13. (d)	14. (a)	15. (a)
16. (c)	17. (c)	18. (d)	19. (d)	20. (d)
21. (b)	22. (b)	23. (d)	24. (c)	25. (d)
26. (d)	27. (c)	28. (c)	29. (c)	30. (d)
31. (b)	32. (c)	33. (d)	34. (a)	35. (b)
36. (a)	37. (b)	38. (c)	39. (b)	40. (a)
41. (b)	42. (d)	43. (d)	44. (a)	45. (d)
46. (b)	47. (b)	48. (c)	49. (b)	50. (a)

JUNE–2012

Note: This paper contains Sixty (60) multiple-choice questions, each question carrying two (2) marks. Candidate is expected to answer any Fifty (50) questions. In case more than Fifty (50) questions are attempted, only the first Fifty (50) questions will be evaluated.

PAPER–I

1. Video-Conferencing can be classified as one of the following types of communication:
   (a) Visual one way
   (b) Audio-Visual one way
   (c) Audio-Visual two way
   (d) Visual two way
2. MC National University of Journalism and Communication is located at
   (a) Lucknow (b) Bhopal
   (c) Chennai (d) Mumbai
3. All India Radio (A.I.R.) for broadcasting was named in the year
   (a) 1926 (b) 1936 (c) 1946 (d) 1956
4. In India for broadcasting TV programmes which system is followed?
   (a) NTCS (b) PAL
   (c) NTSE (d) SECAM
5. The term 'DAVP' stands for
   (a) Directorate of Advertising & Vocal Publicity
   (b) Division of Audio-Visual Publicity
   (c) Department of Audio-Visual Publicity
   (d) Directorate of Advertising & Visual Publicity
6. The term "TRP" is associated with TV shows stands for
   (a) Total Rating Points
   (b) Time Rating Points
   (c) Thematic Rating Points
   (d) Television Rating Points
7. Which is the number that comes next in the following sequence?
   2, 6, 12, 20, 30, 42, 56, _____
   (a) 60 (b) 64 (c) 72 (d) 70
8. Find the next letter for the series YVSP ......
   (a) N (b) M (c) O (d) L
9. Given that in a code language, '645' means 'day is warm'; '42' means 'warm spring' and '634' means 'spring is sunny'; which digit represents 'sunny'?
   (a) 3 (b) 2 (c) 4 (d) 5
10. The basis of the following classification is: 'first President of India', 'author of Godan', 'books in my library', 'blue things' and 'students who work hard'
    (a) Common names
    (b) Proper names
    (c) Descriptive phrases
    (d) Indefinite description
11. In the expression 'Nothing is larger than itself' the relation 'is larger than' is
    (a) antisymmetric (b) asymmetrical
    (c) intransitive (d) irreflexive
12. **Assertion (A):** There are more laws on the books today than ever before, and more crimes being committed than ever before.
    Reason (R): Because to reduce crime we must eliminate the laws.
    Choose the correct answer from below:
    (a) (A) is true, (R) is doubtful and (R) is not the correct explanation of (A).
    (b) (A) is false, (R) is true and (R) is the correct explanation of (A).
    (c) (A) is doubtful, (R) is doubtful and (R) is not the correct explanation of (A).
    (d) (A) is doubtful, (R) is true and (R) is not the correct explanation of (A).
13. If the proposition "All men are not mortal" is true then which of the following inferences is correct? Choose from the code given below:
    1. "All men are mortal" is true.
    2. "Some men are mortal" is false.
    3. "No men are mortal" is doubtful.
    4. "All men are mortal" is false.

Code:

(a) 1, 2 and 3 (b) 2, 3 and 4
(c) 1, 3 and 4 (d) 1 and 3

14. Determine the nature of the following definition: "Abortion" means the ruthless murdering of innocent beings.
(a) Lexical (b) Persuasive
(c) Stipulative (d) Theoretical

15. Which one of the following is not an argument?
(a) Devadutt does not eat in the day so he must be eating at night.
(b) If Devadutt is growing fat and if he does not eat during the day, he will be eating at night.
(c) Devadutt eats in the night so he does not eat during the day.
(d) Since Devadutt does not eat in the day, he must be eating in the night.

16. Venn diagram is a kind of diagram to
(a) represent and assess the validity of elementary inferences of syllogistic form.
(b) represent but not assess the validity of elementary inferences of syllogistic form.
(c) represent and assess the truth of elementary inferences of syllogistic form.
(d) assess but not represent the truth of elementary inferences of syllogistic form.

17. Reasoning by analogy leads to
(a) certainty
(b) definite conclusion
(c) predictive conjecture
(d) surety

18. Which of the following statements are false? Choose from the code given below:
1. Inductive arguments always proceed from the particular to the general.
2. A cogent argument must be inductively strong.
3. A valid argument may have a false premise and a false conclusion.
4. An argument may legitimately be spoken of as 'true' or 'false'.

Codes:

(a) 2, 3 and 4 (b) 1 and 3
(c) 2 and 4 (d) 1 and 2

19. Six persons A, B, C, D, E and F are standing in a circle. B is between F and C, A is between E and D, F is to the left of D. Who is between A and F?
(a) B (b) C (c) D (d) E

20. The price of petrol increases by 25%. By what percentage must a customer reduce the consumption so that the earlier bill on the petrol does not alter?
(a) 20% (b) 25% (c) 30% (d) 33.33%

21. If Ram knows that *y* is an integer greater than 2 and less than 7 and Hari knows that *y* is an integer greater than 5 and less than 10, then they may correctly conclude that
(a) *y* can be exactly determined
(b) *y* may be either of two values
(c) *y* may be any of three values
(d) there is no value of *y* satisfying these conditions

22. Four pipes can fill a reservoir in 15, 20, 30 and 60 hours respectively. The first one was opened at 6 AM, second at 7 AM, third at 8 AM and the fourth at 9 AM. When will the reservoir be filled?
(a) 11 AM (b) 12 Noon
(c) 1 PM (d) 1:30 PM

The total electricity generation in a country is 97 GW. The contribution of various energy sources is indicated in percentage terms in the Pie Chart given below:

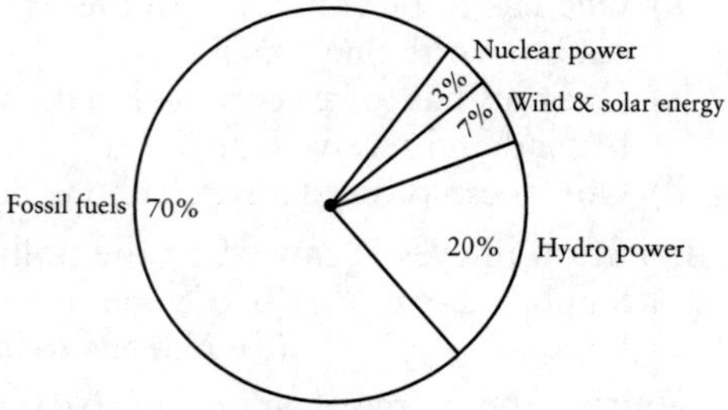

23. What is the contribution of wind and solar power in absolute terms in the electricity generation?
(a) 6.79 GW (b) 19.4 GW
(c) 9.7 GW (d) 29.1 GW

24. What is the contribution of renewable energy sources in absolute terms in the electricity generation?
(a) 29.1 GW (b) 26.19 GW
(c) 67.9 GW (d) 97 GW

25. TCP/IP is necessary if one is to connect to the
    (a) Phone lines (b) LAN
    (c) Internet (d) Server
26. Each character on the keyboard of computer has an ASCII value which stands for
    (a) American Stock Code for Information Interchange
    (b) American Standard Code for Information Interchange
    (c) African Standard Code for Information Interchange
    (d) Adaptable Standard Code for Information Change
27. Which of the following is not a programming language?
    (a) Pascal (b) Microsoft Office
    (c) Java (d) C++
28. Minimum number of bits required to store any 3 digit decimal number is equal to
    (a) 3 (b) 5 (c) 8 (d) 10
29. Internet explorer is a type of
    (a) Operating System (b) Compiler
    (c) Browser (d) IP address
30. POP3 and IMAP are e-mail accounts in which
    (a) One automatically gets one's mail everyday
    (b) One has to be connected to the server to read or write one's mail
    (c) One only has to be connected to the server to send and receive e-mail
    (d) One does not need any telephone lines
31. Irritation in eyes is caused by the pollutant
    (a) Sulphur di-oxide (b) Ozone
    (c) PAN (d) Nitrous oxide
32. Which is the source of chlorofluoro carbons?
    (a) Thermal power plants
    (b) Automobiles
    (c) Refrigeration and Airconditioning
    (d) Fertilizers
33. Which of the following is not a renewable natural resource?
    (a) Clean air (b) Fertile soil
    (c) Fresh water (d) Salt
34. Which of the following parameters is not used as a pollution indicator in water?
    (a) Total dissolved solids (b) Coliform count
    (c) Dissolved oxygen (d) Density
35. S and P waves are associated with
    (a) floods (b) wind energy
    (c) earthquakes (d) tidal energy
36. Match List I and List II and select the correct answer from the codes given below:

List I	List II
(A) Ozone hole	(i) Tsunami
(B) Greenhouse effect	(ii) UV radiations
(C) Natural hazards	(iii) Methane
(D) Sustainable development	(iv) Eco-centrism

Codes:	A	B	C	D
(a)	(ii)	(iii)	(i)	(iv)
(b)	(iii)	(ii)	(i)	(iv)
(c)	(iv)	(iii)	(i)	(ii)
(d)	(iv)	(ii)	(iii)	(i)

37. Indian Institute of Advanced Study is located at
    (a) Dharmshala (b) Shimla
    (c) Solan (d) Chandigarh
38. Indicate the number of Regional Offices of National Council of Teacher Education.
    (a) 04 (b) 05 (c) 06 (d) 08
39. Which of the following rights was considered the "Heart and Soul" of the Indian Constitution by Dr. B.R. Ambedkar?
    (a) Freedom of Speech
    (b) Right to Equality
    (c) Right to Freedom of Religion
    (d) Right to Constitutional Remedies
40. Who among the following created the office of the District Collector in India?
    (a) Lord Cornwallis
    (b) Warren Hastings
    (c) The Royal Commission on Decentralisation
    (d) Sir Charles Metcalfe
41. The Fundamental Duties of a citizen include
    1. Respect for the Constitution, the National Flag and the National Anthem
    2. To develop the scientific temper.
    3. Respect for the Government.
    4. To protect Wildlife.

    Choose the correct answer from the codes given below:

    Codes:
    (a) 1, 2 and 3 (b) 1, 2 and 4
    (c) 2, 3 and 4 (d) 1, 3, 4 and 2

42. The President of India takes oath
(a) to uphold the sovereignty and integrity of India.
(b) to bear true faith and allegiance to the Constitution of India.
(c) to uphold the Constitution and Laws of the country.
(d) to preserve, protect and defend the Constitution and the law of the country.

43. If you get an opportunity to teach a visually challenged student along with normal students, what type of treatment would you like to give him in the class?
(a) Not giving extra attention because majority may suffer.
(b) Take care of him sympathetically in the classroom.
(c) You will think that blindness is his destiny and hence you cannot do anything.
(d) Arrange a seat in the front row and try to teach at a pace convenient to him.

44. Which of the following is not a characteristic of a good achievement test?
(a) Reliability (b) Objectivity
(c) Ambiguity (d) Validity

45. Which of the following does not belong to a projected aid?
(a) Overhead projector (b) Blackboard
(c) Epidiascope (d) Slide projector

46. For a teacher, which of the following methods would be correct for writing on the blackboard?
(a) Writing fast and as clearly as possible.
(b) Writing the matter first and then asking students to read it.
(c) Asking a question to students and then writing the answer as stated by them.
(d) Writing the important points as clearly as possible.

47. A teacher can be successful if he/she
(a) helps students in becoming better citizens
(b) imparts subject knowledge to students
(c) prepares students to pass the examination
(d) presents the subject matter in a well organized manner

48. Dynamic approach to teaching means
(a) Teaching should be forceful and effective
(b) Teachers should be energetic and dynamic
(c) The topics of teaching should not be static, but dynamic
(d) The students should be required to learn through activities

49. The research that aims at immediate application is
(a) Action Research
(b) Empirical Research
(c) Conceptual Research
(d) Fundamental Research

50. When two or more successive footnotes refer to the same work which one of the following expressions is used?
(a) ibid. (b) et al. (c) op. cit. (d) loc. cit.

51. Nine year olds are taller than seven year olds. This is an example of a reference drawn from
(a) Vertical study
(b) Cross-sectional study
(c) Time series study
(d) Experimental study

52. Conferences are meant for
(a) Multiple target groups
(b) Group discussions
(c) Show-casing new Research
(d) All of the above

53. Ex-Post Facto research means
(a) The research is carried out after the incident
(b) The research is carried out prior to the incident
(c) The research is carried out along with the happening of an incident.
(d) The research is carried out keeping in mind the possibilities of an incident.

54. Research ethics do not include
(a) Honesty (b) Subjectivity
(c) Integrity (d) Objectivity

Read the following passage carefully and answer the questions 55 to 60:

James Madison said, "A people who mean to be their own governors must arm themselves with power that knowledge gives." In India, the Official Secrets Act, 1923 was a convenient smokescreen to deny members of the public access to information. Public functioning has traditionally been shrouded in secrecy. But in a democracy in which people govern themselves, it is necessary to have more openness. In the maturing of our democracy, right to information is a major step forward; it enables citizens to participate fully in the decision-making process that affects their lives so profoundly. It is in this context that the address of the Prime Minister in the Lok Sabha is significant. He said, "I would only like to see that everyone, particularly our civil servants, should see the Bill in a positive spirit; not as a draconian law for paralyzing Government, but as an instrument for improving Government-Citizen interface resulting in a friendly, caring and effective Government functioning for the good of our People." He further said, "This is an innovative Bill, where there will be scope to review its functioning as we gain experience. Therefore, this is a piece of legislation, whose working will be kept under constant reviews."

The Commission, in its Report, has dealt with the application of the Right to Information in Executive, Legislature and Judiciary. The judiciary could be a pioneer in implementing the Act in letter and spirit because much of the work that the Judiciary does is open to public scrutiny, Government of India has sanctioned an e-governance project in the Judiciary for about ₹ 700 crores which would bring about systematic classification, standardization and categorization of records. This would help the judiciary to fulfil its mandate under the Act. Similar capacity building would be required in all other public authorities. The transformation from non-transparency to transparency and public accountability is the responsibility of all three organs of State.

55. A person gets power
   (a) by acquiring knowledge
   (b) from the Official Secrets Act, 1923
   (c) through openings
   (d) by denying public information

56. Right to Information is a major step forward to
   (a) enable citizens to participate fully in the decision-making process
   (b) to make the people aware of the Act
   (c) to gain knowledge of administration
   (d) to make the people Government friendly

57. The Prime Minister considered the Bill
   (a) to provide power to the civil servants
   (b) as an instrument for improving Government-citizen interface resulting in a friendly, caring and effective Government
   (c) a draconian law against the officials
   (d) to check the harassment of the people

58. The Commission made the Bill effective by
   (a) extending power to the executive authorities
   (b) combining the executive and legislative power
   (c) recognizing judiciary a pioneer in implementing the act in letter and spirit
   (d) educating the people before its implementation

59. The Prime Minister considered the Bill innovative and hoped that
   (a) It could be reviewed based on the experience gained on its functioning.
   (b) The civil servants would see the Bill in a positive spirit.
   (c) It would not be considered as a draconian law for paralyzing Government.
   (d) All of the above.

60. The transparency and public accountability is the responsibility of three organs of the State. These three organs are
   (a) Lok Sabha, Rajya Sabha and Judiciary
   (b) Lok Sabha, Rajya Sabha and Executive
   (c) Judiciary, Legislature and the Commission
   (d) Legislature, Executive and Judiciary

ANSWERS

1. (c)	2. (b)	3. (b)	4. (b)	5. (d)
6. (a)	7. (c)	8. (b)	9. (a)	10. (c)
11. (d)	12. (a)	13. (b)	14. (b)	15. (b)
16. (a)	17. (c)	18. (c)	19. (c)	20. (a)
21. (a)	22. (c)	23. (a)	24. (b)	25. (c)
26. (b)	27. (b)	28. (d)	29. (c)	30. (c)
31. (c)	32. (c)	33. (d)	34. (d)	35. (c)
36. (a)	37. (b)	38. (a)	39. (d)	40. (b)
41. (b)	42. (d)	43. (d)	44. (c)	45. (b)
46. (d)	47. (a)	48. (d)	49. (a)	50. (a)
51. (b)	52. (d)	53. (a)	54. (b)	55. (a)
56. (a)	57. (b)	58. (c)	59. (d)	60. (d)

PAPER–II

Note: This paper contains fifty (50) objective type questions, each question carrying two (2) marks. All questions are compulsory.

1. Which of the following denote the structural changes in Indian economy?
   (a) Primary sector contribution has gone down.
   (b) Service sector contribution has gone up.
   (c) Secondary sector has not changed much.
   (d) All of the above.
2. Broad Money has to be sensitized through:
   (a) CRR (b) SLR
   (c) Repo Rate (d) All of the above
3. Which one is not an element of legal environment?
   (a) Act of Parliamentarians in Lok Sabha
   (b) Indian Contract Act, 1872
   (c) Indian Partnership Act, 1932
   (d) Negotiable instruments Act, 1881
4. Out of the following, which are four dimensions of Human Development Index?
   (i) Life Expectancy
   (ii) Literacy Level
   (iii) Success Rate of Marriages
   (iv) Standard of Living
   (v) Crime Rate
   (vi) Corruption Level
   (vii) Economic Entitlement
   (viii) Foreign Visits
   Codes:
   (a) (i), (ii), (vi) and (viii)
   (b) (i), (ii), (iv) and (vii)
   (c) (ii), (iii), (vi) and (vii)
   (d) (iii), (v), (vii) and (viii)
5. Public Enterprise is defined as
   (a) An organisation run by joint efforts of Centre and State Governments.
   (b) An organisation which caters to the needs relating to public utilities.
   (c) An organisation in which capital is invested by public.
   (d) An organisation owned and managed by public authorities for definite set of public purposes.
6. Match List-I with List-II and select the correct answer:
   List-I
   (i) Measurement of income
   (ii) Recognition of expense
   (iii) Basis of realization
   (iv) Identification of revenue
   List-II
   (A) Accrues to the equity of owners
   (B) Recognition of revenue
   (C) Matching revenue with expenses
   (D) Accounting period

Codes:	**(i)**	**(ii)**	**(iii)**	**(iv)**
(a)	(A)	(B)	(C)	(D)
(b)	(B)	(A)	(C)	(D)
(c)	(C)	(D)	(A)	(B)
(d)	(C)	(D)	(B)	(A)

7. Consider the following items:
   (i) Debentures (ii) Prepaid rent
   (iii) Interest accrued (iv) Bank overdraft
   Which of them are current liabilities?
   (a) (i), (ii), (iii) and (iv) (b) (iv)
   (c) (ii), (iii) and (iv) (d) (i), (ii) and (iii)
8. Conversion cost is the sum of
   (a) Indirect wages and factory overhead
   (b) Direct wages, direct expenses and factory overhead
   (c) Direct material cost and indirect wages
   (d) Prime cost and selling & distribution overhead
9. **Assertion (A):** Premium received on issue of shares is credited to share premium account but not to Profit and Loss account.
   Reasoning (R): Since share premium is not a trading profit, it is not distributed to shareholders.
   (a) Both (A) and (R) are true but (R) is not correct explanation to (A).
   (b) (A) is false but (R) is correct.
   (c) Both (A) and (R) are true and (R) is correct explanation of (A).
   (d) (A) is correct but (R) is false.
10. Consider the following:
   (i) Basic defensive and interval ratio
   (ii) Current ratio
   (iii) Superquick ratio
   (iv) Quick ratio
   Arrange these ratios in sequence to reflect the liquidity in descending order.
   (a) (ii), (iv), (iii) and (i)
   (b) (i), (ii), (iv) and (iii)

(c) (iv), (ii), (iii) and (i)
(d) (iii), (iv), (i) and (ii)

11. Normally Demand curve slopes
(a) Upward (b) Downward
(c) Horizontal (d) Vertical

12. Which of the following refers to Perfect Competition?
(i) There are restrictions on buyers and sellers
(ii) There are no restrictions on movement of goods
(iii) There are no restrictions on factors of production
Correct one is
(a) only (i) and (ii) (b) only (ii) and (iii)
(c) only (i) and (iii) (d) only (i)

13. **Assertion (A):** Total utility will be maximum when marginal utility to price of respective products are equal.
Reason (R): Deviation from this situation leads to reduction in maximum utility.
(a) (A) and (R) are not correct.
(b) (A) is correct but (R) is not correct.
(c) (A) and (R) are correct.
(d) (A) is incorrect, (R) is correct.

14. Match List-I with List-II and select the correct answer.

List-I	List-II
(A) Survival Objective	(i) Economic
(B) R.O.I.	(ii) Natural Urge
(C) Growth Purpose	(iii) Business
(D) Innovation	(iv) Primary Objective

Codes:	A	B	C	D
(a)	(ii)	(iii)	(iv)	(i)
(b)	(ii)	(i)	(iii)	(iv)
(c)	(i)	(ii)	(iii)	(iv)
(d)	(iv	(iii)	(ii)	(i)

15. Consider the oligopoly models:
(i) Sweezy's kinked demand curve model
(ii) Newman and Morgenstern Game Theory model
(iii) Cournal's duopoly model
(iv) Baumal's sales maximisation model
Arrange them in correct sequence as per order of evolution.
(a) (iv), (iii), (ii), (i) (b) (ii), (i), (iii), (iv)
(c) (iii), (i), (ii), (iv) (d) (i), (iii), (ii), (iv)

16. Which of the following is not a restricted random sampling technique?
(a) Stratified sampling
(b) Simple random sampling
(c) Systematic sampling
(d) Multistage sampling

17. Classification of respondents only on the basis of gender is an application of
(a) Ordinal scale (b) Nominal scale
(c) Interval scale (d) Ratio scale

18. Karl Pearson's co-efficient of correlation between two variables is
(a) the product of their standard deviations
(b) the square root of the product of their regression co-efficients
(c) the co-variance between the variables
(d) None of the above

19. Statistical software packages for research in social sciences include
(a) SPSS (b) STATA
(c) MiniTab (d) All of the above

20. F-test is used to test the significance of the differences between/among
(a) Two sample mean
(b) More than two samples mean
(c) Variance of two samples
(d) (b) and (c)

21. Match the following
List I
(A) The Practice of Management
(B) Philosophy of Management
(C) Scientific Management
(D) General and Industrial Administration
List II
(i) Henry Fayol (ii) F.W. Taylor
(iii) Oliver Sheldon (iv) Peter F Drucker

Codes:	A	B	C	D
(a)	(i)	(ii)	(iii)	(iv)
(b)	(iv)	(iii)	(ii)	(i)
(c)	(iv)	(iii)	(i)	(ii)
(d)	(iii)	(iv)	(ii)	(i)

22. Identify the correct sequence of steps involved in planning:
(i) Selecting the best course of action
(ii) Establishing the sequence of activities
(iii) Establishment of objectives
(iv) Evaluating alternative courses
(v) Determining alternative courses
(a) (i), (ii), (iii), (iv) and (v)
(b) (iii), (v), (iv), (ii) and (i)

(c) (v), (iv), (iii), (ii) and (i)
(d) (iii), (v), (iv), (i) and (ii)

23. **Assertion (A):** One can be sure about future course of actions by making good plans.
Reasoning (R): Planning brings certainty in future course of actions of an organisation.
(a) (R) is correct but (A) is not correct.
(b) (A) is correct but (R) is not correct.
(c) Both (A) and (R) are correct.
(d) Both (A) and (R) are not correct.

24. According to Kieth Devis, which one is not a barrier of communication?
(a) Physical Barriers
(b) Technological Barriers
(c) Personal Barriers
(d) Linguistic Barriers

25. While establishing relation between Maslow's and Herzberg's theories, which Needs of Hierachy Theory will fall under the Hygiene Factors?
(a) Self-actualisation, esteem and social needs
(b) Esteem, social and safety needs
(c) Social, safety and physiological needs
(d) Only social needs

26. Howard-Sueth model of consumer behaviour is popularly known as
(a) Machine Model (b) Human Model
(c) Marketing Model (d) Purchase Model

27. To generate and facilitate any exchange intended to satisfy human needs or wants such that the satisfaction of these wants occur with minimal detrimental impact on the natural environment is known as
(a) Aggressive marketing
(b) Operating marketing
(c) Green marketing
(d) All of the above

28. All the activities involved in selling goods or services directly to final consumers for personal non-business uses are done by
(a) Wholesalers (b) Retailers
(c) Mediators (d) Commission Agents

29. To manage a business well is to manage its future and to manage the future is to manage information is termed as
(a) Management information system
(b) Marketing information system
(c) Future information system
(d) General information system

30. DAGMAR approach in marketing is used to measure
(a) Public relations (b) Advertising results
(c) Selling volume
(d) Consumer satisfaction

31. Which one is not an important objective of Financial Management?
(a) Profit Maximisation
(b) Wealth Maximisation
(c) Value Maximisation
(d) Maximisation of social benefits

32. Which one refers to cash inflow under payback period method?
(a) Cash flow before depreciation and taxes
(b) Cash flow after depreciation and taxes
(c) Cash flow after depreciation but before taxes
(d) Cash flow before depreciation and after taxes

33. The concept of present value is based on the:
(a) Principle of compounding
(b) Principle of discounting
(c) (a) and (b)
(d) None of the above

34. Cost of capital from all the sources of funds is called
(a) Specific cost (b) Composite cost
(c) Implicit cost (d) Simple Average cost

35. Match the following with most suitable option:

(a) Modigiliani-Miller Approach	(i) Commercial papers
(b) Net Operating Income Approach	(ii) Working Capital Management
(c) Short term Money Market Instrument	(iii) Capital Structure
(d) Factoring	(iv) Arbitrage

Codes:	A	B	C	D
(a)	(iv)	(iii)	(i)	(ii)
(b)	(iii)	(iv)	(i)	(ii)
(c)	(iii)	(ii)	(i)	(iv)
(d)	(iii)	(ii)	(iv)	(i)

36. Which four are the factors influencing the Human Resource Management of an organisation?
    (i) Size of workforce
    (ii) Employee expectations
    (iii) Composition of workforce
    (iv) Political influence
    (v) Changes in technology
    (a) (i), (ii), (iii) and (iv)
    (b) (i),(ii), (iii) and (v)
    (c) (i), (ii), (iv) and (v)
    (d) (i), (iii), (iv) and (v)
37. **Assertion (A):** One cannot be sure about the quality of appraisal on the basis of length of service.
    Reasoning (R): Initial appraisal and promotional appraisal are done separately and differently since the length of service is different.
    (a) (R) is correct but (A) is not correct.
    (b) (A) is correct but (R) is not correct.
    (c) (A) and (R) both are correct.
    (d) (A) and (R) both are not correct.
38. Which of the following are covered under the scope of Human Resource Management?
    (i) Forecasting Human Resource Needs
    (ii) Replacement Planning
    (iii) Human Resource Dynamics
    (iv) Human Resource Development Planning
    (v) Human Resource Audit
    (a) (i), (iii), (v)
    (b) (i), (ii), (iii), (iv)
    (c) (iii), (v)
    (d) (i), (ii), (iii), (iv), (v)
39. On which of the following, at the initial stage, the Indian IT companies relying more for getting good IT professionals?
    (a) Job Portals (b) Placement Agencies
    (c) Campus Placement (d) All of the above
40. **Statement (i):** Labour always get a major share of productivity gains.
    Statement (ii): Partial stoppage of work by workers amounts to strike.
    (a) Statement (i) is true but (ii) is false.
    (b) Statement (ii) is true but (i) is false.
    (c) Both statements are true.
    (d) Both statements are false.
41. Imperial Bank was established on January 27, 1921 on the advise of
    (a) J.M. Keynes (b) Lord Illingworth
    (c) King George V (d) Winston Churchill
42. Read the following events:
    (i) Allowing convertibility of rupee at the market rate in the current account
    (ii) Nationalisation of general insurance business
    (iii) Establishment of IDBI
    (iv) Nationalisation of life insurance business
    (v) Capital adequacy norms for commercial banks
    Arrange the events in the ascending order of their occurrence:
    (a) (iv), (iii), (ii), (i), (v)
    (b) (v), (iv), (iii), (ii), (i)
    (c) (i), (ii), (iii), (v), (iv)
    (d) (i), (v), (ii), (iv), (iii)
43. In India, the Commercial Banks are given license of operation by
    (a) The Government of India
    (b) The Ministry of Finance
    (c) Reserve Bank of India
    (d) Banking Companies Regulation Act, 1949
44. The provisions of General Reserve in Banking Companies are made keeping in view the provisions of
    (a) Indian Companies Act, 1956
    (b) Banking Companies Act, 1949
    (c) SEBI Act, 1992
    (d) Statutory Auditor
45. Which among the following is not true with regard to merchant banker?
    (i) It can accept deposits.
    (ii) It can advance loans.
    (iii) It can do other banking activities.
    (iv) It can be manager to a public issue.
    (a) (i), (ii) and (iii) (b) (ii), (iii) and (iv)
    (c) (i), (iii) and (iv) (d) (ii) and (iv)
46. Balance of Payments can be made favourable if
    (a) Exports are increased
    (b) Imports are increased
    (c) Devaluation of money
    (d) (a) and (c)
47. Which one is not an objective of IMF?
    (a) To promote international monetary co-operation
    (b) To ensure balanced international trade

(c) To finance productive efforts according to peace-time requirement
(d) To ensure exchange rate stability

48. EPCG denotes
(a) Export Potential and Credit Guarantee
(b) Earning Promotion and Credit Guarantee
(c) Export Promotion and Credit Guarantee
(d) Export Potential and Credit Goods

49. Which one of the following matches correspond to the Member and Observer countries of the SAARC?
(i) India, Pakistan, Bangladesh, Bhutan, Nepal, Sri Lanka, Afghanistan, Maldive
(ii) Iran, China, Japan, USA, South Korea, European Union
(iii) Pakistan, Nepal, India, Bangladesh, Iran
(iv) UK, USA, North Korea, South Africa
(a) (iii) and (iv) (b) (ii) and (iv)
(c) (i) and (ii) (d) (ii) and (iii)

50. Which one is not an international organisation?
(a) SAARC (b) ASEM
(c) ASEAN (d) CBDT

ANSWERS

1. (d)	2. (d)	3. (a)	4. (b)	5. (d)
6. (d)	7. (b)	8. (b)	9. (c)	10. (a)
11. (b)	12. (b)	13. (c)	14. (a)	15. (c)
16. (b)	17. (b)	18. (b)	19. (d)	20. (d)
21. (b)	22. (d)	23. (a)	24. (b)	25. (c)
26. (a)	27. (c)	28. (b)	29. (a)	30. (d)
31. (d)	32. (d)	33. (b)	34. (b)	35. (a)
36. (c)	37. (d)	38. (d)	39. (c)	40. (b)
41. (a)	42. (a)	43. (c)	44. (b)	45. (a)
46. (d)	47. (c)	48. (c)	49. (c)	50. (d)

PAPER–III

Note: This paper contains Seventy-five (75) objective type questions, each question carrying two (2) marks. All questions are compulsory.

1. If Opening Stock is ₹ 10,000, Net Purchases ₹ 70,000, Wages ₹ 2,500, Carriage inward ₹ 500 and Closing Stock ₹ 15,000, what is the Manufacturing Cost?
(a) ₹ 65,000 (b) ₹ 83,000
(c) ₹ 68,000 (d) ₹ 73,000

2. What does a high payout ratio indicate?
(a) A High Earning Per Share (EPS)
(b) The management is not ploughing back enough profit.
(c) The management is ploughing back profit.
(d) The company is earning high profit.

3. Which one of the following statements is true?
(a) Capital expenditure does not affect the profitability of a concern but revenue expenditure does.
(b) Capital expenditure affects the profitability of a concern directly but revenue expenditure does not.
(c) Capital expenditure affects the profitability of a concern indirectly but revenue expenditure affects directly.
(d) Both capital expenditure and revenue expenditure affect the profitability of a concern directly.

4. Identify the true statement of the following:
(i) Balance Sheet is always prepared from the point of view of the business but not from that of the owners.
(ii) The financial relationship of the business to its owners is shown in the Balance Sheet.
(iii) Balance Sheet is always related to a period of time.

Codes:
(a) (i) and (ii) (b) (ii) and (iii)
(c) (i) and (iii) (d) (i), (ii) and (iii)

5. X and Y are partners in a firm sharing profits in the ratios of 2 : 1. Z is admitted with a 1/3 profit sharing. What will be the new profit sharing ratio of X, Y and Z?
(a) 3 : 3 : 3 (b) 4 : 3 : 2
(c) 4 : 2 : 3 (d) 2 : 3 : 4

6. Which one of the following will not affect the working capital?
(a) Realisation of cash from debtors.
(b) Sale of plant and machinery in cash.
(c) Issue of equity shares.
(d) Redemption of debentures.

7. Given below are two statements, one labelled as Assertion (A) and the other labelled as Reason (R):

   Assertion (A): When a company earns profit prior to its incorporation, it is called capital profit.

   Reason (R): Capital profit cannot be used for distribution as dividend to the shareholders.

   In the context of the above two statements, which one of the following is correct?

   Codes:

   (a) (A) is correct, but (R) is wrong.
   (b) Both (A) and (R) are correct.
   (c) (A) is wrong, but (R) is correct.
   (d) Both (A) and (R) are wrong.

8. Reconstruction of a company takes place when

   (i) the company is undercapitalised
   (ii) company has incurred heavy losses which must be written off
   (iii) the company is overcapitalised

   Which one of the following is correct?

   (a) (i) and (ii) only (b) (i) and (iii) only
   (c) (ii) and (iii) only (d) All the above

9. Match the items of List-I with the items of List-II and select the correct answer using the codes given below the lists:

List-I	List-II
(A) Leverage Ratio	(i) Short-term solvency
(B) Liquidity Ratio	(ii) Earning capacity
(C) Turnover Ratio	(iii) Relationship between debt and equity
(D) Profitability Ratio	(iv) Efficiency of Asset Management

Codes:	A	B	C	D
(a)	(ii)	(i)	(iv)	(iii)
(b)	(iii)	(ii)	(i)	(iv)
(c)	(iv)	(iii)	(i)	(ii)
(d)	(iii)	(i)	(iv)	(ii)

10. Given below are two statements, one labelled as Assertion (A) and the other labelled as Reason (R):

    Assertion (A): Sinking fund is a charge against Profit and Loss Account.

    Reason (R): Sinking fund is created for repayment of a long-term liability.

    In the context of the above two statements, which one of the following is correct?

    Codes:

    (a) (A) is correct, but (R) is wrong.
    (b) Both (A) and (R) are correct.
    (c) (A) is wrong, but (R) is correct.
    (d) Both (A) and (R) are wrong.

11. Match List-I with List-II and select the correct answer using the codes given below the lists:

List-I	**List-II**
(A) Goodwill of a company	(i) Current liability
(B) Overdraft	(ii) Fixed Assets
(C) Preliminary Expenses	(iii) Reserves and Surplus
(D) Premium on Issue of Shares	(iv) Fictitious Assets

Codes:	**A**	**B**	**C**	**D**
(a)	(ii)	(i)	(iv)	(iii)
(b)	(i)	(ii)	(iv)	(iii)
(c)	(i)	(ii)	(iii)	(iv)
(d)	(ii)	(i)	(iii)	(iv)

12. In India, which of the following is prepared on the guidelines of AS-3 (Accounting Standard-3)?

    (a) Balance Sheet of a company
    (b) Funds Flow Statement
    (c) Cash Flow Statement
    (d) Consolidated Financial Statement

13. What is the correct sequence of the following actions required for the preparation of financial accounts?

    (i) Trading accounts
    (ii) Making adjusting entries
    (iii) Balance Sheet
    (iv) Profit and Loss Account

    Select the correct answer from the codes given below:

    Codes:

    (a) (iv), (ii), (i), (iii) (b) (ii), (iv), (iii), (i)
    (c) (ii), (i), (iv), (iii) (d) (iv), (ii), (iii), (i)

14. The main effect of inflation on the financial statement is

    (a) Profits are understated
    (b) Overstatement of assets
    (c) Adequacy of funds for replacement of assets
    (d) Erosion of capital

15. Present value of future earnings is a model of Human Resources Accounting suggested by
   (a) Brauch Lev & ABA Schwartz
   (b) Jaggi & Lau
   (c) S.K. Chakraborty
   (d) Eric Flamhaltz
16. Which element of the promotion mix do wholesalers generally apply to obtain their promotional objective?
   (a) Advertising (b) Personal Selling
   (c) Trade Promotion (d) Direct Marketing
17. Who has given 'Fourteen Principles of Management'?
   (a) Barnard (b) Henry Fayol
   (c) F.W. Taylor (d) Flemming
18. What is M.B.O.?
   (a) Management by Objective
   (b) Multiple Business Organisation
   (c) Management by Organisation
   (d) Multiplicity of Business Operations
19. Match items in List-II with items in List-I:

	List-I		List-II
(A)	Mega Marketing	(I)	Advertising
(B)	Penetration Price	(II)	Kotler
(C)	Promotion Mix	(III)	Low price
(D)	Customer Satisfaction	(IV)	Post Purchase Behaviour

Codes:	A	B	C	D
(a)	I	II	III	IV
(b)	III	I	II	IV
(c)	IV	III	II	I
(d)	III	IV	I	II

20. **Statement (A):** Sales promotion has a strong impact on consumer behaviour in rural India.

   Reason (R): Rural people in India give utmost significance to sales promotion schemes.

   Codes:
   (a) Statement (A) is correct but Reason (R) is incorrect.
   (b) Statement (A) is incorrect, but Reason (R) is correct.
   (c) Both Statement (A) and Reason (R) are correct.
   (d) Both Statement (A) and Reason (R) are incorrect.
21. Market sub-divided on the basis of behavioural characteristics is called
   (a) Segmentation (b) Aggregation
   (c) Precision (d) None of the above
22. What is mass marketing?
   (a) Offering the same products and marketing mix to all consumers.
   (b) Offering variety of products to the entire market.
   (c) Offering differentiated products to all customers.
   (d) Following concentrated marketing strategy.
23. Which concept of marketing is based on the assumption that superior products sell themselves?
   (a) Production (b) Marketing
   (c) Societal (d) Product
24. In broader sense, marketing communication includes
   (a) Product (b) Price (c) Place (d) All
25. Physical distribution provides
   (a) Place utility (b) Time utility
   (c) Place and Time utility (d) Form utility
26. What is relevant to place variable of marketing mix?
   (a) Branding (b) Price penetration
   (c) Sales personnel motivation
   (d) None of these
27. Find incorrect statement.
   (a) Marketers arouse emotional motives
   (b) Marketers satisfy rational motives
   (c) Marketers formulate different sales promotions for different motives
   (d) None of the above
28. Non-store marketing includes
   (a) Home selling (b) V.P.P.
   (c) Vending machines (d) All of the above
29. What is customer delight?
   (a) Performance equal to expectation
   (b) Performance less than expectation
   (c) Performance more than expectation
   (d) Expectation more than performance
30. Which terms are often used interchangeably in marketing literature?
   (a) Concept, method, philosophy
   (b) Concept, approach, technique

(c) Orientation, concept, philosophy
(d) Philosophy, system, concept

31. Which one of the following is not the operative function of HRM?
(a) Development (b) Controlling
(c) Compensation (d) Integration

32. Which one of the following is not in sequence of personnel training procedure?
1. Instructor preparation
2. Present the task
3. Try out performance
4. Training preparation
5. Follow up
(a) 1, 2, 3, 4, 5 (b) 2, 1, 4, 3, 5
(c) 1, 4, 2, 3, 5 (d) 3, 1, 2, 5, 4

33. Under which method of performance appraisal one person is compared with all others for the purpose of placing them in a simple order of work?
(a) Grading
(b) Person-to-person comparison
(c) Ranking
(d) None of the above

34. Which one of the following is not the fundamental procedure that should be considered for the collective bargaining?
(a) Prenegotiation phase
(b) Selection of Negotiators
(c) Tactic and Strategy of Bargaining
(d) None of the above

35. **Assertion (A):** Inevitably the firm must go to the external sources for lower entry jobs.
Reason (R): For positions where required qualification/experience are not met.
Codes:
(a) Both (A) and (R) are not correct.
(b) (A) is true, but (R) is false.
(c) (R) is true, but (A) is false.
(d) Both (A) and (R) are correct.

36. Match the following items of List-I and List-II:

List-I	List-II
A. Asbestos	(1) Lung Cancer
B. Benzene	(2) Cancer
C. Ethylene Disbromide	(3) Leukemia
D. Kerosene	(4) Acute Nervous System Depression

Codes:	A	B	C	D
(a)	4	2	3	1
(b)	4	3	2	1
(c)	1	3	2	4
(d)	3	4	2	1

37. **Assertion (A):** Business Economics is tool centrics facilitating decision making in business.
Reason (R): It provides an analytical understanding of economic activities.
Codes:
(a) Both (A) and (R) are not correct.
(b) Both (A) and (R) are correct.
(c) (A) is true, but (R) is false.
(d) (R) is true, but (A) is false.

38. Demand has the following elements:
(a) Quantity (b) Price
(c) Time (d) All the above

39. A perfectly competitive firm attains equilibrium when
(a) AC = AR (b) MR = MC
(c) MC = AC (d) TC = TR

40. The purpose of job evaluation is
(a) Fixation of Responsibility
(b) Promotion
(c) Wage Determination
(d) Transfer to a better job

41. For testing of hypothesis $H_0 : M_1 = M_2$ and $H_1 : M_1 < M_2$, the critical value of Z at 5% level of significance when size of sample is more than 30 is
(a) 1.96 (b) 2.32 (c) 1.645 (d) 2.5758

42. Which of the following is the non-random method of selecting samples from a population?
(a) Stratified Sampling
(b) Quota Sampling
(c) Systematic Sampling
(d) Cluster Sampling

43. If the two regression coefficients are 0.8 and 0.2, then the value of coefficient of correlation is
(a) + 0.16 (b) – 0.40 (c) – 0.16 (d) + 0.40

44. Which one of the following is a relative measure of dispersion?
(a) Standard deviation
(b) Variance
(c) Coefficient of variation
(d) None of the above

45. **Assertion (A):** Internal factors of business environment are controllable factors.
Reason (R): The company can alter or modify such factors to suit the environment.
Codes:
(a) Both (A) and (R) are correct.
(b) (A) is correct, but (R) is incorrect.
(c) Both (A) and (R) are incorrect.
(d) (A) is incorrect.

46. The concept of 'Rolling Plan' in India was introduced by the
(a) BJP Government
(b) Janta Government
(c) Congress Government
(d) All of the above

47. Which one of the following is an obstacle to globalisation?
(a) Wide base (b) Niche markets
(c) Obsolescence (d) Competition

48. 'VSAT' technology is first followed for on-line trading by
(a) BSE (b) OTCEI (c) NSE (d) ISE

49. Match the following:

List I (Years)	List II (Act)
(A) 1956	(i) Consumer Protection Act
(B) 1986	(ii) Indian Companies Act
(C) 1992	(iii) Securities and Exchange Board of India
(D) 2002	(iv) Securitisation Act

Codes:	A	B	C	D
(a)	(ii)	(i)	(iii)	(iv)
(b)	(i)	(ii)	(iii)	(iv)
(c)	(ii)	(iii)	(i)	(iv)
(d)	(i)	(iv)	(iii)	(ii)

50. The flagship project of Government of India launched for generating guaranteed employment in rural areas is known as
(a) PMRY (b) MNREGA
(c) JRY (d) NREP

51. The conflicts in project ranking in capital budgeting as per NPV and IRR may arise because of
(a) Size disparity (b) Time disparity
(c) Life disparity (d) All the above

52. The degree of financial leverage reflects the responsiveness of
(a) Operating income to changes in total revenue
(b) EPS to changes in EBIT
(c) EPS to changes in total revenue
(d) None of the above

53. The overall capitalisation rate and the cost of debt remain constant for all degrees of financial leverage is advocated by
(a) Traditional Approach
(b) Net Income Approach
(c) Net Operating Income Approach
(d) M-M-Approach

54. Which of the following is not included in the assumptions on which Myron Gordon proposed a model on stock valuation?
(a) Retained earnings, the only source of financing
(b) Finite life of the firm
(c) Taxes do not exist
(d) Constant rate of return on firm's investment

55. Match the following:

List I	List II
(i) Factoring services	(A) Cash Management
(ii) Economic Order Quantity	(B) Receivable Management
(iii) Commercial paper	(C) Inventory Management
	(D) Working Capital Financing

Codes:	(i)	(ii)	(iii)
(a)	(A)	(C)	(B)
(b)	(C)	(B)	(A)
(c)	(B)	(C)	(D)
(d)	(B)	(A)	(C)

56. **Assertion (A):** International business focuses on global resources, opportunities to buy/sell worldwide.
Reason (R): The efforts of IMF, World Bank and WTO to liberalise their economies led to globalisation.
Codes:
(a) Both (A) and (R) are true.
(b) Both (A) and (R) are false.
(c) (A) is true, but (R) is false.
(d) (A) is false, but (R) is true.

57. Match the items of List-I with items of List-II:

List-I	List-II
A. Wider Market	(1) Modes of Entry

B. Turn key Projects	(2) Goal of International Business
C. Expanding the production capacities	(3) Advantages of International Business
D. Geocentric approach	4. Stage of Globalisation

Codes:	A	B	C	D
(a)	4	2	3	1
(b)	3	1	2	4
(c)	1	2	3	4
(d)	4	3	2	1

58. BRICS includes
   (a) Bhutan, Romania, Indonesia, Chile and South Korea
   (b) Brazil, Russia, Indonesia, Chile and Sudan
   (c) Brazil, Russia, India, China and South Africa
   (d) Britain, Russia, India, Czechoslovakia, Sri Lanka

59. Out of the following, one is not related with WTO:
   (a) TRIPS (b) Ministerial Conference
   (c) TRIMS (d) TRAI

60. Balance of Payment includes components
   (a) Current Account, Capital Account, Unilateral Payments Accounts, Official Settlement Account
   (b) Revenue Account, P&L Account, Capital Account, Official Account
   (c) Trade Account, Activity Account, Revenue Account, Currency Account
   (d) Forex Account, Trade Account, Funds Account

61. **Assertion (A):** International Monetary Fund was set up in 1944.

   Reason (R): To promote international monetary cooperation through a permanent institution which provides machinery for consultation and collaboration on international monetary problems.

   Codes:
   (a) Both (A) and (R) are false.
   (b) Both (A) and (R) are true.
   (c) (A) is true, but (R) is false.
   (d) (R) is true, but (A) is false.

62. The commercial banks do not perform one function out of the following:
   (a) Mobilisation of savings
   (b) Giving Loans and Advances
   (c) Issuing Currency Notes
   (d) Financing Priority Sectors

63. There are two lists of items, match the items of List-I with items of List-II:

List-I	List-II
(A) Reserve Bank of India	(1) NPA
(B) EXIM Bank	(2) Facilitating Small Scale Industries
(C) SIDBI	(3) Credit Control
(D) Capital Adequacy	(4) Export/Import Financing

Codes:	A	B	C	D
(a)	1	2	3	4
(b)	4	3	2	1
(c)	2	3	4	1
(d)	3	4	2	1

64. One of the items is not related with e-banking:
   (a) Demand Draft (b) SPNS
   (c) ECS (d) ATM

65. **Assertion (A):** The Treasury Manager uses the derivatives in the Bond market as well as in Forex market.
   Reason (R): It helps risk coverage.
   Codes:
   (a) Both (A) and (R) are false.
   (b) Both (A) and (R) are true.
   (c) (A) is true, but (R) is false.
   (d) (R) is true, but (A) is false.

66. Factoring and forfeiting have not taken off in the Indian economy due to lack of expertise and experience. One is not included in the factoring services rendered.
   (a) Purchase of book debts and receivables.
   (b) Prepayment of debts partially or fully
   (c) Giving advice
   (d) Covering the credit risk of the suppliers

67. Which one is not the form of FDI?
   (a) Purchase of existing assets in foreign currency
   (b) New investment in property, plant, equipment
   (c) Making investment in the mutual funds
   (d) Transfer of many types of assets

68. Match the items of List-I with items of List-II:

	List-I		List-II
(A)	Measures towards globalization	(I)	Globalisation
(B)	Off-shoring	(II)	FEMA
(C)	FERA	(III)	Liberalise the inflow of FDI
(D)	Mr. Aruthur Dunkel	(IV)	Uruguay Round

Codes:	A	B	C	D
(a)	III	I	II	IV
(b)	II	I	III	IV
(c)	IV	II	I	III
(d)	I	II	IV	III

69. Which one of the following is not the advantage of MNCs to the host country?
(a) Increase in social activity
(b) Increase in economic activity
(c) Utilisation of natural resources
(d) R&D efforts enhanced

70. India suffered from deficit balance both in trade balance and net invisibles, hence, took up a number of steps to manage this problem. Which one is not appropriate for this?
(a) Export control
(b) Current Account Convertibility
(c) Liberalised Export Policy
(d) Unified Exchange Rate

71. Mr. James, a citizen of U.S., arrived in India for the first time on 1st July, 2010 and left for Nepal on 15th December 2010. He arrived to India again on 1st January 2011 and stayed till the end of the financial year 2010-11. His residential status for the assessment year 2011-12 is
(a) Resident (ordinarily resident)
(b) Not ordinarily resident
(c) Non-resident
(d) None of the above

72. The value of free accommodation in Delhi provided by employer in the private sector is
(a) 10% of salary (b) 15% of salary
(c) 20% of salary (d) 25% of salary

73. Which of the following is not a capital asset under capital gains head of income?
(a) Stock in trade
(b) Goodwill of business
(c) Agricultural Land in Delhi
(d) Jewellery

74. Match the items of List-I with List-II:

List-I	List-II
A. Tax Planning	(1) Making suitable arrangement of TDS
B. Tax Avoidance	(2) Understatement of Income
C. Tax Evasion	(3) Availing deduction under Section 10A of IT Act.
D. Tax Administration	(4) Misinterpreting the provisions of the IT Act

Codes:	A	B	C	D
(a)	2	1	4	3
(b)	1	4	3	2
(c)	3	4	2	1
(d)	4	1	3	2

75. Under the Income Tax Act, 1961 unabsorbed depreciation can be carried forward for set-off purpose:
(a) For 4 years (b) For 5 years
(c) For 8 years (d) For unspecified period

ANSWERS

1. (c)	2. (b)	3. (c)	4. (a)	5. (c)
6. (a)	7. (b)	8. (c)	9. (d)	10. (c)
11. (a)	12. (c)	13. (c)	14. (d)	15. (a)
16. (c)	17. (b)	18. (a)	19. (b)	20. (a)
21. (a)	22. (a)	23. (d)	24. (d)	25. (c)
26. (c)	27. (d)	28. (d)	29. (c)	30. (c)
31. (b)	32. (c)	33. (c)	34. (d)	35. (d)
36. (c)	37. (b)	38. (d)	39. (b)	40. (c)
41. (c)	42. (b)	43. (d)	44. (c)	45. (a)
46. (b)	47. (c)	48. (c)	49. (a)	50. (b)
51. (d)	52. (b)	53. (c)	54. (b)	55. (c)
56. (a)	57. (b)	58. (c)	59. (d)	60. (a)
61. (b)	62. (c)	63. (d)	64. (a)	65. (b)
66. (c)	67. (c)	68. (a)	69. (a)	70. (a)
71. (b)	72. (b)	73. (a)	74. (c)	75. (d)

DECEMBER–2012

Note: This paper contains Sixty (60) multiple choice questions, each question carrying two (2) marks. Candidate is expected to answer any Fifty (50) questions. In case more than Fifty (50) questions are attempted, only the first Fifty (50) questions will be evaluated.

PAPER–I

1. The English word 'Communication' is derived from the words
   (a) Communis and Communicare
   (b) Communist and Commune
   (c) Communism and Communalism
   (d) Communion and Common sense
2. Chinese Cultural Revolution leader Mao Zedong used a type of communication to talk to the masses is known as
   (a) Mass line communication
   (b) Group communication
   (c) Participatory communication
   (d) Dialogue communication
3. Conversing with the spirits and ancestors is termed as
   (a) Transpersonal communication
   (b) Intrapersonal communication
   (c) Interpersonal communication
   (d) Face-to-face communication
4. The largest circulated daily newspaper among the following is
   (a) *The Times of India*
   (b) *The Indian Express*
   (c) *The Hindu*
   (d) *The Deccan Herald*
5. The pioneer of the silent feature film in India was
   (a) K.A. Abbas (b) Satyajit Ray
   (c) B.R. Chopra (d) Dada Sahib Phalke
6. Classroom communication of a teacher rests on the principle of
   (a) Infotainment (b) Edutainment
   (c) Entertainment (d) Power equation
7. The missing number in the series:
   0, 6, 24, 60, 120, ?, 336, is
   (a) 240 (b) 220 (c) 280 (d) 210
8. A group of 7 members having a majority of boys is to be formed out of 6 boys and 4 girls. The number of ways the group can be formed is
   (a) 80 (b) 100 (c) 90 (d) 110
9. The number of observations in a group is 40. The average of the first 10 members is 4.5 and the average of the remaining 30 members is 3.5. The average of the whole group is
   (a) 4 (b) 15/2 (c) 15/4 (d) 6
10. If MOHAN is represented by the code KMFYL, then COUNT will be represented by
    (a) AMSLR (b) MSLAR
    (c) MASRL (d) SAMLR
11. The sum of the ages of two persons A and B is 50. 5 years ago, the ratio of their ages was 5/3. The present age of A and B are
    (a) 30, 20 (b) 35, 15
    (c) 38, 12 (d) 40, 10
12. Let *a* means minus (–), *b* means multiplied by (×), C means divided by (÷) and D means plus (+). The value of 90 D 9 *a* 29 C 10 *b* 2 is
    (a) 8 (b) 10 (c) 12 (d) 14
13. Consider the Assertion I and Assertion II and select the right code given below:

    Assertion I: Even bank lockers are not safe. Thieves can break them and take away your wealth. But thieves cannot go to heaven. So you should keep your wealth in heaven.

    Assertion II: The difference of skin-colour of beings is because of the distance from the sun and not because of some permanent traits. Skin-colour is the result of body's reaction to the sun and its rays.

Codes:
(a) Both the assertions I and II are forms of argument.
(b) The assertion I is an argument but the assertion II is not.
(c) The assertion II is an argument but the assertion I is not.
(d) Both the assertions are explanations of facts.

14. By which of the following proposition, the proposition 'some men are not honest' is contradicted?
(a) All men are honest.
(b) Some men are honest.
(c) No men are honest.
(d) All of the above.

15. A stipulative definition is
(a) always true
(b) always false
(c) sometimes true sometimes false
(d) neither true nor false

16. Choose the appropriate alternative given in the codes to replace the question mark.
Examiner – Examinee, Pleader – Client, Preceptor – ?
(a) Customer (b) Path-finder
(c) Perceiver (d) Disciple

17. If the statement 'most of the students are obedient' is taken to be true, which one of the following pair of statements can be claimed to be true?
I. All obedient persons are students.
II. All students are obedient.
III. Some students are obedient.
IV. Some students are not disobedient.
Codes:
(a) I & II (b) II & III
(c) III & IV (d) II & IV

18. Choose the right code:
A deductive argument claims that:
I. The conclusion does not claim something more than that which is contained in the premises.
II. The conclusion is supported by the premise/premises conclusively.
III. If the conclusion is false, then premise/premises may be either true or false.
IV. If premise/combination of premises is true, then conclusion must be true.
Codes:
(a) I and II (b) I and III
(c) II and III (d) All the above

On the basis of the data given in the following table, give answers to questions from 19 to 24:

Government Expenditures on Social Services
(As per cent of total expenditure)

Sl.No.	Items	2007-08	2008-09	2009-10	2010-11
	Social Services	11.06	12.94	13.06	14.02
(a)	Education, sports & youth affairs	4.02	4.04	3.96	4.46
(b)	Health & family welfare	2.05	1.91	1.90	2.03
(c)	Water supply, housing, etc.	2.02	2.31	2.20	2.27
(d)	Information & broadcasting	0.22	0.22	0.20	0.22
(e)	Welfare to SC/ST & OBC	0.36	0.35	0.41	0.63
(f)	Labour and employment	0.27	0.27	0.22	0.25
(g)	Social welfare & nutrition	0.82	0.72	0.79	1.06
(h)	North-eastern areas	0.00	1.56	1.50	1.75
(i)	Other social services	1.29	1.55	1.87	1.34
	Total Government expenditure	100.00	100.00	100.00	100.00

19. How many activities in the social services are there where the expenditure has been less than 5 percent of the total expenditures incurred on the social services in 2008-09?
(a) One (b) Three
(c) Five (d) All the above

20. In which year, the expenditures on the social services have increased at the highest rate?

(a) 2007-08 (b) 2008-09
(c) 2009-10 (d) 2010-11

21. Which of the following activities remains almost stagnant in terms of share of expenditures?
(a) North-eastern areas
(b) Welfare to SC/ST & OBC
(c) Information & broadcasting
(d) Social welfare and nutrition

22. Which of the following item's expenditure share is almost equal to the remaining three items in the given years?
(a) Information & broadcasting
(b) Welfare to SC/ST and OBC
(c) Labour and employment
(d) Social welfare & nutrition

23. Which of the following items of social services has registered the highest rate of increase in expenditures during 2007-08 to 2010-11?
(a) Education, sports & youth affairs
(b) Welfare to SC/ST & OBC
(c) Social welfare & nutrition
(d) Overall social services

24. Which of the following items has registered the highest rate of decline in terms of expenditure during 2007-08 to 2009-10?
(a) Labour and employment
(b) Health & family welfare
(c) Social welfare & nutrition
(d) Education, sports & youth affairs

25. ALU stands for
(a) American Logic Unit
(b) Alternate Local Unit
(c) Alternating Logic Unit
(d) Arithmetic Logic Unit

26. A Personal Computer uses a number of chips mounted on a circuit board called
(a) Microprocessor (b) System Board
(c) Daughter Board (d) Mother Board

27. Computer Virus is a
(a) Hardware (b) Bacteria
(c) Software (d) None of these

28. Which one of the following is correct?
(a) $(17)_{10} = (17)_{16}$ (b) $(17)_{10} = (17)_8$
(c) $(17)_{10} = (10111)_2$ (d) $(17)_{10} = (10001)_2$

29. The file extension of MS-Word document in Office 2007 is ______.
(a) .pdf (b) .doc (c) .docx (d) .txt

30. ______ is a protocol used by e-mail clients to download e-mails to your computer.
(a) TCP (b) FTP (c) SMTP (d) POP

31. Which of the following is a source of methane?
(a) Wetlands
(b) Foam Industry
(c) Thermal Power Plants
(d) Cement Industry

32. 'Minamata disaster' in Japan was caused by pollution due to
(a) Lead (b) Mercury
(c) Cadmium (d) Zinc

33. Biomagnification means increase in the
(a) concentration of pollutants in living organisms
(b) number of species
(c) size of living organisms
(d) biomass

34. Nagoya Protocol is related to
(a) Climate change (b) Ozone depletion
(c) Hazardous waste (d) Biodiversity

35. The second most important source after fossil fuels contributing to India's energy needs is
(a) Solar energy (b) Nuclear energy
(c) Hydropower (d) Wind energy

36. In case of earthquakes, an increase of magnitude 1 on Richter Scale implies
(a) a ten-fold increase in the amplitude of seismic waves.
(b) a ten-fold increase in the energy of the seismic waves.
(c) two-fold increase in the amplitude of seismic waves.
(d) two-fold increase in the energy of seismic waves.

37. Which of the following is not a measure of Human Development Index?
(a) Literacy Rate (b) Gross Enrolment
(c) Sex Ratio (d) Life Expectancy

38. India has the highest number of students in colleges after

(a) the U.K. (b) the U.S.A.
(c) Australia (d) Canada

39. Which of the following statement(s) is/are not correct about the Attorney General of India?
   1. The President appoints a person, who is qualified to be a Judge of a High Court, to be the Attorney General of India.
   2. He has the right of audience in all the Courts of the country.
   3. He has the right to take part in the proceedings of the Lok Sabha and the Rajya Sabha.
   4. He has a fixed tenure.
   Select the correct answer from the codes given below:

Codes:
(a) 1 and 4 (b) 2, 3 and 4
(c) 3 and 4 (d) 3 only

40. Which of the following prefix President Pranab Mukherjee desires to be discontinued while interacting with Indian dignitaries as well as in official notings?
   1. His Excellency 2. Mahamahim
   3. Hon'ble 4. Shri/Smt.

Select the correct answer from the codes given below:

Codes:
(a) 1 and 3 (b) 2 and 3
(c) 1 and 2 (d) 1, 2 and 3

41. Which of the following can be done under conditions of financial emergency?
   1. State Legislative Assemblies can be abolished.
   2. Central Government can acquire control over the budget and expenditure of States.
   3. Salaries of the Judges of the High Courts and the Supreme Court can be reduced.
   4. Right to Constitutional Remedies can be suspended.

Select the correct answer from the codes given below:

Codes:
(a) 1, 2 and 3 (b) 2, 3 and 4
(c) 1 and 2 (d) 2 and 3

42. Match List I with List II and select the correct answer from the codes given below:

List I
(A) Poverty Reduction Programme
(B) Human Development Scheme
(C) Social Assistance Scheme
(D) Minimum Need Scheme

List II
(i) Mid-day Meals
(ii) Indira Awas Yojana (IAY)
(iii) National Old Age Pension (NOAP)
(iv) MNREGA

Codes:	**A**	**B**	**C**	**D**
(a)	(iv)	(i)	(iii)	(ii)
(b)	(ii)	(iii)	(iv)	(i)
(c)	(iii)	(iv)	(i)	(ii)
(d)	(iv)	(iii)	(ii)	(i)

43. For an efficient and durable learning, learner should have
   (a) ability to learn only
   (b) requisite level of motivation only
   (c) opportunities to learn only
   (d) desired level of ability and motivation

44. Classroom communication must be
   (a) Teacher centric
   (b) Student centric
   (c) General centric
   (d) Textbook centric

45. The best method of teaching is to
   (a) impart information
   (b) ask students to read books
   (c) suggest good reference material
   (d) initiate a discussion and participate in it

46. Interaction inside the classroom should generate
   (a) Argument (b) Information
   (c) Ideas (d) Controversy

47. "Spare the rod and spoil the child", gives the message that
   (a) punishment in the class should be banned.
   (b) corporal punishment is not acceptable.
   (c) undesirable behaviour must be punished.
   (d) children should be beaten with rods.

48. The type of communication that the teacher has in the classroom, is termed as
   (a) Interpersonal
   (b) Mass communication
   (c) Group communication
   (d) Face-to-face communication

49. Which one of the following is an indication of the quality of a research journal?
 (a) Impact factor (b) h-index
 (c) g-index (d) i10-index

50. Good 'research ethics' means:
 (a) Not disclosing the holdings of shares/stocks in a company that sponsors your research.
 (b) Assigning a particular research problem to one Ph.D./research student only.
 (c) Discussing with your colleagues confidential data from a research paper that you are reviewing for an academic journal.
 (d) Submitting the same research manuscript for publishing in more than one journal.

51. Which of the following sampling methods is based on probability?
 (a) Convenience sampling
 (b) Quota sampling
 (c) Judgement sampling
 (d) Stratified sampling

52. Which one of the following references is written according to American Psychological Association (APA) format?
 (a) Sharma, V. (2010). Fundamentals of Computer Science.
 New Delhi: Tata McGraw Hill
 (b) Sharma, V. 2010. Fundamentals of Computer Science.
 New Delhi: Tata McGraw Hill
 (c) Sharma.V. 2010. Fundamentals of Computer Science,
 New Delhi: Tata McGraw Hill
 (d) Sharma, V. (2010), Fundamentals of Computer Science,
 New Delhi: Tata McGraw Hill

53. Arrange the following steps of research in correct sequence:
 1. Identification of research problem
 2. Listing of research objectives
 3. Collection of data
 4. Methodology
 5. Data analysis
 6. Results and discussion
 (a) 1, 2, 3, 4, 5, 6 (b) 1, 2, 4, 3, 5, 6
 (c) 2, 1, 3, 4, 5, 6 (d) 2, 1, 4, 3, 5, 6

54. Identify the incorrect statement:
 (a) A hypothesis is made on the basis of limited evidence as a starting point for further investigations.
 (b) A hypothesis is a basis for reasoning without any assumption of its truth.
 (c) Hypothesis is a proposed explanation for a phenomenon.
 (d) Scientific hypothesis is a scientific theory.

Read the following passage carefully and answer the questions (55 to 60):

The popular view of towns and cities in developing countries and of urbanization process is that despite the benefits and comforts it brings, the emergence of such cities connotes environmental degradation, generation of slums and squatters, urban poverty, unemployment, crimes, lawlessness, traffic chaos, etc. But what is the reality? Given the unprecedental increase in urban population over the last 50 years from 300 million in 1950 to 2 billion in 2000 in developing countries, the wonder really is how well the world has coped, and not how badly.

In general, the urban quality of life has improved in terms of availability of water and sanitation, power, health and education, communication and transport. By way of illustration, a large number of urban residents have been provided with improved water in urban areas in Asia's largest countries such as China, India, Indonesia and Philippines. Despite that, the access to improved water in terms of percentage of total urban population seems to have declined during the last decade of 20th century, though in absolute numbers, millions of additional urbanites, have been provided improved services. These countries have made significant progress in the provision of sanitation services too, together, providing for an additional population of more than 293 million citizens within a decade (1990-2000). These improvements must be viewed against the backdrop of rapidly increasing urban population, fiscal crunch and strained human resources and efficient and quality-oriented public management.

55. The popular view about the process of urbanization in developing countries is
 (a) Positive (b) Negative
 (c) Neutral (d) Unspecified

56. The average annual increase in the number of urbanites in developing countries, from 1950 to 2000 A.D. was close to
(a) 30 million (b) 40 million
(c) 50 million (d) 60 million

57. The reality of urbanization is reflected in:
(a) How well the situation has been managed.
(b) How badly the situation has gone out of control.
(c) How fast has been the tempo of urbanization.
(d) How fast the environment has degraded.

58. Which one of the following is not considered as an indicator of urban quality of life?
(a) Tempo of urbanization
(b) Provision of basic services
(c) Access to social amenities
(d) All of the above

59. The author in this passage has tried to focus on
(a) Extension of Knowledge
(b) Generation of Environmental Consciousness
(c) Analytical Reasoning
(d) Descriptive Statement

60. In the above passage, the author intends to state
(a) The hazards of the urban life
(b) The sufferings of the urban life
(c) The awareness of human progress
(d) The limits to growth

ANSWERS

1. (a)	2. (d)	3. (a)	4. (a)	5. (d)
6. (b)	7. (d)	8. (b)	9. (c)	10. (a)
11. (a)	12. (d)	13. (a)	14. (a)	15. (d)
16. (c)	17. (c)	18. (d)	19. (d)	20. (d)
21. (c)	22. (d)	23. (d)	24. (b)	25. (d)
26. (d)	27. (c)	28. (d)	29. (b)	30. (d)
31. (a)	32. (b)	33. (a)	34. (d)	35. (c)
36. (a)	37. (c)	38. (b)	39. (d)	40. (c)
41. (c)	42. (a)	43. (d)	44. (b)	45. (d)
46. (c)	47. (c)	48. (c)	49. (a)	50. (a)
51. (d)	52. (a)	53. (b)	54. (d)	55. (b)
56. (a)	57. (a)	58. (a)	59. (d)	60. (d)

PAPER–II

Note: This paper contains fifty (50) objective type questions, each question carrying two (2) marks. All questions are compulsory.

1. GDP at factor cost is
(a) P(Q) + P (S) (b) GDP – TT – S
(c) GDP + DT + S (d) GDP – DT + S

2. Which one is not the main objective of fiscal policy in India?
(a) To increase liquidity in the economy.
(b) To promote price stability.
(c) To minimize the inequalities of income and wealth.
(d) To promote employment opportunities.

3. Which one is not an element of internal environment?
(a) Marketing capability
(b) Operational capability
(c) Money and Capital market
(d) Personnel capability

4. Out of the following, which four benefits are available to host countries from MNCs?
i. Transfer of technology
ii. Learning of business mannerism
iii. Strategic information sharing
iv. Creation of jobs
v. Entertainment
vi. Better utilisation of resources
vii. Enhancing social contacts
viii. Improved competition in local economy
(a) i, iii, v, vii (b) ii, iv, vi, viii
(c) i, iv, vi, viii (d) iii, vi, vii, viii

5. Environmental degradation does not consist of
(a) Land degradation and soil erosion
(b) Problem of overgrazing and ecological degradation
(c) Floods
(d) None of the above

6. Which one of the following concepts is used as fund in the preparation of Funds Flow Statement?
(a) Current Assets
(b) Working Capital
(c) Cash
(d) All Financial Resources

7. Window dressing is prohibited due to
   (a) Conservative Convention
   (b) Convention of Disclosure
   (c) Conventioo of Materiality
   (d) Arrear of book accounts
8. **Assertion (A):** Ratio analysis is one of the tools employed to know the financial the health of a concerm.

   Reason (R): Ratio analysis is not the only technique available to take investment decision.

   Codes:
   (a) Both (A) and (R) are true and (R) is the correct explanation of (A).
   (b) Both (A) and (R) are true, but (R) is incorrect explanation of (A).
   (c) (A) is true, but (R) is false.
   (d) (A) is false, but (R) is true.
9. Which of the following relate to measures of non-financial performance of a concern?
   i. Customer satisfaction
   ii. Business process improvement
   iii. Economic value added
   iv. Learning organisation

   Choose the right combination.
   (a) i, iii, ii, iv (b) ii, iv, iii
   (c) iv, i, iii (d) i, ii, iv
10. Consider the following parties:
    i. Secured creditors
    ii. Unsecured creditors
    iii. Partners who have granted loans
    iv. Partners who have contributed over and above profit sharing ratio.

    Arrange them in correct sequence in the event of dissolution of a firm.
    (a) ii, i, iii, iv (b) i, ii, iii, iv
    (c) i, ii, iv, iii (d) ii, i, iv, iii
11. Which kind of economics explains the phenomenon of cause and effect relationship?
    (a) Normative (b) Positive
    (c) Micro (d) Macro
12. **Assertion (A):** Marginal cost and differential cost do not convey the same meaning in all the circumstances.

    Reason (R): Differential cost increases or decreases due to change in fixed cost.

    Codes:
    (a) (A) is true but (R) is false.
    (b) (A) is false but (R) is true.
    (c) (A) and (R) are correct and (R) is correct explanation of (A).
    (d) Both (A) and (R) are correct, but (R) is not the correct explanation of (A).
13. Consider the following:
    i. Pricing objectives ii. Pricing methods
    iii. Pricing strategies iv. Pricing decisions

    Arrange them in correct sequence:
    (a) i, iii, ii, iv (b) i, iv, iii, ii
    (c) ii, i, iv, iii (d) iv, ii, iii, i
14. A commodity is used for multiple purposes. then the demand for it is known as
    (a) Joint Demand
    (b) Composite Demand
    (c) Direct Demand
    (d) Autonomous Demand
15. Match List-I with List-II and select the correct answer.

List-I	List-II
1. Administered	A. Landed cost price of imports
2. Parity pricing	B. Liberalized economy
3. Competitive price	C. Public enterprise
4. Discriminating price	D. FIXed by Government

Codes:	A	B	C	D
(a)	1	2	3	4
(b)	2	3	4	1
(c)	3	4	2	1
(d)	4	2	1	3

16. Sample design involves the following:
    i. Sampling unit ii. Size of samples
    iii. Type of universe iv. Source list
    v. Sampling procedure

    Which one of the following sequence is correct?
    (a) i, ii, iii, iv, v (b) iii, iv, i, ii, v
    (c) iii, i, iv, ii, v (d) iii, v, i, iv, ii
17. Uruguay Round pertains to
    (a) GATT (b) WTO
    (c) IMF (d) World Bank
18. If bxy = 0.25 and byx = 0.64, correlation coefficient is

(a) 0.16 (b) 0.40 (c) 0.89 (d) 0.30

19. Sturge's rule is used to find out directly
(a) Number of classes in a continuous distribution
(b) Size of class limits
(c) Direction of the classification
(d) None of the above

20. Which of the following software has applications in both Mathematics and Statistics?
(a) SPSS (b) SAS
(c) R (d) None of the above

21. March the following:

A. The Practice of Management	1. Henry Fayol
B. Philosophy of Management	2. F.W. Taylor
C. Scientific Management	3. Oliver
D. General and Industrial Administration	4. Peter F. Drucker

Codes:	A	B	C	D
(a)	1	2	3	4
(b)	4	3	2	1
(c)	4	3	1	2
(d)	3	4	2	1

22. **Assertion (A):** All decisions taken through mental process are rational.
Reason (R): Decision making is a mental process.
Codes:
(a) (R) is correct, but (A) is not correct.
(b) (A) is correct, but (R) is not correct.
(c) Both (A) and (R) are correct.
(d) Both (A) and (R) are not correct.

23. Who among the following developed the technique of Management by Exception?
(a) Joseph L. Massie (b) Lester R. Bittel
(c) L.F. Urwick (d) Peter F Drucker

24. Which among the following are parts of job description?
i. Duties performed
ii. Job summary
iii. Job identification
iv. Supervision given
v. Delegation of authority
(a) i, ii, iii and iv (b) ii, iii, iv and v
(c) i, iii, iv and v (d) i, ii, iii and v

25. Appoimment of independent Directors is the part of Corporate Governance as per the
(a) SEBI
(b) Indian Companies Act
(c) Government of India
(d) RBI

26. A method for achieving maximum market response from limited marketing resources by reorganising differences in the response characteristics of various parts of the market is known as
(a) Market targeting
(b) Market positioning
(c) Market segmentation
(d) Market strategy

27. Who plays their significant role in distribution of goods when they do not sell to ultimate users or consumers?
(a) Retailer (b) Wholeseller
(c) Mediator (d) Commission agent

28. In Marketing Mix, which four Ps are covered?
(a) Product, Price, Place, Promotion
(b) Product, Price, Power, Promotion
(c) Pxoouot, Price, Penetration, Promotion
(d) Product, Price, Positioning, Promotion

29. Which research includes all types of researches into human motives when it refers 10 qualitative research designed to uncover the consumer's subconsciousness or bidden motivatio?
(a) Motivational Research
(b) Marketing Research
(c) Managerial Research
(d) Price Research

30. False and misleading claims and vulgarity in advertisements do not match with
(a) Aggressive advertising
(b) Ethics in advertising
(c) Mass level of advertising
(d) Sales promotion

31. Arrange the following steps involved in capital budgeting in order of their occunence:
i. Project selection
ii. Project appraisal
iii. Project generation

iv. Follow up
v. Project execution
(a) ii, iii, i, v, iv
(b) iii, ii, i, v, iv
(c) i, iii, ii, v, iv
(d) i, ii, iii, v, iv

32. Which method does not consider the time value of money?
(a) Net Present Value
(b) Internal Rate of Return
(c) Average Rate of Return
(d) Profitability Index

33. Which formula is used to measure the degree of Operating leverage?
(a) EBIT / Sales (b) C / EBIT
(c) EBIT / EBT (d) EBIT / C

34. Which one is more appropriate for cost of retained earnings?
(a) Weighted Average Cost of Capital.
(b) Opportunity cost to the firm.
(c) Expected rate of return by the investor.
(d) None of the above.

35. Match the following with the most suitable option.

List-I	List-II
A. Modigliani-Miller approach	1. Commercial paper
B. Net Operating income approach	2. Working capital
C. Short term money market instrument	3. Capital
	4. Structure
D. Factoring	5. Arbitrage

Codes:	A	B	C	D
(a)	4	3	1	2
(b)	3	4	1	2
(c)	3	2	1	4
(d)	4	2	3	1

36. During which plan was the National Apprenticeship Training Scheme introduced?
(a) 1st Five Year Plan
(b) 2nd Five Year Plan
(c) 4th Five Year Plan
(d) Annual Plans

37. Match the following:

List-I	List-II
A. An ordinary person does not want to work on his own.	1. Hierarchy Theory
B. An individual is willing to work on his own	2. Hygiene Theory
C. Motivational Factors	3. X-Theory
D. Esteem Needs	4. Y-Theory

Codes:	A	B	C	D
(a)	1	2	3	4
(b)	3	4	1	2
(c)	1	4	2	3
(d)	3	4	2	1

38. Arrange the following staffing procedures in the correct sequence:
i. Determining sources of personnel supply
ii. Preparing personnel specifications.
iii. Selection of personnel.
iv. Determining personnel.
v. Determining personnel characteristics.
(a) ii, i, iv, iii (b) i, ii, iii, iv
(c) ii, iii, iv (d) ii, iii, i, iv

39. Which among the following is not a voluntary method for prevention and settlement of disputes?
(a) Collective Bargaining
(b) Standing Orders
(c) Joint Consultation
(d) Works Committee

40. **Statement-I:** It is no better to pay employees for little than to pay too much.

Statement-II: Competent employees will remain competent forever.
(a) Statement I is true. but II is false.
(b) Statement II is true, but I is false.
(c) Both Statements I and II are true.
(d) Both Statements I and II are false.

41. Match the following:

A. Credit Control	1. MCA
B. Corporate Control	2. SEBI
C. IPO Control	3. IRDA
D. ULIP Control	4. RBI

Codes:	A	B	C	D
(a)	4	2	3	1
(b)	4	1	2	3
(c)	2	3	4	1
(d)	4	1	3	2

42. Which one among the following has not started Commercial Banking?

(a) SIDBI (b) IDBl
(c) ICICI (d) UTI

43. What is OTP in credit card transactions?
(a) Odd Transaction Password
(b) Owner's Trading Passcode
(c) One Time Password
(d) One Time Pincode

44. The powers of Controller of Capital Issues of India is now shifted to
(a) Ministry of Finance
(b) SEB
(c) AMFl
(d) Ministry of Corporate Affairs

45. The success of E-banking depends upon:
i. Multi-layer Security System
ii. Risk and Surveillance Management
iii. Updated Flawless Softwares
iv. Stringent Legal Frame-work
(a) i and ii (b) i, ii and iii
(c) ii, iii and iv (d) i, ii, iii and iv

46. International liquidity comprises which four of the following?
i. Gold held by Central Banks.
ii. Gold held by families.
iii. Forex Reserve held by Commercial Banks.
iv. Mineral wealth.
v. SDRs.
vi. Borrowing facilities.
vii. NRIs FDRs.
viii. Credit facilities available under SWAP.
(a) i, ii, iii, iv (b) ii, iii, iv, viii
(c) i, iii, v, viii (d) iiii, iv, vii, viii

47. Which among the following are important bodies of WTO?
i. Dispute Settlement Body
ii. NAFTA
iii. Trade Policy Review Body
iv. ASEAN
v. Council for Trade in Goods
vi. IBRD
vii. Council for Trade related aspects of Intellectual Property Rights
viii. GATT
An appropriate combination is
(a) i, ii, iii, iv (b) ii, iii, iv, v
(c) i, iii, v, vii (d) iv, v, vi, viii

48. Which one is not the source of External Finance?
(a) WTO Funds
(b) World Bank Group
(c) Expon Credit
(d) Foreign Direct Investment

49. Which one is called Bretton-Wood Twins?
(a) IBRD and IDA (b) IMF and IFC
(c) IMF and IBRD (d) IDA and IFC

50. UNCTAD stands for
(a) United Nations Committee on Tariff and Development.
(b) United Nations Conference on Trade and Deficit.
(c) United Nations Conference on Trade and Development.
(d) Union of Nations Cause for Trade and Development.

ANSWERS

1. (b)	2. (a)	3. (c)	4. (c)	5. (d)
6. (d)	7. (b)	8. (a)	9. (d)	10. (b)
11. (b)	12. (c)	13. (b)	14. (b)	15. (b)
16. (c)	17. (a)	18. (b)	19. (a)	20. (d)
21. (b)	22. (a)	23. (b)	24. (a)	25. (a)
26. (c)	27. (b)	28. (a)	29. (a)	30. (b)
31. (b)	32. (c)	33. (b)	34. (b)	35. (a)
36. (b)	37. (d)	38. (a)	39. (d)	40. (a)
41. (d)	42. (a)	43. (c)	44. (b)	45. (b)
46. (c)	47. (c)	48. (a)	49. (c)	50. (c)

PAPER–III

Note: This paper contains fifty (50) objective type questions, each question carrying two (2) marks. All questions are compulsory.

1. In accounting, profit prior to incorporation is treated as
(a) Revenue Reserve (b) Secret Reserve
(c) Capital Reserve (d) General Reserve

2. Receipts and Payments Account is prepared by
(a) Manufacturing concerns
(b) Non-Trading concerns
(c) Trading concerns
(d) Companies registered under Companies Act, 1956

3. Owner's equity stands for
   (a) Fixed Assets minus Fixed Liabilities.
   (b) Fixed Assets minus Current Liabilities.
   (c) Current Assets minus Fixed Liabilities.
   (d) Total Assets minus Total outside Liabilities.
4. When the Debt Turnover Ratio is 4, what is the average collection period?
   (a) 5 months (b) 4 months
   (c) 3 months (d) 2 months
5. Which of the following will result into sources of funds?
   (i) Increase in current assets
   (ii) Decrease in current assets
   (iii) Increase in current liabilities
   (iv) Decrease in current liabilities

   Codes:
   (a) (i) and (iv) (b) (ii) and (iii)
   (c) (i) and (iii) (d) (ii) and (iv)
6. In marginal costing, contribution is equal to
   (a) Sales – Fixed cost
   (b) Sales – Variable cost
   (c) Sales – Profit
   (d) Sales – Variable Cost + Fixed cost
7. The funds available with a company after paying all claims including tax and dividend is called
   (a) Net Profit
   (b) Net Operating Profit
   (c) Capital Profit
   (d) Retained Earnings
8. **Assertion (A):** Accounting information refers to only events which are concerned with business firm.

   Reason (R): Accounting information is presented in financial statements.

   Codes:
   (a) (A) is correct, but (R) is wrong.
   (b) Both (A) and (R) are correct.
   (c) (A) is wrong, but (R) is correct.
   (d) Both (A) and (R) are wrong.
9. When average cost is declining
   (a) Marginal cost must be declining.
   (b) Marginal cost must be above average cost.
   (c) Marginal cost must be below average cost.
   (d) Marginal cost must be rising.
10. ABC Ltd. has declared 40% dividend. Which one of the following does it mean?
    (a) The company has declared 40% of net profit as dividend.
    (b) The company has declared 40% of profits after tax as dividend.
    (c) The company will provide dividend 40% on issued capital.
    (d) The company will provide dividend 40% on paid-up capital.
11. The main objective of Accounting Standards is
    (a) To prepare the accounting reports which is easily understood by common man.
    (b) To comply with the legal formalities.
    (c) To harmonise the diversified accounting practices.
    (d) To comply with the requirements of the International Accounting Standards (IAS).
12. Given below are two statements:
    I. Activity ratios show where the company is going.
    II. Balance Sheet ratios show how the company stand.

    Codes:
    (a) I is correct, but II is wrong.
    (b) Both I and II are correct.
    (c) I is wrong, but II is correct.
    (d) Both I and II are wrong.
13. Income and Expenditure Account of non-profit organisation is a
    (a) Real Account
    (b) Nominal Account
    (c) Personal Account
    (d) Representative Personal Account
14. Which of the following statements are correct?
    I. Inventory includes raw materials, finished goods and work-in-progress.
    II. Inventory is a part of the working capital.
    III. Inventory includes goods likely to be purchased.

    Codes:
    (a) I, II and III (b) II and III
    (c) I and III (d) I and II
15. If the current ratio is 2 : 1 and working capital is ₹ 60,000, what is the value of the Current Assets?

(a) ₹ 60,000 (b) ₹ 1,00,000
(c) ₹ 1,20,000 (d) ₹ 1,80,000

16. Which of the following steps of purchase decision process is in sequence?
 1. Problem recognition
 2. Search for alternatives
 3. Evaluation of alternatives
 4. Purchase action
 5. Post purchase action

 Codes:
 (a) 1, 3, 2, 4, 5 (b) 1, 2, 4, 3, 5
 (c) 2, 1, 3, 5, 4 (d) 1, 2, 3, 4, 5

17. What is customer value?
 (a) Ratio between the customer's perceived benefits and the resources used to obtain these benefits.
 (b) Excess of satisfaction over expectation.
 (c) Post purchase dissonance.
 (d) None of the above.

18. Match the items of List-I with items of List-II.

List-I	List-II
A. The silent mental repetition of information.	1. Encoding
B. The process by which we select a word or visual image to represent a perceived object.	2. Rehearsal
C. Where information is kept temporarily before further processing.	3. Working Memory
D. The stage of real memory in which information is processed and held for just a brief period.	4. Store house

Codes:	A	B	C	D
(a)	2	1	4	3
(b)	1	2	3	4
(c)	3	2	1	4
(d)	4	3	2	1

19. Fill in the blanks:

Statements	Alternatives
A. Loyal customers ____ products.	1. Less attention
B. Loyal customers are _____ sensitive.	2. Cheaper
C. Loyal customers pay _____ to competitor's advertising.	3. Less price
D. Serving existing customer is _____.	4. Buy more

Codes:	A	B	C	D
(a)	3	1	2	4
(b)	4	3	1	2
(c)	2	1	3	4
(d)	4	3	2	1

20. **Assertion (A):** High customer expectations lead to dissatisfaction as product performance never matches them.
 Reason (R): Product performance is always customer specific.

 Codes:
 (a) Both (A) and (R) are correct.
 (b) Both (A) and (R) are incorrect.
 (c) (A) is correct, but (R) is incorrect.
 (d) (R) is correct, but (A) is incorrect.

21. Under which concept of marketing do you find greater emphasis on techniques and technology of production?
 (a) Product (b) Selling
 (c) Marketing (d) None

22. Which is used for short-term sales achievement?
 (a) Personal selling (b) Advertising
 (c) Sales Promotion (d) Public Relations

23. Public distribution system relates to
 (a) Marketing system (b) Retailing system
 (c) Industrial system (d) Selling system

24. Who do buy more, complain less, spread positive word of mouth, ensure a large customer base and repeat business?
 (a) Satisfied customers
 (b) Delighted customers
 (c) Industrial customers
 (d) None of the above

25. There are impulses which persuade a customer to buy certain products without evaluating the positive and negative value of the same.
 (a) Emotional motives
 (b) Blind motives

(c) Egoistic motives
(d) All the above

26. Which subject is relevant to the study of consumer behaviour?
(a) Economics (b) Psychology
(c) Sociology (d) All the above

27. Find an incorrect statement.
(a) Consumer attitude can be summarized as evaluation of an object.
(b) Attitudes are learned.
(c) Attitudes are synonymous with behaviour.
(d) Attitudes have motivational qualities.

28. Who is considered Father of Scientific Management?
(a) Peter Drucker (b) F.W. Taylor
(c) Victor Vroom (d) Henry Fayol

29. Who did give the concept of hierarchy of needs?
(a) Fredrick Herzberg (b) Victor Vroom
(c) Douglas McGregor (d) A.H. Maslow

30. **Assertion (A):** Management is a continuous process.
Reason (R): Managers first plan, then organise and finally perform the function of controlling.
Codes:
(a) Both (A) and (R) are correct and (R) is correct explanation of (A).
(b) Both (A) and (R) are correct, but (R) is not a correct explanation of (A).
(c) (A) is correct, but (R) is incorrect.
(d) (A) is incorrect, but (R) is correct.

31. Induction of employees relates to
(a) Organisational awareness
(b) Training programme
(c) Introduction
(d) Assignment of duties

32. 'Kinked' of demand curve is related with
(a) Monopoly
(b) Discriminating monopoly
(c) Oligopoly
(d) Perfect competition

33. Who is not associated with HRM?
(a) Michael J. Jucius (b) Dale Yodar
(c) Edvoin B. Flippo (d) K.K. Devit

34. Merit rating is not known as
(a) Efficiency Rating
(b) Service Rating
(c) Job Rating
(d) Experience Rating

35. Match the items of List-I with the items of List-II.

List-I	List-II
A. FEMA	1. 1986
B. Indian Factories Act	2. 1999
C. Industrial Dispute Act	3. 1948
D. Consumer Protection Act	4. 1947

Codes:	A	B	C	D
(A)	4	2	3	1
(B)	3	1	2	4
(C)	2	3	4	1
(D)	1	4	3	2

36. If price of any commodity decreases by 20% and the demand for that commodity increases by 40%, then elasticity of demand would be
(a) perfectly elastic (b) perfectly inelastic
(c) unit elastic (d) highly elastic

37. Which of the following statements is true?
(a) In case of inferior goods, the income effect is negative, although the substitution effect is positive.
(b) In inferior goods, the income and substitution effects are positive.
(c) In inferior goods, the income and substitution effects are negative.
(d) In case of inferior goods, the income effect is positive although the substitution effect is negative.

38. In perfect competition, the demand curve of a firm is
(a) Vertical (b) Horizontal
(c) Positively sloped (d) Negatively sloped

39. Which one is not non-financial incentive?
(a) Additional bonus on minimum wasteful expenditure.
(b) Permanent job.
(c) Participatory decision making.
(d) Recognition of individuality.

40. HRM does not include
(a) job evaluation
(b) performance appraisal
(c) sales promotion
(d) job enrichment

41. The term (1-B) is called
(a) Level of the test (b) Power of the test
(c) Size of the test (d) None of the above

42. The area under normal distribution covered within $\mu \pm 3\sigma$ limits is
(a) 0.6827 (b) 0.9545 (c) 0.9973 (d) 1.0000

43. Sampling distribution of mean is very close to the standard normal distribution when
(a) Population is normally distributed.
(b) Population is not normally distributed, but sample size is large.
(c) Both (a) and (b).
(d) Neither (a) nor (b).

44. If the value of co-efficient of determination is 0.64, what is the value of coefficient of correlation?
(a) 0.40 (b) 0.80 (c) 0.08 (d) 0.04

45. Which one of the following is not a source of conflict in project ranking in capital budgeting decision as per NPV and IRR?
(a) Independent Investment Project
(b) No Capital Budget Constraints
(c) No time disparity
(d) None of the above

46. Match the following:

List-I	List-II
A. Trade policy	1. Economic conditions
B. Trade flows	2. Economic policies
C. Price trends	3. Global linkages
D. Internal sectoral linkages	4. Structure and Nature of Economy

Codes:	A	B	C	D
(a)	3	1	2	4
(b)	2	3	1	4
(c)	1	2	3	4
(d)	1	2	4	3

47. Which one of the following is not a benefit of privatisation?
(a) Encourage entrepreneurship.
(b) Concentration of economic power.
(c) Better management of enterprise.
(d) Freedom from bureaucracy.

48. 'BOLT' system in the Indian Securities market is related to
(a) National Stock Exchange
(b) Bombay Stock Exchange
(c) Over the Counter Exchange of India
(d) Multi Commodity Stock Exchange

49. Which one of the following is not a money market instrument?
(a) Commercial paper
(b) Participatory certificates
(c) Warrants
(d) Treasury bills

50. Which one is related with microfinancing?
(a) SHG
(b) Anganwadi workers
(c) Women Entrepreneurs
(d) None of the above

51. Which one of the following is not an element of internal environment?
(a) Mission/Objectives
(b) Human Resources
(c) Customers
(d) Shareholders' values

52. The presence of fixed costs in the total cost structure of a firm results into
(a) Financial leverage
(b) Operating leverage
(c) Super leverage
(d) None of the above

53. "The cost of capital declines when the degree of financial leverage increases." Who advocated it?
(a) Net operating income approach
(b) Net income approach
(c) Modigliani-Miller approach
(d) Traditional approach

54. A view that the dividend policy of a firm has a bearing on share valuation advocated by James E. Walter is based on which one of the following assumptions?
(a) Retained earnings is only source of financing.
(b) Cost of capital does not remain constant.
(c) Return on investment fluctuates.
(d) All the above.

55. Match the following:

List-I	List-II
A. Matching approach	1. Dividend Policy

B. Structural ratios	2. Inventory Management
C. Ordering quantity	3. Financing Working Capital
D. Bonus shares	4. Capital Structure

Codes:	A	B	C	D
(a)	1	2	3	4
(b)	3	4	1	2
(c)	3	4	2	1
(d)	2	1	3	4

56. **Assertion (A):** Operating style of the international business can be spread to the entire globe.
Reason (R): The style is limited to the internal economy only.
Codes:
(a) Both (A) and (R) are true.
(b) (A) is true, but (R) is false.
(c) (A) is false, but (R) is true.
(d) Both (A) and (R) are false.

57. The Comparative Cost Advantage Theory was given by
(a) David Ricardo (b) Adam Smith
(c) Raymond Vernon (d) Michael E. Porter

58. The companies globalise their operations through different means:
(a) Exporting directly
(b) Licensing/Franchising
(c) Joint ventures
(d) All the above

59. The components of W.T.O. are
(a) Ministerial Conference
(b) Disputes Settlement Body
(c) Director General
(d) All the above

60. India is not associated with
(a) SAARC (b) NAFTA
(c) BRICS (d) None of the above

61. Which one of the following is true statement?
(a) A balance of trade deals with export and import of invisible items only.
(b) A balance of payment deals with both visible and invisible items.
(c) The current account is not a component of balance of payment.
(d) All the above.

62. SDRs are popularly known as
(a) Currency Notes (b) Paper Gold
(c) Silver Coin (d) Gold Coin

63. Which one is not international institution?
(a) IMF (b) IDA (c) IBRD (d) TRAI

64. **Assertion (A):** Indent may be open or closed. Open indent does not specify the price and other details of the goods. The closed indent specifies the brand, price, number, packing, shipping mode, insurance, etc.
Reason (R): This is required as a part of export procedures.
Codes:
(a) Both (A) and (R) are correct.
(b) Both (A) and (R) are not correct.
(c) (A) is true, but (R) is false.
(d) (R) is true, but (A) is false.

65. Which one of the statements is not true?
(a) Institutional infrastructure facilitates market intelligence.
(b) STC is the chief canalizing agent for export and import of agricultural products.
(c) IIPO organizes trade fairs and exhibitions.
(d) Letter of credit does not indicate that the bank will pay the value of imports to the exporter.

66. Match the items of List-I with items of List-II.

List-I	**List-II**
A. Selective credit control	1. Consumer Credit Regulation
B. Encourage credit for desirable use	2. Cash Reserve Ratio
C. Quantitative credit control	3. Variation in Margin
D. Bank Rate	4. Re-discounting Rate

Codes:	A	B	C	D
(a)	4	2	3	1
(b)	3	1	2	4
(c)	1	3	2	4
(d)	2	1	3	4

67. **Assertion (A):** Use of paper money is replaced by plastic money. The future will see the electronic money clearance through satellite networking.
Reason (R): RBI is encouraging e-banking.

Codes:
(a) (A) is false, but (R) is true.
(b) (A) is true, but (R) is false.
(c) Both (A) and (R) are false.
(d) Both (A) and (R) are true.

68. Which one is not Finance Company?
(a) Hire-Purchase Finance Company
(b) IRDA
(c) Mutual Benefit Finance Companies
(d) Loan Companies

69. The Securities and Exchange Board of India was not entrusted with the function of
(a) Investor Protection.
(b) Ensuring Fair practices by companies.
(c) Promotion of efficient services by brokers.
(d) Improving the earnings of equity holders.

70. Which one is not Non-Marketable Securities?
(a) Corporate Securities
(b) Bank Deposits
(c) Deposits with Companies
(d) Post Office Certificates and Deposits

71. Minimum Alternative Tax (MAT) under Sec. 115 JB of the Income Tax Act is applicable on
(a) Partnership firm
(b) Association of persons
(c) Certain companies
(d) All types of companies

72. For the Assessment Year 2011-12, deduction under Sec. 80G is available without any limit but at the rate of 50% on
(a) Prime Minister's National Relief Fund.
(b) National Foundation for communal Harmany.
(c) Jawaharlal Nehru Memorial Fund.
(d) Chief Minister Relief Fund.

73. Interest on capital paid by a firm to its partners, under the Income Tax Act, 1961, is allowed
(a) 6% (b) 12% (c) 15% (d) 18%

74. Under capital gains head of the Income Tax Act, the income from sale of Household Furniture is
(a) Taxable Income (b) Capital Gain
(c) Revenue Gain (d) Exempted Income

75. Under Section 80E of the Income Tax Act, 1961 deduction in respect of payment of interest on loan taken for higher education shall be allowed up to
(a) ₹ 10,000 (b) ₹ 15,000
(c) ₹ 20,000 (d) Without any limit

ANSWERS

1. (c)	2. (b)	3. (d)	4. (c)	5. (b)
6. (b)	7. (d)	8. (b)	9. (c)	10. (d)
11. (c)	12. (b)	13. (b)	14. (d)	15. (c)
16. (d)	17. (a)	18. (a)	19. (b)	20. (b)
21. (d)	22. (c)	23. (b)	24. (b)	25. (d)
26. (d)	27. (c)	28. (b)	29. (d)	30. (a)
31. (c)	32. (c)	33. (d)	34. (c)	35. (c)
36. (d)	37. (a)	38. (b)	39. (a)	40. (c)
41. (b)	42. (c)	43. (c)	44. (b)	45. (d)
46. (b)	47. (b)	48. (b)	49. (c)	50. (a)
51. (c)	52. (b)	53. (b)	54. (a)	55. (c)
56. (b)	57. (a)	58. (d)	59. (d)	60. (b)
61. (b)	62. (b)	63. (d)	64. (c)	65. (d)
66. (b)	67. (d)	68. (b)	69. (d)	70. (a)
71. (c)	72. (c)	73. (b)	74. (d)	75. (d)

JUNE–2013

Note: This paper contains Sixty (60) multiple-choice questions, each question carrying two (2) marks. Candidate is expected to answer any Fifty (50) questions. In case more than Fifty (50) questions are attempted, only the first Fifty (50) questions will be evaluated.

PAPER–I

1. Which one of the following references is written as per Modern Language Association (MLA) format?
   (a) Hall, Donald. Fundamentals of Electronics, New Delhi: Prentice Hall of India, 2005
   (b) Hall, Donald, Fundamentals of Electronics, New Delhi—Prentice Hall of India, 2005
   (c) Hall, Donald, Fundamentals of Electronics, New Delhi: Prentice Hall of India, 2005
   (d) Hall, Donald. Fundamentals of Electronics. New Delhi: Prentice Hall of India, 2005
2. A workshop is
   (a) a conference for discussion on a topic.
   (b) a meeting for discussion on a topic.
   (c) a class at a college or a university in which a teacher and the students discuss a topic.
   (d) a brief intensive course for a small group emphasizing the development of a skill or technique for solving a specific problem.
3. A working hypothesis is
   (a) a proven hypothesis for an argument.
   (b) not required to be tested.
   (c) a provisionally accepted hypothesis for further research.
   (d) a scientific theory.

Read the following passage carefully and answer the questions (4 to 9):

The Taj Mahal has become one of the world's best known monuments. This domed white marble structure is situated on a high plinth at the southern end of a four-quartered garden, evoking the gardens of paradise, enclosed within walls measuring 305 by 549 metres. Outside the walls, in an area known as Mumtazabad, were living quarters for attendants, markets, serais and other structures built by local merchants and nobles. The tomb complex and the other imperial structures of Mumtazabad were maintained by the income of thirty villages given specifically for the tomb's support. The name Taj Mahal is unknown in Mughal chronicles, but it is used by contemporary Europeans in India, suggesting that this was the tomb's popular name. In contemporary texts, it is generally called simply the Illuminated Tomb (Rauza-i-Munavvara).

Mumtaz Mahal died shortly after delivering her fourteenth child in 1631. The Mughal court was then residing in Burhanpur. Her remains were temporarily buried by the griefstricken emperor in a spacious garden known as Zainabad on the bank of the river Tapti. Six months later her body was transported to Agra, where it was interred in land chosen for the mausoleum. This land, situated south of the Mughal city on the bank of the Jamuna, had belonged to the Kachhwaha rajas since the time of Raja Man Singh and was purchased from the then current raja, Jai Singh. Although contemporary chronicles indicate Jai Singh's willing cooperation in this exchange, extant *farmans* (imperial commands) indicate that the final price was not settled until almost two years after the mausoleum's commencement. Jai Singh's further cooperation was insured by imperial orders issued between 1632 and 1637 demanding that he provide stone masons and carts to transport marble from the mines at Makrana, within his "ancestral domain", to Agra where both the Taj Mahal and Shah Jahan's additions to the Agra fort were constructed concurrently.

Work on the mausoleum was commenced early in 1632. Inscriptional evidence indicates much of the tomb was completed by 1636. By 1643, when Shah Jahan most lavishly celebrated the 'Urs ceremony for Mumtaz Mahal', the entire complex was virtually complete.

4. Marble stone used for the construction of the Taj Mahal was brought from the ancestral domain of Raja Jai Singh. The name of the place where mines of marble is
   (a) Burhanpur (b) Makrana
   (c) Amber (d) Jaipur
5. The popular name Taj Mahal was given by
   (a) Shah Jahan
   (b) Tourists
   (c) Public
   (d) European travellers
6. Point out the true statement from the following:
   (a) Marble was not used for the construction of the Taj Mahal.
   (b) Red sand stone is non-visible in the Taj Mahal complex.
   (c) The Taj Mahal is surrounded by a four-quartered garden known as Chahr Bagh.
   (d) The Taj Mahal was constructed to celebrate the 'Urs ceremony for Mumtaz Mahal'.
7. In the contemporary texts the Taj Mahal is known
   (a) Mumtazabad (b) Mumtaz Mahal
   (c) Zainabad (d) Rauza-i-Munavvara
8. The construction of the Taj Mahal was completed between the period
   (a) 1632 – 1636 A.D. (b) 1630 – 1643 A.D.
   (c) 1632 – 1643 A.D. (d) 1636 – 1643 A.D.
9. The documents indicating the ownership of land, where the Taj Mahal was built, known as
   (a) Farman (b) Sale Deed
   (c) Sale-Purchase Deed (d) None of the above
10. In the process of communication, which one of the following is in the chronological order?
    (a) Communicator, Medium, Receiver, Effect, Message
    (b) Medium, Communicator, Message, Receiver, Effect
    (c) Communicator, Message, Medium, Receiver, Effect
    (d) Message, Communicator, Medium, Receiver, Effect
11. Bengal Gazette, the first Newspaper in India was started in 1780 by
    (a) Dr. Annie Besant
    (b) James Augustus Hicky
    (c) Lord Cripson
    (d) A.O. Hume
12. Press censorship in India was imposed during the tenure of the Prime Minister
    (a) Rajeev Gandhi (b) Narasimha Rao
    (c) Indira Gandhi (d) Deve Gowda
13. Communication via New media such as computers, teleshopping, internet and mobile telephony is termed as
    (a) Entertainment
    (b) Interactive communication
    (c) Developmental communication
    (d) Communitarian
14. Classroom communication of a teacher rests on the principle of
    (a) Infotainment (b) Edutainment
    (c) Entertainment (d) Enlightenment
15. _______ is important when a teacher communicates with his/her student.
    (a) Sympathy (b) Empathy
    (c) Apathy (d) Antipathy
16. In a certain code GALIB is represented by HBMJC. TIGER will be represented by
    (a) UJHFS (b) UHJSF
    (c) JHUSF (d) HUJSF
17. In a certain cricket tournament 45 matches were played. Each team played once against each of the other teams. The number of teams participated in the tournament is
    (a) 8 (b) 10 (c) 12 (d) 14
18. The missing number in the series 40, 120, 60, 180, 90, ?, 135 is
    (a) 110 (b) 270 (c) 105 (d) 210
19. The odd numbers from 1 to 45 which are exactly divisible by 3 are arranged in an ascending order. The number at 6th position is
    (a) 18 (b) 24 (c) 33 (d) 36
20. The mean of four numbers a, b, c, d is 100. If c = 70, then the mean of the remaining numbers is
    (a) 30 (b) 85/2 (c) 170/3 (d) 110
21. If the radius of a circle is increased by 50%, the perimeter of the circle will increase by
    (a) 20% (b) 30% (c) 40% (d) 50%

22. If the statement 'some men are honest' is false, which among the following statements will be true. Choose the correct code given below:
(i) All men are honest.
(ii) No men are honest.
(iii) Some men are not honest.
(iv) All men are dishonest.
Codes:
(a) (i), (ii) and (iii) (b) (ii), (iii) and (iv)
(c) (i), (iii) and (iv) (d) (ii), (i) and (iv)

23. Choose the proper alternative given in the codes to replace the question mark.
Bee – Honey, Cow – Milk, Teacher – ?
(a) Intelligence (b) Marks
(c) Lessons (d) Wisdom

24. P is the father of R and S is the son of Q and T is the brother of P. If R is the sister of S, how is Q related to T?
(a) Wife (b) Sister-in-law
(c) Brother-in-law (d) Daughter-in-law

25. A definition put forward to resolve a dispute by influencing attitudes or stirring emotions is called
(a) Lexical (b) Persuasive
(c) Stipulative (d) Precisions

26. Which of the codes given below contains only the correct statements?
Statements:
(i) Venn diagram is a clear method of notation.
(ii) Venn diagram is the most direct method of testing the validity of categorical syllogisms.
(iii) In Venn diagram method the premises and the conclusion of a categorical syllogism is diagrammed.
(iv) In Venn diagram method the three overlapping circles are drawn for testing a categorical syllogism.
Codes:
(a) (i), (ii) & (iii) (b) (i), (ii) & (iv)
(c) (ii), (iii) & (iv) (d) (i), (iii) & (iv)

27. Inductive reasoning presupposes
(a) unity in human nature
(b) integrity in human nature
(c) uniformity in human nature
(d) harmony in human nature

Read the table below and based on this table answer questions from 28 to 33:

Area under Major Horticulture Crops
(in lakh hectares)

Year	Fruits	Vegetables	Flowers	Total Horti-culture Area
2005-06	53	72	1	187
2006-07	56	75	1	194
2007-08	58	78	2	202
2008-09	61	79	2	207
2009-10	63	79	2	209

28. Which of the following two years have recorded the highest rate of increase in area under the total horticulture?
(a) 2005-06 & 2006-07
(b) 2006-07 & 2008-09
(c) 2007-08 & 2008-09
(d) 2006-07 & 2007-08

29. Shares of the area under flowers, vegetables and fruits in the area under total horticulture are respectively:
(a) 1, 38 and 30 percent
(b) 30, 38 and 1 percent
(c) 38, 30 and 1 percent
(d) 35, 36 and 2 percent

30. Which of the following has recorded the highest rate of increase in area during 2005-06 to 2009-10?
(a) Fruits (b) Vegetables
(c) Flowers (d) Total horticulture

31. Find out the horticultural crop that has recorded an increase of area by around 10 percent from 2005-06 to 2009-10
(a) Fruits (b) Vegetables
(c) Flowers (d) Total horticulture

32. What has been the share of area under fruits, vegetables and flowers in the area under total horticulture in 2007-08?
(a) 53 percent (b) 68 percent
(c) 79 percent (d) 100 percent

33. In which year, area under fruits has recorded the highest rate of increase?
(a) 2006-07 (b) 2007-08
(c) 2008-09 (d) 2009-10

34. 'www' stands for
   (a) work with web (b) word wide web
   (c) world wide web (d) worth while web

35. A hard disk is divided into tracks which is further subdivided into
   (a) Clusters (b) Sectors
   (c) Vectors (d) Heads

36. A computer program that translates a program statement by statement into machine language is called a/an
   (a) Compiler (b) Simulator
   (c) Translator (d) Interpreter

37. A Gigabyte is equal to
   (a) 1024 Megabytes (b) 1024 Kilobytes
   (c) 1024 Terabytes (d) 1024 Bytes

38. A Compiler is a software which converts
   (a) characters to bits
   (b) high level language to machine language
   (c) machine language to high level language
   (d) words to bits

39. Virtual memory is
   (a) an extremely large main memory.
   (b) an extremely large secondary memory.
   (c) an illusion of extremely large main memory.
   (d) a type of memory used in super computers.

40. The phrase 'tragedy of commons' is in the context of
   (a) tragic event related to damage caused by release of poisonous gases.
   (b) tragic conditions of poor people.
   (c) degradation of renewable free access resources.
   (d) climate change.

41. Kyoto Protocol is related to
   (a) Ozone depletion (b) Hazardous waste
   (c) Climate change (d) Nuclear energy

42. Which of the following is a source of emissions leading to the eventual formation of surface ozone as a pollutant?
   (a) Transport sector
   (b) Refrigeration and Airconditioning
   (c) Wetlands
   (d) Fertilizers

43. The smog in cities in India mainly consists of
   (a) Oxides of sulphur
   (b) Oxides of nitrogen and unburnt hydrocarbons
   (c) Carbon monoxide and SPM
   (d) Oxides of sulphur and ozone

44. Which of the following types of natural hazards have the highest potential to cause damage to humans?
   (a) Earthquakes
   (b) Forest fires
   (c) Volcanic eruptions
   (d) Droughts and Floods

45. The percentage share of renewable energy sources in the power production in India is around
   (a) 2-3% (b) 22-25%
   (c) 10-12% (d) < 1%

46. In which of the following categories the enrolment of students in higher education in 2010-11 was beyond the percentage of seats reserved?
   (a) OBC students (b) SC students
   (c) ST students (d) Woman students

47. Which one of the following statements is not correct about the University Grants Commission (UGC)?
   (a) It was established in 1956 by an Act of Parliament.
   (b) It is tasked with promoting and coordinating higher education.
   (c) It receives Plan and Non-Plan funds from the Central Government.
   (d) It receives funds from State Governments in respect of State Universities.

48. Consider the statement which is followed by two arguments (I) and (II):

   Statement: Should India switch over to a two party system?

   Arguments: (I) Yes, it will lead to stability of Government.
   (II) No, it will limit the choice of voters.

   (a) Only argument (I) is strong.
   (b) Only argument (II) is strong.
   (c) Both the arguments are strong.
   (d) Neither of the arguments is strong.

49. Consider the statement which is followed by two arguments (I) and (II):

Statement: Should persons with criminal background be banned from contesting elections?

Arguments: (I) Yes, it will decriminalise politics.
(II) No, it will encourage the ruling party to file frivolous cases against their political opponents.

(a) Only argument (I) is strong.
(b) Only argument (II) is strong.
(c) Both the arguments are strong.
(d) Neither of the arguments is strong.

50. Which of the following statement(s) is/are correct about a Judge of the Supreme Court of India?
1. A Judge of the Supreme Court is appointed by the President of India.
2. He holds office during the pleasure of the President.
3. He can be suspended, pending an inquiry.
4. He can be removed for proven misbehaviour or incapacity.

Select the correct answer from the codes given below:

Codes:
(a) 1, 2 and 3 (b) 1, 3 and 4
(c) 1 and 3 (d) 1 and 4

51. In the warrant of precedence, the Speaker of the Lok Sabha comes next only to
(a) The President
(b) The Vice-President
(c) The Prime Minister
(d) The Cabinet Ministers

52. The blackboard can be utilised best by a teacher for
(a) putting the matter of teaching in black and white
(b) making the students attentive
(c) writing the important and notable points
(d) highlighting the teacher himself

53. Nowadays the most effective mode of learning is
(a) self-study (b) face-to-face learning
(c) e-learning (d) blended learning

54. At the primary school stage, most of the teachers should be women because they
(a) can teach children better than men.
(b) know basic content better than men.
(c) are available on lower salaries.
(d) can deal with children with love and affection.

55. Which one is the highest order of learning?
(a) Chain learning
(b) Problem-solving learning
(c) Stimulus-response learning
(d) Conditioned-reflex learning

56. A person can enjoy teaching as a profession when he
(a) has control over students.
(b) commands respect from students.
(c) is more qualified than his colleagues.
(d) is very close to higher authorities.

57. "A diagram speaks more than 1000 words." The statement means that the teacher should
(a) use diagrams in teaching.
(b) speak more and more in the class
(c) use teaching aids in the class.
(d) not speak too much in the class.

58. A research paper
(a) is a compilation of information on a topic.
(b) contains original research as deemed by the author.
(c) contains peer-reviewed original research or evaluation of research conducted by others.
(d) can be published in more than one journal.

59. Which one of the following belongs to the category of good 'research ethics'?
(a) Publishing the same paper in two research journals without telling the editors.
(b) Conducting a review of the literature that acknowledges the contributions of other people in the relevant field or relevant prior work.
(c) Trimming outliers from a data set without discussing your reasons in a research paper.
(d) Including a colleague as an author on a research paper in return for a favour even though the colleague did not make a serious contribution to the paper.

60. Which of the following sampling methods is not based on probability?
    (a) Simple Random Sampling
    (b) Stratified Sampling
    (c) Quota Sampling
    (d) Cluster Sampling

ANSWERS

1. (d)	2. (d)	3. (c)	4. (b)	5. (d)
6. (c)	7. (d)	8. (c)	9. (a)	10. (c)
11. (b)	12. (c)	13. (b)	14. (b)	15. (b)
16. (a)	17. (b)	18. (b)	19. (c)	20. (d)
21. (d)	22. (b)	23. (d)	24. (b)	25. (b)
26. (b)	27. (c)	28. (d)	29. (a)	30. (c)
31. (b)	32. (b)	33. (a)	34. (c)	35. (b)
36. (d)	37. (a)	38. (b)	39. (c)	40. (c)
41. (c)	42. (a)	43. (b)	44. (d)	45. (c)
46. (a)	47. (d)	48. (c)	49. (a)	50. (d)
51. (c)	52. (c)	53. (d)	54. (d)	55. (d)
56. (b)	57. (c)	58. (c)	59. (b)	60. (c)

PAPER–II

Note: This paper contains fifty (50) objective type questions, each question carrying two (2) marks. All questions are compulsory.

1. Direct supervision over depositories and mutual funds is undertaken by
   (a) NBFCs (b) RBI
   (c) SEBI (d) All of the above

2. In the call/notice money market, which of the following participants is allowed to trade?
   (a) All Banks, Primary Dealers and Mutual Funds
   (b) All Corporates
   (c) Only Commercial Banks
   (d) All of the above

3. Match the items of List-I with the items of List-II and select the correct answer:

List I	List II
(i) Private ownership and Free Enterprise.	(A) Secondary Market
(ii) Government ownership and Central Authority.	(B) Capitalism
(iii) The market for the sale and purchase of previously issued securities.	(C) Primary Market
(iv) The market for new long term capital.	(D) Socialism

Codes:	**(i)**	**(ii)**	**(iii)**	**(iv)**
(a)	(B)	(D)	(A)	(C)
(b)	(A)	(B)	(C)	(D)
(c)	(B)	(D)	(C)	(A)
(d)	(A)	(C)	(B)	(D)

4. The apex consumer court in India is referred to as
   (a) The Consumer Education and Research Centre.
   (b) The Consumer Unity and Trust Society.
   (c) National Consumer Disputes Redressal Commission.
   (d) None of the above

5. Who is Chairman of 13th Finance Commission?
   (a) Dr. C. Rangarajan
   (b) Mr. Vimal Jalan
   (c) Dr. Vijay C. Kelkar
   (d) None of the above

6. Insurance expenses paid to bring an equipment from the place of purchase to the place of installation is a type of
   (a) Revenue expenditure
   (b) Capital expenditure
   (c) Deferred revenue expenditure
   (d) Operating expense

7. ABC Ltd was incorporated with an authorised Share Capital of ₹ 1,00,000 equity shares of ₹ 10 each. The Board of Directors of the company decided to allot 10,000 shares credited as fully paid to the promoters of the company for their services.

Which account should be debited in the books of ABC Ltd.?
(a) Promoters' Account
(b) Services Account
(c) Goodwill Account
(d) Share Capital Account

8. In a reconstruction scheme, the reduction of capital may take the form of
(a) Reducing the liability of the shareholders in respect of any unpaid amount on the shares held by them.
(b) Paying-off any paid-up share capital which is in excess of its requirement.
(c) Cancelling any paid-up share capital which is lost or unrepresented by available assets.
(d) All of the above.

9. While determining the normal rate of return for the valuation of shares in Market Value Method, which of the following should be taken into consideration?
(a) The degree of risk involved.
(b) The current rate of interest on gilt-edged securities.
(c) Weighted average cost of capital.
(d) All of the above.

10. Master budget is a
(a) Functional Budget (b) Operating Budget
(c) Summary Budget (d) Financial Budget

11. **Assertion (A):** Want-satisfying power of a commodity is called its utility.
Reason (R): Utility may not have the characteristic of morality.
Codes:
(a) Both (A) and (R) are correct.
(b) (A) is correct, but (R) is not correct.
(c) Both (A) and (R) are not correct.
(d) (R) is correct, but (A) is not correct.

12. Match the items of List-I with those in List-II and select the correct code for the answer:

List I	List II
(A) Contraction of Demand	(i) Non-Price change effect
(B) Decrease in Demand	(ii) Demand curve remains the same
(C) Increase in Demand	(iii) Price change effect
(D) Expansion of Demand curve	(iv) Shifts the Demand

Codes:	A	B	C	D
(a)	(iii)	(i)	(iv)	(ii)
(b)	(iv)	(iii)	(ii)	(i)
(c)	(i)	(ii)	(iii)	(iv)
(d)	(ii)	(iv)	(i)	(iii)

13. **Assertion (A):** As the proportion of one variable factor in a combination with fixed factor is increased, after a point the marginal product of the factor will diminish.
Reason (R): Beyond the level of optimum combination of inputs leads to this.
Codes:
(a) (R) is appropriate reason of (A).
(b) (R) is not appropriate reason of (A).
(c) (A) and (R) are not related with each other.
(d) (A) is independent of (R).

14. Match the items of List-I with the items of List-II and select the correct answer.

List I	List II
(A) Indifference Curve	(i) Slopes downward to the right
(B) Demand Curve	(ii) P = AR = MR = d
(C) Perfect Competition	(iii) Oligopoly
(D) Price Leadership	(iv) Convex to the origin

Codes:	A	B	C	D
(a)	(ii)	(iii)	(iv)	(i)
(b)	(iii)	(iv)	(i)	(ii)
(c)	(iv)	(i)	(ii)	(iii)
(d)	(i)	(ii)	(iii)	(iv)

15. Price, Marginal Revenue and Elasticity are related to each other. When $e = 1$, then:
(a) MR > 0 (b) MR < 0
(c) MR = 0 (d) MR = 1

16. Consider the following statistical tests:
(i) 'F' test (ii) 't' test
(iii) 'z' test (iv) 'Chi-square' test
Which of these are parametric tests?
(a) (i), (ii) and (iv) (b) (i), (iii) and (iv)
(c) (i), (ii) and (iii) (d) (ii), (iii) and (iv)

17. The difference between sample statistic and its corresponding population parameter is
(a) Sampling error
(b) Measurement error

(c) Coverage error
(d) Non-response error

18. Match the items in List-I with items in List-II.

List I	List II
(i) Level of significance	(A) Sample mean is equal to population mean
(ii) Standard deviation of sampling distribution	(B) Parameters
(iii) Numerical value that describes the characteristics of the population	(C) Type-I error
(iv) Normally distributed population	(D) Standard error

Codes:	(i)	(ii)	(iii)	(iv)
(a)	(D)	(C)	(A)	(B)
(b)	(C)	(D)	(B)	(A)
(c)	(C)	(B)	(D)	(A)
(d)	(D)	(B)	(C)	(A)

19. Kendall's co-efficient of concordance is used to
(a) Test the difference among two or more sets of data.
(b) Test the relationship between variables.
(c) Test the variations in the given data.
(d) Test the randomness of samples.

20. Which of the following softwares are used for data processing?
(i) EXCEL (ii) ACCESS
(iii) SPSS (iv) STAR
(v) PASW
Codes:
(a) (i), (ii), (iii) and (v)
(b) (ii), (iii), (iv) and (v)
(c) (iii) and (iv)
(d) (i), (iii) and (iv)

21. Match the items of List-I with the items of List-II and select the correct answer.

List-I	List-II
(i) Grapevine	(A) Task group
(ii) Formal group	(B) Field force theory
(iii) Informal group	(C) Gossip
(iv) Kurt Lewin	(D) National group

Codes:	(i)	(ii)	(iii)	(iv)
(a)	(C)	(A)	(D)	(B)
(b)	(D)	(C)	(B)	(A)
(c)	(A)	(B)	(C)	(D)
(d)	(B)	(A)	(D)	(C)

22. Who has suggested that achievement motivation among individuals and nations can be developed through training courses?
(a) MeClelland (b) Alderfer
(c) Maslow (d) Herzberg

23. **Assertion (A):** When span of control is wide co-ordination and control becomes difficult.
Reason (R): In a narrow span, levels of authority reduces.
Codes:
(a) Both (A) and (R) are true and (R) is the correct explanation of (A).
(b) Both (A) and (R) are true, but (R) is not a correct explanation of (A).
(c) (A) is true, but (R) is false.
(d) (A) is false, but (R) is true.

24. The general pattern of behaviour, shared belief and values that members have in common is known as
(a) Organisation climate
(b) Organisation culture
(c) Organisation effectiveness
(d) Organisation matrix

25. Which of the following is not a principle of management according to Henri Fayol?
(a) Subordination of individual interest over the organisational interest
(b) Esprit de crops
(c) Unity of Managers
(d) Unity of Direction

26. Which of the following concepts is based on development, design and implementation of marketing programmes, processes and activities that recognise their breadth and interdependence?
(a) Product concept
(b) Sales concept

(c) Societal marketing concept
(d) Holistic marketing concept

27. The concept of marketing-mix, consisting of the 4Ps of marketing, was developed by
(a) E. Jerome McCarthy
(b) Peter F. Drucker
(c) Philip Kotler
(d) William J. Stonton

28. The selling concept is most likely to be used by firms which sell
(a) Convenience goods (b) Shopping goods
(c) Speciality goods (d) Unsought goods

29. Match the items of List-I with those of List-II and select the correct answer from the codes given below:

List I	List II
(A) Everitt M. Rogers	(i) Service Quality Model
(B) J.D. Power	(ii) Three types of marketing for services
(C) Parasuraman, Zeithaml and Berry	(iii) Quality rating of automobiles
(D) Gronroos	(iv) Diffusion of innovation

Codes:	A	B	C	D
(a)	(iii)	(ii)	(i)	(iv)
(b)	(i)	(ii)	(iii)	(iv)
(c)	(ii)	(i)	(iv)	(iii)
(d)	(iv)	(iii)	(i)	(ii)

30. Consumer attitudes and beliefs about diet, health and nutrition are influenced by
(a) Economic environment
(b) Cultural environment
(c) Social environment
(d) Natural environment

31. Positive NPV in project appraised by a firm may not occur an account of
(a) Economics of scale
(b) Market reach
(c) Product differentiation
(d) Intangible benefits

32. In case the projects are divisible under capital rationing an appropriate project appraisal method is
(a) Net Present Value Method
(b) Profitability Index Method
(c) Internal Rate of Return Method
(d) Payback Period Method

33. Permanent working capital is generally financed through
(a) Long-term Capital Funds
(b) Government Assistance
(c) Internal Financing
(d) Short term loans from Banks

34. The appropriate ratio for indicating liquidity crisis is
(a) Operating ratio
(b) Sales turnover ratio
(c) Current ratio
(d) Acid test ratio

35. Who proposed a model to apply economic order quantity concept of inventory management to determine the optimum cash holding in a firm?
(a) Keith V. Smith (b) Miller and Orr
(c) William J. Baumol (d) J.M. Keynes

36. Which of the following is not included in the model of the systems approach to Human Resource Management?
(a) Human Resource Planning
(b) Recruitment and Selection
(c) Performance Appraisal
(d) Departmentation

37. It is generally easy to measure the performance of the
(a) Industrial Relations Manager
(b) Research and Development Manager
(c) Sales person
(d) All of the above

38. Which one of the following is not a monetary incentive to sales people?
(a) Bonus (b) Staff meeting
(c) Travelling allowance (d) Both (b) and (c)

39. **Statement (i):** Sound industrial relations are essential to achieve individual, team goals and organizational goals.

Statement (ii): Congenial labour management relations create an atmosphere of harmony and low rate of absenteeism.
(a) Statement (i) is true, but (ii) is false.
(b) Statement (ii) is true, but (i) is false.
(c) Both statements are true.
(d) Both statements are false.

40. Out of the following, which are the schemes of Social Security?
   (i) Provident Fund Scheme
   (ii) Health Insurance Scheme
   (iii) Job Guarantee Scheme
   (iv) Maternity Benefit Scheme
   (v) Merit Promotion Scheme
   (vi) Compulsory and Voluntary Social Insurance Scheme
   (vii) Child Insurance Scheme

   Codes:
   (a) (i), (ii), (iv) and (vi)
   (b) (ii), (i), (v) and (vii)
   (c) (iii), (v), (iv) and (vi)
   (d) (iv), (vii), (iii) and (ii)

41. RBI ensures that banks operate within the set norms by conducting ______ inspections and _______ monitoring.
   (a) on site, off site (b) off site, on site
   (c) on site, field (d) field, on site

42. Under Section 37 of the Banking (Regulation) Act, a moratorium order can be issued by the High Court for a maximum total period of
   (a) One month (b) Six months
   (c) One year (d) One and a half year

43. Bonds or debentures issued by Securitization company should bear interest not less than
   (a) Bank Rate
   (b) Prime Lending Rate
   (c) 1.5% over the Bank Rate
   (d) 1.5% over the Saving Rate

44. Section 131 of the Negotiable Instruments Act extends protection to the _______
   (a) Collecting Banker (b) Paying Banker
   (c) Advising Banker
   (d) Confirming Banker

45. When a customer, by a letter has advised the bank not to honour/pay a particular cheque, such letter is called ______
   (a) Cancellation letter
   (b) Garnishee letter
   (c) Mandate
   (d) None of the above

46. Flow of foreign loans and investments affect
   (a) Trade balance
   (b) Current Account balance
   (c) Capital Account balance
   (d) None of the above

47. Concessions mainly multinational in character come under the principle of
   (a) Non-discrimination
   (b) Reciprocity
   (c) Market Access
   (d) Fair Competition

48. From the following identify, the one which is not a commercial counter trade?
   (a) Classical barter
   (b) Counter purchase
   (c) Pre-compensation
   (d) Buy-back agreement

49. If the spot price is higher than the strike price in a call option, it is referred to as
   (a) At-the-money
   (b) In-the-money
   (c) Out-of-the-money
   (d) Premium

50. Identity the item which does not include under Current Account transaction?
   (a) Services
   (b) Non-monetary movement of gold
   (c) Unilateral transfer
   (d) Investment income

ANSWERS

1. (c)	2. (c)	3. (a)	4. (c)	5. (c)
6. (b)	7. (c)	8. (d)	9. (d)	10. (c)
11. (a)	12. (a)	13. (a)	14. (c)	15. (c)
16. (c)	17. (a)	18. (b)	19. (b)	20. (a)
21. (a)	22. (a)	23. (c)	24. (b)	25. (c)
26. (d)	27. (a)	28. (d)	29. (d)	30. (b)
31. (d)	32. (b)	33. (a)	34. (d)	35. (c)
36. (d)	37. (c)	38. (d)	39. (c)	40. (a)
41. (a)	42. (b)	43. (c)	44. (a)	45. (d)
46. (c)	47. (b)	48. (d)	49. (b)	50. (b)

PAPER–III

Note: This paper contains Seventy-five (75) objective type questions, each question carrying two (2) marks. All questions are compulsory.

1. Under the provisions of the Industries (Development and Regulation) Act, 1951, a licence is necessary for
   (a) Changing the location of an existing industrial undertaking.
   (b) producing or manufacturing a 'new article' in an existing industrial undertaking.
   (c) Establishing a new undertaking.
   (d) All of the above.

2. Match the items of List-I with the items of List-II and select the correct answer.

	List-I		List-II
(i)	Political and Legal Environment	(A)	Important for industries directly depending on imports or exports.
(ii)	Demographic Environment	(B)	Close relationship with the economic system and economic policy.
(iii)	Economic Environment	(C)	Related to natural resources.
(iv)	Geographical and Ecological Environment	(D)	Occupational and spatial mobilities of population having implications for business.

Codes:	(i)	(ii)	(iii)	(iv)
(a)	(B)	(D)	(C)	(A)
(b)	(B)	(D)	(A)	(C)
(c)	(A)	(B)	(C)	(D)
(d)	(A)	(B)	(D)	(C)

3. Match the items of List-I with the items of List-II and select the correct answer:

	List-I		List-II
(i)	SLR	(A)	Working in the field of consumer protection.
(ii)	SIDBI	(B)	Credit control.
(iii)	CUTS	(C)	Industrial policy.
(iv)	ILPIC	(D)	Facilitating Small Scale Industries.

Codes:	(i)	(ii)	(iii)	(iv)
(a)	(A)	(C)	(D)	(B)
(b)	(B)	(D)	(A)	(C)
(c)	(A)	(B)	(C)	(D)
(d)	(A)	(C)	(B)	(D)

4. Match the following:

	List-I		List-II
(i)	National Stock Exchange	(A)	Marks the beginning of the process of dematerialisation of shares of the participating companies.
(ii)	National Securities Depository Limited	(B)	Facilitation of equal access to investors across the country.
(iii)	Securities and Exchange Board of India	(C)	To foster the development of an active secondary market for government Securities.
(iv)	Securities Trading Corporation	(D)	Abolition of capital issues control and of India retaining the sale authority for new capital issues.

Codes:	(i)	(ii)	(iii)	(iv)
(a)	(B)	(A)	(D)	(C)
(b)	(A)	(B)	(C)	(D)
(c)	(A)	(B)	(D)	(C)
(d)	(D)	(C)	(B)	(A)

5. The United Nations Conference on Trade and Development (UNCTAD) was set up in
   (a) 1944 (b) 1954 (c) 1960 (d) 1964

6. Indicate the ground on which a complaint under the Consumer Protection Act, 1986, shall be invalid.
   (a) A product having short weight.
   (b) A service provided free of cost.
   (c) A misleading advertisement given in newspaper.
   (d) None of the above.

7. Out of the following, which are the four components of food security?
   (i) Food availability (ii) Food market
   (iii) Food accessibility (iv) Food utilization
   (v) Food credit

Codes:
(a) (iii), (iv) and (v) (b) (i), (iii) and (iv)
(c) (i), (ii) and (iii) (d) (i), (ii) and (iv)

8. Performance evaluation of a responsibility centre can be done by
(a) ROI (b) Return on sales
(c) EVA (d) All of the above

9. Social Balance Sheet shows
(a) Social costs
(b) Social revenues
(c) Value of employees of the organisation
(d) All of the above

10. Which of the following comes under efficiency ratios?
(a) Average collection period
(b) Inventory turnover ratio
(c) Fixed assets turnover ratio
(d) All of the above

11. Match the items of the following two lists:

List I	List II
(i) Statement of changes in Working Capital	(A) Cash Flow Statement
(ii) Deferred Tax	(B) Fixed Assets
(iii) Three activities	(C) Funds Flow Statement
(iv) Impairment Loss	(D) Balance Sheet

Codes:	(i)	(ii)	(iii)	(iv)
(a)	(A)	(B)	(C)	(D)
(b)	(C)	(D)	(B)	(A)
(c)	(C)	(D)	(A)	(B)
(d)	(D)	(C)	(A)	(B)

12. Match the items of the following two lists and indicate the correct answer:

List I	List II
(i) Earning ability of firm	(A) Basis of Accounting
(ii) Conservatism	(B) P/V ratio
(iii) Cash profit	(C) Cash flow statement
(iv) Cash and Accrual	(D) Prudence

Codes:	(i)	(ii)	(iii)	(iv)
(a)	(B)	(D)	(C)	(A)
(b)	(B)	(A)	(D)	(C)
(c)	(C)	(D)	(A)	(B)
(d)	(C)	(D)	(B)	(A)

13. Given below are two statements, one labelled as Assertion (A) and the other labelled as Reason (R).
Assertion (A): Only the relevant costs should be taken into consideration for decision making.
Reason (R): All variable costs are relevant costs and all fixed costs are irrelevant costs.
In the above two statements, which one alternative of the following is correct?
Codes:
(a) Both (A) and (R) are correct.
(b) Only (A) is correct, but (R) is wrong.
(c) Only (R) is correct, but (A) is wrong.
(d) Both (A) and (R) are wrong.

14. Given below are two statements, one labelled as Assertion (A) and the other labelled as Reason (R):
Assertion (A): Variance analysis is undertaken for planning and control of costs.
Reason (R): Future costs are taken into consideration in budgeting and standard costing.
In the above two statements, which one alternative of the following is correct?
Codes:
(a) Both (A) and (R) are correct and (R) is the Reason for (R).
(b) Both (A) and (R) are correct and (R) is not the Reason for (A).
(c) (A) is correct, but (R) is wrong.
(d) (A) is wrong, but (R) is correct.

15. **Assertion (A):** Mark-up pricing is a method of determining price.
Reason (R): P = ATC + (m × ATC) is the expression for that.
Codes:
(a) (A) is correct but (R) is not correct.
(b) Both (A) and (R) are correct.
(c) Both (A) and (R) are not correct.
(d) (R) is correct, but (A) is not correct.

16. Match the items of List-I with the items of List-II and select the correct answer.

List-I	List-II
(A) Economic profit	(i) Total Revenue Explicit cost

(B) Accounting profit	(ii) Buyers and Sellers exchanging
(C) Collusion/Cartel	(iii) Total Revenue-Total cost
(D) Market	(iv) Oligopoly

Codes:	A	B	C	D
(a)	(iii)	(i)	(iv)	(ii)
(b)	(i)	(ii)	(iii)	(iv)
(c)	(iv)	(iii)	(ii)	(i)
(d)	(ii)	(iv)	(i)	(iii)

17. Which one is not the item of economic cost to the business?
    (a) Owner supplied resources.
    (b) Market supplied resources.
    (c) Implicit costs.
    (d) Non-monetary opportunity costs of using owner supplied resources.

18. Demand must have the elements
    (a) Desire
    (b) Want
    (c) Quantity, Price and Time
    (d) All of the above

19. Match the items of List-I and items of List-II and select the correct code for the answer.

List-I	List-II
(A) Utilitarian Approach	(i) Marginal Rate of Substitution
(B) Ordinal Approach	(ii) Budget line & Indifference Curve
(C) Price-Consumption Curve	(iii) $U = f(x, y)$
(D) Consumer Equilibrium	(iv) $MRS_{xy} = MRS_{yx}$

Codes:	A	B	C	D
(a)	(i)	(iv)	(iii)	(ii)
(b)	(ii)	(iii)	(iv)	(i)
(c)	(iii)	(i)	(ii)	(iv)
(d)	(iv)	(ii)	(i)	(iii)

20. The Learner Index measures
    (a) Market power (b) Price
    (c) Price-Marginal cost (d) None of the above

21. Match the items of List-I and items of List-II and select the correct answer.

List-I	List-II
(A) Perfect competition	(i) Different prices for the same product
(B) Monopolistic competition	(ii) Dominant strategy
(C) Oligopoly	(iii) Product differentiation
(D) Discriminating Monopoly	(iv) Identical product

Codes:	A	B	C	D
(a)	(iv)	(iii)	(ii)	(i)
(b)	(i)	(ii)	(iii)	(iv)
(c)	(ii)	(iv)	(i)	(iii)
(d)	(iii)	(i)	(iv)	(ii)

22. If there are 8 possible classes under consideration for a goodness of it, the number of degrees of freedom will be
    (a) 8 (b) 7
    (c) 6
    (d) Cannot be determined from the given information.

23. Identify from the following, the test statistic for which the value of numerator should always be greater than that of denominator.
    (a) 'Chi-square' (b) 'F' value
    (c) 'Z' value (d) 't' value

24. Which of the following tests can be applied to ordinal scale data?
    (i) Chi-square test
    (ii) 'Z' test
    (iii) Kruskal-Wallis test
    (iv) Wilcoxon Mann-Whitney test

    Codes:
    (a) (i), (ii) and (iii) (b) (ii), (iv) and (iii)
    (c) (i), (iii) and (iv) (d) (i), (ii) and (iv)

25. Which of the following tests can be based on the normal distribution?
    (a) Difference between independent means
    (b) Difference between dependant means
    (c) Difference between proportions
    (d) All of the above

26. From the following, identify one situation where 'F' test cannot be used?
    (a) To compare more than two population means.
    (b) To test the hypothesis about a single population variance.
    (c) To test the hypothesis about two-population variance.
    (d) To study about randomized block design.

27. Which statistical test should be applied to test the effectiveness of 'special coaching' on the marks scored by the students?
(a) Paired 't' test (b) 'Chi-square' test
(c) 'Z' test (d) 'F' test

28. In a linear equation, $y = a + bx$, 'a' refers to
(a) Slope
(b) Y-intercept
(c) Dependant variable
(d) Independent variable

29. Which among the following is the most popular approach for accomplishing the results?
(a) Management by exception
(b) Reward system
(c) Management by objectives
(d) Mentor system

30. The managerial function of organizing involves
(a) Reviewing and adjusting plan in the light of changing conditions.
(b) Establishing programme for the accomplishment of objectives.
(c) Creating structure of functions and duties to be performed.
(d) Getting things done through others.

31. A leader who identifies what subordinates need to do to achieve objectives, clarify organizational roles and tasks, set up an organization structure, reward performance and provide for the social needs of their followers, is
(a) a transformational leader
(b) a participative leader
(c) a transactional leader
(d) an autocratic leader

32. Which of the following is not an assumption of theory X?
(a) An average human being has an inherent dislike of work and will avoid it if he can.
(b) An average human being prefers to be directed, seeks to avoid responsibility, has relatively little ambition, and wants security above all.
(c) An average human being learns under proper conditions, not only to accept responsibility but also to seek it.
(d) Most people must be coerced, controlled, directed and threatened with punishment to get them put forth adequate effort.

33. If a network of interpersonal relationship that arise when people associate with each other is an informal organization, then find out which of the following is not an informal organization?
(a) The "machine shop" group
(b) Customers' group
(c) The "sixth floor" group
(d) The "Friday evening bowling" gang

34. Which of the following are sources of ethics?
(i) Religion (ii) Legal system
(iii) Economic system (iv) Culture
(v) Family system
Select the correct answer from the codes given below:
(a) (i), (ii), (iii), (v) (b) (i), (ii), (iv)
(c) (i), (iv), (v) (d) (i), (ii), (iii), (iv), (v)

35. Which of the following has refined Maslow's theory of motivation by proposing a hierarchy of three needs?
(a) MeClelland (b) Aldorfer
(c) Herzburg (d) Vroom

36. Which segmentation approach is the most compatible with the spirit of the marketing concept?
(a) Benefit sought (b) Income
(c) Social class (d) Family size

37. The description of a product's quality, features, style, brand name and packaging identifiers the
(a) Actual product (b) Augmented product
(c) Core product (d) Tangible product

38. Consider the following statements and find out the correct alternative from the codes given below:
(i) A firm's marketing information system is a component of its marketing research system.
(ii) The most common forms of marketing researches conducted in most of the firms are the measurement of market potential and the analysis of market share.
(iii) Survey research is seldom used for studying consumer perception and attitudes.

(iv) The concept of cognitive dissonance is relevant to study consumer's post-purchase behaviour.

Codes:
(a) All the statements are true.
(b) All the statements are false.
(c) (i) is false and the rest are true.
(d) (ii) and (iv) are true and the rest are false.

39. In India, which pricing practice is not permissible?
(a) Penetrating pricing (b) Skimming pricing
(c) Predatory pricing (d) None of the above

40. Consider the following statements and find out the correct alternative from the codes given below:
(i) A good salesman is one who can sell refrigerator to an Eskimo.
(ii) Salesmen are born, not made.
(iii) Physical distribution is an area where high cost-savings is possible.

Codes:
(a) (i) and (iii) are correct.
(b) (i) and (ii) are correct.
(c) (ii) and (iii) are correct.
(d) All are correct.

41. Which form of retail outlet has the highest operating costs?
(a) Supermarket
(b) Consumer co-operative store
(c) Department store
(d) Retail chain store

42. Consider the following statements and indicate the correct alternative from the codes given below:
(i) The product management system often turns out to be costly.
(ii) When customers belong to different user groups with distinct buying preferences and practices, a market management organization is not suitable.
(iii) Advertising department has the closest interface with the finance department of the company.

Codes:
(a) (i) and (ii) are correct.
(b) (ii) and (iii) are correct.
(c) Only (i) is correct.
(d) All are correct.

43. Match the statements in List-I with dividend models in List-II as follows:

List-I	**List-II**
(A) Dividend Capitalisation Approach.	(i) Traditional Model
(B) Dividend Policy has a bearing on the share valuation.	(ii) Gardon Model
(C) Stock Market places more weight on dividends than on retain earnings.	(iii) Walter Model
(D) Dividend payout is irrelevant to the value of the firm.	(iv) Modigliani and Miller Model

Codes:	**A**	**B**	**C**	**D**
(a)	(ii)	(iii)	(i)	(iv)
(b)	(i)	(ii)	(iv)	(iii)
(c)	(iv)	(i)	(iii)	(ii)
(d)	(iii)	(iv)	(ii)	(i)

44. Venture capital financing at starting stage is generally not done through
(a) Debt instruments
(b) Deep discount bonds
(c) Equity shares
(d) Conditional loans

45. Match the statements in List-I with the types of lease in the List-II as follows:

List-I	**List-II**
(A) Lessor transfers all risks and rewards of an asset to the lessee	(i) Indirect lease
(B) Lessor transfers the assets to the lessee but bears the cost of maintenance	(ii) Operating lease
(C) The owner of the asset sells it to the lessor who in turn leases it back to the owner (now lessee)	(iii) Finance lease
(D) Lessor owns/ acquires the assets that are leased to a given lessee.	(iv) Direct lease

Codes:	**A**	**B**	**C**	**D**
(a)	(ii)	(iii)	(iv)	(i)
(b)	(i)	(iv)	(ii)	(iii)

(c)	(iii)	(ii)	(i)	(iv)
(d)	(iv)	(i)	(iii)	(ii)

46. Full details for the issue of ADRs by a company must be furnished within 30 days from the date of its closure to
    (a) Securities and Exchange Commission (SEC)
    (b) Reserve Bank of India (RBI)
    (c) Securities and Exchange Board of India (SEBI)
    (d) Company Law Board (CLB)
47. The degree to which the returns of the two securities change together, is reflected by
    (a) Correlation (b) Leverage
    (c) Covariance (d) Beta
48. The transfer by a company of one or more of its business divisions to another newly set up company is called
    (a) Demerger (b) Merger
    (c) Equity Carve-out (d) Disinvestment
49. What combination of the following factors influences the working capital requirement?
    (i) Market Conditions
    (ii) Production Policy
    (iii) Firm's goodwill
    (iv) Supply conditions
    Codes:
    (a) (i), (ii) and (iii) (b) (ii), (iii) and (iv)
    (c) (i), (iii) and (iv) (d) (i), (ii) and (iv)
50. Which of the followings are the modern methods of performance appraisal?
    (i) 360 degree performance appraisal.
    (ii) Graphic rating scale.
    (iii) Management By Objectives (MBO).
    (iv) Forced distribution method.
    (v) Behaviourally Anchored Rating Scales (BARS).
    Select the correct answer from the codes given below:
    (a) (i), (ii), (iii) (b) (ii), (iv), (v)
    (c) (i), (iii), (v) (d) (iv), (ii), (i)
51. Which of the following principle serves as a warning to organisations not to take the selection and promotion process lightly?
    (a) Promotion Principle
    (b) Drucker Principle
    (c) Validity Principle
    (d) Peter Principle
52. According to D. Katz morale has four dimensions:
    (i) Jobs satisfaction.
    (ii) Satisfaction with wages and Promotional opportunities.
    (iii) Identification with company.
    (iv) Pride in the work group.
    (v) Top Management Support.
    Select the correct combination.
    (a) (i), (ii), (iii) and (iv)
    (b) (i), (ii), (iii) and (v)
    (c) (i), (ii), (iv), and (v)
    (d) (i), (iii), (iv) and (v)
53. HRM is viewed as a management process, consisting of four functional activities:
    (i) Acquisition (ii) Motivation
    (iii) Development
    (iv) Resolution of industrial disputes
    (v) Maintenance
    Select the correct combination.
    (a) (i), (ii), (iii) and (iv)
    (b) (i), (ii), (iii) and (v)
    (c) (i), (ii), (iv) and (v)
    (d) (i), (iii), (iv) and (v)
54. OCTAPAC stands for
    (a) Order, Co-ordination, Trust, Authority, Personality and Cooperation.
    (b) Openness, Confrontation, Trust, Authenticity, Pro-action and Collaboration.
    (c) Organisation, Conflict, Team, Authority, People and Collaboration.
    (d) Oneness, Compromise, Tress pass, Authority, Protection and Combination.
55. Technique of 'Transaction Analysis' was developed by
    (a) Elton Mayo (b) Peter Drucker
    (c) Eric Berne (d) Adam Smith
56. Which one of the following methods is not a demand forecasting method of Human Resource Planning?
    (a) Managerial judgement
    (b) Managerial grid
    (c) Work study techniques
    (d) Statistical techniques
57. Transaction of Internet Banking excludes
    (a) Withdrawal of cash anywhere in India.
    (b) Statement of account for a specific period.

(c) Transfer of funds from one account to another account.
(d) Balance enquiry.

58. Which among the following is not a category of Non-Performing Assets?
(a) Substandard Assets (b) Doubtful Debts
(c) Loss Assets (d) Devaluated Assets

59. When a loan will be NPA?
(a) Interest and/or loan instalments overdue for more than 90 days.
(b) Account is out of order for more than 90 days in case of overdraft/cash credit.
(c) Bill remains overdue for more than 90 days.
(d) All of the above.

60. **Assertion (A):** "The problem of rural credit is not primarily one of rural credit, it may be said to be one of rural minded credit."
Reason (R): The Indian economy has yet to come out of rural mentality.
Codes:
(a) Both (A) and (R) are correct.
(b) Both (A) and (R) are incorrect.
(c) (A) is correct, but (R) is incorrect.
(d) (R) is correct, but (A) is incorrect.

61. Match the items of List-I with the items of List-II and select the correct answer:

List-I	List-II
(i) Debit card	(A) Several storage
(ii) Credit card	(B) Online recovery of amount
(iii) Electronic purse	(C) Image processing use
(iv) Cheque function	(D) Revolving credit

Codes:	(i)	(ii)	(iii)	(iv)
(a)	(C)	(A)	(D)	(B)
(b)	(A)	(B)	(D)	(C)
(c)	(D)	(C)	(A)	(B)
(d)	(D)	(C)	(B)	(A)

62. **Assertion (A):** The Indian economy could survive in the recent global recession due to its strong banking system.
Reason (R): The Indian economy contains a large amount of black money.
Codes:
(a) Both (A) and (R) are correct and (R) is the explanation of (A).
(b) Both (A) and (R) are correct, but (R) is not the correct explanation of (A).
(c) (R) is correct, but (A) is not the appropriate assertion of (R).
(d) Both (A) and (R) are incorrect.

63. **Assertion (A):** Most of the development bank in India have setup private commercial banks after the introduction of capital adequacy norms.
Reason (R): Development banks in India have not adhered to their basic objectives.
Codes:
(a) (A) and (R) both are correct, and (R) is correct explanation of (A).
(b) (A) and (R) both are correct, but (R) is not a correct explanation of (A).
(c) (A) is correct, but (R) is incorrect.
(d) (R) is correct, but (A) is incorrect.

64. Match the following items of List-I with List-II:

List-I	List-II
(A) Brettonwoods conference	(i) 1947
(B) General Agreement on Trade and Tariffs	(ii) 1964
(C) ACCRA conference	(iii) 1944
(D) United Nations Conference on Trade and Development	(iv) 2008

Codes:	(i)	(ii)	(iii)	(iv)
(a)	(B)	(D)	(A)	(C)
(b)	(B)	(D)	(C)	(A)
(c)	(B)	(C)	(D)	(A)
(d)	(C)	(A)	(B)	(D)

65. The forces that lend momentum to the process of globalization have been identified by Michael Porter include the following:
(i) Fluid global capital market.
(ii) Technological restructuring.
(iii) Decreasing religious command.
(iv) Ethnic decontrol.
(v) New-global competitors.
(vi) End of the 'cold war' in 1990s.
Codes:
(a) (vi), (v), (iv) and (iii)
(b) (vi), (iii), (ii) and (i)
(c) (vi), (v), (ii) and (i)
(d) (iv), (iii), (ii) and (i)

66. **Statement (I):** Green Box subsidies include amount spent on Government services such as research, disease control, infrastructure and food security.

Statement (II): Blue Box subsidies are certain direct payments made to farmers, to limit production, and are certain government assistance programmes to encourage agriculture and rural development.

Codes:

(a) Statement (I) is correct, but (II) is not correct.
(b) Statement (II) is correct, but (I) is not correct.
(c) Both statement (I) and (II) are correct.
(d) Both statement (I) and (II) are incorrect.

67. **Assertion (A):** The major economic powers have succeeded in creating a new international regime where the profits and the dominance of their transnational corporations will be the decisive consideration.

Reason (R): This regime will legitimise the process of progressive erosion of the sovereign economic space of the third-world countries.

(a) Both (A) and (R) are correct, and (R) is the right explanation of (A).
(b) Both (A) and (R) are correct, but (R) is not the right explanation of (A).
(c) Both (A) and (R) are incorrect.
(d) (R) is correct, but (A) is not correct.

68. **Assertion (A):** The 'Balance of Payments' presents a classified record of all receipts on account of goods exported, services rendered and capital received by 'residents' and payments made by them on account of goods imported and services received from capital transferred to 'non-residents' or 'foreigners'.

Reason (R): The 'Balance of Payments' of a country is a systematic record of all economic transactions between the 'residents' of a country and the rest of the world.

(a) Both (A) and (R) are correct and (R) is the right explanation of (A).
(b) Both (A) and (R) are correct, but (R) is not the right explanation of (A).
(c) (R) is correct, but (A) is not correct.
(d) Both (A) and (R) are incorrect.

69. Which among the following is not rightly explained?

(i) M_1 = Currency with the public + demand deposits of the public.
(ii) $M_2 = M_1$ + Post Office Savings Deposits.
(iii) $M_3 = M_1$ + Time Deposits of the public with Banks.
(iv) $M_4 = M_3$ + Total Post Office Deposits.
(v) M_1 = Narrow money
(vi) M_3 = Broad money

(a) Only (v) and (vi) (b) Only (i) and (iii)
(c) Only (vi) (d) None of the above

70. Which of the following are not effect of dumping on importing country?

(i) Domestic industry might be affected adversely by a decline in sales and profits.
(ii) If dumping is continued for a longer period, survival of the domestic industry may be threatened.
(iii) Dumping may create BOP problems for the country.
(iv) It finds market for its surplus production.

Codes:

(a) (i), (ii), (iii) and (iv) (b) (ii), (iii) and (iv)
(c) (iii) and (iv) (d) Only (iv)

71. Donation to National Children's Fund will come in which of the following deduction under Sec. 80G of Income Tax Act, 1961.

(a) 100 percent deduction without any qualifying limit.
(b) 50 percent deduction without any qualifying limit.
(c) 100 percent deduction subject to qualifying limit.
(d) 50 percent deduction subject to qualifying limit.

72. If the taxable income of a domestic company for the Assessment Year 2011-12 is ₹ 9,00,000, its tax liability will be

(a) ₹ 2,76,800 (b) ₹ 2,78,100
(c) ₹ 3,70,800 (d) ₹ 3,70,880

73. Unabsorbed depreciation which could not be setoff in the same assessment year, can be carried forward upto

(a) 4 years (b) 8 years
(c) 10 years (d) Indefinite period

74. If the book profits of a partnership firm is ₹ 1,10,000, the remuneration admissible to working partners under Sec. 40(b) of the Income Tax Act, 1961 is
    (a) ₹ 1,10,000 (b) ₹1,50,000
    (c) ₹ 99,000 (d) None of the above

75. Which of the following expenses is inadmissible while computing income from other sources?
    (a) Interest paid on amounts borrowed to meet tax liabilities.
    (b) Collection charges paid to the banker or any other person to collect interest/dividend.
    (c) Interest on loan taken to invest in securities.
    (d) Depreciation on let-out machinery and plant

ANSWERS

1. (d)	2. (b)	3. (b)	4. (a)	5. (d)
6. (b)	7. (b)	8. (d)	9. (c)	10. (d)
11. (c)	12. (a)	13. (b)	14. (b)	15. (b)
16. (a)	17. (b)	18. (d)	19. (c)	20. (a)
21. (a)	22. (d)	23. (b)	24. (c)	25. (d)
26. (b)	27. (a)	28. (b)	29. (c)	30. (c)
31. (c)	32. (c)	33. (b)	34. (c)	35. (b)
36. (a)	37. (a)	38. (d)	39. (c)	40. (a)
41. (c)	42. (c)	43. (a)	44. (b)	45. (c)
46. (b)	47. (c)	48. (a)	49. (d)	50. (c)
51. (d)	52. (a)	53. (b)	54. (b)	55. (c)
56. (b)	57. (a)	58. (d)	59. (d)	60. (c)
61. (b)	62. (b)	63. (c)	64. (a)	65. (c)
66. (c)	67. (b)	68. (a)	69. (d)	70. (d)
71. (b)	72. (b)	73. (d)	74. (b)	75. (a)

DECEMBER–2013

Note: This paper contains Sixty (60) multiple-choice questions, each question carrying two (2) marks. Candidate is expected to answer any Fifty (50) questions. In case more than Fifty (50) questions are attempted, only the first Fifty (50) questions will be evaluated.

PAPER–I

1. The post-industrial society is designated as
   (a) Information society
   (b) Technology society
   (c) Mediated society
   (d) Non-agricultural society

2. The initial efforts for Internet-based communication was for
   (a) Commercial communication
   (b) Military purposes
   (c) Personal interaction
   (d) Political campaigns

3. Internal communication within institutions is done through
   (a) LAN (b) WAN (c) EBB (d) MMS

4. Virtual reality provides
   (a) Sharp pictures
   (b) Individual audio
   (c) Participatory experience
   (d) Preview of new films

5. The first virtual university of India came up in
   (a) Andhra Pradesh (b) Maharashtra
   (c) Uttar Pradesh (d) Tamil Nadu

6. Arrange the following books in chronological order in which they appeared. Use the codes given below:
   (i) *Limits to Growth*
   (ii) *Silent Spring*
   (iii) *Our Common Future*
   (iv) *Resourceful Earth*

   Codes:
   (a) (i), (iii), (iv), (ii)
   (b) (ii), (iii), (i), (iv)
   (c) (ii), (i), (iii), (iv)
   (d) (i), (ii), (iii), (iv)

7. Which one of the following continents is at a greater risk of desertification?
   (a) Africa (b) Asia
   (c) South America (d) North America

8. "Women are closer to nature than men." What kind of perspective is this?
   (a) Realist (b) Essentialist
   (c) Feminist (d) Deep ecology

9. Which one of the following is not a matter a global concern in the removal of tropical forests?
   (a) Their ability to absorb the chemicals that contribute to depletion of ozone layer.
   (b) Their role in maintaining the oxygen and carbon balance of the earth.
   (c) Their ability to regulate surface and air temperatures, moisture content and reflectivity.
   (d) Their contribution to the biological diversity of the planet.

10. The most comprehensive approach to address the problems of man-environment interaction is one of the following:
    (a) Natural Resource Conservation Approach
    (b) Urban-industrial Growth Oriented Approach
    (c) Rural-agricultural Growth Oriented Approach
    (d) Watershed Development Approach

11. The major source of the pollutant gas, carbon monooxide (CO), in urban areas is
    (a) Thermal power sector
    (b) Transport sector
    (c) Industrial sector
    (d) Domestic sector

12. In a fuel cell driven vehicle, the energy is obtained from the combustion of
    (a) Methane (b) Hydrogen
    (c) LPG (d) CNG

13. Which one of the following Councils has been disbanded in 2013?
    (a) Distance Education Council (DEC)
    (b) National Council for Teacher Education (NCTE)
    (c) National Council of Educational Research and Training (NCERT)
    (d) National Assessment and Accreditation Council (NAAC)
14. Which of the following statements are correct about the National Assessment and Accreditation Council?
    1. It is an autonomous institution.
    2. It is tasked with the responsibility of assessing and accrediting institutions of higher education.
    3. It is located in Delhi.
    4. It has regional offices.

    Select the correct answer from the codes given below:

    Codes:

    (a) 1 and 3 (b) 1 and 2
    (c) 1, 2 and 4 (d) 2, 3 and 4
15. The power of the Supreme Court of India to decide disputes between two or more States falls under its
    (a) Advisory Jurisdiction
    (b) Appellate Jurisdiction
    (c) Original Jurisdiction
    (d) Writ Jurisdiction
16. Which of the following statements are correct?
    1. There are seven Union Territories in India.
    2. Two Union Territories have Legislative Assemblies
    3. One Union Territory has a High Court.
    4. One Union Territory is the capital of two States.

    Select the correct answer from the codes given below:

    Codes:

    (a) 1 and 3 (b) 2 and 4
    (c) 2, 3 and 4 (d) 1, 2, 3 and 4
17. Which of the following statements are correct about the Central Information Commission?
    1. The Central Information Commission is a statutory body.
    2. The Chief Information Commissioner and other Information Commissioners are appointed by the President of India.
    3. The Commission can impose a penalty upto a maximum of ₹ 25,000
    4. It can punish an errant officer.

    Select the correct answer from the codes given below:

    Codes:

    (a) 1 and 2 (b) 1, 2 and 4
    (c) 1, 2 and 3 (d) 2, 3 and 4
18. Who among the following conducted the CNN-IBN-The Hindu 2013 Election Tracker Survey across 267 constituencies in 18 States?
    (a) The Centre for the Study of Developing Societies (CSDS)
    (b) The Association for Democratic Reforms (ADR)
    (c) CNN and IBN
    (d) CNN, IBN and The Hindu
19. In certain code TEACHER is written as VGCEJGT. The code of CHILDREN will be
    (a) EKNJFTGP (b) EJKNFTGP
    (c) KNJFGTP (d) None of these
20. A person has to buy both apples and mangoes. The cost of one apple is ₹ 7 whereas that of a mango is ₹ 5. If the person has ₹ 38, the number of apples he can buy is
    (a) 1 (b) 2 (c) 3 (d) 4
21. A man pointing to a lady said, "The son of her only brother is the brother of my wife". The lady is related to the man as
    (a) Mother's sister
    (b) Grandmother
    (c) Mother-in-law
    (d) Sister of father-in-law
22. In this series
    6, 4, 1, 2, 2, 8, 7, 4, 2, 1, 5, 3, 8, 6, 2, 2, 7, 1, 4, 1, 3, 5, 8, 6, how many pairs of successive numbers have a difference of 2 each?
    (a) 4 (b) 5 (c) 6 (d) 8
23. The mean marks obtained by a class of 40 students is 65. The mean marks of half of the students is found to be 45. The mean marks of the remaining students is

(a) 85 (b) 60 (c) 70 (d) 65

24. Anil is twice as old as Sunita. Three years ago, he was three times as old as Sunita. The present age of Anil is
    (a) 6 years (b) 8 years
    (c) 12 years (d) 16 years

25. Which of the following is a social network?
    (a) amazon.com (b) eBay
    (c) gmail.com (d) Twitter

26. The population information is called parameter while the corresponding sample information is known as
    (a) Universe (b) Inference
    (c) Sampling design (d) Statistics

Read the following passage carefully and answer questions 27 to 32:

Heritage conservation practices improved worldwide after the International Centre for the Study of the Preservation and Restoration of Cultural Property (ICCROM) was established with UNESCO's assistance in 1959. The inter-governmental organisation with 126 member states has done a commendable job by training more than 4,000 professionals, providing practice standards, and sharing technical expertise. In this golden jubilee year, as we acknowledge its key role in global conservation, an assessment of international practices would be meaningful to the Indian conservation movement. Consistent investment, rigorous attention, and dedicated research and dissemination are some of the positive lessons to imbibe. Countries such as Italy have demonstrated that prioritising heritage with significant budget provision pays. On the other hand, India, which is no less endowed in terms of cultural capital, has a long way to go. Surveys indicate that in addition to the 6,600 protected monuments, there are over 60,000 equally valuable heritage structures that await attention. Besides the small group in the service of Archaeological Survey of India, there are only about 150 trained conservation professionals. In order to overcome this severe shortage the emphasis has been on setting up dedicated labs and training institutions. It would make much better sense for conservation to be made part of mainstream research and engineering institutes, as has been done in Europe.

Increasing funding and building institutions are the relatively easy part. The real challenge is to redefine international approaches to address local contexts. Conservation cannot limit itself to enhancing the art-historical value of the heritage structures, which international charters perhaps overemphasise. The effort has to be broad-based. It must also serve as a means to improving the quality of life in the area where the heritage structures are located. The first task therefore is to integrate conservation efforts with sound development plans that take care of people living in the heritage vicinity. Unlike in western countries, many traditional building crafts survive in India, and conservation practices offer an avenue to support them. This has been acknowledged by the Indian National Trust for Art and Cultural Heritage charter for conservation but is yet to receive substantial state support. More strength for heritage conservation can be mobilised by aligning it with the green building movement. Heritage structures are essentially eco-friendly and conservation could become a vital part of the sustainable building practices campaign in future.

27. The outlook for conservation heritage changed
    (a) after the establishment of the International Centre for the Study of the Preservation and Restoration of Cultural Property.
    (b) after training the specialists in the field.
    (c) after extending UNESCO's assistance to the educational institutions.
    (d) after ASI's measures to protect the monuments.

28. The inter-government organization was appreciated because of
    (a) increasing number of members to 126.
    (b) imparting training to professionals and sharing technical expertise.
    (c) consistent investment in conservation.
    (d) its proactive role in renovation and restoration.

29. Indian conservation movement will be successful if there would be
    (a) Financial support from the Government of India.

(b) Non-governmental organisation's role and participation in the conservation movement.
(c) consistent investment, rigorous attention, and dedicated research and dissemination of awareness for conservation.
(d) Archaeological Survey of India's meaningful assistance.

30. As per the surveys of historical monuments in India, there is very small number of protected monuments. As per given the total number of monuments and enlisted number of protected monuments, percentage comes to
(a) 10 percent (b) 11 percent
(c) 12 percent (d) 13 percent

31. What should India learn from Europe to conserve our cultural heritage?
(i) There should be significant budget provision to conserve our cultural heritage.
(ii) Establish dedicated labs and training institutions.
(iii) Force the government to provide sufficient funds.
(iv) Conservation should be made part of mainstream research and engineering institutes.

Choose correct answer from the codes given below:
(a) (i), (ii), (iii), (iv) (b) (i), (ii), (iv)
(c) (i), (ii) (d) (i), (iii), (iv)

32. INTACH is known for its contribution for conservation of our cultural heritage. The full form of INTACH is
(a) International Trust for Art and Cultural Heritage
(b) Intra-national Trust for Art and Cultural Heritage
(c) Integrated Trust for Art and Cultural Heritage
(d) Indian National Trust for Art and Cultural Heritage

33. While delivering lecture if there is some disturbance in the class, a teacher should
(a) keep quiet for a while and then continue.
(b) punish those causing disturbance.
(c) motivate to teach those causing disturbance.
(d) not bother of what is happening in the class.

34. Effective teaching is a function of
(a) Teacher's satisfaction.
(b) Teacher's honesty and commitment.
(c) Teacher's making students learn and understand.
(d) Teacher's liking for professional excellence.

35. The most appropriate meaning of learning is
(a) Acquisition of skills
(b) Modification of behaviour
(c) Personal adjustment
(d) Inculcation of knowledge

36. Arrange the following teaching process in order:
(i) Relate the present knowledge with previous one
(ii) Evaluation
(iii) Reteaching
(iv) Formulating instructional objectives
(v) Presentation of instructional materials
(a) (i), (ii), (iii), (iv), (v)
(b) (ii), (i), (iii), (iv), (v)
(c) (v), (iv), (iii), (i), (ii)
(d) (iv), (i), (v), (ii), (iii)

37. CIET stands for
(a) Centre for Integrated Education and Technology
(b) Central Institute for Engineering and Technology
(c) Central Institute for Education Technology
(d) Centre for Integrated Evaluation Techniques.

38. Teacher's role at higher education level is to
(a) provide information to students.
(b) promote self-learning in students.
(c) encourage healthy competition among students.
(d) help students to solve their problems.

39. The Verstehen School of Understanding was popularised by
(a) German Social Scientists
(b) American Philosophers
(c) British Academicians
(d) Italian Political Analysts

40. The sequential operations in scientific research are
   (a) Co-variation, Elimination of Spurious Relations, Generalisation, Theorisation
   (b) Generalisation, Co-variation, Theorisation, Elimination of Spurious Relations
   (c) Theorisation, Generalisation, Elimination of Spurious Relations, Co-variation
   (d) Elimination of Spurious Relations, Theorisation, Generalisation, Co-variation.

41. In sampling, the lottery method is used for
   (a) Interpretation (b) Theorisation
   (c) Conceptualisation (d) Randomisation

42. Which is the main objective of research?
   (a) To review the literature
   (b) To summarize what is already known
   (c) To get an academic degree
   (d) To discover new facts or to make fresh interpretation of known facts

43. Sampling error decreases with the
   (a) decrease in sample size
   (b) increase in sample size
   (c) process of randomization
   (d) process of analysis

44. The principles of fundamental research are used in
   (a) action research
   (b) applied research
   (c) philosophical research
   (d) historical research

45. Users who use media for their own ends are identified as
   (a) Passive audience (b) Active audience
   (c) Positive audience (d) Negative audience

46. Classroom communication can be described as
   (a) Exploration
   (b) Institutionalisation
   (c) Unsignified narration
   (d) Discourse

47. Ideological codes shape our collective
   (a) Productions (b) Perceptions
   (c) Consumptions (d) Creations

48. In communication, myths have power, but are
   (a) Uncultural (b) Insignificant
   (c) Imprecise (d) Unpreferred

49. The first multi-lingual news agency of India was
   (a) Samachar (b) API
   (c) Hindustan Samachar (d) Samachar Bharati

50. Organisational communication can also be equated with
   (a) intra-personal communication
   (b) inter-personal communication
   (c) group communication
   (d) mass communication

51. If two propositions having the same subject and predicate terms are such that one is the denial of the other, the relationship between them is called
   (a) Contradictory (b) Contrary
   (c) Sub-contrary (d) Sub-alternation

52. Ananya and Krishna can speak and follow English. Bulbul can write and speak Hindi as Archana does. Archana talks with Ananya also in Bengali. Krishna cannot follow Bengali. Bulbul talks with Ananya in Hindi. Who can speak and follow English, Hindi and Bengali?
   (a) Archana (b) Bulbul
   (c) Ananya (d) Krishna

53. A stipulative definition may be said to be
   (a) Always true
   (b) Always false
   (c) Sometimes true, sometimes false
   (d) Neither true nor false

54. When the conclusion of an argument follows from its premise/premises conclusively, the argument is called
   (a) Circular argument
   (b) Inductive argument
   (c) Deductive argument
   (d) Analogical argument

55. Saturn and Mars are planets like the Earth. They borrow light from the Sun and moves around the Sun as the Earth does. So those planets are inhabited by various orders of creatures as the Earth is.

   What type of argument is contained in the above passage?
   (a) Deductive (b) Astrological
   (c) Analogical (d) Mathematical

56. Given below are two premises. Four conclusions are drawn from those two premises in four codes. Select the code that states the conclusion validly drawn.

Premises:

(i) All saints are religious. (major)
(ii) Some honest persons are saints. (minor)

Codes:

(a) All saints are honest.
(b) Some saints are honest.
(c) Some honest persons are religious.
(d) All religious persons are honest.

Following table provides details about the Foreign Tourist Arrivals (FTAs) in India from different regions of the world in different years. Study the table carefully and answer questions from **57** to **60** based on this table.

Region	**Number of Foreign Tourist Arrivals**		
	2007	**2008**	**2009**
Western Europe	1686083	1799525	1610086
North America	1007276	1027297	1024469
South Asia	982428	1051846	982633
South East Asia	303475	332925	348495
East Asia	352037	355230	318292
West Asia	171661	215542	201110
Total FTAs in India	5081504	5282603	5108579

57. Find out the region that contributed around 20 percent of the total foreign tourist arrivals in India in 2009.
(a) Western Europe (b) North America
(c) South Asia (d) South East Asia

58. Which of the following regions has recorded the highest negative growth rate of foreign tourist arrivals in India in 2009?
(a) Western Europe (b) North America
(c) South Asia (d) West Asia

59. Find out the region that has been showing declining trend in terms of share of foreign tourist arrivals in India in 2008 and 2009.
(a) Western Europe (b) South East Asia
(c) East Asia (d) West Asia

60. Identify the region that has shown hyper growth rate of foreign tourist arrivals than the growth rate of the total FTAs in India in 2008.
(a) Western Europe (b) North America
(c) South Asia (d) East Asia

ANSWERS

1. (a)	2. (b)	3. (a)	4. (c)	5. (d)
6. (c)	7. (a)	8. (b)	9. (a)	10. (d)
11. (b)	12. (b)	13. (a)	14. (b)	15. (c)
16. (d)	17. (c)	18. (a)	19. (b)	20. (d)
21. (d)	22. (c)	23. (a)	24. (c)	25. (d)
26. (d)	27. (a)	28. (b)	29. (c)	30. (b)
31. (b)	32. (d)	33. (c)	34. (c)	35. (b)
36. (d)	37. (c)	38. (b)	39. (a)	40. (a)
41. (d)	42. (d)	43. (b)	44. (b)	45. (b)
46. (d)	47. (b)	48. (c)	49. (c)	50. (c)
51. (a)	52. (c)	53. (d)	54. (c)	55. (c)
56. (c)	57. (b)	58. (d)	59. (a)	60. (c)

PAPER II

Note: This paper contains fifty (50) objective type questions of two (2) marks each. All questions are compulsory.

1. Who is the fiscal agent and advisor to Government in monetary and financial matters?
(a) NABARD (b) SBI
(c) RBI (d) None of the above

2. Match the items of List-I with the items of List-II:

List-I	**List-II**
(A) National Manufacturing Competitiveness Council (NMCC)	(i) Industrial Licensing Policy

(B) National Investment Fund (NIP)		(ii) Eleventh Five Year Plan		
(C) The Industries (Development and Regulation) Act (IDRA), 1951		(iii) The Competition Act, 2002		
(D) Increase in Employment		(iv) Public Sector Undertakings		

Codes:	A	B	C	D
(a)	(iv)	(i)	(ii)	(iii)
(b)	(iii)	(iv)	(i)	(ii)
(c)	(i)	(ii)	(iii)	(iv)
(d)	(iv)	(iii)	(ii)	(i)

3. Kyoto Protocol pertains to
   (a) Capital formulation
   (b) Globalisation
   (c) Environmental protection
   (d) Unemployment reduction
4. Uruguay Round pertains to
   (a) WTO (b) IMF
   (c) GATT (d) World Bank
5. Which of the following are outside the scope of the Consumer Protection Act, 1986?
   (a) Newspaper industry
   (b) Services provided under contract of personal service
   (c) Banking industry
   (d) Both (a) and (b)
6. Which of the following is 'true' regarding the Prudence Principle of Accounting?
   (a) Taking care of the future losses
   (b) Taking care of the future profits
   (c) Taking care of bad debts
   (d) Taking care of inventory and depreciation
7. Which of the following is a non-operating expense?
   (a) Salary of Managing Director
   (b) Depreciation
   (c) Advertisement expenditure
   (d) Interest on loan
8. A and B are partners sharing profits in the ratio of 3 : 2. Their books showed goodwill at ₹ 3,000. C is admitted with 1/4th share of profits and brings ₹ 10,000 as his capital. But he is not able to bring in cash for his share of goodwill ₹ 3,000. How will you treat this?
   (a) Goodwill is raised by ₹ 12,000
   (b) C will remain as debtor for ₹ 3,000
   (c) C's A/c is debited for ₹ 3,000
   (d) Goodwill is raised by ₹ 9,000
9. If there is mutual indebtedness between the transferor company and the transferee company in business combination, which of the following is correct?
   (a) No adjustment is required in the books of the transferor company.
   (b) Adjustment is required in the books of the transferor company.
   (c) No adjustment is required in the books of the transferee company.
   (d) None of the above.
10. Improvement of profit-volume ratio can be done by
    (a) Increasing selling price
    (b) Altering sales mixture
    (c) Reducing variable cost
    (d) All of the above
11. Business Economics is a subject which
    (a) studies economic relationships
    (b) studies economic activities at the aggregate level
    (c) deals with the tools of economics used for decision making in business
    (d) studies optimum allocation of limited resources
12. Match List-I with List-II and select the correct code for the answer:

List-I	List-II
(A) Cross elasticity is zero	(i) Price = AVC
(B) Shut-down point are	(ii) Two commodities
(C) Slutsky	(iii) Transformation theorem line
(D) Production Possibility Curve	(iv) Substitution effect

Codes:	A	B	C	D
(a)	(ii)	(iv)	(i)	(iii)
(b)	(iii)	(ii)	(iv)	(i)
(c)	(i)	(iii)	(ii)	(iv)
(d)	(ii)	(i)	(iv)	(iii)

13. **Assertion (A):** The demand curve has negative slope showing inverse relationship between price and the quantity demanded.
    Reason (R): This applies only to Giffen goods.

Codes:
(a) Both (A) and (R) are true.
(b) (A) is true, but (R) is false.
(c) (A) is false, but (R) is true.
(d) Both (A) and (R) are false.

14. The consumer is said to be in equilibrium when he plans his expenditure on *x*, *y* and *z* commodities in such a way that he ultimately attains:
(a) $MU_x = MU_y = M_z$
(b) $\frac{MU_x}{P_x} = \frac{MU_x}{P_y} = \frac{MU_z}{P_z}$
(c) $\frac{MU_x}{P_x} = \frac{MU_y}{P_y} = \frac{MU_z}{P_z} = MU_m$
(d) $\frac{MU_x}{P_x} < \frac{MU_y}{P_y} < \frac{MU_z}{P_z} < MU_m$

15. Match the items in List-I with those in List-II and select the correct code for the answer:

List-I	List-II
(A) Monopoly	(i) Price taker
(B) Monopolistic competition	(ii) Homogeneous product's price maker
(C) Perfect competition	(iii) Heterogeneous product
(D) Oligopoly	(iv) Price Rigidity

Codes:	A	B	C	D
(a)	(ii)	(iii)	(i)	(iv)
(b)	(i)	(ii)	(iv)	(iii)
(c)	(iii)	(iv)	(ii)	(i)
(d)	(iv)	(i)	(iii)	(ii)

16. Match the following items in List-I with most suitable options in List-II:

List-I	List-II
(A) Fisher	(i) Inverse probability
(B) Karl Pearson	(ii) Normal Distribution
(C) Thomas Baye's	(iii) Correlation Coefficient
(D) Karl Gauss	(iv) Index Numbers

Codes:	A	B	C	D
(a)	(iv)	(iii)	(ii)	(i)
(b)	(iv)	(iii)	(i)	(ii)
(c)	(iv)	(ii)	(iii)	(i)
(d)	(iv)	(ii)	(i)	(iii)

17. The law of statistics, which says 'Moderately large number of items chosen at random from a large group possess the characteristics of the large group', is referred to as:
(a) The Central Limit Theorem
(b) The Law of Statistical Regularity
(c) The Law of Inertia of Large Numbers
(d) None of the above

18. A distribution, where the value of arithmetic mean is maximum as compared to median and mode, is
(a) Normal distribution
(b) Positively-skewed distribution
(c) Negatively-skewed distribution
(d) None of these

19. The most appropriate average to be used to compute the average rate of growth in population is
(a) Arithmetic mean (b) Median
(c) Geometric mean (d) Harmonic mean

20. "The life expectancy of people in Kerala is more than that of Tamil Nadu." This statement is an example of
(a) Descriptive Hypothesis
(b) Causal Hypothesis
(c) Correlational Hypothesis
(d) None of the above

21. Match the items of List-I with the items of List-II and choose the correct answer:

List-I	List-II
(A) Intrapersonal communication	(i) Information sharing
(B) Element of a communication event	(ii) Development of 'will' to work
(C) Objective of organisational communication	(iii) Thinking
(D) Goals of organisational communication	(iv) Purpose

Codes:	A	B	C	D
(a)	(i)	(ii)	(iii)	(iv)
(b)	(iii)	(iv)	(ii)	(i)
(c)	(ii)	(iii)	(i)	(iv)
(d)	(iv)	(iii)	(ii)	(i)

22. According to the Boston Consulting Group, a business which has a high growth rate but a weak market share is referred to as a
(a) Cash Cow (b) Dog
(c) Question Mark (d) Star

23. 'No ideas are ever criticized' and 'the more radical the ideas are the better'—are the rules of which decision-making process?
(a) Programmed decision-making
(b) Non-programmed decision-making
(c) Brainstorming
(d) Group discussion

24. According to McClelland's Needs Theory, which of the following is not a motivating need?
(a) Need for Power
(b) Need for Security
(c) Need for Achievement
(d) Need for Affiliation

25. In the managerial grid, developed by Blake and Mouton, a manager who has high consideration for production but little concern for people is known as
(a) 1.1 Management (b) 1.9 Management
(c) 9.1 Management (d) 5.5 Management

26. Which of the following is not the major component of holistic marketing?
(a) Relationship marketing
(b) Integrated marketing
(c) Customer satisfaction
(d) Socially-responsible marketing

27. Which of the legislations listed below do not form part of the marketing environment of India?
(a) The Drugs and Cosmetics Act, 1940
(b) The Prevention of Food and Adulteration Act, 1954
(c) The Monopolies and Restrictive Trade Practices Act, 1969
(d) Both (b) and (c)

28. The set of all actual and potential buyers of a product is known as
(a) Customer group
(b) Industry
(c) Market
(d) None of the above

29. In the model of consumer behaviour given by Philip Kotler, what constitutes the marketing stimuli?
(a) Marketing environment
(b) Four P's of marketing
(c) Consumer needs and wants
(d) None of the above

30. The factor that exerts the broadest and deepest influence on consumer behaviour is
(a) Culture (b) Sub-culture
(c) Social class (d) Income

31. Which one of the following is not among the assumptions of the Modigliani-Miller model?
(a) Perfect capital market
(b) Equivalent risk classes
(c) Unity for dividend payout ratio
(d) Absence of taxes

32. The most suitable coverage ratio for deciding the debt capacity of a firm is
(a) Interest Coverage Ratio
(b) Cash Flow Coverage Ratio
(c) Debt Service Coverage Ratio
(d) Fixed Assets Coverage Ratio

33. Which one of the following is the most popular method for estimating the cost of equity?
(a) Capital asset pricing model
(b) Dividend yield method
(c) Gordon's dividend discount model
(d) Earnings yield method

34. Which one of the following is not the internal factor affecting the weighted average cost of capital of a firm?
(a) Investment policy of the firm
(b) Capital structure of the firm
(c) Dividend policy followed
(d) Market risk premium for the firm

35. Most common approach for analysing the capital structure of a firm is
(a) Ratio Analysis
(b) Cash Flow Analysis
(c) Comparative Analysis
(d) Leverage Analysis

36. Who propounded "Theory Z"?
(a) William Ouchi (b) Peter F. Drucker
(c) Joseph H. Jurau (d) Douglas McGregor

37. Another name for MATRIX organisation is
(a) Flexible organisation
(b) Geographic organisation
(c) Project organisation
(d) None of the above

38. Which of the following are methods of on-the-job training?

(i) Coaching (ii) Vestibule training
(iii) Demonstration (iv) Role-playing
(v) Apprenticeship training

Select the right answer from the following codes:

(a) (i), (ii), (iii), (iv) (b) (i), (iii), (v)
(c) (ii), (iii), (iv) (d) (i), (ii), (iii), (iv), (v)

39. The idea that a manager tends to be promoted to the level of his incompetence is referred to as
(a) The advancement principle
(b) The Parkinson's law
(c) The Peter principle
(d) The job design principle

40. **Assertion (A):** The emphasis in industrial psychology has shifted from the studies of the isolated individual and the physical environment to the consideration of motivation and morale.

Reason (R): A motivated employee with a high morale will always give high productivity.

Codes:
(a) Both (A) and (R) are correct, and (R) is the right explanation of (A).
(b) (A) is correct, but (R) is not correct.
(c) Both (A) and (R) are incorrect.
(d) Both (A) and (R) are correct, but (R) is not the right explanation of (A).

41. Match the following items of List-I and List-II in terms of functions of commercial banks:

	List-I		**List-II**
(A)	Letter of reference	(i)	Advancing loans
(B)	Sale of gold coins	(ii)	Receiving deposits
(C)	Recurring Account	(iii)	Non-banking function
(D)	Overdrafts	(iv)	Agency function

Codes:	**A**	**B**	**C**	**D**
(a)	(i)	(ii)	(iii)	(iv)
(b)	(iv)	(iii)	(ii)	(i)
(c)	(iv)	(ii)	(iii)	(i)
(d)	(i)	(iii)	(ii)	(iv)

42. Which of the following are included under representation functions of a bank?
(i) Payment of cheques and bills
(ii) Providing remittance facilities
(iii) Underwriting of securities
(iv) Advancing clean credit
(v) Allowing overdrafts on current account
(vi) Purchase and sale of securities

Codes:
(a) (i), (ii), (iii) and (iv)
(b) (iii), (iv), (v) and (vi)
(c) (i), (ii), (iii) and (vi)
(d) (ii), (iii), (v) and (vi)

43. Call money rate is applicable for a very short period to
(a) Inter bank advances
(b) Bank to Reserve Bank advances
(c) Reserve Bank to Bank advances
(d) Commercial Banks to Industrial Banks advances

44. Match the following List-I with List-II:

	List-I (Name of Securities)		**List-II (Type of Securities)**
(A)	Bonds of Land Development Banks	(i)	Semi-Government Securities
(B)	Treasury Bills	(ii)	First Order Securities
(C)	Shares of a Public Ltd. Co.	(iii)	Personal Securities

Codes:	**A**	**B**	**C**
(a)	(i)	(ii)	(iii)
(b)	(ii)	(i)	(iii)
(c)	(iii)	(ii)	(i)
(d)	(i)	(iii)	(ii)

45. Reserve Bank of India controls the activities of some of the following banks in India:
(i) Commercial Banks (ii) Cooperative Banks
(iii) Foreign Banks (iv) Rural Banks

Codes:
(a) (i), (ii) and (iii) (b) (i), (iii) and (iv)
(c) (ii), (iii) and (iv) (d) (i), (ii), (iii) and (iv)

46. Match the following List-I with List-II and select the correct answer:

	List-I		**List-II**
(A)	Comparative Cost Theory of International Trade	(i)	Gottfried Haberler
(B)	International Trade Theory of Opportunity Cost	(ii)	J.S. Mill
(C)	Factor Endowment Theory of International Trade	(iii)	David Ricardo

(D) Doctrine of Reciprocal Demand (iv) Hecksher-Ohlin

Codes:	A	B	C	D
(a)	(iii)	(ii)	(iv)	(i)
(b)	(i)	(iii)	(ii)	(iv)
(c)	(iii)	(i)	(iv)	(ii)
(d)	(ii)	(i)	(iv)	(iii)

47. Identify the one, from the following, which is not a type of disequilibrium in the balance of payments of a country:
(a) Cyclical disequilibrium
(b) Secular disequilibrium
(c) Structural disequilibrium
(d) Sectoral disequilibrium

48. The participants who take advantage of different exchange rates in different markets are
(a) Speculators (b) Arbitrageurs
(c) Hedgers (d) Investors

49. **Assertion (A):** The liability of the option buyer is limited in the currency options market.
Reason (R): Option buyer need not exercise the option if the exchange rate is not favourable for him.
Codes:
(a) (R) is correct and (A) is wrong.
(b) (A) is correct and (R) is wrong.
(c) Both (A) and (R) are correct.
(d) Both (A) and (R) are wrong.

50. An MNC that maintains a balance between the home market and host market-oriented policies is
(a) Ethnocentric firm (b) Polycentric firm
(c) Geocentric firm (d) None of the above

ANSWERS

1. (c)	2. (b)	3. (c)	4. (c)	5. (b)
6. (a)	7. (d)	8. (d)	9. (a)	10. (d)
11. (c)	12. (d)	13. (b)	14. (c)	15. (a)
16. (b)	17. (b)	18. (b)	19. (c)	20. (c)
21. (b)	22. (c)	23. (c)	24. (b)	25. (c)
26. (c)	27. (d)	28. (c)	29. (b)	30. (a)
31. (c)	32. (b)	33. (a)	34. (d)	35. (c)
36. (a)	37. (c)	38. (b)	39. (c)	40. (b)
41. (b)	42. (c)	43. (a)	44. (a)	45. (d)
46. (c)	47. (d)	48. (b)	49. (c)	50. (c)

PAPER III

Note: This paper contains Seventy-five (75) objective type questions of two (2) marks each. All questions are compulsory.

1. The present regime of subsidies can be improved by focussing on
(i) Reducing the overall scale of subsidies.
(ii) Making subsidies as transparent as possible.
(iii) Giving a specific amount to the Member of Parliament for subsidies.
(iv) Setting clear limits on duration of any new subsidy scheme.
(v) Eliminating system of periodic review of subsidies.
(vi) Using subsidies for well-defined economic objectives.
Codes:
(a) (i), (ii), (iii) and (iv)
(b) (ii), (iii), (iv) and (v)
(c) (i), (iii), (iv) and (vi)
(d) (i), (ii), (iv) and (vi)

2. Which of the following is not regulated by The Competition Act, 2002?
(a) Abuse of dominant position
(b) Anti-competitive agreements
(c) Medical negligence
(d) Predatory pricing

3. The freedom of private enterprise is the greatest in the free-market economy. This is characterized by which of the following assumptions?
(i) The factors of production (labour, land, capital) are privately owned and production occurs at the initiative of the private enterprise.
(ii) Income is received in monetary form by the sale of services of the factors of production and from the profits of the private enterprise.

(iii) Members of the free-market economy have freedom of choice in so far as consumption, occupation, savings and investments are concerned.
(iv) The free-market economy is not planned, controlled or regulated by the government.
(v) The free market economy is prone to corrupt practices.

Codes:
(a) (i), (ii) and (iii)
(b) (i), (ii), (iii) and (iv)
(c) (i), (ii), (iii), (iv) and (v)
(d) (ii), (iii), (iv) and (v)

4. The important responsibilities of a business to the customers are
(i) To ensure family welfare of the customers.
(ii) To understand customer needs and to take the necessary measures to satisfy these needs.
(iii) To ensure health condition of the customers.
(iv) To ensure that the product supplied has no adverse effect on the customer.
(v) To provide an opportunity for being heard and to redress genuine grievances.

Codes:
(a) (i), (ii), (iii), (iv) and (v)
(b) (i), (ii), (iii) and (iv)
(c) (ii), (iv) and (v)
(d) (ii), (iii), (iv) and (v)

5. The rationale of expanding role of the public sector stems mainly from which of the following factors?
(i) The failure of the private sector in certain crucial areas
(ii) The exploitation of the society by the private sector
(iii) The revenue need of the Central Government
(iv) The demand of economic justice
(v) The need for accelerating the pace of economic growth

Codes:
(a) (i), (ii), (iii) and (iv)
(b) (ii), (iii), (iv) and (v)
(c) (i), (iii), (iv) and (v)
(d) (i), (ii), (iv) and (v)

6. Which of the following factors may lead to a sick industrial unit?
(i) Shortage of funds and faulty financial management
(ii) Investment by the FIIs in Indian industries
(iii) Unauthorized FDI in Indian industries
(iv) Lack of experience on the part of promoters
(v) Technological factors including obsolete or improper technology

Codes:
(a) (i), (ii), (iii) and (iv)
(b) (ii), (iii), (iv) and (v)
(c) (i), (iv) and (v)
(d) (i), (ii) and (iii)

7. Indicate what is not correct in respect of The Consumer Protection Act, 1986?
(a) No complaint can be entertained in respect of a product purchased more than two years back.
(b) A complaint against medical negligence can be filed by legal heir or representative of the deceased.
(c) A complaint involving a claim of ₹ 15 lakhs is to be filed before the State Commission.
(d) Both (a) and (c)

8. If bonus shares are issued out of preacquisition profit, it will have
(a) Direct effect on the Consolidated Balance Sheet
(b) No effect on the Consolidated Balance Sheet
(c) No effect on Net Profit
(d) None of the above

9. The present value of the future contributions of employees is one of the methods of
(a) HR Accounting
(b) Inflation Accounting
(c) Social Accounting
(d) Responsibility Accounting

10. A standard which can be attained under the most favourable working conditions is called
(a) Attainable Standard
(b) Basic Standard
(c) Current Standard
(d) Ideal Standard

11. Which of the following ratios are taken into consideration by a banker before sanctioning the loan?

(a) Proprietory Ratio
(b) Stock-Turnover Ratio
(c) Debt-Equity Ratio
(d) All of the above

12. Match the items of the following two lists:

List-I	List-II
(i) Zero-base Budgeting	(A) Internal Reconstruction
(ii) Goodwill or Capital Reserve	(B) Earnings Per Share
(iii) Reduction of Capital	(C) Control of Expenditure
(iv) Basic & Diluted	(D) Business Combination

Codes:	(i)	(ii)	(iii)	(iv)
(a)	(C)	(D)	(B)	(A)
(b)	(D)	(C)	(A)	(B)
(c)	(D)	(A)	(C)	(B)
(d)	(C)	(D)	(A	(B)

13. **Assertion (A)**: Dividend paid out of pre-acquisition profit by the subsidiary company to the holding company is deducted from the cost of investment.

Reason (R): Dividend paid out of pre-acquisition profit by the subsidiary company should be treated as a return of capital to the holding company.

Which one of the following is correct?
(a) Both (A) and (R) are correct.
(b) (A) is correct, but (R) is wrong.
(c) (A) is wrong, but (R) is correct.
(d) Both (A) and (R) are wrong.

14. Given below are two statements, one labelled as Assertion (A) and the other labelled as Reason (R):

Assertion (A): Increasing the value of closing inventory increases profit.

Reason (R): Increasing the value of closing inventory reduces cost of goods sold.

In the context of the above two statements, which of the following is correct?

Codes:
(a) Both (A) and (R) are correct.
(b) Only (A) is correct.
(c) Only (R) is correct.
(d) Both (A) and (R) are wrong.

15. Match the items of List-I with the items of List-II and select the correct code for the answer:

List-I	List-II
(A) Multiple plants	(i) $MRP_T = MC = MRP_X = MRP_{PY}$
(B) Cost-plus pricing	(ii) $MRT = MC = MR_1 = MR_2$
(C) Multiple markets	(iii) $MR = MCT = MC_A = MC_B$
(D) Multiple products	(iv) $P = (1 + m)$ ATC

Codes:	A	B	C	D
(a)	(iv)	(ii)	(i)	(iii)
(b)	(i)	(iii)	(iv)	(ii)
(c)	(ii)	(i)	(iii)	(iv)
(d)	(iii)	(iv)	(ii)	(i)

16. A measure of the responsiveness of quantity demanded to changes in the price of a related good is known as
(a) Cross Elasticity of Demand
(b) Substitution Elasticity of Demand
(c) Complementary Elasticity of Demand
(d) Price Elasticity of Demand

17. If the total cost is ₹ 260 and the total variable cost is ₹ 60, what will be total fixed cost if output is (i) 100 units and (ii) 200 units?
(a) ₹ 200 and ₹ 200 (b) ₹ 100 and ₹ 200
(c) ₹ 260 and ₹ 100 (d) ₹ 160 and ₹ 100

18. Optimal input combination to minimize the cost for a given output will be at the point where:
(a) Isocost is tangent to Isoquant
(b) MRTS between inputs is equal
(c) Any movement from optimum point will lead to low level of output
(d) All the above conditions are fulfilled.

19. What kinds of actions can be taken to put the rivals at a disadvantageous position under oligopoly market?
(a) Commitments (b) Threats
(c) Promises (d) All the above

20. There is no exceptions to the law of demand in the case of
(a) Giffen goods
(b) Normal goods

(c) Articles of conspicuous consumption
(d) Ignorance of the buyer

21. What is the degree of elasticity of demand in case the demand is represented by a straight line parallel to the x-axis?
(a) $e > 1$ (b) $e = 0$
(c) $e = \infty$ (d) $e < 1$

22. If a chi-square test is to be performed on a contingency table with 3 rows and 4 columns, how many degrees of freedom should be used?
(a) 6 (b) 12 (c) 8 (d) 9

23. **Assertion (A):** If regression coefficient of X on Y is greater than one, regression coefficient of Y on X must be less than one.
Reason (R): The geometric mean between two regression coefficients is the co-efficient of correlation.
On the basis of the above, choose the appropriate answer:
(a) (A) and (R) are correct.
(b) (A) is correct, but (R) is not correct.
(c) (A) is not correct, but (R) is correct.
(d) Both (A) and (R) are not correct.

24. If the sum of squares of deviations within samples is 140 with 12 degrees of freedom and the sum of squares of deviations between samples is 190 with 2 degrees of freedom, the test statistic will be
(a) 81.4 (b) 12.28 (c) 8.14 (d) 1.22

25. The regression equation of profits (X) on sales (Y) of a firm is given as:
$3Y - 5X + 110 = 0$. If the sales of the firm is ₹ 44,000, the profit will be
(a) ₹ 23,370 (b) ₹ 26,422
(c) ₹ 24,422 (d) ₹ 21,370

26. Cricketer 'A' scores on an average 40 runs with a standard deviation of 5. Scores of players 'B' and 'C', on an average, are 75 and 90 with standard deviations 10 and 18, respectively. Arrange the players in the descending order of consistency.
(a) A, B and C (b) C, B and A
(c) B, A and C (d) C, A and B

27. Among the following, choose the most suitable 'test' that can be applied to examine the influence of one factor on different groups:
(a) 't' test (b) 'F' test
(c) 'Chi-square' test (d) None of the above

28. A machine produced 20 defective articles in a batch of 400. After overhauling, it produced 10% defectives in a batch of 300. Which test of hypothesis can be applied to the above situation to examine whether the machine has improved?
(a) Test of significance of a sample proportion (two-tail test)
(b) Test of significance of a sample proportion (one-tail test)
(c) Test of significance of difference between two sample proportion (two-tail test)
(d) Test of significance of difference between two sample proportion (one-tail test)

29. Strategies and policies
(a) are not closely related
(b) give direction
(c) are the framework for performance appraisal
(d) Both (a) and (b)

30. According to Vroom's Expectancy Theory of Motivation,
(a) Force = valence divided by expectancy
(b) Force = valence × expectancy
(c) Force = strength of an individual preference for an outcome
(d) Valence = probability that a particular action shall lead to a desired outcome

31. In the managerial grid, the managers who have little or no concern for production but are concerned only for people are known as what type of managers?
(a) 1.1 Management (b) 5.5 Management
(c) 9.1 Management (d) 1.9 Management

32. According to the Boston Consulting group, a business, which has a strong market share in a low growth industry is referred to as a
(a) Dog (b) Cash Cow
(c) Star (d) Question mark

33. Which of the following are major principles of leading?
(i) Principle of motivation
(ii) Principle of continuous development
(iii) Principle of harmony of objectives

(iv) Principle of open competition
(v) Principle of communication clarity

Select the correct answer from the codes given below:

Codes:

(a) (i), (ii), (iii), (v) (b) (i), (ii), (iii), (iv), (v)
(c) (i), (iii), (iv), (v) (d) (i), (iii), (v)

34. The following are the steps of management control process:
(i) Taking corrective action from standards
(ii) Establishing standards
(iii) Measuring actual performance
(iv) Comparing performance against standard.

Select the correct sequence of these steps from the codes given below:

Codes:

(a) (i), (ii), (iii), (iv) (b) (ii), (iii), (iv), (i)
(c) (iii), (iv), (i), (ii) (d) (ii), (iv), (i), (iii)

35. Consider the following:
(i) Planning is today's action for tomorrow's decision.
(ii) Planning is forward looking while controlling is looking back.
(iii) Motivation is about getting voluntary willingness of subordinates for action.
(iv) Line and staff organisation is the oldest form of organisation.

Select the correct statements from the codes given below:

Codes:

(a) (ii) and (iii) are correct.
(b) (i), (ii) and (iv) are correct.
(c) (i), (iii) and (iv) are correct.
(d) All are correct.

36. Which is not one of the stages in the consumer buying-decision process?
(a) Purchase decision
(b) Post-purchase behaviour
(c) Problem recognition
(d) Cultural factors

37. At which stage of product-life-cycle are the pricing decisions most complex?
(a) Decline (b) Growth
(c) Introduction (d) Maturity

38. Which one is not an element of market logistics?
(a) Inventory
(b) Order-processing
(c) Warehousing
(d) Supply chain management

39. Under which legislation, the manufacturers and distributors are required to declare Maximum Retail Price (MRP) on packaged commodities?
(a) The Bureau of Indian Standards Act, 1986
(b) The Consumer Protection Act, 1986
(c) The Standards of Weights and Measures Act, 1976
(d) The Essential Commodities Act, 1955

40. In modern marketing, which of the following functions of a distribution middleman is gaining maximum importance?
(a) Making persuasive communication
(b) Price negotiation
(c) Keeping adequate inventory
(d) Gathering market information

41. Which method of setting the advertising budget of a company is considered to be the most scientific?
(a) All-you-can-afford method
(b) Percentage of sales method
(c) Competitive-parity method
(d) Objectives and tasks method

42. Match the items of List-I with those of List-II and indicate the correct combination from the codes given below:

List-I	List-II
(I) AIDA Model	(A) Consumer behaviour
(II) Hierarchy of effects model	(B) Marketing communication
(III) Howard and Sheth model	(C) Consumer buying-decision process
(IV) Information search	(D) Advertising effectiveness

Codes:	I	II	III	IV
(a)	(A)	(B)	(C)	(D)
(b)	(B)	(C)	(D)	(A)
(c)	(B)	(D)	(A)	(C)
(d)	(D)	(A)	(C)	(B)

43. Inability of the firm to meet its obligations results in financial distress which may lead to bankruptcy resulting into the following:
1. Distress sale of assets at lower price.
2. Legal and administrative costs for bankruptcy.

3. Dilution of stakeholders' commitment to the firm.
4. Stretching of payments to suppliers and creditors.

The direct costs of such financial distress may be
(a) 1 and 4 (b) 2 and 3
(c) 1 and 2 (d) 3 and 4

44. Mutually exclusive projects can be more accurately ranked as per
(a) Internal rate of return method
(b) Net Present Value Method
(c) Modified Internal Rate of Returns Method
(d) Accounting or Average Rate of Return Method

45. Which one of the following does not constitute a Standalone Risk Analysis?
(a) Simulation Analysis
(b) Break-even Analysis
(c) Corporate Risk Analysis
(d) Scenario Analysis

46. Financial leverage in a firm is positively affected by
(a) Intensity of tangible assets
(b) Operating leverage
(c) Profitability
(d) Tax Rate

47. Which combination of the following two statements (A) and (R) is correct?

Assertion (A): The IRR of a project is the discount rate which reduces its NPV to zero.

Reason (R): A project is worth accepting if the IRR exceeds the cost of capital.

Codes:
(a) (A) is right, but (R) is wrong.
(b) Both (A) and (R) are correct.
(c) (A) is wrong, but (R) is correct.
(d) Both (A) and (R) are wrong.

48. **Assertion (A):** A company should pay minimum dividend to its shareholders.

Reason (R): Dividends are heavily taxed than capital gains.

Codes:
(a) Both (A) and (R) are correct.
(b) Both (A) and (R) are incorrect.
(c) (A) is not correct, but (R) is correct.
(d) (A) is correct, but (R) is wrong.

49. Dividend irrelevance hypothesis is implied in the
(a) Traditional Model (b) Walter Model
(c) Gordon Model (d) M.M. Model

50. Which one of the following does not serve the main objective of performance appraisal?
(a) Developmental uses
(b) Administrative uses
(c) Ethical and moral values
(d) Organisational objectives

51. **Statement (I):** Job evaluation is a technique of assessing the worth of each job in comparison with others throughout an organization.

Statement (II): Job evaluation and job rating are one and the same for employees' appraisal purposes.

Codes:
(a) Statement (I) is correct, but Statement (II) is incorrect.
(b) Statement (II) is correct, but Statement (I) is incorrect.
(c) Both the Statements (I) and (II) are correct.
(d) Both the Statements (I) and (II) are incorrect.

52. Match the items of List-I with the items of List-II and select the correct answer:

List-I	List-II
(I) Job Rotation	(A) Involves conscious efforts, to organise tasks, duties and responsibilities into a unit of work to achieve certain objectives.
(II) Job Design	(B) Involves movement of employees from job to job.
(III) Job Evaluation	(C) Seeks to improve both task efficiency and human satisfaction and more opportunity for individual growth.
(IV) Job Enrichment	(D) The formal process by which the relative worth of various jobs in the organisation is determined for pay purpose.

Codes:	I	II	III	IV
(a)	(A)	(B)	(C)	(D)
(b)	(D)	(C)	(B)	(A)
(c)	(C)	(D)	(B)	(A)
(d)	(B)	(A)	(D)	(C)

53. **Assertion (A):** Merit rating of an employee is the process of evaluating the employees performance on the job in terms of the requirements of the job.

    Reason (R): Employees' merit rating is a technique for fair and systematic evaluation of an employee's capacities and abilities and performance on the specific job.

    Codes:
    (a) Both (A) and (R) are correct, and (R) is the right explanation of (A).
    (b) Both (A) and (R) are correct, but (R) is not the right explanation of (A).
    (c) Both (A) and (R) are incorrect.
    (d) (R) is correct, but (A) is incorrect.

54. The major provisions for employees' health and safety are contained in
    (a) The Industrial Disputes Act, 1947
    (b) The Factories Act, 1948
    (c) The Industrial Employment (Standing Orders) Act, 1946
    (d) The Employees' Compensation Act, 1923

55. Indicate your choice through the codes given below:
    1. A club is an industry under the Industrial Disputes Act, 1947
    2. Factory as defined under the Factories Act, 1948 includes a mine.
    3. For purpose of the payment of bonus to employees, the gross profits earned by a bank is to be calculated in the manner specified in Schedule I of the Payment of the Bonus Act, 1965.
    4. Various labour laws do not apply to public sector undertakings.

    Codes:
    (a) While 1 and 2 are correct, others are not.
    (b) All the statements are correct.
    (c) Only 1 is correct, others are incorrect.
    (d) Only 1 is incorrect, all others are correct.

56. Match the items of List-I with the items of List-II and select the correct answer:

List-I	List-II
(I) Abraham Maslow	(A) Achievement Motivation Theory
(II) Herzberg	(B) ERG Theory
(III) Alderfer	(C) Two Factor Theory
(IV) McClelland	(D) Need Hierarchy Theory

Codes:	I	II	III	IV
(a)	(A)	(B)	(C)	(D)
(b)	(D)	(C)	(B)	(A)
(c)	(C)	(B)	(A)	(D)
(d)	(D)	(C)	(A)	(B)

57. **Assertion (A):** The Central Bank of the country is responsible to maintain stability of the monetary standard which involves currency circulation.

    Reason (R): The Central Bank is the only authorized entity to do so.

    Codes:
    (a) (A) and (R) both are correct.
    (b) (A) and (R) both are incorrect.
    (c) (A) is correct, but (R) is incorrect.
    (d) (R) is correct, but (A) is incorrect.

58. Identify the quantitative credit control methods among the following:
    (i) Bank Rate
    (ii) Credit Rationing
    (iii) Open Market Operations
    (iv) Variable Reserve Ratio
    (v) Selective Credit Control
    (vi) Liquidity Ratio

    Codes:
    (a) (i), (ii), (iii) and (iv)
    (b) (ii), (iii), (iv) and (v)
    (c) (i), (ii), (v) and (vi)
    (d) (i), (iii), (iv) and (vi)

59. The following activities are mainly related to which organization?
    (i) Micro Finance
    (ii) Rural Finance
    (iii) Self Help Groups
    (iv) Cooperative Banks Finance

    (a) Industrial Finance Corporation of India
    (b) Ministry of Finance
    (c) Reserve Bank of India
    (d) National Bank for Agriculture and Rural Development

60. PIN in banking transaction is known as
 (a) Postal Index Number
 (b) Permanent Identification Number
 (c) Personal Identification Number
 (d) Public Interlocking Numeric

61. Reserve Bank of India was nationalized on
 (a) January 26, 1948 (b) January 01, 1949
 (c) January 26, 1950 (d) January 01, 1956

62. When a banking company is placed under moratorium under Section 45 of the Banking (Regulation) Act, 1949, the RBI must prepare a scheme of
 (a) VRS for staff
 (b) Capital Buy-Back
 (c) Reconstruction of the company or amalgamation with any other bank
 (d) IPO of the bank

63. Match the following items of List-I with List-II:

List-I	List-II
(I) SWIFT	(A) 1996
(II) NEFT	(B) 1988
(III) BASEL I Accord	(C) 1973
(IV) BASEL II Accord	(D) 2004

Codes:	I	II	III	IV
(a)	(A)	(B)	(C)	(D)
(b)	(B)	(C)	(A)	(D)
(c)	(D)	(C)	(B)	(A)
(d)	(C)	(A)	(D)	(B)

64. The main features of TRIMS are:
 (i) All restrictions on foreign capital are imposed.
 (ii) No restriction is imposed on any area of investment.
 (iii) Restrictions on repatriation of dividend is eliminated.
 (iv) Imports of raw material is allowed freely.
 (v) No limit on the extent of foreign investment.

 Indicate the correct combination
 (a) (i), (ii), (iii) and (v)
 (b) (ii), (iii), (iv) and (v)
 (c) (iii), (iv) and (v)
 (d) (iv) and (v)

65. **Assertion (A):** TRIPS requires an understanding about the scope of the new patent regime.

 Reason (R): Patent protection will be extended to micro organisms, non-biological and micro-biological processes and plant varieties.

 Codes:
 (a) (A) and (R) are not related with each other.
 (b) (R) is related with (A).
 (c) (A) is independent of (R).
 (d) While (R) is related with TRIMS, (A) is related with TRIPS.

66. Possible impact of WTO on various aspects of the Indian economy:
 (i) Quantitative restriction will be allowed.
 (ii) Second hand cars will be imported.
 (iii) There will be dumping of Chinese goods.
 (iv) Increase in population.
 (v) Child labour exploitation.
 (vi) Unemployment will increase.

 Which combination is appropriate?
 (a) (i), (ii), (iii) (b) (iii), (iv), (v)
 (c) (ii), (iii), (vi) (d) (iv), (v), (vi)

67. **Assertion (A):** Economic integration abolishes cross-national economic discrimination.

 Reason (R): Geographical proximity is an important reason for economic integration.

 Codes:
 (a) (R) does explain (A).
 (b) Both (A) and (R) are correct.
 (c) Both (A) and (R) are not correct.
 (d) (A) is correct, but (R) is not correct.

68. Match the items of List-I and items of List-II and select the correct answer:

List-I	List-II
(I) Free Trade Area	(A) MERCOSUR
(II) Customs Union	(B) European Union
(III) OEEC	(C) EFTA
(IV) Common Market	(D) Marshall Plan

Codes:	I	II	III	IV
(a)	(A)	(B)	(C)	(D)
(b)	(B)	(D)	(A)	(C)
(c)	(C)	(A)	(D)	(B)
(d)	(D)	(C)	(B)	(A)

69. **Assertion (A):** A futures contract specifies in advance the exchange rate to be used, but it is not as flexible as a forward contract.

 Reason (R): A futures contract is for specific currency amount and a specific maturity date.

Codes:
(a) (R) is a correct explanation of (A).
(b) (R) is not a correct explanation of (A).
(c) (A) and (R) are not related with each other.
(d) (R) is irrelevant for (A).

70. Out of the following, which are the important objectives of IMF?
(i) To promote exchange rate stability
(ii) To create standby reserves
(iii) To print international currency notes
(iv) To establish a multilateral system of payments
(v) To maintain orderly exchange rate stability
(vi) To create employment

Codes:
(a) (ii), (iv), (v), (vi) (b) (iii), (v), (vi)
(c) (i), (ii), (iv), (v) (d) (i), (ii), (v), (vi)

71. Given that:
Fair rent of a let out house property is ₹ 75,000. Its Municipal value is ₹ 60,000, standard rent is ₹ 72,000 and actual rent received is ₹ 63,000.
What is the Gross Annual Value of this house property?
(a) ₹ 60,000 (b) ₹ 63,000
(c) ₹ 72,000 (d) ₹ 75,000

72. Match the items of List-I with the items of List-II

	List-I		List-II
(I)	Amount deposited in PPF	(A)	80-IA
(II)	Profits and gains from undertakings engaged in infrastructure development	(B)	80 G
(III)	Contribution to National Defence Fund	(C)	80-IAB
(IV)	Profits and gains by an undertaking engaged in the development of Special Economic Zone	(D)	80-C

Codes:	I	II	III	IV
(a)	(D)	(C)	(B)	(A)
(b)	(D)	(A)	(B)	(C)
(c)	(D)	(A)	(C)	(B)
(d)	(B)	(A)	(C)	(D)

73. Which of the following deductions will not come under Sec. 80 of the Income Tax Act?
(a) Deduction in the case of a person with disability
(b) Deduction for interest paid on loan taken for pursuing higher education
(c) Deduction for interest on loan taken for the construction/purchase of house property
(d) Deduction for repayment of any instalment of principal amount borrowed for the purchase/ construction of house property

74. X purchased a land in the P.Y. 1997-98 for ₹ 50,000. This land was sold by him during the P.Y. 2009-10 for ₹ 8,00,000. The fair market value of this land on 1-4-81 was ₹ 1,20,000. If the Cost Inflation Index for the A.Y. 2010-11 is 632, his capital gain for the A.Y. 2010-11 will be
(a) ₹ 4,84,000 (b) ₹ 7,50,000
(c) ₹ 6,80,000 (d) ₹ 41,600

75. Any amount of money received in excess of ₹ 50,000 without consideration is fully taxable in the hands of
(a) Individuals
(b) Individuals and HUF
(c) Individuals, HUF and Company
(d) All assessees

ANSWERS

1. (d)	2. (c)	3. (b)	4. (c)	5. (d)
6. (c)	7. (c)	8. (b)	9. (a)	10. (d)
11. (c)	12. (d)	13. (a)	14. (a)	15. (d)
16. (a)	17. (a)	18. (d)	19. (d)	20. (b)
21. (c)	22. (a)	23. (a)	24. (c)	25. (b)
26. (a)	27. (b)	28. (d)	29. (b)	30. (b)
31. (d)	32. (b)	33. (d)	34. (b)	35. (a)
36. (d)	37. (d)	38. (d)	39. (c)	40. (d)
41. (d)	42. (c)	43. (c)	44. (b)	45. (c)
46. (a)	47. (b)	48. (a)	49. (d)	50. (c)
51. (a)	52. (d)	53. (b)	54. (b)	55. (a)
56. (b)	57. (c)	58. (d)	59. (d)	60. (c)
61. (b)	62. (c)	63. (b)	64. (b)	65. (a)
66. (c)	67. (b)	68. (c)	69. (a)	70. (c)
71. (c)	72. (b)	73. (c)	74. (d)	75. (b)

JUNE–2014

Note: This paper contains Sixty (60) multiple-choice questions, each question carrying two (2) marks. Candidate is expected to answer any Fifty (50) questions. In case more than Fifty (50) questions are attempted, only the first Fifty (50) questions will be evaluated.

PAPER–I

1. Break-down in verbal communication is described as
(a) Short circuit (b) Contradiction
(c) Unevenness (d) Entropy

2. The Telephone Model of Communication was first developed in the area of
(a) Technological theory
(b) Dispersion theory
(c) Minimal effects theory
(d) Information theory

3. The Dada Saheb Phalke Award for 2013 has been conferred on
(a) Karan Johar (b) Amir Khan
(c) Asha Bhonsle (d) Gulzar

4. Photographs are not easy to
(a) publish (b) secure
(c) decode (d) change

5. The grains that appear on a television set when operated are also referred to as
(a) sparks (b) green dots
(c) snow (d) rain drops

6. In circular communication, the encoder becomes a decoder when there is
(a) noise (b) audience
(c) criticality (d) feedback

7. In a post-office, stamps of three different denominations of ₹ 7, ₹ 8, ₹ 10 are available. The exact amount for which one cannot buy stamps is
(a) 19 (b) 20 (c) 23 (d) 29

8. In certain coding method, the word QUESTION is encoded as DOMESTIC. In this coding, what is the code word for the word RESPONSE?
(a) OMESUCEM (b) OMESICSM
(c) OMESICEM (d) OMESISCM

9. If the series 4, 5, 8, 13, 14, 17, 22, ... is continued in the same pattern, which one of the following is not a term of this series?
(a) 31 (b) 32 (c) 33 (d) 35

10. Complete the series BB, FE, II, ML, PP, ... by choosing one of the following option given:
(a) TS (b) ST (c) RS (d) SR

11. A man started walking from his house towards south. After walking 6 km, he turned to his left and walked 5 km. Then he walked further 3 km after turning left. He then turned to his left and continued his walk for 9 km. How far is he away from his house?
(a) 3 km (b) 4 km (c) 5 km (d) 6 km

12. One writes all numbers from 50 to 99 without the digits 2 and 7. How many numbers have been written?
(a) 32 (b) 36 (c) 40 (d) 38

13. "If a large diamond is cut up into little bits, it will lose its value just as an army is divided up into small units of soldiers, it loses its strength."
The argument put above may be called as
(a) Analogical (b) Deductive
(c) Statistical (d) Causal

14. Given below are some characteristics of logical argument. Select the code which expresses a characteristic which is not of inductive in character.
(a) The conclusion is claimed to follow from its premises.
(b) The conclusion is based on causal relation.
(c) The conclusion conclusively follows from its premises.
(d) The conclusion is based on observation and experiment.

15. If two propositions having the same subject and predicate terms can both be true but cannot both be false, the relation between those two propositions is called
(a) contradictory (b) contrary
(c) subcontrary (d) subaltern

16. Given below are two premises and four conclusions drawn from those premises. Select the code that expresses conclusion drawn validly from the premises (separately or jointly).
Premises:
(A) All dogs are mammals.
(B) No cats are dogs.
Conclusions:
(i) No cats are mammals.
(ii) Some cats are mammals.
(iii) No dogs are cats.
(iv) No dogs are non-mammals.
Codes:
(a) (i) only (b) (i) and (ii)
(c) (iii) and (iv) (d) (ii) and (iii)

17. Given below is a diagram of three circles A, B and C inter-related with each other. The circle A represents the class of Indians, the circle B represents the class of scientists and circle C represents the class of politicians. p, q, r, s...represent different regions. Select the code containing the region that indicates the class of Indian scientists who are not politicians.

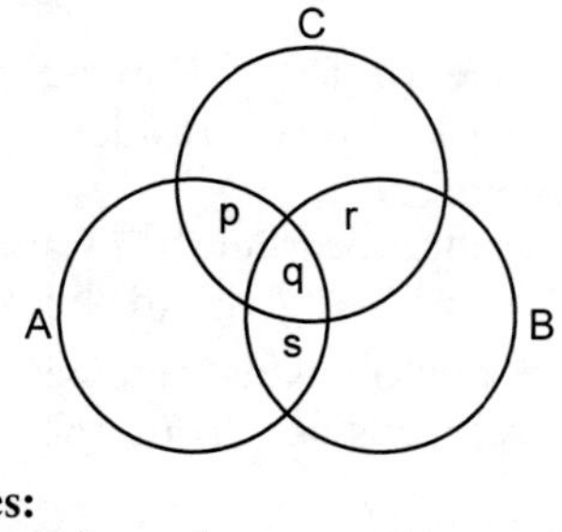

Codes:
(a) q and s only (b) s only
(c) s and r only (d) p, q and s only

Read the following table carefully. Based upon this table answer questions from 18 to 22:

Net Area under Irrigation by sources in a country (Thousand Hectares)

Year	Government canals	Private canals	Tanks	Tube wells & other wells	Other sources	Total
1997-98	17117	211	2593	32090	3102	55173
1998-99	17093	212	2792	33988	3326	57411
1999-00	16842	194	2535	34623	2915	57109
2000-01	15748	203	2449	33796	2880	55076
2001-02	15031	209	2179	34906	4347	56672
2002-03	13863	206	1802	34250	3657	53778
2003-04	14444	206	1908	35779	4281	56618
2004-05	14696	206	1727	34785	7453	58867
2005-06	15268	207	2034	35372	7314	60196

18. Which of the following sources of irrigation has registered the largest percentage of decline in Net area under irrigation during 1997-98 and 2005-06?
(a) Government canals (b) Private canals
(c) Tanks (d) Other sources

19. Find out the source of irrigation that has registered the maximum improvement in terms of percentage of Net irrigated area during 2002-03 and 2003-04.
(a) Government canals
(b) Tanks
(c) Tube wells and other wells
(d) Other sources

20. In which of the following years, Net irrigation by tanks increased at the highest rate?
(a) 1998-99 (b) 2000-01
(c) 2003-04 (d) 2005-06

21. Identify the source of irrigation that has recorded the maximum incidence of negative growth in terms of Net irrigated area during the years given in the table.
(a) Government canals
(b) Private canals
(c) Tube wells and other wells
(d) Other sources

22. In which of the following years, share of the tube wells and other wells in the total net irrigated area was the highest?
(a) 1998-99 (b) 2000-01
(c) 2002-03 (d) 2004-05

23. The acronym FTP stands for
(a) File Transfer Protocol
(b) Fast Transfer Protocol

(c) File Tracking Protocol
(d) File Transfer Procedure

24. Which one of the following is not a/an image/graphic file format?
(a) PNG (b) GIF (c) BMP (d) GUI

25. The first web browser is
(a) Internet Explorer (b) Netscape
(c) World Wide Web (d) Firefox

26. When a computer is booting, BIOS is loaded to the memory by
(a) RAM (b) ROM (c) CD-ROM (d) TCP

27. Which one of the following is not the same as the other three?
(a) MAC address (b) Hardware address
(c) Physical address (d) IP address

28. Identify the IP address from the following:
(a) 300 · 215 · 317 · 3
(b) 302 · 215@ · 417 · 5
(c) 202 · 50 · 20 · 148
(d) 202 - 50 - 20 - 148

29. The population of India is about 1.2 billion. Take the average consumption of energy per person per year in India as 30 Mega Joules. If this consumption is met by carbon based fuels and the rate of carbon emissions per kilojoule is 15×10^6 kgs, the total carbon emissions per year from India will be
(a) 54 million metric tons
(b) 540 million metric tons
(c) 5400 million metric tons
(d) 2400 million metric tons

30. Which of the following cities has been worst affected by urban smog in recent times?
(a) Paris (b) London
(c) Los Angeles (d) Beijing

31. The primary source of organic pollution in fresh water bodies is
(a) run-off urban areas
(b) run-off from agricultural forms
(c) sewage effluents
(d) industrial effluents

32. 'Lahar' is a natural disaster involving
(a) eruption of large amount of material
(b) strong winds
(c) strong water waves
(d) strong winds and water waves

33. In order to avoid catastrophic consequences of climate change, there is general agreement among the countries of the world to limit the rise in average surface temperature of earth compared to that of pre-industrial times by
(a) 1.5°C to 2°C (b) 2.0°C to 3.5°C
(c) 0.5°C to 1.0°C (d) 0.25°C to 0.5°C

34. The National Disaster Management Authority functions under the Union Ministry of
(a) Environment (b) Water Resources
(c) Home Affairs (d) Defence

35. Match List-I and List-II and select the correct answer from the codes given below:

List-I
A. Flood B. Drought
C. Earthquake D. Volcano

List-II
1. Lack of rainfall of sufficient duration
2. Tremors produced by the passage of vibratory waves through the rocks of the earth
3. A vent through which molted substances come out
4. Excess rain and uneven distribution of water

Codes:	A	B	C	D
(a)	4	1	2	3
(b)	2	3	4	1
(c)	3	4	2	1
(d)	4	3	1	2

36. Which one of the following greenhouse gases has the shortest residence time in the atmosphere?
(a) Chlorofluorocarbon (b) Carbon dioxide
(c) Methane (d) Nitrous oxide

37. Consider the following statements and select the correct answer from the code given below:
i. Rajasthan receives the highest solar radiation in the country.
ii. India has the fifth largest installed wind power in the world.
iii. The maximum amount of wind power is contributed by Tamil Nadu.
iv. The primary source of uranium in India is Jaduguda.

Codes:
(a) i and ii (b) i, ii and iii
(c) ii and iii (d) i and iv

38. Who among the following is the de facto executive head of the Planning Commission?
(a) Chairman
(b) Deputy Chairman
(c) Minister of State for Planning
(d) Member Secretary

39. Education as a subject of legislation figures in the
(a) Union List (b) State List
(c) Concurrent List (d) Residuary Powers

40. Which of the following are Central Universities?
1. Pondicherry University
2. Vishwa Bharati
3. H.N.B. Garhwal University
4. Kurukshetra University
Select the correct answer from the code given below:
Codes:
(a) 1, 2 and 3 (b) 1, 3 and 4
(c) 2, 3 and 4 (d) 1, 2 and 4

41. Consider the statement which is followed by two arguments (i) and (ii).
Statement: India should have a very strong and powerful Lokpal.
Arguments: (i) Yes, it will go a long in eliminating corruption in bureaucracy.
(ii) No, it will discourage honest officers from making quick decisions.
Codes:
(a) Only argument (i) is strong.
(b) Only argument (ii) is strong.
(c) Both the arguments are strong.
(d) Neither of the arguments is strong.

42. Which of the following universities has adopted the meta university concept?
(a) Assam University
(b) Delhi University
(c) Hyderabad University
(d) Pondicherry University

43. Which of the following statements are correct about a Central University?
1. Central University is established under an Act of Parliament.
2. The President of India acts as the visitor of the University.
3. The President has the power to nominate some members to the Executive Committee or the Board of Management of the University.
4. The President occasionally presides over the meetings of the Executive Committee or Court.
Select the correct answer from the code given below:
Codes:
(a) 1, 2 and 4 (b) 1, 3 and 4
(c) 1, 2 and 3 (d) 1, 2, 3 and 4

44. Which one of the following is considered a sign of motivated teaching?
(a) Students asking questions
(b) Maximum attendance of the students
(c) Pin drop silence in the classroom
(d) Students taking notes

45. Which one of the following is the best method of teaching?
(a) Lecture (b) Discussion
(c) Demonstration (d) Narration

46. Dyslexia is associated with
(a) mental disorder
(b) behavioural disorder
(c) reading disorder
(d) writing disorder

47. The e-content generation for undergraduate courses has been assigned by the Ministry of Human Resource Development to
(a) INFLIBNET
(b) Consortium for Educational Communication
(c) National Knowledge Commission
(d) Indira Gandhi National Open University

48. Classroom communication is normally considered as
(a) effective (b) cognitive
(c) affective (d) selective

49. Who among the following, propounded the concept of paradigm?
(a) Peter Haggett (b) Von Thunen
(c) Thomas Kuhn (d) John K. Wright

50. In a thesis, figures and tables are included in

(a) the appendix
(b) a separate chapter
(c) the concluding chapter
(d) the text itself

51. A thesis statement is
(a) an observation (b) a fact
(c) an assertion (d) a discussion

52. The research approach of Max Weber to understand how people create meanings in natural settings is identified as
(a) positive paradigm
(b) critical paradigm
(c) natural paradigm
(d) interpretative paradigm

53. Which one of the following is a non-probability sampling?
(a) Simple random (b) Purposive
(c) Systematic (d) Stratified

54. Identify the category of evaluation that assesses the learning progress to provide continuous feedback to the students during instruction.
(a) Placement (b) Diagnostic
(c) Formative (d) Summative

55. The research stream of immediate application is
(a) Conceptual research
(b) Action research
(c) Fundamental research
(d) Empirical research

Read the following passage carefully and answer questions 56 to 60:

Traditional Indian values must be viewed both from the angle of the individual and from that of the geographically delimited agglomeration of peoples or groups enjoying a common system of leadership which we call the 'State'. The Indian 'State's' special feature is the peaceful, or perhaps mostly peaceful, co-existence of social groups of various historical provenances which mutually adhere in a geographical, economic, and political sense, without ever assimilating to each other in social terms, in ways of thinking, or even in language. Modern Indian law will determine certain rules, especially in relation to the regime of the family, upon the basis of how the loin-cloth is tied, or how the turban is worn, for this may identify the litigants as members of a regional group, and therefore as participants in its traditional law, though their ancestors left the region three or four centuries earlier. The use of the word 'State' above must not mislead us. There was no such thing as a conflict between the individual and the State, atleast before foreign governments became established, just as there was no concept of state 'sovereignty' or of any church-and-state dichotomy.

Modern Indian 'secularism' has an admittedly peculiar feature: It requires the state to make a fair distribution of attention and support amongst all religions. These blessed aspects of India's famed tolerance (Indian kings so rarely persecuted religious groups that the exceptions prove the rule) at once struck Portuguese and other European visitors to the West Coast of India in the sixteenth century, and the impression made upon them in this and other ways gave rise, at one remove, to the basic constitution of Thomas More's Utopia. There is little about modern India that strikes one at once as Utopian: but the insistence upon the inculcation of norms, and the absence of bigotry and institutionalized exploitation of human or natural resources, are two very different features which link the realities of India and her tradition with the essence of all Utopians.

56. Which of the following is a special feature of the Indian State?
(a) Peaceful co-existence of people under a common system of leadership
(b) Peaceful co-existence of social groups of different historical provenances attached to each other in a geographical, economic and political sense
(c) Social integration of all groups
(d) Cultural assimilation of all social groups.

57. The author uses the word 'State' to highlight
(a) Antagonistic relationship between the state and the individual throughout the period of history.
(b) Absence of conflict between the state and the individuals upto a point in time.
(c) The concept of state sovereignty.
(d) Dependence on religion.

58. Which one is the peculiar feature of modern Indian 'Secularism'?

(a) No discrimination on religious considerations
(b) Total indifference to religion
(c) No space for social identity
(d) Disregard for social law

59. The basic construction of Thomas More's Utopia was inspired by
(a) Indian tradition of religious tolerance.
(b) Persecution of religious groups by Indian rulers.
(c) Social inequality in India.
(d) European perception of Indian State.

60. What is the striking feature of modern India?
(a) A replica of Utopian State
(b) Uniform laws
(c) Adherence to traditional values
(d) Absence of Bigotry

ANSWERS

1. (d)	2. (d)	3. (d)	4. (c)	5. (c)
6. (d)	7. (a)	8. (c)	9. (c)	10. (a)
11. (c)	12. (a)	13. (a)	14. (c)	15. (c)
16. (c)	17. (b)	18. (c)	19. (d)	20. (d)
21. (a)	22. (c)	23. (a)	24. (d)	25. (c)
26. (b)	27. (d)	28. (c)	29. (b)	30. (d)
31. (c)	32. (a)	33. (a)	34. (c)	35. (a)
36. (c)	37. (d)	38. (b)	39. (c)	40. (a)
41. (a)	42. (b)	43. (c)	44. (a)	45. (c)
46. (c)	47. (b)	48. (c)	49. (c)	50. (d)
51. (c)	52. (d)	53. (b)	54. (c)	55. (b)
56. (b)	57. (d)	58. (a)	59. (a)	60. (d)

PAPER II

Note: This paper contains fifty (50) objective type questions of two (2) marks each. All questions are compulsory.

1. There is acute shortage of electricity in some of the states in India. This reflects a problem in which type of business environment?
(a) Economic (b) Demographic
(c) Politico-legal (d) Socio-cultural

2. Match the items given in List-I and List-II.

List-I	List-II
(A) Economic liberalisation	(i) IT-enabled services
(B) Out sourcing	(ii) SFIO
(C) Corporate frauds	(iii) Macro economic stability
(D) Second generation reforms	(iv) Increased competition

Indicate the correct combination:

Codes:	A	B	C	D
(a)	(i)	(ii)	(iii)	(iv)
(b)	(i)	(iii)	(ii)	(iv)
(c)	(ii)	(iii)	(iv)	(i)
(d)	(iv)	(i)	(ii)	(iii)

3. Which of the following is true?
(a) A consumer court setup under the Consumer Protection Act, does not have the power to punish for its contempt.
(b) Professional services are outside the purview of the CPA.
(c) A consumer court cannot force a person indulging in misleading advertising to confess his quit.
(d) None of the above.

4. Match the items/terms given in List I with those given in and List II.

List I	List II
(A) BIS	(i) Print Media.
(B) CERC	(ii) Minimum support price for agricultural products.
(C) CACP	(iii) Quality of manufactured products.
(D) PCI	(iv) Comparative product testing.

Indicate the correct answer:

Codes:	A	B	C	D
(a)	(iv)	(iii)	(ii)	(i)
(b)	(i)	(ii)	(iii)	(iv)
(c)	(iii)	(iv)	(ii)	(i)
(d)	(ii)	(iii)	(iv)	(i)

5. Which one among the following is not the salient feature of industrial policy since 1991?

(a) Enormous expansion of the private sector.
(b) Redefining the role of public sector.
(c) Limited exposure of Indian industry to foreign competition.
(d) Pruning of the list of items reserved for SSI units.

6. A, a partner in a firm, is drawing ₹ 500 regularly on the 16th of every month. He will have to pay interest at the given rate in a year on ₹ 6000 for the total period of
(a) 5 months (b) 6 months
(c) 7 months (d) 12 months

7. Subsequent expenditures that extend the useful life, improve the quality of output, or reduce operating costs of an existing asset beyond their originally estimated levels are
(a) Capital expenditures
(b) Revenue expenditures
(c) Deferred Revenue expenditures
(d) None of the above

8. Marginal-costing technique is useful for
(a) Make or Buy decisions
(b) Profit planning
(c) Shut-down decisions
(d) All of the above

9. Which one is not a feature of budgetary control?
(a) A tool for management control.
(b) An instrument of delegation and authority.
(c) An instrument for evaluating the overall performance.
(d) A statement of budget and forecasts.

10. The Debt-Equity Ratio of a company is 2 : 1. In this relation, match the following:

List-I	List-II
(A) Issue of equity shares	1. No change on the ratio
(B) Cash received from debtors	2. Reduce the ratio
(C) Redemption of debentures	3. No change on the ratio
(D) Purchased goods on credit	4. Reduce the ratio

Codes:	A	B	C	D
(a)	1	2	3	4
(b)	2	3	4	1
(c)	1	3	4	2
(d)	2	4	1	3

11. Which one of the following does not explain the basic nature of Business economics?
(a) Behaviour of firms in theory and practice.
(b) Distribution theories like rent, wages and interest along with the theory of profit.
(c) Use of the tools of economic analysis in clarifying problems in organising and evaluating information and in comparing alternative courses of action.
(d) Integration of economic theory with business practices for the purpose of facilitating decision-making.

12. At a point of satiety for a commodity the marginal utility is
(a) Negative (b) Positive
(c) Zero (d) Highly positive

13. A rectangular hyperbola-shaped demand curve on all its points has
(a) Equal slopes and equal point elasticities.
(b) Unequal slopes and unequal point elasticities.
(c) Unequal slopes and equal point elasticities.
(d) Equal slopes and unequal point elasticities.

14. **Assertion (A)**: A perfectly competitive firm is not a price-maker but is a price-taker.
Reason (R): The firm is interested in deciding the level of output only.
Codes:
(a) Both (A) and (R) are true.
(b) Both (A) and (R) are false.
(c) (A) is false, while (R) is true.
(d) (A) is true, but (R) is not a correct explanation of (A).

15. Match the items of List-I with the items of List-II.

List-I	List-II
(A) A market having high price elasticity.	I. Skimming pricing
(B) A market having high price inelasticity.	II. Differential pricing
(C) A market having several segments differing prominently with regard to price elasticities of their demand.	III. Penetrating pricing

Codes:	I	II	III
(a)	(B)	(C)	(A)
(b)	(A)	(B)	(C)
(c)	(B)	(A)	(C)
(d)	(A)	(C)	(B)

16. Which one of the following options deals with the process of making estimates, predictions and decisions?
(a) Descriptive statistics
(b) Inferential statistics
(c) Probability theory
(d) None of the above

17. A hypothesis test is being performed for a process in which a Type-I error will be very costly, but a Type-II error will be relatively inexpensive and unimportant. Which of the following would be the best choice for alpha (α) in this test?
(a) 0.10 (b) 0.05 (c) 0.01 (d) 0.50

18. If the dependent variable increases as the independent variable increases in an estimating equation, the coefficient of correlation will be in the range
(a) 0 to (–) 1 (b) 0 to (–) 0
(c) 0 to (–) 0.05 (d) 0 to 1

19. **Assertion (A):** When there is an evidence of a linear relationship between two variables, it may not always mean an independent-dependent relationship between the two variables.
Reason (R): The causal relationship between the two variables may not imply a reasonable theoretical relationship between the two.
Choose the right answer from the following statements:
Codes:
(a) Both (A) and (R) are true and (R) is the correct explanation.
(b) Both (A) and (R) are true, but (R) is not the correct explanation.
(c) (A) is true, but (R) is false.
(d) (A) is false, but (R) is true.

20. **Assertion (A):** User interface is most critical task in DSS design.
Reason (R): DSS is used by outside customers frequently.
(a) (A) is correct, but (R) is wrong.
(b) Both (A) and (R) are wrong.
(c) (A) is wrong, but (R) is correct.
(d) Both (A) and (R) are correct.

21. Which of the following is not true about Matrix Organisation?
(a) It is relatively permanent.
(b) Its project managers authority is distributed reasonably.
(c) There is slow information processing.
(d) Its project heads have to share resources with functional heads.

22. Consider the following leadership styles:
1. Telling 2. Autocratic
3. Selling 4. Motivating
5. Participating 6. Delegating
7. Charismatic
Select the four styles of leadership explained by Hersey and Blauchard.
(a) 1, 2, 6 and 7 (b) 2, 3, 4 and 5
(c) 1, 3, 5 and 6 (d) 4, 5, 6 and 7

23. Given below are two statements, one labelled as Assertion (A), and the other labelled as Reason (R).
Assertion (A): Classical organisations believed in the use of authority to achieve coordination.
Reason (R): Classical thinkers consider organisation is an open system.
Codes:
(a) (A) is correct, but (R) is incorrect.
(b) Both (A) and (R) are correct.
(c) (A) is incorrect, but (R) is correct.
(d) Both (A) and (R) are incorrect.

24. Who has modified Maslow's Hierarchical levels of needs and developed ERG model?
(a) Frederick Herzberg
(b) David C. McClelland
(c) Douglas McGregor
(d) Clayton Alderfer

25. Taylor's differential piece work plan provides that
(a) All labourers should be assigned different amount of work.
(b) All labourers should be put in different time-period.

(c) Those who produce above standard should receive higher wages than those producing below standard.
(d) Payment should be the same on a fixed standard.

26. Which one of the following stages of the marketing research process is most expensive?
(a) Data analysis
(b) Data collection
(c) Developing the research plan
(d) Report writing

27. The people to adopt a new product first are called
(a) Early adopters (b) First users
(c) Initial adopters (d) Innovators

28. A concept in retailing that helps explain the emergence of new retailers is called the ______ hypothesis.
(a) Product life cycle
(b) Service assortment
(c) Retail life cycle
(d) 'Wheel-of-retailing'

29. Manufacturers of cars and motor cycles typically seek _______ distribution.
(a) selective (b) intensive
(c) exclusive (d) restrictive

30. Which method of setting advertising budget is most scientific and logical?
(a) All-you-can afford method
(b) Competitive parity method
(c) Objective-and-task method
(d) Percentage-of-sales method

31. **Assertion (A):** Weighted average cost of capital should be used as a hurdle rate for accepting or rejecting a capital budgeting proposal.
Reason (R): It is because by financing in the proportions specified and accepting the project, yielding more than the weighted average required return, the firm is able to increase the market price of its stock.
Codes:
(a) Both (A) and (R) are false.
(b) Both (A) and (R) are true.
(c) (A) is true, while (R) is false.
(d) (A) is false, while (R) is true.

32. A firm wants to know the Degree of Operating Leverage (DOL) with the following information:
Current level of sales : 6000 units
Break-even point sales : 4000 units
What would be the DOL?
(a) 1.50 (b) 0.67
(c) 3.00 (d) None of the above

33. **Assertion (A):** When two or more investment proposals are mutually exclusive, ranking the proposals on the basis of IRR, NPV and PI methods may give contradictory results.
Reason (R): The contradictory results in the ranking are due to differing dimensions relating to the scale of investments, cash flow patterns and project lives.
Indicate the correct answer:
Codes:
(a) Both (A) and (R) are true.
(b) (a) is true, but (R) is a necessary condition, but not a sufficient condition.
(c) Both (A) and (R) are false.
(d) Both (A) and (R) are true and (R) explains the reason sufficiently.

34. Which one of the following assumptions is not covered in the Walter's Model of the dividend policy?
(a) All financing is done through retained earnings.
(b) Firm's business risk does not change due to additional investments.
(c) The firm has an infinite life.
(d) The key variables like EPS and DPS keep on changing.

35. Which one of the following emphasizes the qualitative aspects of working capital management?
(a) Gross working capital
(b) Quick working capital
(c) Net working capital
(d) None of the above

36. Which of the following training methods exposes the newly recruited employee to the various business functions, divisions and departments?
(a) Orientation (b) Vestibule Training
(c) Transition Analysis (d) Role playing

37. Match the names of the Authors given below with the motivational theories they are associated with

List-I	List-II
1. Herzberg	A. ERG Theory
2. McGregor	B. Three-need theory
3. Alderfer Theory Y	C. Theory X and
4. David McClelland	D. Two-factor theory

Codes:	1	2	3	4
(a)	A	B	C	D
(b)	D	C	B	A
(c)	B	A	D	C
(d)	D	C	A	B

38. Who was closely associated with industrial relations in India?
(a) B. Kurien (b) Gadgil
(c) V.V. Giri (d) Vinoba Bhave

39. Under the Trade Union Act 1926, how many minimum number of members are required for a trade union to be registered?
(a) 5 (b) 7 (c) 9 (d) 11

40. The idea that a manager tends to be promoted to a level of his incompetence is referred to as
(a) the advancement principle
(b) the Paul principle
(c) the Peter principle
(d) the job design principle

41. Which of the following committees is intended to review the working of the monitory system in India?
(a) Narasimham Committee
(b) Tandon Committee
(c) Sukhamoy Chakravarty Committee
(d) Deheja Committee

42. Match the items of List-I with those in List-II and select the correct answer.

List-I	List-II
(A) Bank Rate Policy	1. Involving the shortening of the currency of bills eligible for rediscount.
(B) Credit Rationing	2. Involving the Purchase and sale of securities in the open market.
(C) Variable Reserve System	3. Involving the alteration of discount rate.
(D) Open Market Operations	4. Involving the variation of the minimum reserves.

Codes:	A	B	C	D
(a)	1	4	2	3
(b)	2	1	3	4
(c)	4	2	1	3
(d)	3	1	4	2

43. Match the items of List-I with the items of List-II and select the correct answer using the codes given below the lists.

List-I	List-II
(A) Rural Industries Programme	(i) Meant for various target groups like Rural youth, Ex-serviceman, women and Scheduled Castes/ Tribes.
(B) Mahila Vikas Nidhi Scheme disadvantaged	(ii) Aim at ensuring flow of credit to the sections of the society.
(C) Entrepreneurships Development	(iii) Commercial exploitation of Programme local resources.
(D) Micro Credit Scheme	(iv) Provides assistance to voluntary organizations for the benefit of women.

44. According to the FDI Policy of the Government of India (2012), the FDI in banks is limited to
(a) 20% in Nationalised Banks and 74% in Private Sector Banks.
(b) 20% in Nationalised Banks and 49% in Private Sector Banks.
(c) 16% in Nationalised Banks and 74% in Private Sector Banks.
(d) 49% in Nationalised Banks and 51% in Private Sector Banks.

45. According to the recent guidelines (2013) of the Reserve Bank of India the Private Sector Banks are required to have a minimum paid up equity capital of
(a) ₹ 300 crores (b) ₹ 200 crores
(c) ₹ 400 crores (d) ₹ 500 crores

46. International trade theory which provides that capital intensive country should export labour-intensive goods and import capital goods is referred to as
    (a) Leontief Paradox
    (b) Heckscher-Ohlin Theory
    (c) Mercantilism Theory
    (d) Theory of Comparative Advantage
47. Which of the following is not a form of economic integration in the context of intra-regional trade?
    (a) Customs Union (b) European Union
    (c) Economic Union (d) African Union
48. 'Crawling Peg System' means
    (a) Fixed Exchange Rate System.
    (b) Floating Exchange Rate System.
    (c) Hybrid of Fixed and Floating Exchange System.
    (d) None of the above.
49. From the following modes of international business, identify the mode which involves strategic alliance
    (a) Franchising (b) Leasing
    (c) Turnkey Project (d) Joint venture
50. Which of the following expressions amount to the import restriction measures?
    (i) Currency control
    (ii) Establishment of EPZs
    (iii) Tariff cuts
    (iv) Imposition of tariffs
    (v) Imposition of non-tariff barriers
    Codes:
    (a) (i), (ii) and (iii) (b) (i), (iv) and (v)
    (c) (iii), (iv) and (v) (d) (ii), (iii) and (v)

ANSWERS

1 (a)	2 (d)	3 (a)	4 (c)	5 (c)
6 (b)	7 (a)	8 (d)	9 (d)	10 (b)
11 (b)	12 (c)	13 (c)	14 (d)	15 (a)
16 (b)	17 (c)	18 (d)	19 (a)	20 (a)
21 (c)	22 (c)	23 (a)	24 (d)	25 (a)
26 (b)	27 (d)	28 (d)	29 (d)	30 (c)
31 (b)	32 (c)	33 (b)	34 (d)	35 (c)
36 (a)	37 (d)	38 (c)	39 (b)	40 (c)
41 (c)	42 (d)	43 (d)	44 (a)	45 (d)
46 (a)	47 (d)	48 (c)	49 (d)	50 (b)

PAPER III

Note: This paper contains Seventy-five (75) objective type questions of two (2) marks each. All questions are compulsory.

1. The Competition Act, 2002, seeks to regulate
    (a) Anti-competitive agreements
    (b) Mergers and amalgamation
    (c) Unfair trade practices
    (d) (a) and (b) above
2. Indicate the true statement:
    (a) Large industrial houses are outside the purview of the Competition Act, 2002
    (b) There is no provision for curbing frivolous complaints under the CPA.
    (c) The Trade Marks Act, 1999 does not apply to services.
    (d) All of the above are true.
3. The time limit for filing a complaints before the District forum under the Consumer Protection Act, 1986 is
    (a) one year
    (b) two years
    (c) three years
    (d) There is no such time limit.
4. The Foreign Investment Promotion Board (FIPB) revamps the rules and regulations pertaining to
    (a) Accounting of Foreign Investment
    (b) Investment by NRIs
    (c) Foreign investments
    (d) All of the above
5. Which of the legislation(s) do (does) not form part of the legal environment of business in India?
    (a) The Drugs and Cosmetics Act, 1940
    (b) The Prevention of Food Adulteration Act, 1954
    (c) The Monopolies and Restrictive Trade Practices Act, 1969
    (d) Both (b) and (c) above

6. What is the underlying concept that support the immediate recognition of an estimated loss?
   (a) Substance over form (b) Consistency
   (c) Matching (d) Prudence
7. Which is not the limitation of budgetary control?
   (a) Budgets are based on forecasts which may not be true.
   (b) Installation and operation of a system of budgetary control is costly.
   (c) Budget is a tool of management and not a substitute of management.
   (d) Budgets do not pinpoint the lack of efficiency or the presence of it.
8. Profit volume ratio of an enterprise is 40%. To offset 10% decrease in selling price, how much sales must be increased?
   (a) 10% (b) 20% (c) 25% (d) 40%
9. If debt is ₹ 220, cash balance is ₹ 20 and equity is ₹ 300, then the gearing ratio is
   (a) 20% (b) 40% (c) 50% (d) 30%
10. Responsibility accounting aims to
   (a) ensure that a manager is punished if things go wrong.
   (b) ensure that costs become the responsibility of a specific manager.
   (c) allocate costs to all areas of a business.
   (d) reduce the costs that a department incurs.
11. Find the correct matching of the items of List-I with the items of List-II given below:

List-I	List-II
(A) Normal Profit	(I) Excess of total revenue over total explicit cost
(B) Economic profit	(II) Total revenue equals total economic cost
(C) Accounting	(III) Excess of total revenue profit over total of explicit and implicit costs and a normal rate of return

Codes:	I	II	II
(a)	(C)	(A)	(B)
(b)	(B)	(A)	(C)
(c)	(A)	(B)	(C)
(d)	(A)	(C)	(B)

12. **Assertion (A):** A monopoly firm's revenue curve is downward sloping from left to right.
   Reason (R): The monopoly firm does not simultaneously enjoy the freedom to determine both price and quantity to be sold according to its whims and fancy.
   Codes:
   (a) Both (A) and (R) are true.
   (b) Both (A) and (R) are false.
   (c) (A) is true, but (R) is false.
   (d) (A) is false, but (R) is true.
13. The equilibrium level of output for a perfect competitive firm is given by the point where:
   (a) MR = MC (b) MR < MC
   (c) MR > MC
   (d) MR = MC, and MC starts rising.
14. Match the following:

List-I	List-II
(I) Dumping	(A) Monopolistic competitive firm
(II) Kinked Revenue Curve	(B) Oligopoly firm
(III) Horizontal straight line revenue curve	(C) Perfectively competitive firm
(IV) Large number of buyers and sellers with differentiated products	(D) Discriminatory monopoly

Codes:	I	II	III	IV
(a)	(A)	(D)	(C)	(B)
(b)	(B)	(D)	(A)	(C)
(c)	(D)	(B)	(C)	(A)
(d)	(A)	(B)	(C)	(D)

15. Penetrating pricing strategy is appropriate when
   (a) price elasticity of demand in the market is highly inelastic.
   (b) price elasticity of demand in the market is uncertain.
   (c) price elasticity of demand in the market is highly elastic.
   (d) income elasticity of demand in the market is negatively elastic.
16. **Assertion (A):** The expected values should be atleast 5 to apply the chi-square test.

Reason (R): The chi-square distribution provides an adequate approximation of the sampling distribution.

Indicate the correct answer from the following:

Codes:

(a) Both (A) and (R) are true, and (R) is the right explanation.
(b) Both (A) and (R) are true, but (R) is not the correct explanation.
(c) (A) is true, but (R) is false.
(d) (A) is false, but (R) is true.

17. In a decision problem having four possible alternative decisions and six possible states of nature, the pay-off table will include
(a) Four payoffs (b) Six payoffs
(c) Twenty-four payoff (d) Ten payoff

18. The mathematical formula for joint probabilities P(AB) = P(A/B) × P(B), holds when
(a) The events are statistically independent.
(b) The events are statistically dependent.
(c) The event is either independent or dependent.
(d) None of the above

19. Which one of the following statements is the correct interpretation of P-value of less than 0.01 in hypothesis testing?
(a) There is overwhelming evidence to infer that the alternative hypothesis is true.
(b) There is strong evidence to infer that the alternative hypothesis is true.
(c) There is weak evidence to indicate that the alternative hypothesis is true.
(d) There is no evidence to infer that the alternative hypothesis is true.

20. Two lists of items are given below:

List-I	List-II
(I) Charles Babbage	(A) Mossai
(II) Herbert A. Simon	(B) HTML
(III) Tim Berners Lee	(C) Computer Design
(IV) Maarc Andreessen	(D) Decision model

Which one of the following is the correct match?

Codes:	I	II	III	IV
(a)	(C)	(B)	(A)	(D)
(b)	(A)	(C)	(D)	(B)
(c)	(B)	(A)	(C)	(D)
(d)	(C)	(D)	(B)	(A)

21. Which of the following statements are true about informal organization?
1. It arises spontaneously.
2. It reflects individual and group goals.
3. It tends to be permanent and stable.
4. It tends to be small and manageable.
5. Its basic purpose is to improve human relations.
6. Its basic purpose is to achieve organisation's goals.

Codes:
(a) 1, 2, 3 and 5 (b) 1, 2, 4 and 6
(c) 1, 2, 4 and 5 (d) 2, 3, 5 and 6

22. Which of the following is not true about an employee-centered leader as identified by Michigan researchers?
(a) Treats subordinates as human beings.
(b) Shows concern for their well-being.
(c) Focuses on work standards and close supervision.
(d) Encourages and involves them in goal setting.

23. According to Talcott Parson, organizations can be classified primarily into four categories, based on functions. Which of the following is not an organization in Parson's scheme?
(a) Political organisations
(b) Integrative organisations
(c) Pattern maintenance organisations
(d) Commercial organisations

24. An MBO programme usually involves the following steps:
1. Establishing unit's objectives
2. Establishing organisational goals
3. Negotiating or agreeing
4. Reviewing the performance
5. Creating action plans

Indicate the correct sequence of the above steps from the following codes:
(a) 1, 2, 3, 4, 5 (b) 2, 1, 3, 5, 4
(c) 2, 3, 1, 4, 5 (d) 5, 4, 3, 2, 1

25. Match the following:

List-I	List-II
(A) Fayol	(1) Economy and Society
(B) Taylor	(2) General and Industrial Administration
(C) Weber	(3) Principles of Organization

(D)	Mooney and Reilly	(4) Shop Management

Codes:	A	B	C	D
(a)	(3)	(4)	(1)	(2)
(b)	(2)	(4)	(1)	(3)
(c)	(1)	(3)	(2)	(4)
(d)	(4)	(3)	(2)	(1)

26. A primary group influencing the buyer behaviour is a
   (a) Family
   (b) Professional association
   (c) Religious group
   (d) Trade Union

27. After conducting the business analysis for developing a new product, a company must do
   (a) Idea generation
   (b) Product positioning
   (c) Product development and testing
   (d) Test marketing

28. Match the items in List I with those in List II:

	List I		List II
(A)	Post purchase behaviour	(i)	AIDA
(B)	Personal selling	(ii)	ACMEE
(C)	Everitt M. Rogers	(iii)	Diffusion of Innovation
(D)	Salesperson training	(iv)	Cognitive dissonance

Indicate the correct matching:

Codes:	A	B	C	D
(a)	(i)	(ii)	(iii)	(iv)
(b)	(iv)	(ii)	(iii)	(i)
(c)	(iii)	(ii)	(i)	(iv)
(d)	(iv)	(i)	(iii)	(ii)

29. Which type of retail stores generally has the highest operating costs?
   (a) Department store
   (b) Supermarket
   (c) Chain store
   (d) Co-operative store

30. Indicate the correct statement:
   (a) India has been a pioneer in social marketing.
   (b) Advertising Standards Council of India is a statutory body set up by the Government of India.
   (c) Both (a) and (b) are incorrect.
   (d) Both (a) and (b) are correct.

31. Match the items of List-I with the items of List-II:

	List-I		List-II
(A)	Trade credit and other payables that arise in the firm's day today operations	(i)	Maturity Financing
(B)	Financing and asset needs over time	(ii)	Factoring
(C)	A tool for accelerating the collection from the customers	(iii)	Spontaneous financing
(D)	Seeking financial service to finance on its debtors balances'	(iv)	Lockbox system

Codes:	A	B	C	D
(a)	(iv)	(iii)	(ii)	(i)
(b)	(iii)	(ii)	(iv)	(i)
(c)	(ii)	(iv)	(i)	(iii)
(d)	(i)	(ii)	(iii)	(iv)

32. Indicate the cost of equity capital, based on capital asset pricing model, with the following information:

   Beta coefficient–1.40

   Risk-free rate of interest–9%

   Expected Rate of Return on equity in the market–16%

   (a) 9.8% (b) 18% (c) 18.8% (d) 16%

33. The degree of super-leverage would be calculated by:
   (a) Adding DOL (Degree of Operating Leverage) and DFL (Degree of Financial Leverage)
   (b) Dividing DOL with DFL
   (c) Multiplying DOL and DFL
   (d) Subtracting DOL from DFL

34. Interim cash in flows are reinvested at a rate of return equal to the internal rate of return is the built-in mechanism for
   (a) Net Present Value Method
   (b) Internal Rate of Return Method

(c) Profitability Index Method
(d) None of the above

35. Who formulated the following model for estimating the market price of equity share?

$$P = \frac{R + \frac{R_a}{R_c}(E - D)}{R_c}$$

Where, P = Market price of equity share
D = DPS
E = EPS
E – D = Retained earning per share
R_a = Internal rate of return on investment
R_c = Cost of capital
(a) Modigliani-Miller (b) Myron-Gordon
(c) James E. Walter (d) Clarkson and Elliot

36. Indicate the quantitative methods of job evaluation
(a) Ranking methods and Job comparison method
(b) Point rating method and Factor comparison method
(c) Grading method and Job classification method
(d) Factor comparison method and Ranking method

37. Match the items of List-I with those List-II:

List-I	List-II
1. Career goals	(A) The process where in an executive serves as a guide
2. Career path	(B) The future positions one strives to reach as part of career
3. Career counseling	(C) The sequential pattern of jobs that form a career
4. Mentoring	(D) Guiding people on their possible career path

Codes:	1	2	3	4
(a)	(B)	(C)	(D)	(A)
(b)	(A)	(B)	(C)	(D)
(c)	(D)	(C)	(B)	(A)
(d)	(C)	(B)	(A)	(D)

38. The process of receiving and welcoming an employee when he first joins a company and giving him the basic information he needs to settle down quickly and happily and starts working, is referred to as
(a) Placement (b) Orientation
(c) Job Rotation (d) Counseling

39. Which is not relevant of succession planning?
(a) Analysis of the demand for managers
(b) Review of existing executives
(c) Planning individuals career paths
(d) Recruitment to meet immediate needs

40. Where does recognition of an Employee fall in Maslow's hierarchy of needs theory ?
(a) Self-actualisation (b) Security needs
(c) Social needs (d) Esteem needs

41. The profitability of public-sector banks is low due to
(i) Over-cautions approach to lending
(ii) Reserve Bank Policies
(iii) High Overhead Costs
(iv) Social-sector lending
Identify the correct code:
Codes:
(a) (i) and (ii) (b) (i) and (iv)
(c) (i), (iii) and (iv) (d) (ii) and (iii)

42. Match the items of List-I with those List-II and select correct answer:

List-I	List-II
1. Narasimham Committe	(A) Lending under consortium arrangement
2. Shetty Committee	(B) Frauds and Malpractices in banks
3. Ghosh Committee	(C) Securities operations of banks and financial institutions
(D) Janakiraman Committee	(D) Financial system in India

Codes:	A	B	C	D
(a)	(3)	(4)	(2)	(1)
(b)	(2)	(3)	(4)	(1)
(c)	(4)	(2)	(3)	(1)
(d)	(3)	(4)	(1)	(2)

43. Which of the following financial institutions is not with in the Supervisory Purview of Reserve Bank of India?
(a) Foreign Commercial Banks Operating in India
(b) Regional Rural Banks
(c) Mutual Funds
(d) State Co-operative Banks

44. The Repo and Reserve Repo rates are resorted to by the RBI as a tool of
(a) Credit Control
(b) Settlement Systems
(c) Currency Management
(d) Liquidity Control

45. Which one of the following institutions is promoted by the IFCI:
(a) Credit Analysis and Research Ltd. (CARE)
(b) Rashtriya Gramin Vikas Nidhi (RGVN)
(c) Clearing Corporation of India Ltd (CCIL)
(d) Small Industries Development Bank of India (SIDBI)

46. Indicate the right sequence of the stages of internationalization:
(i) Multinational Company
(ii) Global Company
(iii) Transnational Company
(iv) International Company

Codes:

(a)	(i)	(iv)	(ii)	(iii)
(b)	(iv)	(i)	(iii)	(ii)
(c)	(i)	(iv)	(iii)	(ii)
(d)	(iv)	(i)	(ii)	(iii)

47. Which of the following is not one of the components of 'International Reserve'?
(a) Special Drawing Rights
(b) Reserve Position in IMF
(c) Monetary Gold
(d) Money Market Instruments

48. Match the items given in List-I with the most appropriate items in List-II:

List-I	List-II
(A) UNCTAD	(i) Foreign investment
(B) WTO	(ii) Developing countries
(C) TRIMS	(iii) UNDP
(D) ITC	(iv) General Council

Codes:	A	B	C	D
(a)	(ii)	(iv)	(i)	(iii)
(b)	(iii)	(iv)	(i)	(ii)
(c)	(iv)	(ii)	(i)	(iii)
(d)	(iii)	(ii)	(i)	(iv)

49. Duty levied on the value of goods imported is referred to as
(a) Ad valorem Duty (b) Compound Duty
(c) Specific Duty (d) Import Duty

50. Which of the following can be included in the current account of the balance of payments?
(i) Purchase of goods from abroad
(ii) Sale of services abroad
(iii) Workers' remittances from aboard
(iv) Sale of copyright to foreigners
(v) Direct investment in equity capital

Codes:
(a) (i), (ii) and (iii)
(b) (i), (ii) and (iv)
(c) (i), (ii), (iii) and (v)
(d) (i), (ii), (iii) and (iv)

51. Which of the following items would be specifically included in the statement of cash flows constructed in compliance with AS-3?
(a) Conversion of debt to equity
(b) Acquiring an asset through lease
(c) Operating and non-operating cash flow information
(d) Purchasing a building by giving a mortgage to the seller

52. Fixing the value of an employee depending upon his productivity, promotability, transferability and retainability is the core of the
(a) Certainty equivalent model
(b) Stochastic Reward Valuation model
(c) Human asset multiplier model
(d) Present value of future earnings model

53. Which of the following refers to a situation in which the merger of companies results in over 25% of the market in the hands of the merged companies?
(a) 'Gateway' condition
(b) Restrictive practice
(c) 'Share of supply' test
(d) 'Asset' test

54. Which of the following is true?
(a) Systematic risk is diversifiable but unsystematic risk is non-diversifiable.
(b) Systematic risk is non-diversifiable but unsystematic risk is diversifiable.
(c) Both systematic and unsystematic risks are diversifiable.
(d) Both systematic and unsystematic risks are non-diversifiable.

55. Match the following:

List-I (Explanation)	List-II (Term)
(A) It involves using the version of master file and the update	(1) Audit Trail Controls

	transactions used to create the current file to recreate the current master file if it becomes damaged.		
(B)	It involves copying the whole or a portion of the database to some back up medium, typically magnetics tape.	(2)	Dumping
(C)	It stores current and historical data extracted from various operations systems and consolidates for management reporting and analysis.	(3)	Grandfather, Father, Son
(D)	It maintains the chronology of events that occur either to the database definition or the database itself.	(4)	Data warehouse for Accounting

Codes:	A	B	C	D
(a)	(3)	(2)	(4)	(1)
(b)	(3)	(1)	(2)	(4)
(c)	(1)	(3)	(2)	(4)
(d)	(4)	(3)	(2)	(1)

56. Which one is not a major component of holistic marketing?
(a) Relationship marketing
(b) Integrated marketing
(c) Internal marketing
(d) Socially responsible marketing

57. The final step in target marketing is
(a) Market Analysis
(b) Market Positioning
(c) Market Segmentation
(d) Market Targeting

58. The most recent consideration in product packaging is
(a) Cost effectiveness (b) Product protection
(c) Product promotion (d) Economy

59. Distribution logistics (also termed as 'market logistics') does not include
(a) Distribution channel (b) Inventory
(c) Transportation (d) Warehouses

60. Most of the money spent in measuring the effectiveness of advertising is spent on
(a) Communication-response research
(b) Pre-testing the advertisements
(c) Post-testing the advertisements
(d) Sales-response research

61. Which of the following is not included in the model of the systems approach to human resource management?
(a) Departmentation
(b) Recruitment
(c) Performance Appraisal
(d) Promotion

62. Which one of the following is not an example of Herzberg's hygiene factors?
(a) Advancement
(b) Interpersonal relations
(c) Job security
(d) Work conditions

63. Which of the following two forms of collective bargaining were identified by Chamberlain and Kuhn?
(a) Integrative Bargaining and Distributive Bargaining
(b) Conjunctive Bargaining and Cooperative Bargaining
(c) Integrative Bargaining and Cooperative Bargaining
(d) Distributive Bargaining and Conjunctive Bargaining

64. Who observed that a worker's behaviour and sentiments are closely related?
(a) Peter Drucker (b) Elton Mayo
(c) F.W. Taylor (d) Dale Yoder

65. What is not an operative function of HRM?
(a) Procurement (b) Development
(c) Organising (d) Integration

66. The total number of Special Economic Zones notified by the Government of India till March 2011 under the SEZ Act, 2005 is
(a) 154 (b) 184 (c) 286 (d) 386

67. The different forms of IMF assistance are given below. Identify the one which is mainly meant for Less Developed Countries (LDCs)
(a) Credit Tranche Drawing
(b) Extended Fund Facility
(c) Compensatory Financing Facility
(d) Structural Adjustment Facility

68. In the context of globalization, 'Levitt Thesis' means

(a) Standardisation strategy to respond to the worldwide homogenised market and expand the market through aggressive low pricing
(b) Customise products to regional markets
(c) Customise products to meet the national market
(d) None of the above

69. Which one of the following is an internal hedging technique?
(a) Leading (b) Netting
(c) Both (a) and (b) above (d) Swap

70. Business conglomerates have different names in different countries. Which country's conglomerates are called 'Chaebols'?
(a) Japan (b) South Korea
(c) Germany (d) China

71. Mr. X, a non-resident, earned ₹ 36,000 as interest on German Development Bonds. Of this, he received one-sixth in India. The amount to be included as interest for the computation of his Gross Total Income is
(a) ₹ 36,000 (b) ₹ 30,000
(c) ₹ 6,000 (d) Nil

72. Consider the following problem relating to a let-out house property:
Municipal value–₹ 60,000
Fair rent–₹ 68,000
Standard rent under the Rent Control Act–₹ 62,000
Annual Rent received–₹ 65,000
The Gross Annual Value of the property will be
(a) ₹ 68,000 (b) ₹ 62,000
(c) ₹ 65,000 (d) ₹ 60,000

73. From the following, identify by the web-based financial software:
(a) Private Equity Software
(b) Share Accounting Software
(c) Wealth Management Software
(d) WINGS 2013

74. Which of the following are true in tax planning?
(i) It is futuristic in its approach.
(ii) It has limited scope compared to tax management.
(iii) The benefits arising from it are limited particularly in the short run.
(iv) Its main objective is to reduce the tax liability.

Codes:
(a) (i), (ii) and (iii) (b) (i) and (ii)
(c) (i) and (iv) (d) (ii), (iii) and (iv)

75. The benefits of debt financing over equity financing are likely to be highest in which of the following situations?
(a) High marginal tax rates and low non-interest tax benefits
(b) Low marginal tax rates and low non-interest tax benefits
(c) High marginal tax rates and high non-interest tax benefits
(d) Low marginal tax rates and high non-interest tax benefits.

ANSWERS

1. (d)	2. (c)	3. (b)	4. (c)	5. (d)
6. (c)	7. (c)	8. (b)	9. (a)	10. (d)
11. (c)	12. (d)	13. (a)	14. (a)	15. (d)
16. (a)	17. (a)	18. (d)	19. (d)	20. (b)
21. (c)	22. (a)	23. (a)	24. (c)	25. (b)
26. (a)	27. (b)	28. (d)	29. (b)	30. (b)
31. (d)	32. (b)	33. (d)	34. (b)	35. (a)
36. (d)	37. (d)	38. (d)	39. (c)	40. (d)
41. (d)	42. (c)	43. (c)	44. (b)	45. (c)
46. (a)	47. (b)	48. (a)	49. (d)	50. (c)
51. (a)	52. (d)	53. (b)	54. (b)	55. (a)
56. (b)	57. (c)	58. (d)	59. (d)	60. (c)
61. (b)	62. (c)	63. (b)	64. (b)	65. (a)
66. (c)	67. (b)	68. (c)	69. (a)	70. (c)
71. (c)	72. (b)	73. (c)	74. (d)	75. (b)

DECEMBER–2014

Note: This paper contains Sixty (60) multiple-choice questions, each question carrying two (2) marks. Candidate is expected to answer any Fifty (50) questions. In case more than Fifty (50) questions are attempted, only the first Fifty (50) questions will be evaluated.

PAPER–I

1. The term 'Yellow Journalism' refers to
   (a) sensational news about terrorism and violence
   (b) sensationalism and exaggeration to attract readers/viewers
   (c) sensational news about arts and culture
   (d) sensational news prints in yellow paper

2. In the classroom, the teacher sends the message either as words or images. The students are really
   (a) Encoders (b) Decoders
   (c) Agitators (d) Propagators

3. Media is known as
   (a) First Estate (b) Second Estate
   (c) Third Estate (d) Fourth Estate

4. The mode of communication that involves a single source transmitting information to a large number of receivers simultaneously, is called
   (a) Group Communication
   (b) Mass Communication
   (c) Intrapersonal Communication
   (d) Interpersonal Communication

5. A smart classroom is a teaching space which has
   (i) Smart portion with a touch panel control system
   (ii) PC/Laptop connection and DVD/VCR player
   (iii) Document camera and specialized software
   (iv) Projector and screen

   Select the correct answer from the codes given below:
   (a) (i) and (ii) only (b) (ii) and (iv) only
   (c) (i), (ii) and (iii) only (d) (i), (ii), (iii) and (iv)

6. Digital Empowerment means
   (i) Universal digit literacy
   (ii) Universal access to all digital resources.
   (iii) Collaborative digital platform for participative governance.
   (iv) Probability of all entitlements for individuals through cloud.

   Choose the correct answer from the codes given below:
   Codes:
   (a) (i) and (ii) only (b) (ii) and (iii) only
   (c) (i), (ii) and (iii) only (d) (i), (ii), (iii) and (iv)

7. The next term in the series:
   2, 7, 28, 63, 126, _______ is
   (a) 215 (b) 245 (c) 276 (d) 296

8. The next term in the series:
   AB, ED, IH, NM, _______ is
   (a) TS (b) ST (c) TU (d) SU

9. If STREAMERS is coded as UVTGALDQR, then KNOWLEDGE will be coded as
   (a) MQPYLCDFD (b) MPQYLDCFD
   (c) PMYQLDFCD (d) YMQPLDDFC

10. A is brother of B. B is the brother of C. C is the husband of D. E is the father of A. D is related to E as
    (a) Daughter (b) Daughter-in-law
    (c) Sister-in-law (d) Sister

11. Two numbers are in the ratio 3 : 5. If 9 is subtracted from the numbers, the ratio becomes 12 : 23. The numbers are
    (a) 30, 50 (b) 36, 60 (c) 33, 55 (d) 42, 70

12. The mean of the ages of father and his son is 27 years. After 18 years, father will be twice as old as his son. Their present ages are
    (a) 42, 12 (b) 40, 14 (c) 30, 24 (d) 36, 18

Read the following passage carefully and answer questions 13 to 17:

The literary distaste for politics, however, seems to be focused not so much on the largely murky practice of politics in itself as a subject of literary representation but rather more on how it is often depicted in literature, i.e., on the very politics of such representation. A political novel often turns out to be not merely a novel about politics but a novel with a politics of its own, for it seeks not merely to show us how things are but has fairly definite ideas about how things should be, and precisely what one should think and do in order to make things move in that desired direction. In short, it seeks to convert and enlist the reader to a particular cause or ideology; it often is (in an only too familiar phrase) not literature but propaganda. This is said to violate the very spirit of literature which is to broaden our understanding of the world and the range of our sympathies rather than to narrow them down through partisan commitment. As John Keats said, 'We hate poetry that has a palpable design upon us'.

Another reason why politics does not seem amenable to the highest kind of literary representation seems to arise from the fact that politics by its very nature is constituted of ideas and ideologies. If political situations do not lend themselves to happy literary treatment, political ideas present perhaps an even greater problem in this regard. Literature, it is argued, is about human experiences rather than about intellectual abstractions; it deals in what is called the 'felt reality' of human flesh and blood, and in sap and savour (rasa) rather than in arid and lifeless ideas. In an extensive discussion of the matter in her book Ideas and the Novel, the American novelist Mary McCarthy observed that 'ideas are still today felt to be unsightly in the novel' though that was not so in 'former days', i.e., in the 18th and 19th centuries. Her formulation of the precise nature of the incompatibility between ideas on the one hand and the novel on the other betrays perhaps a divided conscience in the matter and a sense of dilemma shared by many writers and readers: 'An idea cannot have loose ends, but a novel, I almost think, needs them. Nevertheless, there is enough in common for the novelists to feel...the attraction of ideas while taking up arms against them—most often with weapons of mockery.'

13. According to the passage, a political novel often turns out to be a
    (a) Literary distaste for politics
    (b) Literary representation of politics
    (c) Novel with its own politics
    (d) Depiction of murky practice of politics
14. A political novel reveals
    (a) Reality of the things
    (b) Writer's perception
    (c) Particular ideology of the readers
    (d) The spirit of literature
15. The constructs of politics by its nature is
    (a) Prevalent political situation
    (b) Ideas and Ideologies
    (c) Political propaganda
    (d) Understanding of human nature
16. Literature deals with
    (a) Human experiences in politics
    (b) Intellectual abstractions
    (c) Dry and empty ideas
    (d) Felt reality of human life
17. The observation of the novelist, Mary McCarthy reveals
    (a) unseen felt ideas of today in the novel
    (b) dichotomy of conscience on political ideas and novels
    (c) compatibility between idea and novel
    (d) endless ideas and novels
18. When in a group of propositions, one proposition is claimed to follow from the others, that group of propositions is called
    (a) An argument
    (b) A valid argument
    (c) An explanation
    (d) An invalid argument
19. Namita and Samita are brilliant and studious. Anita and Karabi are obedient and irregular. Babita and Namita are irregular but brilliant. Samita and Kabita are regular and obedient. Who among them is/are brilliant, obedient, regular and studious?
    (a) Samita alone (b) Namita and Samita
    (c) Kabita alone (d) Anita alone
20. Warrior is related to sword, carpenter is related to saw, farmer is related to plough. In the same way, the author is related to
    (a) Book (b) Fame
    (c) Reader (d) Pen

21. Given below is a diagram of three circles A, B and C over-lapping each other. The circle A represents the class of honest people, the circle B represents the class of sincere people and circle C represents the class of politicians. p, q, r, s, U, X, Y represent different regions. Select the code that represents the region indicating the class of honest politicians who are not sincere.

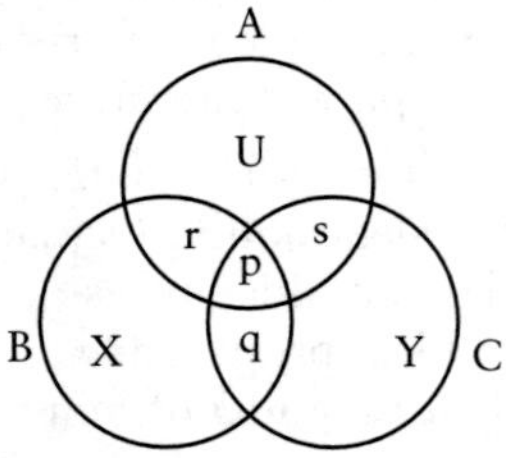

Codes:
(a) X (b) q (c) p (d) s

22. "A man ought no more to value himself for being wiser than a woman if he owes his advantage to a better education, than he ought to boast of his courage for beating a man when his hands were tied."
The above passage is an instance of
(a) Deductive argument
(b) Hypothetical argument
(c) Analogical argument
(d) Factual argument

23. By which of the following proposition, the proposition 'wise men are hardly afraid of death' is contradicted?
(a) Some wise men are afraid of death.
(b) All wise men are afraid of death.
(c) No wise men is afraid of death.
(d) Some wise men are not afraid of death.

For a country CO_2 emissions (million metric tons) from various sectors are given in the following table. Answer the questions (24 to 29) based on the data given:

CO_2 emissions (million metric tons)					
Sector / Year	Power	Industry	Commercial	Agriculture	Domestic
2005	500	200	150	80	100
2006	600	300	200	90	110
2007	650	320	250	100	120
2008	700	400	300	150	150
2009	800	450	320	200	180

24. What is the percentage (%) growth of CO_2 emissions from power sector during 2005 to 2009?
(a) 60 (b) 50 (c) 40 (d) 80

25. Which sector has recorded maximum growth in CO_2 emissions during 2005 to 2009?
(a) Power (b) Industry
(c) Commercial (d) Agriculture

26. By what percentage (%), the total emissions of CO_2 have increased from 2005 to 2009?
(a) ~89.32% (b) ~57.62%
(c) ~40.32% (d) ~113.12%

27. What is the average annual growth rate of CO_2 emissions in power sector?
(a) ~12.57% (b) ~16.87%
(c) ~30.81% (d) ~50.25%

28. What is the percentage contribution of power sector to total CO_2 emissions in the year 2008?
(a) ~30.82% (b) ~41.18%
(c) ~51.38% (d) ~60.25%

29. In which year, the contribution (%) of industry to total sectoral CO_2 emissions was minimum?
(a) 2005 (b) 2006 (c) 2007 (d) 2009

30. Symbols A-F are used in which one of the following?
(a) Binary number system
(b) Decimal number system
(c) Hexadecimal number system
(d) Octal number system

31. Which one of the following is not a search engine?
(a) Google (b) Chrome
(c) Yahoo (d) Bing

32. CSS stands for
(a) Cascading Style Sheets
(b) Collecting Style Sheets
(c) Comparative Style Sheets
(d) Comprehensive Style Sheets

33. MOOC stands for
(a) Media Online Open Course
(b) Massachusetts Open Online Course
(c) Massive Open Online Course
(d) Myrind Open Online Course

34. Binary equivalent of decimal number 35 is
(a) 100011 (b) 110001
(c) 110101 (d) 101011

35. gif, jpg, bmp, png are used as extensions for files which store
(a) audio data (b) image data
(c) video data (d) text data

36. Which of the anthropogenic activity accounts for more than 2/3rd of global water consumption?
(a) Agriculture
(b) Hydropower generation
(c) Industry
(d) Domestic and Municipal usage

37. One of the anthropogenic sources of gaseous pollutants chlorofluorocarbons (CFCs) in air is
(a) Cement industry (b) Fertiliser industry
(c) Foam industry (d) Pesticide industry

38. In terms of total CO_2 emissions from a country, identify the correct sequence:
(a) U.S.A. > China > India > Russia
(b) China > U.S.A. > India > Russia
(c) China > U.S.A. > Russia > India
(d) U.S.A. > China > Russia > India

39. Match List I and List II and identify the correct code:

List I	List II
A. World Health Day	i. 16th September
B. World Population Day	ii. 1st December
C. World Ozone Day	iii. 11th July
D. World AIDS Day	iv. 7th April

Codes:	A	B	C	D
(a)	i	ii	iii	iv
(b)	iv	iii	i	ii
(c)	ii	iii	iv	i
(d)	iii	iv	ii	i

40. The cyclone 'Hudhud' hit the coast of which State?
(a) Andhra Pradesh (b) Karnataka
(c) Kerala (d) Gujarat

41. Which of the following is not a renewable natural resource?
(a) Clean air (b) Fresh water
(c) Fertile soil (d) Salt

42. The maximum number of fake institutions/universities as identified by the UGC in the year 2014 are in the State/Union territory of
(a) Bihar (b) Uttar Pradesh
(c) Tamil Nadu (d) Delhi

43. Which of the following institutions are empowered to confer or grant degrees under the UGC Act, 1956?
(i) A university established by an Act of Parliament.
(ii) A university established by an Act of Legislature.
(iii) A university/institution established by a linguistic minority.
(iv) An institution which is a deemed to be university.

Select the correct answer from the codes given below:

Codes:
(a) (i) and (ii) (b) (i), (ii) and (iii)
(c) (i), (ii) and (iv) (d) (i), (ii), (iii) and (iv)

44. Which of the following are the tools of good governance?
(i) Social Audit
(ii) Separation of Powers
(iii) Citizen's Charter
(iv) Right to Information

Select the correct answer from the codes given below:

Codes:
(a) (i), (iii) and (iv) (b) (ii), (iii) and (iv)
(c) (i) and (iv) (d) (i), (ii), (iii) and (iv)

45. Which of the following powers, the President has in relation to Lok Sabha?
(i) Summoning
(ii) Adjournment–sine die
(iii) Prorogation
(iv) Dissolution

Select the correct answer from the codes given below:

Codes:
(a) (i) and (iv) (b) (i), (ii) and (iii)
(c) (i), (iii) and (iv) (d) (i), (ii), (iii) and (iv)

46. The interval between two sessions of parliament must not exceed
(a) 3 months (b) 6 months
(c) 4 months (d) 100 days

47. Right to Privacy as a Fundamental Right is implied in

(a) Right to Freedom
(b) Right to Life and Personal Liberty
(c) Right to Equality
(d) Right against Exploitation

48. Which of the following organizations deals with 'capacity building program' on Educational Planning?
(a) NCERT (b) UGC
(c) NAAC (d) NUEPA

49. "Education is the manifestation of perfection already in man" was stated by
(a) M.K. Gandhi (b) R.N. Tagore
(c) Swami Vivekanand (d) Sri Aurobindo

50. Which of the following is not a prescribed level of teaching?
(a) Memory (b) Understanding
(c) Reflective (d) Differentiation

51. Maximum participation of students during teaching is possible through
(a) Lecture method
(b) Demonstration method
(c) Inductive method
(d) Textbook method

52. Diagnostic evaluation ascertains
(a) Students performance at the beginning of instructions.
(b) Learning progress and failures during instructions.
(c) Degree of achievement of instructions at the end.
(d) Causes and remedies of persistent learning problems during instructions.

53. Instructional aids are used by the teacher to
(a) glorify the class
(b) attract the students
(c) clarify the concepts
(d) ensure discipline

54. Attitude of the teacher that affects teaching pertains to
(a) Affective domain
(b) Cognitive domain
(c) Connative domain
(d) Psychomotor domain

55. When planning to do as social research, it is better to
(a) approach the topic with an open mind
(b) do a pilot study before getting stuck into it
(c) be familiar with literature on the topic
(d) forget about theory because this is a very practical

56. When academicians are called to deliver lecture or presentation to an audience on certain topics or a set of topics of educational nature, it is called
(a) Training Program (b) Seminar
(c) Workshop (d) Symposium

57. The core elements of a dissertation are
(a) Introduction; Data Collection; Data Analysis; Conclusions and Recommendations
(b) Executive Summary; Literature review; Data gathered; Conclusions; Bibliography
(c) Research Plan; Research Data; Analysis; References
(d) Introduction; Literature Review; Research Methodology; Results; Discussion and Conclusion

58. What is a Research Design?
(a) A way of conducting research that is not grounded in theory.
(b) The choice between using qualitative or quantitative methods.
(c) The style in which you present your research findings, e.g. a graph.
(d) A framework for every stage of the collection and analysis of data.

59. 'Sampling Cases' means
(a) Sampling using a sampling frame
(b) Identifying people who are suitable for research
(c) Literally the researcher's brief case
(d) Sampling of people, newspapers, television programmes, etc.

60. The frequency distribution of a research data which is symmetrical in shape similar to a normal distribution but center peak is much higher, is
(a) Skewed (b) Mesokurtic
(c) Leptokurtic (d) Platykurtic

ANSWERS

1. (b)	2. (b)	3. (d)	4. (b)	5. (d)
6. (d)	7. (a)	8. (a)	9. (b)	10. (b)
11. (c)	12. (a)	13. (c)	14. (b)	15. (b)

16. (d)	17. (a)	18. (a)	19. (a)	20. (d)
21. (d)	22. (c)	23. (b)	24. (a)	25. (d)
26. (a)	27. (a)	28. (b)	29. (a)	30. (c)
31. (b)	32. (a)	33. (c)	34. (a)	35. (b)
36. (a)	37. (c)	38. (b)	39. (b)	40. (a)
41. (d)	42. (b)	43. (c)	44. (d)	45. (c)
46. (b)	47. (b)	48. (d)	49. (c)	50. (d)
51. (b)	52. (d)	53. (c)	54. (a)	55. (c)
56. (b)	57. (d)	58. (d)	59. (d)	60. (c)

PAPER–II

Note: This paper contains fifty (50) objective type questions, each question carrying two (2) marks. All questions are compulsory.

1. The responsibility of the organization to the workers includes:
   (i) The payment of fair wages
   (ii) Arrangement of proper training and education of the workers
   (iii) The installation of an efficient grievance handling system
   (iv) Welfare of family members
   (v) The provision of the best possible working conditions

   Identify the correct combination:
   (a) (i), (ii), (iii) and (v)
   (b) (ii), (iii), (iv) and (v)
   (c) (i), (ii), (iii) and (iv)
   (d) (i), (iii), (iv) and (v)

2. Match the items of List-I with List-II:

   List-I
   A. Industries Development Regulation Act
   B. Import and Export Control Act
   C. Foreign Exchange Management Act
   D. Factories Act

   List-II
   i. 1947 ii. 1948 iii. 1951 iv. 1999

   Identify the correct combination:

Codes:	**A**	**B**	**C**	**D**
(a)	i	iii	iv	ii
(b)	iii	i	ii	iv
(c)	iii	i	iv	ii
(d)	iii	iv	ii	i

3. Which among the following is not a correct sequential combination?
   (a) Macro Environment → Economic Environment → National Income → Pattern of Income Distribution
   (b) Business Environment → Internal Environment → Business Ethics → Payment of Fair Wages
   (c) Business Environment → External Environment → Micro Environment → Suppliers
   (d) Macro Environment → External Environment → Customers → Prospects of Business Development

4. Which among the following is not a correct combination?
   (a) Industrial Policy – 1948
   (b) Industrial Policy Statement – 1977
   (c) Industrial Policy Statement – 1980
   (d) Industrial Policy Statement – 1991

5. **Statement–I:** The industrial policy of the Government of India is aimed at increasing the tempo of industrial development.

   Statement–II: After the New Industrial Policy–1991, the Balance of Trade for India has always been positive.

   Codes:
   (a) Statement (I) is correct, but (II) is incorrect.
   (b) Statement (II) is correct, but (I) is incorrect.
   (c) Both Statements (I) and (II) are correct.
   (d) Both Statements (I) and (II) are incorrect.

6. Current Ratio 2.5, Liquid Ratio 1.5 and Working Capital ₹ 60,000. What is Current Assets?
   (a) ₹ 60,000 (b) ₹ 80,000
   (c) ₹ 1,00,000 (d) ₹ 1,20,000

7. X, Y, Z are sharing profits in the ratio of 6 : 5 : 3. A is admitted into partnership for 1/8th share. The sacrificing ratio of X, Y and Z is
   (a) Equal (b) 6 : 5 : 3
   (c) 5/14, 4/14, 5/14 (d) 4 : 5 : 5

8. Accounting information given by a company:

Total assets turnover	3 times
Net profit margin	10%
Total assets	₹ 1,00,000

The net profit is

(a) ₹ 10,000 (b) ₹ 15,000
(c) ₹ 25,000 (d) ₹ 30,000

9. "Make sufficient provisions for future losses, but do not anticipate future profits." This statement is in accordance to the concept of:

(a) Matching (b) Objectivity
(c) Conservatism (d) Materiality

10. When a firm is dissolved, profit or loss on realisation is shared by the partners

(a) Equal
(b) In the ratio of their capital balances
(c) In the profit sharing ratio
(d) In the ratio laid down in Garner Vs. Murray

11. The inverse relationship between variations in the price and quantity demanded is not due to

(a) Income Effects
(b) Substitution Effects
(c) Future Expectations
(d) Law of Diminishing Marginal Utility

12. Consumer is said to be in equilibrium, maximizing his total utility, when

(a) the marginal utilities of the two goods consumed are equal.
(b) the proportions of the marginal utilities and respective prices are equal.
(c) the consumer gets full satisfaction from the consumption.
(d) the consumer feels satisfied with his expenditure on the various goods.

13. Match the items of the following two lists and suggest the correct code:

List-I

A. Zero Income Elasticity
B. Unit Cross Elasticity
C. Positive Cross Elasticity
D. Negative Cross Elasticity

List-II

i. Substitute goods
ii. Complementary goods
iii. Indifferent goods
iv. Independent goods

Choose the correct option:

Codes:	**A**	**B**	**C**	**D**
(a)	iii	ii	i	iv
(b)	ii	iii	iv	i
(c)	iii	iv	i	ii
(d)	iv	i	ii	iii

14. **Statement (A):** The isoquant curves are drawn convex to the origin due to diminishing technical rate of substitution.

Statement (B): The lesser the convexity of the isoquant curve the greater the possibility of the complementarity of the two inputs.

Codes:

(a) Statements (A) and (B) both are correct.
(b) Statement (A) is correct but (B) is incorrect.
(c) Statement (A) is incorrect but (B) is correct.
(d) Statements (A) and (B) both are incorrect.

15. Match the items of the List-I with those of List-II and suggest the correct code:

List-I

A. Constant average cost over a range of output
B. Average cost becomes constant momentarily
C. Normal average cost is a U-shaped curve
D. Modern Long-run average cost is L-shaped

List-II

i. Economic capacity
ii. Reserve capacity
iii. Production and Managerials costs effects
iv. Economies and Diseconomies

Codes:	**A**	**B**	**C**	**D**
(a)	i	ii	iii	iv
(b)	ii	iii	iv	i
(c)	iii	iv	ii	i
(d)	ii	i	iv	iii

16. Which one of the following is not probability sampling method?

(a) Simple Random Sampling
(b) Cluster Sampling
(c) Judgemental Sampling
(d) Systematic Sampling

17. The research carried out to expand the knowledge of a particular field is known as

(a) Applied research
(b) Qualitative research
(c) Quantitative research
(d) Basic research

18. In univariate data analysis t-test is used when the data are in the form of

(a) Metric data with one sample
(b) Non-metric data

(c) Non-metric data with independent variable
(d) Metric data with independent two sample

19. To show the trend for a variable, which one of the presentation method is used?
(a) Histogram (b) Frequency polygon
(c) Line graph (d) Scatter graph

20. Which one of the following objectives is not the objective of secondary data collection?
(a) Identify the problem
(b) Test the hypotheses of the relevant present problem
(c) Better define the problem
(d) Interpret primary data more insightfully

21. The structure of an organisation in which there is separation of ownership and management is called
(a) Sole proprietorship
(b) Partnership
(c) Company
(d) Cooperative society

22. When a person transacts with a company on matters which is beyond the power of the company, the person will be governed by the Doctrine of
(a) Management by Exception
(b) Constructive Notice
(c) Indoor Management
(d) Self Management

23. **Assertion (A)**: MBO is effective way of planning and organizing the work.
Reason (R): Employees participate in setting the objectives.
Codes:
(a) Both (A) and (R) are true.
(b) Both (A) and (R) are false.
(c) (A) is true, but (R) is false.
(d) (A) is false, but (R) is correct.

24. The appropriate sequence of the formation of a company are in the following order:
(a) Promotion, commencement of business and incorporation
(b) Promotion, incorporation, capital subscription and commencement of business
(c) Capital subscription, promotion, incorporation and commencement of business
(d) Incorporation, capital subscription, commencement of business and promotion

25. Delegation of authority makes the size of the organization:
(a) Smaller organization
(b) Larger organization
(c) Very big organization
(d) It does not affect the size of the organization

26. Managerial Grid suggests the following as the best leader behaviour:
(a) High structure and high consideration
(b) Low structure and low consideration
(c) High concern both for production and people
(d) Low concern both for production and people

27. Marketing strategy development is also known as
(a) Marketing Control
(b) Marketing Exercise
(c) Marketing Planning
(d) Situation Analysis

28. For most people, the purchase of cheese for daily use can be described as a
(a) Completely novel buy
(b) Modified re-buy
(c) Routine re-buy
(d) High involvement product

29. The promotion mix of a company consists of these—
(a) Marketing communication, promotion decisions
(b) Personal selling, product objectives
(c) Advertising, personal selling, sales promotion, publicity and public relations
(d) Consumer psychology, buyers motives, brand equity

30. Rational buying motives that determine purchase decisions are mostly based on
(a) Price factor (b) Psychological factors
(c) Quality of product
(d) Advertisement

31. **Statement–I:** Capital structure refers to composition of long-term funds.
Statement–II: These include equity share capital, preference share capital, debentures, all debts and all reserves.

(a) Both Statements I and II are correct.
(b) Statement I is correct but Statement II is incorrect.
(c) Statement I is incorrect but Statement II is correct.
(d) Both statements are incorrect.

32. Match the items of the following two lists and suggest the correct code:

List-I
A. Pay-back Rate of Return
B. Internal Rate of Return
C. Benefit Cost Ratio
D. Net Terminal Value Method

List-II
i. Discounted Cash Flow Technique
ii. Compounded values of investments and returns
iii. Crude method for project evaluation
iv. Varying sized projects evaluation

Codes:	A	B	C	D
(a)	ii	iii	i	iv
(b)	iii	i	iv	ii
(c)	i	iv	ii	iii
(d)	iv	ii	iii	i

33. Match the items of the following two lists and suggest the correct code:

List-I
A. Realised yield method
B. Taxation
C. Cost of total capital employed
D. Dividend growth is a consideration

List-II
i. Cost of equity share capital
ii. Cost of equity capital
iii. Cost of debt capital
iv. Weighted cost of capital

Codes:	A	B	C	D
(a)	iv	iii	ii	i
(b)	ii	iv	i	iii
(c)	ii	iii	iv	i
(d)	i	ii	iii	iv

34. Cash Flow Management involves:
I. Lock-box system
II. Marketable securities
III. Playing the float
IV. Concentration Bank Account

Codes:
(a) I, II and III only (b) II, III and IV only
(c) I, III and IV only (d) I, II and IV only

35. Dividend capitalisation model was developed by
(a) Ezra Solomon
(b) Myron J. Gordon
(c) James E. Walter
(d) Merton H. Miller and Franco Modigliani

36. The process of narrowing a large number of candidates to a smaller field is called
(a) Rushing (b) Recruitment
(c) Selection (d) Enrollment

37. According to which theory, people are motivated to the extent to which they expect that their actions will help in achievement of goals?
(a) Vroom's Vector Valence Theory
(b) Need Theory
(c) Z Theory
(d) X Theory

38. Match the items of List-I with List-II and select the correct code:

List-I
A. Getting Effective Leadership in the Industrial Organization
B. The Nature of Leadership, Organization and Management
C. Industrial Management
D. Personnel Management

List-II
i. Dale Yoder ii. Alford and Beatty
iii. Douglas McGregor iv. Chester I. Bernard

Codes:	A	B	C	D
(a)	i	ii	iii	iv
(b)	iii	iv	ii	i
(c)	iii	iv	i	ii
(d)	iv	iii	ii	i

39. Match the items of List-I with List-II:

List-I	List-II
A. AITUC	i. Indian National Congress
B. BMS	ii. Socialists
C. INTUC	iii. Rashtriya Swayamsevak Sangh
D. CITU	iv. Communist Party of India

Identify the correct combination:

Codes:	A	B	C	D
(a)	iv	iii	ii	i
(b)	iv	i	ii	iii
(c)	iv	iii	i	ii
(d)	iv	i	iii	ii

40. The main characteristics of Weber's bureaucracy are:
(a) Specialization (b) Hierarchy of authority
(c) System of rules (d) All of the above

41. Match the items of List-I with List-II:
List-I
A. RBI Nationalization
B. Imperial Bank Nationalization
C. Nationalization of 14 Commercial Banks
D. Establishment of IDBI
List-II
i. 1964 ii. 1949 iii. 1955 iv. 1969
Identify the correct combination:

Codes:	A	B	C	D
(a)	i	ii	iii	iv
(b)	ii	iii	i	iv
(c)	iii	ii	iv	i
(d)	ii	iii	iv	i

42. As per the RBI Act, 1934, the following functions are described as the functions of a Central Bank:
(i) Banking functions
(ii) Advisory functions
(iii) Supervisory functions
(iv) Promotional functions
Identify the correct combination:
(a) (i), (iii) and (iv) (b) (i), (ii) and (iv)
(c) (ii), (iii) and (iv) (d) Only (i) and (iii)

43. Phishing is an attempt to acquire:
(a) Loan from unauthorized firms
(b) Sensitive information such as username, password, etc.
(c) Personal information from banks
(d) None of the above

44. What is Call Money?
(a) Money borrowed or lent for a day or overnight.
(b) Money borrowed for more than one day but upto 3 days.
(c) Money borrowed for more than one day but upto 7 days.
(d) Money borrowed for more than one day but upto 14 days.

45. The Regulatory Authority of Regional Rural Banks is
(a) NABARD (b) Central Government
(c) State Government (d) Sponsor Bank

46. Which of the following is not ensured to the consumer in the globalization?
(a) Lower prices
(b) Better selection
(c) Clear origin of goods and services
(d) Improved services

47. In international trade which of the following is a non-tariff trade barrier?
(a) Quotas (b) Import bans
(c) Export controls (d) Anti dumping laws

48. Match the items of List-I with items in List-II and select a correct code:
List-I
A. Current Account
B. Capital Account
C. Unilateral Payments
D. Official Statement Account
List-II
i. Official Capital
ii. Reserves from foreign countries
iii. Reparations
iv. Visible Exports and Imports

Codes:	A	B	C	D
(a)	i	iii	ii	iv
(b)	iv	i	ii	iii
(c)	iv	i	iii	ii
(d)	iii	ii	i	iv

49. Match the items of List-I with the items in List-II and select a correct code:
List-I
A. Vishesh Krishi Upaj Yojana B. EPCG
C. DFRC D. DEPB
List-II
i. Scheme intended to reduce difficulties of exporters
ii. Duty Entitlement Pass Book
iii. To boost exports of fruits, vegetables, flowers, minor forest produce, etc.
iv. Relating to import of duty free fuel

Codes:	A	B	C	D
(a)	iv	i	ii	iii
(b)	iv	iii	i	ii
(c)	iii	iv	ii	i
(d)	iii	i	iv	ii

50. Which of the following is not the agency of World Bank?
(a) MIGA (b) ICSID (c) ADB (d) IDA

ANSWERS

1. (a)	2. (c)	3. (d)	4. (d)	5. (a)
6. (c)	7. (b)	8. (d)	9. (c)	10. (c)
11. (c)	12. (b)	13. (c)	14. (b)	15. (d)
16. (c)	17. (d)	18. (d)	19. (c)	20. (b)
21. (c)	22. (b)	23. (a)	24. (b)	25. (b)
26. (c)	27. (c)	28. (c)	29. (c)	30. (b)
31. (b)	32. (b)	33. (c)	34. (c)	35. (b)
36. (c)	37. (a)	38. (b)	39. (c)	40. (d)
41. (d)	42. (a)	43. (b)	44. (a)	45. (a)
46. (c)	47. (b)	48. (c)	49. (d)	50. (c)

PAPER–III

Note: This paper contains seventy-five (75) objective type questions of two (2) marks each. All questions are compulsory.

1. Match the items of List-I with List-II:

   List-I (International Economic Groups)
   A. European Union (EU)
   B. European Free Trade Association (EFTA)
   C. Caribbean Community (CARICOM)
   D. South Asian Association for Regional Cooperation (SAARC)

   List-II (Year of Establishment)
   i. 1973 ii. 1992 iii. 1985 iv. 1960

Codes:	A	B	C	D
(a)	ii	iv	iii	i
(b)	ii	iv	i	iii
(c)	iv	ii	i	iii
(d)	iii	i	ii	iv

2. The important objectives of WTO are:
   (i) To improve the quality of technology in the member countries.
   (ii) To improve the standard of living of people in the member countries.
   (iii) To ensure full employment and broad increase in effective demand.
   (iv) To enlarge production and trade of goods.
   (v) To increase trade of services.

   Codes:
   (a) (i), (ii), (iii) and (iv)
   (b) (ii), (iii), (iv) and (v)
   (c) (i), (ii), (iii) and (v)
   (d) (i), (iii), (iv) and (v)

3. **Assertion (A):** The industrial growth in India has been hampered by the burden of many controls and regulations.

   Reason (R): The New Industrial Policy seeks to liberate the industry from the shackles of Licensing System.

   Codes:
   (a) Assertion (A) is correct, but Reason (R) is not correct.
   (b) Assertion (A) is correct and Reason (R) is right explanation of (A).
   (c) Both Assertion (A) and Reason (R) are correct.
   (d) Both Assertion (A) and Reason (R) are incorrect.

4. Internal environment of a business includes:
   (i) Business ethics and moral standards
   (ii) Business and managerial policies
   (iii) Prospects of business development
   (iv) Government rules and regulations
   (v) Industrial relations

   Codes:
   (a) (i), (ii), (iv) and (v)
   (b) (ii), (iii), (iv) and (v)
   (c) (i), (ii), (iii) and (iv)
   (d) (i), (ii), (iii) and (v)

5. Identify the incorrect combination from the following:

Finance Commission	Constituted (Year)	Report Submitted (Year)	Chairman
(a) 1st	1951	1953	K.C. Neogi
(b) 7th	1977	1978	J.M. Shelat
(c) 11th	1998	2000	N.K.P. Salve
(d) 13th	2007	2009	V.L. Kelkar

6. A flexible budget requires careful study and classification of expenses into
   (a) Product expenses and period expenses
   (b) Past and current expenses
   (c) Administrative, selling and factory expenses
   (d) Fixed, semi-variable and variable expenses

7. Responsibility accounting aims at collecting and reporting costing information

(a) Department-wise (b) Cost centre-wise
(c) Function-wise (d) Product-wise

8. Return on Investment (RoI) is computed as
(a) Net Profit Ratio × Capital Turnover Ratio
(b) Operating Net Profit Ratio × Shareholders Fund
(c) Net Profit / Sales
(d) Cost of Sales / Capital Employed

9. Margin of Safety is calculated by using
(a) Profit / (P/V Ratio)
(b) Fixed Cost / Contribution
(c) Break Even Sales / Sales
(d) Profit / Sales

10. Pre-acquisition profit in subsidiary company is considered as
(a) Revenue profit (b) Capital profit
(c) Goodwill (d) Minority interest

11. **Assertion (A):** The financial statements prepared on historical cost basis result into an erosion of capital in the long run.

Reason (R): Maintaining the books of accounts as per Current Purchasing Power Technique only may contain the inflationary pressure.

In the context of above two statements, which one of the following is correct one?
(a) Both (A) and (R) are true and (R) is the correct explanation of (A).
(b) Both (A) and (R) are true, but (R) is not the correct explanation of (A).
(c) (A) is true, but (R) is false.
(d) (A) is false, but (R) is true.

12. Secondary market intermediaries for corporate securities in India are
I. Investors
II. Jobbers
III. Brokers and sub-brokers
IV. Portfolio consultants

Codes:
(a) I, II and III only (b) II, III and IV only
(c) II and III only (d) III and IV only

13. The type of lease requiring an agreement between the financier and lessor is known as
(a) Financial lease (b) Sale and lease back
(c) Leveraged lease (d) Operating lease

14. Match the various stock exchanges in List-I with the years of their establishment in List-II as follows and suggest the correct code:

List-I
A. National Stock Exchange (NSE)
B. MCX Stock Exchange (MCX-SX)
C. Bombay Stock Exchange (BSE)
D. Interconnected Stock Exchange of India (ISEI)

List-II
i. 1875 ii. 1992
iii. 2000 iv. 2008

Codes:	**A**	**B**	**C**	**D**
(a)	ii	iv	i	iii
(b)	ii	iii	iv	i
(c)	i	iii	ii	iv
(d)	iii	ii	iv	i

15. Monopolists prefer to sell the products in the markets with
(a) Elastic demand
(b) Unitary elastic demand
(c) Inelastic demand
(d) Absence of elasticity of demand

16. **Assertion (A):** In long run under Perfect Competition all firms invariably get only normal profit.

Reason (R): All firms incur minimum average cost and incur no selling cost due to absence of product differentiation.

Codes:
(a) Assertion (A) and Reason (R) both are correct.
(b) Assertion (A) is correct, but Reason (R) is incorrect.
(c) Assertion (A) is incorrect, but Reason (R) is correct.
(d) Assertion (A) and Reason (R) both are incorrect.

17. **Assertion (A):** Differential pricing structure is designed to accommodate the various categories of buyers.

Reason (R): It aims at increasing sales and revenues and driving the competitors out from the market.

Codes:
(a) Assertion (A) and Reasoning (R) both are correct.

(b) Assertion (A) is correct, but Reasoning (R) is incorrect.
(c) Assertion (A) is incorrect, but Reasoning (R) is correct.
(d) Assertion (A) and Reasoning (R) both are incorrect.

18. Cost-plus pricing is considered appropriate for:
I. Product Tailoring
II. Public Utility Pricing
III. Refusal Pricing
IV. Monopoly Pricing

Codes:
(a) I and II only (b) I, II and III only
(c) II, III and IV only (d) III and IV only

19. For promoting sales advertising endeavours may be made as per
I. Competitive parity
II. Objective and task
III. Tied sales
IV. All-one-can-Afford

Codes:
(a) I and II only (b) II, III and IV only
(c) I, II and IV only (d) III and IV only

20. In the hypothesis testing procedure a researcher may commit type II error in which of the following conditions?
(a) When the true null hypothesis is rejected.
(b) When the alternative hypothesis is accepted.
(c) When the false null hypothesis is accepted.
(d) When the true null hypothesis is accepted.

21. Which one of the following tenets is not correct in the context of Central Limit Theorem?
(a) If a population from which a sample is drawn is normally distributed the sampling distribution of mean (SDM) will be normal for all sample sizes.
(b) The mean of the SDM is the population mean.
(c) If the population is not normal from which the sample is drawn, the SDM is not normal for any sample size.
(d) If the population is not normal from which a sample is drawn, the SDM approaches normality as the sample size increases.

22. Which one of the following is not an example of tax evasion?
(a) Submitting misleading documents.
(b) Not maintaining proper accounts of income earned.
(c) Suppression of facts.
(d) Interpreting the tax law in ones own way to minimise tax liability.

23. Which one of the following is not the purpose of performance-monitoring research?
(a) To provide feedback for evaluation and control.
(b) To indicate things that are not going as planned.
(c) To help the organisation to plan various activities.
(d) It is required to explain why something went wrong.

24. The transformation of raw data into a form that will make them easy to understand and interpret, rearranging and manipulating data to generate information is called
(a) Descriptive research
(b) Descriptive analysis
(c) Causal research
(d) Exploratory research

25. **Assertion (A):** The span of management at the upper level is generally narrow while at the lower level span is wide.

Reason (R): The task allocated to subordinates at the lower level of management are more specific and precise and thus making supervision easy and simple.

Suggest correct code:
(a) (A) is correct, but (R) is wrong.
(b) (A) is wrong, but (R) is correct.
(c) Both (A) and (R) are correct.
(d) Both (A) and (R) are wrong.

26. Match the following:

List-I
A. To check the quality of work
B. To see that work is completed in time
C. To check absenteeism of workers
D. To issue instructions regarding methods of work

List-II

i. Speed loss ii. Inspector
iii. Instruction and check iv. Shop discipline

Select the code:

Codes:	A	B	C	D
(a)	iii	ii	i	iv
(b)	ii	i	iv	iii
(c)	ii	i	iii	iv
(d)	iv	iii	i	ii

27. F.W. Taylor called "The Military type of Foreman" to
(a) Unity of Command
(b) Span of Control
(c) Delegated Legislature
(d) Department

28. Match the items of List-I with List-II:

List-I

A. Commentary Four Chambault
B. Midvale Steel Works
C. Charleton Twist Company
D. Credit Mobilier

List-II

i. F.W. Taylor
ii. Claud Henry Saint Simon
iii. Henry Fayol
iv. Robert Owen

Codes:	A	B	C	D
(a)	iii	ii	iv	i
(b)	i	ii	iii	iv
(c)	iii	i	ii	iv
(d)	iii	i	iv	ii

29. **Assertion (A)**: The risk condition exists when decision-makers have absolutely no idea of what the results of an implemented alternative would be.

Reason (R): When operating under complete uncertainty condition, decision-makers usually find that sound decisions are a matter of chance.

In the context of the two statements, which one of the following is correct?

Codes:
(a) Both (A) and (R) are correct.
(b) Both (A) and (R) are wrong.
(c) (A) is correct, but (R) is wrong.
(d) (A) is wrong, but (R) is correct.

30. **Assertion (A)**: In product concept, focus is on innovating and improving products.

Reason (R): In selling concept, consumers are persuaded to buy products.

Codes:
(a) Both (A) and (R) are true.
(b) (A) is true, but (R) is false.
(c) (A) is false, but (R) is true.
(d) Both (A) and (R) are false.

31. Which of the following is not a method of segmenting a market?
(a) Behavioural segmentation
(b) Psychographic segmentation
(c) Benefits segmentation
(d) Customer segmentation

32. Consumer attitudes and beliefs about diet, health and nutrition are influenced by
(a) Economic environment
(b) Cultural environment
(c) Social environment
(d) Natural environment

33. Select the phases of Product Life Cycle:

1. Initiation 2. Decline
3. Boom 4. Introduction
5. Maturity 6. Growth

Codes:
(a) 1, 3, 5, 6 (b) 1, 2, 3, 4
(c) 4, 6, 5, 2 (d) 2, 3, 5, 6

34. Which of the following is not a product-mix strategy?
(a) Trading up (b) Alteration
(c) Simplification (d) Value addition

35. "Relationship" in marketing means
(a) Relation between buyer and seller
(b) Relation between sales person
(c) Relation between company and consumers
(d) All of the above

36. Match the items of List-I with the items of the List-II:

List-I (Company Name)	List-II (Brand)
A. HUL	i. Cerelac
B. ITC	ii. Eclares
C. Nestle	iii. Vivel
D. Cadbury	iv. Sunsilk

Codes:	A	B	C	D
(a)	iv	iii	i	ii
(b)	i	ii	iii	iv
(c)	iv	ii	iii	i
(d)	iv	iii	ii	i

37. The following are the steps in designing the market driven distribution:
    1. Know what customers want
    2. Determine the costs
    3. Review assumptions
    4. Decide on the outlet
    5. Compare alternatives
    6. Implement changes

    Select the right sequence of the steps from the codes given below:
    (a) 1, 4, 2, 5, 3, 6 (b) 1, 2, 3, 5, 4, 6
    (c) 1, 3, 4, 5, 2, 6 (d) 2, 3, 4, 5, 6, 1
38. Which of the following are consumption values that customers look for in any product or service in a society?
    1. Functional value 2. Social value
    3. Money value 4. Emotional value
    5. Maximum value

    Codes:
    (a) 1, 2, 3, 5 (b) 1, 3, 4, 5
    (c) 5, 4, 3, 2, 1 (d) 1, 2 and 4
39. Franchising is a practice of:
    (a) Leasing for a prescribed period of time, the right to use firm's successful business model and brand.
    (b) Selling out a successful business model and brand.
    (c) Hiring a firm's successful business model and brand.
    (d) None of the above.
40. Underwriters of the security issues are required to
    (a) Purchase the securities underwritten
    (b) Work as agent of the company for marketing the securities
    (c) Manage the issues of the securities
    (d) Take up securities not subscribed by investors
41. The optimum capital structure of a company is planned as per considerations of
    I. Profitability
    II. Solvency
    III. Marketability of shares
    IV. Control

    Codes:
    (a) I, II and IV only (b) II, III and IV only
    (c) I and II only (d) III and IV only
42. **Assertion (A):** Investors in capital market seem to be inclined for fixed income securities.

    Reason (R): Debt instruments now have active secondary market.

    Codes:
    (a) Assertion (A) and Reason (R) both are correct and (R) is correct explanation of (A).
    (b) Assertion (A) and Reason (R) both are correct, but (R) is not correct explanation of (A).
    (c) Assertion (A) is correct, but Reason (R) is incorrect.
    (d) Assertion (A) is not correct, but Reason (R) is correct.
43. Insufficient working capital in any enterprise may also result into
    I. Failure to adapt to changes
    II. Overcapitalisation
    III. Reduced availability of trade and cash discounts
    IV. Reduced volume of production and sales

    Codes:
    (a) I, II and III only (b) I, III and IV only
    (c) II and III only (d) I and IV only
44. **Assertion (A):** Arbitrage keeps the cost of capital constant despite change in the capital structure.

    Reason (R): It ensures compensating inverse change in cost of equity capital with a change in the cost of debt capital.

    Codes:
    (a) Assertion (A) and Reason (R) both are correct and (R) is correct explanation of (A).
    (b) Assertion (A) and Reason (R) are correct, but (R) is not correct explanation of (A).
    (c) Assertion (A) is correct, but Reason (R) is incorrect.
    (d) Assertion (A) is not correct, but Reason (R) is correct.
45. **Assertion (A):** High morale and high productivity go hand-in-hand.

    Reason (R): Workers do not have their own ways for relief from fatigue and monotony.

Codes:
(a) Both (A) and (R) are true.
(b) (A) is true, but (R) is false.
(c) (A) is false, but (R) is true.
(d) Both (A) and (R) are false.

46. Relationship at work is the source of
(a) Status anxiety (b) Managerial stress
(c) Legitimate power (d) Expert power

47. Match the group of words in List-I with the group of words in List-II:

List-I
A. Grievances
B. Impact of technology
C. Adjustment to technology
D. Morale improvement

List-II
i. Profit sharing
ii. Effective planning
iii. Index of low morale
iv. Changes in occupation

Codes:	A	B	C	D
(a)	i	ii	iii	iv
(b)	iv	iii	ii	i
(c)	iii	ii	iv	i
(d)	iii	iv	ii	i

48. **Assertion (A):** Functional conflict is a type of institutionalised conflict.

Reason (R): Politics is a kind of emergent conflict.

Codes:
(a) Both (A) and (R) are true.
(b) (A) is true, but (R) is false.
(c) (A) is false, but (R) is true.
(d) Both (A) and (R) are false.

49. Formal conflict is a kind of
(a) Goal Conflict (b) Organisational Conflict
(c) Role Conflict (d) Emergent Conflict

50. One of the objectives of organisational change is
(a) Increased motivation
(b) Greater innovation
(c) Solving inter-group problems
(d) Changes in an organisation's level of adaptation to its environment

51. **Assertion (A):** Job design relates to the manner in which tasks are put together to form complete job.

Reason (R): The matrix organisation is a project organisation plus a functional organisation.
(a) Both (A) and (R) are true.
(b) (A) is true, but (R) is false.
(c) (A) is false, but (R) is true.
(d) Both (A) and (R) are false.

52. HRD as a total system includes the following major sub-systems:
1. Performance Appraisal
2. Career Planning
3. Role Analysis
4. ABC Analysis
5. Rewards

Select the correct answer from the codes.

Codes:
(a) 1, 2, 3, 4 (b) 1, 2, 3, 5
(c) 2, 3, 4, 5 (d) 1, 3, 4, 5

53. Which of the following is not true about employee grievances?
(a) Grievance is a sign of employee's discontent with job or its nature.
(b) Grievance provides a downward channel of communication.
(c) Grievance arises only when an employee feels that injustice has been done to him.
(d) Grievance can be real or imaginary.

54. Which of the following is not a component of Job Analysis?
(a) Job Description (b) Role Analysis
(c) Job Summary (d) Job Specification

55. As per the Master Circular on "Prudential Norms on Capital Adequacy—Basel I Framework", elements of Tier I capital include:
(i) Authorised Capital (Ordinary shares), statutory reserves, all other free reserves (disclosed), if any.
(ii) Paid-up capital (Preference shares).
(iii) Perpetual Non-Cumulative Preference Shares (PNCPS).
(iv) Innovative Perpetual Debt Instruments (IPDI).

Codes:
(a) (i) and (ii) only (b) (ii) and (iii) only
(c) (i) and (iii) only (d) (iii) and (iv) only

56. What is true about the Basel Committee on Banking Supervision (BCBS)?

(i) BCBS is an Indian National Committee of banking supervisory authority.
(ii) BCBS was established by a group of 19 nationalized commercial banks.
(iii) BCBS was established in 1996.
(iv) It provides a forum for regular cooperation on banking supervisory matters.

Codes:
(a) (i) and (ii) only (b) (ii) and (iii) only
(c) (iii) and (iv) only (d) (iv) only

57. Under the Cooperative Bank structure, the apex institution is
(a) National Cooperative Bank
(b) State Cooperative Bank
(c) District Cooperative Bank
(d) IDBI Bank

58. What is SLR ratio of a bank?
(a) Ratio of total deposits against total investments.
(b) Amount deposited by the bank with the Central Bank in the form of cash, gold and securities.
(c) Amount that commercial banks are required to maintain before providing credit to customers.
(d) Amount that commercial banks deposit with the foreign banks.

59. **Assertion (A)**: The USA remains the world's largest FDI recipient country.

Reason (R): The global economic crisis of 2009, causes a reduction of global FDI flows took place to USA.

Select the correct code:

Codes:
(a) Both (A) and (R) are correct and (R) is the correct explanation of (A).
(b) (A) is correct, but (R) is not correct.
(c) Both (A) and (R) are incorrect.
(d) Both (A) and (R) are correct, but (R) is not correct explanation of (A).

60. As per the South Asia Free Trade Agreement, 1993 of SAARC, the member countries have to bring their duties down to
(a) 25 percent by 2006
(b) 15 percent by 2006
(c) 10 percent by 2007
(d) 20 percent by 2007

61. Which of the following is the correct combination?
(i) A GSA allows an MNE to enter into activities that might too costly and risky to pursue on its own.
(ii) A GSA does not allow a firm to enhance economics of scale.
(iii) A GSA does not allow a firm to bypass entry barriers into a target foreign country.
(iv) A GSA allows a firm to acquire partner knowledge.

Codes:
(a) (i), (iv) are correct.
(b) (i), (ii) are correct.
(c) (i), (ii), (iii) and (iv) are correct.
(d) (ii) and (iii) are correct.

62. Which of the following are the outcomes of the Sixth Ministerial Conference of WTO which was held at Hong Kong in December 2005?

Select the correct combination:
(i) Resolve to complete the Doha Work Programme fully and to conclude negotiations in 2006.
(ii) Amendments to TRIPS agreement reaffirmed to address public health concerns of developing countries.
(iii) To continue export subsidies in agriculture upto 2018.
(iv) Duty free, quota free market access for all LDC's products to all developed countries.

Codes:
(a) (i), (ii) and (iv) (b) (i), (ii), (iii) and (iv)
(c) (i) and (iii) only (d) (ii) and (iv) only

63. Which of the following is not a function of Foreign Exchange Market?
(a) Stabilization function
(b) Hedging function
(c) Credit function
(d) Transfer function

64. **Assertion (A)**: The impact of depreciating Indian Rupee leads to less competition for Indian firms from imports.

Reason (R): The depreciating Indian Rupee results in downward pressure on inflation.

Select the correct code:

Codes:
(a) Both (A) and (R) are correct.
(b) (A) is false, but (R) is correct.
(c) Both (A) and (R) are false.
(d) (A) is true, but (R) is false.

65. In which of the following Stock Exchanges the GDR's are listed?
(i) London Stock Exchange
(ii) New York Stock Exchange
(iii) Luxembourg Stock Exchange
(iv) Bombay Stock Exchange
(v) Singapore Stock Exchange
(vi) Hong Kong Exchange
Identify the correct combination:
(a) (i), (ii) and (iii)
(b) (i), (iv), (v) and (vi)
(c) (iii), (iv), (v) and (vi)
(d) (i), (iii), (v) and (vi)

66. **Statement I:** FIIs do not invest in unlisted entities. They participate only through stock exchanges.
Statement II: FIIs cannot invest at the time of initial allotment. Select the correct code:
Codes:
(a) Statements I and II are correct.
(b) Statement I is true and II is false.
(c) Statement I is false and II is correct.
(d) Statements I and II are false.

67. ADRs' and GDRs' are an excellent means of investment to invest in India for
(a) NRIs' (b) Foreign nationals
(c) Both (a) & (b) (d) None of the above

68. Which of the following is not provided by EXIM Bank, for financing overseas investments?
(a) Term loans to Indian Companies upto 80% of their equity investment in overseas JV/WOS.
(b) Term loans to Indian Companies towards upto 100% of loan extended by them to the overseas JV/WOS.
(c) Term loan to overseas JV/WOS towards part financing.
(d) Guarantee facility to the overseas JV/WOS for raising term loan/working capital

69. Under Section 271 C of the Income Tax Act, 1961 the amount of penalty for failure to deduct tax at source is
(a) 10% of tax which is otherwise deductible under Section 194 C.
(b) 100% of tax which is otherwise deductible under Section 194 C.
(c) 200% of tax which is otherwise deductible under Section 194 C.
(d) 300% of tax which is otherwise deductible under Section 194 C.

70. Match the following items of List-I and List-II and select the correct answer from the codes given below:
List-I (Sections)
A. Section 80C of I.T. Act
B. Section 80D of I.T. Act
C. Section 80 DDB of I.T. Act
D. Section 80 TTA of I.T. Act
List-II (Maximum Deduction)
i. ₹ 10,000 ii. ₹ 40,000
iii. ₹ 1,00,000 iv. ₹ 15,000

Codes:	A	B	C	D
(a)	iii	i	iv	ii
(b)	iii	iv	ii	i
(c)	iv	iii	ii	i
(d)	ii	iii	i	iv

71. In which of the following cases, income of previous year is assessable in the previous year itself?
(a) A person in employment.
(b) A person engaged in illegal business.
(c) A person who is running charitable business.
(d) A person leaving India permanently.

72. Long term capital loss can be set off from which of the following?
(a) Short term capital gain only
(b) Long term capital gain only
(c) Income from business and profession
(d) Capital gain head of income

73. In which of the following long term assets, cost indexation benefit is allowed?
(a) Debentures issued by a company
(b) Self generated goodwill of a business
(c) Bonus shares allotted on 1-4-2000
(d) Jewellery

74. Calculate the Gross Annual Value from the following details:
Municipal Value – ₹ 45,000
Fair Rental Value – ₹ 50,000

Standard Rent – ₹ 48,000
Actual Rent – ₹ 42,000

(a) ₹ 50,000 (b) ₹ 48,000
(c) ₹ 45,000 (d) ₹ 42,000

75. Minimum Alternate Tax (MAT) is imposed on
(a) All companies
(b) Public Limited Companies only
(c) Private Limited Companies only
(d) Partnership Firms and Companies

ANSWERS

1. (b)	2. (b)	3. (a)	4. (d)	5. (c)
6. (d)	7. (b)	8. (a)	9. (a)	10. (b)
11. (b)	12. (b)	13. (c)	14. (a)	15. (a)
16. (a)	17. (b)	18. (b)	19. (c)	20. (c)
21. (c)	22. (d)	23. (c)	24. (b)	25. (c)
26. (b)	27. (a)	28. (d)	29. (d)	30. (a)
31. (d)	32. (b)	33. (c)	34. (d)	35. (c)
36. (a)	37. (a)	38. (d)	39. (a)	40. (d)
41. (z)	42. (c)	43. (b)	44. (a)	45. (d)
46. (b)	47. (d)	48. (a)	49. (b)	50. (d)
51. (a)	52. (b)	53. (b)	54. (c)	55. (d)
56. (d)	57. (b)	58. (c)	59. (a)	60. (d)
61. (a)	62. (a)	63. (a)	64. (d)	65. (d)
66. (d)	67. (c)	68. (b)	69. (b)	70. (b)
71. (d)	72. (b)	73. (d)	74. (b)	75. (a)

z → All options are correct.

JUNE–2015

Note: This paper contains Sixty (60) multiple-choice questions, each question carrying two (2) marks. Candidate is expected to answer any Fifty (50) questions. In case more than Fifty (50) questions are attempted, only the first Fifty (50) questions will be evaluated.

PAPER–I

1. Which of the following is the highest level of cognitive ability?
   (a) Knowing (b) Understanding
   (c) Analysing (d) Evaluating

2. Which of the following factors does not impact teaching?
   (a) Teacher's knowledge
   (b) Class room activities that encourage learning
   (c) Socio-economic background of teachers and students
   (d) Learning through experience

3. Which of the following statements about teaching aids are correct?
   I. They help in retaining concepts for longer duration.
   II. They help students learn better.
   III. They make teaching-learning process interesting.
   IV. They enhance rote learning.

   Select the correct answer from the codes given below:

   Codes:
   (a) I, II, III and IV (b) I, II and III
   (c) II, III and IV (d) I, II and IV

4. Techniques used by a teacher to teach include:
   I. Lecture II. Interactive lecture
   III. Group work IV. Self study

   Select the correct answer from the codes given below:

   Codes:
   (a) I, II and III (b) I, II, III and IV
   (c) II, III and IV (d) I, II and IV

5. Achievement tests are commonly used for the purpose of:
   (a) Making selections for a specific job
   (b) Selecting candidates for a course
   (c) Identifying strengths and weaknesses of learners
   (d) Assessing the amount of learning after teaching

6. A good teacher is one who:
   (a) gives useful information
   (b) explains concepts and principles
   (c) gives printed notes to students
   (d) inspires students to learn

7. Which of the following statements regarding the meaning of research are correct?
   I. Research refers to a series of systematic activity or activities undertaken to find out the solution of a problem.
   II. It is a systematic, logical and an unbiased process wherein verification of hypothesis, data analysis, interpretation and formation of principles can be done.
   III. It is an intellectual enquiry or quest towards truth.
   IV. It leads to enhancement of knowledge.

   Select the correct answer from the codes given below:

   Codes:
   (a) I, II and III (b) II, III and IV
   (c) I, III and IV (d) I, II, III and IV

8. A good thesis writing should involve:
   I. reduction of punctuation and grammatical errors to a minimum.
   II. careful checking of references.
   III. consistency in the way the thesis is written.
   IV. a clear and well written abstract.

Select the correct answer from the codes given below:

(a) I, II, III and IV (b) I, II and III
(c) I, II and IV (d) II, III and IV

9. Jean Piaget gave a theory of cognitive development of humans on the basis of his:
(a) Fundamental Research
(b) Applied Research
(c) Action Research
(d) Evaluation Research

10. "Male and female students perform equally well in a numerical aptitude test." This statement indicates a:
(a) research hypothesis
(b) null hypothesis
(c) directional hypothesis
(d) statistical hypothesis

11. The conclusions/findings of which type of research cannot be generalized to other situations?
(a) Historical Research
(b) Descriptive Research
(c) Experimental Research
(d) Causal Comparative Research

12. Which of the following steps are required to design a questionnaire?
I. Writing primary and secondary aims of the study.
II. Review of the current literature.
III. Prepare a draft of questionnaire.
IV. Revision of the draft.

Select the correct answer from the codes given below:

Codes:

(a) I, II and III (b) I, III and IV
(c) II, III and IV (d) I, II, III and IV

Read the following passage carefully and answer questions 13 to 18.

Story telling is not in our genes. Neither it is an evolutionary history. It is the essence of what makes us Human.

Human beings progress by telling stories. One event can result in a great variety of stories being told about it. Sometimes those stories differ greatly. Which stories are picked up and repeated and which ones are dropped and forgotten often determines how we progress. Our history, knowledge and understanding are all the collections of the few stories that survive. This includes the stories that we tell each other about the future. And how the future will turn out depends partly, possibly largely, on which stories we collectively choose to believe.

Some stories are designed to spread fear and concern. This is because some story-tellers feel that there is a need to raise some tensions. Some stories are frightening, they are like totemic warnings: "Fail to act now and we are all doomed." Then there are stories that indicate that all will be fine so long as we leave everything upto a few especially able adults. Currently, this trend is being led by those who call themselves "rational optimists". They tend to claim that it is human nature to compete and to succeed and also to profit at the expense of others. The rational optimists however, do not realize how humanity has progressed overtime through amiable social networks and how large groups work in less selfishness and in the process accommodate rich and poor, high and low alike. This aspect in story-telling is considered by the 'Practical Possibles', who sit between those who say all is fine and cheerful and be individualistic in your approach to a successful future, and those who ordain pessimism and fear that we are doomed.

What the future holds for us is which stories we hold on to and how we act on them.

Answer the following questions:

13. Our knowledge is a collection of:
(a) all stories that we have heard during our life-time
(b) some stories that we remember
(c) a few stories that survive
(d) some important stories

14. Story telling is:
(a) an art (b) a science
(c) in our genes
(d) the essence of what makes us human

15. How the future will turn out to be, depends upon the stories?
(a) We collectively choose to believe in
(b) Which are repeatedly narrated
(c) Designed to spread fear and tension
(d) Designed to make prophecy

16. Rational optimists:
    I. Look for opportunities.
    II. Are sensible and cheerful.
    III. Are selfishly driven.

    Identify the correct answer from the codes given below:

    Codes:

    (a) I, II and III (b) I only
    (c) I and II only (d) II and III only

17. Humans become less selfish when:
    (a) they work in large groups
    (b) they listen to frightening stories
    (c) they listen to cheerful stories
    (d) they work in solitude

18. 'Practical Possibles' are the ones who:
    (a) follow Midway Path
    (b) are doom-mongers
    (c) are self-centred
    (d) are cheerful and carefree

19. Effectiveness of communication can be traced from which of the following?
    I. Attitude surveys
    II. Performance records
    III. Students attendance
    IV. Selection of communication channel

    Select the correct answer from the codes given below:

    Codes:

    (a) I, II, III and IV (b) I, II and III
    (c) II, III and IV (d) I, II and IV

20. **Assertion (A) :** Formal communication tends to be fast and flexible.

    Reason (R): Formal communication is a systematic and orderly flow of information.

    (a) Both (A) and (R) are correct and (R) is correct explanation of (A)
    (b) Both (A) and (R) are correct, but (R) is not correct explanation of (A)
    (c) (A) is correct but, (R) is false
    (d) (A) is false but, (R) is correct

21. Which of the following are the characteristic features of communication?
    I. Communication involves exchange of ideas, facts and opinions.
    II. Communication involves both information and understanding.
    III. Communication is a continuous process.
    IV. Communication is a circular process.

    Select the correct answer from the codes given below:

    Codes:

    (a) I, II and III (b) I, II and IV
    (c) II, III and IV (d) I, II, III and IV

22. The term 'grapevine' is also known as:
    (a) Downward communication
    (b) Informal communication
    (c) Upward communication
    (d) Horizontal communication

23. Which of the following is not a principle of effective communication?
    (a) Persuasive and convincing dialogue
    (b) Participation of the audience
    (c) One-way transfer of information
    (d) Strategic use of grapevine

24. In communication, the language is:
    (a) The verbal code
    (b) Intrapersonal
    (c) The symbolic code
    (d) The non-verbal code

25. The next term in the series is:

    2, 5, 9, 19, 37,?

    (a) 73 (b) 75 (c) 78 (d) 80

26. In certain code MATHURA is coded as JXQEROX. The code of HOTELS will be:
    (a) LEQIBP (b) ELQBIP
    (c) LEBIQP (d) ELIPQB

27. One day Prakash left home and walked 10 km towards south, turned right and walked 5 km, turned right and walked 10 km and turned left and walked 10 km. How many km will he have to walk to reach his home straight?

    (a) 10 (b) 20 (c) 15 (d) 30

28. A girl introduced a boy as the son of the daughter of the father of her uncle. The boy is related to the girl as:
    (a) Brother (b) Uncle
    (c) Nephew (d) Son

29. In an examination 10,000 students appeared. The result revealed the number of students who have:

passed in all five subjects	=	5583
passed in three subjects only	=	1400
passed in two subjects only	=	1200
passed in one subject only	=	735

failed in English only = 75
failed in Physics only = 145
failed in Chemistry only = 140
failed in Mathematics only = 200
failed in Bio-science only = 157

The number of students passed in at least four subjects is:
(a) 6300 (b) 6900 (c) 7300 (d) 7900

30. At present a person is 4 times older than his son and is 3 years older than his wife. After 3 years the age of the son will be 15 years. The age of the person's wife after 5 years will be:
(a) 42 (b) 48 (c) 45 (d) 50

31. If we want to seek new knowledge of facts about the world, we must rely on reason of the type:
(a) Inductive (b) Deductive
(c) Demonstrative (d) Physiological

32. A deductive argument is invalid if:
(a) Its premises and conclusions are all false
(b) Its premises are true but its conclusion is false
(c) Its premises are false but its conclusion is true
(d) Its premises and conclusions are all true

33. Inductive reasoning is grounded on:
(a) Integrity of nature
(b) Unity of nature
(c) Uniformity of nature
(d) Harmony of nature

34. Among the following statements two are contradictory to each other. Select the correct code that represents them:
Statements:
(i) All poets are philosophers.
(ii) Some poets are philosophers.
(iii) Some poets are not philosophers.
(iv) No philosopher is a poet.
Codes:
(a) (i) and (ii) (b) (i) and (iv)
(c) (i) and (iii) (d) (ii) and (iii)

35. Which of the codes given below contains only the correct statements? Select the code:
Statements:
(i) Venn diagram represents the arguments graphically.
(ii) Venn diagram can enhance our understanding.
(iii) Venn diagram may be called valid or invalid.
(iv) Venn diagram is clear method of notation.
Codes:
(a) (i), (ii) and (iii) (b) (i), (ii) and (iv)
(c) (ii), (iii) and (iv) (d) (i), (iii) and (iv)

36. When the purpose of a definition is to explain the use or to eliminate ambiguity the definition is called
(a) Stipulative (b) Theoretical
(c) Lexical (d) Persuasive

Question numbers 37 to 42 are based on the tabulated data given below:

A company has 20 employees with their age (in years) and salary (in thousand rupees per month) mentioned against each of them:

S.No.	Age (in years)	Salary (in thousand rupees per month)	S.No.	Age (in years)	Salary (in thousand rupees per month)
1.	44	35	11.	33	30
2.	32	20	12.	31	35
3.	54	45	13.	30	35
4.	42	35	14.	37	40
5.	31	20	15.	44	45
6.	53	60	16.	36	35
7.	42	50	17.	34	35
8.	51	55	18.	49	50
9.	34	25	19.	43	45
10.	41	30	20.	45	50

37. Classify the data of age of each employee in class interval of 5 years. Which class interval of 5 years has the maximum average salary?
(a) 35 - 40 years (b) 40 - 45 years
(c) 45 - 50 years (d) 50 - 55 years

38. What is the frequency (%) in the class interval of 30-35 years?
(a) 20% (b) 25% (c) 30% (d) 35%

39. What is the average age of the employees?
(a) 40.3 years (b) 38.6 years
(c) 47.2 years (d) 45.3 years

40. What is the fraction (%) of employees getting salary $\geq$ 40,000 per month?
(a) 45% (b) 50% (c) 35% (d) 32%

41. What is the average salary (in thousand per month) in the age group 40-50 years?
(a) 35 (b) 42.5 (c) 40.5 (d) 36.5

42. What is the fraction of employees getting salary less than the average salary of all the employees?
(a) 45% (b) 50% (c) 55% (d) 47%

43. Encoding or scrambling data for transmission across a network is known as:
(a) Protection (b) Detection
(c) Encryption (d) Decryption

44. Which of the following is not an output device?
(a) Printer (b) Speaker
(c) Monitor (d) Keyboard

45. Which of the following represents one billion characters?
(a) Kilobyte (b) Megabyte
(c) Gigabyte (d) Terabyte

46. Which of the following is not open source software?
(a) Internet explorer
(b) Fedora Linux
(c) Open office
(d) Apache HTTP server

47. Which one of the following represents the binary equivalent of the decimal number 25?
(a) 10101 (b) 01101 (c) 11001 (d) 11011

48. Which is an instant messenger that is used for chatting?
(a) Altavista (b) MAC
(c) Microsoft Office (d) Google Talk

49. In which of the countries per capita use of water is maximum?
(a) USA (b) European Union
(c) China (d) India

50. India's contribution to total global carbon dioxide emissions is about:
(a) ~ 3% (b) ~ 6% (c) ~ 10% (d) ~ 15%

51. Two earthquakes A and B happen to be of magnitude 5 and 6 respectively on Richter Scale. The ratio of the energies released E_B/E_A will be approximately:
(a) ~ 8 (b) ~ 16 (c) ~ 32 (d) ~ 64

52. Which of the following combinations represent renewable natural resources?
(a) Fertile soil, fresh water and natural gas
(b) Clean air, phosphates and biological diversity
(c) Fishes, fertile soil and fresh water
(d) Oil, forests and tides

53. In the recently launched Air Quality Index in India, which of the following pollutants is not included?
(a) Carbon monoxide
(b) Fine particulate matter
(c) Ozone
(d) Chlorofluorocarbons

54. The factors which are most important in determining the impact of anthropogenic activities on environment are:
(a) Population, affluence per person, land available per person
(b) Population, affluence per person and the technology used for exploiting resources
(c) Atmospheric conditions, population and forest cover
(d) Population, forest cover and land available per person

55. The session of the parliament is summoned by:
(a) The President
(b) The Prime Minister
(c) The Speaker of the Lok Sabha
(d) The Speaker of the Lok Sabha and the Chairman of the Rajya Sabha

56. Civil Service Day is celebrated in India on:
(a) 21st April (b) 24th April
(c) 21st June (d) 7th July

57. The South Asia University is situated in the city of:
(a) Colombo (b) Dhaka
(c) New Delhi (d) Kathmandu

58. The University Grants Commission was established with which of the following aims?
I. Promotion of research and development in higher education
II. Identifying and sustaining institutions of potential learning
III. Capacity building of teachers
IV. Providing autonomy to each and every higher educational institution in India

Select the correct answer from the codes given below:

Codes:
(a) I, II, III and IV (b) I, II and III
(c) II, III and IV (d) I, II and IV

59. The Gross Enrolment Ratio (GER) in institutions of higher education in India at present (2015) is about:
(a) 8 percent (b) 12 percent
(c) 19 percent (d) 23 percent

60. The total number of central universities in India in April 2015 was:
(a) 08 (b) 14 (c) 27 (d) 43

ANSWERS

1. (d)	2. (c)	3. (b)	4. (a)	5. (d)
6. (d)	7. (d)	8. (a)	9. (a)	10. (b)
11. (a)	12. (d)	13. (c)	14. (d)	15. (a)
16. (a)	17. (a)	18. (a)	19. (b)	20. (d)
21. (d)	22. (b)	23. (c)	24. (a)	25. (b)
26. (b)	27. (c)	28. (a)	29. (a)	30. (d)
31. (a)	32. (b)	33. (c)	34. (c)	35. (b)
36. (c)	37. (d)	38. (d)	39. (a)	40. (a)
41. (b)	42. (c)	43. (c)	44. (d)	45. (c)
46. (a)	47. (c)	48. (d)	49. (b)	50. (b)
51. (c)	52. (c)	53. (d)	54. (b)	55. (a)
56. (a)	57. (c)	58. (b)	59. (c)	60. (t)

t →No option is correct.

PAPER–II

Note: This paper contains fifty (50) objective type questions, each question carrying two (2) marks. All questions are compulsory.

1. The world's first electronic stock market is:
(a) KOSPI (b) Nikkie
(c) NASDAQ (d) Dow Jones

2. The Human Development Index (HDI) is introduced by:
(a) UNDP (b) UNICEF
(c) IMF (d) World Bank

3. Examine the following statements and choose the correct code:

Assertion (A): American style option, compared to European style, provides more freedom to option holders in exercising the option.

Reason (R): American style option can be exercised only at a specified date which is generally the expiration date.

Codes:
(a) Both (A) and (R) are correct.
(b) Both (A) and (R) are wrong.
(c) (A) is correct, but (R) is wrong.
(d) (A) is not correct, but (R) is correct.

4. From the statements given below, identify the correct code:

Statement (I): The key strategy behind acquiring a company is to create share holder's value.

Statement (II): Conglomeration is a merger between two companies that have common business areas.

Statement (III): MRTP Act got replaced by the Competition Act, 2002 in India.

Codes:
(a) All the three statements are correct.
(b) Statements (I) and (II) only are correct.
(c) Statements (I) and (III) only are correct.
(d) Statement (II) only is correct.

5. From the following, identify the tools of fiscal policy:
(i) Public expenditure
(ii) Open market operations
(iii) Deficit financing
(iv) Taxation
(v) Reserve requirements

Codes:
(a) (i), (iii), (iv) and (v)
(b) (i), (ii), (iv) and (v)
(c) (ii) and (v)
(d) (i), (iii) and (iv)

6. The basic difference between a static budget and flexible budget is that:
(a) A flexible budget considers only variable costs but a static budget considers all costs.
(b) Flexible budgets allow management latitude in meeting goals, whereas static budget is based on fixed standards.

(c) A flexible budget is applicable for a single department only but a static budget for entire production facility.
(d) A flexible budget can be prepared for any production level within a relevant range but a static budget is based on one specific level of production.

7. A retiring partner continues to be liable for obligations incurred after his retirement:
(a) If unpaid amount is transferred to his loan account.
(b) If he does not give public notice.
(c) If he starts a similar business elsewhere.
(d) In all the situations till he survives.

8. In what order, the following assets are shown in the balance sheet of a company?
(i) Trade receivables
(ii) Cash
(iii) Furniture and fittings
(iv) Investment in shares and debentures

Codes:

(a) (ii), (i), (iv), (iii) (b) (i), (ii), (iii), (iv)
(c) (iii), (iv), (i), (ii) (d) (iv), (iii), (ii), (i)

9. When opening stock is ₹ 50,000, closing stock is ₹ 60,000 and the cost of goods sold is ₹ 2,20,000, the stock turnover ratio is:
(a) 2 times (b) 3 times (c) 4 times (d) 5 times

10. If: Stock turnover ratio is = 6 times
Average stock = ₹ 8,000
Selling price = 25% above cost
What is the amount of gross profit?
(a) ₹ 2,000 (b) ₹ 4,000
(c) ₹ 10,000 (d) ₹ 12,000

11. A rectangular hyperbola shaped demand curve on all its points has:
(a) Equal slopes of the price demand curve
(b) Price elasticity equal to unity
(c) Varying price elasticity
(d) Both slope and price elasticity equal

12. In case of short-run equilibrium, a perfectly competitive firm while earning abnormal profits operates at an output level where:
(a) Marginal cost is the minimum
(b) Average cost is the minimum
(c) Both marginal cost and average cost are equal
(d) Marginal cost is higher than average cost

13. Which one of the following statements is false?
(a) Normally, a price demand curve slopes downward from left to right.
(b) Economies of scale and economies of scope are the same.
(c) For optimization, equality between marginal cost and marginal revenue is a necessary condition but it is not a sufficient one.
(d) Law of variable proportions denotes input-output relationship during short-run.

14. Match the items of List I with the items of List II:

List I
A. Law of diminishing marginal utility
B. Relationship between price of one commodity and demand for other commodity
C. Skimming the cream policy
D. Price rigidity

List II
(i) Cross demand (ii) Oligopoly
(iii) Cardinal approach (iv) Pioneer pricing

Codes:	**(A)**	**(B)**	**(C)**	**(D)**
(a)	(i)	(ii)	(iii)	(iv)
(b)	(iii)	(i)	(ii)	(iv)
(c)	(ii)	(iv)	(i)	(iii)
(d)	(iv)	(iii)	(ii)	(i)

15. The following are the demand and supply equations in a perfectly competitive market:
$P = 12 + 0.3\ Q_s$
$P = 40 - 0.4\ Q_d$
The equilibrium market price would be:
(a) 24 (b) 10 (c) 40 (d) 20

16. Which of the following is not an accounting software package?
(a) Quick Books (b) Sage one
(c) Sage M (c) Sage 50

17. Which one of the following formula is used to calculate probable error of correlation-coefficient between two variables of 'n' pairs of observations?

(a) $0.6745\left[\frac{1-r^2}{\sqrt{n}}\right]$ (b) $0.5758\left[\frac{1-r^2}{\sqrt{n}}\right]$

(c) $0.675\left[\frac{1-r^2}{n}\right]$ (d) $0.5758\left[\frac{1-r^2}{n}\right]$

18. If the population is heterogeneous, which one of the following probability sampling methods is more appropriate?
 (a) Sequential sampling
 (b) Quota sampling
 (c) Double sampling
 (d) Stratified sampling

19. Which of the following relating to normal distribution are not correct?
 (i) Co-efficient of skewness is three.
 (ii) It is mesokurtic.
 (iii) Mean deviation for it is $2/3\sigma$.
 (iv) $\mu \pm 2\sigma$ covers 95.45% area.
 (v) Mean, median and mode are equal.
 (vi) The standard normal variate z has mean one and SD zero.

 Codes:
 (a) (i), (iii) and (vi) (b) (iii), (iv) and (v)
 (c) (i), (iii) and (v) (d) (i), (iii) and (iv)

20. Which one of the following statements is false?
 (a) Both correlation and regression co-efficients have same sign.
 (b) Arithmetic mean of the regression co-efficients is always more than the correlation co-efficient.
 (c) Regression co-efficients are independent of both the origin and scale.
 (d) Correlation co-efficient is the square root of two regression co-efficients.

21. Match the items of List I with List II:

 List I
 A. "He who can manage, can manage anything".
 B. "Due to these experiments, a factory does not remain a factory, it is converted into a laboratory".
 C. "Management succeeds or fails as human relations in business are intelligently or unintelligently handled".
 D. "A place for everything, and everything in its place".

 List-II
 (i) Henry Fayol (ii) William B. Cornell
 (iii) F.W. Taylor (iv) Lawrance A. Appley

Codes:	**(A)**	**(B)**	**(C)**	**(D)**
(a)	(i)	(ii)	(iii)	(iv)
(b)	(i)	(ii)	(iv)	(iii)
(c)	(iv)	(iii)	(ii)	(i)
(d)	(iii)	(ii)	(i)	(iv)

22. **Assertion (A):** Management is mainly associated with economic affairs.
 Reasoning (R): Big business houses are the result of effective financial management.

 Codes:
 (a) (A) is correct and (R) is the right explanation of (A).
 (b) Both (A) and (R) are correct but (R) is not the right explanation of (A).
 (c) (A) is incorrect but (R) is correct in isolation.
 (d) Both (A) and (R) are incorrect.

23. Areas of establishing objectives under MBO are:
 (i) Market Standing
 (ii) Innovation
 (iii) Industrial Relations
 (iv) Public Accountability
 (v) Productivity
 (vi) Industrial Policy

 Codes:
 (a) (iii), (iv), (v) and (vi)
 (b) (i), (ii), (iv) and (v)
 (c) (i), (ii), (v) and (vi)
 (d) (ii), (iii), (iv) and (v)

24. Match the items of List I with List II:

 List I
 A. Management of Tomorrow
 B. Motivation and Personality
 C. The Motivation of Work
 D. Personality and Organisation

 List II
 (i) Chris Argyris (ii) Fredrick Hergberg
 (iii) L.F. Urwick (iv) A.H. Maslow

Codes:	**(A)**	**(B)**	**(C)**	**(D)**
(a)	(i)	(iv)	(ii)	(iii)
(b)	(iii)	(iv)	(i)	(ii)
(c)	(iv)	(iii)	(ii)	(i)
(d)	(iii)	(iv)	(ii)	(i)

25. Narayan Murthy Committee revised its recommendations on Corporate Governance as on 29th October 2004 which diluted the following areas:
 (i) Independence of Directors
 (ii) Whistle Blower Policy
 (iii) Performance evaluation of Non-Executive Directors

(iv) Mandatory training of Non-Executive Directors

Codes:

(a) (i), (ii) and (iii) only
(b) (i) and (iii) only
(c) (i), (ii) and (iv) only
(d) All (i), (ii), (iii) and (iv)

26. The service marketing mix is an extended marketing mix and includes:
(i) People (ii) Process
(iii) Service (iv) Physical evidence

Codes:

(a) (ii), (iii) and (iv) (b) (i), (ii) and (iii)
(c) (i), (ii) and (iv) (d) (i), (iii) and (iv)

27. Black box model in marketing relates to:
(a) Marketing planning
(b) Marketing mix
(c) Marketing control
(d) Consumer behaviour

28. Items, considered part of the augmented product, do not include:
(a) Guarantee
(b) Warranty
(c) Complementary products
(d) Channels of distribution

29. Which of the following is not a type of direct marketing?
(a) Direct mail marketing
(b) Retail marketing
(c) Telemarketing
(d) Email direct marketing

30. 'Press release' is a part of:
(a) Public relations (b) Advertising
(c) Sales promotion (d) None of the above

31. In capital budgeting, the term capital rationing implies:
(a) that no retained earnings are available.
(b) that limited funds are available for investment.
(c) that no external funds can be raised.
(d) that no fresh investment is required in current year.

32. In certainty equivalent approach, adjusted cash flows are discounted at:
(a) Accounting Rate of Return
(b) Internal Rate of Return
(c) Hurdle Rate
(d) Risk Free Rate

33. Combined leverage is calculated as:
(a) Operating Leverage + Financial Leverage
(b) Operating Leverage – Financial Leverage
(c) Operating Leverage × Financial Leverage
(d) Operating Leverage ÷ Financial Leverage

34. Which of the following is not true with reference to capital budgeting?
(a) Capital budgeting is related to asset replacement decisions.
(b) Cost of capital is equal to minimum required return.
(c) Existing investment in a project is not treated as sunk cost.
(d) Timing of cash flows is relevant.

35. What is Economic Order Quantity?
(a) Cost of an order
(b) Cost of stock
(c) Reorder level
(d) Optimum order size

36. Which of the following is not a basic objective of HRM?
(a) To attract HR into the organisation
(b) To develop and motivate HR for better performance
(c) To have the reward and punishment system for HR
(d) To integrate and maintain HR in the organisation

37. What is 'gate hiring'?
(a) To select people who approach on their own for employment in the organisation.
(b) To select people who are recommended by the employees.
(c) To select people from public employment exchanges.
(d) To select people supplied by labour contractors.

38. Matching essential managers and essential positions is a step in the process of:
(a) Career Cycle (b) Succession Planning
(c) Career Planning (d) Career Stages

39. The barriers to effective performance appraisal are:
(i) Psychological blocks of managers
(ii) Faulty assumptions of the parties concerned
(iii) Technical pitfalls

(iv) Faulty written communications

Codes:

(a) All are correct.
(b) Only (ii) and (iii) are correct.
(c) Only (i) and (ii) are correct.
(d) Only (i), (ii) and (iii) are correct.

40. Who has developed the 'Systems Approach' of industrial relations?
(a) John Dunlop (b) Garry S. Becker
(c) Michael J. Jucius (d) Edwin B. Flippo

41. In 1992, the banking sector reforms were introduced as per:
(a) C. Rangarajan Committee Report
(b) M. Narasimham Committee Report
(c) Suresh Tandulkar Committee Report
(d) Sukhamoy Chakrabarty Committee Report

42. For the purpose of extending rural banking and agro finance, the NABARD:
(a) Directly lends and monitors the rural borrowers
(b) Refinances the banks extending rural finance
(c) Refinances the rural borrowers obtaining credit from banks
(d) Directly finances the rural borrowers and gets refinance from government

43. When RBI grants loan to commercial banks and charges interest on it, it is called:
(a) Rapo rate
(b) Reverse Rapo rate
(c) Sweep stack rate, basic rate
(d) Bank rate

44. E-banking business is essentially regulated by the Information Technology Act, 2000, under which personal signature is replaced by:
(a) Encrypted signature (b) Image signature
(c) Digital signature (d) Online signature

45. In order to control inflation and ensure stability in money market:
(a) The RBI works under the direction of ministry of finance, government of India.
(b) The RBI acts independently and can refuse the government directive.
(c) The RBI acts under the board of directors.
(d) The RBI's board of governors shall abide by the government directive.

46. In respect of international business, a project is called a turnkey project because:
(a) The licensee agrees to construct an entire plant in his home county and hands over the key.
(b) The licensor starts the operation and hands over the key of the operating plant to the licensee.
(c) The licensor starts the operation and then invites the licensee and hands over the key to complete the remaining work.
(d) The licensor and the licensee jointly carry out the project and agree to share profit equally.

47. Match the items in List I with the items in List II:

List I

A. Bretton woods conference
B. Soft loan window
C. Geneva
D. Loan to private sector

List II

(i) WTO (ii) World Bank
(iii) IFC (iv) IDA

Codes:	(A)	(B)	(C)	(D)
(a)	(i)	(iii)	(ii)	(iv)
(b)	(iv)	(iii)	(ii)	(i)
(c)	(ii)	(iv)	(i)	(iii)
(d)	(iv)	(ii)	(iii)	(i)

48. **Assertion (A):** The member nations, consistently finding balance of payments crisis, may approach the World Bank seeking financial accommodation to mitigate the crisis.

Reasoning (R): The member nations facing balance of payments crisis can approach the IMF seeking redressal of the BOP crisis.

Codes:

(a) (A) is correct and (R) is correct explanation of (A).
(b) (A) is correct but (R) is wrong.
(c) (R) is correct and (A) is wrong.
(d) Both (A) and (R) are wrong.

49. In computation of balance of payments, overall balance of payments =
(a) Balance of current account + Balance of capital account + Statistical discrepancy

(b) Export of goods and invisibles – Import of goods
(c) Foreign exchange inflow – Foreign exchange outflow
(d) Export of goods and invisibles + Import of goods and invisibles

50. The instrument chosen for enhancement of international liquidity is:
(a) Society for World wide Inter bank Financial Telecommunications (SWIFT)
(b) Special Drawing Rights (SDRs)
(c) Multilateral Netting
(d) Netting of Payments

ANSWERS

1. (c)	2. (a)	3. (c)	4. (c)	5. (d)
6. (d)	7. (b)	8. (c)	9. (c)	10. (d)
11. (b)	12. (d)	13. (b)	14. (c)	15. (a)
16. (c)	17. (a)	18. (d)	19. (a)	20. (c)
21. (c)	22. (c)	23. (b)	24. (d)	25. (d)
26. (c)	27. (d)	28. (d)	29. (b)	30. (a)
31. (b)	32. (d)	33. (c)	34. (c)	35. (d)
36. (c)	37. (a)	38. (b)	39. (d)	40. (a)
41. (b)	42. (b)	43. (a)	44. (c)	45. (b)
46. (b)	47. (c)	48. (c)	49. (a)	50. (b)

PAPER–III

Note: This paper contains seventy-five (75) objective type questions of two (2) marks each. All questions are compulsory.

1. GNP at market prices – Indirect taxes + subsidies is referred to as:
(a) GNP at factor cost (b) GDP at factor cost
(c) NNP at factor cost (d) NDP at factor cost

2. EDI system got legal recognition under which one of the following Acts?
(a) Electronics Act, 1996
(b) Right to Data Act, 1998
(c) DGFT Act, 1999
(d) Information Technology Act, 2000

3. Following statements are related to futures contracts. Choose the statements that are not true:
(i) Purchase of a futures contract is called short position.
(ii) Currency futures are traded on an exchange in standardised form and in fixed quantity.
(iii) Default risk in futures contract is high compared to forward contract.

Codes:
(a) only (i) and (ii) (b) only (i) and (iii)
(c) (i), (ii) and (iii) (d) only (ii)

4. From the following, identify the trading blocks in the world and choose the correct code:
A. European Union
B. North American Free Trade Agreements
C. South Asian Association of Regional Co-operation
D. Central American Common Market
E. Central African Customs Union

Codes:
(a) A, B and C (b) A, B, C and D
(c) A, B, C, D and E (d) A, B and E

5. Match the items of List I with items of List II and choose the correct code:

List I
A. Carroll Model
B. Corlett - Hague Rule
C. Hecksher Ohlin Theorem
D. Knut Wick sell's Theory

List II
(i) International trade
(ii) Interest rate
(iii) Principles of taxation
(iv) Social responsibility of business

Codes:	**(A)**	**(B)**	**(C)**	**(D)**
(a)	(iv)	(iii)	(i)	(ii)
(b)	(iii)	(ii)	(i)	(iv)
(c)	(iii)	(i)	(ii)	(iv)
(d)	(ii)	(iii)	(i)	(iv)

6. Labour Rate of Pay Variance can be calculated by which one of the following equations?
(a) Budgeted Labour Costs – Actual Labour Costs
(b) (Standard Hours – Actual Hours) × Actual Wage Rate
(c) (Standard Wage Rate – Actual Wage Rate) × Actual Hours Worked

(d) (Standard Wage Rate – Actual Wage Rate) × Standard Hours Worked

7. Given :

Margin of Safety	₹ 80,000
Profit	₹ 20,000
Sales	₹ 3,00,000

What is the amount of Fixed Cost?
(a) ₹ 1,00,000 (b) ₹ 75,000
(c) ₹ 55,000 (d) ₹ 20,000

8. Preparation of consolidated statement of accounts as per AS - 21 is:
(a) Optional
(b) Mandatory for Private Ltd. Companies
(c) Mandatory for Listed Companies
(d) Mandatory for all Companies

9. Which one of the following is not true of cash Budget?
(a) The shortage or excess of cash would appear in a particular period.
(b) All inflows would arise before outflows for those periods.
(c) Only revenue nature cash flows are shown.
(d) Proceeds from issue of share capital is shown as an inflow.

10. Study the following transactions:
A. Raising of short term loans
B. Goods purchased for cash
C. Payment of bonus in the form of shares
D. Issue of shares in lieu of raw materials

Flow of funds is:
(a) A, B, C, and D (b) B, C, and D
(c) C and D (d) Only D

11. When a consumer increases units of X - commodity by giving up some units of Y - commodity and even to attain the same level of satisfaction, the marginal rate of substitution, will be calculated by:
(a) Change in X - Commodity divided by change in Y - Commodity
(b) Change in X - Commodity divided by marginal utility of Y - Commodity
(c) Change in Y - Commodity divided by change in X - Commodity
(d) Change in Y - Commodity divided by marginal utility of X - Commodity

12. The following is the demand function in the small market:

$Q = 50 - 5P$

Where 'Q' denotes quantity in physical units and 'P' denotes price of the commodity. At price ₹ 5, the point price elasticity of demand would be:
(a) Zero (b) Equal to unity
(c) Highly elastic (d) Highly inelastic

13. Match the items of List I with the items of List II and find out the correct matching.

List I (Production functions)
A. $Q = 10.2\ K^{0.19}\ L^{0.88}$
B. $Q = 1.01\ L^{0.75}\ K^{0.25}$
C. $Q = 0.84\ L^{0.63}\ K^{0.3}$

List II (Name of the shapes of returns to scale)
(i) Constant Returns to scale
(ii) Diminishing Returns to scale
(iii) Increasing Returns to scale

Codes:	**(A)**	**(B)**	**(C)**
(a)	(i)	(ii)	(iii)
(b)	(ii)	(i)	(iii)
(c)	(ii)	(iii)	(i)
(d)	(i)	(iii)	(ii)

14. In the short-run, when a simple monopoly firm attains equilibrium and earns only normal profit, its level of output will correspond to:
(a) Lowest average cost
(b) Average cost above optimum level of output
(c) Average cost equals marginal cost
(d) Marginal cost much below average cost

15. Which one of the following is a false statement?
(a) Ramsey pricing rates to the methodology of pricing to situations where firms are regulated and the maximization of allocative efficiency is the objective of pricing together with the objective of profit-maximization.
(b) Peak-load pricing is a pricing practice where price varies with time of the day.
(c) Value-pricing is the practice of pricing where the price is set based on its value to the customer.
(d) Two - part tariff refers to a price structure which has two parts - a lump sum charge and a variable charge.

16. All the properties of order, interval and zero origin are simultaneously possessed by:

(a) Nominal Data (b) Interval Data
(c) Ratio Data (d) Ordinal Data

17. Under which of the following situations, chi-square test is applicable?
   A. testing homogenity
   B. testing goodness of fit
   C. testing equality of two sample means
   D. testing equality of two sample proportions
   E. testing independence of attributes

   Codes:
   (a) Only A, B and C (b) Only A, B and E
   (c) Only C, D and E (d) Only A, C and E

18. Which one of the following is not the correct statement regarding sampling distribution of mean?
   (a) Sampling distribution of mean is normally distributed for large sized samples.
   (b) Sampling distribution of mean is normally distributed for small sized samples drawn from not normally distributed population.
   (c) 't' distribution is not normally distributed.
   (d) Mean of the sampling distribution of mean is equal to the parametric value of mean.

19. Consider the following statements and identify the wrong statements:

   Statement I: Accepting null hypothesis, when it is false, is called a level of significance.

   Statement II: $1 - \alpha$ is called power of a test.

   Statement III: Critical value of Z - static for two-tailed test at 5% level of significance is 1.96.

   Codes:
   (a) Statements I, II and III
   (b) Statements I and III
   (c) Statements II and III
   (d) Statements I and II

20. The process of thoroughly checking the collected data to ensure optimal quality level is referred to as:
   (a) Validation (b) Editing
   (c) Classification (d) Entry

21. **Statement - (I):** Management is the art of knowing what you want to do and then seeing that it is done in the best and the cheapest way.

   Statement - (II): Management is the process of planning and regulating the activities of an enterprise.
   (a) Statement (I) is correct, but (II) is incorrect
   (b) Statement (II) is correct, but (I) is incorrect
   (c) Both the statements (I) and (II) are incorrect
   (d) Both the statements (I) and (II) are correct

22. **Assertion (A):** No business runs itself, even on momentum.....every business needs repeated stimulus.

   Reasoning (R): The management is the dynamic, life giving element in every business, without its leadership, the resources of production remain as resources and never become production.
   (a) Assertion (A) and Reasoning (R), both are correct, and (R) is the correct explanation of (A).
   (b) Assertion (A) and Reasoning (R), both are correct, but (R) is not the correct explanation of (A).
   (c) Assertion (A) is correct, but Reasoning (R) is incorrect.
   (d) Reasoning (R) is correct, but Assertion (A) is incorrect.

23. Match the items of List I with List II:

   List I
   A. Credit Mobilier
   B. Charleton Twist Company
   C. Difference Engine
   D. Commentry Four Chambault

   List II
   (i) Charles Babbage
   (ii) Henry Fayol
   (iii) Claud Henri Saint Simon
   (iv) Robert Owen

Codes:	**(A)**	**(B)**	**(C)**	**(D)**
(a)	(iii)	(iv)	(i)	(ii)
(b)	(iii)	(i)	(iv)	(ii)
(c)	(i)	(iii)	(iv)	(ii)
(d)	(ii)	(i)	(iv)	(iii)

24. Find out the correct combination of statements with regards to business ethics:
   A. Business ethics is the behaviour that a business adheres to in its daily dealings.
   B. The ethics of a particular business can be diverse.
   C. Business ethics has normative and descriptive dimensions.
   (a) Only A and B (b) Only A and C
   (c) Only B and C (d) All A, B and C

25. Which one of the following is not correct about business ethics?
   (a) Business ethics reflects the philosophy of business.
   (b) Business ethics is a form of applied ethics.
   (c) Business ethics are governed by the Government Policies.
   (d) Ethics are the standards which govern decisions on daily basis.
26. A marketing network consists of:
   (a) The tasks to devise marketing activities.
   (b) The tasks of hiring, training and motivating employees.
   (c) The activities that help in designing and implementing the marketing programmes.
   (d) The company and its supporting stakeholders with whom it has built mutually profitable business relationships.
27. Target marketing involves which of the following activities?
   A. Market positioning
   B. Market targeting
   C. Market behaviour
   D. Market segmentation

   Codes:
   (a) A and B (b) B and D
   (c) A, B and D (d) B, C and D
28. The pricing strategy which adjusts the basic price to accommodate differences in customers, products and locations is called:
   (a) Differentiated pricing
   (b) Promotional pricing
   (c) Geographical pricing
   (d) Price discounts and allowances
29. Horizontal marketing system comprises of:
   (a) the producer, wholesaler and retailer acting in a unified system.
   (b) multichannel marketing.
   (c) two or more marketing channels to reach one or more customer segments.
   (d) two or more unrelated companies put together resources to exploit an emerging market.
30. Match the items of List I with the items of List II:

   List I
   A. Face-to-face interaction with one or more prospective purchasers
   B. Any paid form of nonpersonal promotion
   C. Short-term incentives to encourage purchase
   D. Programmes to promote company's image

   List II
   (i) Sales promotion (ii) Public relations
   (iii) Personal selling (iv) Advertising

Codes:	**(A)**	**(B)**	**(C)**	**(D)**
(a)	(iii)	(iv)	(ii)	(i)
(b)	(iii)	(iv)	(i)	(ii)
(c)	(ii)	(i)	(iii)	(iv)
(d)	(ii)	(iii)	(i)	(iv)

31. Which of the following techniques for appraisal of investment proposals are based on time value of money?
   A. Accounting Rate of Return
   B. Internal Rate of Return
   C. Profitability Index Method
   D. Earnings Per Share

   Codes:
   (a) A and B (b) B and C
   (c) A and D (d) A, B and D
32. On the basis of the following information, what will be the EBIT corresponding to financial indifference point?

   Total capital outlay ₹ 60,00,000

   Financing Plans
   A. 100% Equity @ ₹ 10/- per share
   B. Debt - equity ratio 2 : 1

   Rate of interest 18% p.a., corporate tax rate 40%
   (a) ₹ 10,00,000 (b) ₹ 12,00,000
   (c) ₹ 10,80,000 (d) ₹ 12,80,000
33. Which one of the following assumptions is not included in the James E. Walter Valuation model?
   (a) All financing by retained earnings only
   (b) No change in the key variables such as EPS and DPS
   (c) The firm has finite life
   (d) All earnings are either distributed as dividends or invested internally immediately
34. Match the items of List I with the items of List II and find out the correct matching.

   List I (Formulae)
   A. Contribution/EBIT
   B. EBIT/Earnings before Tax (EBT)

C. Contribution/EBT

List II (Type of leverages)

(i) Financial leverage (ii) Super-leverage
(iii) Operating leverage

Codes:	**(A)**	**(B)**	**(C)**
(a)	(ii)	(iii)	(i)
(b)	(i)	(ii)	(iii)
(c)	(iii)	(ii)	(i)
(d)	(ii)	(i)	(iii)

35. **Statement - I:** Working capital leverage measures the responsiveness of Return on Equity for changes in current Assets.

Statement - II: When the annual demand for an item is 3200 units, unit cost ₹ 6, inventory carrying charges 25% p.a. and cost of one procurement ₹ 150, the economic ordering quantity would be 700 units.

Codes:

(a) Both statements are correct
(b) Both statements are incorrect
(c) Statement - I is correct and Statement - II is incorrect
(d) Statement - I is incorrect and Statement - II is correct

36. Match the items of List I with the items of List II:

List I (Conventional HRM)

A. Staff specialists B. Slow and reactive
C. Capital and products D. Cost centre

List II (Strategic HRM)

(i) Fast and proactive
(ii) People and knowledge
(iii) Line managers
(iv) Investment centre

Codes:	**(A)**	**(B)**	**(C)**	**(D)**
(a)	(ii)	(i)	(iii)	(iv)
(b)	(ii)	(iii)	(i)	(iv)
(c)	(iii)	(ii)	(i)	(iv)
(d)	(i)	(ii)	(iii)	(iv)

37. Which one of the following is a traditional method for selection of personnel?
(a) Interview (b) Selection Test
(c) Phrenology (d) Aptitude Test

38. The method of training in crafts, trades and technical areas is known as:
(a) Vestibule training (b) Coaching
(c) Mentoring (d) Apprenticeship

39. Behaviourally Anchored Rating Scale is a technique used for:
(a) Selection
(b) Succession Planning
(c) Performance appraisal
(d) Recruitment

40. Which one of the following is not a mechanism of managing stress?
(a) Rust out (b) Cognitive therapy
(c) Job enrichment (d) Networking

41. Interest earned by a depositor against a deposit with a commercial bank for custodial service:
(a) is a fund based income
(b) is a fee based income
(c) is a combination of fund and fee based gain
(d) is a commitment based gain

42. Match the items in List I with the items in List II:

List I

A. ATM card
B. Debts due for more than 30 days
C. Micro finance
D. State level finance corporations

List II

(i) NPA
(ii) John Shephard Barron
(iii) State Finance Corporations Act
(iv) NABARD

Codes:	**(A)**	**(B)**	**(C)**	**(D)**
(a)	(i)	(iii)	(ii)	(iv)
(b)	(ii)	(i)	(iv)	(iii)
(c)	(iv)	(iii)	(ii)	(i)
(d)	(ii)	(i)	(iii)	(iv)

43. **Assertion (A):** A well developed money market is the basis for an effective monetary policy. It is in the money market that the Central Bank comes into contact with the financial sectors of the economy as a whole and it is through the liquidity in the market that influence the cost and availability of credit.

Reasoning (R): A well organised money market is an essential condition for the successful operation of the Central Banking policies, and for holding the conditions of

liquidity within the bounds of what the monetary authorities consider desirable.
(a) (A) is true but (R) is false
(b) (R) is true but (A) is false
(c) (A) is true and (R) offers correct explanation to (A)
(d) Both (A) and (R) are false

44. The operations of banks and financial institutions are regulated by:
(a) The RBI Act 1934 only
(b) The Banking Regulation Act 1949 only
(c) Information Technology Act 2000 only
(d) All of the above

45. To operationalise online, internet, mobile banking, debit card and credit card tools, some of the essential ingredients are:
(a) Compliance with the Information Technology Act 2000
(b) Satellite connection
(c) Selection of a portal and server
(d) All of the above

46. Any country consistently facing balance of payment deficiency can approach:
(a) The World Bank
(b) The Smithsonian Institute
(c) IMF
(d) The IMF and the IBRD

47. Counter-trade means:
(a) A sort of bilateral trade where one set of goods is exchanged for another set of goods and a seller provides a buyer with deliveries.
(b) A company takes full responsibility for making its goods available in the target market by selling directly to the end-users.
(c) The companies in two separate sovereigns agree to exchange one set of goods for another set of goods.
(d) A set of multilateral trade where one of goods and services may be exchanged for another set of goods and services among the trading partners.

48. The floating rate system is characterised by:
(a) the market forces that determine the exchange rate between two currencies.
(b) the central banking authorities of the two countries mutually agree upon the rate.
(c) help realigning the par value of major currencies.
(d) the rate of exchange mutually agreed upon between IMF and its member nations.

49. A practice of selling a commodity in a foreign market at a price lower than the domestic price; and even at equal to the cost of production to capture foreign market is known as:
(a) Gouging (b) Forging
(c) Dumping (d) Forfeiting

50. The highest percentage of export from India went to which of the following regions in 2013-14?
(a) OECD countries (b) USA
(c) SAARC (d) Latin America

51. Match the items of List I with the items of List II and select a correct code:

List I
A. SEBI B. RBI C. STCI D. OTCEI

List II
(i) Exchange for small companies
(ii) Secondary market in treasury bills
(iii) Regulation of secondary market
(iv) Ad-hoc treasury bills

Codes:	(A)	(B)	(C)	(D)
(a)	(iv)	(ii)	(iii)	(i)
(b)	(iii)	(iv)	(ii)	(i)
(c)	(iii)	(i)	(ii)	(iv)
(d)	(ii)	(iii)	(i)	(iv)

52. X Ltd. goes into liquidation and a new company Z Ltd. purchases the business of X Ltd. It is a case of:
(a) Amalgamation
(b) Absorption
(c) Internal reconstruction
(d) External reconstruction

53. When the cost incurred on recruiting, training and developing the employees is considered for determining the value of employees, it is called:
(a) The replacement cost approach
(b) The historical cost approach
(c) The opportunity cost approach
(d) None of the above

54. In India, NIFTY and SENSEX are calculated on the basis of:

(a) Market capitalisation
(b) Paid up capital
(c) Free-float market capitalisation
(d) Authorized share capital

55. Financial Instruments which are issued with detachable warrants and are redeemable after certain period is known as:
(a) Deep Discount Bonds
(b) Secured Premium Notes
(c) Bunny Bonds
(d) Junk Bonds

56. Which of the following can be used by a company as communication mix to reach the target customers?
(A) Advertising
(B) Sales promotion
(C) Events and experiences
(D) Public relations
(E) Direct marketing
(F) Personal selling

Codes:
(a) (A), (B), (D) and (F)
(b) (A), (B), (E) and (F)
(c) (A), (B), (D), (E) and (F)
(d) (A), (B), (C), (D), (E) and (F)

57. In addition to motivation, learning and memory, which one of the following is included in the main psychological processes affecting consumer behaviour?
(a) Perception (b) Life cycle
(c) Lifestyle (d) Social class

58. Match the items of List I with the items of List II:

List I
A. Geographic Segmentation
B. Demographic Segmentation
C. Psychographic Segmentation
D. Behavioural Segmentation

List II
(i) Gender, income, religion
(ii) Knowledge, attitude, response
(iii) Regions, cities, neighbourhoods
(iv) Lifestyle, personality traits, values

Codes:	(A)	(B)	(C)	(D)
(a)	(ii)	(iv)	(iii)	(i)
(b)	(ii)	(iv)	(i)	(iii)
(c)	(iv)	(ii)	(i)	(iii)
(d)	(iv)	(i)	(ii)	(iii)

59. Which one of the following is not a stage in the product life cycle?
(a) Introduction (b) Growth
(c) Equilibrium (d) Decline

60. Which one of the following is correct statement in respect of co-branding?
(a) Co-branding is an umbrella branding of goods of a company.
(b) In co-branding, two or more well-known existing brands are combined into a joint product.
(c) Co-branding is the process of combining two brands for promoting brand equity.
(d) All of the above

61. Which one of the following is not a major punishment?
(a) Withholding of increments (b) Demotion
(c) Transfer (d) Suspension

62. **Assertion (A):** Job evaluation is essentially a job rating process, not unlike the rating of employees.
Reasoning (R): Job evaluation is a practice which seeks to provide a degree of objectivity in measuring the comparative value of jobs within an organisation and among similar organisations.
(a) Both Assertion (A) and Reasoning (R) are correct
(b) Both Assertion (A) and Reasoning (R) are incorrect
(c) Assertion (A) is correct, but Reasoning (R) is incorrect
(d) Reasoning (R) is correct, but Assertion (A) is incorrect

63. Identify the correct combinations from the following:

	Skills	Training and Development Methods	Target Trainees
A.	Knowledge	Deliberation/Lecture	Managerial
B.	Multi-skills	Vestibule training	Operative
C.	Decision-making skills	Management game	Managerial
D.	Behavioural skills	Sensitivity training	Supervisory

Codes:
(a) (A), (B) and (C) (b) (A), (C) and (D)
(c) (B), (C) and (D) (d) (A), (B) and (D)

64. Which among the following are not part of staffing process?

(A) Human Resource Planning
(B) Recruitment
(C) Selection
(D) Induction and Orientation
(E) Training and Development
(F) Performance Appraisal
(G) Transfers
(H) Separations

Codes:
(a) (E), (F), (G) and (H)
(b) (G) and (H)
(c) (F) and (H)
(d) None of the above

65. Match the items of List I with List II:

List I	List II
(A) INTUC	(i) 1920
(B) AITUC	(ii) 1947
(C) CITU	(iii) 1955
(D) BMS	(iv) 1970

Codes:	(A)	(B)	(C)	(D)
(a)	(i)	(ii)	(iii)	(iv)
(b)	(ii)	(i)	(iv)	(iii)
(c)	(ii)	(i)	(iii)	(iv)
(d)	(iii)	(i)	(iv)	(ii)

66. **Assertion (A):** Amended Patent Act, in compliance with WTO, provides for grant of product patent as well as a process patent for a period of 20 years from the date of application.

Reasoning (R): Under the Act, patent may be granted to an invention which means a new product or process involving an inventive step and capable of industrial application, a technical advance over existing knowledge.

Codes:
(a) Both (A) and (R) are true but (R), is not correct explanation to (A).
(b) (A) is false but (R) is correct.
(c) Both (A) and (R) are true and (R), is correct explanation to (A).
(d) (A) is correct but (R) is false.

67. Which of the following have been recognised under the intellectual property eligible for creation of rights as per WTO mandate?
(A) Computer software, music disc, performing art
(B) Geographical indicator
(C) Global positioning system
(D) Journals, books, seeds, design, brand

Codes:
(a) A, B and C (b) D, C and A
(c) A, B and D (d) C, A and B

68. NAFTA came into force from January, 1994 embracing:
(a) The USA, Canada, Cuba, Trinidad and Tobago
(b) The USA, Canada, Mexico
(c) Cuba, Mexico, USA, Havana
(d) Trinidad, The USA, Mexico

69. A common market is one where:
(a) all the trading nations agree commonly to levy a common and uniform tariff rate for all goods.
(b) all the trading nations agree commonly to rationalise tariff and non-tariff barriers mutually to promote intra-region trade.
(c) there is a customs union along with free intra-union movement of factors of production.
(d) there is an economic union along with free intra-union movement of residents.

70. The Maastricht Treaty of February, 1992 renamed the European Community (EC) as:
(a) the European Union (EU)
(b) the European Economic Union (EEU)
(c) the European Monetary Union (EMU)
(d) the European Economic Community (EEC)

71. In which of the following cases, Assessing officer has the discretion to assess the income of the previous year in the previous year or in the subsequent assessment year?
(a) Shipping business of non-residents
(b) Association of Persons (AOP) or Body of Individuals (BOI) formed for a particular event or purpose
(c) Assessment of persons likely to transfer property to avoid tax
(d) Discontinued business

72. Rental income received by a foreign individual, from another foreign individual, in respect of the property situated in Delhi is taxable in the hands of:
(a) Resident and Ordinarily Resident (OR) only

(b) Ordinarily Resident (OR) and Not Ordinarily Resident (NOR) only
(c) Non Resident (NR) only
(d) Ordinarily Resident (OR), Not Ordinarily Resident (NOR) and Non Resident (NR)

73. Which of the following income is not chargeable under the head 'income from business and profession'?
(a) Profits and Gains carried on by an assessee during the previous year.
(b) Income derived by a trade professional or similar association from specific services performed for its members.
(c) Income from the activity of owning or owning and maintaining race horses.
(d) Salary received by a partner of a firm from the same firm.

74. Mr. A earned a capital gain of ₹ 100 lakhs on 31-2-2014 from the sale of a long term capital asset (land) within the limits of Jaipur corporation. If he invests ₹ 60 lakhs, out of ₹ 100 lakhs, in Rural Electricity Corporation Bonds approved under Sec. 54 EC in 20-2-2014, what is the amount of exemption he can claim under Sec. 54 EC of Income Tax Act for the AY 2014-15?
(a) ₹ 60 lakhs (b) ₹ 50 lakhs
(c) ₹ 100 lakhs (d) ₹ 30 lakhs

75. Under which of the following situations, the Appellate Tribunal can rectify the mistake in the order passed by it under Sec. 254 (2) of Income Tax Act?
A. If subsequent decision of the Supreme Court/High Court is available on the subject after the Appellate Tribunal's order
B. If an assessee apply for rectification of the Tribunal's order by raising fresh grounds before the Tribunal
C. If the omission or mistake is on the part of Appellate Tribunal
D. If the order is passed by the Appellate Tribunal under an erroneous impression of fact or law

Codes:
(a) A, B and C (b) B, C and D
(c) A, C and D (d) only C and D

ANSWERS

1. (a)	2. (d)	3. (b)	4. (c)	5. (a)
6. (c)	7. (c)	8. (c)	9. (c)	10. (d)
11. (c)	12. (b)	13. (c)	14. (d)	15. (a)
16. (c)	17. (b)	18. (b)	19. (d)	20. (a)
21. (d)	22. (a)	23. (a)	24. (d)	25. (c)
26. (d)	27. (c)	28. (a)	29. (d)	30. (b)
31. (b)	32. (c)	33. (c)	34. (a)	35. (b)
36. (b)	37. (c)	38. (d)	39. (c)	40. (a)
41. (a)	42. (d)	43. (c)	44. (d)	45. (d)
46. (c)	47. (a)	48. (a)	49. (c)	50. (a)
51. (b)	52. (d)	53. (b)	54. (c)	55. (b)
56. (d)	57. (a)	58. (z)	59. (c)	60. (b)
61. (c)	62. (a)	63. (b)	64. (d)	65. (b)
66. (c)	67. (c)	68. (b)	69. (c)	70. (a)
71. (d)	72. (d)	73. (c)	74. (z)	75. (c)

z → All options are correct.

DECEMBER–2015

Note: This paper contains Sixty (60) multiple-choice questions, each question carrying two (2) marks. Candidate is expected to answer any Fifty (50) questions. In case more than Fifty (50) questions are attempted, only the first Fifty (50) questions will be evaluated.

PAPER–I

1. Greater the handicap of the students coming to the educational institutions, greater the demand on the:
   (a) Family (b) Society
   (c) Teacher (d) State
2. What are the characteristics of Continuous and Comprehensive Evaluation?
   (i) It increases the workload on students by taking multiple tests.
   (ii) It replaces marks with grades.
   (iii) It evaluates every aspect of the student.
   (iv) It helps in reducing examination phobia.
   Select the correct answer from the codes given below:
   Codes:
   (a) (i), (ii), (iii) and (iv) (b) (ii) and (iv)
   (c) (i), (ii) and (iii) (d) (ii), (iii) and (iv)
3. Which of the following attributes denote great strengths of a teacher?
   (i) Full-time active involvement in the institutional management
   (ii) Setting examples
   (iii) Willingness to put assumptions to the test
   (iv) Acknowledging mistakes
   Select the correct answer from the codes given below:
   Codes:
   (a) (i), (ii) and (iv) (b) (ii), (iii) and (iv)
   (c) (i), (iii) and (iv) (d) (i), (ii), (iii) and (iv)
4. Which one of the following statements is correct in the context of multiple-choice type questions?
   (a) They are more objective than true-false type questions.
   (b) They are less objective than essay type questions.
   (c) They are more subjective than short-answer type questions.
   (d) They are more subjective than true-false type questions.
5. As Chairman of an independent commission on education, Jacques Delors report to UNESCO was titled:
   (a) International Commission on Education Report
   (b) Millennium Development Report
   (c) Learning: The Treasure Within
   (d) World Declaration on Education for All
6. What are required for good teaching?
   (i) Diagnosis (ii) Remedy
   (iii) Direction (iv) Feedback
   Select the correct answer from the codes given below:
   Codes:
   (a) (i), (ii), (iii) and (iv) (b) (i) and (ii)
   (c) (ii), (iii) and (iv) (d) (iii) and (iv)
7. Which of the following statements is not true in the context of participatory research?
   (a) It recognizes knowledge as power.
   (b) It emphasises on people as experts.
   (c) It is a collective process of enquiry.
   (d) Its sole purpose is production of knowledge.
8. Which of the following statements is true in the context of the testing of a hypothesis?
   (a) It is only the alternative hypothesis, that can be tested.
   (b) It is only the null hypothesis, that can be tested.
   (c) Both, the alternative and the null hypotheses can be tested.
   (d) Both, the alternative and the null hypotheses cannot be tested.
9. Which of the following are the basic rules of APA style of referencing format?

(i) Italicize titles of shorter works such as journal articles or essays
(ii) Invert authors' names (last name first)
(iii) Italicize titles of longer works such as books and journals
(iv) Alphabetically index reference list

Select the correct answer from the codes given below:

Codes:

(a) (i) and (ii) (b) (ii), (iii) and (iv)
(c) (iii) and (iv) (d) (i), (ii), (iii) and (iv)

10. Which of the following are the characteristics of a seminar?
(i) It is a form of academic instruction.
(ii) It involves questioning, discussion and debates.
(iii) It involves large groups of individuals.
(iv) It needs involvement of skilled persons.

Select the correct answer from the codes given below:

Codes:

(a) (ii) and (iii) (b) (ii) and (iv)
(c) (ii), (iii) and (iv) (d) (i), (ii) and (iv)

11. A researcher is interested in studying the prospects of a particular political party in an urban area. What tool should he prefer for the study?
(a) Rating scale (b) Interview
(c) Questionnaire (d) Schedule

12. Ethical norms in research do not involve guidelines for:
(a) Thesis format (b) Copyright
(c) Patenting policy (d) Data sharing policies

Read the following passage carefully and answer question numbers 13 to 17.

I did that thing recently where you have to sign a big card—which is a horror unto itself, especially as the keeper of the Big Card was leaning over me at the time. Suddenly I was on the spot, a rabbit in the headlights, torn between doing a fun message or some sort of in-joke or a drawing. Instead overwhelmed by the myriad options available to me, I decided to just write "Good luck, best, Joel".

It was then that I realised, to my horror, that I had forgotten how to write. My entire existence is "tap letters into computer". My shopping lists are hidden in the notes function of my phone. If I need to remember something I send an e-mail to myself. A pen is something I chew when I'm struggling to think. Paper is something I pile beneath my laptop to make it a more comfortable height for me to type on.

A poll of 1,000 teens by the stationers, Bic found that one in 10 don't own a pen, a third have never written a letter, and half of 13 to 19 years - old have never been forced to sit down and write a thank you letter. More than 80% have never written a love letter, 56% don't have letter paper at home. And a quarter have never known the unique torture of writing a birthday card. The most a teen ever has to use a pen is on an exam paper.

Bic, have you heard of mobile phones? Have you heard of e-mail, facebook and snap chatting? This is the future. Pens are dead. Paper is dead. Handwriting is a relic.

"Handwriting is one of the most creative outlets we have and should be given the same importance as other art forms such as sketching, painting or photography."

Answer the following questions:

13. When confronted with signing a big card, the author felt like "a rabbit in the headlight".
What does this phrase mean?
(a) A state of confusion (b) A state of pleasure
(c) A state of anxiety (d) A state of pain

14. According to the author, which one is not the most creative outlet of pursuit?
(a) Handwriting (b) Photography
(c) Sketching (d) Reading

15. The entire existence of the author revolves round:
(i) Computer (ii) Mobile phone
(iii) Typewriter

Identify the correct answer from the codes given below:

Codes:

(a) (ii) only (b) (i) and (ii) only
(c) (i), (ii) and (iii) (d) (ii) and (iii) only

16. How many teens, as per the Bic survey, do not own a pen?
(a) 800 (b) 560 (c) 500 (d) 100

17. What is the main concern of the author?

(a) That the teens use social networks for communication.
(b) That the teens use mobile phones.
(c) That the teens use computer.
(d) That the teens have forgotten the art of handwriting.

18. The main objectives of student evaluation of teachers are:
(i) To gather information about student weaknesses.
(ii) To make teachers take teaching seriously.
(iii) To help teachers adopt innovative methods of teaching.
(iv) To identify the areas of further improvement in teacher traits.

Identify the correct answer from the codes given below:

Codes:
(a) (i) and (ii) only
(b) (ii), (iii) and (iv) only
(c) (i), (ii) and (iii) only
(d) (i) only

19. Using the central point of the classroom communication as the beginning of a dynamic pattern of ideas is referred to as:
(a) Systemisation (b) Problem-orientation
(c) Idea protocol (d) Mind mapping

20. Aspects of the voice, other than the speech are known as:
(a) Physical language (b) Personal language
(c) Para language (d) Delivery language

21. Every type of communication is affected by its:
(a) Reception (b) Transmission
(c) Non-regulation (d) Context

22. Attitudes, actions and appearances in the context of classroom communication are considered as:
(a) Verbal (b) Non-verbal
(c) Impersonal (d) Irrational

23. Most often, the teacher-student communication is:
(a) Spurious (b) Critical
(c) Utilitarian (d) Confrontational

24. In a classroom, a communicator's trust level is determined by:
(a) the use of hyperbole
(b) the change of voice level
(c) the use of abstract concepts
(d) eye contact

25. The next term in the series
2, 5, 10, 17, 26, 37, ? is:
(a) 50 (b) 57 (c) 62 (d) 72

26. A group of 210 students appeared in some test. The mean of 1/3rd of students is found to be 60. The mean of the remaining students is found to be 78. The mean of the whole group will be
(a) 80 (b) 76 (c) 74 (d) 72

27. Anil after travelling 6 km towards East from his house realized that he has travelled in a wrong direction. He turned and travelled 12 km towards West, turned right and travelled 8 km to reach his office. The straight distance of the office from his house is:
(a) 20 km (b) 14 km (c) 12 km (d) 10 km

28. The next term in the series:
B2E, D5H, F12K, H27N, ___? is:
(a) J56I (b) I62Q (c) Q62J (d) J58Q

29. A party was held in which a grandmother, father, mother, four sons, their wives and one son and two daughters to each of the sons were present. The number of females present in the party is:
(a) 12 (b) 14 (c) 18 (d) 24

30. P and Q are brothers. R and S are sisters. The son of P is brother of S. Q is related to R as:
(a) Son (b) Brother (c) Uncle (d) Father

31. Consider the argument given below:
'Pre-employment testing of teachers is quite fair because doctors, architects and engineers who are now employed had to face such a testing.'
What type of argument it is?
(a) Deductive (b) Analogical
(c) Psychological (d) Biological

32. Among the following propositions two are related in such a way that they can both be true although they cannot both be false. Which are those propositions? Select the correct code.

Propositions:
(i) Some priests are cunning.
(ii) No priest is cunning.

(iii) All priests are cunning.
(iv) Some priests are not cunning.

Codes:

(a) (i) and (ii) (b) (iii) and (iv)
(c) (i) and (iii) (d) (i) and (iv)

33. A Cluster of propositions with a structure that exhibits some inference is called:
(a) An inference (b) An argument
(c) An explanation (d) A valid argument

34. Consider the following assertion (A) and reason (R) and select the correct code given below:

Assertion (A): No man is perfect.

Reason (R): Some men are not perfect.

(a) Both (A) and (R) are true but (R) does not provide sufficient reason for (A).
(b) Both (A) and (R) are true and (R) provides sufficient reason for (A).
(c) (A) is true but (R) is false.
(d) (A) is false but (R) is true.

35. A definition that has a meaning that is deliberately assigned to some symbol is called:
(a) Lexical (b) Precising
(c) Stipulative (d) Persuasive

36. If the proposition 'No men are honest' is taken to be false which of the following proposition/propositions can be claimed certainly to be true?

Propositions:

(a) All men are honest
(b) Some men are honest
(c) Some men are not honest
(d) No honest person is man

Given below in the table is the decadal data of Population and Electrical Power Production of a country.

Year	Population (million)	Electrical Power Production (GW)*
1951	20	10
1961	21	20
1971	24	25
1981	27	40
1991	30	50
2001	32	80
2011	35	100
		* 1 GW = 1000 million watt

Based on the above table, answer the questions from Sl. No. 37 to 42.

37. Which decade registered the maximum growth rate (%) of population?
(a) 1961-1971 (b) 1971-1981
(c) 1991-2001 (d) 2001-2011

38. Average decadal growth rate (%) of population is:
(a) ~ 12.21% (b) ~ 9.82%
(c) ~ 6.73% (d) ~ 5%

39. Based on the average decadal growth rate, what will be the population in the year 2021?
(a) 40.34 million (b) 38.49 million
(c) 37.28 million (d) 36.62 million

40. In the year 1951, what was the power availability per person?
(a) 100 W (b) 200 W (c) 400 W (d) 500 W

41. In which decade, the average power availability per person was maximum?
(a) 1981-1991 (b) 1991-2001
(c) 2001-2011 (d) 1971-1981

42. By what percentage (%) the power production increased from 1951 to 2011?
(a) 100% (b) 300% (c) 600% (d) 900%

43. NMEICT stands for:
(a) National Mission on Education through ICT
(b) National Mission on E-governance through ICT
(c) National Mission on E-commerce through ICT
(d) National Mission on E-learning through ICT

44. Which of the following is an instant messaging application?
(i) WhatsApp (ii) Google Talk
(iii) Viber
Select the correct answer from the codes given below:

Codes:

(a) (i) and (ii) only (b) (ii) and (iii) only
(c) (i) only (d) (i), (ii) and (iii)

45. In a Computer a byte generally consists of:
(a) 4 bits (b) 8 bits (c) 16 bits (d) 10 bits

46. Which of the following is not an input device?
(a) Microphone (b) Keyboard
(c) Joystick (d) Monitor

47. Which of the following is an open source software?
(a) MS Word (b) Windows
(c) Mozilla Firefox (d) Acrobat Reader

48. Which of the following enables us to send the same letter to different persons in MS Word?
(a) Mail join (b) Mail copy
(c) Mail insert (d) Mail merge

49. Inside rural homes, the source/sources of Nitrogen Oxide Pollution may be:
(i) Unvented gas stoves
(ii) Wood stoves
(iii) Kerosene heaters

Choose the correct code:

Codes:
(a) (i) and (ii) only (b) (ii) and (iii) only
(c) (ii) only (d) (i), (ii) and (iii)

50. Which of the following pollutants can cause cancer in humans?
(a) Pesticides (b) Mercury
(c) Lead (d) Ozone

51. **Assertion (A):** People population control measures do not necessarily help in checking environmental degradation.

Reason (R): The relationship between population growth and environmental degradation is rather complex.

Choose the correct answer from the following:
(a) Both (A) and (R) are true and (R) is the correct explanation of (A).
(b) Both (A) and (R) are true but (R) is not the correct explanation of (A).
(c) (A) is true but (R) is false.
(d) (A) is false but (R) is true.

52. Which of the following phenomena is not a natural hazard?
(a) Wildfire
(b) Lightning
(c) Landslide
(d) Chemical contamination

53. As part of National Climate Change Policy, Indian government is planning to raise the installed capacity of renewable energy by the year 2030 to:
(a) 175 GW (b) 200 GW
(c) 250 GW (d) 350 GW

54. At present, in terms of per capita energy consumption (kWh/year), identify the correct sequence.
(a) Brazil > Russia > China > India
(b) Russia > China > India > Brazil
(c) Russia > China > Brazil > India
(d) China > Russia > Brazil > India

55. Which of the following are the objectives of Rashtriya Uchchatar Shiksha Abhiyan (RUSA)?
(i) To improve the overall quality of state institutions.
(ii) To ensure adequate availability of quality faculty.
(iii) To create new institutions through upgradation of existing autonomous colleges.
(iv) To downgrade universities with poor infrastructure into autonomous colleges.

Select the correct answer from the codes given below:

Codes:
(a) (i), (ii), (iii) and (iv) (b) (i), (ii) and (iii)
(c) (i), (iii) and (iv) (d) (i), (ii) and (iv)

56. The grounds on which discrimination in admission to educational institutions is constitutionally prohibited are:
(i) Religion (ii) Sex
(iii) Place of birth (iv) Nationality

Select the correct answer from the codes given below:

Codes:
(a) (ii), (iii) and (iv) (b) (i), (ii) and (iii)
(c) (i), (ii) and (iv) (d) (i), (ii), (iii) and (iv)

57. Which of the following statements are correct about Lok Sabha?
(i) The Constitution puts a limit on the size of the Lok Sabha.
(ii) The size and shape of the Parliamentary Constituencies is determined by the Election Commission.
(iii) First-past-the Post electoral system is followed.

(iv) The Speaker of Lok Sabha does not have a casting vote in case of an equality of votes.

Select the correct answer from the codes given below:

Codes:

(a) (i) and (iii) (b) (i), (ii) and (iii)
(c) (i), (iii) and (iv) (d) (i), (ii), (iii) and (iv)

58. Public Order as an item in the Constitution figures in
(a) the Union List
(b) the State List
(c) the Concurrent List
(d) the Residuary Powers

59. The term of office of the Advocate General of a State is
(a) 4 years
(b) 5 years
(c) 6 years or 65 years of age whichever is earlier
(d) not fixed

60. Which among the following States has the highest number of seats in the Lok Sabha?
(a) Maharashtra (b) Rajasthan
(c) Tamil Nadu (d) West Bengal

ANSWERS

1. (c)	2. (d)	3. (b)	4. (a)	5. (c)
6. (a)	7. (d)	8. (b)	9. (b)	10. (d)
11. (c)	12. (a)	13. (a)	14. (d)	15. (b)
16. (d)	17. (d)	18. (c)	19. (d)	20. (c)
21. (d)	22. (b)	23. (c)	24. (d)	25. (a)
26. (d)	27. (d)	28. (d)	29. (b)	30. (c)
31. (b)	32. (d)	33. (b)	34. (a)	35. (c)
36. (b)	37. (a)	38. (b)	39. (b)	40. (d)
41. (c)	42. (d)	43. (a)	44. (d)	45. (b)
46. (d)	47. (c)	48. (d)	49. (d)	50. (a)
51. (a)	52. (d)	53. (d)	54. (c)	55. (b)
56. (b)	57. (a)	58. (b)	59. (d)	60. (a)

PAPER–II

Note: This paper contains fifty (50) objective type questions, each question carrying two (2) marks. All questions are compulsory.

1. Environmental degeneration does not consist of:
(a) Land degeneration and soil erosion
(b) Problem of over grazing and ecological degeneration
(c) Floods
(d) None of the above

2. Which of the following is not the main objective of "Fiscal Policy of India"?
(a) To increase liquidity in economy
(b) To promote price stability
(c) To minimize the in-equality in income and wealth
(d) To promote employment opportunities

3. Liberalization means:
(a) Reducing number of reserved industries from 17 to 8
(b) Liberating the industry, trade and economy from unwanted restriction
(c) Opening up economy to the world by attaining international competitiveness
(d) Free determination of interest rate

4. **Assertion (A):** Industrialization of an economy is considered synonymous with growth.

Reasoning (R): The transfer of resources from agrarian to industrial may be capital or labour or both.

Codes:
(a) Both (A) and (R) are true and (R) is correct explanation of (A).
(b) Both (A) and (R) are true but (R) is not the correct explanation of (A).
(c) (A) is true but (R) is false.
(d) (A) is false but (R) is true.

5. Globalization is the term used to describe process of removal of restriction on which one of the following?
(a) Foreign trade (b) Investment
(c) Both (a) and (b) (d) None of the above

6. Interest on loan taken for the purchase of fixed assets is a:
(a) Revenue Expenditure
(b) Capital Expenditure
(c) Deferred Revenue Expenditure
(d) Capital Loss

7. Dual Aspect Concept results in the following accounting equation:

(a) Revenue = Expenses
(b) Capital + Profits = Assets + Expenses
(c) Capital + Liabilities = Assets
(d) Capital + Drawings = Owner's Equity

8. Match the items in Column 1 with the items in Column 2:

Column 1
A. Materiality Concept
B. Going Concern Concept
C. Historical Cost Concept
D. Consistency Concept

Column 2
(i) The same accounting method used by a firm from one period to another
(ii) An inappropriate assumption of a firm being bankrupt
(iii) A normal basis used for accounting assets
(iv) Relates to the importance of an item or event

Codes:	**(A)**	**(B)**	**(C)**	**(D)**
(a)	(iv)	(ii)	(iii)	(i)
(b)	(i)	(ii)	(iii)	(iv)
(c)	(ii)	(iii)	(iv)	(i)
(d)	(iv)	(ii)	(i)	(iii)

9. 'X' Ltd. has a liquid ratio of 2 : 1. If its stock is ₹ 40,000 and its current liabilities are of ₹ 1 Lac, its current ratio will be:
(a) 1.4 times (b) 2.4 times
(c) 1.2 times (d) 3.4 times

10. 'Comparison of the financial statements of the current year with the performance of previous years of the same firm', is known as:
(a) Trend Analysis
(b) Horizontal Analysis
(c) Intra - firm comparison
(d) All of the above

11. The Marshallian utility analysis is based on a less valid assumption of:
(a) cardinal measurability of the utility
(b) given marginal utility of money
(c) diminishing marginal utility of the goods
(d) additivity of the utility

12. Match the items of the List-I with those of the List-II and indicate the correct code:

List-I
(A) Convexity of the indifferences curve to origin
(B) Quantity of certain goods sacrificed for a large quantity of other goods
(C) Equality of the ratio of the marginal utilities with that of the prices of the two goods
(D) Separation of substitution and income effects from the total price effect

List-II
(i) Indifference curve analysis
(ii) Consumer's equilibrium
(iii) Substitutability/complementarity of the two goods
(iv) Marginal rate substitution

Codes:	**(A)**	**(B)**	**(C)**	**(D)**
(a)	(iv)	(ii)	(i)	(iii)
(b)	(iii)	(iv)	(ii)	(i)
(c)	(iii)	(i)	(iv)	(ii)
(d)	(i)	(iii)	(ii)	(iv)

13. Firms producing and selling a large variety of goods will generally follow:
(a) Cost plus pricing
(b) Marginal pricing
(c) Skimming pricing
(d) Product line pricing

14. For the following two statements of Assertion (A) and Reasoning (R) indicate the correct code:

Assertion (A): All firms under perfect competition in long run earn only normal profit.

Reasoning (R): All firms under perfect competition in long run operate at the minimum average cost level.

Codes:
(a) (A) and (R) both are correct.
(b) (A) is correct but (R) is not correct.
(c) (A) is not correct but (R) is correct.
(d) (A) and (R) both are incorrect.

15. Match the items of List-I with those of List-II and indicate the correct code:

List-I
A. Substitute Goods
B. Complementary Goods
C. Giffen Goods
D. High Income Group Consumption Goods

List-II
(i) Negative Cross Elasticity
(ii) Low Price Elasticity

(iii) Positive Cross Elasticity
(iv) Positive Price Elasticity

Codes:	(A)	(B)	(C)	(D)
(a)	(iii)	(iv)	(ii)	(i)
(b)	(iii)	(i)	(iv)	(ii)
(c)	(ii)	(iii)	(i)	(iv)
(d)	(i)	(ii)	(iii)	(iv)

16. Which one of the following is not a method of studying association of attributes?
(a) Concurrent Deviation Method
(b) Proportion Method
(c) Yule's Method
(d) Coefficient of Contingency

17. Identify which of the following steps would be included in hypothesis testing:
(A) State the null and alternative hypothesis.
(B) Set the significance level before the research study.
(C) Eliminate all outliers.
(D) Obtain the probability value using a computer program such as SPSS.
(E) Compare the probability value to the significance level and make the statistical decision.

Codes:
(a) A, C and D (b) C, D, and E
(c) A, B, D and E (d) B, C, D and E

18. Select the methods of finding out correlation from the following:
A. Karl Pearson's Method
B. Spearman's Rank Method
C. Yule's Method
D. Coefficient of Contingency
E. Concurrent Deviation Method

Codes:
(a) A, B, C (b) A, B, C, D
(c) A, B, E (d) C, D, E

19. A set of data can be distinguished from other set of data by means of:
(a) Central value and dispersion
(b) Central value, dispersion and skewness
(c) Central value, dispersion, skewness and Kurtosis
(d) None of the above

20. The advent of computers in research has led to:
(a) Limitations of options in analysis
(b) Tremendous amount of flexibility with marginal increase in cost
(c) Myopic exposure of statistics to the researcher
(d) None of the above

21. Who among the following is not related to the planning function given by Taylor?
(a) Route clerk (b) Time and cost clerk
(c) Inspector (d) Disciplinarian

22. Match the following:

Book
A. *Functions of the Executive*
B. *On the Economy of Machinery and Manufactures*
C. *The Effective Executive*
D. *General and Industrial Administration*

Author
(i) Charles Babbage (ii) Henri Fayol
(iii) Chester Barnard (iv) Peter Drucker

Codes:	(A)	(B)	(C)	(D)
(a)	(i)	(ii)	(iii)	(iv)
(b)	(iii)	(i)	(iv)	(ii)
(c)	(iv)	(iii)	(i)	(ii)
(d)	(iii)	(iv)	(i)	(ii)

23. The classical organisation theory treats organisation as a/an:
(a) Open system (b) Closed system
(c) Technical system (d) Macro system

24. Which of the following is a systematic interactive forecasting method that relies on a panel of experts?
(a) Pay-off matrix (b) Game theory
(c) Queing theory (d) Delphi technique

25. According to Hersey and Blanchard's situational approach to leadership, the 'participating style' of leadership has:
(a) High task and low relationship orientation
(b) High task and high relationship orientation
(c) Low task and high relationship orientation
(d) Low task and low relationship orientation

26. Which of the following is not a reason for the failure of new products?
(a) Good idea but overestimated market size.
(b) Correctly positioned new product, not promoted effectively or overpriced.
(c) Development costs are lower than or equal to estimated or expected.
(d) Competitors fight back harder than expected.

27. Which one of the following is true for the calculation of overall market share?
    (a) (Customer penetration) × (Customer loyalty) × (Price selectivity)
    (b) (Customer loyalty) × (Customer selectivity) × (Price selectivity)
    (c) (Customer selectivity) × (Price selectivity) × (Customer penetration)
    (d) (Customer penetration) × (Customer loyalty) × (Customer selectivity) × (Price selectivity)
28. _____is wielded by a manufacturer that threatens to withdraw a resource or terminate a relationship if intermediaries fail to cooperate.
    (a) Coercive Power (b) Legitimate Power
    (c) Expert Power (d) Reference Power
29. When the consumers favour those products which offer the most quality, performance or innovative features, then it is called as:
    (a) Production concept
    (b) Product concept
    (c) Sales concept
    (d) Marketing concept
30. Match the items of List-I with List-II where the PLC curve patterns are given for different categories:

    List-I
    A. Product category B. Product forms
    C. Products D. Branded Products

    List-II
    (i) One of several variant shapes
    (ii) Longest PLC
    (iii) Standard PLC
    (iv) Short or long PLC

Codes:	**(A)**	**(B)**	**(C)**	**(D)**
(a)	(iii)	(iv)	(ii)	(i)
(b)	(i)	(ii)	(iv)	(iii)
(c)	(iv)	(ii)	(i)	(iii)
(d)	(ii)	(iii)	(i)	(iv)

31. The term 'capital structure' implies:
    (a) Share Capital + Reserves + Long-Term Debts
    (b) Share Capital + Long and Short-Term Debts
    (c) Share Capital + Long-Term Debts
    (d) Equity and Preference Share Capital
32. A company has issued 10 percent perpetual debt of ₹ 1 lac at 5 percent premium. If tax rate is 30 percent, then the cost of debt will be:
    (a) 10 percent (b) 15 percent
    (c) 6.66 percent (d) 8.21 percent
33. "Dividend is not relevant in determining the value of the company". Who among the following held this opinion?
    (a) J.E. Walter (b) Ezra Soloman
    (c) Modigliani-Miller (d) M.J. Gordon
34. The formula Q/2 is used to compute the:
    (a) Total ordering cost (b) Total carrying cost
    (c) Opportunity cost (d) Re-order point
35. Financial Leverage is measured by:
    (a) EBIT / EAT (b) EBIT / EBT
    (c) EAIT / EBT (d) C / EBIT
36. Which of the following is a key role of HR Manager as defined by Ulrich et al. (2009)?
    (a) Personnel Administrator
    (b) Business Ally
    (c) Payroll Advisor
    (d) Organizational Geographer
37. Which of the following is the most serious problem that might arise due to excessive reliance on internal recruitment?
    (a) reduced job performance
    (b) high labour turnover
    (c) lack of motivation
    (d) internal resistance
38. Match the methods of performance appraisal given in List-I with the explanations given in the List-II:

    List-I
    A. Behaviourally Anchored Rating Scale (BARS)
    B. Management by Objectives (MBO)
    C. Critical incident method
    D. Behaviour observation scale

    List-II
    (i) Evaluator keeps a log of critical incidents to evaluate performance
    (ii) Evaluator indicates on a scale how often the appraise was actually observed engaging in the specific behaviours already identified
    (iii) Evaluator rates on the scale described in the form of critical incidents

(iv) Systematic and organized approach that allows management to focus on achievable goals

Codes:	(A)	(B)	(C)	(D)
(a)	(ii)	(iv)	(i)	(iii)
(b)	(i)	(iv)	(ii)	(iii)
(c)	(iii)	(iv)	(i)	(ii)
(d)	(ii)	(i)	(iv)	(iii)

39. The internal factors affecting the wage mix include:
(A) Relative worth of the job
(B) Area wage rates
(C) Employer's ability to pay
(D) Manpower market conditions

Codes:
(a) (A), (B) and (C) (b) (A) and (C)
(c) (B), (C) and (D) (d) All of the above

40. Match the items of List-I with the items of List-II:

List-I
A. Giri Approach
B. Industrial Sociology Approach
C. Gandhian Approach
D. Human Relations Approach

List-II
(i) The utility of non-violence as the means of conflict resolution.
(ii) Organizations are made up of people and the success of management lies in its dealing with these people.
(iii) Voluntary negotiations between employers and employees are a means of settling disputes.
(iv) Investigating the underlying trends and patterns in the cause and effect of industrial disputes.

Codes:	(A)	(B)	(C)	(D)
(a)	(ii)	(iii)	(i)	(iv)
(b)	(iii)	(iv)	(i)	(ii)
(c)	(i)	(iii)	(ii)	(iv)
(d)	(i)	(ii)	(iv)	(iii)

41. **Assertion (A):** Taking of deposits and granting of loans single out banks.

Reasoning (R): Banks act as intermediaries when they mobilize savings from surplus units to shortage units in order to finance productive activities.

Codes:
(a) Assertion (A) is correct and Reasoning (R) is the correct explanation of (A).
(b) Both Assertion (A) and Reasoning (R) are correct but (R) is not the correct explanation of (A).
(c) Assertion (A) is correct but Reasoning (R) is incorrect.
(d) Reasoning (R) is correct but Assertion (A) is incorrect.

42. "Skimming" in e-banking refers to:
(a) Identifying fraudsters copying vital information from credit cards
(b) Multiple transactions by one credit card
(c) Conversion of a debit card into credit card
(d) None of the above

43. Match the items of List-I with List-II in terms of functions of a bank:

List-I (Activities)	List-II (Functions)
A. Underwriting	(i) Primary Functions
B. Transfer of funds	(ii) Granting Advances
C. Overdraft	(iii) Utility Functions
D. Recurring Deposits	(iv) Agency Functions

Codes:	(A)	(B)	(C)	(D)
(a)	(i)	(ii)	(iv)	(iii)
(b)	(iv)	(iii)	(ii)	(i)
(c)	(iii)	(iv)	(ii)	(i)
(d)	(ii)	(iv)	(iii)	(i)

44. Which among the following is not a subsidiary of Reserve Bank of India?
A. Deposit Insurance and Credit Gaurantee Corporation of India.
B. Bharatiya Reserve Bank Note Mudran Private Limited.

Codes:
(a) Only (A) (b) Only (B)
(c) Both (A) and (B) (d) Neither (A) nor (B)

45. Which among the following is not associated with NABARD?
A. NIEAF B. BIRD C. RIDF D. SHPI

Codes:
(a) (A) only (b) (B) only
(c) (B) and (C) only (d) None of the above

46. Examine the following statements and choose the correct code:

Statement (I): Companies with Low cash reserves normally prefer Licensing mode rather than Foreign Direct Investment.

Statement (II): Cash rich firms normally prefer Foreign Direct Investment.

Codes:

(a) Both (I) and (II) are correct
(b) Both (I) and (II) are wrong
(c) (I) is correct but (II) is wrong
(d) (I) is not correct but (II) is correct

47. Which one of the following is not a feature of Business Process Outsourcing (BPO)?
(a) It enables executives to concentrate on strategy
(b) It improves process and saves money
(c) It decreases organizational capabilities
(d) None of the above

48. The major outcome of the Bretton Woods Conference was:
(a) Establishment of IMF and IFC
(b) Establishment of IBRD and IFC
(c) Establishment of IBRD and ADB
(d) Establishment of IMF and IBRD

49. Which one of the following is an important activity of the World Bank borrowings?
(a) It borrows in the international capital market
(b) It borrows on currency on swap agreements
(c) It borrows under the discount net programme
(d) All of the above

50. Which one of the following statements is false?
(a) IFC was established in July 1956
(b) IFC encourages the growth and development of Public Sector Enterprises in member countries
(c) IFC is an affiliate of the World Bank
(d) IFC encourages the growth of productive private enterprises in member countries

ANSWERS

1. (d)	2. (a)	3. (c)	4. (b)	5. (c)
6. (b)	7. (c)	8. (a)	9. (b)	10. (d)
11. (b)	12. (b)	13. (d)	14. (a)	15. (b)
16. (a)	17. (c)	18. (c)	19. (c)	20. (b)
21. (c)	22. (b)	23. (b)	24. (d)	25. (c)
26. (c)	27. (d)	28. (a)	29. (b)	30. (d)
31. (a)	32. (c)	33. (c)	34. (b)	35. (b)
36. (b)	37. (d)	38. (c)	39. (b)	40. (b)
41. (a)	42. (a)	43. (c)	44. (d)	45. (d)
46. (a)	47. (c)	48. (d)	49. (d)	50. (b)

PAPER–III

Note: This paper contains seventy-five (75) objective type questions of two (2) marks each. All questions are compulsory.

1. The method being used for Transferring Complex Technology is known as:
(a) Licensing Agreement
(b) Transfer of Technology
(c) Turnkey Contract
(d) None of the above

2. Which of the following is not a 'force' in the "Porter Five Forces Model"?
(a) Buyers
(b) Suppliers
(c) Complementary produce
(d) Industry rivalry

3. LIBOR term is used for:
(a) Deposit rate in European market
(b) Interest rate in Euro currency market
(c) Deposit rate applicable to interbank loans in London
(d) Interest rate in Euro bond market

4. Which of the following characterises the early stage financial crises?
(a) Falling the price of residential properties
(b) Excessive euphoria about the future price of certain assets
(c) Excessive pessimism about future assets price
(d) Stragnating share price

5. **Assertion (A):** In 1991 Government decided to allow all foreign investments to any industry without any restrictions.

Reason (R): Government has enhanced the investment limit of small scale industrial units.

Codes:

(a) Both (A) and (R) are true and (R) is the correct explanation of (A).

(b) Both (A) and (R) are true but (R) is not the correct explanation of (A).
(c) (A) is true but (R) is false.
(d) (A) is false but (R) is true.

6. When a business is purchased, any amount paid in excess of the total of assets, minus the liabilities taken, is called:
(a) Share Premium (b) Goodwill
(c) Capital Employed (d) Working Capital

7. Indicate the correct code as regards the sources of funds for a Funds Flow Statement from the following:
A. Increase in working capital
B. Decrease in working capital
C. Writing off the intangible/fictitious assets
D. Issuing equity shares for acquisition of a building for office
E. Charging depreciation on fixed assets
Codes:
(a) (A), (C), (D) (b) (B), (C), (E)
(c) (A), (D), (E) (d) (B), (C), (D)

8. Which of the following statements are correct?
A. Analysis and interpretation of financial statements, is a function of accounting.
B. Profit and Loss account is prepared for ascertaining financial position of a firm.
C. Goodwill is a wasting asset.
D. Balance Sheet is prepared for ascertaining financial position of a firm.
Select the correct answer using the codes given below:
Codes:
(a) A and B (b) A and C
(c) A and D (d) B and C

9. Match the items of List-I with those of the List-II and indicate the correct code for the following:
List-I
A. Debtors Turnover Ratio
B. Proprietary Ratio
C. Operating Ratio
D. Acid Test Ratio
List-II
(i) Solvency Ratio (ii) Liquidity Ratio
(iii) Activity Ratio (iv) Profitability Ratio

Codes:	(A)	(B)	(C)	(D)
(a)	(ii)	(iv)	(iii)	(i)
(b)	(iii)	(ii)	(i)	(iv)
(c)	(iii)	(i)	(iv)	(ii)
(d)	(iv)	(iii)	(ii)	(i)

10. For the following two statements of Assertion (A) and Reasoning (R), indicate the correct code:
Assertion (A): Cash Flow Statement as per the financial statements as well is incapable in revealing the overall financial position of a firm.
Reasoning (R): Cash is an important constituent of the working capital based on the recorded facts only.
Codes:
(a) (A) and (R) both are correct and (R) is an explanation of (A).
(b) (A) is correct but (R) is not correct.
(c) (A) is not correct but (R) is correct
(d) (A) and (R) both are incorrect

11. For the following two statements of Assertion (A) and Reasoning (R), indicate the correct code:
Assertion (A): The quantity of a commodity demanded invariably changes inversely to changes in its price.
Reasoning (R): The price effect is the net result of the positive substitution effect and negative income effect.
Codes:
(a) (A) and (R) both are correct.
(b) (A) is correct but (R) is incorrect.
(c) (A) is incorrect but (R) is correct.
(d) (A) and (R) both are incorrect.

12. Economic capacity of a plant represents its:
(a) maximum physical output level
(b) average output level over a period
(c) break-even output and sales level
(d) output level that equates the average and the marginal costs

13. Match the items of List-I with those of the List-II and indicate the correct code:
List-I
A. Excess capacity of the plant
B. Resorting to New Technology
C. Setting up of the Training Institutions
D Reserve capacity of the plant
List-II
(i) Cost reduction with output expansion
(ii) Constant cost with output expansion

(iii) Internal economies
(iv) External economies

Codes:	(A)	(B)	(C)	(D)
(a)	(i)	(iii)	(iv)	(ii)
(b)	(iii)	(i)	(iv)	(ii)
(c)	(ii)	(iii)	(i)	(iv)
(d)	(iv)	(ii)	(iii)	(i)

14. In case the elasticity of demand on an average revenue curve is equal to unity, the marginal revenue will be:
(a) more than unity
(b) equal to unity
(c) equal to a fraction of unity
(d) equal to zero

15. Match the items of the List-I with those of the List-II and indicate the correct code:

List-I

A. Trade Channel Discount
B. Loss Leadership
C. Pricing being non-responsive to changes in the demand and the cost
D. Basing Point Pricing

List-II

(i) Oligopoly Pricing
(ii) Locational Price Differentials
(iii) Differential Pricing
(iv) Product-Line Pricing

Codes:	(A)	(B)	(C)	(D)
(a)	(iv)	(iii)	(ii)	(i)
(b)	(iii)	(iv)	(i)	(ii)
(c)	(ii)	(iii)	(iv)	(i)
(d)	(i)	(ii)	(iii)	(iv)

16. **Statement I:** When a null hypothesis gets rejected in statistical hypothesis testing, it is known as II type-error in hypothesis testing.
Statement II: When a sample is small sized and parametric value of the standard deviation is not known, z-test is the most appropriate test for hypothesis testing.
Codes:
(a) Both statements are correct
(b) Both statements are incorrect
(c) Statement I is correct while statement II is incorrect
(d) Statement I is incorrect while statement II is correct

17. The following are the estimated regression equations for x and y variables:
$x = 0.85y$
$y = 0.89x$
With this information, the value of the coefficient of correlation would be:
(a) 0.87 (b) 0.86 (c) 0.89 (d) 0.75

18. The power of the statistical hypothesis testing is denoted by:
(a) α (alpha) (b) β (beta)
(b) 1 - α (c) 1 - β

19. Match the items of List-I and List-II and indicate the code of correct matching of the items:

List-I

(A) $\frac{z^2 . \sigma_p^2}{e^2}$ (B) $\frac{|\overline{X}_1 - \overline{X}_2|}{\sqrt{\sigma_p^2\left(\frac{1}{n_1}+\frac{1}{n_2}\right)}}$

(C) $\frac{\mu_4}{\mu_2^2}$ (D) $\frac{\sigma_{s_1}^2}{\sigma_{s_2}^2}$

List-II

(i) Measurement for Kurtosis
(ii) Calculated value of F ratio
(iii) Statistical approach to find out the size of sample
(iv) Calculated z value of mean differences

Codes:	(A)	(B)	(C)	(D)
(a)	(i)	(ii)	(iii)	(iv)
(b)	(ii)	(iv)	(iii)	(i)
(c)	(iii)	(iv)	(ii)	(i)
(d)	(iii)	(iv)	(i)	(ii)

20. **Assertion (A):** A reasonably large sized sample drawn randomly from a given population contains almost all the characteristics of the population.
Reason (R): As per the sampling theory, the assertion is based only on the 'Law of Inertia of Large Numbers'.
Codes:
(a) Assertion (A) is correct and Reason (R) as per the sampling theory is also fully correct.
(b) Assertion (A) is correct but the Reason (R) as per the sampling theory is not fully correct.
(c) Both Assertion (A) and Reason (R) are incorrect.

(d) Assertion (A) is incorrect but the Reason (R) is sufficient as per the sampling theory.

21. Which of the following approaches of team building is based on the belief that each person possesses positive and negative characteristics that must be owned up to a permitted expression?
(a) Process approach
(b) Gestalt approach
(c) Role analysis approach
(d) Parallel learning structure approach

22. Which of the following factors lead to group cohesiveness?
A. agreement on group goals
B. high intra-group competition
C. frequent interaction of members
D. personal attractiveness
Codes:
(a) A and B (b) A, B and C
(c) A, C and D (d) A, B and D

23. **Assertion (A)**: 'Uncertainty Avoidance' is one of the dimensions of cultural differences, as identified by Geert Hofstede.

Reasoning (R): 'Uncertainty Avoidance' is the extent to which people feel threatened by ambiguous situations. To avoid such situations, organisations provide greater career stability, make more formal rules and reject deviant behaviours.
Codes:
(a) (A) is wrong (R) is right
(b) Both (A) and (R) are wrong
(c) Both (A) and (R) are right and (R) is the correct explanation of (A)
(d) Both (A) and (R) are right but (R) is not the correct explanation of (A)

24. Which of the following is the internal conflict or anxiety that occurs when people receive information incompatible with their value systems, prior decisions and knowledge?
A. Polarisation
B. Cognitive dissonance
C. Premature evaluation
D. Projection
Codes:
(a) A and B (b) Only B
(c) Only D (d) A, B, C and D

25. Matrix organisation structure is essentially a violation of the principle of:
(a) Unity of Command
(b) Scalar Chain
(c) Unity of Direction
(d) Division of Labour

26. Which of the following statements is not true?
(a) One sided messages work best with audiences those are initially predisposed to communicator's position.
(b) Two sided arguments work best with audiences who are similar and not opposed.
(c) Two sided messages tend to be more effective with better educated audiences.
(d) Two sided messages tend to be more effective with audiences those are likely to be exposed to counter propaganda.

27. In the course of converting to a marketing-oriented company, a company may face which of the following hurdles?
(a) Organised resistance (b) Slow learning
(c) Fast forgetting (d) All of the above

28. A person's distinguishing psychological characteristics that lead to relatively consistent and enduring responses to his or her environment is called:
(a) Lifestyle (b) Self-concept
(c) Personality (d) Attitude

29. When electronic markets permit prices to change faster even daily as a function of demand and supply then this practice is called:
(a) competitive pricing
(b) e-marketing pricing
(c) yield management pricing
(d) None of the above

30. Match the strategies given in List-I with the examples given in List-II:
List-I (Strategies)
(A) Differential Pricing
(B) Complimentary Service
(C) Reservation System
(D) Non-peak Demand Cultivation
List-II (Examples)
(i) Customer lounges to sit in while waiting for a table at service centres, etc.

(ii) Breakfast service by McDonald's and mini vacation and weekends by hotels
(iii) Low prices for early and evening movies, weekend discounts for car parking rentals
(iv) Airlines, Hotels and Physicians employ extensively

Codes:	**(A)**	**(B)**	**(C)**	**(D)**
(a)	(i)	(iii)	(ii)	(iv)
(b)	(iv)	(ii)	(i)	(iii)
(c)	(ii)	(i)	(iv)	(iii)
(d)	(iii)	(i)	(iv)	(ii)

31. From investor's point of view, the cost of capital is:
(a) Interest Rate
(b) Market Value
(c) Yield of Capital Sacrifice
(d) Stock Exchange Value

32. Formula for net cash inflow of a project is:
(a) Sales-Operating Expenses – Interest-Tax
(b) Sales-Operating Expenses
(c) Net Profit after tax + Depreciation
(d) Gross Profit + Depreciation

33. Concentration Banking is a method of:
(a) Decentralised collection
(b) Centralised collection
(c) Direct collection
(d) Payment only through cheques

34. In case, cost of capital is 10%, EPS ₹ 10, IRR 8% and Retention Ratio is 60%, then the value of equity share as per Gordon's Model will be:
(a) ₹ 100 (b) ₹ 87 (c) ₹ 90 (d) ₹ 77

35. A firm with high operating leverage has:
(a) Low fixed cost in its production process
(b) High variable cost in its production process
(c) High fixed cost in its production process
(d) Low variable cost in its production process

36. Match the items of List-I with List-II according to 'The Harvard Framework' developed for HRM:

List-I
A. Stakeholder's interest
B. Situational factor
C. HRM policy choice
D. HR outcome
E. Long-term consequence

List-II
(i) Work systems (ii) Cost-effectiveness
(iii) Individual well-being
(iv) Government
(v) Business strategy

Codes:	**(A)**	**(B)**	**(C)**	**(D)**	**(E)**
(a)	(iv)	(i)	(ii)	(iii)	(v)
(b)	(v)	(iv)	(ii)	(i)	(iii)
(c)	(iv)	(v)	(i)	(ii)	(iii)
(d)	(i)	(v)	(ii)	(iii)	(iv)

37. The committees which promote worker's participation in management are usually established only at the:
(a) Corporate level (b) Plant level
(c) Shop-floor level (d) All of the above

38. Choose the correct code for the statements given below:
Statement (I): T-group and sensitivity training are not the same.
Statement (II): T-group participants belong to a diverse groups and may not be familiar with each other.
Statement (III): T-group training sessions are well structured.
Codes:
(a) Statements (I) and (II) only are correct
(b) Only (II) and (III) statements are correct
(c) All the three statements are correct
(d) Only statement (II) is correct

39. A review is heavily influenced only by any one characteristic of the employee whose performance is being reviewed is known as:
(a) Recency of Events Error
(b) Central Tendency
(c) Logical Error
(d) Halo Effect

40. Which one of the following tests is not recommended for the top level positions?
(a) Presentations (b) Role plays
(c) Interviews
(d) Leaderless group discussions

41. Select the major principles which banks strive to incorporate in their working from the following:
A. Profitability B. Labour welfare
C. Social welfare D. Safety
E. HRD F. Liquidity

Codes:
(a) A, B, D, E (b) A, C, D, F
(c) C, D, E, F (d) A, B, C, D

42. Identify the years in which different phases of Bank Nationalisation took place in India:
A. 1950 B. 1955 C. 1969 D. 1949 E. 1980
Codes:
(a) A, B, C, D (b) B, C, E
(c) B, D, E (d) C, D, E

43. 'SWIFT' stands for:
(a) Society for Worldwide Inter-bank Fund Transfer
(b) Society for Worldwide Inter-bank Fast Transmission
(c) Society for Worldwide Inter-bank Financial Telecommunications
(d) None of the above

44. Select the techniques of monetary control adopted by RBI from the following:
A. Cash Reserve Ratio
B. Statutory Liquidity Ratio
C. Bank Rate D. Currency Rate
Codes:
(a) A, B, C, D (b) B, C, D
(c) A, C, D (d) A, B, C

45. Which of the following is not a development banking institution?
(a) IDBI (b) IFCI (c) EXIM Bank (d) ICICI

46. Which of the following is not a characteristic of bartering internationally?
(a) Bartering can be time-consuming.
(b) Bartering can be expensive.
(c) Bartering is a type of service export and import.
(d) Bartering can be risky.

47. **Assertion (A):** International business has grown in more recent years at a faster pace than global production.
Reason (R): Growth through trade has increased, but growth through foreign direct investment has not.
Codes:
(a) Both (A) and (R) are correct
(b) (A) is correct but (R) is incorrect
(c) (A) is incorrect but (R) is correct
(d) Both (A) and (R) are incorrect

48. Identify the multinational corporations (MNCs) from the following:
A. IOCL B. GAIL C. SBI
D. SAIL E. Tata Steel F. Bharat Petroleum
Codes:
(a) A, B, C, D (b) B, C, D, E
(c) C, D, E, F (d) A, C, E, F

49. **Statement I:** Legal agreements between two countries govern how both the countries tax earnings.
Statement II: International Law may determine how and whether companies can operate in a certain locale.
Codes:
(a) Both the statements are true
(b) Both the statements are false
(c) Statement I is true but Statement II is false
(d) Statement I is false but Statement II is true

50. Which of the following is an example of an issue for which an agreement has not been made between two or more countries?
(a) Restricting harmful emissions
(b) Deep-sea mining in non-coastal areas of the oceans
(c) Preserving endangered species
(d) Banning the use of certain pesticides

51. Match the items of List-I with List-II:
List-I
A. Intangible Assets
B. Impairment of Assets
C. Interim Financial Reporting
D. Interests in Joint Ventures
List-II
(i) Ind AS 31 (ii) Ind AS 34
(iii) Ind AS 36 (iv) Ind AS 38

Codes:	(A)	(B)	(C)	(D)
(a)	(i)	(ii)	(iii)	(iv)
(b)	(iv)	(iii)	(ii)	(i)
(c)	(iv)	(i)	(ii)	(iii)
(d)	(iv)	(ii)	(i)	(iii)

52. **Assertion (A):** Human Resource Accounting is the measurement of the cost and value of people to the organization.
Reasoning (R): Human Resource Accounting involves measuring costs incurred by the organizations to recruit, select, hire, train and develop employees and judge their economic value to the organization.
Codes:
(a) Assertion (A) and Reasoning (R) are correct and (R) is the right explanation of (A)

(b) Assertion (A) and Reasoning (R) are correct and (R) is not the right explanation of (A)
(c) Assertion (A) is correct but Reasoning (R) is incorrect
(d) Both Assertion (A) and Reasoning (R) are incorrect

53. For the discharge of its functions efficiently, SEBI has been vested with the following powers:
A. to approve by-laws of stock exchanges
B. to direct the stock exchanges to amend their by-laws
C. inspect the books of accounts and call for periodical returns from recognized stock exchanges
D. inspect the books of accounts of financial intermediaries
E. compel certain companies to list their shares in one or more stock exchanges
F. registration of brokers

Codes:
(a) A, B, C and F (b) A, C, D and F
(c) B, C, D, E and F (d) A, B, C, D, E and F

54. Consider the following characteristics:
A. High risk high return opportunity
B. Small and medium size enterprise
C. Private equity stakes in start-ups
D. Investment fund

The above attributes are found in:
(a) Mutual Funds
(b) Venture Capital Funds
(c) Qualified Institutional Buyers
(d) Domestic Institutional Investors

55. Identify the incorrect statement(s), regarding money market, among the following:
(A) The call money market deals in short term finance repayable on demand, with a maturity period varying from one day to 14 days.
(B) Treasury bills are instruments of short-term borrowing by the Government of India, issued as promissory notes under discount.
(C) A reduction in the repo rate helps banks to get money at a cheaper rate.
(D) Money market mutual funds invest money in specifically, high-quality and very short maturity-based money market instruments.

Codes:
(a) A and C (b) B
(c) D (d) None of these

56. "Buyers are less price sensitive when they cannot easily compare the quality substitutes".

Which of the following factors of price sensitivity is reflected from this statement?
(a) Substitute - awareness effect
(b) Unique value effect
(c) Price quality effect
(d) None of the above

57. The model of decision support where there is recommendation of the type of advertisement with humourous and 'slice of life' kinds of appeals to use for given marketing goals and characteristics of products, target markets and competitive situations is known as:
(a) MEDIAC (b) PROMOTOR
(c) ADCAD (d) COVERSTORY

58. Which of the following statements is not true?
(a) Marketing profitability analysis measures the profitability of different marketing activities.
(b) Marketing efficiency studies try to determine how various marketing activities could be carried out more efficiently.
(c) Each company needs to reassess periodically its marketing effectiveness through a control instrument called marketing audit.
(d) All the above are true

59. Industry boundaries are blurring at an incredible rate as companies are recognizing that the new opportunities lie at the intersection of two or more industries, it is called:
(a) Globalization (b) Customization
(c) Industry convergence (d) Acquisition

60. A picture of two characters is presented, with one making a statement. Respondents are asked to identify with the other and fill in the empty balloon.

This description belongs to which one of the following projective techniques?

(a) Thematic Apperception Test
(b) Picture Completion Test
(c) Sentence Completion Test
(d) Story Completion Test

61. Match the items of List-I with the items of List-II:

List-I (Job Analysis)

A. Task B. Element C. Duty
D. Position E. Job F. Occupation

List-II (Examples)

(i) Payroll processing
(ii) Compensation policy administrator
(iii) Compensation design manager
(iv) Compensation specialist
(v) Preparing forms
(vi) Signing pay-cheques

Codes:	**(A)**	**(B)**	**(C)**	**(D)**	**(E)**	**(F)**
(a)	(i)	(ii)	(iii)	(iv)	(v)	(vi)
(b)	(v)	(vi)	(i)	(ii)	(iii)	(iv)
(c)	(vi)	(v)	(iv)	(ii)	(iii)	(i)
(d)	(vi)	(i)	(ii)	(iii)	(iv)	(v)

62. In which of the following types of collective bargaining, one party gains at the expense of the other?
(a) Distributive bargaining
(b) Integrative bargaining
(c) Centralized bargaining
(d) None of the above

63. Which one of the following dispute settlers cannot make a binding decision?
(a) Arbitrator (b) Adjudicator
(c) Conciliator
(d) Industrial tribunal member

64. Ensuring the safety, health and welfare of the employee is the primary purpose of which one of the following Acts?
(a) The Factories Act, 1948
(b) The Payment of Wages Act, 1936
(c) The Equal Remuneration Act, 1976
(d) The Industrial Disputes Act, 1947

65. Match the items of List-I with the items of List-II and select the correct code:

List-I

A. Pension scheme B. Personal security
C. Financial assistance D. Allowance

List-II

(i) Health Care for family
(ii) Severance Pay
(iii) Provident Fund
(iv) Transport Allowance

Codes:	**(A)**	**(B)**	**(C)**	**(D)**
(a)	(i)	(ii)	(iii)	(iv)
(b)	(iii)	(i)	(ii)	(iv)
(c)	(iii)	(ii)	(i)	(iv)
(d)	(i)	(iv)	(ii)	(iii)

66. Examine the following statements and choose the correct answer:

Statement I: FIIs do not invest in unlisted securities. They participate only through Stock Exchanges.

Statement II: FIIs cannot invest at the time of initial allotment.

Codes:

(a) Both the statements are wrong
(b) Both the statements are correct
(c) Statement-I is correct but the statement-II is wrong
(d) Statement-I is wrong but the statement-II is correct

67. Which one of the following is not a member country in the Association of South-East Asian Nations (ASEAN)?
(a) Singapore (b) Malaysia
(c) Thailand (d) Vietnam

68. Match the items of List-I with the items of List-II and select the correct answer with the codes given below:

List-I	**List-II**
A. SAARC	(i) Philippines
B. ASEAN	(ii) Canada
C. EU	(iii) Afghanistan
D. NAFTA	(iv) Hungary

Codes:	**(A)**	**(B)**	**(C)**	**(D)**
(a)	(ii)	(iv)	(i)	(iii)
(b)	(iv)	(ii)	(i)	(iii)
(c)	(iii)	(i)	(iv)	(ii)
(d)	(iii)	(iv)	(ii)	(i)

69. Which among the following are criticisms given against World Trade Organization (WTO)?
A. It is not a democratic and transparent institution.
B. It has domination of international trade by rich countries for the benefit of their individual interests.
C. It encourages a 'race to the bottom' in wages by pitting workers against

each other rather than promoting internationally recognized labor standards.

D. It is seeking to privatize essential public services.

Codes:

(a) B, C and D (b) A, B and C
(c) A, B and D (d) A, B, C and D

70. Domestic Currency tends to depreciate owing to:
(a) Constant inflation rate
(b) Lowering of inflation rate
(c) High inflation rate
(d) All of the above

71. Consider the following conditions:
A. An individual is in India for a period of 182 days in the financial year in which he is getting his salary income.
B. An individual is in India for a period of 60 days or more during financial year in which he gets his salary and 365 days or more during 4 years immediately preceding to that financial year.

If one of the above conditions is satisfied, as per the provisions of Income Tax Act, 1961, he is:
(a) Resident but not ordinarily resident of India
(b) Non-resident citizen of India
(c) Resident and categorised citizen of India U/S 29
(d) Ordinary resident of India

72. Agriculture income is exempted from income tax under the following section of Income Tax Act, 1961:
(a) 2 (1A) (b) 10 (1) (c) 10 (2) (d) 10 (4)

73. Match the items of List-I with List-II:

List-I

(A) When the assessee is in default or is deemed to be in default in making payment of tax, including the tax deducted at source
(B) Failure to pay the advance tax as directed by the Assessing Officer
(C) Concealment of particulars of income or furnishing of inaccurate particulars of income

List-II

(i) Section 271 (1) (c) (ii) Section 273 (1)
(iii) Section 201 (1)

Codes:	**(A)**	**(B)**	**(C)**
(a)	(i)	(ii)	(iii)
(b)	(iii)	(ii)	(i)
(c)	(iii)	(i)	(ii)
(d)	(ii)	(i)	(iii)

74. **Assertion (A):** Tax evasion is undertaken by employing unfair means.
Reasoning (R): Payment of tax is avoided through illegal means or fraud for tax evasion.

Codes:
(a) Assertion (A) is correct and Reasoning (R) is the right explanation of (A).
(b) Assertion (A) is correct but Reasoning (R) is not the right explanation of (A).
(c) Both Assertion (A) and Reasoning (R) are correct independently and (R) may be considered as an explanation of (A).
(d) Both Assertion (A) and Reasoning (R) are incorrect.

75. Which among the following are necessary documents to file Income Tax Return for an employed person in India?
A. Adhar Card B. PAN Card
C. Form No. 16 issued by employer

Codes:
(a) A only (b) A and B
(c) A, B and C (d) B and C

ANSWERS

1. (c)	2. (c)	3. (c)	4. (b)	5. (d)
6. (b)	7. (b)	8. (c)	9. (c)	10. (a)
11. (c)	12. (d)	13. (a)	14. (d)	15. (b)
16. (b)	17. (b)	18. (d)	19. (d)	20. (b)
21. (b)	22. (c)	23. (c)	24. (b)	25. (a)
26. (b)	27. (d)	28. (c)	29. (c)	30. (d)
31. (c)	32. (c)	33. (a)	34. (d)	35. (c)
36. (c)	37. (d)	38. (a)	39. (d)	40. (b)
41. (b)	42. (b)	43. (c)	44. (d)	45. (c)
46. (c)	47. (b)	48. (d)	49. (a)	50. (b)
51. (b)	52. (a)	53. (d)	54. (b)	55. (d)
56. (d)	57. (c)	58. (d)	59. (c)	60. (b)
61. (b)	62. (a)	63. (c)	64. (a)	65. (b)
66. (a)	67. (t)	68. (c)	69. (d)	70. (c)
71. (d)	72. (b)	73. (b)	74. (a)	75. (d)

t → No option is correct.

JULY–2016

Note: This paper contains Sixty (60) multiple-choice questions, each question carrying two (2) marks. Candidate is expected to answer any Fifty (50) questions. In case more than Fifty (50) questions are attempted, only the first Fifty (50) questions will be evaluated.

PAPER–I

1. Select the alternative which consists of positive factors contributing to effectiveness of teaching:

   List of factors:

   (i) Teacher's knowledge of the subject.
   (ii) Teacher's socio-economic background.
   (iii) Communication skill of the teacher.
   (iv) Teacher's ability to please the students.
   (v) Teacher's personal contact with students.
   (vi) Teacher's competence in managing and monitoring the classroom transactions.

   Codes:

   (a) (ii), (iii) and (iv) (b) (iii), (iv) and (vi)
   (c) (ii), (iv) and (v) (d) (i), (iii) and (vi)

2. The use of teaching aids is justified on the grounds of

   (a) attracting students' attention in the class room.
   (b) minimising indiscipline problems in the classroom.
   (c) optimising learning outcomes of students.
   (d) effective engagement of students in learning tasks.

3. **Assertion (A):** The purpose of higher education is to promote critical and creative thinking abilities among students.

   Reason (R): These abilities ensure job placements.

   Choose the correct answer from the following code:

   (a) Both (A) and (R) are true and (R) is the correct explanation of (A).
   (b) Both (A) and (R) are true but (R) is not the correct explanation of (A).
   (c) (A) is true but (R) is false.
   (d) (A) is false but (R) is true.

4. Match the items of the first set with that of the second set in respect of evaluation system.

   Choose the correct code:

   Set I

   (A) Formative evaluation
   (B) Summative evaluation
   (C) Continuous and comprehensive evaluation
   (D) Norm and criterion referenced tests

   Set II

   (i) Evaluating cognitive and co-cognitive aspects with regularity
   (ii) Tests and their interpretations based on a group and certain yardsticks
   (iii) Grading the final learning outcomes
   (iv) Quizzes and discussions

Codes:	(A)	(B)	(C)	(D)
(a)	(iv)	(iii)	(i)	(ii)
(b)	(i)	(ii)	(iii)	(iv)
(c)	(iii)	(iv)	(ii)	(i)
(d)	(i)	(iii)	(iv)	(ii)

5. A researcher intends to explore the effect of possible factors for the organization of effective mid-day meal interventions. Which research method will be most appropriate for this study?

   (a) Historical method
   (b) Descriptive survey method
   (c) Experimental method
   (d) Ex-post-facto method

6. Which of the following is an initial mandatory requirement for pursuing research?

   (a) Developing a research design
   (b) Formulating a research question
   (c) Deciding about the data analysis procedure
   (d) Formulating a research hypothesis

7. The format of thesis writing is the same as in
   (a) preparation of a research paper/article
   (b) writing of seminar presentation
   (c) a research dissertation
   (d) presenting a workshop/conference paper
8. In qualitative research paradigm, which of the following features may be considered critical?
   (a) Data collection with standardised research tools.
   (b) Sampling design with probability sample techniques.
   (c) Data collection with bottom-up empirical evidences.
   (d) Data gathering to take place with top-down systematic evidences.
9. From the following list of statements identify the set which has negative implications for 'research ethics':
   (i) A researcher critically looks at the findings of another research.
   (ii) Related studies are cited without proper references.
   (iii) Research findings are made the basis for policy making.
   (iv) Conduct of practitioner is screened in terms of reported research evidences.
   (v) A research study is replicated with a view to verify the evidences from other researches.
   (vi) Both policy making and policy implementing processes are regulated in terms of preliminary studies.

   Codes:
   (a) (i), (ii) and (iii) (b) (ii), (iii) and (iv)
   (c) (ii), (iv) and (vi) (d) (i), (iii) and (v)
10. In a research on the effect of child-rearing practices on stress-proneness of children in completing school projects, the hypothesis formulated is that 'child-rearing practices do influence stress-proneness'. At the data-analysis stage a null hypothesis is advanced to find out the tenability of research hypothesis. On the basis of the evidence available, the null hypothesis is rejected at 0.01 level of significance. What decision may be warranted in respect of the research hypothesis?
   (a) The research hypothesis will also be rejected.
   (b) The research hypothesis will be accepted.
   (c) Both the research hypothesis and the null hypothesis will be rejected.
   (d) No decision can be taken in respect of the research hypothesis.

Read the following passage carefully and answer question numbers from 11 to 16:

In terms of labour, for decades the relatively low cost and high quality of Japanese workers conferred considerable competitive advantage across numerous durable goods and consumer-electronics industries (e.g. Machinery, automobiles, televisions, radios). Then labour-based advantages shifted to South Korea, then to Malaysia, Mexico and other nations. Today, China appears to be capitalizing best on the basis of labour. Japanese firms still remain competitive in markets for such durable goods, electronics and other products, but the labour force is no longer sufficient for competitive advantage over manufacturers in other industrializing nations. Such shifting of labour-based advantage is clearly not limited to manufacturing industries. Today, a huge number of IT and service jobs are moving from Europe and North America to India, Singapore, and like countries with relatively well-educated, low-cost workforces possessing technical skills. However, as educational levels and technical skills continue to rise in other countries, India, Singapore, and like nations enjoying labour-based competitive advantage today are likely to find such advantage cannot be sustained through emergence of new competitors.

In terms of capital, for centuries the days of gold coins and later even paper money restricted financial flows. Subsequently regional concentrations were formed where large banks, industries and markets coalesced. But today capital flows internationally at rapid speed. Global commerce no longer requires regional interactions among business players. Regional capital concentrations in places such as New York, London and Tokyo still persist, of course, but the capital concentrated there is no longer sufficient for competitive advantage over other capitalists distributed worldwide. Only if an organization is able to combine, integrate and apply its resources (e.g. Land, labour, capital, IT) in an effective manner that is not readily imitable by competitors can such an organization enjoy competitive advantage sustainable overtime.

In a knowledge-based theory of the firm, this idea is extended to view organizational knowledge as a resource with atleast the same level of power and importance as the traditional economic inputs. An organization with superior knowledge can achieve competitive advantage in markets that appreciate the application of such knowledge. Semiconductors, genetic engineering, pharmaceuticals, software, military warfare, and like knowledge-intensive competitive arenas provide both time-proven and current examples. Consider semiconductors (e.g. computer chips), which are made principally of sand and common metals. These ubiquitous and powerful electronic devices are designed within common office buildings, using commercially available tools, and fabricated within factories in many industrialized nations. Hence, land is not the key competitive resource in the semiconductor industry.

Based on the passage answer the following questions:

11. Which country enjoyed competitive advantages in automobile industry for decades?
 (a) South Korea (b) Japan
 (c) Mexico (d) Malaysia
12. Why labour-based competitive advantages of India and Singapore cannot be sustained in IT and service sectors?
 (a) Due to diminishing levels of skill.
 (b) Due to capital-intensive technology making inroads.
 (c) Because of new competitors.
 (d) Because of shifting of labour-based advantage in manufacturing industries.
13. How can an organisation enjoy competitive advantage sustainable overtime?
 (a) Through regional capital flows.
 (b) Through regional interactions among business players.
 (c) By making large banks, industries and markets coalesced.
 (d) By effective use of various instrumentalities.
14. What is required to ensure competitive advantages in specific markets?
 (a) Access to capital
 (b) Common office buildings
 (c) Superior knowledge
 (d) Common metals
15. The passage also mentions about the trend of
 (a) Global financial flow
 (b) Absence of competition in manufacturing industry
 (c) Regionalisation of capitalists
 (d) Organizational incompatibility
16. What does the author lay stress on in the passage?
 (a) International commerce
 (b) Labour-Intensive industries
 (c) Capital resource management
 (d) Knowledge-driven competitive advantage
17. Imagine you are working in an educational institution where people are of equal status. Which method of communication is best suited and normally employed in such a context?
 (a) Horizontal communication
 (b) Vertical communication
 (c) Corporate communication
 (d) Cross communication
18. Identify the important element a teacher has to take cognizance of while addressing students in a classroom.
 (a) Avoidance of proximity
 (b) Voice modulation
 (c) Repetitive pause
 (d) Fixed posture
19. What are the barriers to effective communication?
 (a) Moralising, being judgemental and comments of consolation.
 (b) Dialogue, summary and self-review.
 (c) Use of simple words, cool reaction and defensive attitude.
 (d) Personal statements, eye contact and simple narration.
20. The choice of communication partners is influenced by factors of
 (a) Proximity, utility, loneliness
 (b) Utility, secrecy, dissonance
 (c) Secrecy, dissonance, deception
 (d) Dissimilarity, dissonance, deviance
21. As a teacher, select the best option to ensure your effective presence in the classroom.

(a) Use of peer command
(b) Making aggressive statements
(c) Adoption of well-established posture
(d) Being authoritarian

22. Every communicator has to experience
(a) Manipulated emotions
(b) Anticipatory excitement
(c) The issue of homophiles
(d) Status dislocation

23. In certain code, SELECTION is coded as QCJCARGML. The code of AMERICANS will be
(a) YKCPGAYLQ (b) BNFSJDBMR
(c) QLYAGPCKY (d) YQKLCYPAG

24. In the series
3, 11, 23, 39, 59, ...
The next term will be
(a) 63 (b) 73 (c) 83 (d) 93

25. Two railway tickets from city A to B and three tickets from city A to C cost ₹ 177. Three tickets from city A to B and two tickets from city A to C cost ₹ 173. The fare for city B from city A will be ₹
(a) 25 (b) 27 (c) 30 (d) 33

26. A person walks 10 m infront and 10 m to the right. Then every time turning to his left, he walks 5, 15 and 15 m respectively. How far is he now from his starting point?
(a) 20 m (b) 15 m (c) 10 m (d) 5 m

27. A is sister of B. F is daughter of G. C is mother of B. D is father of C. E is mother of D. A is related to D as
(a) Grand daughter (b) Daughter
(c) Daughter-in-law (d) Sister

28. In the series
AB, EDC, FGHI, ...?...., OPQRST, the missing term is
(a) JKLMN (b) JMKNL
(c) NMLKJ (d) NMKLJ

29. Among the following propositions two are related in such a way that one is the denial of the other. Which are those propositions? Select the correct code:
Propositions:
(i) All women are equal to men
(ii) Some women are equal to men
(iii) Some women are not equal to men
(iv) No women are equal to men
Codes:
(a) (i) and (ii) (b) (i) and (iv)
(c) (iii) and (iv) (d) (i) and (iii)

30. If the proposition 'All thieves are poor' is false, which of the following propositions can be claimed certainly to be true?
Propositions:
(a) Some thieves are poor.
(b) Some thieves are not poor.
(c) No thief is poor.
(d) No poor person is a thief.

31. Consider the following statement and select the correct code stating the nature of the argument involved in it:
To suppose that the earth is the only populated world in the infinite space is as absurd as to assert that in an entire field of millet only one grain will grow.
(a) Astronomical (b) Anthropological
(c) Deductive (d) Analogical

32. Select the code which is not correct about Venn diagram:
(a) Venn diagram represents propositions as well as classes.
(b) It can provide clear method of notation.
(c) It can be either valid or invalid.
(d) It can provide the direct method of testing the validity.

33. Select the code which is not correct in the context of deductive argument with two premises:
(a) An argument with one true premise, one false premise and a false conclusion may be valid.
(b) An argument with two true premises and a false conclusion may be valid.
(c) An argument with one true premise, one false premise and a true conclusion may be valid.
(d) An argument with two false premises and a false conclusion may be valid.

34. Given below are two premises and four conclusions are drawn from them (taking singly or together). Select the code that states the conclusions validly drawn.

Premises: (i) All religious persons are emotional.
(ii) Ram is a religious person.

Conclusions: (A) Ram is emotional.
(B) All emotional persons are religious.
(C) Ram is not a non-religious person.
(D) Some religious persons are not emotional.

Codes:
(a) (A), (B), (C) and (D) (b) (A) only
(c) (A) and (C) only (d) (B) and (C) only

The following table shows the percentage profit (%) earned by two companies A and B during the years 2011-15. Answer questions 35-37 based on the data contained in the table:

Profit earned by two companies

Year	Percentage Profit (%)	
	A	B
2011	20	30
2012	35	40
2013	45	35
2014	40	50
2015	25	35

Where, percent (%) Profit

$$= \frac{\text{Income} - \text{Expenditure}}{\text{Expenditure}} \times 100$$

35. If the total expenditure of, the two companies was ₹ 9 lakh in the year 2012 and the expenditure of A and B were in the ratio 2: 1, then what was the income of the company A in that year?
(a) ₹ 9.2 lakh (b) ₹ 8.1 lakh
(c) ₹ 7.2 lakh (d) ₹ 6.0 lakh

36. What is the average percentage profit earned by the company B?
(a) 35% (b) 42% (c) 38% (d) 40%

37. In which year, the percentage profit earned by the company B is less than that of company A?
(a) 2012 (b) 2013 (c) 2014 (d) 2015

The following table shows the number of people in different age groups who responded to a survey about their favourite style of music. Use this information to answer the questions that follow: (Question 38-40) to the nearest whole percentage

Style of Music ↓ / Age →	Number of people (Years) 15-20	(Years) 21-30	(Years) 31+
Classical	6	4	17
Pop	7	5	5
Rock	6	12	14
Jazz	1	4	11
Blues	2	3	15
Hip-Hop	9	3	4
Ambient	2	2	2

38. Approximately what percentage of the total sample were aged 21-30?
(a) 31% (b) 23% (c) 25% (d) 14%

39. Approximately what percentage of the total sample indicates that Hip-Hop is their favourite style of music?
(a) 6% (b) 8% (c) 14% (d) 12%

40. What percentage of respondents aged 31+ indicated a favourite style other than classical music?
(a) 64% (b) 60% (c) 75% (d) 50%

41. The statement "the study, design, development, implementation, support or management of computer-based information systems, particularly software applications and computer Hardware" refers to
(a) Information Technology (IT)
(b) Information and Collaborative Technology (ICT)
(c) Information and Data Technology (IDT)
(d) Artificial Intelligence (AI)

42. If the binary equivalent of the decimal number 48 is 110000, then the binary equivalent of the decimal number 51 is given by
(a) 110011 (b) 110010
(c) 110001 (d) 110100

43. The process of copying files to a CD-ROM is known as
(a) Burning (b) Zipping
(c) Digitizing (d) Ripping

44. An unsolicited e-mail message sent to many recipients at once is a
(a) Worm (b) Virus (c) Threat (d) Spam

45. ________ is a type of memory circuitry that holds the computer's start-up routine.
(a) RIM (Read Initial Memory)
(b) RAM (Random Access Memory)
(c) ROM (Read Only Memory)
(d) Cache Memory

46. An ASCII is a character-encoding scheme that is employed by personal computers in order to represent various characters, numbers and control keys that the computer user selects on the keyboard. ASCII is an acronym for
(a) American Standard Code for Information Interchange
(b) American Standard Code for Intelligent Information
(c) American Standard Code for Information Integrity
(d) American Standard Code for Isolated Information

47. Identify the air pollutant in urban areas which irritates eyes and also respiratory tract of human beings.
(a) Particulate matter
(b) Oxides of nitrogen
(c) Surface ozone
(d) Carbon monoxide

48. Which of the following is the largest source of water pollution in major rivers of India?
(a) Untreated sewage
(b) Agriculture run-off
(c) Unregulated small scale industries
(d) Religious practices

49. Sustainable development goals have specific targets to be achieved by
(a) 2022 (b) 2030 (c) 2040 (d) 2050

50. Indian government's target of producing power from biomass by the year 2022, is
(a) 50 MW (b) 25 MW
(c) 15 MW (d) 10 MW

51. **Assertion (A):** Conserving our soil resources is critical to human survival.
Reason (R): Soil is home to many micro-organisms and contains minerals.
Choose the correct code:
(a) Both (A) and (R) are correct and (R) is the correct explanation of (A).
(b) Both (A) and (R) are correct but (R) is not the correct explanation of (A).
(c) (A) is true and (R) is false.
(d) (A) is false and (R) is true.

52. World Meteorological Organisation's (WMO) objective has been to reduce the number of deaths due to hydrometeorological disasters over the decade 2010-2019 by (with reference to the decade 1994-2003)
(a) 25% (b) 50% (c) 75% (d) 80%

53. Which of the following core values among the institutions of higher education are promoted by the NAAC (National Assessment and Accreditation Council)?
I. Contributing to national development.
II. Fostering global competencies among the students.
III. Inculcating a value system among students and teachers.
IV. Promoting the optimum utilization of the infrastructure.

Select the correct answer from the codes given below:

Codes:
(a) II, III and IV (b) I, II and III
(c) I, III and IV (d) I, II, III and IV

54. The best way for providing value education is through
(a) discussions on scriptural texts
(b) lectures/discourses on values
(c) seminars/symposia on values
(d) mentoring/reflective sessions on values

55. The National Judicial Appointments Commission (NJAC) has been declared unconstitutional by
(a) The Supreme Court of India
(b) The High Court
(c) The High Court and the Supreme Court both
(d) The President of India

56. Which of the following statements about the Indian political system is/are correct?
I. The President is both Head of the State and Head of the Government.
II. Parliament is Supreme.

III. The Supreme Court is the guardian of the Constitution.
IV. The Directive Principles of State Policy are justiciable.

Select the correct answer from the codes given below:

(a) I, II, III and IV (b) II, III and IV
(c) II and III (d) III only

57. Which of the following are the fundamental duties?
I. To respect the National Flag.
II. To protect and improve the natural environment.
III. For a parent to provide opportunities for education to his/her child.
IV. To protect monuments and places of national importance.

Select the correct answer from the codes given:

Codes:

(a) I, II and III (b) I, II and IV
(c) I, III and IV (d) I, II, III and IV

58. Which of the following statements are correct in respect of Niti Aayog?
I. It is a constitutional body.
II. It is a statutory body.
III. It is neither a constitutional body nor a statutory body.
IV. It is a think tank.

Select the correct answer from the codes given below:

(a) I and IV (b) II and IV
(c) III and IV (d) II, III and IV

59. A college level assistant professor has planned his/her lectures with an intent to develop cognitive dimensions of students centered on skills of analysis and synthesis. Below, given are two sets of items Set I consisting of levels of cognitive interchange and Set II comprising basic requirements for promoting them. Match the two sets and indicate your answer by choosing the correct alternative from the code:

Set I (Levels of Cognitive Interchange)

(A) Memory level (B) Understanding level
(C) Reflective level

Set II (Basic requirements for promoting cognitive interchange)

(i) Giving opportunity for discriminating examples and non-examples of a point.
(ii) Recording the important points made during the presentations.
(iii) Asking the students to discuss various items of information.
(iv) Critically analyzing the points to be made and discussed.

Codes:	**(A)**	**(B)**	**(C)**
(a)	(ii)	(iv)	(i)
(b)	(iii)	(iv)	(ii)
(c)	(ii)	(i)	(iv)
(d)	(i)	(ii)	(iii)

60. Which set of learner characteristics may be considered helpful in designing effective teaching-learning systems? Select the correct alternative from the codes given below:
I. Prior experience of learners in respect of the subject.
II. Interpersonal relationships of learner's family friends.
III. Ability of the learners in respect of the subject.
IV. Student's language background.
V. Interest of students in following the prescribed dress code.
VI. Motivational-orientation of the students.

Codes:

(a) I, II, III and IV (b) I, III, IV and VI
(c) II, III, IV and V (d) III, IV, V and VI

ANSWERS

1. (d)	2. (c)	3. (b)	4. (a)	5. (d)
6. (b)	7. (c)	8. (c)	9. (c)	10. (b)
11. (b)	12. (c)	13. (d)	14. (c)	15. (a)
16. (d)	17. (a)	18. (b)	19. (a)	20. (a)
21. (c)	22. (b)	23. (a)	24. (c)	25. (d)
26. (d)	27. (a)	28. (c)	29. (d)	30. (b)
31. (d)	32. (c)	33. (b)	34. (c)	35. (b)
36. (c)	37. (b)	38. (c)	39. (d)	40. (c)
41. (a)	42. (a)	43. (a)	44. (d)	45. (c)
46. (a)	47. (c)	48. (a)	49. (b)	50. (d)
51. (b)	52. (b)	53. (b)	54. (d)	55. (a)
56. (d)	57. (a)	58. (c)	59. (c)	60. (b)

PAPER–II

Note: This paper contains fifty (50) objective type questions, each question carrying two (2) marks. All questions are compulsory.

1. For the following statements of Assertion (A) and Reasoning (R) indicate the correct code from the alternatives given:

   Assertion (A): Liberalization means corporatisation of departmental undertakings and public undertakings.

   Reasoning (R): Freedom to public sector undertakings to access capital market.

   Codes:
   (a) Both (A) and (R) are true and (R) is correct explanation of (A).
   (b) Both (A) and (R) are true but (R) is not a correct explanation of (A).
   (c) (A) is true but (R) is false.
   (d) (A) is false but (R) is true.

2. Match the items of List I with List II and indicate the correct code:

   List I
   A. Fiscal Policy
   B. Technology Policy
   C. Macro-Economic Policy
   D. Monetary Policy

   List II
   i. Mitigation of National hazards
   ii. Balance of Payment
   iii. Fiscal Federalism
   iv. Inflation

Codes:	A	B	C	D
(a)	i	ii	iii	iv
(b)	iii	i	ii	iv
(c)	iv	iii	i	ii
(d)	ii	i	iv	iii

3. Which of the following factor is not directly responsible for slowing down the growth of infrastructure?
   (a) High level of perceived political risk.
   (b) High level of sunk cost.
   (c) High probability of time and cost over-run.
   (d) Introduction of competition in all sectors.

4. Out of the following which is not a major component of Gross Domestic Product (GDP)?
   (a) Personal Consumption Expenditure
   (b) Gross Private Domestic Investment
   (c) Net Personal Income
   (d) Net Exports

5. Which of the following is not a forum of Consumer Dispute Redressal System?
   (a) Local forum
   (b) District forum
   (c) State Forum (State Commission)
   (d) National Commission

6. X Ltd. purchased 70 percent of the shares of Y Ltd. at a price of ₹ 1,00,000. Share capital of Y Ltd. was of ₹ 70,000 and its accumulated profits amounted to ₹ 90,000. What would be the amount of Minority Interest in the consolidated Balance Sheet?
   (a) ₹ 25,000 (b) ₹ 70,000
   (c) ₹ 1,00,000 (d) ₹ 40,000

7. Match the items in Column-I with the items in Column-II and indicate the correct code:

   Column-I
   A. Debt-Equity Ratio
   B. Proprietary Ratio
   C. Interest coverage ratio
   D. Capital gearing ratio

   Column-II
   (i) Net Profit before interest and tax / Interest on long term loans
   (ii) (Equity share capital + Reserves) / (Preference share capital + Interest bearing finance)
   (iii) Long term debts / Shareholder's Funds
   (iv) Shareholder's Funds / Total Assets

Codes:	A	B	C	D
(a)	i	ii	iii	iv
(b)	iii	iv	i	ii
(c)	iii	iv	ii	i
(d)	ii	iii	iv	i

8. Ram and Shyam are partners in a firm with capital of ₹ 4,80,000 and ₹ 3,10,000, respectively. They admitted Ganesh as a partner with 1/4th share of profit. Ganesh brings ₹ 3,00,000 as his capital. Ganesh's share of goodwill will be
   (a) ₹ 1,10,000 (b) ₹ 27,500
   (c) ₹ 17,500 (d) ₹ 70,000

9. Which of the following is a deferred revenue expenditure?
   (a) Legal expenses incurred on the purchase of land.

(b) Expenses on a mega advertisement campaign while launching a new product.
(c) Expenses incurred on installation of a new machine.
(d) Wages paid for construction of an additional room in the building.

10. The amount of depreciation charged to Profit and Loss Account varies every year under:
(a) Fixed instalment method
(b) Annuity method
(c) Diminishing balance method
(d) Insurance policy method

11. Ordinal utility analysis of the consumer's behaviour is considered superior to the cardinal utility analysis mainly due to
(a) assumption of the rationality of the consumer's behaviour.
(b) possibility of the derivation of the consumer's demand.
(c) bifurcation of price effects into income and substitution effects.
(d) consideration of the available limited resources for satisfying consumer's demand.

12. For the following statements of Assertion (A) and Reasoning (R) indicate the correct code:

Assertion (A): Price reduction normally leads to an increase in the demand for a commodity.

Reason (R): Price reduction leads to the entry of new buyers of the commodity in the market.

Codes:
(a) (A) is correct but (R) is not correct.
(b) (A) is not correct but (R) is correct.
(c) Both (A) and (R) are correct and (R) offers full explanation of (A).
(d) Both (A) and (R) are correct but (R) does not offer full explanation of (A).

13. The minimum Long Run Average Cost (LAC) can be determined on a
I. LAC curve for a normal production function
II. LAC curve for a linear production function
III. Planning curve
IV. Envelope curve

Codes:

(a)	I	II	III
(b)	II	III	IV
(c)	I	III	IV
(d)	I	II	IV

14. Monopoly is not considered desirable from the point of view of the society mainly because the monopolist endeavours to
(a) earn net revenue on sale of all goods including those involving no cost of production.
(b) earn net revenue on sale of goods in short run as well as long run.
(c) charge different prices for the same product from the different categories of buyers.
(d) produce below economic capacity level when he exhibits satisfaction with normal profit only.

15. Product-line pricing strategy includes which combination of the following?
I. Public utility pricing
II. Complementary goods pricing
III. Spare parts pricing
IV. Load factor pricing

Codes:

(a)	I	II	III
(b)	II	III	IV
(c)	I	II	IV
(d)	I	III	IV

16. When the data are classified only on the basis of descriptive characteristics which cannot be quantified is known as
(a) Geographical classification
(b) Chronological classification
(c) Qualitative classification
(d) Quantitative classification

17. Which one of the following is a false description?
(a) In a moderately asymmetrical distribution, the empirical relationship between Mean, Mode and Median suggested by Karl Pearson is Mean – Mode = 3 (Mean – Median)
(b) Coefficient of variation is an absolute measure of dispersion.
(c) Measure of skewness indicates the direction and extent of skewness in the

distribution of numerical values in the data set.

(d) Kurtosis refers to the degree of flatness or peakedness in the region around the mode of a frequency curve.

18. Match the items of List I with the items of List II and indicate the code of correct matching:

List I

A. Coefficient of determination
B. Spearman's Rank correlation coefficient
C. Regression coefficient of x on y variable
D. Karl Pearson's formula of calculating γ

List II

(i) $\gamma_{xy}\dfrac{\sigma_x}{\sigma_y}$ (ii) $1-\dfrac{6\sum d^2}{n(n^2-1)}$

(iii) $\dfrac{\sum xy}{n\sigma_x\sigma_y}$ (iv) γ^2

Codes:	A	B	C	D
(a)	i	ii	iii	iv
(b)	i	iv	ii	iii
(c)	iv	iii	ii	i
(d)	iii	ii	iv	i

19. **Statement-I:** When the null hypothesis is true but as per the hypothesis-testing, it is rejected, it is known as beta type error in hypothesis testing.

Statement-II: Chi-square test is exclusively a non-parametric test.

Codes:

(a) Both the statements are true.
(b) Both the statements are false.
(c) Statement-I is true while Statement-II is false.
(d) Statement-I is false while Statement-II is true.

20. Computers that recognize data as discrete signals are called?

(a) Analog computers (b) Digital computers
(c) Hybrid computers (d) Super computers

21. Herbert Simon's concept of administrative man assumes that

(A) He has satisfying approach in decision-making rather than the maximising approach.
(B) He can make decisions without determining all possible alternatives.
(C) He is completely rational in decision-making.

(a) (A) only (b) (B) only
(c) Both (A) and (B) (d) (A), (B) and (C)

22. Which of the following statement(s) is/are correct about scalar chain principle as given by Fayol?

(A) Each communication, going up or down, must flow through each position in the line authority.
(B) Chain of communication cannot be broken under any circumstances.

(a) Only (A) is correct.
(b) Only (B) is correct.
(c) Neither (A) nor (B) is correct.
(d) Both (A) and (B) are correct.

23. A mission statement should be

A. Self-explanatory B. Elaborate
C. Distinctive D. Feasible

Codes:

(a) (A) only (b) (A) and (B)
(c) (A), (B) and (C) (d) (A), (C) and (D)

24. Match List I and List II and indicate the correct code:

List I

A. Equity theory
B. Vroom's theory
C. Porter and Lawler model
D. Herzberg's theory

List II

i. Motivation depends on ratios of inputs and outcomes of self and others.
ii. People are motivated to achieve a goal to the extent that they expect that certain action will help them to reach the goal.
iii. There exists a complex relationship among motivation, performance and satisfaction.
iv. A challenging job that has opportunities for achievement, recognition, responsibility and growth will motivate employees.

Codes:	A	B	C	D
(a)	i	ii	iii	iv
(b)	ii	i	iii	iv
(c)	iii	ii	i	iv
(d)	i	iii	ii	iv

25. **Assertion (A)**: 'Grapevine' tends to be more active during periods of change, excitement, anxiety and sagging economic conditions.

    Reason (R): Employees use this communication to fill in important information gaps and clarify management decisions.

    Codes:
    (a) (A) is right and (R) is wrong.
    (b) (A) is wrong and (R) is right.
    (c) Both (A) and (R) are right and (R) explains (A).
    (d) Both (A) and (R) are right but (R) does not explain (A).

26. Which type of differentiation is used to gain competitive advantage through the way a firm designs its distribution coverage, expertise and performance?
    (a) Channel differentiation
    (b) Services differentiation
    (c) People differentiation
    (d) Product differentiation

27. Which one of the following is the most likely result of a marketing strategy that attempts to serve all potential customers?
    (a) All customers will be delighted.
    (b) Customer-perceived value will be increased.
    (c) The company will need to follow up with a demarketing campaign.
    (d) Not all customers will be satisfied.

28. Which of the following is not a primary activity in Michael Porter's value chain?
    (a) Inbound logistics (b) Operations
    (c) Outbound logistics (d) Procurement

29. Which of the following represents consistency of results when the test instrument is used repeatedly?
    (a) Validity (b) Reliability
    (c) Relativity (d) Sensitivity

30. **Assertion (A)**: Too many stimuli make a person accommodated to those sensations. Sensory adaptation is a problem that concerns many advertisers, which is why they try to change their advertising campaigns regularly.

    Reason (R): To cut through advertising clutter and to ensure that consumers perceive advertisement, marketers try to increase sensory input.

    Codes:
    (a) (A) is right and (R) is wrong.
    (b) (A) is wrong and (R) is right.
    (c) Both (A) and (R) are right but (R) does not explain (A).
    (d) Both (A) and (R) are right and (R) explains (A).

31. Which of the following is not a feature of payback period method?
    (a) It is simply a method of cost recovery and not of profitability.
    (b) It does not consider the time value of money.
    (c) It does not consider the risk associated with the projects.
    (d) It is very difficult to calculate.

32. Which of the following is not a source of credit information of prospective customers?
    (a) Letter of credit (b) Bank Reference
    (c) Trade Enquiry (d) Credit Bureau

33. The portion of earnings which is distributed among shareholders in the form of dividend is called
    (a) Proprietary Ratio (b) Earnings-yield Ratio
    (c) Payout Ratio (d) Retention Ratio

34. Select the correct code regarding motives for holding inventories by firms:
    (A) Transaction motive
    (B) Environmental motive
    (C) Precautionary motive
    (D) Speculative motive
    (E) Competitive motive

    Codes:
    (a) (A), (B), (C), (D) (b) (A), (B), (D), (E)
    (c) (A), (D), (E) (d) (A), (C), (D)

35. Which of the following formulae is related to operating leverage?
    (a) Contribution / Operating Profit
    (b) (Sales – Variable Cost) / Earnings before Interest and tax
    (c) Percentage change in EBIT / Percentage change in sales
    (d) All of the above

36. Which of the following is not true in case of HRM?
    (a) Employees are seen as an investment to be nurtured as well as a cost to be controlled.
    (b) Conflicts are dealt with by team members within their teams.

(c) Preference is for collective bargaining of pay and working conditions.
(d) Emphasis is on competitive pay and conditions to stay ahead of competitors.

37. Which one of the following is an advantage of Magazines as a source of recruitment?
(a) Less expensive
(b) Long lead time for advertisement placement
(c) Reach a diverse audience
(d) Many unmotivated applicants

38. Examine the following statements and choose the correct code:

Assertion (A): Human Resource planning must always be seen within the strategy making context.

Reason (R): Human Resource planning process removed from the realities of the business will be a waste of time.

Codes:
(a) Both (A) and (R) are correct.
(b) Both (A) and (R) are wrong.
(c) (A) is correct, but (R) is wrong.
(d) (A) is not correct, but (R) is correct.

39. Match the items of List I with the items of List II and select the correct code:

List I
A. Golden parachutes B. Gain sharing
C. Stock-option D. Annual bonus

List II
i. The right to purchase a stated number of shares of a company stock at today's price at some time in the future.
ii. An incentive plan that engages employees in a common effort to achieve productivity objectives and share the gains.
iii. Payments companies make in connection with a change in ownership or control of a company.
iv. Plans designed to motivate short term performance of managers and are tried to company profitability.

Codes:	A	B	C	D
(a)	iii	i	ii	iv
(b)	i	ii	iii	iv
(c)	ii	iii	i	iv
(d)	iii	ii	i	iv

40. Which one of the following is not a function of plant council?
(a) Recommend and improve safety, health and welfare measures.
(b) Determination of productivity schemes taking into consideration the local conditions.
(c) Planning, implementation and review of monthly targets and schedules.
(d) Review of working of shop level bodies.

41. **Assertion (A):** "Banks globally are facing more challenges now, and Macro sustainability is a necessity but not sufficient for sustainable economic growth."

Reason (R): "Putting regulations in place is only one part and their implementation is equally important for achieving growth and sustainability."

Codes:
(a) (A) and (R) both are true and (R) is correct explanation of (A).
(b) (A) and (R) both are true but (R) is not the correct explanation of (A).
(c) (A) is true and (R) is false.
(d) (A) is false and (R) is true.

42. Banking on telephone service includes:
(i) Automatic balance voice out
(ii) Inquiry all term deposit account
(iii) Direct cash withdrawl
(iv) Utility bill payment
(v) Voice out last five transactions

Codes:
(a) (i), (ii), (iii) and (v)
(b) (i), (ii), (iv) and (v)
(c) (ii), (iii), (iv) and (v)
(d) All of the above

43. Which one of the following banks currently ranks number one in India in terms of market capitalization?
(a) State Bank of India (b) I.C.I.C.I. Bank
(c) U.T.I. Bank (d) I.D.B.I. Bank

44. Match the items of Column-I with the items in Column-II and suggest the correct code:

Column-I
A. Interbank call market
B. Commercial bills
C. Commercial paper market
D. Treasury bills

i. Money market
ii. Promissory note
iii. Short-term maturity
iv. Government papers

Codes:	A	B	C	D
(a)	i	ii	iv	iii
(b)	iii	i	ii	iv
(c)	i	iii	iv	ii
(d)	iv	iii	ii	i

45. Match the items of List I with List II with regard to the BASEL III norms and select the correct code:

List I
A. Pillar 1 B. Pillar 2
C. Pillar 3

List II
i. Supervisory review process
ii. Market discipline
iii. Minimum regulatory capital requirements based on Risk Weighted Assets (RWAs)

Codes:	A	B	C
(a)	i	ii	iii
(b)	i	iii	ii
(c)	iii	ii	i
(d)	iii	i	ii

46. **Assertion (A):** Comparative cost theory is static in character.
Reason (R): Comparative cost theory is based on fixed supplies of factors of production.
Codes:
(a) (A) is correct, but (R) is incorrect.
(b) (R) is correct, but (A) is incorrect.
(c) (A) and (R) both are correct, but (R) is not the correct explanation of (A).
(d) (A) and (R) both are correct and (R) is the correct explanation of (A).

47. Match the items of List I with List II with regard to Balance of Payments equilibrium:

List I
A. Exchange control
B. Trade Policy Measure
C. Expenditure reducing policy
D. Expenditure switching policy

List II
i. Exporters surrender foreign exchange to the central bank
ii. Bank rate raised by the central bank
iii. Reduction in foreign exchange rate
iv. Enhancing exports by granting subsidies

Codes:	A	B	C	D
(a)	i	iv	ii	iii
(b)	i	ii	iii	iv
(c)	iii	ii	iv	i
(d)	iv	iii	ii	i

48. Which among the following is closely associated with intellectual property rights?
(a) GATS (b) TRIMS (c) TRIPS (d) MFN

49. What is not correct about International Development Association (IDA)?
(A) Following earthquake in 2015, IDA has helped Nepal rebuild and recover.
(B) IDA ranks as the highest performing multilateral development bank in 2016.
(C) IDA is a subsidiary bank of IBRD.
(D) India has procured highest amount of international loan from IDA.
Codes:
(a) (A) and (B) (b) (C)
(c) (D) (d) (A) and (C)

50. As per the Foreign Trade Policy 2015-2020, a three star export house should have:
(a) Export performance (FOB/FOR) of US $ 100 million during current and previous two years.
(b) Export performance (FOB/FOR) of US $ 500 million during current and previous two years.
(c) Export performance (FOB/FOR) of US $ 1000 million during current and previous two years.
(d) Export performance (FOB/FOR) of US $ 2000 million during current and previous two years.

ANSWERS

1. (a)	2. (b)	3. (d)	4. (c)	5. (a)
6. (t)	7. (b)	8. (b)	9. (b)	10. (c)
11. (c)	12. (d)	13. (c)	14. (d)	15. (b)
16. (c)	17. (b)	18. (t)	19. (b)	20. (b)
21. (c)	22. (a)	23. (d)	24. (a)	25. (c)
26. (a)	27. (d)	28. (d)	29. (b)	30. (d)
31. (d)	32. (a)	33. (c)	34. (d)	35. (d)

36. (c)	37. (c)	38. (a)	39. (d)	40. (a)
41. (a)	42. (b)	43. (a)	44. (b)	45. (d)
46. (d)	47. (a)	48. (c)	49. (c)	50. (a)

t → No option is correct.

PAPER–III

Note: This paper contains seventy-five (75) objective type questions of two (2) marks each. All questions are compulsory.

1. Read the following and select the right code:
   Statement-I: A custom to be valid should be proved to be immemorial but may not be ancient.
   Statement-II: The principle of judicial decision which is only authoritative is known as 'ratio decidendi'.
   (a) Both the statements are true.
   (b) Both the statements are false.
   (c) Statement-I is true but Statement-II is false.
   (d) Statement-II is true but Statement-I is false.
2. To become a director in a company the person must obtain
   (a) Business Licence (b) Director's Licence
   (c) TIN (d) DIN
3. Which of following is not a "Maharatna" industry in India?
   (a) CIL (b) SAIL (c) OIL (d) GAIL
4. Match the items of Column-I with those of Column-II:
   Column-I
   (A) Exchange control (B) Price control
   (C) Import control (D) Legislative control
   Column-II
   i. Adverse BOP
   ii. Domestic firms
   iii. Mass consumption product
   iv. Industrial location

Codes:	A	B	C	D
(a)	ii	i	iii	iv
(b)	iv	ii	iii	i
(c)	iii	ii	i	iv
(d)	ii	iii	i	iv

5. Match the items of List I with those of List II and choose the correct code:
   List I
   A. Provision for taxation
   B. Live-stock
   C. Sundry Debtors
   D. Interest accrued on unsecured loans
   List II
   i. Current Assets ii. Unsecured loans
   iii. Fixed Assets iv. Provisions

Codes:	A	B	C	D
(a)	iv	iii	i	ii
(b)	iv	iii	ii	i
(c)	iii	iv	ii	i
(d)	ii	i	iii	iv

6. A, B and C are partners in a firm sharing profits and losses in the ratio of 4 : 3 : 2. They agreed to take D into partnership and gave him 1/8 share. What will be their new profit sharing ratio?
   (a) 4 : 3 : 2 : 1 (b) 28 : 21 : 14 : 9
   (c) 28 : 21 : 14 : 8 (d) 4 : 1 : 2 : 1
7. From the following information, find out the number of units that must be sold by the firm to earn profit of ₹ 80,000 per year.
   Sales price : ₹ 25 per unit
   Variable manufacturing costs – ₹ 12 per unit
   Variable selling costs – ₹ 3 per unit
   Fixed factory overheads – ₹ 5,00,000
   Fixed selling costs – ₹ 3,00,000
   (a) 60,000 units (b) 88,000 units
   (c) 98,000 units (d) 1,00,000 units
8. Which of the following is not a cash inflow?
   (a) Decrease in creditors
   (b) Decrease in debtors
   (c) Issue of shares
   (d) Sale of a fixed asset
9. Match the items of List I with those of List II and indicate the correct code from the following:
   List I
   A. Postage stamp pricing
   B. Loss leader
   C. Economic capacity
   D. Reserve capacity
   List II
   i. Equality of marginal and average cost
   ii. Constant average and marginal cost
   iii. Product line pricing
   iv. Differential pricing

Codes:	**A**	**B**	**C**	**D**
(a)	iii	iv	ii	i
(b)	iv	iii	i	ii
(c)	ii	i	iii	iv
(d)	i	ii	iv	iii

10. For the following two statements of Assertion (A) and Reasoning (R) indicate the correct code:

Assertion (A): Low initial pricing for new products is regarded as the principal instrument for entering into mass markets.

Reasoning (R): Firms generally go for production of new products with excess capacity initially.

Codes:

(a) Assertion (A) and Reasoning (R) both are correct but (R) does not offer full explanation for (A).
(b) Assertion (A) and Reasoning (R) both are wrong.
(c) Assertion (A) is correct but Reasoning (R) is wrong.
(d) Assertion (A) and Reasoning (R) both are correct and (R) offers full explanation for (A).

11. For the following two statements of Assertion (A) and Reasoning (R) indicate the correct code:

Assertion (A): Gossen's first law of consumption is invariably applicable in case of individuals' consumption behaviour.

Reasoning (R): It serves as an important determinant of demand for the goods and services in the market.

Codes:

(a) Assertion (A) and Reasoning (R) both are correct.
(b) Assertion (A) and Reasoning (R) both are incorrect.
(c) Assertion (A) is correct but Reasoning (R) is incorrect.
(d) Assertion (A) is incorrect but Reasoning (R) is correct.

12. Production function for a product is based on certain assumptions. Indicate the correct code from the following:

(A) Complementarity (B) Substitutability
(C) Product elasticity (D) Specificity

Codes:			
(a)	A	B	C
(b)	B	C	D
(c)	A	C	D
(d)	A	B	D

13. Which one of the following is not the characteristic of normal distribution?

(a) Mean, median and mode for the normal distribution are equal.
(b) The two tails of the normal curve extend to infinity in both directions but never touch the horizontal axis.
(c) For different values of standard deviation, the height of the mean ordinate remains the same.
(d) The number of independent constraints of normal distribution are N, $\overline{X}$ and σ.

14. Which one of the following formulae is used to calculate the standard error of coefficient of correlation between 25 paired observations of a sample?

(a) $\dfrac{\left(1-r^2\right)}{\sqrt{n}}$ (b) $\sqrt{\dfrac{\left(1-r^2\right)}{(n-2)}}$

(c) $(0.6745)\left(\dfrac{1-r^2}{\sqrt{n}}\right)$ (d) $\sqrt{\dfrac{(n-2)}{\left(1-r^2\right)}}$

15. Read the following statements and choose the correct code:

Statement-I: Non-parametric tests are based on some assumptions about the parent population from which the sample has been drawn.

Statement-II: The standard deviation of the sampling distribution of mean is called standard error of mean.

Codes:

(a) Both statements are true.
(b) Both statements are false.
(c) Statement-I is true while Statement-II is false.
(d) Statement-I is false while Statement-II is true.

16. Match the items of List I with the items of List II and indicate the code of correct matching:

List I

i. Contingency coefficient for any size of contingency table

ii. Statistical approach to decide size of a sample
iii. Finite population multiplier
iv. Standard error of mean

List II

A. $\sqrt{\frac{N-n}{N-1}}$ B. $\frac{\sigma_p}{\sqrt{n}}$

C. $\sqrt{\frac{x^2}{x^2+n}}$ D. $\frac{z^2 \cdot \sigma_p^2}{e^2}$

Codes:	A	B	C	D
(a)	i	ii	iii	iv
(b)	iii	iv	i	ii
(c)	i	iii	ii	iv
(d)	iii	ii	iv	i

17. Which of the following is a deterioration of mental efficiency, reality testing and moral judgement that results from in-group pressure?
(a) Harassment (b) Group think
(c) Group burnout (d) Group control

18. According to Fiedler's contingency model of leadership, favourableness of situation depends on which combination of the following?
(A) Leader-member relationship
(B) Member-member relationship
(C) Leader's position power
(D) Degree of task structure
(E) Degree of training
Codes:
(a) (A), (B) and (C) (b) (A), (C) and (D)
(c) (C), (D) and (E) (d) (A), (B) and (E)

19. The apex body at the highest level of the unit/ division, which oversees the functioning of quality circles, is called
(a) Facilitator
(b) Coordinator
(c) Steering committee
(d) Supervisory committee

20. Which of the following is related to the practical means of determining a moral course of action?
(a) Meta ethics (b) Virtue ethics
(c) Normative ethics (d) Applied ethics

21. Match List I and List II and indicate the correct code:

List I
A. Convenience goods B. Shopping goods
C. Speciality goods D. Unsought goods

List II
i. Consumer purchases them frequently, immediately and with minimal effort.
ii. Consumer compares them on the basis of suitability, quality, price and style.
iii. These are goods with unique characteristics or brand identification.
iv. Consumers are not aware of them and normally do not think of buying them.

Codes:	A	B	C	D
(a)	i	iv	ii	iii
(b)	i	ii	iii	iv
(c)	iv	iii	ii	i
(d)	ii	i	iii	iv

22. Which of the following marketing strategies is/are not used in 'growth stage' of the product life cycle?
(a) Improving quality and adding new features.
(b) Adding new models of product.
(c) Entering new market segments.
(d) Using awareness and trial communications.

23. Who among the following take(s) both title to and possession of goods from the preceding member(s) and channelize them to the subsequent members?
(A) Agent intermediaries
(B) Merchant intermediaries
(a) (A) only (b) (B) only
(c) Both (A) and (B) (d) Neither (A) nor (B)

24. Which of the following is not a determinant of service quality?
(a) Reliability (b) Responsiveness
(c) Sensitivity (d) Assurance

25. Sales of a firm are ₹ 74 lakh, variable costs ₹ 40 lakh, fixed costs ₹ 8 lakh. Operating leverage of the firm will be
(a) 1.48 (b) 1.78 (c) 1.31 (d) 2.42

26. From the following techniques of capital budgeting decision, indicate the correct combination of discounting techniques:
I. Profitability index
II. Net present value
III. Accounting rate of return
IV. Internal rate of return

Codes:

(a)	I	II	III
(b)	II	III	IV
(c)	I	II	IV
(d)	I	III	IV

27. Insufficient working capital may result into which combination of the following?
    I. Failures to adapt to changes.
    II. Enhancement in credit-worthiness of the firm.
    III. Reduced availability of trade and cash discounts.
    IV. Reduced volume of sales.

Codes:
(a) I, II, III, IV (b) I, III, IV
(c) I, II, IV (d) I, II, III

28. Which combination of the following represents the assumptions of the Walter's dividend model?
    I. The company has a very long or perpetual life.
    II. All earnings are either reinvested internally or distributed as dividend.
    III. There is no floatation cost for the company.
    IV. Cost of capital of the company is constant.

Codes:

(a)	I	II	III
(b)	II	III	IV
(c)	I	II	IV
(d)	I	III	IV

29. Match the items of List I with the items of List II and indicate the correct code:

List I
A. Job specifications B. Job description
C. Job analysis

List II
i. The procedure for determining the duties and skill requirements of a job and the kind of person who should be hired for it.
ii. A list of human requirements
iii. A list of job's duties, responsibilities, reporting relationships, working conditions and supervisory responsibilities.

Codes:	A	B	C
(a)	i	ii	iii
(b)	ii	iii	i
(c)	iii	ii	i
(d)	ii	i	iii

30. A training technique in which trainees are first shown good management techniques in a film, are asked to play roles in a simulated situation, and are then given feedback and praise by their supervisor is known as
    (a) Behaviour modelling
    (b) Role playing
    (c) In-house development center
    (d) Management game

31. Which combination of the following statements is correct about the code of discipline in industry?
    (A) It aims at preventing disputes by providing for outside agency or adjudication.
    (B) It is a government imposed involuntary principle of discipline.
    (C) It restrains the parties from unilateral action.

Codes:
(a) (A), (B) and (C) (b) (B) and (C)
(c) (A) only (d) (C) only

32. A conciliation proceeding is deemed to be pending until any combination of the following conditions is fulfilled:
    (A) a settlement is arrived at a memorandum of settlement is signed by parties to the dispute.
    (B) no settlement is arrived at, the report of conciliation officer is received by the appropriate government.
    (C) a reference is made to the court of Inquiry, Labour Court, Tribunal or National Tribunal during the pendency of conciliation proceedings.

Codes:
(a) only (A) is correct.
(b) only (B) is correct.
(c) (A) and (C) are correct.
(d) (A), (B) and (C) are correct.

33. Identify the correct combination of statements with regard to banking in India.
    A. For many years the presidency banks had acted as quasi-central banks.
    B. The Bank of Hindustan was liquidated during 1829-32.
    C. General Bank of India was an unsuccessful bank and was dissolved in 1791.
    D. Bank of Calcutta was renamed as Bank of Bengal in 1921.

Codes:

(a) (A), (B) and (C) (b) (B), (C) and (D)
(c) (A), (B) and (D) (d) (A), (B), (C) and (D)

34. Which combination of the following methods indicates quantitative methods of control of credit creation practiced by the Reserve Bank of India?
(A) Bank Rate
(B) Open Market Operations
(C) Variable Reserve Ratios
(D) Credit Rationing

Codes:

(a) (A), (B) and (C) (b) (A), (B) and (D)
(c) (B), (C) and (D) (d) (A), (C) and (D)

35. Which one of the following development financial institutions in India has started the special refinance scheme for the resettlement and rehabilitation of voluntary retired workers of the National Textile Corporation of India?
(a) IDBI (b) SIDBI
(c) ICICI (d) None of the above

36. Read the following statements and choose the correct code:

Statement-I: Small Industry Development Bank of India (SIDBI) was set up as a wholly owned subsidiary of RBI.

Statement-II: SIDBI has taken over the responsibility of administering small industry development fund managed by IDBI.

Codes:

(a) Only (I) is correct.
(b) Only (II) is correct.
(c) Both (I) and (II) are correct.
(d) Both (I) and (II) are wrong.

37. Under the Foreign Trade Policy 2015-2020, following additional ports are allowed for export and import:
A. Calicut Airport, Kerala
B. Rajkot Airport, Gujarat
C. Arakonam ICD, Tamil Nadu
D. Ludhiana Airport, Punjab

Codes:

(a) (A) and (C) (b) (A) and (D)
(c) (B) and (D) (d) (C) and (D)

38. **Assertion (A):** Under FEMA, the receiver of laundered money is to be made culpable, instead of sender/distributor.

Reasoning (R): FEMA differs from the earlier exchange regulation Act FERA with regard to penalties and punishment in case of violation of the Act.

Codes:

(a) (A) is correct but (R) is not correct.
(b) (A) and (R) both are correct but (R) is not the right explanation of (A).
(c) (A) and (R) both are correct and (R) is the right explanation of (A).
(d) (A) and (R) both are incorrect.

39. Match the items of List I with those of List II with regard to international monetary fund's various schemes:

List I

A. Extended Fund Facility (EFF)
B. Stan Arrangements
C. Supplemented Reserve Fund (SRF)
D. Poverty Reduction and Growth Facility (PRGF)

List II

i. Repayment period 4 to 10 years
ii. Repayment period 3 to 5 years
iii. Repayment period 2 to 5 years
iv. Repayment period 10 years

Codes:	**A**	**B**	**C**	**D**
(a)	i	ii	iii	iv
(b)	iv	iii	ii	i
(c)	iv	ii	iii	i
(d)	i	iv	ii	iii

40. Which combination of the following is correct with regard to World Trade Organization (WTO):
A. WTO initiates peace process among the member countries to enhance international trade.
B. WTO avoids the task of "Settlement of Disputes" among the member countries.
C. WTO administers the "Trade Review Mechanism".
D. WTO cooperates in an appropriate manner with the IMF and the World Bank.

Codes:

(a) (B), (C) and (D) (b) (A) and (C)
(c) (C) and (D) (d) (A), (B) and (D)

41. Choose the code representing the correct sequence of steps in a merging transaction:
    (I) Screening and investigation of merger proposal.
    (II) Approval of Central Government
    (III) Approval of respective High Courts
    (IV) Negotiation Stage
    (V) Approval of proposal by Board of Directors, Shareholders and Creditors

    Codes:
    (a) (I) → (V) → (IV) → (III) → (II)
    (b) (I) → (IV) → (V) → (III) → (II)
    (c) (I) → (IV) → (III) → (V) → (II)
    (d) (I) → (III) → (V) → (II) → (IV)

42. Which of the following are the important features of option contracts?
    (I) Buyers of option have limited liability.
    (II) Options have high degree of risk to option-writers.
    (III) Options are exercisable only by buyers of option.
    (IV) Buyers of option have all rights which are available to equity shareholders of the concerned companies.

    Codes:
    (a) (I), (II), (III) (b) (I), (II), (III), (IV)
    (c) (I), (II), (IV) (d) (I), (III), (IV)

43. Which of the following approaches is adopted for the valuation of human resource according to economic concept?
    (a) Replacement cost approach
    (b) Opportunity cost approach
    (c) Historical cost approach
    (d) None of the above

44. Match the items of List I with those of List II and select the correct code:

    List I
    A. High levered fund B. Increase in bank rate
    C. Inflation D. Political instability

    List II
    i. Market risk
    ii. Purchasing power risk
    iii. Financial risk
    iv. Interest rate risk

Codes:	A	B	C	D
(a)	iii	i	ii	iv
(b)	i	iii	iv	ii
(c)	iii	iv	ii	i
(d)	ii	iii	i	iv

45. Which of the following are the instruments of money market?
    (i) Call money market
    (ii) Commercial bill market
    (iii) Industrial securities market
    (iv) Short-term loans market
    (v) Treasury bill market

    Codes:
    (a) (i), (ii), (iv), (v) (b) (i), (ii), (v)
    (c) (i), (ii), (iii), (iv), (v) (d) (i), (ii), (iii), (iv)

46. Accounting Standard-6 is meant for
    (a) Accounting for Fixed Assets
    (b) Accounting treatment for goodwill
    (c) Depreciation Accounting
    (d) Disclosure of Accounting policies

47. Which of the following is not a feature of OTCEI?
    (a) Quick transfer and disposal system
    (b) Nationalised computerised networking
    (c) Ringless trading system
    (d) Fragmentation of regional stock exchanges

48. Which of the following requires consumers to interpret ambiguous stimuli?
    (a) Focus group method
    (b) Projective techniques
    (c) Rejective techniques
    (d) Semantic differential scales

49. Which of the following passes through the four stages of distinctiveness, emulation, mass fashion and decline?
    (a) Style (b) Fashion
    (c) Fad (d) Style and Fashion

50. Which of the following positioning strategies is adopted by marketers to position their product in two categories simultaneously?
    (a) Point of Difference
    (b) Point of Parity
    (c) Straddle Positioning
    (d) Emotional Positioning

51. **Statement (I):** Marketing is the process by which a firm profitably translates customer needs into revenue.

    Statement (II): Marketing is the messages and/or actions that causes messages and/or actions.

    Codes:
    (a) (I) is correct but (II) is not correct.
    (b) (II) is correct but (I) is not correct.

(c) (I) and (II) both are correct.
(d) (I) and (II) both are incorrect.

52. **Assertion (A):** Odd pricing aims at maximising profit by making micro-adjustments in pricing structure.

Reasoning (R): Odd pricing refers to a price ending in 1, 3, 5, 7, or 9. When examining a price, the first digits carry more weight than the last ones.

Codes:
(a) (A) is right and (R) is wrong.
(b) (A) is wrong and (R) is right.
(c) Both (A) and (R) are right.
(d) Both (A) and (R) are wrong.

53. Name the process in which a buyer posts its interest in buying a certain quantity of item and sellers compete for the business by submitting lower bid until there is only one seller left.
(a) Internet (b) Reverse auction
(c) B2B market place (d) B2C market place

54. Advertising method in which an advertisement is broadcasted simultaneously on several radio stations and/or television channels is known as
(a) Black-out (b) Consolidation
(c) Road-block (d) Cornering

55. Which of the following is the mental condition or attitude of individuals and groups which determines their willingness to cooperate?
(a) Motivation (b) Morale
(c) Excitement (d) Delight

56. Which of the following is not provided under the Factories Act, 1948?
(a) The certificate of fitness is granted by a certifying surgeon on the application of any young person or a parent or a guardian.
(b) An adolescent who has not been granted a certificate of fitness shall be deemed to be a child for the purpose of the act.
(c) The certificate of fitness granted or renewed remains valid for a period of six months from the date of issue.
(d) Any fee payable for the certificate of fitness shall be paid by occupier and not by the young person or his parent or guardian.

57. Arrange the following steps of developing Behaviourally Anchored Rating Scales (BARS) in the right sequence:
A. Developing performance dimensions
B. Generate critical incidents
C. Scale the incidents
D. Reallocate the incidents
E. Develop the final instrument

Codes:
(a) (A), (B), (C), (D), (E)
(b) (B), (A), (D), (C), (E)
(c) (A), (B), (D), (C), (E)
(d) (A), (C), (B), (D), (E)

58. Within how much period from the close of accounting year, bonus must be paid, if there is no dispute about the payment of bonus?
(a) Two months (b) Six months
(c) Eight months (d) Ten months

59. Which of the following statements is correct about Wage Boards in India?
A. A Wage Board is a tripartite body.
B. Labour and management representatives on a Wage Board can be selected from industries other than the one which is investigated.
C. Wage Boards are always statutory in nature.
D. Wage Boards work on the principle of living wage.

Codes:
(a) (A) only (b) (B) and (C)
(c) (C) and (D) (d) (A), (B), (C) and (D)

60. Who gave the surplus value theory of wage?
(a) David Ricardo (b) Karl Marx
(c) Adam Smith (d) F.A. Walker

61. Who gave the systems approach to industrial relations?
(a) Beatrice Webb (b) John Dunlop
(c) Eric Trist (d) Henry Fayol

62. Which among the following are multinational corporations?
A. A multinational, decentralized corporation with strong home country presence.
B. A global, centralized corporation that acquires cost advantage through centralized production when cheaper resources are available.

C. An international company that builds on the parent corporations technology and R&D.
D. A transnational enterprise that combines the (A), (B) and (C).

Codes:

(a) (A) and (B) (b) (B) and (C)
(c) (A), (B) and (C) (d) (A), (B), (C) and (D)

63. Which among the following are full member countries of ASEAN?
A. Brunei Darussalam B. Cambodia
C. Vietnam D. Myanmar
E. Sri Lanka

Codes:

(a) (A), (B) and (E)
(b) (A), (B), (C) and (E)
(c) (B), (C), (D) and (E)
(d) (A), (B), (C) and (D)

64. **Assertion (A):** Capital Account convertibility is introduced only sometime after the introduction of convertibility on current account when exchange rate of currency of a country is relatively stable.

Reasoning (R): Capital Account convertibility is necessary for faster growth and development of economy and it makes foreign exchange rate more stable.

Codes:

(a) (A) is correct but (R) is not correct.
(b) (A) and (R) both are correct and (R) is the right explanation of (A).
(c) (A) and (R) both are correct but (R) is not the right explanation of (A).
(d) Both (A) and (R) are incorrect.

65. **Statement (I):** WTO is only international organization which deals with the rules of trade between organizations.

Statement (II): The limit of holding by individual foreign institutional investors in a company has been raised from 5 to 10% of company's share while the aggregate limit has been increased from 24 to 34%.

Codes:

(a) Statement (I) is correct but Statement (II) is false.
(b) Statement (II) is correct but Statement (I) is false.
(c) Statements (I) and (II) both are correct.
(d) Statements (I) and (II) both are false.

66. In case a farmer in India buys a wheat option on future:
A. The farmer must accept a wheat futures contract and not take physical possession of wheat.
B. The farmer must accept delivery of the wheat at a higher price.
C. The farmer has the right to deliver the wheat and will do so only if the price is favourable.
D. The farmer must deliver the wheat at market price.

Codes:

(a) (A) and (D) (b) (D) only
(c) (C) only (d) (B) and (C)

67. Sector specific policy of Government of India in case of B2B is when
(a) FDI is upto 100%
(b) FDI is upto 49%
(c) FDI is upto 100% subject to condition that the investment in favour of Indian public to the tune of 20% within 5 years to be done.
(d) FDI is upto 100% subject to condition that the investment in favour of Indian public to the tune of 26% within 10 years to be done.

68. **Statement I:** In India a "copyright" of an unpublished book can be registered under copyright Act of India.

Statement II: Once granted by the European Patent Office, the proprietor has a patent which is effective in all contracting states of the patent cooperation treaty and the agreement on the trade related aspects of IPR.

Codes:

(a) Statement (I) is correct and (II) is false.
(b) Statement (II) is correct and (I) is false.
(c) Statements (I) and (II) both are correct.
(d) Statements (I) and (II) both are false.

69. As per the Income Tax Act, 1961 for the assessment year 2015-16, a deduction u/s 80 QQB for authors of books of literacy, artistic or scientific nature is allowed upto

(a) ₹ 1,00,000 (b) ₹ 2,00,000
(c) ₹ 2,40,000 (d) ₹ 3,00,000

70. Gratuity received by a government employee is
(a) exempted upto ₹ 3,50,000
(b) exempted upto ₹ 10,00,000
(c) fully exempted
(d) fully taxable

71. Match the items of the List I with those of the List II and indicate the correct code:

List I
A. Residential status of an individual
B. Agricultural income
C. House rent allowance
D. Gratuity

List II
i. Section 10 (13A) ii. Section 10 (10)
iii. Section 6 iv. Section 10 (1)

Codes:	A	B	C	D
(a)	i	iii	ii	iv
(b)	iii	iv	i	ii
(c)	ii	i	iii	iv
(d)	iv	ii	i	iii

72. Match the items of the List I with List II and indicate the correct code:

List I
A. House rent allowance
B. Casual income
C. Collection charges of interest on securities
D. Best judgement assessment

List II
i. A deduction from income
ii. A step taken by tax authorities
iii. Taxable income
iv. Partly taxable allowance

Codes:	A	B	C	D
(a)	iv	iii	ii	i
(b)	iv	iii	i	ii
(c)	iii	iv	i	ii
(d)	ii	iv	i	iii

73. The statutory limit for deduction u/s 80 GG of Income tax Act, 1961, for the assessment year 2015-16 is
(a) ₹ 2,000 per month (b) ₹ 3,000 per month
(c) ₹ 2,500 per month (d) ₹ 5,000 per month

74. For the purpose of assessment under Income Tax Act, 1961, which combination of the following represent income?
(I) Tax-free salary from the private sector employer.
(II) Pin money received by a family member.
(III) Awards received by the sports persons.
(IV) Loss incurred by the assessee.
(V) Perquisites received by employees.

Codes:
(a) (I), (II), (III), (IV) (b) (II), (III), (IV), (V)
(c) (I), (III), (IV), (V) (d) (I), (II), (IV), (V)

75. Indicate the correct code for forms for filing income tax return from the following Income Tax Return Forms:
(A) ITR-4S (B) ITR-2 (C) ITR-2B (D) ITR-3

Codes:
(a) (A), (B) and (C) (b) (B), (C) and (D)
(c) (A), (B) and (D) (d) (A), (C) and (D)

ANSWERS

1. (d)	2. (d)	3. (c)	4. (d)	5. (a)
6. (b)	7. (b)	8. (a)	9. (b)	10. (a)
11. (d)	12. (d)	13. (c)	14. (b)	15. (d)
16. (b)	17. (b)	18. (b)	19. (c)	20. (c)
21. (b)	22. (d)	23. (b)	24. (c)	25. (c)
26. (c)	27. (b)	28. (c)	29. (b)	30. (a)
31. (d)	32. (d)	33. (a)	34. (a)	35. (a)
36. (b)	37. (a)	38. (c)	39. (a)	40. (c)
41. (b)	42. (a)	43. (b)	44. (c)	45. (a)
46. (c)	47. (d)	48. (b)	49. (b)	50. (c)
51. (c)	52. (c)	53. (b)	54. (c)	55. (b)
56. (c)	57. (b)	58. (c)	59. (a)	60. (b)
61. (b)	62. (d)	63. (d)	64. (a)	65. (c)
66. (c)	67. (c)	68. (c)	69. (d)	70. (c)
71. (b)	72. (b)	73. (a)	74. (c)	75. (c)

PRACTICE PAPERS

MOCK TEST–1
PAPER–I

1. A teacher is called the leader of the class because
   (a) he is autocratic emperor of his class
   (b) he masters the art of oratory like a political leader
   (c) he is a maker of the future of his students
   (d) he belongs to a recognised teachers' union
2. The aim of introducing career courses in schools and colleges is to
   (a) increase G.K. in students
   (b) develop the ability to make the intelligent choice of jobs
   (c) provide professional knowledge to students
   (d) All of the above
3. The most effective attribute for a teacher is
   (a) teaching skills (b) knowledge
   (c) feedback (d) management
4. Those teachers are preferred most by students who
   (a) are themselves disciplined
   (b) give important questions before examination
   (c) dictate notes in the class
   (d) can clear their difficulties regarding subject-matter
5. The quality/qualities of a teacher is/are:
   (i) He must not give any false promise
   (ii) He must not have any bad habits
   (iii) He should be mentally and physically fit
   (iv) He must not be superstitious about his class and students
   (a) Only (iii), (iv) and (ii)
   (b) Only (iv), (i) and (ii)
   (c) Only (i), (iii) and (iv)
   (d) All of the above
6. A teacher is more effective who can
   (a) motivate students to learn
   (b) control the class
   (c) correct the assignments carefully
   (d) give more information in less time
7. A teacher ought to know the problems prevalent in the field of education because
   (a) he can tell the government about it
   (b) with this knowledge, he can have information about education
   (c) he can tell about the same to another teacher
   (d) only he can do something about solving them
8. We can judge the quality of a research by the
   (a) experience of researcher
   (b) relevance of research
   (c) depth of the research
   (d) methodology followed in conducting the research
9. The theory or model developed through the fundamental research to the actual solution of the problems is applied in
   (a) educational research
   (b) action research
   (c) applied research
   (d) basic research
10. A write-up based on studies of the census data of a given area is called
    (a) Research paper (b) Article
    (c) Research report (d) Thesis

Direction (Q. Nos. 11-16): Study the following passage and give answer to the questions based on it.

Knowledge creation in many cases requires creativity and idea generation. This is especially important in generating alternative decision support solutions. Some people believe that an individual's creative ability stems primarily from personality traits such as inventiveness, independence, individuality, enthusiasm, and flexibility. However, several studies have found that creativity is not so much a function of individual traits as was once believed, and that individual creativity can be learned and improved. This understanding has led innovative companies to recognise that the key to fostering creativity may be the development of an idea-nurturing work environment. Idea-generation methods and techniques, to be used by individuals or in groups, are consequently being developed. Manual methods for supporting idea generation, such as brain-storming in a group, can be very successful in certain situations. However, in other situations, such an approach is either not economically feasible or not possible. For example, manual methods in group creativity sessions will not work or will not be effective when: (a) there is no time to conduct a proper idea-generation session; (b) there is a poor facilitator (or no facilitator at all); (c) it is too expensive to conduct an idea-generation session; (d) the subject matter is too sensitive for a face-to-face session; or (e) there are not enough participants, the mix of participants is not optimal, or there is no climate for idea generation. In such cases, computerised idea-generation methods have been tried, with frequent success. Idea-generation software is designed to help stimulate a single user or a group to produce new ideas, options and choices. The user does all the work, but the software encourages and pushes, something like a personal trainer. Although idea-generation software is still relatively new, there are several packages on the market. Various approaches are used by idea-generating software to increase the flow of ideas to the user. Idea Fisher, for example, has an associate lexicon of the English language that cross-references words and phrases. These associative links, based on analogies and metaphors, make it easy for the user to be fed words related to a given theme. Some software packages use questions to prompt the user towards new, unexplored patterns of thought. This helps users to break out of cyclical thinking patterns, conquer mental blocks, or deal with bouts of procrastination.

11. The author, in this passage, has focused on
    (a) individual traits (b) knowledge creation
    (c) creativity (d) idea-generation
12. Idea-generation software works as if it is a
    (a) user-friendly trainer
    (b) stimulant
    (c) climate creator
    (d) knowledge package
13. Which among the following personality traits is not believed to be a factor contributing to an individual's creative ability?
    (a) Flexibility (b) Individuality
    (c) Sophistication (d) Enthusiasm
14. In certain occasions, manual methods for the support of idea-generation
    (a) can be less expensive
    (b) do not need a facilitator
    (c) require a mix of optimal participants
    (d) are alternatively effective
15. Mental blocks, bouts of procrastination and cyclical thinking patterns can be won when
    (a) idea-generation software prompts questions
    (b) individuals acquire a neutral attitude towards the software
    (c) manual methods are removed
    (d) innovative companies employ electronic thinking methods
16. Fostering creativity needs an environment of
    (a) decision support systems
    (b) alternative individual factors
    (c) idea-nurturing
    (d) decision support solutions
17. For controlling noise in a classroom, the best method of communication is
    (a) remaining calm and just looking at student
    (b) saying 'don't talk'
    (c) continue teaching without caring for noise
    (d) raising one's voice above students voice
18. In India, Education TV was first introduced in the year
    (a) 1978 (b) 1959 (c) 1987 (d) 1998
19. The failure of the teacher to communicate his ideas well to students may result into:
    I. Classroom indiscipline.
    II. Decrease in attendance in class.
    III. Loss of student's interest in class.
    (a) Only II (b) Only III
    (c) Only I (d) All of these
20. Visualisation in the instructional process cannot increase

(a) curiosity and concentration
(b) interest and motivation
(c) stress and boredom
(d) retention and adaptation

21. Communication helps in
(a) entertainment
(b) integration of country
(c) cultural promotion
(d) All of these

22. "Because you deserve to know" is the punchline used by
(a) *Hindustan Times* (b) *The Telegraph*
(c) *The Times of India* (d) *India Today*

23. Find the odd man out from the following groups of letters:
(a) UlmnE (b) AbcdE (c) ApqrL (d) IfghO

24. The ambitious computerisation program of the Government of India aimed at connecting 60,000 government schools through internet is known as
(a) Vidya Vahini (b) Gyan Vahini
(c) Kalpana project (d) Vidya Vani

25. Find the wrong number in the following sequence.
225, 336, 447, 557, 669, 771
(a) 669 (b) 557 (c) 336 (d) 771

26. In this question two words are given which have certain relationship followed by four paired lettered words. Select the paired words, that has the same relation as original pair.
ROOF : FOUNDATION
(a) Plateau: Valley (b) Peak: Valley
(c) Mountain: Grassland (d) Hill: Mountain

27. "Communication is a verbal process by which we understand each other and reduce uncertainty through the use of symbol." Who is the author of this statement?
(a) David K. Barlo (b) Dance
(c) P.S.K. Serichavenko (d) K.J. Newman

Direction: Find out the missing number (Q 28-30)

28. 8 24 12 ? 18 54
(a) 28 (b) 32 (c) 36 (d) 38

29. A D C F
C F E H
O R ? ?
(a) J K (b) R N (c) S U (d) Q T

30. 3, 12, 27, 48, 75, (?), 147.
(a) 111 (b) 108 (c) 117 (d) 122

31. In this question four words have been given, out of which three are alike in some manner and the fourth one is different. Choose the odd one out.
(a) Epigraphy (b) Ecology
(c) Archaeology (d) Palaeontology

32. Which of the following figures will represent the right relationship between, societies, societies who run schools, DPS society.

(a)  (b) 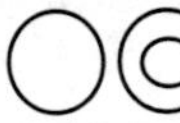

(c)  (d) 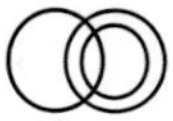

33. **Read the following and choose the correct option.**
Statements:
I. All students are ambitious.
II. All ambitious persons are hard working.
Conclusions:
(i) All students are hard-working.
(ii) All hardly working people are not ambitious.
Which of the following is correct?
(a) Only (i) is correct
(b) Only (ii) is correct
(c) Both (i) and (ii) are correct
(d) Neither (i) nor (ii) is correct

34. In a certain code language:
'pit dit mit' means: 'Reena went to Delhi'.
'dit ket set' means: 'Delhi is closing'.
'mit set un' means: 'Reena' is educated.
Then what is the code for 'went'?
(a) dit (b) mit (c) pit (d) None of these

35. EDITOR : MAGAZINE
Choose the pair from the answer choices that best expresses the relationship similar to that expressed by the question pair.
(a) Novel : Writer (b) Director : Film
(c) Poem : Poet (d) Chair : Carpenter

36. Should education in India be made free?

Arguments:

I. Yes, this is the only way to improve the level of literacy.

II. No, this would add already heavy burden on the exchequer.

(a) Only argument I is strong
(b) Only argument II is strong
(c) Both the arguments are strong
(d) None of these

Direction: (37-41) Study the table and answer the questions:

Export of Pulses and Import of Onion (in ₹ crores)

Year	Export of Pulses (in ₹ crores)	Import of Onion (in ₹ crores)
1998-99	44	58
1999-00	45	50
2000-01	60	54
2001-02	56	60
2002-03	92	68
2003-04	100	78
2004-05	68	60

37. During which year there was a maximum fall in export?
(a) 2004-05 (b) 2001-02
(c) 2003-04 (d) None of these

38. The percent of increase of imports in 2003-04 over 2002-03 is
(a) 14.9% (b) 14.7%
(c) 18.4% (d) 18.9%

39. In 1999-2000, the ratio of export to the import is
(a) 19:11 (b) 11:9 (c) 13:17 (d) 9:10

40. During which year there was maximum increase in import over its preceding year?
(a) 2003-04 (b) 2000-01
(c) 2001-02 (d) 2002-03

41. During which year there was minimum increase in import over its preceding year?
(a) 2003-04 (b) 2002-03
(c) 2001-02 (d) None of these

42. The sum of a positive number and its reciprocal is twice the difference of the number and its reciprocal. The number is:
(a) $\sqrt{3}$ (b) $\sqrt{2}$
(c) $\frac{1}{\sqrt{2}}$ (d) $\frac{1}{\sqrt{3}}$

43. Which one of the following states has the maximum number of Wildlife Sanctuaries (National Parks and Sanctuaries)?
(a) Madhya Pradesh (b) Rajasthan
(c) Uttar Pradesh (d) West Bengal

Directions (44-48): Answer the following questions based on the graph given below:

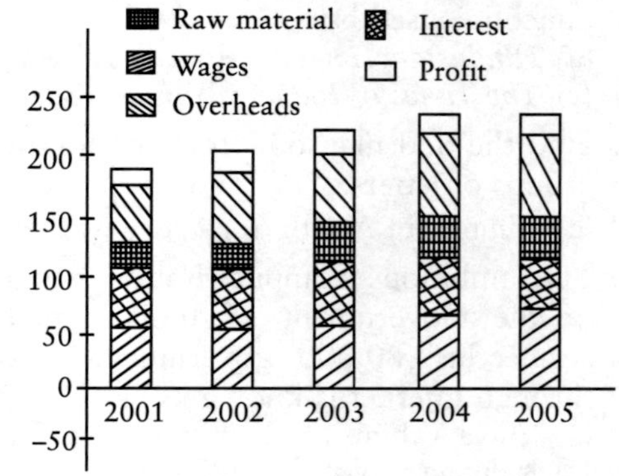

44. Which component of the cost of production has remained almost unchanged over the period 2001-05?
(a) Wages (b) Interest
(c) Raw material (d) Overheads

45. In which year was the increase in raw material maximum?
(a) 2004 (b) 2002 (c) 2003 (d) 2001

46. What percent of costs did the profits form over the period?
(a) 7% (b) 5% (c) 2% (d) 1%

47. In which period was the change in profit maximum?
(a) 2002-03 (b) 2001-02
(c) 2004-05 (d) 2003-04

48. If the interest component is not included in the total cost calculation, which year would show the maximum profit per unit cost?
(a) 2001 (b) 2002 (c) 2003 (d) 2005

49. How many types of emergencies have been envisaged by the Constitution?
(a) One (b) Two (c) Three (d) Four

50. Photocopying and other electrical equipments produce

(a) methane (b) ethane
(c) ozone (d) hydrogen dioxide

PAPER–II

1. A stable and dynamic political environment is indispensable for
   (a) enhancement of the export.
   (b) business growth.
   (c) Both (a) and (b).
   (d) None of the above.
2. A mixed economy is necessarily an ____ economy.
   (a) Organised (b) Controlled
   (c) Planned (d) None of the above
3. In the three and a half decades of industrialisation, the gross domestic product increased
   (a) Near about 15 per cent
   (b) 10 per cent
   (c) 20 per cent exact
   (d) 18 per cent
4. The most promising source of saving to finance development is
   (a) profits of railway.
   (b) the profits of organised sector.
   (c) only the profit of private sector.
   (d) profits of government sector.
5. Choose the correct statement.
   (a) The public sector will have responsibility for meeting social need.
   (b) The public sector would play useful in augmenting basic resources of country like land, forest and water.
   (c) Both (a) and (b).
   (d) Public sector would not play a useful role in population controls.
6. Which English alphabet is similar to the shape of an account?
   (a) H (b) I
   (c) T (d) None of these
7. Overcasting of purchases journal would affect
   (a) Supplier's account and purchase account
   (b) Sales account
   (c) Purchase account
   (d) None of the above
8. Purchase journal is kept to record
   (a) all credit purchases.
   (b) all purchases of goods.
   (c) all credit purchases of goods.
   (d) None of the above.
9. Payment of compensation to a worker who has been discharged from service is a
   (a) revenue expenditure.
   (b) capital expenditure.
   (c) non-business expenditure.
   (d) referred revenue expenditure.
10. If net profit is ₹ 30,000 after writing off goodwill ₹ 6000 and depreciation on furniture ₹ 2000, fund from operation will be
    (a) ₹ 32,000 (b) ₹ 36,000
    (c) ₹ 38,000 (d) ₹ 26,000
11. The fall in the price of one commodity leads to fall in demand for other commodity and vice versa for
    (a) Complementaries (b) Substitutes
    (c) Both (a) and (b) (d) None of these
12. Under total outlay or total expenditure method, the elasticity of demand can be measured as
    (a) $\dfrac{\Delta p/(q_1+q_2)}{\Delta p/(P_1+P_2)}$ (b) $1-\dfrac{\Delta Exp}{\chi\Delta p}$
    (c) $\dfrac{\Delta Q}{\Delta P}$ (d) $\dfrac{\Delta p}{\Delta q}\times\dfrac{p}{q}$
13. Two conditions are required to be there for the equilibrium under monopoly. These are
    (a) MC = MR and MR cuts the MC from below.
    (b) MR = MC and MC cuts the MR from above.
    (c) MR = MC and MC cuts the MR from below.
    (d) MC = AR and MC cuts the MR from below.
14. In case of giffen goods, price effect is
    (a) Positive (b) Zero
    (c) Negative (d) None of these
15. If demand curve is rectangular hyperbola, e_p is equal to
    (a) 1 (b) ∞ (c) 0 (d) 2
16. The graphical method can be used to solve
    (a) A linear programming problem with two decision variables.

(b) A linear programming problem with all integer database.
(c) Any linear programming problem.
(d) A transportation problem with two origins and two destinations.

17. Personnel activity reports are produced from the
(a) applicant file
(b) jobs files
(c) personnel transactions file
(d) employee file

18. A machine on the average produces 5% defective items. What are the mean and variance in a set of 32 items?
(a) 4, 16 (b) 16, 4
(c) 16, 8 (d) None of these

19. Marketing research data is gathered by
(a) controlled experiment
(b) observation
(c) in-depth interviews
(d) All of the above

20. Relation between two variables is determined by
(a) Dispersion (b) Correlation
(c) Mean (d) Regression

21. Management by exception introduces
(a) requirement of full reports on performance.
(b) selective, responsibility-oriented reporting.
(c) computation of actuals in different spheres of performance.
(d) reporting of significant variances.

22. Five Ms of management are
(a) Man, Money, Materials, Machinery and Methods
(b) Manager, Muscle, Machinery, Methods and Marketing
(c) Marketing, Monitoring, Motivation, Machinery and Methods
(d) Marketing, Manpower, Muscle power, Motivation and Methods

23. Management is
(a) a science (b) an art
(c) Both (a) and (b) (d) None of these

24. Esprit de corps principle of management states that
(a) labour turnover should be minimised.
(b) there is a need for teamwork.
(c) there should be only one superior for each subordinate.
(d) discipline should be maintained.

25. 'Matrix organisation' refers to a term of
(a) mathematical arrangement of events in columns and rows.
(b) organisation where authority and responsibility coexist.
(c) organisation in which two or more basic types of departmentation are combined.
(d) None of the above.

26. Role of marketing has become vital because of changes and increased ______.
(a) competition (b) technological
(c) Both (a) and (b) (d) None of these

27. Promotional activities involve establishing contact with the ____ and ____ customers.
(a) prospective (b) existing
(c) Both (a) and (b) (d) None of these

28. In credit sales payment of price is postponed for _____ after the sale takes place.
(a) one year (b) five year
(c) postponed (d) a period

29. ______ refers to the division concerning product line or which product will be offered in different markets.
(a) Market mix (b) Ratio analysis
(c) Product mix (d) None of these

30. Role of the middlemen is to ______ out buyers and sellers and match goods to the requirements of market.
(a) find (b) search
(c) Both (a) and (b) (d) None of these

31. Banks ask for ______ security while granting cash credit.
(a) fixed (b) collateral
(c) bilateral (d) None of these

32. Enumerate the various points of difference between cash credit and bank overdraft.
(a) The amount of credit in case of cash credit depends upon the value of securities offered. But overdraft limits is decided on the average balance of the customers in his account.
(b) Overdraft is granted without the security of tangible assets. But for cash credit security of tangible assets is an essential requirement.

(c) In case of cash credit, the amount of credit is placed in a separate account of the borrower. Overdraft limit is generally granted to an existing account of the customer.
(d) All of the above.

33. In case of good profits, company pays higher dividend.
(a) Merits to management
(b) Demerits to management
(c) Merits to shareholders
(d) Demerits to shareholders

34. Which of the following is a method for accounting of risk in capital budgeting?
(a) Sensitivity technique
(b) Probability technique
(c) Decision tree analysis
(d) All of the above

35. Which of the factors do not influence the level of working capital?
(a) Operating capital (b) Nature of business
(c) Profit (d) Sales

36. Data obtained from job analysis has utility for all but which of the following human resource management activities?
(a) Labour relations (b) Selection
(c) Training (d) Job redesign

37. The Human Relations Theory can be termed as
(a) Socio-economic theory
(b) Humanistic theory
(c) Either (a) or (b)
(d) Both (a) and (b)

38. Which of the following is not a reason for the increased use of human resources department in the strategic planning process?
(a) A workforce that is becoming most demanding with regard to job satisfaction and the quality of work life.
(b) Changes in the composition of work force.
(c) The societal shift towards greater conservation.
(d) None of the above.

39. Which of the following is the external source of recruitment?
(a) Unsolicited applicants.
(b) Promotion from within.
(c) Transfer of employees.
(d) None of the above.

40. Vestibule training is provided
(a) training department
(b) on the job
(c) in the class room
(d) None of the above

41. How many banks were nationalized in the first phases in India?
(a) 14 (b) 12 (c) 8 (d) 18

42. Expansion of deposit through expanding loans and advances by commercial banks is known as ______
(a) Trade discount (b) Credit creation
(c) Bank advances (d) Deposit

43. If interest is charged on full amount of loan (principal) throughout the entire tenure of the loan is
(a) Flat rate (b) Float rate
(c) Diminishing rate (d) Fixed rate

44. Which part of the Constitution of India is known as “Code of Administrators”?
(a) Part I (b) Part II (c) Part III (d) Part IV

45. In which year the first central bank in the world was established?
(a) 1680 (b) 1668 (c) 1660 (d) 1670

46. In which year was the EXIM Bank established?
(a) 1982 (b) 1985 (c) 1986 (d) 1988

47. Letter of credit is now becoming an increasingly popular method of financing
(a) Distribution of dividend
(b) Fixed capital needs
(c) Working capital needs
(d) Redemption of debentures

48. Globalization of financial services is being promoted by
(a) International Bank for Reconstruction and Development
(b) World Trade Organization
(c) International Monetary Fund
(d) International Finance Corporation

49. Mercantilism originated in
(a) Britain (b) Span
(c) France (d) Germany

50. Physiocracy which developed as commercial capitalism was yielding place to

(a) Communism (b) Socialism
(c) Industrial capitalism (d) Feudalism

PAPER–III

1. What was the rate of growth of industrial production during the Sixth Plan?
(a) 4.5% (b) 7% (c) 5.5% (d) 6%
2. What are the important external factors that constitute the economic environment of business?
(a) Economic system
(b) Economic condition
(c) Economic policy
(d) All of the above
3. When did the population policy in India receive a new impetus?
(a) In April 1976 (b) In May 1976
(c) In May 1977 (d) In June 1977
4. A vacancy caused by resignation of an auditor is filled by
(a) general meeting
(b) board of directors
(c) managing director
(d) None of the above
5. Membership of the Institute of Company Secretaries of India is a qualification which a person shall possess in order to be eligible for appointment as a secretary in the case of
(a) all public sector undertakings.
(b) a company having a paid-up capital of ₹ 20 lakhs or less.
(c) companies in which public are substantially interested.
(d) a company having a paid-up share capital of ₹ 25 lakhs or more.
6. Goodwill of a firm of A and B is valued at ₹ 30,000. It is appearing in the books at ₹ 12,000. C is admitted for 1/4 share, what amount he is supposed to bring for goodwill?
(a) ₹ 7,500 (b) ₹ 10,500
(c) ₹ 3,000 (d) ₹ 4,500
7. A firm earns a profit of ₹ 15,000 per year. In the same business a 10% return is generally expected. The total assets of the firm are ₹ 1,70,000. The value of other liabilities is ₹ 60,000. What is the value of goodwill?
(a) ₹ 40,000 (b) ₹ 50,000
(c) ₹ 20,000 (d) ₹ 30,000
8. Redeemable preference shares are
(a) Current assets
(b) Non-current assets
(c) Current liabilities
(d) Non-current liabilies
9. Project Engineering Ltd. has an adverse current ratio which one of the following would improve this ratio?
(a) Collection of some of the current accounts receivables.
(b) Sale of fixed assets for cash.
(c) Collection from sundry debtors.
(d) Use of cash to pay off some long term debts.
10. The ratios which measure relative contribution of financing by owners and financing provided by outsiders are called
(a) Leverage Ratio
(b) Liquidity Ratio
(c) Profitability Ratio
(d) Activity Ratio
11. Total utility is maximum when marginal utility is
(a) zero (b) rising (c) positive (d) negative
12. In case of demand curve, if lower segment is greater than upper segment, then e_p will be
(a) 3 (b) 2
(c) greater than one (d) lower than one
13. Total revenue is maximum when elasticity of demand is
(a) 1 (b) 3 (c) 0 (d) 0.5
14. Which of the following dimensions is external to the leaders?
(a) Relations (b) Task
(c) Attitude (d) Style
15. Imperfect competition was introduced by
(a) Keynes (b) Marshall
(c) Chamberlaine (d) None of these
16. As the value of x increases, if y also increases, then coefficient of correlation will be

(a) zero (b) negative
(c) positive (d) none of these

17. Relationship of two or more variables is examined excluding some other variables in case of
(a) multiple correlation (b) total correlation
(c) partial correlation (d) none of the above

18. Karl Pearson's coefficient of correlation is based on the assumption by
(a) Platykurtic (b) Leptokurtic
(c) Normality (d) None of these

19. Coefficient of correlation in case of frequency distribution could not be calculated in case of
(a) least square method (b) Karl Pearson
(c) Spearman (d) none of the above

20. ______ is the original hypothesis.
(a) Statistical analysis (b) Probability
(c) Null hypothesis (d) None of these

21. When jobs are broadened in scope and complexity so that the person's overall area of job responsibility increases, it is a case of
(a) job enrichment (b) job rotation
(c) job enlargement (d) job specification

22. An important aspect of control is that the
(a) manager sets as effective management information system.
(b) plans are checked before implementation against predetermined measures of performance.
(c) performance is checked against predetermined standards.
(d) manager motivates his subordinates to give better performance.

23. Scalar principle refers to the
(a) existence of a clear line of authority in all parts of the organization.
(b) responsibility of a subordinate to a superior.
(c) delegation of authority at all levels of an organization.
(d) conflict of instructions from two or more superiors.

24. The internal mail implies
(a) the letters posted within India.
(b) the written messages transmitted within the organisation.
(c) the letters posted in the same city.
(d) None of the above.

25. Indexing is an important
(a) method of maintaining statistical books.
(b) aid to filing.
(c) method of maintaining account books.
(d) method of filing.

26. Informing buyers of new brand and new package is the ______ of sales promotion.
(a) application (b) objective
(c) method (d) None of these

27. By advertising copy is meant the ______, contents, colour and presentation of the message of advertisement.
(a) shape (b) size
(c) quality (d) None of these

28. Salesman explains to the customers by giving a ______ of how to use it.
(a) demonstration (b) action
(c) Both (a) and (b) (d) None of these

29. Which of the following is/are not factors of the demand variable, according to Philip Kotler?
(a) Competition variable
(b) Environment variable
(c) Customer variable
(d) All of the above

30. Which one of the following is/are not element of marketing mix?
(a) Product (b) Promotion
(c) Place (d) None of these

31. Which of these is not an essential element of optimum or ideal capital structure?
(a) Minimum risk (b) Flexibility
(c) Simplicity (d) Minimumcontrol

32. The third stage of change in capital structure shows the
(a) Constant value (b) Declining value
(c) Optimum value (d) Increasing value

33. Operating costs of the firm include
(a) those costs which vary directly with the sales volume.
(b) those costs which are partly fixed and partly variable.
(c) those costs which do not vary with sales volume.
(d) All of the above.

34. Which among these is not a specific cost?
    (a) Cost of retained earnings
    (b) Cost of an asset
    (c) Cost of debt
    (d) None of the above
35. Which of the following pairs will give consistent results in terms of acceptance or rejection of an investment proposal?
    (a) ARR: Profitability Index
    (b) IRR and NPV (Net Present Value)
    (c) Pay-back: IRR (Internal Rate of Return) Method
    (d) None of the above
36. Which of the following is classified in the category of the developmental research?
    (a) Philosophical research
    (b) Action research
    (c) Descriptive research
    (d) All of the above
37. Job analysis should always be done
    (a) at the time of placement
    (b) before recruitment
    (c) after recruitment
    (d) None of the above
38. Where the work can't be measured the working force can be easily controlled the wage payment must be
    (a) according to time (b) according to pieces
    (c) Any of the above (d) None of these
39. "No temptation to increase the quantity at the cost of quality" is
    (a) piece rate system (b) time rate system
    (c) Both of the above (d) None of these
40. The Human Relations Theory does not lay emphasis on
    (a) human motivations (b) principles
    (c) informal group (d) people functions
41. "Cash credit granted to a customer is drawn by him as and when needed and not all at once." Do you agree with this?
    (a) Can't say (b) No
    (c) Yes (d) None of these
42. When was the Reserve Bank of India Act passed?
    (a) March 6, 1934 (b) March 6, 1930
    (c) March 6, 1937 (d) March 6, 1935
43. RBI introduced ______ scheme in 1969.
    (a) Lead Bank (b) DIRE
    (c) SAA (d) Village Adaptation
44. The Schedule of Banking Act is related with
    (a) Fixed Assets (b) Interest
    (c) Capital (d) Investments
45. The financial position of a commercial bank is reflected in its
    (a) Cash Flow Statement
    (b) Profit and Loss Account
    (c) Fund Flow Statement
    (d) Balance Sheet
46. India should export according to H-O Theory
    (a) labour intensive goods
    (b) capital intensive goods
    (c) Both (a) and (b)
    (d) None of the above
47. Leontief tested his hypothesis with the help of
    (a) input-output table (b) demand curve
    (c) cost curve (d) none of the above
48. Prebisch's argument is concerned with deterioration in terms of trade against
    (a) oil producing countries
    (b) developed countries
    (c) undeveloped countries
    (d) developing countries
49. Protection creates
    (a) corruption (b) inefficiency
    (c) vested interest (d) all of the above
50. Immersing growth refers to a situation where
    (a) gains from trade is more than offset by deterioration in terms of trade.
    (b) deterioration in terms of trade more than offset gains from trade.
    (c) a country promotes exports.
    (d) None of the above.

ANSWER SHEET

PAPER–I

1. (c)	2. (c)	3. (a)	4. (d)	5. (d)
6. (a)	7. (d)	8. (b)	9. (d)	10. (b)
11. (d)	12. (a)	13. (c)	14. (c)	15. (a)

16. (c)	17. (a)	18. (b)	19. (a)	20. (c)
21. (d)	22. (a)	23. (c)	24. (a)	25. (b)
26. (b)	27. (b)	28. (c)	29. (d)	30. (b)
31. (b)	32. (c)	33. (a)	34. (c)	35. (b)
36. (b)	37. (a)	38. (b)	39. (d)	40. (a)
41. (d)	42. (c)	43. (a)	44. (b)	45. (c)
46. (b)	47. (d)	48. (b)	49. (c)	50. (c)

PAPER–II

1. (b)	2. (c)	3. (a)	4. (c)	5. (c)
6. (c)	7. (c)	8. (c)	9. (a)	10. (c)
11. (b)	12. (b)	13. (c)	14. (a)	15. (a)
16. (a)	17. (c)	18. (d)	19. (d)	20. (b)
21. (d)	22. (a)	23. (c)	24. (b)	25. (a)
26. (c)	27. (c)	28. (d)	29. (c)	30. (c)
31. (b)	32. (d)	33. (c)	34. (d)	35. (a)
36. (a)	37. (c)	38. (a)	39. (a)	40. (a)
41. (a)	42. (b)	43. (a)	44. (d)	45. (b)
46. (a)	47. (a)	48. (d)	49. (d)	50. (a)

PAPER–III

1. (c)	2. (d)	3. (a)	4. (a)	5. (b)
6. (d)	7. (a)	8. (d)	9. (b)	10. (a)
11. (a)	12. (c)	13. (a)	14. (d)	15. (c)
16. (c)	17. (c)	18. (c)	19. (c)	20. (c)
21. (c)	22. (c)	23. (a)	24. (b)	25. (b)
26. (b)	27. (c)	28. (a)	29. (d)	30. (d)
31. (d)	32. (b)	33. (b)	34. (b)	35. (b)
36. (a)	37. (b)	38. (a)	39. (b)	40. (b)
41. (c)	42. (a)	43. (a)	44. (d)	45. (d)
46. (a)	47. (c)	48. (c)	49. (a)	50. (c)

MOCK TEST–2
PAPER–I

1. Minimum program of guidance includes
   (a) occupational information service
   (b) data collector service
   (c) counselling service
   (d) All of these
2. If majority of students in a class is weak, a teacher should
   (a) not care about intelligent students
   (b) keep his speed of teaching fast so that students' comprehension level may increase
   (c) keep his teaching slow which can also be helpful-to bright students
   (d) keep his teaching slow along with some extra guidance to bright students
3. If the principal of your institution is not satisfied with your performance and charges you with the act of negligence of duties, how would you behave with him?
   (a) You would neglect him
   (b) You would take revenge by giving physical and mental agony to him
   (c) You would keep yourself alert and make his efforts unfruitful
   (d) You would take a tough stand against the charges
4. What makes people to undertake research?
   (a) Desire to get intellectual joy of doing some creative work
   (b) Desire to get a research degree along with its consequential benefits
   (c) Desire to face the challenge in solving the unsolved problems
   (d) All of these
5. Which of the following aims at probing into the phenomenon to formulate a more precise research problem or to develop a new hypothesis?
   (a) Descriptive research
   (b) Conclusive research
   (c) Diagnostic research
   (d) Exploratory research
6. Which of the following is not instructional material?
   (a) Transparency (b) Overhead projector
   (c) Printed material (d) Audio cassette
7. Of great importance in determining the amount of transference that occurs in the process of learning is the

(a) knowledge of the teacher
(b) IQ of the teacher
(c) presence of identical elements
(d) use of appropriate elements

8. The characteristic(s) of hypothesis is/are:
   I. It can be tested.
   II. It must consist of known facts.
   III. It must be objective and specific.
   (a) Only I and III (b) Only I and II
   (c) Only I (d) All of these

9. The guide for the research requires which of the following qualities?
   (a) Interdisciplinary expertise
   (b) Subject matter expertise
   (c) Methodological expertise
   (d) All of these

10. Which of the following indicates evaluation?
   (a) Seema got 195 marks out of 200
   (b) Sapna got 72 percent marks in English
   (c) Asha got First Division in final examination
   (d) All of the above

Direction (11-16): Study the following passage and give answer to the questions based on it.

Much of the theoretical literature of archeology in the 1980s devotes considerable energy to bashing the 1970s, and the target often turns out to be the so-called New or Processual Archeology. While many of the attacks come from recent theorists who are attempting to replace it with post-processual archeology, some criticism comes from within what was New Archeology even from the hand of its original champion, Lewis Binford. If scholars from both outside and inside the theoretical developments of the 1970s are rejecting the New Archeology, why am I defending its importance to us today? The answer is very simple...for better or worse, it is us! As Alison Whylie has recently said the New Archeology of the 1960s quickly became everybody's archeology in the 1970s. Most of today's faculty members and senior archeologists were the people who, in one way or another, adopted the teachings of New Archeology. Although most archeologists did not claim to agree with all aspects of New Archeology nor could more than two or three people agree on what it was, virtually one rejected it outright. Typically, each one presented her or his version, often using a New Archeology text as a starting point for pedagogical purposes. Few wanted to be left out of the exciting new theoretical movement of those years, and New Archeology was passed on to the succeeding generation of students who reached maturity in the 1980s and are today's young professionals.

Criticisms now leveled against the New Archeology of the seventies do have merit, but by discounting that era as misguided, critics have overlooked its crucial importance. New Archeology has an important historical role in the developments of the field we have today and it has continuing importance because it is still guiding archeology's trajectory into the future. Equally troubling is that some critics ask us to reject the basic tenets of New Archeology and to replace them with a system often called post processualist archeology. I believe this is rhetoric that not only misrepresents the achievements of the New Archeology of the seventies, but also does not successfully articulate the potential contributions of its own position.

To put the New Archeology of the seventies into perspective, it is important to review the decades leading up to its development. In the first years following World War II, archeology was still a small field, but by the fifties and the sixties, it was expanding rapidly and taking itself quite seriously. Since the launching of Sputnik in 1957 there had emerged a frenzy in the United States to make all disciplines more scientific. Great strides were made in bringing science into archeology through new dating techniques a multidisciplinary approach, early experiments with the use of statistics, and devoting substantial attention to increasing the precision of artifact classification. The sixties provided the nation with both the optimistic Kennedy years, with an emphasis on science and the conviction that we were capable of accomplishing wondrous; things, and the cynical Vietnam era. Coming on the heels of a decade of civil rights unrest, the widespread dissatisfaction with the Vietnam conflict in the late sixties molded a generation of young Americans who were distrustful of established authority. In academic life, there was an increasing emphasis on environment, other cultures, and people-oriented disciplines. Anthropology and archeology grew markedly because of these trends. Archeologists were urged to become concerned with sociological issues—the people behind the artifacts.

It was during these decades of rapid change that many of the core concepts of the New Archeology entered the literature. However, they were not, at first, assembled into a program for action that attracted a solid following. Water Taylor advocated the conjuctive approach with little effect, while Leslie White's evolutionism and Julian Styeward's cultural ecology attracted some attention, but largely among cultural anthropologists. Albert Spaulding led a one-man campaign to bring science and statistics into archeology. But the individual whose work catalyzed the New Archeology movement was Lewis Binford, who incorporated these earlier lines of thinking together with an explicit concern for scientific methods and field research designs. Much of Binford's thinking probably crystallised while he was at the University of Michigan, but was during his relatively few years at the University of Chicago that he changed the direction of modern archeology.

11. New Archeology refers to
    (a) newer techniques used in Archeology
    (b) newer inventions used in Archeology
    (c) newer theoretical foundations in Archeology
    (d) None of these
12. The author defends the Archeology of the 1970s because
    (a) he has a nostalgic feeling about it
    (b) it has research value
    (c) it paved way for newer traditions
    (d) it has historical value
13. The author suggests that
    (a) We should respect new Archeology as a movement in Archeology
    (b) We should go back to the tenets of processual Archeology
    (c) We should treat tenets of new Archeology with respect
    (d) All of the above
14. The importance of Archeology arose from
    (a) the end of World War II
    (b) an increasing scientific outlook
    (c) the launch of Sputnik in 1957
    (d) All of these
15. Which one of the following is not an area of focus for archeologist?
    (a) Study the interaction of people of small group
    (b) Studying cultures of other people
    (c) Study the social structure of the past societies
    (d) Study the man-environment relationship in the past
16. An archeologist is concerned with
    (a) classification of artefacts
    (b) maintenance of museums
    (c) digging of ancient cities
    (d) All of these
17. Rhetorics means
    (a) study of the technique and rules for using language effectively
    (b) using language effectively to please or persuade
    (c) excessive use of verbal ornamentation
    (d) All of the above
18. If a receiver replying on 'hmm-mm' or 'Isee'. This type of reply is known as
    (a) positive feedback
    (b) ambiguous feedback
    (c) negative feedback
    (d) None of these
19. Which of the following FM radio stations is owned by the Times of India group?
    (a) AIR (b) Radio Rainbow
    (c) Radio Mirchi (d) Red FM
20. Find the next number in the following sequence:
    9, 8, 25, 12, 49, 18, 121, 26, ?, ?
    (a) 142, 36 (b) 169, 36
    (c) 225, 36 (d) 196, 36
21. **Read the following and Choose the correct option.**

    Statement: Should there be complete ban on pouched tobacco products (like Gutka) in India?

    Arguments:
    (i) Yes, it is the most important cause of mouth cancer and mouth ulcer in our country.
    (ii) No, there are many people employed in this industry right from manufacturing

to retailing. This ban will hamper their livelihood.

(a) Only argument (i) is strong
(b) Only argument (ii) is strong
(c) Both the arguments (i) and (ii) are strong
(d) Neither (i) nor (ii) is strong

22. The relationship between Animal, Cows, Dogs can be shown by

(a) 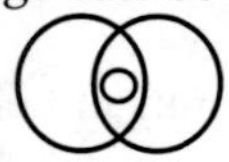 (b) 

(c) 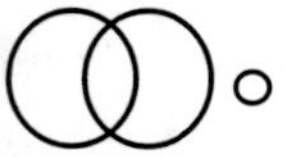 (d) 

23. If in a certain code:

'nso prt kli chn' means 'sharma gets marriage gift'.

'pit lnm wop chn' means 'wife gives marriage gift'. 'tti wop nhi' means 'he gives nothing'. What would mean gives:

(a) kli (b) tti (c) wop (d) lnm

24. Characteristics of all informal and formal communications are

(a) same (b) structured
(c) different (d) none of these

25. Three of the following four are alike in a certain way and so form a group. Find the one which doesn't belong to that group?

(a) Dog (b) Tiger (c) Horse (d) Lion

26. What is research design?

(a) The methods used in analysis and finding the final conclusion is known as research design
(b) A researcher needs to prepare a plan of action for his study which is known as research design
(c) The presentation of final data is known as research design
(d) None of these

27. Recording a television program on a Set Top Box is an example of

(a) content reference
(b) time-shifting
(c) media synchronisation
(d) mechanical clarity

28. Which of the following statements say the same thing?

(i) "I am a teacher" (said by Arvind)
(ii) "I am a teacher" (said by Binod)
(iii) "My son is a teacher" (said by Binod's father)
(iv) "My brother is a teacher" (said by Binod's sister)
(v) "My brother is a teacher" (said by Binod's only sister)
(vi) "My sole enemy is a teacher" (said by Binod's only enemy)

Choose the correct answer from the codes given below:

Codes:

(a) (v) and (vi) (b) (i) and (ii)
(c) (ii) and (vi) (d) (ii), (iii), (iv) and (v)

29. In this question there are two statements followed by four conclusions numbered I, II, III and IV.

Statements:

A. All books are trees. B. All trees are lions.

Conclusions:

I. All books are lions.
II. All lions are books.
III. All trees are books.
IV. Some lions are books.

Choose the correct answer.

(a) Only I and IV follow
(b) Only II and III follow
(c) None of conclusions follow
(d) All conclusions follow

Directions (30-34): Answer the questions based on following table.

Machines X and Y can independently produce either product P or product Q. The time taken by machines X and Y (in minutes) to produce one unit of product P and Q are given in the table below. (Each machine works 8 hours per day.)

Product	X	Y
P	10	8
Q	6	6

30. If the number of units of P is to be three times that of Q, what is the maximum idle time to maximise total units manufactured?

(a) 8 minutes (b) 0 minute
(c) 12 minutes (d) None of these

31. If X works at half its normal efficiency, what is the maximum number of units produced, if at least one unit of each must be produced?

(a) 119 (b) 135 (c) 127 (d) 136

32. What is the maximum number of units that can be manufactured in one day?
(a) 250 (b) 160 (c) 270 (d) 195

33. If equal quantities of both are to be produced, then out of four choice given below the least efficient way would be
(a) 59 of each with 8 min. idle
(b) 71 of each with 9 min. idle
(c) 53 of each with 10 min. idle
(d) 48 of each with 4 min. idle

34. What is the least number of machine hours required to produce 30 pieces of P and 25 pieces of Q respectively?
(a) 6 hr 30 min. (b) 9 hr 30 min.
(c) 6 hr 40 min. (d) 8 hr 30 min.

35. Telematic is a combination of
(a) Telecommunication and computer
(b) Telecommunication and information
(c) Television and computer
(d) All of the above

36. Following is a part of balance sheet of Timas Pvt. Ltd. Study the table and choose the correct option:

(All values in ₹ crore)

Year	Expenditure	Income
1990	3400	4000
1995	3800	4500
2000	4500	5400
2005	6400	8000

Which of the following conclusions is not true?
(a) There has been a steady growth in % profit of the company
(b) There is around 90% increase in expenditure of the firm from 1990 to 2005
(c) Income of the company is doubled in 15 years
(d) Percentage profit in 2000 was 18%

37. If EFGHUK is coded as VUTSRQ then LIMIT can be coded as
(a) KNRNC (b) ORNRG
(c) JKOKG (d) RSTSG

38. The more is 'Resolution Power' of a printer better is its
(a) Speed (b) Colour
(c) Memory (d) Quality

39. Laterite soil develops due to
(a) deposits of alluvial
(b) deposition of losses
(c) leaching
(d) continued vegetation cover

40. Line access and avoidance of collision are the main functions of
(a) network protocols
(b) wide area networks
(c) the CPU
(d) the monitor

41. Communication satellites are placed in
(a) Geostationary Orbit (b) Polar Orbit
(c) Both (a) and (b) (d) None of these

42. DLL stands for
(a) Data Deriving Language
(b) Data Definition Language
(c) Data Design Language
(d) All of the above

43. Transistors were first used in
(a) 2nd generation computers
(b) 3rd generation computers
(c) 4th generation computers
(d) None of these

44. Which of the following is not provided in the constitution?
(a) Planning Commission
(b) Election Commission
(c) Finance Commission
(d) Public Service Commission

45. The 1st satellite launched in space was
(a) Early Bird (b) Sputnik-1
(c) Skylab (d) Aryabhatta-1

46. At what time between 5.30 and 6.00 will the hands of a clock be at right angles?
(a) 45 minutes past 5
(b) 478/11 minutes past 5
(c) 480/11 minutes past 5
(d) 40 minutes past 5

47. A person can be a member of Council of Ministers without being a member of Parliament for a maximum period of
(a) 45 days (b) 90 days
(c) 180 days (d) one year

48. Many engineers and architects use a different type of pen called a
(a) Pointer pen (b) Computer pen
(c) Light pen (d) Logical pen

49. Which of the following are wrongly matched?

Name of Volcano	Country
(a) Mt. Spur	USA
(b) Mt. Fuego	Guatemala
(c) Mt. Ag'ung	Indonesia
(d) Mt. Lascor	Equador

50. How many types of emergency can be declared by the President of India?
(a) 1 (b) 2 (c) 3 (d) 4

PAPER–II

1. The factors included in the total environment of business are
(a) Economic (b) Political-legal
(c) Social culture (d) All of the above
2. The new economic policy has components
(a) Privatisation (b) Globalisation
(c) Liberalisation (d) All of the above
3. The feature of the industrial policy is
(a) liberalisation of foreign investment and technological participation.
(b) delicensing with certain exceptions.
(c) Both (a) and (b).
(d) None of the above.
4. The expanded production of fertilizers, textiles and buildings require some
(a) economical growth.
(b) power production.
(c) domestic production of the necessary capital goods.
(d) None of the above.
5. In which industry, units in the co-operative sector account for over half of the total production?
(a) Petrochemical industry
(b) Steel industry
(c) Sugar industry
(d) None of the above
6. How many sides does an account have?
(a) One (b) Two (c) Three (d) None
7. Sales to Benson ₹ 500 posted to his account as ₹ 50 would affect
(a) Benson's account (b) Cash account
(c) Sales account (d) None of the above
8. Sales journal is used to record
(a) credit sales of assets.
(b) credit sales of goods.
(c) cash sales.
(d) None of the above.
9. Goods sold for cash is an example of
(a) Revenue (b) Expenses
(c) Loss (d) Liability
10. Purchase of typewriter would result in _____ of fund.
(a) service (b) no flow
(c) change (d) application
11. When a commodity with many uses is demanded then it is called
(a) direct demand (b) composite demand
(c) joint demand (d) None of the above
12. For the relationship between AC and MC, which of the following statement is wrong?
(a) If AC rises, MC also rises.
(b) Both AC and MC are calculated from TC.
(c) For the minimum point of AC, average cost is equal to marginal cost.
(d) If AC Falls, MC will rise.
13. Demand curve was drawn with empirical evidence by
(a) indifference curve (b) utility
(c) revealed preference (d) None of these
14. The reason behind goods could not be explained by
(a) indifference curve (b) utility theory
(c) Both (a) and (b) (d) None of these
15. In case of veblen goods, demand curve will slope
(a) Vertically (b) Horizontally
(c) Downward (d) Upward
16. Choose the methods of sampling
(a) Non-probability sampling or non-random sampling
(b) Probability sampling or random sampling
(c) Both (a) and (b)
(d) None of the above
17. Data integrity refers to the
(a) privacy of data (b) simplicity of data
(c) security of data (d) validity of data
18. A model in which one physical property is used to represent another physical property is known as

(a) ionic model
(b) decision theory model
(c) deterministic model
(d) analog model

19. Quantitative techniques used to solve business problems are called
(a) operation science
(b) operation management
(c) operation research
(d) None of the above

20. Range of the coefficient of correlation is
(a) +1 (b) 0.25 (c) +2 (d) 0.5

21. Memory unit is a part of
(a) electronic data processing.
(b) punched card system.
(c) both electronic data processing and punched card system.
(d) both punched card system and manually operated accounting machines.

22. An analogue computer makes
(a) measurements but not calculations.
(b) calculations but not measurement.
(c) both measurements and calculations.
(d) None of the above.

23. Partnership may come into existence
(a) by an express agreement only.
(b) by the operation of the law.
(c) by inheritance of property.
(d) by an express or implied agreement only.

24. An association of persons becomes partnership
(a) when its purpose is to carry on business for profit motive.
(b) when its purpose is to carry on some charitable work.
(c) when its purpose is to render services for general welfare of mankind.
(d) All of the above.

25. A nominal partner is
(a) entitled to equal share in the profits unless there is an agreement to any other profit showing ratio.
(b) not liable to third parties.
(c) not entitled to share the profits of the concern.
(d) not liable for the acts of other partners.

26. Some retailers provide free home delivery service to their
(a) consumers (b) customer
(c) Both (a) and (b) (d) None of these

27. Retail demonstrations are supplied by manufacturers for preparing and distributing the products as retail
(a) price (b) sample
(c) products (d) None of these

28. Newspapers happen to be suitable media for advertising ______ products used by masses.
(a) wholesaler (b) retailer
(c) consumer (d) customer

29. Which concept of marketing is/are customer oriented?
(a) Entity concept of business
(b) Modern concept of marketing
(c) Old concept of marketing
(d) All of the above

30. Sub-division marketing is called
(a) Allocation of marketing
(b) Decision of market
(c) Only segmentation
(d) Market segmentation

31. Discounted cash flow technique involves
(a) accounting rate of return
(b) net present value
(c) payback method
(d) None of the above

32. The minimum amount of current assets needed to conduct a business even during the dullest season of that year is known as
(a) variable working capital
(b) fixed working capital
(c) net working capital
(d) gross working capital

33. Which among the following is an assumption of the NOI approach?
(a) The cost of capital is dynamic.
(b) The capitalisation rate is constant.
(c) The value of equity is not a residual value.
(d) All of the above.

34. Financial leverage can be measured in
(a) flow term (b) stock term
(c) Both (a) and (b) (d) None of the above

35. Historical weight takes into account
(a) the past benefits accruing due to investment in assets.

(b) the long-term implications of firm's current finaricing.
(c) the market value of assets.
(d) None of the above.

36. In Emerson plan
(a) minimum wages are guaranteed.
(b) payments are on the basis of output.
(c) minimum wages are not guaranteed.
(d) None of the above.

37. Behavioural factors consist of
(a) physical fitness
(b) personal attitudes
(c) behaviour patterns and work habits
(d) None of the above

38. The purpose of induction of training is
(a) to receive the earlier learning in the minds of employees.
(b) to enable the trainee to overcome nervousness and get the best out of training.
(c) to finalise the new entrants to the organisation, its objectives, rules and working conditions.
(d) None of the above.

39. Incentives given on psychological base
(a) monetary and non-monetary
(b) are not financial
(c) are financial
(d) None of the above

40. Human resource can be valued like any other asset.
(a) False (b) True
(c) Both (a) and (b) (d) None of these

41. Which one of the following banks was the first public banking institution in world?
(a) Bank of Venice (b) Bank of Japan
(c) Bank of England (d) Bank of Hindustan

42. Indian coastal areas experienced Tsunami disaster in the year
(a) 2005 (b) 2004 (c) 2006 (d) 2007

43. The RBI was nationalised in
(a) 1948 (b) 1950 (c) 1940 (d) 1942

44. Apex bank for rural credit is
(a) LDB (b) NABARD
(c) RRB (d) PACS

45. Which of the following is the name of the asset reconstruction company created by various banks in India?
(a) SBI (b) HCR (c) AMFI (d) ARCIL

46. According to Heckscher-Ohlin theory, capital abundant country will export
(a) labour intensive goods
(b) capital intensive goods
(c) Both (a) and (b)
(d) None of the above

47. Factor price equalisation takes place when
(a) factor intensity in different countries is same.
(b) marginal productivity of factors of production in different countries is same.
(c) Both (a) and (b).
(d) None of the above.

48. Net barter terms of trade is
(a) $\frac{P_x}{P_m} \times 100$ (b) $P_x \cdot P_m$
(c) $\frac{P_m}{P_x}$ (d) None of these

49. Adam Smith advocated
(a) custom duty (b) quantitative restriction
(c) free trade (d) None of the above

50. Korea had followed
(a) export promotion policy.
(b) import substitution policy.
(c) Both (a) and (b).
(d) None of the above.

PAPER–III

1. A qualified company secretary is needed to be appointed as secretary to a company only on the basis of the
(a) paid-up capital of the company.
(b) business of the company.
(c) listing of the company on any stock exchange.
(d) location of the company.

2. In verification of assets, the duty of the auditor is
(a) to satisfy himself that they are properly valued.
(b) to satisfy himself with regard to the existence, ownership and value of the assets.
(c) to ensure that assets have actually been acquired.
(d) to ensure that they are clearly stated in the balance sheet.

3. Which one of the following describes the correct effect when a registered partnership firm is dissolved?
   (a) The partners cannot start any other business within one year of dissolution.
   (b) One or two of the old partners can continue the business of the firm with a new name.
   (c) The partners will not be entitled to any personal loans from banks.
   (d) All the partners will be relieved from the debt obligations of the firm.
4. When a statement in lieu of prospectus is to be filed with the Registrar of Companies, it must be drafted in accordance with the particulars set out in which of the following?
   (a) Schedule III (b) Rule 4-CCCA
   (c) Table E (d) Schedule II
5. To whom, is the auditor's report pursuant to a special audit of a company furnished?
   (a) Board of directors of the company
   (b) Shareholders of the company
   (c) Concerned State Government(s)
   (d) Central Government
6. Payment of interim dividend is a
   (a) no flow of fund (b) service of fund
   (c) application of fund (d) all of the above
7. Which one in the following statements is correct?
   (a) An increase in current liabilities causes a decrease in the working capital.
   (b) A decrease in current liabilities causes an increase in the working capital.
   (c) An increase in the current assets cause a decrease in the working capital.
   (d) A decrease in the current assets an increase in the working capital.
8. Prepaid expenses appearing in trial balance will appear in
   (a) Depreciation Account
   (b) Balance Sheet
   (c) Profit and Loss Account
   (d) Trading Account
9. Cost of goods sold = purchases + stock ________ + direct expenses – stock ______.
   (a) closing, valued (b) opening, closing
   (c) closing opening (d) opening, valued
10. Which is the adjustment entry for interest on capital?
   (a) Capital A/C Dr.
   To Interest A/C
   (b) Interest A/C Dr.
   To Capital A/C
   (c) Capital A/C Dr.
   To Interest on Capital
   (d) Interest on Capital A/C Dr.
   To Capital A/C
11. Profit = Total revenue – (?). Choose the suitable answer for blank.
   (a) Total price (b) Total sale
   (c) Total cost (d) None of these
12. Which one of the following statements is incorrect?
   (a) Marginal Product—The decrease in output that arises from an additional unit of input.
   (b) Marginal Product—The increase in output that arises from an additional unit of input.
   (c) Accounting Profit = Total revenue – Total explicit cost.
   (d) Economic Profit = Total revenue – Total cost, including both explicit and implicit costs.
13. A curve on which various combinations of labour and capital show the same output, is called
   (a) Capital (b) Isoquant/Isoproduct
   (c) Factor (d) Cost
14. Which one of the characteristics is not of competitive market?
   (a) The goods offered by the various sellers are largely the same.
   (b) There are many buyers and many sellers in the market.
   (c) Firms cannot freely enter or exit the market.
   (d) Firms can freely enter or exit the market.
15. A cost that has already been committed and cannot be recovered is known as
   (a) Full cost (b) Variable cost
   (c) Sunk cost (d) Total cost
16. These decisions are original and the product of managerial wisdom. These decisions are known as

(a) unprogrammed decision
(b) programmed decision
(c) top-level decisions
(d) middle-level decisions

17. ____ describes the magnitude of difference between observed frequencies and expected frequencies.
(a) F-value (b) t-value
(c) z-value (d) Chi-square value

18. Chi-square test was first used by
(a) Frank Wicoxon (b) Karl Pearson
(c) Simeon Denis Poisson (d) R.A. Fischer

19. It is a business situation in a capsule form. Its purpose is to reduce the complex reality into smaller and manageable dimensions without mutilating the character of the reality.
(a) System (b) Political variables
(c) Economic variables (d) OR model

20. What is mimeography?
(a) A process of blue printing.
(b) A method of photocopying.
(c) A process of digital photography.
(d) A method of stencil duplication.

21. The minimum number of directors in a public limited company is
(a) 7 (b) 10 (c) 2 (d) 3

22. In the case of companies with ability limited by guarantee, the liability of members is limited
(a) to the additional amount payable in addition to the amount of share as laid down in the Memorandum of Association needs to arise.
(b) to the nominal values of shares.
(c) to the called up value of shares.
(d) None of the above.

23. A private limited company can commence business
(a) only when it receives both the certificate of incorporation and certificate of commencement of business.
(b) immediately on receiving a certificate of incorporation.
(c) only when it receives certificate of commencement of business.
(d) without receiving a certificate of incorporation.

24. The life of a co-operative society is
(a) affected by the insolvency of a member.
(b) affected by the withdrawal by a member from membership.
(c) not affected by death, insolvency, etc. of members.
(d) affected by the death of member.

25. Profits earned by a co-operative society are distributed
(a) to members in the ratio of capital held by them.
(b) by declaring dividend at a specific rate and transferring remaining to general reserves.
(c) by providing a nominal rate of interest on capital contribution by members and remaining the ratio of purchases made by members.
(d) to members in the ratio of purchases made by them.

26. Communications model is a representation of the flow of information in a message from its sources to ______ and of the audience's reaction to the message.
(a) customers (b) business firms
(c) audiences (d) none of these

27. A letter of credit means
(a) A bank agreeing to accept and pay on due date
(b) A letter containing conditions of credit purchase or sale
(c) A letter sent by exporter to importer sanctioning credit deal
(d) A letter sent by importer to exporter sanctioning credit deal

28. Which one of the formula may be used for setting prices under cost plus pricing method?
(a) Selling price = Unit total cost + Selling expenses
(b) Selling price = Unit total cost + Desired unit profit
(c) Selling price = Unit total cost + Profit
(d) None of the above

29. Channels of distribution is known as
(a) Proper channel (b) Trade channel
(c) Path channel (d) None of these

30. Which is the primary aim of social marketing?

(a) Service (b) Maximization of profit
(c) Minimization of loss
(d) Social of goods

31. A person insured his property worth ₹ 2,00,000 for ₹ 1,50,000 against fire. His actual loss is ₹ 1,00,000. His claim is
(a) ₹ 1,50,000 (b) ₹ 1,00,000
(c) ₹ 2,00,000 (d) Nil

32. Risk that translation effects of unexpected changes in exchange rates could increase tax liabilities is known as
(a) Economic exposure (b) Finance Exposure
(c) Tax exposure (d) None of the above

33. The factors affecting P/E multiple are
(a) Required return and expected growth rate
(b) Dividend pay-out ratio and required return
(c) Dividend pay-out ratio, required return and expected growth rate
(d) Dividend pay-out ratio and expected growth rate

34. The term current assets does not include
(a) furniture (b) stock
(c) cash (d) advance payment

35. A provision is a
(a) specific reserve (b) capital reserve
(c) general reserve (d) None of these

36. Grievance is affecting one or more individual workers in respect of their conditions of work and not disputes over matters of general applicability to all
(a) information (b) claims
(c) complaint (d) order

37. Personality test includes
(a) Objective tests (b) Projective tests
(c) Training method (d) Both (a) and (b)

38. The career planning and development process is also part of comprehensive organisation development
(a) Communication (b) Process
(c) Finn (d) Project

39. Which of the following includes under techniques of training?
(a) Role playing method
(b) On the job training method
(c) Informal training
(d) All of the above

40. Executive employee training method involves
(a) Transactional analysis training method
(b) Management game method
(c) Understudy
(d) Programme training method

41. The SBI was set-up in
(a) 1935 (b) 1955 (c) 1921 (d) 1949

42. The Bank of England was nationalised in
(a) 1946 (b) 1945 (c) 1949 (d) 1947

43. ______ is the first specialist institution to be established in India soon after independence, in July 1948.
(a) General Insurance Corporation
(b) State Bank of India
(c) The Industrial Finance Corporation of India
(d) Reserve Bank of India

44. Unit Banking means a system of banking under which banking services are provided a single banking organisation. Do you agree with this statement?
(a) Sometimes (b) Can't say
(c) No (d) Yes

45. ____ controls the monetary system and the over all credit operation of the banks.
(a) Reserve Bank of India
(b) Central Government
(c) Finance Minister
(d) State Bank of India

46. Expressions/abbreviations with their respective definitions and the obligations that each implies for the buyer and the seller is called
(a) Harmonised system (b) Loading
(c) Incoterm (d) None of the above

47. Accommodating capital flows are
(a) Planned (b) Unplanned
(c) Both (a) and (b) (d) Either (a) or (b)

48. Imbalance in the balance of payment can be corrected through policy changes in
(a) Current account (b) Capital account
(c) Both (a) and (b) (d) Either (a) or (b)

49. Gold standard is an example of
(a) floating exchange rate
(b) fixed exchange rate
(c) Both of the above
(d) None of the above

50. The Swan diagram explains

(a) both internal and external equilibrium.
(b) either internal or external equilibrium.
(c) internal equilibrium.
(d) external equilibriurn.

ANSWER SHEET

PAPER–I

1. (d)	2. (d)	3. (c)	4. (d)	5. (d)
6. (a)	7. (b)	8. (d)	9. (d)	10. (d)
11. (d)	12. (c)	13. (c)	14. (b)	15. (a)
16. (d)	17. (d)	18. (b)	19. (c)	20. (b)
21. (a)	22. (b)	23. (c)	24. (c)	25. (c)
26. (b)	27. (b)	28. (c)	29. (b)	30. (b)
31. (a)	32. (b)	33. (c)	34. (a)	35. (b)
36. (d)	37. (b)	38. (d)	39. (c)	40. (a)
41. (a)	42. (b)	43. (a)	44. (a)	45. (b)
46. (c)	47. (c)	48. (c)	49. (d)	50. (c)

PAPER–II

1. (d)	2. (d)	3. (c)	4. (c)	5. (c)
6. (a)	7. (a)	8. (b)	9. (c)	10. (d)
11. (b)	12. (d)	13. (c)	14. (b)	15. (d)
16. (c)	17. (d)	18. (d)	19. (b)	20. (c)
21. (a)	22. (a)	23. (d)	24. (a)	25. (c)
26. (c)	27. (b)	28. (c)	29. (b)	30. (d)
31. (a)	32. (b)	33. (b)	34. (c)	35. (b)
36. (a)	37. (c)	38. (c)	39. (c)	40. (d)
41. (a)	42. (b)	43. (a)	44. (d)	45. (d)
46. (b)	47. (c)	48. (a)	49. (c)	50. (c)

PAPER–III

1. (a)	2. (b)	3. (b)	4. (a)	5. (d)
6. (a)	7. (b)	8. (b)	9. (b)	10. (d)
11. (c)	12. (a)	13. (b)	14. (c)	15. (c)
16. (a)	17. (d)	18. (b)	19. (d)	20. (d)
21. (c)	22. (a)	23. (b)	24. (c)	25. (c)
26. (c)	27. (a)	28. (b)	29. (b)	30. (d)
31. (b)	32. (c)	33. (c)	34. (c)	35. (a)
36. (c)	37. (d)	38. (b)	39. (d)	40. (d)
41. (a)	42. (b)	43. (c)	44. (d)	45. (a)
46. (c)	47. (b)	48. (c)	49. (b)	50. (a)

MOCK TEST–3
PAPER–I

1. In the large group communications, effectively used media is
   (a) Radio (b) Television
   (c) Overhead Projector (d) Computer
2. A child may be suffering from hearing impairment if
   (a) he generally says 'please repeat' to the teacher
   (b) he speaks loudly unusually
   (c) he comes nearer to the speaker during conversation
   (d) All of the above
3. If a student is absent from the classes for a long time
   (a) Teacher should try to know the cause of his absence
   (b) Teacher should try to solve his problems or help him
   (c) Teacher should go to his home to meet him
   (d) Both (a) and (b)
4. The telecast materials are used to
   (a) increase retention power
   (b) enhance concentration and learning
   (c) reduce the burden of the teacher
   (d) All of the above
5. The main function of educational psychology is to provide prospective teacher with
   (a) how to deal with students and everyday class situation
   (b) research procedures for evaluating current teaching procedure
   (c) insight into the needs, problems and styles of behaviour of teacher
   (d) insight into various aspects of modern teaching education
6. Which of the following is not a method of research?
   (a) Historical (b) Observation
   (c) Philosophical (d) Survey

7. The communication which transpires inside a person is known as
   (a) group communication
   (b) intrapersonal communication
   (c) interpersonal communication
   (d) mass communication
8. The word research is derived from
   (a) Greek word (b) French word
   (c) Spanish word (d) Latin word
9. Educational quality is
   (a) Only a legal right
   (b) Fundamental right
   (c) Only a customary right
   (d) None of these
10. A good teacher is one who
   (a) has genuine interest in his student
   (b) is highly intelligent
   (c) lives simple life
   (d) has mastery over his teaching subject
11. Which of the following institutions is responsible for the implementation of reforms in teaching profession?
   (a) National Institute of Educational Planning and Administration
   (b) University Grants Commission
   (c) National Council for Teacher's Education
   (d) National Council for Educational Research and Training
12. The most important characteristic of Open Book Examination system is that
   (a) it compels students to think
   (b) students become serious
   (c) it improves attendance in the classroom
   (d) it reduces examination anxiety amongst students
13. Discussion in the class will be more effective if the topic of discussion is
   (a) informed to the student well in advance
   (b) not introduced
   (c) stated before the start of discussion
   (d) written on the board without introducing it
14. A person is not a successful communicator
   (a) who presents material in a precise and clear way
   (b) who sometimes becomes informal before the receiver and develops rapport
   (c) who knows a lot but is somewhat reserve in his attitude
   (d) who is able to adapt himself according to the language of communication
15. Which of the following provides more freedom for the learners to interact actively?
   (a) Small group discussions
   (b) Lecture by experts
   (c) Viewing of the TV
   (d) Use of film projector
16. In this question, four words are given, out of which three are alike in some manner and one is different. Choose the odd one out.
   (a) Diamond (b) Graphite
   (c) Coal (d) Pearl
17. Two objects or events are related in some way. Pick out that option which has the same type of relationship stated in the given two words:

   HANDS : FINGERS :: ?
   (a) Competition : Victory (b) Head : Hair
   (c) Skin : Colour (d) Machine:Tools
18. Human ear is most sensitive to noise in the range
   (a) 1-2 kHz (b) 100-500 Hz
   (c) 10-12 kHz (d) 13-16 kHz

Direction (19-23): Study the following passage and give answer to the questions based on it.

A recent report in *Newsweek* says that in American colleges, students of Asian origin outperform not only the minority group students but the majority Whites as well. Many of these students might be of Indian origin, and their achievement is something that we can be really proud of. It is unlikely that these talented youngsters will come back to India, and that is the familiar brain drain problem. However, recent statements by the nation's policymakers indicate that the perception of this issue is changing. 'Brain Bank' and not the 'Brain Drain' is the more appropriate idea, they suggest that since the expertise of Indians abroad is only deposited in other places and not lost.

This may be so, but this brain bank, like most of other banks, is one that primarily serves customers in its neighbourhood. The skills of Asians now excelling in America's colleges will mainly help the USA. No matter how significant, what non-resident Indians do for India and what their counterparts do for other Asian lands is only a by-product.

But it is also necessary to ask, or be reminded why Indians study more fruitfully when abroad. The Asians whose accomplishments *Newsweek* records would have probably had a very different fate if they had studied in India. In America, they found an elbow room, books and facilities not available and not likely to be available here. The need to prove themselves in their new country and the competition of an international standard they faced there must have cured mental and physical laziness. But other things helping them in America can be obtained if we achieve a change in social attitudes, especially towards youth.

We need to learn to value individuals and their unique qualities more than conformity and respectability. We need to learn the language of encouragement to add to our skill in flattery. We might also learn to be less liberal with blame and less tight-fisted with appreciation, especially to those showing signs of independence.

19. It is a general belief that the talented young Indians studying in America
    (a) will not return to pursue their careers in India
    (b) have a reputation for being hard-working
    (c) have an opportunity to contribute in India's development
    (d) can solve the brain drain problem because of recent changes in policy
20. Among the many groups of students in American colleges, Asian students
    (a) have only a minority status like the blacks
    (b) are often written about in magazines like *Newsweek*
    (c) are the most successful academically
    (d) have proved that they are as good as Whites
21. There is talk of the 'Brain Bank'; this idea
    (a) is based on plan to utilise foreign exchange remittances to stimulate research and development
    (b) is a solution to the brain drain problem
    (c) is a new problem caused partly by the brain drain
    (d) is a new way of looking at the role of qualified Indians living abroad
22. The students of Asian origin in America include
    (a) Indians who are the most hard- working of all
    (b) a fair number from India
    (c) a small group from India
    (d) persons from India who are very proud
23. Which of the following most appropriately sums up the intent of the author?
    (a) USA has excelled just because of the contributions from talented immigrants
    (b) We need to look at 'Brain Drain' in a positive way as 'Brain Bank'
    (c) Indians should take pride in the fact that fellow Indians have excelled in foreign lands against all odds
    (d) We need to think of the ways to help grow and retain the talent of our land
24. What should come in place of the question mark (?) in the following series?
    102, 99, 104, 97, 106, ?
    (a) 106 (b) 59 (c) 95 (d) 64
25. **Read the following and choose the correct option (Q 25-26).**
    Statement: Let us increase the taxes to cover the deficit.
    Conclusions:
    I. If the taxes are not increased, the deficit cannot be met.
    II. The present taxes are very low.
    III. Deficit in the budget are not desirable.
    (a) Only II and III are implicit
    (b) Only I and III are implicit
    (c) Only I and II are implicit
    (d) All are implicit
26. **Statements:**
    A. Some dogs are cats.
    B. None of the cats is a cow.
    Conclusions:
    I. Some cats are not dogs.
    II. Some cats are dogs.
    III. Some cows are dogs.
    IV. No dog is a cow.
    (a) Only II follows (b) Only III follows
    (c) Only I and III follow (d) Only IV follows

Directions (27-30): Using the following table and choose the correct option:

Yearly income (in ₹ '000)

Name/Year	2008	2009	2010	2011
Mahesh	1200	1600	2000	2400
Suresh	1000	1400	1600	2000
Ganesh	900	1200	1500	2000
Seema	2000	2500	3000	3700
Sapna	1200	1200	1500	1700

27. Whose average income for all the four years is ₹ 1400000?
    (a) Mahesh alone
    (b) Ganesh and Sapna both
    (c) Mahesh and Suresh
    (d) Sapna alone
28. How high is the total average income for four years of men as compared to that of women?
    (a) 2133340 (b) 3500440
    (c) 4320540 (d) 5440820
29. What is the round figure, the ratio between the total income of men and that of women for all years?
    (a) 16:14 (b) 14:15 (c) 15:16 (d) 23:21
30. Can we say women earn more than men?
    (a) No
    (b) Yes
    (c) Not sure
    (d) Difference is not so significant

Directions (31-35): Using the following graph, choose the correct option.

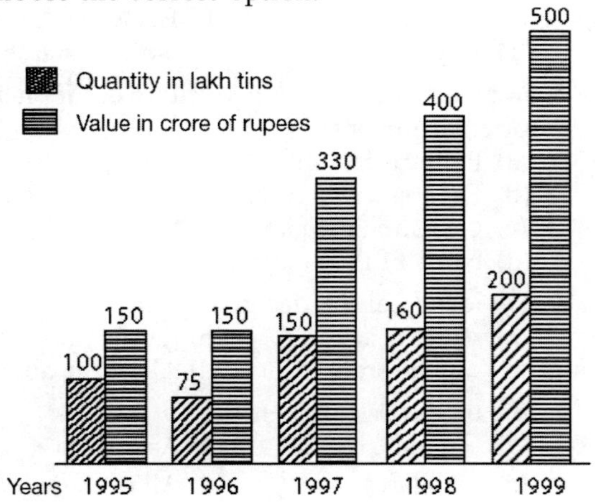

31. What was the approximate percentage increase in export value from 1995 to 1999?
    (a) 435 (b) 395.5
    (c) 422.8 (d) None of these
32. If in 1998, the tins were exported at the same rate per tin as that in 1997, what would be the value (in ₹ crores) of export in 1998?
    (a) 375 (b) 352 (c) 395 (d) 392
33. In which year the value per tin was minimum?
    (a) 1996 (b) 1998 (c) 1995 (d) 1999
34. What was the percentage drop in export quantity from 1995 to 1996?
    (a) 25 (b) 46
    (c) 52 (d) None of these
35. What was the difference between the tins exported in 1997 and 1998?
    (a) 10 (b) 1000
    (c) 100000 (d) 1000000
36. Which of the following statements is/are true about ozone layer?
    (a) It is depleting due to human activities
    (b) It is found in upper atmosphere, which absorbs UV rays
    (c) It causes skin cancer and genetic disorder
    (d) Both (a) and (b)
37. Study the figure and find the region which represents the students who study Physics and Chemistry but not Mathematics.

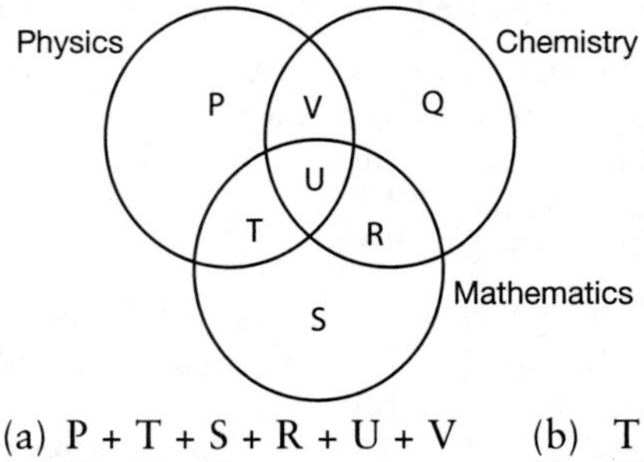

    (a) P + T + S + R + U + V (b) T
    (c) P + T + S (d) V
38. Which of the following is a non-point source of water pollution?
    (a) Factories (b) Lawn
    (c) Coal mines (d) None of these
39. The depletion of ozone layer causes
    I. Skin cancer.

II. Damage to our immune system.
III. Damage to our eyes.

(a) Only III (b) I and II
(c) I and III (d) All of the above

40. **Read the following statements and choose the correct option.**

Statements:

I. All the fruits are stones.
II. No tree is fruit.
III. All stones are rains.

Conclusion:

(a) Some rain is fruit (b) No stone is a tree
(c) No rain is a tree (d) None is true

41. Web designer is also known as
(a) Web maintainer (b) Web editor
(c) Web master (d) Web author

42. Which of the following schedule of our constitution is related to languages?
(a) Sixth (b) Eighth (c) Seventh (d) Tenth

43. In the hypermedia database, information bits are stored in the form of
(a) symbols (b) signals
(c) cubes (d) nodes

44. Explosive volcanic eruption is caused by
(a) high water content in ground
(b) low viscosity of magma
(c) high viscosity of magma
(d) none of these

45. The VIRUS is a
(a) device (b) software program
(c) hardware (d) anti-piracy software

46. Appropriation Act of the General Budget is
(a) a Constitution Amendment Bill
(b) a Finance Bill
(c) a Money Bill
(d) an Ordinary Bill

47. If in a certain language, GERMANY is coded as HGUQFTF then how will you code NEOMAN?
(a) OFQQFT (b) OFQPES
(c) OGRQFT (d) None of these

48. Which of the following is biggest fresh-water lake in India?
(a) Loktak (b) Dal
(c) Sukhna (d) None of these

49. Different memories can be classified according to the concept of
(a) Transfer Rate
(b) Access mode/capacity
(c) Access Time
(d) All of the above

50. Which of the following diagrams represents the relation between red, clothes and roses most appropriately?

(a) 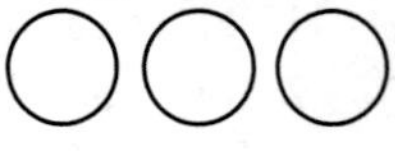 (b) 

(c)  (d) 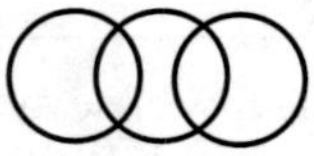

PAPER–II

1. If a partnership firm is not registered with the registrar of firms
(a) the members can enforce their rights among themselves.
(b) it has to pay penalty for non-registration.
(c) the members can file suit against the third party.
(d) None of the above.

2. The most important clause in the Memorandum of Association of a company is
(a) Liability clause.
(b) Objects clause.
(c) Registered office clause.
(d) Name clause.

3. Audit of company accounts is
(a) unnecessary (b) compulsory
(c) advisable (d) all of the above

4. *Introduction to Business* is written by
(a) Schoell (b) Reincke
(c) Copen (d) Both (a) and (b)

5. Which of the following is not a component of environment?
(a) Political factors
(b) Economical factors
(c) Geographical factors
(d) None of the above

6. Dividend can be declared from
(a) secret reserve (b) revenue profit
(c) capital profit (d) All of the above

7. Balance is a statement of
(a) Capital (b) Assets
(c) Liabilities (d) All of these

8. Which of the following statements is true?
   (a) The statement showing the result is known as Profit and Loss Account.
   (b) The statement disclosing status of investment is known as Balance Sheet.
   (c) The Balance Sheet comprises a list of assets, liabilities and capital as given date.
   (d) The preparation of the financial statements is the responsibility of top management.
9. Which one of the following formula would apply for the calculation of Interest on Drawings?
   (a) $\frac{\text{Amount of drawing} \times \text{Rate of interest}}{100}$
   (b) $\frac{\text{Rate of interest}}{100 \times \text{Amount of drawing}}$
   (c) $\frac{\text{Total of product} \times \text{Rate of interest}}{100 \times 12}$
   (d) None of the above
10. Unrecorded liability, when paid by a firm on its dissolution is debited to
   (a) partner's capital account
   (b) realisation account
   (c) unrecorded liability account
   (d) None of the above
11. Goods with negative income elasticities are defined as
   (a) Competitive goods (b) Inferior goods
   (c) Selective goods (d) All of the above
12. Cross elasticity is defined as
   (a) $\frac{\text{Percentage change in quantity demanded of one goods caused by a 1 per cent}}{\text{Change in the price of someother goods}}$
   (b) $\frac{\text{Percentage change in quantity}}{1 + \text{Price}}$
   (c) $\frac{\text{Price} + 1}{\text{Change in quantity demanded}}$
   (d) $\frac{1 + \text{Price}}{\text{Percentage change in quantity}}$
13. In a market where there are a large number of small buyers and individual firms _____ has little control over price
   (a) Firm (b) Market (c) Buyer (d) Seller
14. If one input is variable and all other inputs are fixed the firm's production function exhibits the
   (a) Law of capital (b) Law variable
   (c) Law of demand (d) Law of supply
15. A company is planning to develop a new packaging for its consumer product. In order to ensure that the packaging is attractive and easy to handle, the company must conduct _______ test.
   (a) association (b) engineering
   (c) dealer (d) Inquiry
16. In which files are the records organised in sequence and an index table is used to speed up access to the records without requiring a search of the entire file?
   (a) Indexed sequential files
   (b) Direct files
   (c) Sequential files
   (d) None of the above
17. Files held on a storage device are identified by a special block of data held as the first block on the file. This block called the
   (a) File maintenance (b) File lable
   (c) File scratch (d) None of these
18. If all the points of a scatter diagram lie on a straight line falling from the lower left-hand corner to the upper right-hand corner, the correlation is said to be
   (a) Perfect negative correlation
   (b) Zero correlation
   (c) Perfect positive correlation
   (d) High degree of positive correlation
19. When three or more variables are studied simultaneously for correlation analysis it is called
   (a) Partial correlation
   (b) Multiple correlation
   (c) Simple correlation
   (d) All of the above
20. If the plotted points of a scatter diagram fall on a narrow band, it indicates a _____ degree of correlation.
   (a) high (b) low
   (c) Both (a) and (b) (d) None of these
21. Setting the mission which encompasses objectives, policies and goals is known as

(a) strategic planning
(b) operational planning
(c) contingency planning
(d) tactical planning

22. The primary responsibility for the teacher's adjustment lies with
(a) The children (b) The principal
(c) The teacher himself (d) The community

23. Which of the following is not a dual mode university?
(a) Delhi University
(b) Bangalore University
(c) Madras University
(d) Indira Gandhi National Open University

24. Which of the following is true about the British rule in India?
(a) It was behind the modernisation of the Indian society.
(b) India gained economically during that period.
(c) Various establishments were formed for the purpose of progress.
(d) None of these.

25. The enrolment in higher education in India is contributed both by Formal System of Education and by System of Distance Education. Distance education contributes
(a) 50% of formal system
(b) 25% of formal system
(c) 10% of the formal system
(d) Distance education system's contribution is not taken into account while considering the figures of enrolment in higher education

26. A departmental store offers a wide range of products in an organised fashion and is easily accessible to the
(a) Firm (b) Suppliers
(c) Consumers (d) Governments

27. The process of advertising in business begins with market situation analysis conducted to assess the marketing _____ for the product in the existing state of business in the market.
(a) assessibility (b) functioning
(c) opportunities (d) difficulty

28. Which cost is known as periodical cost?
(a) Variable cost (b) Sunk cost
(c) Fixed cost (d) Total cost

29. ______ are those cost items which can be traced logically and conveniently, in their entirety, to a cost object.
(a) Fixed costs (b) Make cost
(c) Direct costs (d) Indirect costs

30. ______ are those costs which are incurred to perform the marketing functions.
(a) Full costs (b) Sale of goods
(c) Transfer cost (d) Distribution costs

31. Which of the following is a document of the title of sale of goods?
(a) Certificate of Origin (b) Letter of Credit
(c) Bill of Lading (d) Bill of Entry

32. The purpose of depreciation is to
(a) reduce fixed assets to nil as soon as possible.
(b) reduce fixed assets to market value each year.
(c) allocate the cost of fixed assets to expense over their working lives.
(d) save income tax and wealth tax.

33. A company has inadvertently overstated its ending inventory. This will
(a) decrease the income of the current year.
(b) increase the income of the succeeding year.
(c) decrease the income of the succeeding year.
(d) have no effect on the income of the succeeding year.

34. The bonds where the coupon can be adjusted at pre-determined intervals are
(a) Convertible bonds
(b) Floating rate bonds
(c) Euro bonds
(d) Putable bonds

35. An asset is purchased for ₹ 50,000 on which depreciation is to be provided annually according to the straight line method. The useful life of the asset is 10 years and the residual value is ₹ 10,000. The rate of depreciation is
(a) 18% (b) 8% (c) 20% (d) 10%

36. When was 3 Factories Act introduced?
(a) 1950 (b) 1961 (c) 1948 (d) 1949

37. Elimination of hazardous conditions involves
(a) Insufficient work space
(b) Placement hazard
(c) Use of improper tools
(d) All of the above

38. Social security (minimum standards) convention includes
(a) Employment injury benefit
(b) Invalidity benefit
(c) Survivors' benefits
(d) All of the above

39. The Mica Mines Labour Welfare Fund Act was introduced from
(a) 1970 (b) 1963 (c) 1946 (d) 1960

40. Work Motivation Theory involves
(a) Herzberg (b) Human Relations
(c) Maslow (d) All of the above

41. The first development financial institution in India that has got merged with a bank is
(a) IDFC (b) UTI (c) IDBI (d) ICICI

42. According to the principle of subrogation,
(a) the actual amount of loss, not exceeding the amount of the policy, shall be paid.
(b) the insured must take all necessary steps to minimise the loss.
(c) on making good the loss, the insurer is entitled to succeed to all the rights of the insured regarding the subject matter of insurance.
(d) the actual amount of loss, should be distributed among the different insurers of the same risk.

43. Exchange risk in case of foreign currency non resident (banks) scheme (FCNB) is borne by
(a) Concerned Bank (b) RBI
(c) Depositor (d) Govt. of India

44. The definition of the term 'banker' can be found in
(a) the Negotiable Instruments Act, 1881.
(b) the Banking Companies (Acquisition and Transfer of Undertakings Act, 1971).
(c) the Banking Regulation Act, 1949.
(d) None of the above.

45. The fiscal deficit in 2001-02 was ______ of GDP.
(a) 5.4% (b) 5.3% (c) 5.2% (d) 5.1%

46. The appropriate expenditure-switching policy to correct a deficit in the balance of payment is
(a) Monetary policy (b) Fiscal policy
(c) Revaluation (d) Devaluation

47. Mint parity theory is applicable only when countries are on
(a) different metallic standard.
(b) bimetallic standard.
(c) same metallic standard.
(d) None of the above.

48. Under balance of payment theory, foreign exchange rate is determined by
(a) Price of gold
(b) Demand and supply of foreign exchange
(c) Change in inflation
(d) None of the above

49. Shape of the offer curve is determined by
(a) Supply conditions
(b) Demand conditions
(c) Both (a) and (b)
(d) None of the above

50. Expenditure switching policies primarily work by changing
(a) Investment (b) Relative prices
(c) National income (d) Consumption

PAPER–III

1. M.M. Approach is similar to ____ approach.
(a) Net Income Approach
(b) Net Operating Income Approach
(c) Both (a) and (b)
(d) None of the above

2. The Indian Contract Act, 1872 applies upon
(a) Delhi (b) Mumbai
(c) Jaipur (d) All of these

3. Capital economic system consists of
(a) existence of competition.
(b) right to own private property.
(c) profit motive.
(d) All of the above.

4. Which one of the following is not the characteristic of socialist economic system?
(a) Goal of social welfare
(b) Market mechanism

(c) Restriction on production
(d) Collectivist economy

5. The minute books of company's meeting can be examined by
(a) debentureholders on payment of fee.
(b) shareholders without paying any fee.
(c) any person on payment of fee.
(d) All of the above.

6. β-error in hypothesis testing refers to
(a) Type-I error (b) Type-II error
(c) Both (a) and (b) errors
(d) None of the above

7. The net profits will be maximised when contribution is
(a) Minimised (b) Equal
(c) Maximised (d) None of these

8. Which one of the item is not of capital nature?
(a) Expenditure incurred on issue of equity shares.
(b) Money raised by issue of equity shares.
(c) Carriage paid on goods purchased.
(d) Cost of formation of a new company.

9. A and B are partners sharing profit in the ratio of 3 : 2. They admit a new partner R with 1/5 share in the profit which he takes equally from A and B. The new profit sharing ratio between the partners will be
(a) 5 : 3 : 2 (b) 8 : 12 : 5
(c) 2 : 2 : 1 (d) None of these

10. In the event of dissolution of firm, the partner's assets are first used for payment of the
(a) Firm's liabilities (b) External liabilities
(c) Personal liabilities (d) None of these

11. The additional cost that will be incurred by the firm if it undertakes a new project or produces an additional batch of output known as
(a) Fixed cost (b) Variable cost
(c) Incremental cost (d) All of the above

12. Average product is
(a) $\dfrac{\text{Total output}}{100 + \text{Number of use quantity}}$
(b) $\dfrac{\text{Total output}}{\text{The number of units of the input in use}}$
(c) $\dfrac{\text{Total output}}{\frac{2}{100} \times \text{Total number of input}}$
(d) $\dfrac{\text{Total outut}}{\frac{100}{2} \times \text{Total number of input}}$

13. The additional revenue which a firm will receive by undertaking a particular project is known as
(a) Profit (b) Incremental revenue
(c) Revenue (d) All of the above

14. Marginal private cost + Marginal external costs is defined as
(a) Variable cost (b) Marginal Social cost
(c) Social cost (d) All of the above

15. Total revenue – Total costs (including opportunity cost) is expressed as
(a) Profit (b) Net profit
(c) Total profit (d) All of the above

16. A basic limitation of this method is that it is sometimes difficult to master all the data with the degree of precision required by the mathematical equations.
(a) The Model (b) Experience
(c) Experiment (d) Any of the above

17. The technique of analysis of variance is developed by
(a) Frank Wilcoxon (b) James Bernoulli
(c) R.A. Fischer (d) Kruskal

18. This approach is similar to the marginal analysis except that it takes a total view of the plus and minus of the two alternatives after the decision is taken.
(a) Cost-benefit analysis
(b) Differential analysis
(c) Limiting factor analysis
(d) None of the above

19. The two major dimension, viz. (i) the peripheral dimension, and (ii) the time dimension are relevant in this approach.
(a) The cost-benefit analysis
(b) The limiting factor analysis
(c) The marginal analysis
(d) The differential analysis

20.

List I	List II
A. Probable error	1. $\sqrt{bxy.byx}$

B. Standard error 2. $1 - r^3 / \sqrt{N}$

C. Correlation 3. $\frac{2}{3}\left(1 - r^3 / \sqrt{N}\right)$

Codes:	A	B	C
(a)	2	3	1
(b)	2	1	3
(c)	3	2	1
(d)	1	2	3

21. Establishment of management by objectives presupposes
    (a) unlimited freedom to set goals.
    (b) unlimited freedom to operate in the assigned task.
    (c) that the employees are provided with result expected.
    (d) that limits of authority are not defined.
22. Theory X and theory Y was originated by
    (a) McClelland (b) Herzberg
    (c) Maslow (d) McGregor
23. The idea of MBO originally come from
    (a) P.F. Drucker (b) McGregor
    (c) Maslow (d) Taylor
24. Three necessary and sufficient conditions that must be satisfied if traits should be unique determinants of the Leadership Index are
    1. the trait quality should follow a descending order as one traverses from the highest to the lowest levels.
    2. there must be a high correlation between the level of traits and the level of success.
    3. the achievement trait curve should be convex to the trait axis as one travels from the low to the high trait terminals.

    The above conditions have been suggested by
    (a) Elton Mayo (b) F.W. Taylor
    (c) Dorvvin Cartwright (d) Edwin E. Ghiselli
25. What is the order of the performance of the following functions of management?
    1. Planning 2. Directing
    3. Organising 4. Controlling

    Codes:
    (a) 1, 3, 2, 4 (b) 1, 3, 4, 2
    (c) 1, 2, 3, 4 (d) 1, 4, 2, 3
26. Which of the following functions is/are involved under marketing management's functions?
    1. Collection of marketing sources
    2. Marketing co-ordination
    3. Marketing controlling
    4. Marketing direction

    Codes:
    (a) 2 and 3 (b) 1, 2, 3 and 4
    (c) 1 only (d) 2 only

Match the following lists.

Direction: Read the following and choose the correct option from the given codes (Q 27-33)

27. **List I**
    A. W.J. Stanton B. Paul Mazur
    C. H.L. Hansen D. E. Jerome Mc Carthy
    E. Malcolm Menair

    List II (Statements)
    1. Marketing is a total system of interacting business activities designed to plan, price, promote and distribute want satisfying products and services to present and potential customers.
    2. Marketing is the delivery of a standard of living.
    3. Marketing is the process of discovering and translating consumer needs and wants into product and service specifications, creating demand for these products and services and then in turn expanding this demand.
    4. Marketing is the responses of businessmen to the need to adjust production capabilities to the requirements of consumer demands.

Codes:	A	B	C	D
(a)	4	2	3	1
(b)	1	2	4	3
(c)	1	2	3	4
(d)	2	1	3	4

28. **List I (Marketing sub-plan)**
    A. Baseline research
    B. Technical plan
    C. Organisational plan
    D. Contingency plan

    List II (Variables of marketing sub-plan)
    1. Customer service 2. Packaging
    3. Regulation 4. Risk management

Codes:	A	B	C	D
(a)	2	3	1	4
(b)	1	3	2	4

(c)	4	2	3	1
(d)	1	2	3	4

29. **List I (Types of wholesalers)**
   A. Manufacturer wholesalers
   B. Retailer wholesalers
   C. Wholesalers proper
   D. Single line wholesalers

   List II (Their qualities)
   1. A wholesaler who engages in manufacturing activities to some extent.
   2. These wholesalers purchase goods in large parcle from the manufacturers and retail them to the consumers through their own shops.
   3. The wholesalers who are, however, those merchants who concentrate entirely on the functions of buying and selling in large lots, and do not engage in the manufacturing or retailing activities.
   4. The wholesalers deal in different varieties in a particular line of goods and sell goods to many types of buyers of such goods.

Codes:	**A**	**B**	**C**	**D**
(a)	2	1	3	4
(b)	1	2	3	4
(c)	2	3	1	4
(d)	3	4	1	2

30. **List I (Marketing management thinker)**
   A. Tousley, Clark and Clark
   B. Stanton
   C. Richard Buskrik
   D. Mc Carthy

   List II (Their statements)
   1. Re-sale price maintenance is the marketing policy under which the manufacturer or owner of a commodity by brand trademark, copyright, or patent, places restrictions on the price at which that commodity shall be sold by purchasers and sub-purchasers.
   2. A channel of distribution for a product is the route taken by the title to the goods as they move from the producer to the ultimate consumer or industrial user.
   3. Distribution channels are systems of economic institutions, through which a producer of goods delivers them into the hands of their users.
   4. Any sequence of institutions from the producer to the consumer, including one or any number of middlemen, is called a channel of distribution.

Codes:	**A**	**B**	**C**	**D**
(a)	1	2	3	4
(b)	1	2	4	3
(c)	3	1	2	4
(d)	4	3	1	2

31. Rate of return on investment is meaningful to
   1. Shareholders 2. Creditors
   3. Management

   Codes:
   (a) 1 and 3 are true (b) 1 alone is true
   (c) 1, 2 and 3 are true (d) 2 and 3 are true

32. **List I (Appointment of auditor)**
   A. First auditor of a non-government limited company
   B. Reappointment of a retiring auditor of a non-government limited company
   C. Auditor of a government company
   D. Auditor of a non-government limited company, when shareholders fail to appoint or reappoint an auditor

   List II (Appointing authority)
   1. Shareholders of the company
   2. Board of Directors of the company
   3. Central Government on the advice of the Comptroller and Auditor General of India
   4. Central Government

Codes:	**A**	**B**	**C**	**D**
(a)	1	2	3	4
(b)	2	1	4	3
(c)	1	2	4	3
(d)	2	1	3	4

33. **List I**
   A. Balance of debenture redemption fund account.
   B. Balance of sinking fund account for replacement of an asset.
   C. On dissolution of a firm, the provisions made for doubtful debts appearing in balance sheet.
   D. Financial consequences of business operations.

   List II
   1. Realisation account
   2. Funds-flow statement

3. General reserve
4. Asset account

Codes:	A	B	C	D
(a)	1	2	4	3
(b)	3	4	2	1
(c)	1	2	3	4
(d)	3	4	1	2

Read the following and choose the correct option:

34. **Assertion (A):** The matching concept requires that costs should be recognised as expenses in the period in which revenue is realised.

Reason (R): There may not be a matching between expenditure and expense over a short period.

(a) Both A and R are true and R is the correct explanation of A.
(b) Both A and R are true but R is not the correct explanation of A.
(c) A is true but R is false.
(d) A is false but R is true.

35. Purchase of fixed assets is a day-to-day expense.

(a) False (b) True
(c) Can't say
(d) It depends on the value of asset

Read the following and choose the correct option from the given codes (Q. 36-40)

36. **List I (Management educationist)**

A. William P. Anthony
B. Richard W. Woodman and John J. Sherwood
C. Jean Jones, and Thomas A. De caltis
D. Herbert G. Zollitsch and Adolph

List II (Their books)

1. *The Human Resource Information System*
2. *A Comprehensive Look at Job Design*
3. *Job Analysis—National Survey Finding*
4. *Wages and Salary Administration*

Codes:	A	B	C	D
(a)	3	1	2	4
(b)	4	2	1	3
(c)	1	2	4	3
(d)	1	2	3	4

37. **List I (Years)**

A. 1923 B. 1918 C. 1901 D. 1890

List II (Growth of HRM in India)

1. Workmen's Compensation Act passed
2. Massive industrial unrest prevailed following the end of World War I
3. The Mines Act
4. The First Labour Organisation

Codes:	A	B	C	D
(a)	4	3	1	2
(b)	3	1	2	4
(c)	1	2	3	4
(d)	1	3	2	4

38. **List I (Thinkers of management)**

A. Omit Oscar
B. Myers C.A.
C. T.K. Richardson
D. Institute of Personnel Management

List II (Their books/articles)

1. *Jobs and Workers*
2. *Industrial Relations in India*
3. *Industrial Relations*
4. *Personnel Management in India*

Codes:	A	B	C	D
(a)	1	2	3	4
(b)	1	2	4	3
(c)	4	3	1	2
(d)	2	3	1	4

39. **List I (Components of human resource planning)**

A. Demographics
B. Community attitudes
C. Replacement summaries
D. Human resource planning

List II (Their qualities)

1. Demographic trends are another long- term development that affects the availability of external supply
2. Community attitudes also affect the nature of the labour market
3. The list is likely for replacements for each job and indicate their relative strengths and weeknesses
4. The planning requires considerable time, staff and financial resources

Codes:	A	B	C	D
(a)	2	3	4	1
(b)	1	2	3	4
(c)	4	3	1	2
(d)	2	4	3	1

40. **List I (Specific training methods)**
   A. On-the-job training
   B. Off-the-job training
   C. Understudy method
   D. Role playing method

   List II (Their qualities)
   1. Mostly the executive training is done on the job. An executive is expected to learn his work while working.
   2. That method can also be used to train the executives.
   3. The method under this executive is assigned an understudy or an assistant who, in addition to his regular duties, is expected to acquire some familiarity with the tasks and practices of his superior.
   4. The method under which an employee learns by playing a role in dramatic setting which corresponds to his work.

Codes:	**A**	**B**	**C**	**D**
(a)	4	2	3	1
(b)	2	3	1	4
(c)	1	2	3	4
(d)	1	2	4	3

41. A banker is under statutory obligation to honour his customer's cheques provided that
   (a) there is no legal bar to such payment.
   (b) they are drawn in proper form and presented during banking hours.
   (c) there is sufficient balance in the account to meet the cheque or arrangements have been made for an overdraft.
   (d) All of the above.
42. The Banking Regulation Act, 1949, does not at all apply to
   (a) Foreign banks having their offices in India.
   (b) State Bank of India and its subsidiaries.
   (c) Primary agricultural credit societies and co-operative and mortagagee banks.
   (d) Nationalized banks.
43. A customer has a right to ask the bank to return him a paid instrument, before the expiry of period of preservation of such instrument, under
   (a) Section 45Z of the Banking Regulation Act, 1949.
   (b) Section 131 of the Negotiable Instruments Act, 1881.
   (c) Section 34 of Reserve Bank of India Act, 1934.
   (d) None of the above.
44. In accordance with [under Section 23(10)] Banking Regulation Act, 1949 a banking company is exempted from obtaining prior permission of Reserve Bank of India for
   (a) opening a temporary branch on the occasion of an exhibition, a conference or a mela for a period not exceeding three months.
   (b) change of premises within the same city town or village.
   (c) opening a branch in a foreign country.
   (d) opening an extension counter.
45. What does third party confirmation in auditing mean?
   (a) Confirmation of bank balances.
   (b) Confirmation of balances of sundry debtors or creditors.
   (c) Confirmation of security deposits.
   (d) Confirmation of contingent liabilities.
46. The World Bank gives financial assistance only to its
   (a) Staff (b) Member countries
   (c) Governor (d) Managing director
47. The authorised capital of the IFC is
   (a) ₹ 1000 lakh (b) 5000 SDRs
   (c) ₹ 50 crores (d) 100 million US dollars
48. The IFC is affiliated to the
   (a) ADB (b) RBI
   (c) United States (d) World Bank
49. The spot rate of exchange is quoted for the immediate delivery of
   (a) Foreign rate (b) Foreign treasury
   (c) Foreign transaction (d) Foreign exchange
50. GATT was the substitute of
   (a) ECM (b) WTO (c) ITO (d) IMF

ANSWER SHEET

PAPER–I

1. (c)	2. (d)	3. (d)	4. (b)	5. (a)
6. (c)	7. (b)	8. (d)	9. (d)	10. (a)
11. (a)	12. (d)	13. (a)	14. (c)	15. (b)

16. (d)	17. (b)	18. (a)	19. (a)	20. (c)
21. (d)	22. (b)	23. (d)	24. (c)	25. (b)
26. (a)	27. (b)	28. (a)	29. (a)	30. (c)
31. (d)	32. (b)	33. (c)	34. (a)	35. (d)
36. (d)	37. (d)	38. (b)	39. (d)	40. (d)
41. (d)	42. (b)	43. (d)	44. (c)	45. (b)
46. (c)	47. (c)	48. (d)	49. (d)	50. (d)

PAPER–II

1. (d)	2. (b)	3. (b)	4. (d)	5. (d)
6. (b)	7. (d)	8. (d)	9. (c)	10. (b)
11. (b)	12. (a)	13. (d)	14. (b)	15. (a)
16. (a)	17. (b)	18. (c)	19. (b)	20. (a)
21. (b)	22. (b)	23. (b)	24. (c)	25. (b)
26. (c)	27. (b)	28. (b)	29. (b)	30. (d)
31. (c)	32. (c)	33. (c)	34. (b)	35. (b)
36. (c)	37. (d)	38. (d)	39. (c)	40. (d)
41. (d)	42. (c)	43. (a)	44. (c)	45. (a)
46. (d)	47. (c)	48. (b)	49. (c)	50. (b)

PAPER–III

1. (a)	2. (a)	3. (d)	4. (c)	5. (b)
6. (c)	7. (c)	8. (c)	9. (a)	10. (c)
11. (c)	12. (b)	13. (b)	14. (b)	15. (c)
16. (a)	17. (c)	18. (b)	19. (a)	20. (d)
21. (c)	22. (d)	23. (a)	24. (d)	25. (a)
26. (b)	27. (c)	28. (d)	29. (b)	30. (a)
31. (b)	32. (d)	33. (c)	34. (c)	35. (a)
36. (c)	37. (d)	38. (d)	39. (d)	40. (b)
41. (d)	42. (c)	43. (a)	44. (c)	45. (b)
46. (b)	47. (d)	48. (d)	49. (d)	50. (c)

MOCK TEST–4
PAPER–I

1. Dewey defines education as a
   (a) theoretical need (b) social need
   (c) personal need (d) psychological need

2. All of the following statements about a teacher are correct except the one.
   (a) A teacher changes his/her attitudes and behaviour according to the need of the society
   (b) A teacher is a friend, guide and philosopher
   (c) A teacher distinguishes between students
   (d) A teacher is the leader in the class

3. A person cannot be an effective teacher if he
   (a) teaches moral values
   (b) is a strict disciplinarian
   (c) knows his subject well
   (d) has no interest in teaching

4. The most important signal factor in underlying the success of a teacher is
   (a) organisational ability
   (b) scholarship
   (c) communicative ability
   (d) personality and his ability to relate to the class and to the pupils

5. Which of the following is correct statement?
   (a) Under perfect competition, a firm determines its price where AR=MR
   (b) In perfect competitive industry, a firm is in equilibrium in the short run only when its AC=AR=MR=MC
   (c) The short-run supply curve has a negative slope
   (d) A firm is price-taken under perfect competition

6. The term 'SITE' stands for
   (a) Satellite Instructional Teachers Education
   (b) Satellite International Television Experiment
   (c) Satellite Instructional Television Experiment
   (d) Satellite Indian Television Experiment

7. Team teaching has the potential to develop
   (a) highlighting the gaps in each other's teaching
   (b) competitive spirit
   (c) cooperation
   (d) the habit of supplementing the teaching of each other

8. In any research one should
   (a) not try out anything blindly but wait until a sudden flash appears in his mind

(b) know everything in the area without bothering to learn the details of any
(c) know more and more about less and less in certain specific sub-area
(d) None of these

9. Determine the nature of the following definition:
'Poor' means having an annual income of ₹ 10,000.
(a) Lexical (b) Persuasive
(c) Precising (d) Stipulative

10. Which of the following methods implies the collection of information by way of investigators own examination without interviewing the respondents?
(a) Random probability sampling
(b) Observation
(c) Posting questionnaire
(d) Schedule method

11. Why do teachers use teaching aid?
(a) For students' attention
(b) To make teaching fun-filled
(c) To make students attentive
(d) To teach within understanding level of students

12. On which of the following statements there is consensus among educators?
(a) Disciplinary cases should be totally neglected in the class
(b) Disciplinary cases should be sent to the principal only when other means have failed
(c) Disciplinary cases should never be sent to principal's office
(d) None of these

13. Good evaluation of written material should not be based on
(a) logical presentation
(b) comprehension of subject
(c) linguistic expression
(d) ability to reproduce whatever is read

14. A good researcher lays his hands on
(a) any area so long as manpower and fundings are available in plenty
(b) a specific area and tries to understand in minute details
(c) several areas and tries to understand them at fundamental level
(d) None of these

15. The basis on which assumptions are formulated
(a) Universities
(b) Cultural background of the country
(c) Specific characteristics of the castes
(d) All of these

Read the following passage and answer the questions 16 to 20:

India is dedicated to free institutions and principles of democracy. We are striving to give everyone an opportunity and raise the standard of living for all. A democracy is one where people have the right to live their own lives and develop themselves in their own way under the guidance of their chosen representatives. If our political democracy is to succeed, it is essential that it be buttressed by steps towards economic equality or what has been referred to as the 'socialistic pattern of society'. Poverty and unemployment hold the biggest threat to the successful working of our democratic system.

16. One may infer from the paragraph that in a socialistic pattern of society
(a) to provide employment to all is the greatest problem
(b) the socialist party dominates
(c) all the inhabitants are treated equal
(d) None of these

17. The successful working of Indian democratic system is under a threat of
(a) economic inequality (b) poverty
(c) unemployment (d) All the above

18. In a democratic system
(a) commodities are freely bought and sold
(b) government serves the people
(c) the government is run by the people themselves
(d) people do not have political freedom

19. The word buttressed in the paragraph means
(a) Supported (b) Dictating
(c) Declared (d) Guided

20. Democracy can fail if there is
(a) opportunity for development
(b) a weak government
(c) economic inequality
(d) unemployment

21. The aspect ratio of TV screen is
(a) 4:3 (b) 3:4 (c) 2:3 (d) 2:4

22. Which of the following is not a product of learning?
(a) Knowledge (b) Attitudes
(c) Maturation (d) Concepts

23. The first paper for the human beings was developed by
(a) The Aryans (b) The Babilonians
(c) The Chinese (d) The Sumerians

24. Which sequence in turn will lead one to face the west direction from which one starts turning?
(a) Right, right, left, right, left right
(b) Left, right, left, left, right, right
(c) Right, right left, left, right, right
(d) Left, left, right, left, right, left

25. Fill in the blank with the most appropriate choice.
_____ is the supreme medium to express yesterday, today and tomorrow with its own unique language.
(a) Television (b) Cinema
(c) Radio (d) Newspaper

26. In which language the newspapers have highest circulation?
(a) Tamil (b) English
(c) Bengali (d) Hindi

27. Amit is the son of Rahul. Sarika, Rahul's sister has a son Sonu and a daughter Rita. Raja is the maternal uncle of Sonu. How is Rita related to Raja.
(a) Aunt (b) Sister
(c) Daughter (d) Niece

28. **Statement:** A man must be wise to be a good wrangler. Good wrangler's are all talkative and boring.

Conclusions:
I. All the wise persons are boring.
II. All the wise persons are good wranglers.

Choose the correct option.
(a) Only conclusion I follows
(b) Only conclusion II follows
(c) Both I and II follow
(d) None of these

29. What is the number that comes next in the sequence?
2, 5, 9, 19, 37, ...
(a) 74 (b) 75 (c) 76 (d) 78

30. Match List I with List II and select the correct answer using the codes given below:

List I	List II
(A) Pandit Jasraj	(1) Hindustani vocalist
(B) Kishan Maharaj	(2) Sitar
(C) Ravi Shankar	(3) Tabla
(D) Udai Shankar	(4) Dance

Codes:	A	B	C	D
(a)	1	2	3	4
(b)	1	3	4	2
(c)	1	3	2	4
(d)	3	2	1	4

31. Who developed the ability to speak?
(a) Aryans (b) Neanderthal
(c) Cro-Magnon (d) Dravidians

32. In what way does communication in small group differ from that in the large group?
(a) Large group communication provides better feedback
(b) Small group provides far more interaction among the participants
(c) Interaction in small group is more restrictive
(d) Small group takes less time to convey the message

33. What is the main aim and objective of provision for feedback in communication system?
(a) Understand more about the content
(b) To make communication better by adjusting at both ends of Encoder and Decoder
(c) Identify the defect of communication
(d) Make necessary modification in communication system

34. Communications bandwidth that has the highest capacity and is used by microwave, cable and fibre optics lines is known as
(a) Carrier wave (b) Hyper-link
(c) Broadband (d) Bus width

35. In a certain code, CLOCK is written as KCOLC. How would STEPS be written in that code?
(a) SPETS (b) SPEST (c) SPSET (d) SEPTS

36. Which one of the following is not an argument?

(a) Ram is not at home, so he must have gone to town
(b) Ram insulted me so I punched him in the nose
(c) If today is Tuesday, tomorrow will be Wednesday
(d) Since today is Tuesday, tomorrow will be Wednesday.

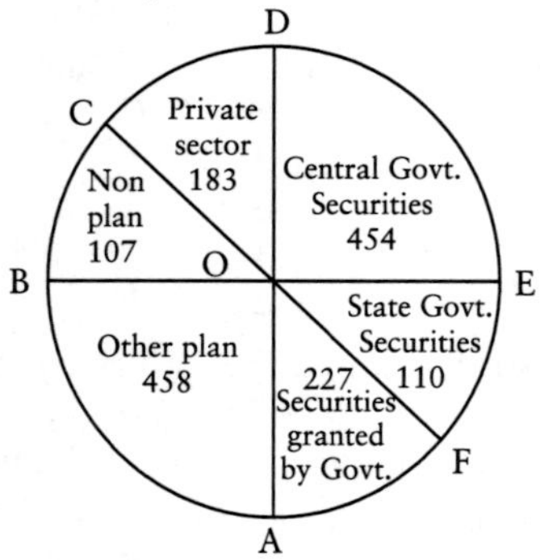

Direction (37-41): Study the following pie chart and answer the questions based on it. Following pie chart represents the investment done by Timas Finance Ltd. in the various sectors. (All investments are in ₹ crores)

37. The percentage or gross investment in state government securities is nearly
(a) 7.1% (b) 9.2% (c) 8.6% (d) 7.8%

38. The investment in plan and non-plan sector together is more or less than the investment in government securities (Central and State) by
(a) less, 106 crores (b) more, 4 crores
(c) more, 1 crores (d) more, 111 crores

39. The magnitude of ∠AOC is nearly
(a) 132° (b) 123° (c) 126° (d) 115°

40. The ratio of area of the circle above ∠COF to the area of the circle below it is about
(a) 1 (b) 0.92 (c) 0.94 (d) 0.96

41. The investment in private sector is nearly what percent higher than the investment in State Government Security?
(a) 44% (b) 66% (c) 54% (d) 46%

42. How many numbers between 100 and 300 begin or end with 2?
(a) 120 (b) 110 (c) 100 (d) 180

43. Which of the following operating system is used on mobile phones?
(a) Windows XP (b) Windows Vista
(c) Android (d) All of the above

44. Structure of logical argument is based on
(a) Linguistic expression
(b) Material truth
(c) Formal validity
(d) Aptness of examples

45. HTML is used to create
(a) machine language program
(b) high level program
(c) web page
(d) web server

46. Which of the following pollutants affects the respiratory tract in humans?
(a) Aerosols (b) Sulphur dioxide
(c) Nitric oxide (d) Carbonmonoxide

47. Which of the following sources of energy has the maximum potential in India?
(a) Wind energy (b) Solar energy
(c) Ocean thermal energy (d) Tidal energy

48. In a deductive argument conclusion is
(a) Additional to the premises
(b) Entailed by the premises
(c) Summing up of the premises
(d) Not necessarily based on premises

49. What is the range of the numbers which can be stored in an eight bit register?
(a) –127 to + 128 (b) –127 to + 127
(c) –128 to + 128 (d) –128 to + 127

50. Universal Product Code (UPC), a pattern of bars printed on merchandise can be read by
(a) Product Code Reader
(b) Bar Code Reader
(c) Code Reader
(d) Card Reader

PAPER–II

1. Income of previous year is chargeable to tax in the
(a) immediately succeeding assessment year.
(b) immediately preceding assessment year.
(c) current year.
(d) same previous year.

2. Allowances received by Indian nationals outside India from the Government of India are

(a) dependent upon fact and circumstances of the case.
(b) chargeable to tax in India.
(c) exempt from tax in India.
(d) None of the above.

3. As per the provisions of Section 115(7)A, in case of a company having total income less than 30 per cent of book profit, the total income shall be deemed to be
(a) 40 per cent of book profit.
(b) 30 per cent of book profit.
(c) 30 per cent of net profit as per Profit and Loss A/c.
(d) None of the above.

4. The relevant form in which declaration is to be furnished in the case of interest other than interest on securities is
(a) Form No. 15 (b) Form No. 15H
(c) Form No. 13 (d) Form No. 15F

5. Credit rating means—(under SEBI guide lines, 2000)
(a) if the rating has been obtained from one credit rating agencies, disclosure shall be made of all ratings including unaccepted rating.
(b) all the credit ratings obtained during the previous three years before filling of the offer document for any of its listed debt—Securities at the time of accessing the market through a rated debt—Security shall be disclosed.
(c) the credit rating obtained from a credit rating agency for the proposed issue of debt security including convertible instruments.
(d) All of the above.

6. Conservatism concept represents.
(a) An auditor is not valuer.
(b) Anticipate no profit and provide for all losses.
(c) Stock should be valued at cost price and market price whichever is less.
(d) For every debit, there is a credit.

7. Which of the following is not concept of accounting?
(a) Entity concept (b) Cost concept
(c) Matching concept (d) Stock valuation

8. Methods of analysis and interpretation of financial statement are
(a) Average analysis
(b) Preparation of comparative statements
(c) Ratio analysis
(d) All of the above

9. Average disbursement period can be find out as
(a) $\frac{\text{Accounts Payable}}{\text{Net Credit Purchases}} \times \text{No. of working days}$
(b) $\frac{\text{Net Credit Purchases}}{\text{Accounts Payable}} \times \text{No. of working days}$
(c) $\frac{\text{Net Credit + Purchases}}{\text{No. of working days}} \times \text{Accounts Payable}$
(d) $\frac{\text{Net Credit Purchases}}{\text{Opening Balance of Accounts}} \times 365$

10. Revised AS-3 issued by
(a) Company
(b) The Institute of Chartered Accountant of India
(c) The Institute of Company Secretaries of India
(d) The President of India

11. The World Bank gives financial assistance only to its
(a) Staff (b) Member countries
(c) Governor (d) Managing director

12. The market demand is the sum of individual demand for a product at a price per unit of
(a) Quantity (b) Time
(c) Demand (d) All of the above

13. That goods which are demanded in increasing quantities as consumer's income rises?
(a) Substitute goods (b) Inferior goods
(c) Normal goods (d) All of the above

14. Which of the following is/are the determinants of price elasticity of demand?
(a) Weightage in the total consumption
(b) Availability of substitutes
(c) Nature of commodity
(d) All of the above

15. Which of the following statement is true?

(a) If price elasticity < 1, MR < 0
(b) If price elasticity = 1, MR = 0
(c) If price elasticity > 1, MR > 0
(d) All of the above

16. Vertical filing is used in
(a) Medium size offices (b) Big offices
(c) Small offices (d) All of the above

17. 1. Feedback.
2. Evaluation.
3. Identification of discrepancies.
4. Correcting the system to reality.

Above are the features of
(a) Application of a model
(b) Formulation of a model
(c) Testing a model
(d) Monitoring a model

18. Mathematical solutions suffer from some limitations which are often classified as inherent limitations and empirical limitations. Below are given a few important limitations.

Read them and choose the correct option from the codes:
1. It is almost impossible to identify and incorporate all the variables of the reality situation into the model.
2. There are many intangible variables to which only notional values can be assigned.
3. The functional relations between the variables are often too vague and elusive for precision and qualification.
4. The mathematical tools should not choose the real-life problems.
5. The communication gap between the manager and the O.R. specialist is difficult to bridge.
6. The level of basic management in most enterprises is still crude and unrefined.
7. Imprecision in the input information spoils the precision of the mathematical solution.
8. The data and information base available is often inadequate.

Codes:
(a) 3, 4, 5 and 6 (b) 4, 5, 6 and 7
(c) 1, 2, 5 and 6 (d) 1, 2, 3 and 4

Read the following and choose the correct option from the given codes (Q. 19-21):

19. **List I (Systems)**
A. Procedural Test
B. Stratified Random Test
C. Substantive Test
D. Depth Test

List II (Events)
1. Population is divided into two or more than two groups
2. Verification of sampling procedures and their implementation
3. Tracing through the system all aspects of a transaction
4. Obtaining an evidence as to the completeness and accuracy of data

Codes:	A	B	C	D
(a)	4	3	2	1
(b)	2	1	4	3
(c)	4	1	2	3
(d)	2	3	4	1

20. **List I**
A. Relation between price standard
B. Relation between income and demand
C. Relation between rainfall and population

List II
1. Negative 2. Positive
3. Zero

Codes:	A	B	C
(a)	2	1	3
(b)	3	2	1
(c)	2	3	1
(d)	1	2	3

21. Staffing function of management includes
1. Training 2. Recruitment
3. Placement 4. Appraisal

Codes:
(a) 2, 3 and 4 (b) 1, 2, 3 and 4
(c) 1, 2 and 4 (d) 1, 2 and 3

22. Consider the following statements and choose the correct option.
1. Planning is looking ahead
2. Controlling is looking back
3. Delegation multiplies leadership
4. Life insurance is a contract of indemnity

Codes:
(a) 1, 3 and 4 are correct
(b) 1, 2 and 4 are correct
(c) 2, 3 and 4 are correct
(d) 1, 2 and 3 are correct

23. Which of the following constitute manpower planning? Choose the correct from the given codes:
    1. Determining human resource requirements both quantitatively and qualitatively.
    2. Finding the sources of talented individuals.
    3. Planning for the human resource needs of an organization.
    4. Reaching out to the right source for procuring the right people.

    Codes:
    (a) 1, 2, 3 and 4 (b) 1 and 3
    (c) 2 and 3 (d) 1, 2 and 4

24. Consider the following elements in a feedback loop. Choose the correct from the given codes:
    1. Identification of deviations
    2. Measurement of actual performance
    3. Actual performance
    4. Comparison of actual against standards

    Codes:
    (a) 2, 3, 1, 4 (b) 2, 3, 4, 1
    (c) 3, 2, 1, 4 (d) 3, 2, 4, 1

25. Decentralisation of an organization is commanded on account of which of the following advantages? Choose the correct from the given codes:
    1. Reduced burden on top executives
    2. Executive development
    3. Improvement of morale
    4. Solves problems of coordination

    Codes:
    (a) 1, 2 and 3 (b) 3 and 4
    (c) 2 and 3 (d) 1, 2 and 4

26. **List I (Marketing management thinkers)**
    A. Mason and Rath
    B. Cundiff and Still
    C. William J. Stanton
    D. James Stephenson

    List II (Books and articles)
    1. *Marketing and Distribution*
    2. *Basic Marketing*
    3. *Fundamental of Marketing*
    4. *Principles and Practice of Commerce*

Codes:	A	B	C	D
(a)	1	2	3	4
(b)	2	1	3	4
(c)	3	1	2	4
(d)	1	2	4	3

27. Which of the following is the basic objective of the World Bank?
    (a) To provide social services
    (b) To provide financial assistance
    (c) To promote economic growth
    (d) To eradicate poverty

Read the following and choose the correct options from the given codes (Q. 28-30)

28. **List I (Promotion mix tools)**
    A. Personal selling B. Publicity
    C. Sales Promotion D. Advertising

    List II (Sources of message)
    1. Telemarketing 2. News stories
    3. Trade shows 4. Billboard ads

Codes:	A	B	C	D
(a)	2	3	4	1
(b)	1	2	3	4
(c)	1	4	3	2
(d)	2	1	3	4

29. **List I (Product categories)**
    A. Bread B. Biscuits
    C. Butter D. Soap

    List II (Brand names)
    1. Modern 2. Britannia
    3. Amul 4. Lux

Codes:	A	B	C	D
(a)	3	4	1	2
(b)	1	2	4	3
(c)	1	2	3	4
(d)	2	1	3	4

30. **List I (Marketing management educationists)**
    A. Kaldor A.G. B. Mckitterick J.B.
    C. Levitt. T. D. Lazo H. and A. Corbin

    List II (Books and Articles)
    1. *Imbricative Marketing*
    2. *What is the Marketing Management Concept?*
    3. *Innovation in Marketing*
    4. *Management in Marketing*

Codes:	A	B	C	D
(a)	1	2	3	4
(b)	2	3	1	4
(c)	1	3	4	2
(d)	3	1	2	4

31. Capital gearing is the ratio between
    (a) equity capital and preference capital.
    (b) equity capital and fixed interest securities.

(c) equity capital and debentrues.
(d) All of the above.

32. What is quick ratio?
(a) Immediate realisable assets/current liabilities.
(b) Current assets/immediately realisable liabilities.
(c) Current assets/current liabilities.
(d) None of the above.

33. Which of the following increases the working capital? Choose the correct option from the codes:
1. Cash received from debtors
2. B/R realised
3. Issue of debenture
4. Issue of shares
5. Conversion of debenture into shares

Codes:
(a) 3, 4, 5 (b) 1, 2, 3
(c) 3 and 5 (d) All of the above

34. By adopting which of the following tactics, return on investment of a company can be enhanced? Choose the correct option from the codes.
1. Postponing the replacement.
2. Valuing closing stock on LIFO basis during rising prices.
3. Providing less depreciation.
4. Making higher provisions.

Codes:
(a) 1, 3 and 4 (b) 1, 2, 3 and 4
(c) 1 and 3 (d) 2 and 4

35. To test the liquidity of a concern which of the following ratios are useful? Choose the correct option from the codes.
1. Acid test ratio
2. Capital turnover ratio
3. Bad debts to sales ratio
4. Inventory turnover ratio

Codes:
(a) 2 and 4 (b) 2 and 3
(c) 1 and 3 (d) 1 and 4

Read the following and choose the correct option from the codes (Q 36-37):

36. **List I**
A. Man power planning
B. Selection and placement
C. Reinforcement and advancement
D. Industrial relations

List II
1. Forecast man power needs based on the policies and strategies of the company trend
2. Use the criteria and measures developed for selection procedures and placement
3. Promotion
4. Job analysis

Codes:	A	B	C	D
(a)	2	1	3	4
(b)	1	2	3	4
(c)	1	3	2	4
(d)	3	1	4	2

37. **List I (Psychologist needs)**
A. Physiological B. Security
C. Social D. Ego
E. Self-realisation

List II (Basic needs)
1. Eating 2. Accidents
3. Need for association with other
4. Reputation 5. Confidence

Codes:	A	B	C	D	E
(a)	3	1	2	4	5
(b)	4	2	3	1	5
(c)	1	2	4	3	5
(d)	1	2	3	4	5

Read the following statements and choose the correct option from the codes (Q. 38-39):

38. **Statement (A):** Performance appraisal is a critical activity of personnel management.

Statement (B): Its goal is to provide an accurate picture of a past and future employee performance.

Codes:
(a) Statement 'A' and statement 'B' both are true
(b) Statement 'A' is true but statement 'B' is explanation of statement 'A'
(c) Statement 'A' and statement 'B' both are false
(d) Statement 'A' is true but statement 'B' is not explanation of statement 'B'

39. **Statement (A):** A job description defines what the job is. It is a profile of the job.

Statement (B): A job specification describes what the job demands of employees who do it and the human skills that are required.

Codes:

(a) Only statement 'A' is true
(b) Statement 'A' is true but 'B' is not true
(c) Statement 'A' and 'B' are true
(d) Statement 'A' is not true but statement B is true

40. Training Information System included the following choose the correct option from the codes:
   1. training resources
   2. internal and external faculty
   3. training aids
   4. training needs
   5. opportunities

   Codes:

   (a) 1 only (b) 2 only
   (c) 3 and 4 (d) All of the above

41. Principle of indemnity does not apply for
   (a) Marine insurance. (b) Fire insurance.
   (c) Theft insurance. (d) Life insurance.

42. When the shares of a company are listed on the stock exchange, it indicates
   (a) company is financially sound.
   (b) that the stock exchange guarantees the financial soundness of the company.
   (c) the company is legally organised.
   (d) All of the above.

43. In India, all insurance companies are
   (a) privately owned but regulated by government.
   (b) government owned.
   (c) privately owned.
   (d) All of the above.

Read the following and choose the correct option from the codes:

44. **List I (Types of mutual fund)**
   (a) Open-ended mutual fund
   (b) Interval fund
   (c) Close-ended mutual fund
   (d) Balanced fund

   List II (Explanations)
   1. They are open for sale or redemption during pre-determind intervals at NAV related prices.
   2. The fund is open for subscription only during a specified period.
   3. Provides both growth and regular income.
   4. One that is available for subscription all through out the year.

Codes:	**A**	**B**	**C**	**D**
(a)	3	2	1	4
(b)	4	1	2	3
(c)	3	1	2	4
(d)	4	2	1	3

45. Fiscal policy relates to the government decision in respect of
   1. Taxation
   2. Government spending
   3. Government borrowing
   4. Public Debt

   Choose the correct option from the following codes:

   Codes:

   (a) 3 and 4 are correct
   (b) 2, 3 and 4 are correct.
   (c) 1 and 2 are correct
   (d) All the above are correct.

46. USA's deficit in balance of payment and surplus of Japan and Germany led to the problem of
   (a) Devaluation (b) Depreciation
   (c) Seignorange (d) None of these

47. International Bank for Reconstruction and Development was also called as
   (a) World Bank
   (b) African Bank
   (c) Asian Development Bank
   (d) None of the above

48. Most favoured nation clause was introduced by
   (a) ADB (b) IBRD (c) WTO (d) GATT

49. Dunkel proposal was discussed in
   (a) Asian Development Bank
   (b) World Bank
   (c) IMF
   (d) WTO

50. GATT is a
   (a) Binding contract (b) Organisation
   (c) Corporate body (d) Institution

PAPER–III

1. Conversion of a private company into a public company may be grouped under
   (a) conversion by operation of law
   (b) conversion by choice
   (c) conversion by default
   (d) All of the above
2. The memorandum of a limited company consists of
   (a) the name of the state, in which the registered office of the company is to be situated.
   (b) the object of the company.
   (c) the name of the company with 'Limited' or 'Private Limited' as the last word(s) of the name in the case of a Public Company or a Private Company as the case may be.
   (d) All of the above.
3. Minimum issued equity capital of a company should be
   (a) Two crores (b) Five crores
   (c) Six crores (d) Ten thousands
4. The appointment of a banker is necessary as it has to receive the share application along with
   (a) Allotment Money
   (b) Application Money
   (c) Second Call
   (d) First Call
5. The offer document shall also contain the information and statement specified in chapter VI of
   (a) SEBI guideline - 2000
   (b) SEBI guideline - 2001
   (c) SEBI guideline - 2002
   (d) SEBI guideline - 2003
6. The liabilities of shareholders of a public company is limited to the extent of
   (a) called up value of the share.
   (b) paid up value of the share.
   (c) the face value of the share.
   (d) All of the above.
7. A public company having a share capital
   (a) may file a statement in lieu of prospectus.
   (b) must issue a prospectus.
   (c) cannot file a statement in lieu of prospectus.
   (d) None of the above.
8. What does water in Balance Sheet indicate?
   (a) Over trading
   (b) Excess of liquidity
   (c) Part of capital not represented by assets
   (d) Under trading
9. "Higher the ratio, the more favourable it is" does not apply to
   (a) operating profit ratio
   (b) stock turnover ratio
   (c) gross profit ratio
   (d) operating ratio
10. Z Ltd. forfeited 20 shares of ₹ 10 each, on which ₹ 4 share were paid. What is the minimum price for reissue of these shares as fully paid?
    (a) ₹ 4 per share (b) ₹ 2 per share
    (c) ₹ 8 per share (d) ₹ 6 per share
11. When the disturbing positions do not bring back to, nor drive it from the original position it is called
    (a) Neutral equilibrium (b) Stable equilibrium
    (c) Both (a) and (b) (d) None of the above
12. The equilibrium of a single consumer is
    (a) Partial equilibrium
    (b) General equilibrium
    (c) Both (a) and (b)
    (d) None of the above
13. The necessary condition for the resources to be employed is the existence of
    (a) General equilibrium
    (b) Abundant resources
    (c) Exploitation of resources
    (d) None of the above
14. The marginal utility of money goes on increasing
    (a) with the decrease of money.
    (b) with the desire for money remaining constant.
    (c) with the increasing of money.
    (d) None of the above.
15. Marginal utility is a function of
    (a) Supply (b) Demand
    (c) Both (a) and (b) (d) None of these

16. It is the variable that sets limit to achieving the goal or extending the goal horizon.
(a) Cost factor
(b) Marginal factor
(c) Differential factor
(d) Limiting factor

17. This approach states that once the key factor is located, management can plan matching resources which together then constitute the system.
(a) The cost-benefit approach
(b) The marginal approach
(c) The limiting factor approach
(d) The differential approach

18. Chi-square value ranges from 0 to
(a) –1 (b) +1 (c) 10 (d) Infinity

19. Determine the order in which the following were developed
1. Fisher's F-test of significance of differences between the means of more than two samples.
2. Gosset's t-test of difference between the means of two samples.
3. Pearson's correlation coefficient.
4. Spearman's rank correlation coefficient.

Choose the correct option from the following codes:

Codes:
(a) 1, 2, 3, 4 (b) 2, 1, 3, 4
(c) 3, 2, 1, 4 (d) 4, 1, 2, 3

20. Which of the following advantages could be derived from the use of Franking machine?
1. It saves time because of its speed
2. Valuable facts and figures can be obtained
3. It is very convenient to use
4. In ensures much greater accuracy.

Choose the correct option from the following codes:

Codes:
(a) 1 and 2 (b) 2 and 3
(c) 1 and 4 (d) 1 and 3

21. An informal organisation is
(a) not written and manualised.
(b) not portrayed in organisational charts.
(c) a set of work relationship that grow out of the mutual interactions of persons working together over a period of time.
(d) customary, not enacted.

Choose the correct option from the following codes:

Codes:
(a) 1, 2 and 3 (b) 1, 2, 3 and 4
(c) 1 only (d) 1 and 2

22. The Human Relations Theory does not lay emphasis on
1. Principles
2. People
3. Human motivations
4. Informal group functions

Choose the correct option from the following codes:

Codes:
(a) 1, 2 and 3 (b) 1, 2, 3 and 4
(c) 1 only (d) 1 and 2

23. Which of the following are devices to bring about co-ordination
1. Cabinet Committees
2. Union Government
3. Zonal Councils
4. National Development Council

Choose the correct option from the following codes:

Codes:
(a) 2 only (b) 1 and 2
(c) 1, 2, 3 and 4 (d) 1, 3 and 4

24. Decentralization of an organisation is commended on account of which of the following advantages?
1. Reduced burden on top executives
2. Executive development
3. Improvement of morale
4. Solves problems of coordination.

Choose the correct option from the following codes:

Codes:
(a) 1, 2 and 3 (b) 3 and 4
(c) 2 and 3 (d) 1, 2 and 4

25. Directing function of management implies
1. Planning 2. Staffing
3. Leadership 4. Motivation

Choose the correct option from the following codes:

Codes:
(a) 2 and 4 (b) 2, 3 and 4
(c) 1 and 2 (d) 3 and 4

26. Which of the following factor affects the pricing decisions?
    1. Demand of the product
    2. Product characteristics
    3. Cost of the product
    4. Distribution channels of the product
    5. Customers characteristics

    Choose the correct option from the following codes:

    Codes:

    (a) 3 and 4 (b) 1 only
    (c) 3 only (d) All of the above
27. A marketing plan is composed of three basic components, namely
    1. Objective 2. Policies
    3. Program 4. Procedure
    5. Hints 6. Decision
    7. Command 8. Periodic
    9. Diversification

    Choose the correct option from the following codes:

    Codes:

    (a) 5, 7 and 9 (b) 6, 7 and 8
    (c) 1, 2 and 3 (d) 2, 3 and 9
28. The net profit will be maximised when
    (a) Contribution is maximised
    (b) Contribution is minimised
    (c) Fixed cost remains same
    (d) Fixed cost is increased
29. Decision-making is a future-oriented activity. It involves forecasting and planning. The function of decision-making is to choose alternatives for the
    (a) Profit (b) Loss
    (c) Future (d) Present
30. If fixed costs are expected to remain unaltered, that would be irrelevant in
    (a) Sales planning
    (b) Product mix decision
    (c) Production decision
    (d) The make or buy decision
31. In operating cycle method of working capital, the first step will be taken as
    (a) estimation of total amount of annual operating expenses.
    (b) estimation of required working.
    (c) computation of duration of the operating cycle.
    (d) None of the above.
32. Which factor is responsible for over-capitalization?
    (a) Liberal dividend policy
    (b) High promotion expenses
    (c) Wrong estimate of earning at the time of promotion
    (d) All of the above
33. Depreciation and write off intangible assets are included in
    (a) non-cash expenses
    (b) operating expenses
    (c) capital expenses
    (d) None of the above
34. The duration of operating cycle is computed in
    (a) Weeks (b) Days (c) Years (d) Months
35. A bearer of a share warrant of a company is
    (a) A member subject to certain conditions
    (b) A creditor of the company
    (c) A member of the company
    (d) Not a member of the company
36. When was The Employees' State Insurance Act started?
    (a) 1947 (b) 1950 (c) 1940 (d) 1948
37. Social security (minimum standards) convention covers
    (a) Sickness benefit
    (b) Unemployment benefit
    (c) Medical care
    (d) All of the above
38. Satisfaction is an attitude of mind and it is not the same as
    (a) Communication (b) Performance
    (c) Motivation (d) None of these
39. Equity theory of work motivation has been developed by
    (a) R. Thesis (b) Dr. L.N. Koli
    (c) J. Stacy Adams (d) J. Arun Kaul
40. The object of employees appraisal is
    (a) To help determine promotions and transfers.
    (b) To identify areas which require further training.
    (c) To improve job performance.
    (d) All of the above.
41. Which one of the following is not a commercial risk?

(a) Change in the exchange rate
(b) Insolvency of the buyer
(c) New restrictions placed on import-export trade
(d) Damage to goods in transit

42. The average clause in a fire policy states that the insured can get back
(a) the entire amount of the total loss suffered.
(b) the entire amount of partial loss suffered.
(c) a fixed percentage of loss suffered.
(d) only that portion of the actual loss suffered as the sum insured bears to total value.

43. Average clause in a fire policy
(a) penalises under-insurance.
(b) average the claim on the different policies taken by the insured.
(c) insures the property at average premium paid for the last three years.
(d) insures the property at the average rate of premium received.

44. The rate of which discounting the bills of first class banks is done by RBI is called
(a) Discounting Rate (b) Bank Rate
(c) Prime Lending Rate (d) Loan Rate

45. What is USGAAP?
(a) Union State Generous Agreement & Accounting Principles
(b) United States Generally Accepted Accounting Principles
(c) Union State Generous Accounts & Affairs and Practices
(d) United State General Allies & Army Practices

46. Consider.
1. Export duty
2. Export subsidy
3. Liberal import entitlement
4. Revaluation of currency

Which of the above policy measures would lead to an expansion of exports?

Codes:
(a) 3 and 4 (b) 2 and 4
(c) 1 and 3 (d) 1, 2, and 4

47. Which one of the following statements are correct? Choose the correct option.
1. Bills of lading is a document of file.
2. Green shipping bill is used for export of goods entitled to duty drawback.
3. An airway bills is not a document of title.
4. A consular invoice and a performa invoice are one and the same.

Codes:
(a) 1, 3 and 4 (b) 1, 2 and 3
(c) 2 and 4 (d) 1, 2 and 4

Read the following and choose the correct option:

48.

List I	List II
A. Mercantilism	1. France
B. Cameralism	2. Spain
C. Physiocrats	3. England
	4. Germany

Codes:	A	B	C
(a)	3	4	1
(b)	1	2	3
(c)	4	2	3
(d)	2	3	4

49. The following steps are normally taken in an import trade. Choose the correct option.
1. Indent and letter of credit
2. Ship's report
3. Delivery and customs formalities
4. Exchange and bill of exchange

Codes:
(a) 4, 1, 3, 2 (b) 1, 4, 3, 2
(c) 1, 4, 2, 3 (d) 4, 1, 2, 3

50. Which of the following is not the example of only upward Communication?
(a) Reports (b) Interviews
(c) Grapevine (d) Circulars

ANSWER SHEET

PAPER–I

1. (b)	2. (c)	3. (d)	4. (d)	5. (a)
6. (c)	7. (d)	8. (c)	9. (c)	10. (b)
11. (b)	12. (b)	13. (a)	14. (b)	15. (b)
16. (c)	17. (d)	18. (b)	19. (a)	20. (c)
21. (a)	22. (c)	23. (c)	24. (b)	25. (b)
26. (b)	27. (d)	28. (d)	29. (b)	30. (c)
31. (c)	32. (b)	33. (b)	34. (c)	35. (a)
36. (b)	37. (a)	38. (c)	39. (a)	40. (c)
41. (b)	42. (b)	43. (c)	44. (b)	45. (c)
46. (c)	47. (b)	48. (b)	49. (d)	50. (b)

PAPER–II

1. (d)	2. (b)	3. (b)	4. (d)	5. (d)
6. (b)	7. (d)	8. (d)	9. (a)	10. (b)
11. (c)	12. (b)	13. (c)	14. (d)	15. (d)
16. (b)	17. (d)	18. (d)	19. (b)	20. (d)
21. (b)	22. (d)	23. (b)	24. (c)	25. (a)
26. (a)	27. (b)	28. (b)	29. (c)	30. (a)
31. (b)	32. (a)	33. (c)	34. (c)	35. (d)
36. (b)	37. (d)	38. (b)	39. (c)	40. (d)
41. (d)	42. (c)	43. (b)	44. (b)	45. (d)
46. (c)	47. (a)	48. (d)	49. (d)	50. (a)

PAPER–III

1. (d)	2. (d)	3. (b)	4. (b)	5. (a)
6. (c)	7. (a)	8. (d)	9. (d)	10. (d)
11. (a)	12. (a)	13. (a)	14. (c)	15. (a)
16. (d)	17. (c)	18. (d)	19. (c)	20. (d)
21. (b)	22. (c)	23. (c)	24. (d)	25. (d)
26. (d)	27. (c)	28. (b)	29. (c)	30. (d)
31. (a)	32. (d)	33. (a)	34. (b)	35. (d)
36. (d)	37. (d)	38. (c)	39. (c)	40. (d)
41. (c)	42. (d)	43. (a)	44. (b)	45. (b)
46. (b)	47. (a)	48. (a)	49. (d)	50. (b)

MOCK TEST–5
PAPER–I

1. Which among the following gives more freedom to the learner to interact?
   (a) Small group discussion
   (b) Lectures by experts
   (c) Use of film
   (d) Viewing country-wide classroom program on TV
2. While designing communication strategy feed-forward studies are conducted by
   (a) Media (b) Audience
   (c) Communicator (d) Satellite
3. A theory is correct because
   (a) its derivations match with most observations
   (b) its advocate has written a big volume to establish it
   (c) it is supported by a large number of scholars
   (d) it has a large number of followers
4. Which of the following are true about the concepts?
   I. Concepts have different meanings in different contents.
   II. Concepts are the blocks from which theories are built.
   III. Concepts are ideas, abstractions, that do not have meaning in themselves.
   (a) Only II (b) I and III
   (c) I and II (d) All of these
5. The most sensible idea about teaching and research is that
   (a) they interfere with each other
   (b) they are two entirely different kinds of activities
   (c) they cannot go together
   (d) they are two sides of the same coin
6. Which of the following is quality of a teacher?
   (a) He should know the child psychology
   (b) He should evoke curiosity of the pupils by presenting the subject matter in an effective manner with clear explaining leading to better understanding of the matter
   (c) He should be trained in various teaching methodologies
   (d) All of these
7. Which of the following is/are true about research?
   (i) Gives emphasis to the development of theories, principles and generalisation, which are very helpful in accurate prediction regarding the variable understudy.
   (ii) It is always directed towards the solution of a problem.
   (iii) It is always based upon empirical or observable evidences.
   (a) Both (i) and (ii) (b) Both (i) and (iii)
   (c) Both (ii) and (iii) (d) All of the above
8. Which of the following methods of teaching encourages the use of maximum senses?

(a) Team teaching method
(b) Problem-solving method
(c) Laboratory method
(d) Self-study method

9. A non-fictional literary composition that forms an independent part of a publication, as a newspaper or magazine is known as
(a) Symposium (b) Paper
(c) Article (d) None of these

10. Photo bleeding means
(a) Photo placement (b) Photo cropping
(c) Photo colour adjustment
(d) Photo cutting

11. Attitudes, concepts, skills and knowledge are products of
(a) Explanation (b) Learning
(c) Research (d) Heredity

12. To study the relationship of family size with income a researcher classifies his population into different income slabs and then takes a random sample from each slab. Which technique of sampling does he adopt?
(a) Systematic Sampling
(b) Random Sampling
(c) Stratified Random Sampling
(d) Cluster Sampling

13. In business communication, the major obstacles arise because of the
(a) psychological barriers
(b) physical barriers
(c) organisational barriers
(d) mechanical barriers

14. The most important question that a researcher is interested to use statistical techniques in his problem then he has to see
(a) whether worthwhile inferences could be drawn
(b) whether the data could be quantified
(c) whether appropriate statistical techniques are available
(d) whether analysis of data would be possible

15. How can the objectivity of the research be enhanced?
(a) Through its validity
(b) Through its impartiality
(c) Through its reliability
(d) All of these

16. Which one of the following is not correct? A belief becomes a scientific truth when it
(a) can be replicated
(b) is established experimentally
(c) is arrived logically
(d) is accepted by many people

17. **Statement:** All cars are ducks. All ducks are birds.

Conclusions:
(i) All birds are cars. (ii) All cars are birds.

Choose the correct one.
(a) Only conclusion (i) follows
(b) Only conclusion (ii) follows
(c) Both (i) and (ii) follow
(d) Neither (i) nor (ii) follows

18. Research can be conducted by a person who
(a) is a hard worker
(b) has studied research methodology
(c) holds a postgraduate degree
(d) possesses thinking and reasoning ability

19. Action-research is
(a) A longitudinal research
(b) An applied research
(c) A research carried out to solve immediate problems
(d) All of the above

Read the following passage and answer the questions 20 to 24:

The genesis of service tax emanates from the ongoing structural transformation of the Indian economy, whereby presently more than one-half of GDP originates from the services sector. Despite the growing presence of the services sector in the Indian economy it remained out of the tax net prior to 1994-95, leading to a steady deterioration in tax-GDP ratio. The service tax was introduced in 1994-95 on a select category of services at a low rate of five percent. While the service tax rate and the coverage of services being taxed have increased ever since, the combined tax-GDP ratio of the Centre and States, nevertheless, deteriorated from 16.4 percent in 1985-86 to 14.1 percent in 1999-2000. It may be noted that between 1990-91 and 1998-99, the share of industrial sector in GDP dropped by 6.4 percentage points whereas almost 64 percent of the tax revenue was generated by indirect taxes for which industrial sector continues to be the principal tax base. On the other hand, during the same period, the share of services sector in GDP has increased by 10 percentage points and this sector has still remained poorly taxed.

The rationale for service tax, therefore, lies not only in arresting the falling tax-GDP ratio but also in *ipso facto* improving allocative efficiency in the economy as well as promoting equity. Against this backdrop, the service tax needs to be designed taking into account the fact that (i) the share of services in GDP is expanding; (ii) failure to tax services distorts consumer choices and encourages spending on services at the expense of goods; (iii) untaxed service traders are unable to claim Value Added Tax (VAT) on service inputs, which encourages businesses to develop in-house services, creating further distortions; and (iv) most services that are likely to become taxable are positively correlated with expenditure of high-income households and, therefore, service tax improves equity.

In the Indian context, taxation of services assumes importance in the wake of the need for improving the revenue system, ensuring a measure of neutrality in taxation between goods and services and eventually helping to evolve an efficient system of domestic trade taxes, both at the Central and the State levels.

20. What, according to the passage, was the impact of exclusion of service tax till the first half of the last decade of the past century?
    (a) Service sector used to flourish exorbitantly
    (b) There was no impact as there was no service tax
    (c) There was a steady deterioration in the GDP
    (d) Tax-GDP ratio had steadily and gradually aggravated
21. Levying service tax is most likely to achieve which of the following?
    (i) Promoting equity.
    (ii) Check on reducing tax-GDP ratio.
    (iii) Enhancement in allocative efficiency.
    (a) Both (ii) and (iii) (b) Both (i) and (iii)
    (c) Both (i) and (ii) (d) All the three
22. The origin of service tax is attributed to
    (a) metamorphosis of our country's economy
    (b) increase in Gross Domestic Product (GDP)
    (c) existence of service sector
    (d) tax of the future
23. Which of the following factors helps service tax to improve fairness across different economic strata of society?
    (a) It improves revenue system
    (b) Taxable services are mostly those that are utilised by the rich
    (c) Untaxed service traders are prevented from claiming value added tax
    (d) Encouragement to in-house services is effected
24. Which of the following is most likely to provide neutrality to various economic activities?
    (a) Consistency in tax structure and revenue buoyancy
    (b) Increase in revenue buoyancy
    (c) fairness in tax administration
    (d) Equity and efficiency in various activities
25. Which of the following is classified in the category of the developmental research?
    (a) Descriptive research
    (b) Philosophical research
    (c) Action research
    (d) All the above
26. The education aims at the fullest realisation of all the potentialities of children. It implies that
    I. it is necessary that their attitudes are helpful, encouraging and sympathetic.
    II. teacher and parents must know what children are capable of and what potentialities they possess.
    III. they should provide suitable opportunities and favourable environmental facilities which are conducive to the maximum growth of children.

    Choose the correct one.
    (a) II and III (b) I and III
    (c) I and II (d) All of them
27. How many times has the preamble of Indian constitution been amended so far?
    (a) Once (b) Twice (c) Thrice (d) Never
28. The relationship between earth, mountains and forests can be represented as

(a)  (b) 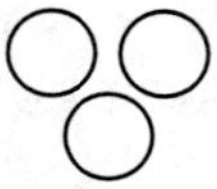

(c)  (d) 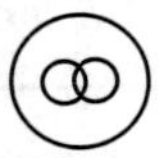

29. Central Fuel Research Institute is situated in
    (a) Pune (b) Jadugoda
    (c) Lucknow (d) Kolkata
30. The letters in the first set have certain relationship. On the basis of this relationship what is the right choice for the second set?
    AST : BRU :: NQV : ?
    (a) OPW (b) ORW (c) MPU (d) MRW
31. The number of students in four classes A, B, C, D and their respective mean marks obtained by each of the class are given below:

	Class A	Class B	Class C	Class D
Number of students	10	40	30	20
Arithmetic mean	20	30	50	15

The combined mean of the marks of four classes together will be
(a) 15 (b) 32 (c) 50 (d) 20

32. Communication with oneself is known as
    (a) Organisational communication
    (b) Interpersonal communication
    (c) Intrapersonal communication
    (d) Grapewine communication
33. The number system which is not a positional notation system is
    (a) Binary (b) Octal
    (c) Roman (d) Decimal
34. Which of the following options will complete the series?
    AZ, GT, MN, ?, YB.
    (a) TS (b) KF (c) RX (d) SH
35. If '367' means 'I am happy'; '748' means 'You are sad' and '469' means 'Happy and sad' in a given code, then which of the following represents 'and' in that code?
    (a) 4 (b) 6 (c) 3 (d) 9
36. What is the excess 3 code?
    (a) self-algebraic code
    (b) cyclic complimenting code
    (c) cyclic algebraic code
    (d) self-complimenting code
37. Which of the following is not created by the Act of Parliament?
    (a) Railway Board
    (b) Atomic Energy Commission
    (c) Backward Class Commission
    (d) University Grants Commission
38. Which of the following is radioactive pollutant?
    (a) Nickel (b) Iron
    (c) Chlorine (d) Thorium
39. The first Indian experimental geostationary communication satellite was
    (a) Skylab (b) Apple
    (c) INSAT-1A (d) INSAT-1B
40. Which one of the following is a research tool?
    (a) Diagram (b) Questionnaire
    (c) Graph (d) Illustration
41. Which article of the constitution provides safeguards to Naga Customary and their social practices against any act of Parliament?
    (a) Article 371B (b) Article 371A
    (c) Article 263 (d) Article 371C
42. **Statement:** Although the city was under kneedeep water for a week in this monsoon, there is no outbreak of any water borne disease.
    Assumptions:
    (i) Waterborne disease usually spreads in monsoon.
    (ii) Water concentration at a place leads to waterborne disease.

    Choose the correct option.
    (a) Only assumption (i) is implicit
    (b) Only assumption (ii) is implicit
    (c) Both (i) and (ii) are implicit
    (d) Neither (i) nor (ii) is implicit
43. Books and records are the primary sources of data in
    (a) laboratory research
    (b) historical research
    (c) participatory research
    (d) clinical research

44. The Kothari Commission's report was entitled on
(a) Learning to be Adventure
(b) Education and National Development
(c) Education and Socialisation in Democracy
(d) Diversification of Education

45. What is the term used for a half byte?
(a) word (b) bit (c) nibble (d) bug

46. C-band transponder in satellites uses the frequency range
(a) 12 GHz to 14 GHz (b) 4 GHz to 6 GHz
(c) 2 GHz to 4 GHz (d) None of these

47. Which of the following water pollutants is the cause of sterility in human beings?
(a) Manganese (b) Mercury
(c) Arsenic (d) None of these

48. Controlled group condition is applied in
(a) Descriptive Research
(b) Survey Research
(c) Experimental Research
(d) Historical Research

49. Match List I with List II and select the correct answer using the codes given below.

List I (Institutes)
(A) Central Arid Zone Institute
(B) Space Application Centre
(C) Indian Institute of Public Administration
(D) Headquarters of Indian Science Congress

List II (Cities)
(1) Kolkata (2) New Delhi
(3) Ahmedabad (4) Jodhpur

Codes:	A	B	C	D
(a)	4	3	2	1
(b)	4	2	1	3
(c)	3	1	2	4
(d)	1	2	4	3

The total CO_2 emissions from various sectors are 5 mmt. In the Pie Chart given below, the percentage contribution to CO_2 emissions from various sectors is indicated.

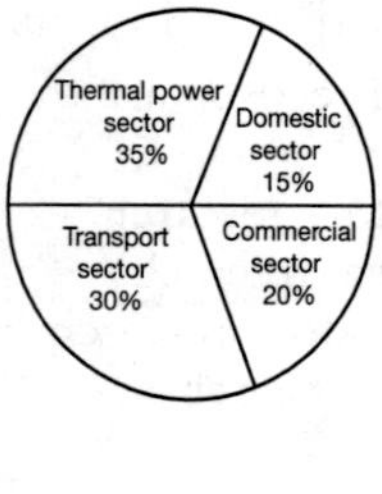

50. What is the absolute CO_2 emission from domestic sector?
(a) 1.75 mmt (b) 0.75 mmt
(c) 1.5 mmt (d) 2.5 mmt

PAPER–II

1. A minor
(a) can be admitted to the loss of partnership as a partner.
(b) can become a partner of firm.
(c) cannot be partner of firm.
(d) can be admitted to the benefits of partnership.

2. Whether the liability of a partner is
(a) Joint
(b) Limited
(c) Unlimited, Joint and Several
(d) Unlimited

3. Income Tax Act came into force from
(a) 1961 (b) 1960 (c) 1965 (d) 1962

4. The term 'Person' includes (in case of Income Tax, Act 1961)
(a) a Firm.
(b) a Company.
(c) a Hindu Undivided Family.
(d) All of the above.

5. The tax rate applicable in case of domestic company is
(a) 22 per cent (b) 48 per cent
(c) 35 per cent (d) 38.5 per cent

6. Which of the following assets would be taken into account for working capital turnover ratio?
1. Plant 2. Stock 3. Mortgage
4. Sales 5. Reserve 6. Bank

Choose the correct one.

Codes:
(a) 2, 4, and 6 (b) 3, 5, and 6
(c) 1, 5, and 6 (d) 4, 5, and 6

7. Consider the following information.
1. Gross sales ₹ 20,00,000
2. Sales tax 7% on gross sales
3. Income tax 40%
4. Profit before tax 400,000

What is net profit before tax ratio?

Codes:
(a) 23.5% (b) 24.5% (c) 21.5% (d) 22.5%

8. What is the amount of goodwill in the following case? Three year's purchase of the last four year's average profits. The profits and losses for the last four years are
   1. Year ₹ 5,000 2. Year ₹ 8,000
   3. Year ₹ 3,000 (Loss) 4. Year ₹ 6,000
   (a) ₹ 11,000 (b) ₹ 12,000
   (c) ₹ 9,000 (d) ₹ 10,000
9. Given the following data.

Net profit during the year	₹ 30,000
Total purchase	₹ 70,000
Creditors in the beginning	₹ 24,000
Creditors at the end	₹ 36,000

   Cash from operations is
   (a) ₹ 22,000 (b) ₹ 42,000
   (c) ₹ 100,000 (d) ₹ 30,000

Match List I with List II and select the correct answer using the codes given below.

10. **List I**
    A. Mutual fund
    B. Public issue of capital
    C. Forward trading
    D. Option pricing

    List II
    1. Stock exchange
    2. Assets management company
    3. Merchant banking
    4. Forex market

Codes:	A	B	C	D
(a)	2	3	1	4
(b)	2	3	4	1
(c)	3	2	4	1
(d)	3	2	1	4

11. The marginal utility falls when the quantity of the commodity with the consumer
    (a) Remains constant (b) Increases
    (c) Decreases (d) None of these
12. The Law of Diminishing Marginal Utility holds goods if the persons are
    (a) Eccentric (b) Normal
    (c) Irrational (d) All of the above
13. A consumer goes on purchasing a commodity till the marginal utility is
    (a) equal to price (b) less than the price
    (c) zero (d) None of the above
14. Among following which are conditions of price discrimination
    1. market must be segmentable
    2. price elasticity of demand is different in different markets
    3. income disparity exists

    Choose the correct one.

    Codes:
    (a) 1 and 2 (b) only 2
    (c) All of these (d) None of these

Match List I with List II and select the correct answer using the codes given below.

15. **List I**
    A. H. Wold and L. Jurren
    B. A.C. Harberger
    C. Cobb. H. Douglas
    D. Henry Schultz

    List II
    1. Demand analysis
    2. The demand for durable goods
    3. A theory of production
    4. Theory and measurement of demand

Codes:	A	B	C	D
(a)	2	3	1	4
(b)	1	2	3	4
(c)	2	1	3	4
(d)	2	1	4	2

16. Non-parametric test
    (a) Does not make assumption about the form of distribution
    (b) Not concerned with parameter
    (c) Distribution free statistical test
    (d) All of the above
17. Memory unit in an electronic computer performs the function of
    (a) Making calculations
    (b) Storing the data
    (c) Giving out the end product
    (d) Controlling the other operating units
18. Franking machine is used for
    (a) fixing stamps on outward letters and envelopes.
    (b) producing a typewritten document in multiple copies.
    (c) printing addresses on envelopes, wrappers, etc.
    (d) None of the above.
19. Computer hardware refers to
    (a) punch cards, magnetic tapes or paper tapes.

(b) data required for processing.
(c) the end product obtained from computer.
(d) all the equipment required for proper functioning of a programme.

20. Signed rank test was developed by
(a) Kolmogrov (b) Frank Wilcoxon
(c) Karl Pearson (d) Kruskal

21. The three main objectives of Scientific Management are
1. Standardization of working conditions
2. Standardization of working methods
3. Planning of large daily tasks
4. Maximisation of employment
Choose the correct one.
Codes:
(a) 2, 3 and 4 (b) 1, 2 and 4
(c) 1, 2 and 3 (d) 1, 3 and 4

22. Dorwin Cartwright and Alvin Zander identified the following two variables
1. Employee-oriented
2. Production-oriented
3. Goal-oriented
4. Group-oriented
Choose the correct one.
Codes:
(a) 3 and 4 (b) 1 and 4
(c) 1 and 2 (d) 2 and 3

23. In line and staff organisation, the authority lies in
(a) Staff (b) Line
(c) Both (a) and (b) (d) All of the above

24. Decentralisation
(a) decreases the importance of superiors.
(b) increases the importance of superiors.
(c) decreases the importance of subordinates.
(d) increases the importance of subordinates.

25. In the field of management some of the important techniques, relate to budgeting, cost accounting, planning and control through
(a) Budgetary Control
(b) Operational Research
(c) Financial Administration
(d) PERT and CPM

Match List I with List II and select the correct answer using the codes given below.

26. **List I (Motivation models)**
A. Economic model
B. Learning model
C. Psycho analytic model
D. Organisational model

List II (Elements)
1. Attractive design 2. Inspiration
3. Sex 4. Cost of product

Codes:	A	B	C	D
(a)	1	2	3	4
(b)	1	2	4	3
(c)	1	3	2	4
(d)	2	1	4	3

26. **List I (Products on the basis of Psychology)**
A. Prestige products
B. Maturity products
C. Anxiety product
D. Hedonic product

List II (Products)
1. Ownership on the car, bus, house
2. Bidi, cigareatte, cold drink
3. Soap, Blades
4. Biscuit, double-roti, bread and butter

Codes:	A	B	C	D
(a)	2	1	3	4
(b)	1	2	3	4
(c)	4	3	1	2
(d)	1	2	4	3

27. **List I (Functions of a marketing process)**
A. Functions of exchanges
B. Transfer of ownership
C. Functions of physical supply
D. Facilitating functions

List II (Their sub-functions)
1. Selling 2. Buying and selling
3. Transportation 4. Financing

Codes:	A	B	C	D
(a)	2	3	1	4
(b)	1	2	3	4
(c)	4	2	3	1
(d)	3	1	2	4

28. **List I (Instrument of marketing)**
A. Product B. Promotion
C. Price D. Place

List II (Their qualities)
1. Shape, design
2. Advertising, publicity

3. Discount, policies regarding pricing
4. Layout of stores, location

Codes:	A	B	C	D
(a)	2	1	3	4
(b)	1	2	3	4
(c)	2	3	1	4
(d)	3	4	1	2

30. **List I (Promotion mix tools)**
A. Advertising
B. Sales Promotion
C. Personal selling
D. Publicity

List (Sources of message)
1. Print ads 2. Couponing
3. Telemarketing 4. Print media

Codes:	A	B	C	D
(a)	3	1	2	4
(b)	1	2	3	4
(c)	3	2	4	1
(d)	2	3	1	4

31. Cost of machine ₹ 1,00,000, scrap value ₹ 10,000. Life is 4 years. What will be the amount of depreciation according to sum of years digit method in the first year?
(a) 36,000 (b) 25,000
(c) 40,000 (d) 60,000

32. The underwriting commission on share capital should not exceed
(a) 4% (b) 7% (c) 5% (d) 2%

33. Under which method of depreciation, the value of machinery never comes to zero?
(a) Diminishing value (b) Straight line
(c) Sinking fund (d) Sum of years digit

34. Charging of capital expenditure to revenue results in
(a) Capital reserve (b) Secret reserve
(c) Revenue reserve (d) None of these

35. Secret reserves serve the purpose of
(a) meeting exceptional losses.
(b) increasing the working capital.
(c) enabling the directors to tide over unfavourable times.
(d) None of the above.

36. When was a Tripartite Committee on fair wages appointed?
(a) In 1949 (b) In 1950
(c) In 1948 (d) In 1947

37. The Tripartite Committee on fair wages examined the question of fare wages at length and adopted its draft report on
(a) 6th of July 1949
(b) 6th of September 1949
(c) 6th of June 1949
(d) None of the above

38. The provisions of the Payment of Bonus Act, 1965 take effect from the accounting year commencing on
(a) 7th July 1965 (b) 6th April 1966
(c) 7th August 1960 (d) Any day in 1964

39. The Trade Union activity in India made a beginning even before the end of the ____ century.
(a) 16th (b) 20th (c) 18th (d) 19th

40. Who started an agitation to draw the attention of the government to the deplorable condition of women and child labour in Indian industry?
(a) Mahatma Gandhi
(b) Mr. Sorabjee Shapurjee
(c) Madan Mohan Malviya
(d) Pt. Jawaharlal Nehru

41. When a customer gives standing instructions to the bank for remitting a specified sum of money every month towards payment to his rent to a person, the banks acts as
(a) an agent of the customer.
(b) a servant of the customer.
(c) a debtor of the customer's landlord.
(d) pledgor.

42. A banker is duty-bound to observe secrecy of a customer's account. However, disclosure would be justified when
(a) the bank replies to a status enquiry from a party who desires to supply some machinery on credit to the customer.
(b) it is under compulsion of law.
(c) the banker indicates the credit balance in the account at the time of returning a cheque for want of funds.
(d) None of the above.

43. While collecting cheques/bills, etc. for a customer the bank acts as
(a) a debtor
(b) a pledgor

(c) an agent of the customer
(d) a trustee of the customer

44. Upon the banker's allowing an overdraft to a customer in his current account, the relationship between the two will be that of
(a) Principal and agent
(b) Trustee and beneficiary
(c) Creditor and debtor
(d) None of the above

45. When a customer deposits a sealed box with bank for safe custody, the relationship between the two is that of
(a) bailor and bailee
(b) trustee and beneficiary
(c) principal and agent
(d) debtor and creditor

46. Managerial decisions which increase the importance of subordinates are linked with
(a) Centralised authority
(b) Decentralised authority
(c) Both (a) and (b)
(d) None of the above

47. The World Bank is an
(a) International agency
(b) International money fund
(c) International office
(d) International market

48. LIBOR means
(a) London Interbank Bid Rate
(b) London Interbank Offered Rate
(c) London Interbank Original Rate
(d) London Interbank Banking Rate

49. A US dollar deposited with a bank in London is a
(a) Euro dollar deposit
(b) US dollar deposit
(c) Pound US dollar deposit
(d) None of these

50. For political co-operation which body came into existence?
(a) Reserve Bank of India
(b) World Bank
(c) International Monetary Fund
(d) United Nations Organisation

PAPER–III

1. Which of the following statements are correct?
   1. A minor is not competent to become a member of a company.
   2. A firm cannot be treated as a member of a company.
   3. A foreigner may become a member of a company.
   4. A partnership firm cannot hold shares in a company in the individual names of partners as joint holders.

   Choose the correct one.

   Codes:
   (a) 1, 3 and 4 (b) 1, 2 and 3
   (c) 1 and 2 (d) 2, 3 and 4

2. Which of the following statements are correct?
   1. Compare the lists of debtors and creditors.
   2. Check the total of cash book.
   3. Ensure that no entry remained unposted.
   4. Check the trial balance.

   What is the correct balance of these functions to be performed by an auditor to locate errors?
   Choose the correct one.

   Codes:
   (a) 4, 3, 1, 2 (b) 1, 2, 4, 3
   (c) 4, 2, 1, 3 (d) 1, 3, 4, 2

Match List I with List II and select the correct answer using the codes given below.

3. **List I (Economic systems)**
   A. Capitalism B. Socialism
   C. Communism D. Mixed

   List II (Features)
   1. Managers are selected on the basis of ability
   2. Profits recognised
   3. No depreciation permitted
   4. Public and private sector

Codes:	A	B	C	D
(a)	4	3	2	1
(b)	1	2	3	4
(c)	3	4	2	1
(d)	2	1	3	4

4. **List I (Year)** / **List II (Annual Rate of Growth of GDP)**

A. 2007-08 — 1. 9-3%
B. 2008-09 — 2. 6-8%
C. 2009-10 — 3. 8-0%
D. 2010-11 — 4. 8-6%

Codes:	A	B	C	D
(a)	4	3	2	1
(b)	1	2	3	4
(c)	3	2	4	1
(d)	4	1	3	2

5. **List I**
   A. Partners and Firm
   B. Sole Proprietorship
   C. Public Limited Company
   D. Nominal Partnership

   List II
   1. Agent and principle relationship
   2. Prospectus
   3. Personal Supervision
   4. Firm image

Codes:	A	B	C	D
(a)	4	2	3	1
(b)	1	2	4	3
(c)	1	3	2	4
(d)	2	3	1	4

6. From the following statements related insolvency account mark your answer according to the answer code given
   1. List A contains particulars relating to unsecured creditors.
   2. All taxes due are considered preferential creditors.
   3. Properties held by the insolvent in the fiduciary capacity can be distributed amongst his creditors.
   4. List D contains the particulars relating to assets and properties.

   Codes:
   (a) 2 and 4 are correct (b) 1 and 4 are correct
   (c) 1 and 3 are correct (d) 1 and 2 are correct

7. Consider the following statements.
   1. Operational loss is a source of fund.
   2. Decrease in working capital is a source of fund.
   3. Additions to fixed assets are an application of fund.
   4. Fresh introduction of capital is an application of funds.

   Which of the above statements are applicable while preparing the funds flow statements?
   Choose the correct one.
   Codes:
   (a) 2 and 3 (b) 1, 3 and 4
   (c) 1 and 2 (d) 1 and 3

8. In what order the following items are shown on the liability side of the balance sheet?
   1. Share capital 2. Debentures
   3. Sundry creditors 4. Proposed dividends

   Choose the correct one.
   Codes:
   (a) 2, 3, 4, 1 (b) 1, 4, 2, 3
   (c) 1, 2, 3, 4 (d) 1, 3, 2, 4

9. Which group of the following items are application of funds?
   1. Loss from operations
   2. Loan from financial institutions
   3. Redemption of debentures
   4. Sale of fixed assets
   5. Payment of dividends

   Choose the correct one.
   Codes:
   (a) 1, 2 and 4 (b) 3, 4 and 5
   (c) 1, 3 and 4 (d) 1, 3 and 5

10. In what order the following items in respect of share capital are shown in the balance sheet of a company?
    1. Paid up capital
    2. Issued capital
    3. Authorised capital
    4. Subscribed capital

    Choose the correct one.
    Codes:
    (a) 3, 2, 4, 1 (b) 4, 3, 1, 2
    (c) 4, 1, 3, 2 (d) 3, 4, 2, 1

11. The National Museum at New Delhi is attached to
    (a) Delhi University
    (b) a Deemed University
    (c) a Subordinate Office of the JNU
    (d) Part of Ministry of Tourism and Culture

12. Human relations approach of management is associated with:
    (a) Abraham Maslow (b) Peter F. Drucker
    (c) Elton Mayo (d) Herzberg

13. The total utility of a quantity of a commodity is maximum when the marginal utility is
   (a) Zero (b) Maximum
   (c) Minimum (d) All of these

14. With every diminution of one's stock the marginal utility will go on
   (a) Remaining constant (b) Decreasing
   (c) Increasing (d) All of the above

15. Marginal utility analysis assumes that the marginal utility of money
   (a) varies according to price fluctuations.
   (b) remains constant.
   (c) varies according to consumer behaviour.
   (d) None of the above.

16. Internal check serves the purpose of
   (a) detection and prevention of errors.
   (b) detection of errors.
   (c) prevention of errors.
   (d) None of the above.

17. Who is the majority investor in insurance companies?
   (a) Individual Policy-holder or Retail Customer
   (b) Corporate Sector
   (c) Government Sector
   (d) Semi-Government Sector

18. Break-Even analysis deals with:
   (a) relationship between cost and cost mix
   (b) relationship between cost, output and profits
   (c) relationship between cost and sales
   (d) relationship between profit and sales

19. Ohil state model suggests the following as the best leader-behaviour.
   (a) High concern both for production and people.
   (b) Low structure and low consideration.
   (c) High structure and high consideration.
   (d) Low concern both for production and people.

20. Computer system accessible to non-specialists to assist in planning and decision-making is called
   (a) Expert System
   (b) Disk Operating System
   (c) Management Information System
   (d) Decision Support System

21. Which of the following constitute man-power planning?
   1. Determining human resource requirements both quantitatively and qualitatively.
   2. Finding the sources of talented individuals.
   3. Planning for the human resource needs of an organisation.
   4. Reaching out to the right source for procuring the right people.

   Choose the correct one.

   Codes:
   (a) 1 and 3 (b) 1, 2, 3 and 4
   (c) 1, 2 and 4 (d) 2 and 3

22. Consider the following statements. The social responsibility of business is to
   1. do a business as per the public policy.
   2. obey all the rules and regulations of the government.
   3. make payment of the taxes imposed by the government.
   4. provide not necessarily adequate but good quality of goods.

   Choose the correct one.

   Codes:
   (a) 1 and 4 are correct.
   (b) 2 and 3 are correct.
   (c) 1, 2, 3 and 4 are correct.
   (d) 1, 2 and 3 are correct.

23. What is the order of the performance of the following functions of management?
   1. Planning 3. Organising
   2. Directing 4. Controlling

   Choose the correct one.

   Codes:
   (a) 1, 3, 2, 4 (b) 1, 3, 4, 2
   (c) 1, 2, 3, 4 (d) 1, 4, 2, 3

24. Consider the following statements.
   1. MBO is a control technique in which managers devote time only on the areas of deviation.
   2. MBO integrates the individual with the organisation and the organisation with the environment.
   3. In MBO the control over people is shifted to control over operations.
   4. The MBO principle must be accompanied in practice by the principle of critical-point control.

Choose the correct one.

Codes:

(a) 3 and 4 are correct (b) 1 and 4 are correct
(c) 1 and 2 are correct (d) 2 and 3 are correct

25. The strategic approach to total compensation involved splitting the total compensation into three parts as under
 1. Variable pay 2. Indirect pay
 3. Base pay

 Choose the correct one.

 Codes:

 (a) 1, 2 and 3 (b) 2 and 3
 (c) 1 only (d) 1 and 2

Match List I with List II and select the correct answer using the codes given below (Q 26-27).

26. **List I (Marketing Sub-plans)**
 A. Contingency plan
 B. Organisational plan
 C. Technical plan
 D. Baseline research

 List II (Variables of Marketing Sub-plan)
 1. Diversification
 2. Public relations
 3. Quality control
 4. Customer service

Codes:	A	B	C	D
(a)	1	2	3	4
(b)	1	3	2	4
(c)	4	2	3	1
(d)	2	4	3	1

27. **List I (Market Segmentations)**
 A. Geographic B. Demographic
 C. Psychographic D. Behavioural

 List II (Factors of Segmentation)
 1. Habitat
 2. Sex
 3. Nationality
 4. Personal preferences

Codes:	A	B	C	D
(a)	2	3	1	4
(b)	1	2	3	4
(c)	2	1	3	4
(d)	2	1	4	3

28. A firm producing a large number of products will follow the pricing strategy known as:
 (a) Cost-plus pricing
 (b) Differential pricing
 (c) Product-line pricing
 (d) Price leadership

29. Which of the following is/are not stage of the marketing management process?
 1. Assessment of business opportunity
 2. Organising research market surveys
 3. Selecting target markets
 4. Strategy formulation
 5. Planning marketing programmes
 6. Implementation
 7. Controlling marketing efforts
 8. Accounting information system

 Choose the correct one.

 Codes:

 (a) 1, 4 and 6 (b) 1, 2 and 4
 (c) 8 only (d) None of these

30. Which of the following factors affects the choice of channels of distribution?
 1. Size of manufacturer
 2. Desire to control the channel
 3. Perishability of product
 4. Weight of product
 5. Number of customers

 Choose the correct one.

 Codes:

 (a) 3 and 4 (b) 4 and 5
 (c) 2 only (d) All of the above

31. Consider the steps in Risk Management.
 1. Risk Evaluation 2. Risk Avoidance
 3. Risk Identification 4. Risk Elimination
 5. Risk Reduction 6. Risk Financing

 Choose the correct one.

 Codes:

 (a) 3, 4, 2, 5, 6, 1 (b) 4, 1, 2, 3, 5, 6
 (c) 2, 4, 5, 1, 6, 3 (d) 3, 1, 2, 4, 5, 6

32. Consider the following conditions to be fulfilled by a company regarding issue of sweat equity shares.
 1. The issue of sweat equity shares is authorised by an ordinary resolution passed by the company in the general meeting.
 2. Not less than six months should have, at the date of the issue elapsed since the date on which the company was entitled to commence business.

3. All the limitations shall be applicable to such sweat equity shares.

Choose the correct one.

Codes:

(a) 3 only (b) 1, 2 and 3
(c) 1 only (d) 1 and 2

33. The tax shield would result in
 1. increase in tax liability
 2. increase in EPS
 3. decrease in EPS
 4. decrease in tax liability

Choose the correct one.

Codes:

(a) 2 and 4 (b) 1 and 3
(c) 1 and 4 (d) 3 and 4

34. Which of the following ratios are used for measuring profitability of a business?
 1. Acid test ratio 2. ROI
 3. Net profit ratio 4. Interest coverage ratio

Choose the correct one.

Codes:

(a) 2 and 3 (b) 1, 2, 3 and 4
(c) 3 only (d) 1 and 3

35. Sinking fund for depreciation is created
 (a) to provide funds for replacement of asset.
 (b) to write off depreciation.
 (c) to provide for increased price of new asset to be purchased.
 (d) None of the above.

36. Methods of training is
 1. the telling method
 2. the showing method
 3. the role playing method
 4. the discussion technique

Choose the correct one.

Codes:

(a) 2 and 3 (b) 2 only
(c) 1, 2 and 3 (d) 1, 2, 3 and 4

37. McGehee and Thayer recommend which of the following three tier approach to determine the training needs?
 1. Organisational analysis
 2. Operational analysis
 3. Man analysis
 4. Assets analysis
 5. Inventory analysis

Choose the correct one.

Codes:

(a) 1, 2 and 3 (b) 4 and 5
(c) 1, 3 and 5 (d) 2 and 3

38. Which of the following need does/do not fall under needs of training and development?
 1. Technological advances
 2. Organisational complexity
 3. Organisational tenure
 4. Human relation movement
 5. Performance evaluation

Choose the correct one.

Codes:

(a) 3 only (b) 2 only
(c) 4 and 5 (d) 1, 2, 3 and 4

39. Which of the following points is/are not important for training?
 1. Reduction in supervision
 2. Reduction in cost and wastage
 3. Increased stability and flexibility
 4. Convenience in co-ordination
 5. Improvement in Industrial Relations

Choose the correct one.

Codes:

(a) 1 only (b) 5 only
(c) 3 and 4 (d) All of the above

40. Methods of securing workers' participation in management involves
 1. Co-partnership
 2. Suggestions scheme
 3. Joint consultation
 4. Employees representations on the Board of Directors

Choose the correct one

Codes:

(a) 1, 2, 3 and 4 (b) 1, 2 and 4
(c) 1, 3 and 4 (d) 2, 3 and 4

41. Identify sources of agricultural credit in India from the code given below:
 1. Commercial Banks
 2. Money Lender
 3. Regional Rural Bank
 4. Small Industries Development Bank of India

Codes:

(a) 1, 4 and 3 (b) 1, 2, 3 and 4
(c) 1, 2 and 3 (d) 2, 3 and 1

42. Consider the following statements regarding grey market in the context of security exchange, and choose the correct options from the given codes.
    1. It is a market wherein trading in a security takes place before it is officially listed.
    2. It is legal and a form of private placement business.
    3. Securities are sold through prospectus.

    Choose the correct one.

    Codes:
    (a) 3 only (b) 1, 2 and 3
    (c) 1 only (d) 2 and 3
43. The biggest stock exchange of India is
    (a) Calcutta (b) Bombay
    (c) Madras (d) Delhi
44. Short sales in a stock exchange means
    (a) signing transfer deed without filling in the name of the transferee.
    (b) selling those shares which one does not have.
    (c) selling shares and then buying the same shares.
    (d) All of the above.
45. Principle of indemnity does not apply to
    (a) theft insurance
    (b) life insurance
    (c) fire insurance
    (d) marine insurance
46. Which one of the following best explains the term 'Duty Drawback'?
    (a) Payment of duties in rupees and not in foreign currency.
    (b) Refund of customs duty paid on imports and excise duty on customs purchases.
    (c) Duty free import of raw materials and refund of excise duty on other indigenous purchases.
    (d) Refund of excise duty for manufacture of goods exported out of the country.
47. A foreign company means
    (a) a company incorporated outside India and having established place of business in India.
    (b) a company incorporated in India and having a place of business outside India.
    (c) Both of (a) and (b).
    (d) All of the above.
48. When a full ship is hired, the shipping company issues
    (a) Bill of entry (b) Shipping order
    (c) R/R (d) Charter party
49. In the context of foreign trade, the CTF cost may be obtained by
    (a) deducting freight and marine insurance premium for the FOB price.
    (b) adding freight and marine insurance premium to the FOB price.
    (c) deducting customs duties, freight and marine insurance premium from the price.
    (d) adding customs duties, freight and marine insurance premium to the cost.
50. Consider the following passage: "In a system of freely flexible exchange rates each country must be prepared to let the exchange rate fall or rise to whatever level is required to clear the foreign exchange market The authorities must not intervene. Only if these conditions are met will autonomous equilibrium in foreign exchange market and its equivalent (that is balance of payments equilibrium) be consistently achieved."

    According to this passage, under freely flexible exchange rate
    (a) foreign exchange market cannot bring about equilibrium.
    (b) equilibrium of balance of payments is automatic.
    (c) gold standard is required for equilibrium.
    (d) Government's interference is necessary for equilibrium.

ANSWER SHEET

PAPER–I

1. (c)	2. (c)	3. (a)	4. (d)	5. (d)
6. (a)	7. (d)	8. (b)	9. (c)	10. (b)
11. (d)	12. (a)	13. (c)	14. (c)	15. (a)
16. (c)	17. (a)	18. (b)	19. (a)	20. (c)
21. (d)	22. (a)	23. (c)	24. (a)	25. (b)
26. (b)	27. (b)	28. (c)	29. (d)	30. (b)

31. (b) 32. (c) 33. (a) 34. (c) 35. (b)
36. (b) 37. (a) 38. (b) 39. (d) 40. (a)
41. (d) 42. (c) 43. (a) 44. (b) 45. (c)
46. (b) 47. (d) 48. (b) 49. (c) 50. (c)

PAPER–II

1. (d) 2. (c) 3. (a) 4. (d) 5. (d)
6. (a) 7. (c) 8. (b) 9. (b) 10. (b)
11. (b) 12. (c) 13. (a) 14. (d) 15. (b)
16. (c) 17. (b) 18. (a) 19. (d) 20. (b)
21. (a) 22. (b) 23. (b) 24. (d) 25. (d)
26. (a) 27. (b) 28. (b) 29. (b) 30. (b)
31. (a) 32. (c) 33. (a) 34. (b) 35. (d)
36. (c) 37. (c) 38. (d) 39. (d) 40. (b)
41. (a) 42. (b) 43. (c) 44. (c) 45. (a)
46. (b) 47. (a) 48. (b) 49. (a) 50. (d)

PAPER–III

1. (c) 2. (a) 3. (b) 4. (b) 5. (c)
6. (a) 7. (a) 8. (c) 9. (d) 10. (a)
11. (b) 12. (b) 13. (a) 14. (c) 15. (b)
16. (c) 17. (a) 18. (c) 19. (c) 20. (d)
21. (a) 22. (c) 23. (a) 24. (d) 25. (c)
26. (b) 27. (b) 28. (b) 29. (c) 30. (d)
31. (d) 32. (a) 33. (a) 34. (a) 35. (a)
36. (d) 37. (a) 38. (d) 39. (d) 40. (a)
41. (c) 42. (c) 43. (b) 44. (b) 45. (b)
46. (d) 47. (d) 48. (d) 49. (d) 50. (b)